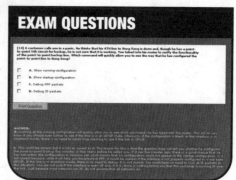

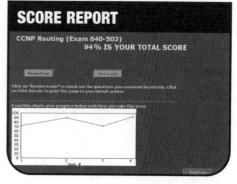

CCNP™ Routing
Study Guide

(Exam 640-503)

Osborne/**McGraw-Hill**
2600 Tenth Street
Berkeley, California 94710
U.S.A.

For information on translations or book distributors outside the U.S.A.,
or to arrange bulk purchase discounts for sales promotions, premiums, or fund-raisers, please
contact Osborne/**McGraw-Hill** at the above address.

CCNP™ Routing Study Guide (Exam 640-503)

1234567890 MMN MMN 019876543210

Book p/n: 0-07-212541-1 and CD p/n: 0-07-212542-X
parts of ISBN: 0-07-212543-8

Publisher	**Editorial Management**	**Technical Reviewer**
Brandon A. Nordin	Syngress Media, Inc.	Frank Jimenez
Vice President and	**Project Editor**	**Copy Editor**
Associate Publisher	Maribeth A. Corona	Darlene Bordwell
Scott Rogers		
	Acquisitions Coordinator	**Production and Editorial**
Editorial Director	Jessica Wilson	Black Hole Publishing Services
Gareth Hancock		
	Series Editor	**Series Design**
Associate Acquisitions Editor	Mark Buchmann	Roberta Steele
Timothy Green		
	Technical Editor	**Cover Design**
	Paul Hogrell	Greg Scott

This book was published with Corel VENTURA™ Publisher.

CISCO® CERTIFIED NETWORK PROFESSIONAL

CCNP™ Routing
Study Guide

(Exam 640-503)

Syngress Media, Inc.

Osborne/McGraw-Hill

Berkeley New York St. Louis San Francisco Auckland Bogotá Hamburg London Madrid Mexico City
Milan Montreal New Delhi Panama City Paris São Paulo Singapore Sydney Tokyo Toronto

About Syngress Media

Syngress Media creates books and software for Information Technology professionals seeking skill enhancement and career advancement. Its products are designed to comply with vendor and industry standard course curricula, and are optimized for certification exam preparation. You can contact Syngress via the Web at www.sygnress.com.

Contributors

Micah Bartell (CCIE #5069) is currently a Network Consulting Engineer at Cisco Systems in Dallas, TX. He specializes in large-scale network design and service provider architectures. Micah is an acknowledged expert in IP routing protocols.

Ricardo Daza (CISSP, CCNP (LAN-ATM, Voice Access), CCDA, SCNA (Solaris 7), IBM CSE (AIX 4.3 Sys Admin, AIX Firewall), MCSE+I, MCT, CNA) is a Channel Systems Engineer for Cisco Systems (http://www.cisco.com/), working out of Cisco's Seattle, WA office. He has over 10 years of computer consulting experience and has passed nine Cisco Certified Exams including the CCIE Written Qualification Exam (lab scheduled for later this year). During his career, Ricardo has worked on many extensive and diverse projects, including, network infrastructure and security analysis, network design and implementation, network management and documentation, project management and end-user training. He is proficient in a number of different vendor products ranging from Cisco, Microsoft, Sun, Novell, IBM, Bay, and 3Com to name a but a few.

Benoit Durand (CCNA, CCDA, CCNP, CCDP, CCIE #5754) is the Midwest Region network engineer for Tivoli Systems (www.tivoli.com), located in Indianapolis, IN. Ben designs and integrates high-end network solutions for Tivoli's worldwide operations while maintaining his own Cisco powered network in Indianapolis. He has over 10 years of networking engineering experience in a wide range of environments. Prior to working at Tivoli, Ben worked on many high-profile military projects for the Canadian Air Force, deploying wide-area network solutions to peacekeeping forces in Kuwait, Yugoslavia, and other exotic locations. His latest projects involve Voice-over-ATM, Virtual Private Network solutions and Wide-Area Network switching.

Ben lives with his wife Dr. Christy Snider in Kingston, GA and can be reached at ccie5754@hotmail.com.

Richard A. Holland (MCSE, MCP+I, CCNP, CSE) is one of the key members of the data/voice integration division of Telec Inc. (http://www.telecinc.com), located in Springfield, MO. He handles both voice and data tasks, and helps develop cost effective solutions that combine voice, data, and video across one network infrastructure as well as Cisco router/switch configuration, Windows NT administration and PBX configuration and maintenance.

Richard lives in Springfield, MO and can be reached at rholland@classicnet.net or rholland@freon.republic.k12.mo.us.

Damon Merchant (CCDP, CCNP, CCNA, CCDA, MCSE, MCP, CNE, and CNA) is the President of Corbus Systems, Inc., an information technology firm in Detroit, MI. He has about 10 years experience in networking. Not only is he a network engineering guru, he is also a seasoned software developer. His most recent application, Touch-Tone Administrator for NT, allows network administrators to manage their Windows NT networks from a telephone. Damon also provides training and technical workshops for IT professionals. In his spare time, Damon enjoys playing basketball, ping pong, video games, weight lifting, and candlelight dinners with his wife, Lortensia.

More information about Damon Merchant and his software products can be found at his company's Web site, www.corbus-systems.com. Damon can be e-mailed at damon@corbus-systems.com.

Tony Olzak (CCNP, MCSE) presently works as a consultant at Frontway in Toledo, OH. He specializes in the planning, design, and implementation of enterprise networks and is working towards the CCIE certification. In his free time Tony likes to play guitar and write music.

Ronald A. Panus (CCIE 5823, CCNP, CCNA, CCDA, MCSE, MCP + Internet, CNA) is employed by SBC Datacomm (Pacific Bell) as a Professional Services Senior Consultant. Ron's primary work related responsibilities include assessing, designing, and implementing Wide Area Networks for large corporations. He also mentors SBC associates that are striving to rise the technological ladder at SBC Datacomm. Ron has over 16 years of experience in the computer/networking industry. During his career, Ron has worked on a variety of projects in industries such as NASA's space program, several of the major U.S. airlines, and many startup and established Dot Com company's.

Ron currently lives in Concord, CA with his wife Kathy and their two daughters Kasey Renee and Taylor Ann.

Charles Riley (CCNP, MCSE, CNE) is a Technical Solutions Consultant with Sprint Enterprise Network Services (Sprint Paranet) in Fort Worth, TX. He designs and implements networking solutions for Sprint customers. Charles has over 10 years of IT experience, much of it in networking and Cisco products. He worked for the U.S Army in many capacities, including assignments in Germany. He is currently working on his CCIE. Charles is grateful to his wife René, and his daughter Tess, for understanding and supporting his work. He can be reached at ceriley@sprintparanet.com.

Leland Vandervort (BA, CCNP, CCDA, CNE3.x) is Director of Network Operations of MultiMania (http://www.multimania.fr/), a web-based community and E-commerce hosting and application provider located in Paris, France, which is positioned among the top four most visited sites in France. He specializes in the design, implementation, and management of large-scale, high-performance network infrastructures for services demanding high availability, based primarily on routing and switching equipment by Cisco Systems and Foundry Networks, as well as a variety of UNIX-based platforms. He has accumulated 10 years of network design, administration, and teaching experience, ranging from radio and satellite telemetry systems, X.25 over radio and land-based links, as well as IPX and IP over a myriad of Internet architectures and technologies.

He spends his spare with aviation, playing flamenco guitar, listening to music, and teaching. He can be contacted at leland@mmania.com or leland@taranta.discpro.org.

Derek S. Winchester (CCNP, CCNA, MCSE, MCP+I) is a Senior Network Engineer for a major healthcare insurance provider, located in Columbia, MD. He has 9 years experience in the information systems field, the last 4 being solely dedicated to WAN and LAN technologies. Derek is currently working on his CCIE certification and his Network Security certification. Derek currently resides in Baltimore, MD with his wife Larissa and children Mataya, William, Joy, and Tarell.

Technical Editor

Paul Hogrell (CCIE, CCSI, CCNP) is the Director of Internetworking Services for CertaNet, Inc. (http://www.certanet.com/). He is the Global Knowledge course director for Cisco's BSCN course and is the author and course director for the Border Gateway Protocol course. Paul teaches a variety of Cisco courses including ICND, BSCN, BCRAN, BCMSN, CIT, and CID. For the past 10 years, Paul has been a consultant helping large organizations design and implement complex routing environments. He is considered especially knowledgeable in the Border Gateway Protocol and has worked with several Tier One ISPs on their BGP peering policies.

Paul lives with his wife Kelly and their son Patrick in Canal Winchester, OH and can be reached at hogrell@certanet.com.

Technical Reviewer

Frank Jimenez (CCIE #5738, CCDP, CCNP, MCNE, MCSE, MCP+I) is employed as a Systems Architect at CompuCom Systems, Inc. (http://www.compucom.com), headquartered in Dallas, TX. He has over eight years of experience designing networks to support corporate internetworking, messaging, and management solutions. Frank lives with his wife Diana and three children in Dallas, and can be contacted via email at ccie5738@hotmail.com.

Series Editor

Mark Buchmann (CCIE, CCSI) is a Cisco Certified Internetworking Expert (CCIE) and has been a Certified Cisco Systems Instructor (CCSI) since 1995. He is the owner of MAB Enterprises, Inc., a company providing consulting, network support, training, and various other services. Mark is also a co-owner of www.CertaNet.com, a company providing on-line certification assistance for a variety of network career paths including all the various Cisco certifications.

In his free time he enjoys spending time with his family and boating. He currently lives in Raleigh, NC. Mark is Series Editor for Syngress Cisco books.

ACKNOWLEDGMENTS

W e would like to thank the following people:

- All the incredibly hard-working folks at Osborne/McGraw-Hill: Brandon Nordin, Scott Rogers, Timothy Green, Gareth Hancock, and Jessica Wilson.

- The Black Hole Publishing Services staff for their help in fine tuning the project.

CONTENTS AT A GLANCE

CONTENTS

T his book's primary objective is to help you prepare for and pass the CCNP Routing Exam 640-503. We believe that the only way to do this is to help you increase your knowledge and build your skills. After completing this book, you should feel confident that you have thoroughly reviewed all of the objectives that Cisco has established for the exam.

In This Book

This book is organized around the topics covered within the CCNP Routing Exam administered at Sylvan Testing Centers.

In Every Chapter

We've created a set of chapter components that call your attention to important items, reinforce important points, and provide helpful exam-taking hints. Take a look at what you'll find in the chapters:

- Each chapter begins with the **Certification Objectives**—what you need to know in order to pass the section on the exam dealing with the chapter topic. The Certification Objective headings identify the objectives within the chapter, so you'll always know an objective when you see it!

EXERCISE 1-1

- **Certification Exercises** are interspersed throughout the chapters. These are step-by-step exercises. They help you master skills that are likely to be an area of focus on the exam. Don't just read through the exercises; they are hands-on practice that you should be comfortable completing. Learning by doing is an effective way to increase your competency with the language.

- **From the Classroom** sidebars describe the issues that come up most often in the training classroom setting. These sidebars give you a valuable perspective into certification- and product-related topics. They point out common mistakes and address questions that have arisen from classroom discussions.

■ S & S sections lay out specific scenario questions and solutions in a quick-to-read format.

SCENARIO & SOLUTION

You have just taken over as the network administrator and have no information on the password for one of your 3600 series routers. What is a possible solution?	Perform the password recovery process on the 3600 series router.
You have been informed that a new remote location needs connectivity. It will require ISDN access and a four-port hub. What model of router would provide a solution here?	The 803 and 804 both provide for ISDN with a four-port hub.?
An OC-1 connection is being installed at your central location that now employs a 2600 series router. What changes will need to be made at the central site to accommodate this connection?	A 3600 series with the HSSI port will be needed here.

■ The **Certification Summary** is a succinct review of the chapter and a re-statement of salient points regarding the exam.

 ■ The **Two-Minute Drill** at the end of every chapter is a checklist of the main points of the chapter. It can be used for last-minute review.

 ■ The **Self Test** offers questions similar to those found on the certification exam. The answers to these questions, as well as explanations of the answers, can be found in Appendix A. By taking the Self Test after completing each chapter, you'll reinforce what you've learned from that chapter, while becoming familiar with the structure of the exam questions.

Some Pointers

Once you've finished reading this book, set aside some time to do a thorough review. You might want to return to the book several times and make use of all the methods it offers for reviewing the material:

1. *Re-read all the Two-Minute Drills,* or have someone quiz you. You also can use the drills as a way to do a quick cram before the exam.

2. *Review all the S & S scenarios* for quick problem solving.

3. *Re-take the Self Tests.* Taking the tests right after you've read the chapter is a good idea, because it helps reinforce what you've just learned. However, it's an even better idea to go back later and do all the questions in the book in one sitting. Pretend you're taking the exam. (For this reason, you should mark your answers on a separate piece of paper when you go through the questions the first time.)

4. *Complete the exercises.* Did you do the exercises when you read through each chapter? If not, do them! These exercises are designed to cover exam topics, and there's no better way to get to know this material than by practicing.

INTRODUCTION

How to Take a Cisco Certification Examination

This introduction covers the importance of your CCNP certification and prepares you for taking the actual examination. It gives you a few pointers on methods of preparing for the exam, including how to study and register, what to expect, and what to do on exam day.

Catch the Wave!

Congratulations on your pursuit of Cisco certification! In this fast-paced world of networking, few certification programs are as valuable as the one offered by Cisco.

The networking industry has virtually exploded in recent years, accelerated by nonstop innovation and the Internet's popularity. Cisco has stayed at the forefront of this tidal wave, maintaining a dominant role in the industry.

The networking industry is highly competitive, and evolving technology only increases in its complexity, so the rapid growth of the networking industry has created a vacuum of qualified people. There simply aren't enough skilled networking people to meet the demand. Even the most experienced professionals must keep current with the latest technology in order to provide the skills that the industry demands. That's where Cisco certification programs can help networking professionals succeed as they pursue their careers.

Cisco started its certification program many years ago, offering only the designation Cisco Certified Internetwork Expert (CCIE). Through the CCIE program, Cisco provided a means to meet the growing demand for experts in the field of networking. However, the CCIE tests are brutal, with a failure rate of over 80 percent. (Fewer than 5 percent of candidates pass on their first attempt.) As you might imagine, very few people ever attain CCIE status.

In early 1998, Cisco recognized the need for intermediate certifications, and several new programs were created. Four intermediate certifications were added: CCNA (Cisco Certified Network Associate), CCNP (Cisco Certified Network Professional), CCDA (Cisco Certified Design Associate), and CCDP (Cisco

Certified Design Professional)In addition, several specialties were added to the CCIE certifications; currently CCIE candidates can receive their CCIE in five areas: Routing and Switching, WAN Switching, ISP-Dial, SNA/IP Integration, and Design.

CCNP
@dvice

I would encourage you to take beta tests when they are available. Not only are the beta exams less expensive than the final exams (some are even free!), but also, if you pass the beta, you will receive credit for passing the exam. If you don't pass the beta, you will have seen every question in the pool of available questions, and can use this information when you prepare to take the exam for the second time. Remember to jot down important information immediately after the exam, if you didn't pass. You will have to do this after leaving the exam area, since materials written during the exam are retained by the testing center. This information can be helpful when you need to determine which areas of the exam were most challenging for you as you study for the subsequent test.

Why Vendor Certification?

Over the years, vendors have created their own certification programs because of industry demand. This demand arises when the marketplace needs skilled professionals and an easy way to identify them. Vendors benefit because it promotes people skilled in their product. Professionals benefit because it boosts their careers. Employers benefit because it helps them identify qualified people.

In the networking industry, technology changes too often and too quickly to rely on traditional means of certification, such as universities and trade associations. Because of the investment and effort required to keep network certification programs current, vendors are the only organizations suited to keep pace with the changes. In general, such vendor certification programs are excellent, with most of them requiring a solid foundation in the essentials, as well as their particular product line.

Corporate America has come to appreciate these vendor certification programs and the value they provide. Employers recognize that certifications, like university degrees, do not guarantee a level of knowledge, experience, or performance; rather, they establish a baseline for comparison. By seeking to hire vendor-certified employees, a company can assure itself that not only has it found a person skilled in networking, but also it has hired a person skilled in the specific products the company uses.

Technical professionals have also begun to recognize the value of certification and the impact it can have on their careers. By completing a certification program, professionals gain an endorsement of their skills from a major industry source. This endorsement can boost their current position, and it makes finding the next job even easier. Often a certification determines whether a first interview is even granted.

Today a certification may place you ahead of the pack. Tomorrow it will be a necessity to keep from being left in the dust.

CCNP advice

Signing up for an exam has become easier with the new Web-based test registration system. To sign up for the CCNP exams, access http://www.2test.com, and register for the Cisco Career Certification path. You will need to get an Internet account and password, if you do not already have one for 2test.com. Just select the option for first-time registration, and the Web site will walk you through that process. The registration wizard even provides maps to the testing centers, something that is not available when you call Sylvan Prometric on the telephone.

Cisco's Certification Program

Cisco now has a number of certifications for the Routing and Switching career track, as well as for the WAN Switching career track. While Cisco recommends a series of courses for each of these certifications, they are not required. Ultimately, certification is dependent upon a candidate's passing a series of exams. With the right experience and study materials, you can pass each of these exams without taking the associated class.

Table i-1 shows the Cisco CCNP 2.0 exam track.

The Foundation Routing and Switching exam (640-509) can be taken in place of the Routing, Switching, and Remote Access exams.

As you can see, the CCNA is the foundation of the Routing and Switching track, after which candidates can pursue the Network Support path to CCNP and CCIE, or the Network Design path to CCDA, CCDP, and to CCIE Design.

TABLE i-1	Exam Name	Exam #
CCNP 2.0 Track	CCNA 2.0	640-507
	Routing	640-503
	Switching	640-504
	Remote Access	640-505
	Support	640-506

Please note that if you have taken CCNP exams from the 1.0 track (Exam #'s 640-403, 640-404, 640-405, 640-440) you may take the remainder of your exams from the 2.0 track, but you will be certified as a CCNP 1.0.

CCNP
@dvice

In addition to the technical objectives that are being tested for each exam, you will find much more useful information on Cisco's Web site at http://www.cisco.com/warp/public/10/wwtraining/certprog. You will find information on becoming certified, exam-specific information, sample test questions, and the latest news on Cisco certification. This is the most important site you will find on your journey to becoming Cisco certified.

CCNP
@dvice

When I find myself stumped answering multiple-choice questions, I use my scratch paper to write down the two or three answers I consider the strongest, and then underline the answer I feel is most likely correct. Here is an example of what my scratch paper looks like when I've gone through the test once:

21. B or C
33. A or C

It is extremely helpful to you mark the question and then continue. You can return to the question and immediately pick up your thought process where you left off. Use this technique to avoid having to reread and rethink questions.
You will also need to use your scratch paper during complex, text-based scenario questions to create visual images to help you understand the question. For example, during the CCNP exam you will need to draw multiple networks and the connections between them or calculate a subnet mask for a given network. By drawing the layout or working the calculation while you are interpreting the question, you may find a hint that you would not have found without your own visual aid. This technique is especially helpful if you are a visual learner.

Computer-Based Testing

In a perfect world, you would be assessed for your true knowledge of a subject, not simply how you respond to a series of test questions. But life isn't perfect, and it just isn't practical to evaluate everyone's knowledge on a one-to-one basis. (Cisco actually does have a one-to-one evaluation, but it's reserved for the CCIE Laboratory exam, and the waiting list is quite long.)

For the majority of its certifications, Cisco evaluates candidates using a computer-based testing service operated by Sylvan Prometric. This service is quite popular in the industry, and it is used for a number of vendor certification programs, including Novell's CNE and Microsoft's MCSE. Thanks to Sylvan Prometric's large number of facilities, exams can be administered worldwide, generally in the same town as a prospective candidate.

For the most part, Sylvan Prometric exams work similarly from vendor to vendor. However, there is an important fact to know about Cisco's exams: They use the traditional Sylvan Prometric test format, not the newer adaptive format. This gives the candidate an advantage, since the traditional format allows answers to be reviewed and revised during the test. (The adaptive format does not.)

CCNP
@dvice

Many experienced test takers do not go back and change answers unless they have a good reason to do so. You should change an answer only when you feel you may have misread or misinterpreted the question the first time. Nervousness may make you second-guess every answer and talk yourself out of a correct one.

To discourage simple memorization, Cisco exams present a different set of questions every time the exam is administered. In the development of the exam, hundreds of questions are compiled and refined, using beta testers. From this large collection, a random sampling is drawn for each test.

Each Cisco exam has a specific number of questions and test duration. Testing time is typically generous, and the time remaining is always displayed in the corner of the testing screen, along with the number of remaining questions. If time expires during an exam, the test terminates, and incomplete answers are counted as incorrect.

CCNP
@dvice

I have found it extremely helpful to put a check next to each objective as I find it is satisfied by the proposed solution. If the proposed solution does not satisfy an objective, you do not need to continue with the rest of the objectives. Once you have determined which objectives are fulfilled you can count your check marks and answer the question appropriately. This is a very effective testing technique!

At the end of the exam, your test is immediately graded, and the results are displayed on the screen. Scores for each subject area are also provided, but the system will not indicate which specific questions were missed. A report is automatically printed at the proctor's desk for your files. The test score is electronically transmitted back to Cisco.

In the end, this computer-based system of evaluation is reasonably fair. You might feel that one or two questions were poorly worded; this can certainly happen, but you shouldn't worry too much. Ultimately, it's all factored into the required passing score.

Question Types

Cisco exams pose questions in a variety of formats, most of which are discussed here. As candidates progress toward the more advanced certifications, the difficulty of the exams is intensified, through both the subject matter and the question formats.

CCNP *In order to pass these challenging exams, you may want to talk with other* **advice** *test takers to determine what is being tested, and what to expect in terms of difficulty. The most helpful way to communicate with other CCNP hopefuls is the Cisco mailing list. With this mailing list, you will receive e-mail every day from other members, discussing everything imaginable concerning Cisco networking equipment and certification. Access http://www.cisco.com/warp/public/84/1.html to learn how to subscribe to this source of a wealth of information.*

True/False

The classic true/false question format is not used in the Cisco exams, for the obvious reason that a simple guess has a 50 percent chance of being correct. Instead, true/false questions are posed in multiple-choice format, requiring the candidate to identify the true or false statement from a group of selections.

Multiple Choice

Multiple choice is the primary format for questions in Cisco exams. These questions may be posed in a variety of ways.

Select the Correct Answer   This is the classic multiple-choice question, in which the candidate selects a single answer from a minimum of four choices. In addition to the question's wording, the choices are presented in a Windows radio button format, in which only one answer can be selected at a time. The question will instruct you to "Select the best answer" when they are looking for just one answer.

Select the Three Correct Answers   The multiple-answer version is similar to the single-choice version, but multiple answers must be provided. This is an all-or-nothing format; all the correct answers must be selected, or the entire question is incorrect. In this format, the question specifies exactly how many answers must be selected. Choices are presented in a check box format, allowing more than one answer to be selected. In addition, the testing software prevents too many answers from being selected.

Select All That Apply   The open-ended version is the most difficult multiple-choice format, since the candidate does not know how many answers should be selected. As with the multiple-answer version, all the correct answers must be selected to gain credit for the question. If too many answers or not enough answers are selected, no credit is given. This format presents choices in check box format, but the testing software does not advise the candidates whether they've selected the correct number of answers.

CCNP
@dvice

Make it easy on yourself and find some "braindumps." These are notes about the exam from test takers, which indicate the most difficult concepts tested, what to look out for, and sometimes even what not to bother studying. Several of these can be found at http://www.dejanews.com. Simply do a search for CCNP and browse the recent postings. Another good resource is at http://www.groupstudy.com. Beware however of the person that posts a question reported to have been on the test and its answer. First, the question and its answer may be incorrect. Second, this is a violation of Cisco's confidentiality agreement, which you as a candidate must agree to prior to taking the exam. Giving out specific information regarding a test violates this agreement and could result in the revocation of your certification status.

Freeform Response

Freeform responses are prevalent in Cisco's advanced exams, particularly where the subject focuses on router configuration and commands. In the freeform format, no choices are provided. Instead, the test prompts for user input, and the candidate must type the correct answer. This format is similar to an essay question, except the response must be specific, allowing the computer to evaluate the answer.

For example, the question

Type the command for viewing routes learned via the EIGRP protocol.

requires the answer

show ip route eigrp

For safety's sake, you should completely spell out router commands, rather than using abbreviations. In this example, the abbreviated command **SH IP ROU EI** works on a real router, but is counted as wrong by the testing software. The freeform response questions almost always are answered by commands used in the Cisco IOS. As you progress in your track for your CCNP you will find these freeform response question increasingly prevalent.

Fill in the Blank

Fill-in-the-blank questions are less common in Cisco exams. They may be presented in multiple-choice or freeform response format.

Exhibits

Exhibits, usually showing a network diagram or a router configuration, accompany many exam questions. These exhibits are displayed in a separate window, which is opened by clicking the Exhibit button at the bottom of the screen. In some cases, the testing center may provide exhibits in printed format at the start of the exam.

Scenarios

While the normal line of questioning tests a candidate's "book knowledge," scenarios add a level of complexity. Rather than asking only technical questions, they apply the candidate's knowledge to real-world situations.

Scenarios generally consist of one or two paragraphs and an exhibit that describes a company's needs or network configuration. This description is followed by a series of questions and problems that challenge the candidate's ability to address the situation. Scenario-based questions are commonly found in exams relating to network design, but they appear to some degree in each of the Cisco exams.

You will know when you are coming to a series of scenario questions, because they are preceded by a blue screen, indicating that the following questions will have the same scenario, but different solutions. You must remember that the scenario will be the same during the series of questions, which means that you do not have to spend time reading the scenario again.

Studying Techniques

First and foremost, give yourself plenty of time to study. Networking is a complex field, and you can't expect to cram what you need to know into a single study session. It is a field best learned over time, by studying a subject and then applying your knowledge. Build yourself a study schedule and stick to it, but be reasonable about the pressure you put on yourself, especially if you're studying in addition to your regular duties at work.

One easy technique to use in studying for certification exams is the 30-minutes-per-day effort. Simply study for a minimum of 30 minutes every day. It is a small but significant commitment. On a day when you just can't focus, then give up at 30 minutes. On a day when it flows completely for you, study longer. As long as you have more of the flow days, your chances of succeeding are extremely high.

Second, practice and experiment. In networking, you need more than knowledge; you need understanding, too. You can't just memorize facts to be effective; you need to understand why events happen, how things work, and (most important) how and why they break.

The best way to gain deep understanding is to take your book knowledge to the lab. Try it out. Make it work. Change it a little. Break it. Fix it. Snoop around "under the hood." If you have access to a network analyzer, like Network Associate Sniffer, put it to use. You can gain amazing insight to the inner workings of a network by watching devices communicate with each other.

Unless you have a very understanding boss, don't experiment with router commands on a production router. A seemingly innocuous command can have a nasty side effect. If you don't have a lab, your local Cisco office or Cisco users' group may be able to help. Many training centers also allow students access to their lab equipment during off-hours.

Another excellent way to study is through case studies. Case studies are articles or interactive discussions that offer real-world examples of how technology is applied to meet a need. These examples can serve to cement your understanding of a technique or technology by seeing it put to use. Interactive discussions offer added value because you can also pose questions of your own. User groups are an excellent source of examples, since the purpose of these groups is to share information and learn from each other's experiences.

The Cisco Networkers conference is not to be missed. Although renowned for its wild party and crazy antics, this conference offers a wealth of information. Held every year in cities around the world, it includes three days of technical seminars and presentations on a variety of subjects. As you might imagine, it's very popular. You have to register early to get the classes you want.

Then, of course, there is the Cisco Web site. This little gem is loaded with collections of technical documents and white papers. As you progress to more advanced subjects, you will find great value in the large number of examples and reference materials available. But be warned: You need to do a lot of digging to find the really good stuff. Often your only option is to browse every document returned by the search engine to find exactly the one you need. This effort pays off. Most CCIEs I know have compiled six to ten binders of reference material from Cisco's site alone.

Scheduling Your Exam

The Cisco exams are scheduled by calling Sylvan Prometric directly at (800) 829-6387. For locations outside the United States, your local number can be found on Sylvan's Web site at http://www.prometric.com. Sylvan representatives can schedule your exam, but they don't have information about the certification programs. Questions about certifications should be directed to Cisco's training department.

This Sylvan telephone number is specific to Cisco exams, and it goes directly to the Cisco representatives inside Sylvan. These representatives are familiar enough with the exams to find them by name, but it's best if you have the specific exam number handy when you call. After all, you wouldn't want to be scheduled and charged for the wrong exam (for example, the instructor's version, which is significantly harder).

Exams can be scheduled up to a year in advance, although it's really not necessary. Generally, scheduling a week or two ahead is sufficient to reserve the day and time you prefer. When you call to schedule, operators will search for testing centers in your area. For convenience, they can also tell which testing centers you've used before.

Sylvan accepts a variety of payment methods, with credit cards being the most convenient. When you pay by credit card, you can even take tests the same day you call—provided, of course, that the testing center has room. (Quick scheduling can be handy, especially if you want to retake an exam immediately.) Sylvan will mail you a receipt and confirmation of your testing date, although this generally arrives after the test has been taken. If you need to cancel or reschedule an exam, remember to call at least one day before your exam, or you'll lose your test fee.

When you register for the exam, you will be asked for your ID number. This number is used to track your exam results back to Cisco. It's important that you use the same ID number each time you register, so that Cisco can follow your progress. Address information provided when you first register is also used by Cisco to ship certificates and other related material. In the United States, your Social Security number is commonly used as your ID number. However, Sylvan can assign you a unique ID number if you prefer not to use your Social Security number.

Table i-2 shows the available CCNP 2.0 exams and the number of questions and duration of each. This information is subject to change as Cisco revises the exams, so it's a good idea to verify the details when you register for an exam.

In addition to the regular Sylvan Prometric testing sites, Cisco also offers facilities for taking exams free of charge at each Networkers Conference in the United States. As you might imagine, this option is quite popular, so reserve your exam time as soon as you arrive at the conference.

| TABLE i-2 | Cisco Exam Lengths and Question Counts |

Exam Title	Exam Number	Number of Questions	Duration (minutes)	Exam Fee (US$)
Routing 2.0	640-503	80	90	$100
Switching 2.0	640-504	80	90	$100
Remote Access 2.0	640-505	80	90	$100
Support 2.0	640-506	80	90	$100

Arriving at the Exam

As with any test, you'll be tempted to cram the night before. Resist that temptation. You should know the material by this point, and if you're too groggy in the morning, you won't remember what you studied anyway. Instead, get a good night's sleep.

Arrive early for your exam; it gives you time to relax and review key facts. Take the opportunity to review your notes. If you get burned out on studying, you can usually start your exam a few minutes early. On the other hand, I don't recommend arriving late. Your test could be canceled, or you might be left without enough time to complete the exam.

When you arrive at the testing center, you'll need to sign in with the exam administrator. In order to sign in, you need to provide two forms of identification. Acceptable forms include government-issued IDs (for example, passport or driver's license), credit cards, and company ID badge. One form of ID must include a photograph.

Aside from a brain full of facts, you don't need to bring anything else to the exam. In fact, your brain is about all you're allowed to take into the exam. All the tests are closed book, meaning that you don't get to bring any reference materials with you. You're also not allowed to take any notes out of the exam room. The test administrator will provide you with paper and a pencil. Some testing centers may provide a small marker board instead.

Calculators are not allowed, so be prepared to do any necessary math (such as hex-binary-decimal conversions or subnet masks) in your head or on paper. Additional paper is available if you need it.

Leave your pager and telephone in the car, or turn them off. They only add stress to the situation, since they are not allowed in the exam room, and can sometimes still be heard if they ring outside the room. Purses, books, and other materials must be left with the administrator before you enter. While you're in the exam room, it's important that you don't disturb other candidates; talking is not allowed during the exam.

In the exam room, the exam administrator logs onto your exam, and you have to verify that your ID number and the exam number are correct. If this is the first time you've taken a Cisco test, you can select a brief tutorial for the exam software. Before the test begins, you will be provided with facts about the exam, including the duration, the number of questions, and the score required for passing. Then the clock starts ticking, and the fun begins.

The testing software is Windows-based, but you won't have access to the main desktop or to any of the accessories. The exam is presented in full screen, with a single question per screen. Navigation buttons allow you to move forward and backward between questions. In the upper right corner of the screen, counters show the number of questions and time remaining. Most important, there is a Mark check box in the upper left corner of the screen—this will prove to be a critical tool in your testing technique.

Test-Taking Techniques

One of the most frequent excuses I hear for failing a Cisco exam is "poor time management." Without a plan of attack, candidates are overwhelmed by the exam or become sidetracked and run out of time. For the most part, if you are comfortable with the material, the allotted time is more than enough to complete the exam. The trick is to keep the time from slipping away when you work on any one particular problem.

Your obvious goal in taking an exam is to answer the questions effectively, although other aspects of the exam can distract from this goal. After taking a fair number of computer-based exams, I've developed a technique for tackling the problem, which I share with you here. Of course, you still need to learn the material. These steps just help you take the exam more efficiently.

Size Up the Challenge

First take a quick pass through all the questions in the exam. "Cherry-pick" the easy questions, answering them on the spot. Briefly read each question, noticing the type of question and the subject. As a guideline, try to spend less than 25 percent of your testing time in this pass.

This step lets you assess the scope and complexity of the exam, and it helps you determine how to pace your time. It also gives you an idea of where to find potential answers to some of the questions. Often the answer to one question is shown in the exhibit of another. Sometimes the wording of one question might lend clues or jog your thoughts for another question.

Imagine that the following questions are posed in this order:

Question 1: Review the router configurations and network diagram in exhibit XYZ (not shown here). Which devices should be able to ping each other?

Question 2: If RIP routing were added to exhibit XYZ, which devices would be able to ping each other?

The first question seems straightforward. Exhibit XYZ probably includes a diagram and a couple of router configurations. Everything looks normal, so you decide that all devices can ping each other.

Now consider the hint left by Question 2. When you answered Question 1, did you notice that the configurations were missing the routing protocol? Oops! Being alert to such clues can help you catch your own mistakes.

If you're not entirely confident with your answer to a question, answer it anyway, but check the Mark check box to flag it for later review. If you run out of time, at least you've provided a first-guess answer, rather than leaving it blank.

Take on the Scenario Questions

Second, go back through the entire test, using the insight you gained from the first go-through. For example, if the entire test looks difficult, you'll know better than to spend more than a minute or so on each question. Break down the pacing into small milestones; for example, "I need to answer 10 questions every 15 minutes."

At this stage, it's probably a good idea to skip past the time-consuming questions, marking them for the next pass. Try to finish this phase before you're 50 to 60 percent through the testing time.

By now, you probably have a good idea where the scenario questions are found. A single scenario tends to have several questions associated with it, but they aren't necessarily grouped together in the exam. Rather than rereading the scenario every time you encounter a related question, save some time by answering the questions as a group.

Tackle the Complex Problems

Third, go back through all the questions you marked for review, using the Review Marked button in the question review screen. This step includes taking a second look at all the questions you were unsure of in previous passes, as well as tackling the time-consuming ones you postponed until now. Chisel away at this group of questions until you've answered them all.

If you're more comfortable with a previously marked question, unmark it now. Otherwise, leave it marked. Work your way now through the time-consuming questions, especially those requiring manual calculations. Unmark them when you're satisfied with the answer.

By the end of this step, you've answered every question in the test, despite your reservations about some of your answers. If you run out of time in the next step, at least you won't lose points for lack of an answer. You're in great shape if you still have 10 to 20 percent of your time remaining.

Review Your Answers

Now you're cruising! You've answered all the questions, and you're ready to do a quality check. Take yet another pass (yes, one more) through the entire test, briefly rereading each question and your answer. Be cautious about revising answers at this point unless you're sure a change is warranted. If there's a doubt about changing the answer, I always trust my first instinct and leave the original answer intact.

Trick questions are rarely asked, so don't read too much into the questions. Again, if the wording of the question confuses you, leave the answer intact. Your first impression was probably right.

Be alert for last-minute clues. You're pretty familiar with nearly every question at this point, and you may find a few clues that you missed before.

The Grand Finale

When you're confident with all your answers, finish the exam by submitting it for grading. After what will seem like the longest ten seconds of your life, the testing software will respond with your score. This is usually displayed as a bar graph, showing the minimum passing score, your score, and a PASS/FAIL indicator.

If you're curious, you can review the statistics of your score at this time. Answers to specific questions are not presented; rather, questions are lumped into categories, and results are tallied for each category. This detail is also given on a report that has been automatically printed at the exam administrator's desk.

As you leave the exam, you'll need to leave your scratch paper behind or return it to the administrator. (Some testing centers track the number of sheets you've been given, so be sure to return them all.) In exchange, you'll receive a copy of the test report.

This report will be embossed with the testing center's seal, and you should keep it in a safe place. Normally, the results are automatically transmitted to Cisco, but occasionally you might need the paper report to prove that you passed the exam. Your personnel file is probably a good place to keep this report; the file tends to follow you everywhere, and it doesn't hurt to have favorable exam results turn up during a performance review.

Retesting

If you don't pass the exam, don't be discouraged—networking is complex stuff. Try to have a good attitude about the experience, and get ready to try again. Consider yourself a little more educated. You know the format of the test a little better, and the report shows which areas you need to strengthen.

If you bounce back quickly, you'll probably remember several of the questions you might have missed. This will help you focus your study efforts in the right area. Serious go-getters will reschedule the exam for a couple of days after the previous attempt, while the study material is still fresh in their minds.

Ultimately, remember that Cisco certifications are valuable because they're hard to get. After all, if anyone could get one, what value would it have? In the end, it takes a good attitude and a lot of studying, but you can do it!

CISCO® CERTIFIED NETWORK PROFESSIONAL

1

IP Routing
Fundamentals

Congratulations! If you are reading this chapter, you have already taken the first step toward passing Exam 641-503 (Building Scalable Cisco Networks). Whether you are a CCNP 1.0 or an aspiring CCNP 2.0, the basics remain the same. This chapter will provide you with those basics and give you the foundation you need to gain an understanding of the knowledge that lies ahead.

This chapter will provide you with an introduction to routing protocols and their placement in the IP protocol stack. You will also learn the key information that routers need to actually route data. Later in the chapter, you will be given an in-depth comparison of distance-vector protocols to link-state protocols. So, without further delay, let's get down to basics!

CERTIFICATION OBJECTIVE 1.01

Routing Protocols and Their Placement in the IP Stack

This section covers various Internet Protocol (IP) routing protocols and their placement in the IP protocol stack. You will be introduced to the distance-vector protocols RIP and Cisco's proprietary IGRP. You will also learn about Cisco's hybrid routing protocol, EIGRP. You will then be introduced to OSPF and BGP.

Before we can jump into a discussion on routing protocols in the IP protocol stack, you must first know that the *IP protocol stack* is a group of protocols used to transport data from one location to another. Different combinations of protocols within the stack can provide this function. For example, the Transmission Control Protocol (TCP) can be used with IP to provide connection-oriented communication. TCP/IP was originally designed by the U.S. Department of Defense and is based on a model similar to the Open System Interconnection (OSI) reference model. The Department of Defense IP model has four layers: Application, Host-to-Host, Internet, and Network Access. The two models are diagrammed in Figure 1-1.

The Application layer of the DOD IP model performs the functions of the top three layers of the OSI model: Application, Presentation, and Session. The

DOD MODEL

OSI MODEL

DOD MODEL	OSI MODEL
	APPLICATION
APPLICATION	PRESENTATION
	SESSION
HOST-TO-HOST	TRANSPORT
INTERNET	NETWORK
NETWORK ACCESS	DATA LINK
	PHYSICAL

Application layer contains protocols such as Telnet, Network File System (NFS), File Transfer Protocol (FTP), Trivial File Transport Protocol (TFTP), Simple Mail Transfer Protocol (SMTP), Simple Network Management Protocol (SNMP), Line Printer Daemon (LPD), and X-Windows. The DOD Application layer allows applications and processes on different hardware or operating system platforms to communicate with one another. For example, an FTP session started on a PC running Windows 98 attaches to a UNIX workstation to download a file.

The Host-to-Host layer performs the functions of the OSI Transport layer. The TCP and UDP (User Datagram Protocol) protocols operate within this layer. The Host-to-Host layer is responsible for transporting data between the upper and lower layers. The protocols in the Host-to-Host layer also determine whether communication will be connectionless or connection-oriented. *Connectionless communication* occurs when using UDP with IP, which means stations receiving data do not send an acknowledgment back to the sender. The sending station has no way of knowing whether or not the data arrived successfully. On the other hand, *connection-oriented communication* occurs when TCP is used with IP to cause receiving stations to send an acknowledgment back to the sender.

The DOD Internet layer mirrors the OSI Network layer. IP and the following protocols function at this layer: BOOTP, Internet Control Message Protocol (ICMP), Address Resolution Protocol (ARP), and Reverse Address Resolution Protocol (RARP). The DOD Internet layer is where the all-important task of routing occurs. Since no other layer handles routing, an understanding of this layer is critical to your success as a CCNP.

The DOD Network Access layer combines the functions of the OSI Data Link and Physical layers, as shown in Figure 1-2. Protocols at the Network Access layer define the physical transmission of data. Protocols operating at this layer are Ethernet, Fast Ethernet, Gigabit Ethernet, Token Ring, and Fiber Distributed Data Interface (FDDI).

FIGURE 1-2 DOD and IP Protocol Suite

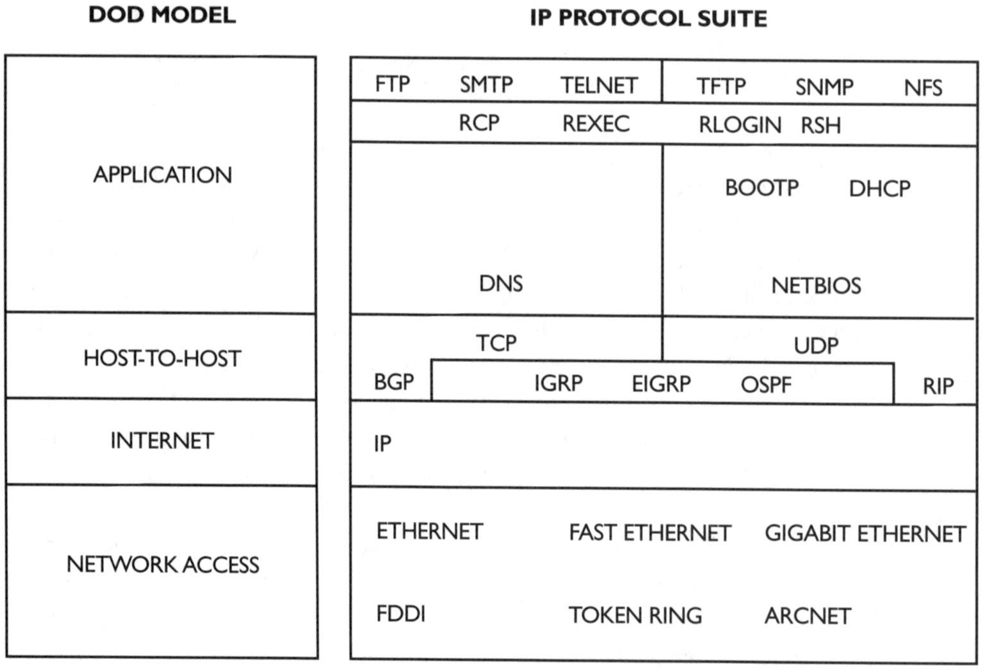

Routing Information Protocol

Routing Information Protocol, or RIP, is a distance-vector routing protocol used to route packets through an internetwork. There are actually two implementations of RIP for IP: IP RIP version 1 and IP RIP version 2. Only IP RIPv1 is discussed in this chapter. For more information on IP RIP version 2, see RFC 1723.

RIP is an interior gateway protocol that operates at the Internet layer of the DOD model and the Network layer of the OSI model. Being an interior gateway protocol means that RIP routes packets only within a single autonomous system. RIP is commonly used in small internetwork environments. RIP fulfills its routing responsibilities by maintaining a routing table and sending the entire table to each of its neighbors in 30-second intervals. This can be a problem in large internetworks because significant bandwidth would be consumed by multiple router broadcasts. Another reason that RIP would not work well in a large internetwork is its hop-count limitation of 15 hops. In other words, any route to a destination that must cross more than 15 routers is unreachable by RIP. Additional information on IP RIPv1 can be found in RFC 1058.

exam
ⓦatch

Because Exam 641-503 covers objectives that include the operation of RIP, it is imperative that you understand the 15-hop count limitation of RIP.

To get an idea of how RIP routers communicate with each other, Figure 1-3 displays a RIP packet. The following list defines the fields in the RIP packet:

- **Command** Indicates whether the packet is a request or a response
- **Version Number** Simply specifies the RIP version being used
- **Zero** Is not used by RIP
- **Address-Family Identifier (AFI)** Indicates the type of address being used; when IP is in use, the AFI is 2
- **Address** Indicates the sending entry's IP address
- **Metric** Indicates the number of routers, or hops, that have to be crossed through this advertising router on the way to the destination; 16 indicates that the destination was unreachable

FIGURE 1-3 A RIP packet

1	1	2	2	2	4	4	4	4
C O M M A N D	V E R S I O N	ZERO	AFI	ZERO	ADDRESS	ZERO	ZERO	METRIC

24 BYTES

Interior Gateway Routing Protocol

Interior Gateway Routing Protocol, or IGRP, is Cisco's proprietary distance-vector protocol that operates at the Internet layer of the DOD model and the Network layer of the OSI model. IGRP was designed to replace RIP in Cisco internetworks by providing a more scalable routing protocol.

IGRP supports a maximum of 255 hops, surpassing the 15-hop limitation of RIP. Another enhancement of IGRP over RIP is the additional routing metrics available to calculate route selection. IGRP metrics consist of bandwidth, delay, reliability, load, and Maximum Transmission Unit (MTU). This is a major improvement over RIP because slow links can be differentiated from fast links. In contrast, the RIP routing metric for a 56K link to a network is equal to the RIP routing metric for a T3 link. Regardless of the link speed, one link equates to 1 hop metric. IGRP metric calculations would view the previous links as unequal.

Another improvement over RIP is the frequency of routing updates. IGRP route updates occur every 90 seconds, by default. This frequency utilizes less bandwidth on larger internetworks in comparison to RIP 30-second routing updates. In addition to update timers, IGRP uses the following configurable timers to control network performance:

- **Invalid timer** Specifies how long a router should wait without receiving a specific route update before declaring a route invalid. The default is 270, or three times the update timer.

- **Hold-down timer** Specifies the hold-down period. The default is 280, or 10 plus 3 x the update timer.

■ **Flush timer**   Specifies how long a router should wait without receiving a specific route update before flushing the route from the routing table. The default is 7 x the update timer.

The following fields are present in an IGRP packet:

■ **Version**   Protocol version number

■ **Opcode**   Indicates the message type: 1 = Update message, 2 = Request message

■ **Edition**   Serial number that increments whenever a route change occurs

■ **Asystem**   Autonomous system number

■ **Ninterior**   Number of subnets in local network

■ **Nsystem**   Number of networks within the autonomous system (AS)

■ **Nexterior**   Number of networks outside the AS

■ **Checksum**   Checksum of IGRP header and data

When the Opcode field is 1, indicating an IGRP Update message, the IGRP packet includes the following fields:

■ **Number**   First three significant octets of IP address

■ **Delay**   Delay, in tens of microseconds, in reaching the network

■ **Bandwidth**   Bandwidth, in units of 1Kbps

■ **MTU**   MTU, in octets

■ **Reliability**   Percentage of packets successfully transmitted and received; 255 equals 100 percent

■ **Load**   Percentage of channel occupied; 255 equals 100 percent

■ **Hopcount**   Number of hops to network

Although these fields do not need to be memorized for the exam, this information will help you better understand how these protocols work.

Now that you have a better understanding of RIP and IGRP, the following are some possible design scenarios and their solutions.

SCENARIO & SOLUTION

When implementing an internetwork less than 16 hops in diameter, what protocol should I use?	Use RIP.
When implementing an internetwork more than 16 hops in diameter but much less than 255, what protocol should I use?	Use IGRP. EIGRP or OSPF could also be used.

Enhanced Interior Gateway Routing Protocol

Enhanced Interior Gateway Routing Protocol, or *EIGRP,* is Cisco's proprietary hybrid routing protocol that operates at the Internet layer of the DOD model and the Network layer of the OSI model. It combines the advantages of distance-vector and link-state protocols. EIGRP is an enhancement over its predecessor, IGRP, because it sends incremental routing updates instead of the entire routing table. This method uses less network bandwidth than previous distance-vector protocols, making EIGRP more scalable than IGRP and much more scalable than RIP. EIGRP performs its routing tasks by maintaining the following tables:

- **Route table**   Stores the best routes from the topology table
- **Topology table**   Stores information on all routes
- **Neighbor table**   Stores information about other EIGRP neighbor routers

In addition to IP, EIGRP can be used to route IPX and AppleTalk protocols. This means an additional six tables would be maintained if both IPX and AppleTalk were also configured on the EIGRP router.

exam
ⓦatch
Because Exam 641-503 covers EIGRP, a proprietary Cisco protocol, you should remember its versatility with routed protocols such as IPX and AppleTalk as well as IP.

When an EIGRP router comes online, it attempts to establish neighbor relationships with neighboring, or adjacent, routers. An EIGRP router accomplishes this by sending out hello packets to adjacent EIGRP routers to determine the state of the connection between them. Once the neighbor relationship has been established, the two EIGRP routers can exchange route information to populate their topology and route tables. Details of each neighbor reside in the Neighbor table.

The following steps outline the EIGRP neighbor establishment process:

1. The EIGRP router is powered on and multicasts hello packets from all its interfaces.

2. Neighboring EIGRP routers respond to the hello packets by sending all routes and metrics in their topology tables.

3. The originating EIGRP router acknowledges the response and route updates by sending the neighboring EIGRP router an ACK packet.

4. The originating EIGRP router updates its topology table with the new information.

5. The originating EIGRP router advertises its entire topology table to all its new neighbors.

6. Neighboring EIGRP routers acknowledge the originating router's topology table by sending back ACK packets.

on the **Job**

Organizations with large internetworks connected exclusively via Cisco equipment typically run EIGRP. EIGRP is used because it is recommended by Cisco when your Cisco routers do not have to connect with non-Cisco routers. In cases in which routers from multiple vendors, such as Cisco and Nortel, need to connect, Open Shortest Path First (OSPF) is the logical choice.

Open Shortest Path First Protocol

Open Shortest Path First (OSPF) protocol is an industry-standard link-state routing protocol that operates at the Internet layer of the DOD model and the Network layer of the OSI model. OSPF is a highly robust protocol that surpasses even EIGRP in network scalability. It is also far more complex to configure than RIP. It exceeds the 255-hop count limit of IGRP with an upper metric limit of 65,535. Unlike distance-vector protocols such as RIP and IGRP, OSPF sends routing updates only when a route change has been detected. Similar to EIGRP, OSPF maintains the following three databases:

- **Adjacency**   Stores Information about other OSPF neighbor routers
- **Topology**   Stores information on all routes
- **Route**   Stores the best routes from the topology table

Before OSPF can participate in routing, it must first initialize and establish an adjacency according to the following steps:

1. The new OSPF router multicasts hello packets from every interface.

2. The *Init state* occurs. This means that the new OSPF router is added to the OSPF adjacency table of the listening routers.

3. Routers reply to the hello packet by sending back OSPF multicast information.

4. The *two-way state* occurs. This means that the new OSPF router adds all the replying routers to the adjacency tables.

5. The *Exstart state* occurs. Two routers agree to exchange database information. In the Exstart state, we elect the router that is in charge of the exchange (called the *master*) and which sequence number to start with for the exchange of the database summary.

6. The *Exchange state* occurs. The new OSPF router exchanges link-state and complete route information with the other router.

7. The *Full state* occurs. This state indicates that a successful router adjacency has been established. To maintain this status, OSPF routers exchange hello packets periodically.

OSPF supports four types of routers:

- **Internal**   Interfaces are defined on the same area
- **Backbone**   Has one or more interfaces connected to area 0

- **Area border router (ABR)** Has interfaces connected to multiple OSPF areas
- **Autonomous system boundary router (ASBR)** Has an interface connected to an external network or a different autonomous system

OSPF routers send routing updates with the use of *link-state advertisements,* or *LSAs.* LSAs contain a list of active links and are sent to neighboring routers. The following list defines the LSAs used by OSPF:

- **Type 1 LSA (router link entry)** Broadcast only in its defined area; contains links to neighbor routers
- **Type 2 LSA (network entry)** Multicast to all area routers by designated router; contains list of routers connected to a network segment
- **Type 3 LSA (summary entry)** Sent to backbone routers by ABR; contains route information for internal networks
- **Type 4 LSA (summary entry)** Sent to backbone routers by ABR; contains information about ASBRs
- **Type 5 LSA (autonomous system entry)** Originates from the ASBR; contains information about external networks

exam
ⓦatch *Because Exam 641-503 covers the operation of OSPF, it is imperative that you understand the purpose of each LSA and where each of them originates.*

OSPF can be a very complex protocol to configure. For this reason, you should always be able to justify its deployment in lieu of a less complex distance-vector protocol such as RIP or IGRP. You can find more information about OSPF in RFC 1247.

EXERCISE 1-1

Routing Protocols

Given the following requirements and the network diagram, select the appropriate routing solution for this scenario.

Twisted Pears Current Network Topology

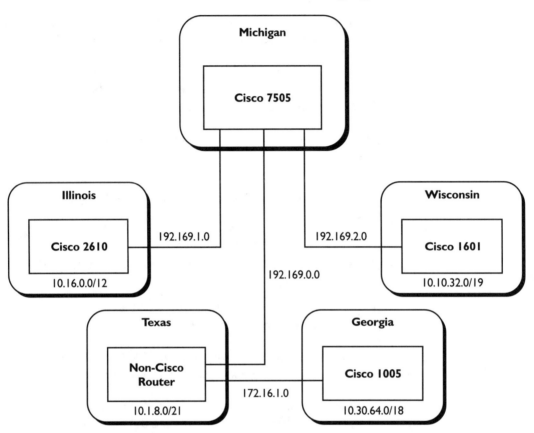

A new company called Twisted Pears is in need of some network consultation. The company requires that the final solution be scalable and compatible with current and future locations.

Currently, the network has only five routers. The company has $50 billion in the bank and is going on a buying spree to be the largest fruit-flavored pretzel maker in the world. The company will have distribution sites for its dough in all 50 states within three years and plans to be in the top 50 worldwide markets within six years. The company does not know what equipment it needs to purchase or what equipment exists in other companies it plans to acquire.

Your task is to recommend a routing protocol and describe why that routing protocol's features would support Twisted Pears' needs.

Solution:

The best choice for a routing protocol is OSPF. Since OSPF supports VLSM (Variable-Length Subnetwork Mask, it will be able to reach each 10.0.0.0 subnetwork. This is accomplished by the inclusion of subnet information in OSPF routing updates. Another reason OSPF is a good choice is its scalability. OSPF will easily scale to accommodate the predicted growth of Twisted Pears' network.

RIPv1 would not be a good choice because it does not support VLSM. It would view all the 10.0.0.0 subnetworks as the same network, which would cause a serious routing failure. IGRP and EIGRP would not be wise choices, either, because they are proprietary to Cisco routers. This means that the Texas and Georgia facilities would not be able to participate in Twisted Pears' wide area network. Even though Georgia uses Cisco equipment, it still would have to route through the non-Cisco router in Texas. Finally, Twisted Pears does not know what internetworking equipment with which it will need to integrate in the future.

Border Gateway Protocol

Border Gateway Routing Protocol, or *BGP,* is an exterior gateway routing protocol that functions at the Host-to-Host layer of the DOD model and at the Transport layer of the OSI model. The term *exterior gateway* defines routing protocols that perform routing between multiple autonomous systems. Due to BGP's scalability, it is the routing protocol of choice for the Internet.

Just like the previous routing protocols mentioned in this chapter, BGP maintains a forwarding table consisting of paths to networks. A BGP router does not update the IP routing table until a peer BGP router sends an incremental update. Like OSPF, BGP's incremental updates are an improvement over distance-vector protocols sending the entire routing table. Unlike RIP, BGP uses multiple metrics to determine the best possible path to a network. A BGP metric is assigned to each BGP router link on an internetwork.

Additional information on BGP can be found in the following RFCs: RFC 1105, RFC 1163, RFC 1267, RFC 1654, and RFC 1771.

on the
()o b

Internet service providers (ISPs) deploy BGP to connect to other ISPs and the rest of the Internet.

FROM THE CLASSROOM

Configuring Routing Protocols

Just as important as knowing how routing protocols work is knowing how to actually configure them. Some routing protocols are easier to configure than others. In general, link-state routing protocols are more difficult to configure than distance-vector routing protocols because more parameters must be set to make it all happen. Furthermore, link-state protocols are normally deployed on very large internetworks that require a high degree of implementation planning.

The following information will assist you in configuring some of the IP routing protocols. The configuration commands used here provide the bare minimum necessary to simply enable these routing protocols. For further configurations and more complex implementations, more complex commands and parameters must be added.

RIP

- **router rip**   Enables the RIP routing process and starts the RIP router configuration mode
- **network** *network-number*   Adds a network to the RIP routing process

IGRP

- **router igrp** *autonomous-system*   Enables the IGRP routing process and starts the IGRP router configuration mode

- **network** *network-number*   Adds a network to the IGRP routing process

EIGRP

- **router eigrp** *autonomous-system*   Enables the EIGRP routing process and starts the EIGRP router configuration mode
- **network** *network-number*   Adds a network to the EIGRP routing process

OSPF

- **router ospf** *process-id*   Enables the OSPF routing process and starts the OSPF router configuration mode
- **network** *address wildcard-mask* **area** *area-id*   Adds a network to the OSPF routing process

BGP

- **router bgp** *autonomous-system*   Enables the BGP routing process and starts the BGP router configuration mode
- **network** *network-number* **mask** *network-mask*   Adds a network to the BGP routing process

—*Damon Merchant, CCDP, CCNP, CCDA, CCNA, MCSE, CNE*

CERTIFICATION OBJECTIVE 1.02

Key Information for Routers to Route Data

This section discusses the key information that is required for routers to route data. Before we continue, though, a better understanding of routing is in order. After we define routing and routing requirements, we examine an overview of the two main functions of routing.

What Is Routing?

Routing protocols behave much like the postal service, which takes your mail and routes it through the post office to its destination. The function of a routing protocol is to route data from one network to another. Routing protocols accomplish this task by maintaining routing tables. Just like the post office maintains information on how to reach different homes, routing tables contain a list of networks and how to reach them.

For example, Network XYZ is reachable from Serial Interface 1 on the router. When source nodes attempt to pass data to destination nodes on remote networks, the router's routing protocols look up the destination network in its routing table. If the destination network is the same as the source network, the routing protocol drops and ignores the data packet. Otherwise, it routes the data out the appropriate router interface to either the destination network or another router that is connected or closer to the destination network. If the destination network is not found in the routing table, it is unknown and unreachable. If a default route is configured on the router, routing protocols will route all unknown destinations to the IP address or interface designated by the default route.

Routing protocols should not be confused with *routed protocols*. Remember: Routing protocols route data from one network to another. Routed protocols are protocols that are routed by routing protocols. For example, IP is a routed protocol that can be routed by the routing protocol OSPF.

Routing Metrics

When there is more than one route to a destination network, a router needs to determine which path to take. This decision is accomplished using routing metrics.

TABLE 1-1	Routing Protocol	Metric
Routing Protocol Metrics	RIP Version 1 and RIP Version 2	Hops
	IGRP	Bandwidth, delay, reliability, load, and MTU
	EIGRP	Bandwidth, delay, reliability, load, and MTU
	OSPF	Bandwidth
	BGP	Weight, local preference, multiexit discriminator

Routing metrics are assigned to router links to determine which route to a destination is the shortest. The route with the lowest metric is deemed the shortest and is used until another route to the same destination has a lower metric. In cases in which the route with the lowest metric is down, or offline, the route with the next lowest metric is used. If there is no other route to the destination, the destination network will be unreachable until the route comes back up.

Different routing protocols calculate routing metrics in different ways. RIP, for instance, uses hops to determine the routing metric. EIGRP, on the other hand, uses multiple attributes to calculate routing metrics. By default, EIGRP uses link bandwidth and delay to calculate routing metrics. Table 1-1 shows routing protocols and the metrics they use.

Now that you have a better idea of the routing metrics used by routing protocols, let's look at some possible scenarios and their solutions.

SCENARIO & SOLUTION

When implementing an internetwork of fewer than 16 hops with links having equal bandwidth, which protocol should I use?	Use RIP.
When implementing an internetwork of fewer than 16 hops with links having unequal bandwidth, which protocol should I use?	Use IGRP, EIGRP, or OSPF.

Default Route

When a workstation on a network needs to send data to a workstation on another network, a router is usually involved in making the communication possible. A router's function is to route data between networks. It does this by looking up the destination network in its routing table and routing the data to it out of the appropriate interface. What if the router does not find the destination network in its table? In that case, the network is unreachable. If a default route has been configured, all packets destined for unknown destination networks will be routed out the interface corresponding to the default route.

To add a route to a routing table, you issue the IP ROUTE command. Similarly, to add a default route, you again issue the IP ROUTE command. The following example configures a default route that sends all packets destined for unknown networks to 148.98.30.1:

```
ip route 0.0.0.0 0.0.0.0 148.98.30.1
```

Notice that all zeros were used. Zeros indicate unknown values. If we were adding a specific route to the routing table, the zeros would have been replaced with a valid IP address and subnet mask.

Load Balancing

In mission-critical environments, redundancy could be necessary. *Redundancy* refers to having multiple links to the same destination. If the primary link fails, the second link will take over.

Unfortunately, even though redundancy is a great benefit, it can also be a waste of network bandwidth. For example, if you have two redundant full T1 links to a remote network, one of the full T1 links will be in use while the other one remains idle. The bandwidth of a full T1 would be wasted.

To eliminate the bandwidth wastefulness of redundancy while maintaining its benefits, load balancing should be implemented. *Load balancing* allows multiple links to be used simultaneously. Using our redundant T1 example again, load balancing would provide us with the combined throughput of two T1 lines to the remote network. This allows all our available bandwidth to be used, if necessary, when both links are operational. If one of the links goes offline, the other link handles all the traffic. When the offline link comes back online, the traffic load is once again shared by the two T1 links.

Administrative Distance

On large internetworks, having multiple routing protocols is commonplace. For example, an organization might be running both OSPF and RIP. What happens if both routing protocols find a route to the same destination? Which route will the router use to transport the data?

In our example, the route found by OSPF would be used because OSPF has a smaller administrative distance than RIP. *Administrative distance* is a number from 0 to 255 that indicates the reliability of the route's source. The lower the administrative distance, the more reliable the source.

Let's say that a pro basketball coach gave you instructions on how to dribble a basketball. Then you were given instructions on the same action from a high school basketball coach. Of course, the pro basketball coach is a more reliable source for basketball information. In our previous example that used OSPF and RIP, OSPF is similar to the pro basketball coach, while RIP is like the high school basketball coach.

Table 1-2 shows the administrative distances for various routing protocols, according to Cisco. In a later chapter, you will learn how to modify these values.

TABLE 1-2	Route Source	Administrative Distance
Administrative Distances for Various Route Sources	Directly connected interface	0
	Static route	1
	EIGRP summary route	5
	External BGP	20
	Internal EIGRP	90
	IGRP	100
	OSPF	110
	IS-IS	115
	RIP	120
	EGP	140
	External EIGRP	170
	Internal BGP	200
	Unknown route	255

In an internetworking environment, it might be necessary to view the contents of a router's routing table. This view would assist you in troubleshooting routing protocol problems. For example, viewing the routing table would allow you to verify that a particular routing protocol is accurately discovering routes.

To view a router's routing table, issue the SHOW IP ROUTE command. This command displays the IP address of the remote network, administrative distance, route metric, next-hop address, and other route-specific information. The following output was generated by the SHOW IP ROUTE command:

```
CORBUS>sh ip route
Codes: C - connected, S - static, I - IGRP, R - RIP, M - mobile,
B - BGP
        D - EIGRP, EX - EIGRP external, O - OSPF, IA - OSPF inter
area
        N1 - OSPF NSSA external type 1, N2 - OSPF NSSA external
type 2
        E1 - OSPF external type 1, E2 - OSPF external type 2, E -
EGP
        i - IS-IS, L1 - IS-IS level-1, L2 - IS-IS level-2, * -
candidate default
        U - per-user static route, o - ODR

Gateway of last resort is 147.97.10.68 to network 0.0.0.0

C       147.97.3.0/24 is directly connected, Ethernet1/2
C       147.97.2.0/24 is directly connected, ATM1/0.1
D EX 214.113.180.0/24 [170/313344] via 149.89.2.14, 1d17h,
ATM0/0.3
                        [170/313344] via 149.89.13.6, 1d17h,
ATM0/0.4
O    215.201.128.0/24 [110/10542080] via 150.98.21.96, 2d07h,
ATM0/0.2
S    0.0.0.0/0 [1/1] via 147.97.10.68, 1d11h, ATM0/0.1
D EX    158.175.39.218/30 [170/288256] via 138.78.11.69, 2d08h,
ATM1/1.1
```

The first section of the output displays the codes for the routing protocols. The letters next to the route entries correspond to a code that indicates which routing protocol discovered the route. The line after the code key displays the gateway of last resort. In this case, any traffic destined for an unknown network will be routed to 147.97.10.68. The first two route entries are networks that are directly connected to one of the router's interfaces. The letter C in front of each entry means that the network is directly connected. Network 147.97.3.0 is directly connected to one of the router's Ethernet interfaces. Network 147.97.2.0 is directly connected to one of the router's asynchronous transfer mode (ATM) interfaces.

The next route entry, prefixed with D EX, indicates that network 214.113.180.0 was externally discovered by EIGRP. The administrative distance is 170, with a metric of 313344. This particular entry also shows load balancing in action. Both 149.89.2.14 and 149.89.13.6 load balance and route traffic to network 214.113.180.0. In this case, load balancing occurs through equal-cost OC-3 links.

The next route entry was discovered by OSPF. The O in front of the entry indicates this. The administrative distance of this entry is 110. The next entry is a statically created default route. This entry defined the gateway of last resort. The last route entry is another externally discovered EIGRP network. Notice that the entry's subnet mask, indicated by /30, is not using a standard Class B subnet mask. Network 158.175.39.218 is subnetted, leaving only 2 bits for host addresses.

To get even more information on a specific route entry, add the IP address at the end of the SHOW IP ROUTE command:

```
CORBUS>sh ip route 147.97.3.0
Routing entry for 147.97.3.0/24
  Known via "connected", distance 0, metric 0 (connected)
  Redistributing via eigrp 1329
  Routing Descriptor Blocks:
  * directly connected, via Ethernet1/0
      Route metric is 0, traffic share count is 1
```

Requirements for IP Routing

Unfortunately, IP routing is not Plug and Play technology. You cannot plug in a brand new Cisco 2610 router and expect it to fulfill your IP routing needs right out of the box. It requires some effort and configuration on your part. The following tasks must be accomplished in order for IP routing to work:

- IP routing must be turned on
- The IP address must be assigned to each router interface that will use IP
- The destination network must be present in the routing table

exam
ⓦatch

Since Exam 641-503 is a test on routing, you should know the requirements in order for routing to work. You should also know how to turn on IP routing.

Enabling IP Routing

Before any IP routing can occur, IP routing must first be enabled on the router. This is accomplished using the global configuration command IP ROUTING. To disable IP routing, use the global configuration command NO IP ROUTING. IP routing must be enabled on every router that will route IP packets. By default, IP routing is already enabled on Cisco routers. When IP routing is disabled, the running-config will have an entry that says NO IP ROUTING. Otherwise, there is no entry for IP routing.

Assigning an IP Address

After IP routing has been enabled, you are ready to assign an IP address to each router interface that will be connected to an IP network. This is accomplished using the interface configuration command IP ADDRESS *IP-ADDRESS MASK*. To remove an IP address from a router interface, use the interface configuration command NO IP ADDRESS *IP-ADDRESS MASK*.

Making Sure the Destination Network Is Present in the Routing Table

After IP routing has been enabled and IP addresses assigned, a final requirement must be fulfilled before IP routing will work: the destination network must be present in the routing table. Without this requirement, the router would have no idea where to route traffic.

Routing tables are the key to routing and are accessed by routers when making traffic routing decisions. It is important that routes exist in the routing table so that remote networks can be reached. Before a route shows up in the routing table, a couple of requirements must be met:

- The router interface must be up
- The route must be current

Making IP Routing Work

This exercise demonstrates the steps needed to make IP routing work. A Cisco router with a serial interface and an Ethernet interface is required. The IOS version should be up to at least 11.0.

1. Log in to the router's console.

2. Type **enable** to enter privileged mode.

3. Type **config terminal** to enter Global Configuration mode.

4. Type **ip routing** to turn on IP routing.

5. Type **interface ethernet0** to enter Configuration mode for the Ethernet interface.

6. Type **ip address 192.168.0.1 255.255.255.0** to assign an IP address to the Ethernet interface.

7. Type **interface serial0** to enter Configuration mode for the Serial interface.

8. Type **ip address 10.0.0.1 255.0.0.0** to assign an IP address to the Serial interface.

9. Type **exit** to return to Global Configuration mode.

10. Type **exit** again to return to Privileged mode.

11. Type **show ip route** to view the directly connected routes in the routing table.

The Two Major Functions of Routing

These days, routers are responsible for voice, video, and data. Although routers perform a multitude of functions, two major functions underlie the entire routing process:

■ Gathering and disseminating routing information

■ Switching packets from an inbound interface to an outbound interface

Without these two functions, other routing features would not be possible.

Gathering and Disseminating Routing Information

The first major function of routing is to gather and disseminate routing information. Depending on the routing protocol used, routing information can be processed in a number of ways. Routers use routing protocols to gather information about routes to networks by receiving updates from other routers. Routers also gather information about the network by monitoring the network's links for failure. Some routing protocols disseminate routing information by sending the entire routing table to multiple routers. Other routing protocols disseminate routing information by sending only updates of the routing table to multiple routers.

Switching Packets from Inbound Interface to Outbound Interface

The second major function of routing is to switch packets from the inbound interface to the outbound interface. When a router receives a packet on its inbound interface, it determines the best path to its destination. The packet is then forwarded to the outbound interface that connects to the best path. The outbound interface then sends the packet to its destination. The packet-switching process happens very quickly.

CERTIFICATION OBJECTIVE 1.03

Comparing Distance-Vector Protocols to Link-State Routing Protocols

Ultimately, there are two main types of routing protocols: distance vector and link state. Both types have their place in internetworks. Distance-vector protocols were created when internetworks spanning hundreds of routers were uncommon. Link-state protocols, on the other hand, were specifically designed for these larger internetworks.

This section explores and compares the two routing protocol types and provides examples of each. This section also introduces the topics of classful and classless routing.

Classful vs. Classless Routing

Before we can compare classful and classless routing, you must first understand the three main classes of IP addressing: Class A, Class B, and Class C. These IP classes allow for different network and host capacities. Each IP class has its own bit pattern that is used to denote its class and create the IP address. The first bit in an IP address octet represents 128 when the bit is on, or 1. Table 1-3 shows the value of each bit in a single IP address octet.

Class A addresses start with a bit pattern of 0, making 127 the highest number possible in the first octet of the IP address. The first 8 bits of the IP address represent the network; the remaining 24 bits represent the host. For example, the IP address 127.63.0.32 has a bit representation of 01111111.00111111.00000000.00100000. The network would be 127; the host would be 63.0.32. The standard subnet mask for a Class A address is 255.0.0.0, or 11111111.00000000.00000000.00000000.

Class B addresses start with a bit pattern of 10, making 191 the highest number possible in the first octet of the IP address. The first 16 bits of the IP address represent the network; the remaining 16 bits represent the host. For example, the IP address 191.24.0.2 has a bit representation of 10111111.00011000.00000000.00000010. The network would be 191.24; the host would be 0.2. The standard subnet mask for a Class B address is 255.255.0.0, or 11111111. 11111111.00000000.00000000.

TABLE 1-3	IP Octet	Value
IP Octet Values	00000000	0
	00000001	1
	00000010	2
	00000100	4
	00001000	8
	00010000	16
	00100000	32
	01000000	64
	10000000	128

Class C addresses start with a bit pattern of 110, making 223 the highest number possible in the first octet of the IP address. The first 24 bits of the IP address represent the network; the remaining 8 bits represent the host. For example, the IP address 223.96.0.128 has a bit representation of 11011111.01100000.00000000.10000000. The network would be 223.96.0; the host would be 128. The standard subnet mask for a Class C address is 255.255.255.0, or 11111111. 11111111. 11111111.00000000.

What Is Classful Routing?

Classful routing is the process of sending routing updates without advertising the subnet masks as an explicit part of the routing update per network. Classful routing protocols read the starting bit pattern of the IP address to determine its class. The subnet mask is automatically assigned to the IP address based on class standards. This means that a network with an IP address of 10.1.1.0 and a subnet mask of 255.255.255.0 would be advertised as 10.0.0.0 by classful routing protocols. The subnet mask would not be in the routing update. Routers that receive the routing update would recognize that the address was a Class A IP address and would assume that the subnet mask was the Class A standard 255.0.0.0, unless the receiving router were using that same network on one of its interfaces—say, 10.2.2.0 with a mask of 255.255.255.0. The receiving router would use the interface's network mask associated with that classful network.

Although classful routing is sufficient for most small internetworks, it has severe limitations on internetworks that implement subnetting. *Subnetting* does not conform to the standard class subnet masks. Subnetting allows a network designer more flexibility with the network implementation. For example, a single Class B network address can be subnetted into multiple networks according to the requirements of the network design.

Classful routing protocols do not handle subnetting very well. One problem is discontinuous subnets. Remember, classful routing protocols do not advertise subnet addresses.

Let's say that you have a single Class B network address of 191.148.0.0. The standard Class B subnet mask is 255.255.0.0. You would like to expand the number of networks and decrease the number of hosts per network. You decide to modify your subnet mask to 255.255.224.0. This gives you up to six subnets. You design your network as shown in Figure 1-4. As you can see, if we use a classful routing protocol, Router A and Router C advertise the same network address of

FIGURE 1-4

Classful routing
dilemma

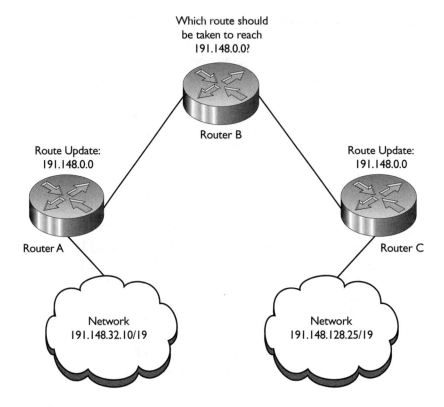

191.148.0.0, thus confusing Router B. This occurs because the classful routing protocols running on the routers advertise the standard Class B address without the subnet mask of 255.255.224.0 or /19. Router B assumes the subnet mask is 255.255.0.0 and fails to make a proper routing decision. This limitation prevents the implementation of subnets in this manner.

What Is Classless Routing?

Classless routing provides routers with the ability to advertise the subnet mask with each network address. This advertisement prevents classless routing protocols from making assumptions about the subnet mask. A Class B network with an IP address of 128.10.32.0 and a subnet mask of 255.255.224.0 would be advertised as 128.10.32.0/19 by classless routing protocols. The /19 indicates that the first 19 bits of the IP address will be used for the subnet mask. In bit notation, /19 represents 11111111.11111111.11100000.00000000.

Unlike classful routing protocols, classless routing protocols allow you to be more flexible with subnetting. The benefits of subnetting include the ability to expand a single network into multiple subnetworks and divide the network into more manageable pieces. Figure 1-5 demonstrates how classless routing protocols solve the classful routing dilemma.

Router A and Router C both advertise the subnet mask with their route updates. Router B receives the updates and updates its routing table with the appropriate path and subnet information. Router B can now route traffic successfully to networks 191.148.32.10 and 191.148.128.25.

Table 1-4 displays some of the classful and classless routing protocols.

FIGURE 1-5

Classless routing solution

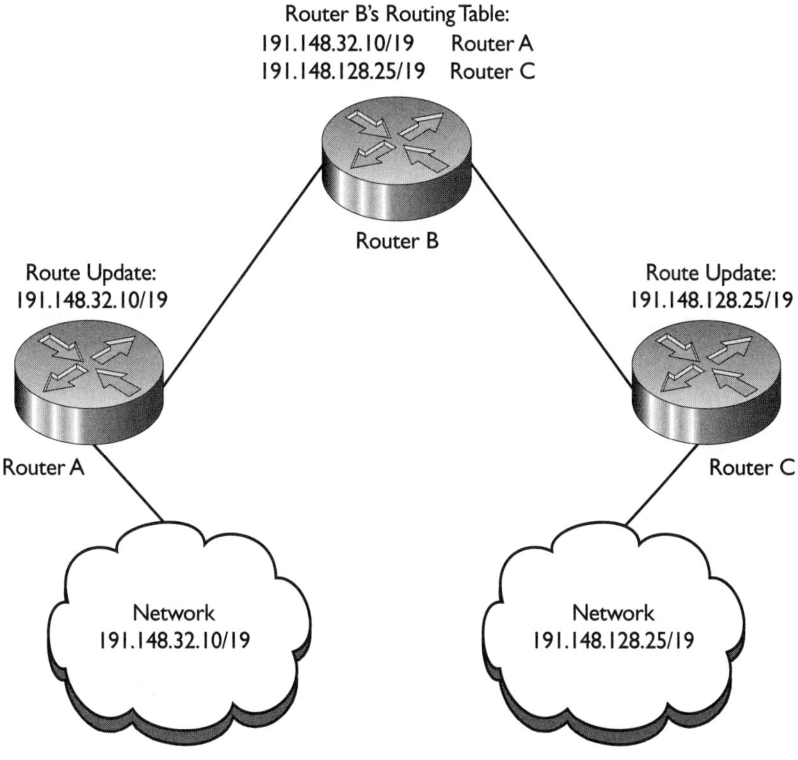

Router B's Routing Table:
191.148.32.10/19   Router A
191.148.128.25/19   Router C

Router B

Route Update:
191.148.32.10/19

Route Update:
191.148.128.25/19

Router A

Router C

Network
191.148.32.10/19

Network
191.148.128.25/19

TABLE 1-4	Protocol	Type
Classful and Classless Routing Protocols	RIPv1	Classful
	IGRP	Classful
	RIPv2	Classless
	EIGRP	Classless
	OSPF	Classless
	BGP	Classless

The IP CLASSLESS Command

When using the RIP routing protocol with subnets, a few problems arise. For example, the following output displays the routing table of a router running both RIP and EIGRP:

```
Corbus>sh ip route
Codes: C - connected, S - static, I - IGRP, R - RIP, M - mobile, B - BGP
       D - EIGRP, EX - EIGRP external, O - OSPF, IA - OSPF inter area
       N1 - OSPF NSSA external type 1, N2 - OSPF NSSA external type 2
       E1 - OSPF external type 1, E2 - OSPF external type 2, E - EGP
       i - IS-IS, L1 - IS-IS level-1, L2 - IS-IS level-2, * - candidate default
       U - per-user static route, o - ODR

Gateway of last resort is 10.1.1.3

C       147.97.3.0/24 is directly connected, Ethernet1/2
C       147.97.2.0/24 is directly connected, ATM1/0.1
172.24.0.0/16 is variably subnetted, 2 subnets, 2 masks
D       172.24.32.0/20 [90/10545152] via 10.1.1.1
D       172.24.32.0/24 [90/314368] via 10.1.1.2
S*      0.0.0.0/0 [1/0] via 10.1.1.3
```

If the router received a packet with a destination address of 172.24.33.1, the packet would be forwarded to 10.1.1.1. Likewise, a packet destined for 172.24.32.1 would be forwarded to 10.1.1.2. Packets destined for networks other than 172.24.0.0, such as a packet with a destination address of 192.168.1.1, would be forwarded to 10.1.1.3, the default route. So far, so good, right?

The problem arises when the router receives a packet destined for a subnet on 172.24.0.0 that is not defined in the routing table. When this happens, the packet is dropped. It is not forwarded through the default route, because the router believes it knows about all possible subnets for the 172.24.0.0 network. It simply does not know how to get to the unknown subnet of 172.24.0.0.

The IP CLASSLESS Global Configuration command resolves this problem by allowing the router to forward packets to subnetworks without being discarded. The IP CLASSLESS command informs the routing process to use the longest match in selecting the best route. The destination address 172.24.33.12 does not match the first 24 bits of the 172.24.0.0 subnetworks, so it cannot take those pathways to the next-hop address. The default route says that any packet that matches 0 bits can go to its next hop. When only classless routing protocols are used, the IP CLASSLESS command is not necessary. You can use the NO IP CLASSLESS command to turn off this feature.

Classless routing protocols inherently know about subnetworks. Classful routing protocols, on the other hand, require the IP CLASSLESS command to resolve the classful routing dilemma.

exam
ⓦatch

Because Exam 641-503 covers objectives relating to both classless and classful routing protocols, you need to know when it is necessary to use the IP CLASSLESS command on a router.

Distance-Vector Routing Protocol Characteristics

Distance-vector protocols perform well in small internetworks fewer than 15 hops wide. Distance-vector protocols are preferred over link-state protocols in internetworks of this size due to their easy configuration. In addition, distance-vector protocols are easier to troubleshoot and understand. Problems do not arise until the internetwork becomes larger and more complex.

To understand the limitations of distance-vector protocols, you must first understand how they work. When a network change, such as a down link, is detected, a distance-vector protocol updates its routing table and broadcasts the entire routing table to all other routers every 30 to 90 seconds when operating in a steady state. As the internetwork grows, you can expect to see the following problems when using distance-vector protocols:

- Convergence time increases
- Routing loops occur

■ Networks become unreachable

■ Broadcast traffic increases

Increased Convergence Time

Convergence takes so long because the routers now have to wait until another router volunteers a pathway to the down network. But before another router can volunteer a pathway, the routers must wait a set time limit to prevent routing loops. Convergence time increases as the network grows, because more routers need to be updated with route information. The more time it takes for the internetwork to converge, the slower the internetwork is perceived by end users. This is not a problem when there are only a few routers that need to be updated.

Routing Loops

Routing loops occur because routers on an internetwork are not updated at close to the same time. This causes routers to send outdated route information as though the information were new.

Figure 1-6 shows a network before and after a link failure was detected. When Router 2 detects a link failure to network 10.1.5.0, it updates its routing table and sends its entire route table to the other routers on the internetwork. Router 3 receives the update from Router 2 and updates its routing table. At this point, any packets received on Router 3 destined for 10.1.5.0 will not be sent to Router 2.

Router 1 still has not received an update for network 10.1.5.0. Since Router 1 thinks 10.1.5.0 can still be reached via Router 4, this incorrect route information is sent in the route update to the other routers on the internetwork. Router 4 receives the update from Router 1 and updates its routing table. Before Router 1 receives an update that network 10.1.5.0 is down, it has already sent out updates letting other routers know that it has a live route to 10.1.5.0. The other routers send packets destined for 10.1.5.0 to Router 1, while Router 1 sends the same packets to Router 4. This creates a routing loop. This is not a problem on small internetworks with a few routers, because the routers are updated at close to the same time.

Unreachable Networks

If distance-vector routing protocols are in use, internetwork growth can cause some networks to be unreachable. This is due to the hop-count limitation of distance-vector protocols. For example, RIP has a maximum hop count of 15. Any

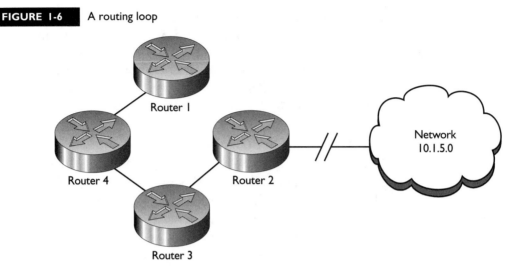

FIGURE 1-6 A routing loop

Before Link Down Detected:

Router 1 Route Table:	Router 2 Route Table:	Router 3 Route Table:	Router 4 Route Table:
10.1.5.0 via Router 4	10.1.5.0 via local interface	10.1.5.0 via Router 2	10.1.5.0 via Router 3

After Link Down Detected:

Router 1 Route Table:	Router 2 Route Table:	Router 3 Route Table:	Router 4 Route Table:
10.1.5.0 via Router 4	10.1.5.0 via Router 3	10.1.5.0 via Router 4	10.1.5.0 via Router 1

network more than 15 hops away is considered unreachable by RIP. Network growth should be monitored closely and a periodic re-evaluation of routing protocols should be done.

Increased Broadcasts

Distance-vector protocols are known for being "chatty." In other words, they put a constant flow of traffic on the internetwork. This traffic comes in the form of periodic broadcasts containing the entire route tables sent from routers running distance-vector protocols. The larger a network gets, the more routers there are to load the internetwork with broadcasts. Eventually, this process can cause varying degrees of slowness on the internetwork as network devices and end stations compete for bandwidth.

Organizations with large internetworks steer clear of protocols that operate using excessive broadcasts. The reason for this avoidance is that too many broadcasts can degrade network performance. When designing large internetworks, use routed protocols such as IP and routing protocols such as EIGRP or OSPF. This solution will allow your design to be more scalable and lacking in excessive broadcasts.

Distance-Vector Routing Protocols

Even though distance-vector protocols are plagued with routing issues as an internetwork grows, these protocols do have methods for functioning in these larger environments. These methods include the usage of timers and rules for preventing routing loops. Of course, if an internetwork grows too large and too complex, link-state routing protocols should be considered.

One method that distance-vector routing protocols use to manage routing loops is a *maximum hop count*. What this means for RIP is that a packet that has reached more than 15 hops in a routing loop will cause the router to mark the destination network as down in its routing table. This does not prevent a routing loop from occurring. It does, however, prevent a routing loop from continuing into infinity.

Split horizon is another method that distance-vector protocols use to solve the routing loop problem. Split horizon is basically a rule that states that route information cannot be sent back in the direction from which that information was received.

The last method that distance-vector protocols employ to defeat routing loops is *hold-downs*, which prevent periodic route updates from reinstating a route that has gone down. Hold-downs accomplish this using timers, allowing enough time for either the downed route to come back online or the network to stabilize before switching to the next best route. Hold-down timers are reset by triggered updates under the following circumstances:

- The hold-down timer expires
- The router receives a processing task that is proportional to the number of links in the internetwork
- The router receives another update indicating a change in the network's status.

Table 1-5 outlines the distance-vector protocols that are used to route IP

TABLE 1-5		RIPv1 and RIPv2	IGRP
Distance-Vector Protocols	Route update interval (seconds):	30	90
	Invalid timer (seconds):	180	270
	Hold-down timer (seconds):	180	280
	Flush timer (seconds):	240	630
	Maximum hop count:	15	255

EXERCISE 1-3

Configuring IGRP

This exercise provides you with a step-by-step method for configuring IGRP on a Cisco router.

1. Log in to the router's console.

2. Type **enable** to enter Privileged mode.

3. Type **configure terminal** to enter Global Configuration mode.

4. Type **router igrp 10** to start an IGRP process and enter Router Configuration mode.

5. Type **network 172.16.0.0** to associate the network with the IGRP routing process.

6. Type **show running-configuration** to view your new router configuration.

Link-State Routing Protocol Characteristics

Link-state routing protocols are very complex and can be extremely difficult to configure and troubleshoot in large, complex internetworks. Link-state protocols send *link-state packets (LSPs)* to other routers to inform them about the state of their links. This allows routers running link-state protocols to compile all of the LSPs received to create a complete topology map of the entire internetwork. The complexity of link-state protocols is not needed on small internetworks because network convergence happens so quickly. On larger internetworks, link-state protocols speed up convergence by sending updates immediately after a change has been detected.

The Link-State Routing Protocols

Link-state routing protocols do not have the same problems that distance-vector protocols have with routing loops. Link-state routing protocols prevent routing loops by employing a shortest-path-first (SPF) algorithm. Link-state algorithms allow the router to view the network topology as an upside-down tree with itself as the root. Table 1-6 outlines the link-state and hybrid routing protocols.

Link-State Routing Protocols vs. Older Distance-Vector Protocols

When comparing link-state routing protocols to distance-vector protocols, it is important to understand that both types of protocols have their place in internetworks. In other words, one type of protocol is not always better than another type.

For example, as a rule, distance-vector protocols should be deployed instead of link-state protocols for small internetworks. However, link-state protocols are preferred for large internetworks. One reason for this preference is that link-state protocols send a single change as a route update, but distance-vector protocols sending their entire route table minus split-horizon routes. This allows link-state protocols to more efficiently utilize bandwidth on internetwork links.

One of the drawbacks of using link-state protocols is that they require more processor and memory utilization on the router than do their older distance-vector counterparts. Table 1-7 compares link-state protocols to distance-vector protocols.

Now that you have a better idea of the pros and cons of the various routing protocols, refer to the following Scenario & Solution questions

TABLE 1-6	Protocol	Keepalive/Hello Timer (Seconds)	Hold Time (Seconds)
Link-State and Hybrid Protocols	EIGRP	5 (60 for low-speed links)	15 (180 for low-speed links)
	OSPF	10	5
	BGP	60	180

SCENARIO & SOLUTION

When routers have low memory but are connected to fast links . . .	Use a distance-vector routing protocol.
When routers have an abundance of memory but are connected to slow links . . .	Use link-state routing protocols.

Convergence Issues for IP Routing Protocols

Convergence is the time it takes for a link change to be detected and updated on every router in the internetwork. Three timers affect the speed at which most routing protocols converge:

- **Hold-down timers**   Used to avoid routing loops
- **Invalid timers**   Specifies how long a router should wait without receiving an update about a specific route before marking that route as invalid
- **Flush timers**   Specifies how long a router should wait without receiving an update about a specific route before flushing, or purging, the route from the route table

TABLE 1-7   Distance-Vector vs. Link-State Protocols

Distance-Vector Protocol	Link-State Protocol
Must trust route tables of other routers; not always accurate	Compiles an accurate topology map
Calculates best path using hops	Uses bandwidth analysis and other metrics for best-path calculation
Updates only occur at preset intervals	Updates occur whenever there is a link change
Requires less memory	Requires more memory
Requires less processor utilization	Requires more processor utilization
Requires more bandwidth	Requires less bandwidth
Less complex configuration	More complex configuration
Sufficient for small internetworks	Sufficient for large internetworks

RIP Convergence

RIP convergence consists of the following steps:

1. A link change is detected by the RIP router.

2. The RIP router waits for an update interval before broadcasting its routing table to other RIP routers. This can take approximately 30 to 90 seconds.

The size of the internetwork is the true determiner of full convergence time.

IGRP Convergence

IGRP convergence consists of the following steps:

1. A link change is detected. This process is instantaneous for FDDI, Token Ring, or carrier loss. Other media add a delay of about two to three times the keepalive timer.

2. The triggered update about the network change is sent to adjacent routers.

3. Routers send the entire routing table using periodic updates.

The size of the internetwork is the true determiner of full convergence time.

EIGRP Convergence

EIGRP convergence consists of the following steps:

1. A link change is detected. This process is instantaneous for FDDI, Token Ring, or carrier loss. Other media add a delay of about three times the 5-second hello timer.

2. The router looks for an alternate route in local and neighbor routing tables.

3. If an alternate route is found in local or neighbor routing tables, the router will use it.

4. If an alternate route is not found in local or neighbor routing tables, the router queries neighbors for an alternate route.

5. EIGRP routers update their routing tables with the updated route information.

In general, EIGRP convergence takes less than 1 second for normal failures of FDDI, Token Ring, and carrier loss. Of course, the size of the internetwork will ultimately impact convergence time.

OSPF Convergence

OSPF convergence consists of the following steps:

1. A link change is detected. This process is instantaneous for FDDI, Token Ring, or carrier loss. Ethernet and serial add a delay of about two to three times the keepalive timer.

2. OSPF routers exchange route information using LSAs.

   OSPF routers build new routing tables using the Dijkstra, or shortest-path-first (SPF), algorithm. This takes approximately 1 second.

3. There is also a built-in delay of about 5 seconds for the SPF delay timer.

The size of the internetwork is the true determiner of full convergence time.

CERTIFICATION SUMMARY

The beginning of this chapter provided you with the foundation to tackle the more complex concepts of this book. At this point, you have learned about IP routing protocols and their place in the IP protocol stack, as well as the OSI and DOD models. You should now have an understanding of how routing works and the elements that are required to make it happen.

In this chapter, you were introduced to distance-vector protocols and the concept of classful routing. RIP and IGRP were discussed as examples of distance-vector and classful routing protocols. You should now have an understanding of the benefits and limitations of these types of protocols.

You were also introduced to link-state protocols and the concept of classless routing. OSPF and BGP were the examples we used for link-state and classless routing. Additionally, the hybrid protocol, EIGRP, was introduced and defined as a cross between the best attributes of both distance-vector and link-state protocols. The pros and cons of each routing protocol were discussed and compared with the attributes of other routing protocols.

✓ TWO-MINUTE DRILL

Here are some of the key points from each certification objective in Chapter 1.

Routing Protocols and Their Placement in the IP Stack

❑ DOD model consists of four layers: Application, Host-to-Host, Internet, and Network Access.

❑ RIP and IGRP are interior gateway, distance-vector routing protocols.

❑ EIGRP is Cisco's proprietary, interior gateway, hybrid routing protocol.

❑ OSPF and BGP are link-state routing protocols.

Key Information for Routers to Route Data

❑ Default routes are used for packets with unknown destinations.

❑ Routing metrics are used to calculate route selection.

❑ The following tasks are required for routing to work:

  ❑ IP routing must be turned on.

  ❑ The IP address must be assigned.

  ❑ There must be a destination in the routing table.

❑ The following requirements must be met before a route can show up in a routing table:

  ❑ Interface up

  ❑ Route is current

Comparing Distance-Vector Protocols to Link-State Routing Protocols

❑ Classful routing is the process of sending routing updates without advertising the subnet masks.

❑ Classless routing allows routers to advertise the subnet mask of each network in route updates.

❑ Routing loops can occur when routers are not being updated at close to the same time.

❑ Link-state routing protocols require more memory and processor utilization than do distance-vector protocols.

❑ Distance-vector protocols are effective on small internetworks; link-state protocols are the choice for large internetworks requiring scalability for future growth.

❑ Convergence is the time it takes for a link change to be detected and updated on every router in the internetwork.

❑ Hold-down timers are used to avoid routing loops.

SELF TEST

The following questions will help you measure your understanding of the material presented in this chapter. Read all the choices carefully because there might be more than one correct answer. Choose all correct answers for each question.

Routing Protocols and Their Placement in the IP Stack

1. What are the layers of the DOD model? Choose all that apply.

    A. Application

    B. Host-to-Host

    C. Internet

    D. Data Link

    E. Network Access

2. What type of protocol is RIP? Choose all that apply.

    A. Distance vector

    B. Link state

    C. Interior gateway

    D. Exterior gateway

3. You are designing an IP network that will be 25 routers in diameter across links of various speeds. What routing protocol should you use?

    A. RIP

    B. IGRP

    C. RTMP

    D. NLSP

4. You have been commissioned to merge two networks. The first network uses only IP. The second network uses both IPX and AppleTalk. Which single routing protocol should you implement?

    A. IP RIP

    B. IGRP

    C. EIGRP

    D. OSPF

5. Which OSPF table stores the best routes from the topology table?

    A. Adjacency

    B. Topology

    C. BestPath

    D. Route

6. You are troubleshooting an OSPF problem on a router and want to verify that LSAs are broadcasting links to neighbor routers. What type of LSA would you be investigating?

    A. Type 1 LSA

    B. Type 2 LSA

    C. Type 3 LSA

    D. Type 5 LSA

Key Information for Routers to Route Data

7. What routing metrics do IGRP and EIGRP use? Choose all that apply.

    A. Bandwidth

    B. Cost

    C. Delay

    D. Reliability

    E. Load

    F. MTU

8. You are managing a network that is connected to the Internet via a router. What should you do to allow your users access to networks that are unknown to the router?

    A. Add a route entry for every network on the Internet.

    B. Configure a default route.

    C. Create an access list denying all traffic.

    D. There is no solution.

9. Currently, your company's network has redundant T1 links between the main office and a branch office. Management would like to take advantage of the inactive link's bandwidth. What should you do?

   A. Add more memory to the router

   B. Upgrade the router's processor

   C. Implement load balancing

   D. Load balancing is automatic on all routing protocols

10. What has the lowest administrative distance?

   A. OSPF

   B. IGRP

   C. RIP

   D. Directly connected interface

   E. Static route

11. You are troubleshooting a router problem in which a particular router is not routing IP. What could be the problem?

   A. A PC on the network is running both IP and IPX

   B. IP routing is not enabled on the router

   C. The router interface does not have an IP address

   D. The Windows 2000 server recently rebooted

12. What command enables IP routing?

   A. IP ROUTING

   B. ROUTING IP

   C. IPX ROUTING

   D. ROUTING IPX

13. What are the requirements for a network to be in the routing table?

   A. The interface must be up

   B. The interface must be down

   C. The route has to be current

   D. The IP CLASSLESS command must be executed

Comparing Distance-Vector Protocols to Link-State Routing Protocols

14. What type of routing sends updates without advertising subnet masks?

    A. Upperclass routing

    B. Lowerclass routing

    C. Classful routing

    D. Classless routing

15. You are designing a network that will use network 10.0.0.0 and have subnets of different sizes, such as 254 users on the Ethernet and a bunch of HDLC serial links which only need two IP addresses. What type of routing protocol should you use?

    A. Upperclass routing

    B. Lowerclass routing

    C. Classful routing

    D. Classless routing

16. Which are *not* classless protocols? Choose all that apply.

    A. BGP

    B. RIP

    C. EIGRP

    D. OSPF

    E. IGRP

17. You are using classful protocols on your network and need the ability to forward packets to subnetworks that do not appear in the routing table but should be forwarded to the default network without being discarded. What command should you use?

    A. IP CLASSLESS (Global Configuration command)

    B. IP CLASSLESS (Interface Configuration command)

    C. IP CLASSFUL (Global Configuration command)

    D. IP CLASSFUL (Interface Configuration command)

18. Your network staff wants to implement distance-vector protocols for their ease of use. What do you tell them is the trade-off for ease of use as the network grows? Choose all that apply.

    A. Convergence time increases

    B.   Bandwidth utilization decreases

    C.   Routing loops occur

    D.   Networks become unreachable

    E.   Broadcasts increase

19. What causes routing loops?

    A.   Routers being updated at the same time

    B.   Routers not being updated at close to the same time

    C.   Use of the shortest-path-first (SPF) algorithm

    D.   NetWare 5.1 server running Pure IP

20. What methods are used to prevent or alleviate routing loops? Choose all that apply.

    A.   Maximum hop count

    B.   Split horizon

    C.   Slow routing updates

    D.   Hold-downs

LAB QUESTION

Your customer is using both Cisco and Nortel routers in a large internetwork. What routing protocol should you use? Configure a Cisco router with the appropriate protocol.

SELF TEST ANSWERS

Routing Protocols and Their Placement in the IP Stack

1. ☑   A, B, C, and E. Application, Host-to-Host, Internet, and Network Access.
   ☒   D is incorrect because the Data Link layer is part of the OSI reference model.

2. ☑   A and C. Distance vector and interior gateway are correct because RIP is a distance-vector and interior gateway protocol similar to IGRP.
   ☒   B and D are incorrect because RIP is not a link-state or exterior gateway routing protocol.

3. ☑   B. IGRP. IGRP has a maximum hop count of 255, which will support the 25-hop network.
   ☒   A is incorrect because using RIP, networks that are more than 15 hops away would be unreachable. C is incorrect because RTMP routes AppleTalk, not IP. D is incorrect because NLSP routes IPX, not IP.

4. ☑   C. EIGRP can be used to route IP, IPX, and AppleTalk.
   ☒   A, B, and D are incorrect because IP RIP, IGRP, and OSPF route IP exclusively.

5. ☑   D. Route is correct, because OSPF uses the route table to store the best paths learned from the topology table.
   ☒   A is incorrect because the adjacency table shows information about neighboring routers. B is incorrect because the topology table contains all routes learned. C is incorrect because OSPF does not maintain a table called BestPath.

6. ☑   A. Type 1 LSAs contain links to neighbor routers.
   ☒   B is incorrect because Type 2 LSAs contain a list of routers connected to a network segment. C is incorrect because Type 3 LSAs contain route information for internal networks. D is incorrect because Type 5 LSAs contain information about ASBRs.

Key Information for Routers to Route Data

7. ☑   A, C, D, E, and F. Bandwidth, delay, reliability, load, and MTU are used by both IGRP and EIGRP as routing metrics.
   ☒   B is incorrect because cost is a routing metric configured by OSPF rather than IGRP or EIGRP.

8. ☑   B. Configure a default route. Default routes allow packets with unknown destinations to be routed to the next hop.

☒ **A** is incorrect because it is simply not feasible to manually add static routes to every network on the Internet. **C** is incorrect because an access list denying Internet traffic would defeat the purpose of being connected to an ISP. **D** is incorrect because a default route is a solution.

9. ☑ **C.** Implement load balancing. Load balancing would take advantage of the inactive link's bandwidth.
☒ **A** and **B** are incorrect because extra memory and processing power would not take advantage of the inactive link's bandwidth. **D** is incorrect because load balancing is not automatic on all router configurations—specifically, BGP, Apple's RTMP, and IPX RIP.

10. ☑ **D.** Directly connected interface. This answer is correct because a directly connected interface has an administrative distance of 0.
☒ **A** is incorrect because OSPF has an administrative distance of 110. **B** is incorrect because IGRP has an administrative distance of 100. **C** is incorrect because RIP has an administrative distance of 120. **E** is incorrect because a static route has an administrative distance of 1.

11. ☑ **B** and **C.** IP routing is not enabled on the router, and the router interface does not have an IP address. Routing requires that IP routing be turned on, with an IP assigned to an interface.
☒ **A** is incorrect because a PC running both IP and IPX would not prevent a router from routing. **D** is incorrect because a Windows 2000 server reboot would not prevent a router from routing.

12. ☑ **A.** IP ROUTING uses the proper syntax to enable IP routing.
☒ **B** and **D** are incorrect because ROUTING IP and ROUTING IPX do not use proper syntax. **C** is incorrect because IPX ROUTING enables IPX routing rather than IP routing.

13. ☑ **A** and **C.** The interface must be up, and the route has to be current. The interface must be up and the route current for a network to be in the routing table.
☒ **B** is incorrect because a down interface would prevent a network from being in the route table. **D** is incorrect because IP CLASSLESS is not a required command for a network to be in the route table.

Comparing Distance-Vector Protocols to Link-State Routing Protocols

14. ☑ **C.** Classful routing sends routing updates without advertising the subnet masks.
☒ **A** and **B** are incorrect because there is no such thing as upperclass or lowerclass routing. **D** is incorrect because classless routing advertises subnets with routing updates.

15. ☑ **D.** Classless routing advertises subnets with routing updates.
☒ **A** and **B** are incorrect because there is no such thing as upperclass or lowerclass routing. **C** is incorrect because classful routing sends routing updates without advertising the subnet masks.

16. ☑ **B** and **E.** RIP and IGRP are classful routing protocols.
☒ **A, C,** and **D** are incorrect because BGP, EIGRP, and OSPF are classless routing protocols.

17. ☑ **A.** This command allows a router to forward packets to subnetworks when classful routing protocols are in use.
☒ **B** is incorrect because there is no such Interface Configuration command as IP CLASSLESS. **C** and **D** are incorrect because these IP CLASSFUL commands do not exist.

18. ☑ **A, C, D,** and **E.** Convergence time increases, routing loops occur, networks become unreachable, and broadcasts increase as the network grows.
☒ **B** is incorrect because bandwidth utilization increases as a network grows.

19. ☑ **B.** Routing loops can occur when routers are not updated at close to the same time.
☒ **A** is incorrect because routers being updated at the same time would be optimal and would prevent routing loops. **C** is incorrect because the SPF algorithm is used by OSPF to prevent routing loops. **D** is incorrect because a NetWare 5.1 server running Pure IP would not cause routing loops.

20. ☑ **A, B,** and **D. A** is correct because maximum hop counts alleviate routing loops by ending them after a packet's TTL has exceeded the maximum hop count. **B** and **D** are correct because split horizon and hold-downs prevent routing loops.
☒ **C** is incorrect because slow routing updates can cause routing loops.

LAB ANSWER

You should use OSPF as the routing protocol because it is an industry standard that can be configured across routers in a multivendor environment. The following is a sample configuration for OSPF:

```
router ospf 5
network 10.0.0.0 0.0.0.255
area 100
```

2

IP Addressing
Issues

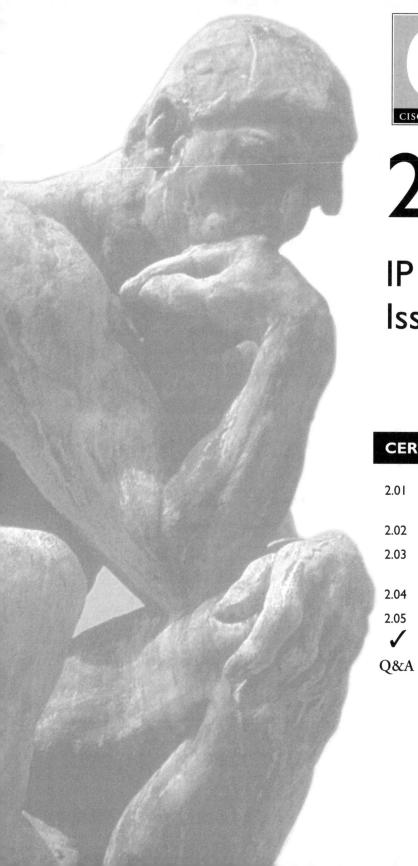

I n Chapter 1, we learned the differences between distance-vector and link-state routing protocols. You learned what information a router needs to actually route packets across the network. You also learned about classless and classful routing. We build on this knowledge in this chapter, which discusses IP addressing.

IP addressing is not a complex topic, yet it can be difficult to fully understand. IP addressing has several components that, if not presented properly, can create confusion. We start by discussing the basics of IP addresses, moving along to complex techniques such as subnetting, variable-length subnet mask (VLSM), and classless interdomain routing (CIDR).

First, we need to look at a few request-for-comment (RFC) documents. These are basically technical documents covering a given concept relating to the Internet. The RFCs can be viewed at http://www.faqs.org/rfcs; it is recommended you accustom yourself to reading RFCs. As a network engineer, you must read these beasts often, especially if you go for your CCIE.

CERTIFICATION OBJECTIVE 2.01

Requests for Comments Dealing with IP Addressing Issues

Internet-related RFCs were started in 1969 as a way to discuss the many aspects of the Internet. Protocols, programs, procedures, and various other topics were discussed. Today, thousands of these documents exist. This section points a few out pertaining to material in this chapter; it is recommended that you read them all along with this chapter.

RFC 950: IP Subnet Masking

Based on RFC 917, RFC 950 defines the proper usage of subnetting an IP address space. The procedures are for host nodes (workstations, for example), as opposed to in-between subnet gateways such as routers.

RFC 1518: Route Summarization

This RFC provides an architecture and plan for allocating IP addresses on the Internet. Basically, this RFC discusses the war on IP address exhaustion. The idea is to get all network managers to utilize CIDR (which is discussed in detail later in this chapter).

RFCs 1519 and 2050: Classless Interdomain Routing

Like RFC 1518 (discussed in the preceding subsection), RFCs 1519 and 2050 discuss concepts related to CIDR.

RFC 1519 is concerned with efficiently assigning the existing address space. CIDR is discussed to combat the depletion of IP addresses. RFC 2050 discusses IP address assignment policies and registry guidelines. Again, CIDR is discussed. All three of these RFCs discuss route aggregation/summarization and CIDR as ways to maximize the use of available address space.

RFC 1631: Network Address Translation

RFC 1631 discusses Network Address Translation (NAT). NAT can map a block of locally unique or private addresses to global public addresses. This way you can allocate a bunch of private addresses to your local area network (LAN). (Guidelines for private addressing can be found in RFC 1918, discussed in a subsequent section.) You can then map the private addresses to a few global IP addresses for Internet use. NAT, as you can probably see, is a good way to conserve address space.

RFC 1812: Variable-Length Subnet Masks

RFC 1812 is actually the updated version of RFC 1716 (*Requirements for Internet Routers*). RFC 1812 defines the proposed requirements of an IP version 4 router. Issues regarding VLSM are introduced here. (VLSM is discussed in detail later in this chapter.)

RFC 1918: Address Allocation for Private Internets

RFC 1918 gives guidelines on assigning private address space to your network. The advantages of making such assignments (not having to renumber devices when another network is added through a company acquisition, for example) are outlined in this RFC.

CERTIFICATION OBJECTIVE 2.02

IP Addressing

IP addresses, 32 bits long, are represented in the dotted-decimal format of A.B.C.D (for example, 192.168.1.2). The 32-bit address space is split into two parts: the network portion and the host portion. The boundary between the network and the host portion is defined by either the class of the address or the subnet mask associated with the address. This is a good time to bring up the fact that IP addresses are one of the only address types for which the network and host portion of the address can be different sizes. When you determine the network and node portions using the various classes of IP address, you are using a *classful* addressing model. When you simply apply a subnet mask to the IP address, you are using a *classless* addressing model.

We'll look first at the various classes of IP address, moving on to using subnet masks to split IP address spaces to fit your needs.

IP Address Classes

In the beginnings of Transmission Control Protocol/Internet Protocol (TCP/IP), the IP address's first octet determined the network (RFC 760). This system allowed only 254 IP networks to exist. Nobody expected the Internet to grow as big or as fast as it did; eventually, 254 networks simply weren't enough, so five "classes" of IP addresses were created (RFC 791); these five classes are A, B, C, D, and E. Of the five classes, two were experimental, leaving three common classes.

Each class has a range of addresses associated with it. You can determine the class of an IP address by examining the value of its first octet. A Class A IP address's first bit of the first octet is always 0, a Class B's first two bits is always 10, and a Class C's first three bits is always 110. Class D is used for multicast applications, and Class E is purely experimental. Our discussion is concerned only with Classes A through C. With this in mind, we can tell the beginning and ending value of the first octet for each class. As we know, there are 8 bits per octet, so a Class A's beginning value is 00000000, and its maximum value is 0111111. This gives us a value of 0–127 for our first octet (0 and 127 are reserved values, so we actually have 1–126). So 10.1.2.1 is a Class A address. A Class B address is 1000000 through 10111111, giving us a first octet of 128–191. Finally, the Class C address is 11000000 through 11011111, giving us a first octet of 192–223.

The idea behind the various classes was to split the address space into chunks of different network and host address spaces, providing networks that cater to a wide range of needs. Let's examine each class in detail. Class D and E addresses are not actually used to provide address space, so we do not discuss the number of networks and hosts for these classes here.

The Class A Range

The Class A address space uses 8 bits for the network portion, giving us 128 total networks, each having 16,777,214 allowed hosts. Remember, 0 and 127 are reserved, so we really have 126 Class A networks. Within these networks are 24 host bits, which give us 16,777,216 hosts, but each network needs a network number and broadcast address, so, not counting these two addresses, we have 16,777,216 allowed hosts.

As you can see, a Class A address provides an organization with a vast amount of hosts. Only the biggest organizations are assigned Class A addresses.

The Class B Range

The Class B address space uses 16 bits of network address space, giving us 16,384 networks, each having 65,534 allowed hosts. A Class B address is smaller than a Class A address, yet you are still allowed quite a large number of hosts. Class B addresses are suitable for medium-sized organizations.

The Class C Range

The Class C address space uses a 24-bit network address space, giving us 2,097,152 networks, each having 256 allowed hosts. The Class C address is perfect for small businesses and organizations; 2,097,152 networks is a pretty large number, but thinking globally, you can see how this number could be eaten up quickly.

The Class D Range

Class D addresses' first four bits are 1110, giving us 11100000 through 11101111 (224–239). Class D address space is used for multicast applications.

The Class E Range

Class E addresses have their first four bits set to 1111, giving us 11110000 through 11111111 (240–255). Class E address space is for experimental use only. You probably won't run into these addresses often.

RFC 1918: Private Address Space

Now that we've defined the various classes of IP networks, we can look at the address rangers specified in RFC 1918. RFC 1918 specifies address ranges for each class of network for private use. The ranges break down like this:

Class A: 10.0.0.0 255.0.0.0
Class B: 172.16.0.0 255.255.0.0 through 172.31.0.0 255.255.0.0
Class C: 192.168.0.0 255.255.255.0 through 192.168.255.0 255.255.255.0

You can see that this breakdown provides an organization with ample private address space. You'll notice all the examples use RFC 1918 private addressing; you should know these address ranges like your own phone number.

Subnetting Overview

Looking at the various classes of IP addresses, you can tell that splitting the network and host space in this way is not very efficient. A person has little control over how many IP addresses he or she gets. For example, if Company A needed 300 hosts, two Class C addresses would be the company's best bet. However, two Class C addresses provide close to 500 hosts, wasting around 200 IP addresses. A way to provide the right number of addresses had to be discovered. This is where *subnetting* comes into play.

Subnetting, in a nutshell, is using (or *stealing*) bits beyond the normal classful boundary, extending the subnet mask. This practice further divides a classful address space. You accomplish this task using subnet masks, defined in the following discussion.

exam
ⓦatch

Subnetting is a review for a CCNP candidate. Subnetting was covered under your CCNA studies. The exam will assume that you already know simple and complex subnetting, so topics such as VLSM, route summarization, and CIDR will be covered heavily on the exam, whereas subnetting will not. Of course, VLSM, route summarization, and CIDR build on subnetting, so it's essential you know this topic.

Subnetting and Its Benefits

Subnetting should be a review topic for you, but we start from the beginning to make this chapter's discussion complete.

Subnet masks are applied to a given IP address to distinguish the network address portion from the host portion. Subnet masks are written in dotted-decimal notation and are 32-bits long, just like an IP address. (Subnet masks are not addresses; they are masks that you apply to an IP address, bitwise.) It's vitally important to examine the exercises and examples in binary form to fully understand what this discussion. Here is how you examine a subnet mask in binary form: where you see a 1, the corresponding bit in the IP address belongs to the network portion of the address, and where you see a 0, the corresponding bit in the IP address belongs to the host portion. You must have contiguous subnet masks, which means that you have to have a steady line of 1s followed by 0s. You cannot have 0s between 1s. Each class of IP address has a default, or a natural subnet mask, associated with it. A Class A address has a mask of 255.0.0.0, a Class B address has a mask of 255.255.0.0, and a Class C has a mask of 255.255.255.0. To determine the network portion of an address using a subnet mask, as opposed to thinking classfully, you can write the IP in binary format and write the subnet mask in binary format directly below it. Take, for example, 192.168.1.3, with the subnet mask of 255.255.255.0 (see Figure 2-1).

Now you perform a Boolean (logical) AND function on the IP address and its mask for every bit position. The AND function compares two bits. The result is one and only one if the two bits are one; otherwise, the result is zero.

As you can see from Figure 2-1, 11000000.10101000.00000001.00000000 is our network address (192.168.1.0) written in binary format.

You can tell from our example why they call it a subnet *mask*: You "throw it over" an IP like a face mask, and it lets only the network portion through.

Subnetting creates greater flexibility in deploying IP addresses. For example, you might steal 3 additional bits in our example, making a subnet mask of 11111111.11111111.11111111.11100000 and creating additional space for network addresses. Notice we have fewer 0s available for the host portion now. It's important to realize that when you steal bits to extend the subnet mask, you leave less space for host addresses.

Throughout the book, you'll see IP addresses that look like this:

```
192.168.1.34/30
```

This is an alternate way of writing an IP address with its subnet mask. The /30 tells us that we apply a subnet mask that is 30 bits long to 192.168.1.34

FIGURE 2-1

The logical AND process

192.168.4.3 in binary is 11000000.10101000.00000001.00000011
255.255.255.0   =   11111111.11111111.11111111.00000000

After you AND =   11000000.10101000.00000001.00000000

(11111111.11111111.11111111.11111100, or 255.255.255.252). The slash (/) basically separates the IP address from the subnet mask length. You'll see this notation frequently when dealing with CIDR, discussed later in this chapter.

Let's look at subnetting a bit more closely now. As stated previously, you steal bits from the host portion to add to the subnet mask. It's important to realize that subnetting is equally dividing a classful network with X number of hosts. (VLSM is dividing an address space into different-sized chunks, as discussed later in this chapter.) You can think of this as similar to a pie chart. If you're assigned a Class C address space, think of it as the total pie, and when you subnet, you cut the whole pie into smaller, equal pieces (see Figure 2-2).

FIGURE 2-2

This network has four subnets; we need to split our Class C address into at least four sections

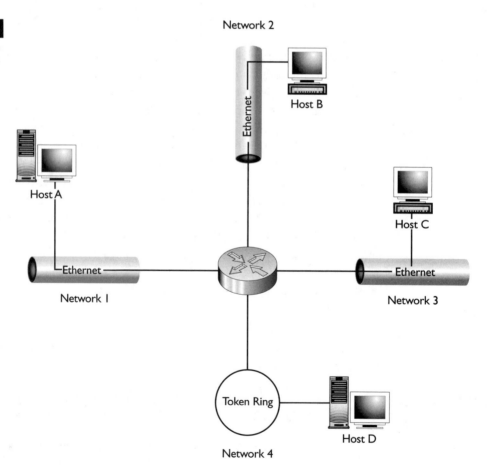

Now that we understand the theory behind subnetting, let's work through some subnetting examples. Say that you work for Acme Distribution, Inc. You administer a medium-sized LAN running TCP/IP. Your organization has one large Token Ring LAN segment and plans to remove a large number of hosts from the Token Ring, creating three 100Mbps Ethernet segments and keeping some SNA hosts on the Token Ring segment. We know that each segment is a network and will need its own network address. You were assigned the Class C network of 192.168.1.0. This was fine when you had the one Token Ring network, but your Class C network does not provide for four segments. You could use three more Class C networks, but in the real world, this is hardly ever an option. The answer is to subnet your Class C, cutting it into smaller but equal divisions. In this example, you need a minimum of four subnets, with no restrictions on the number of hosts in each. (Obviously, you would have a specific need for so many hosts per subnet, but for simplicity's sake, we'll assume you'll have the space.)

First, let's look at how we convert binary to decimal so we can decide how many bits we need to steal from the host portion of our Class C to provide at least four subnets. IP addresses have four octets (remember, an octet is a group of 8 bits). Each bit position of an IP address's octet has a decimal value associated with it. Starting at the rightmost bit, the value is 1 and rises in powers of two. For example:

1	1	1	1	1	1	1	1
128	64	32	16	8	4	2	1

The next octet repeats that formation, adding 128 + 64 + 32 + 16 + 8 + 4 + 2 + 1 = 255. So, to convert an octet written in binary to decimal format, you take any field that has a bit value of 1 and note the number that lines up with it, adding all these values together. For example, 10000001 has the first and last bits set, and we can see from the chart that the first bit is 128 and the last is 1, so this is 129 in decimal format.

When designing subnets and their masks, the number of available subnets under a major network address (a classful address) and the number of hosts in each subnet are both calculated with the same formula: $2 \wedge n - 2$, where n is the number of bits in the subnet or host space, and 2 is subtracted to account for the unavailable all-zeros or all-ones addresses such as the broadcast and subnet addresses. So, given the Class A network address of 12.0.0.0 with a subnet mask of 16 bits (255.255.0.0), we count only the bits passed to the natural subnet mask for the class. Since a Class A address space has an 8-bit network mask by definition, we have 8 bits of subnetting. So, we insert our 8 bits into our formula, $2 \wedge 8 - 2$, which yields 254 available subnets. We then have 16 bits left for host allocation, so we insert those bits into our formula, $2 \wedge 16 - 2$, giving us 65,534 hosts per subnet.

In the Acme scenario discussed previously, we needed at least four subnets to satisfy the requirements of the network. Use the formula $2 \wedge n - 2$ to determine the number of bits we need for the network or host portion. Since we're trying to find the number of bits to steal in order to create at least four subnets, we insert the number of bits of subnetting into the formula. Trying several values in place of n, we discover that 3 bits of subnetting is sufficient. Therefore, $2 \wedge 3 - 2 = 6$, so we get six possible subnets using 3 bits of subnetting; using just 2 bits gives us two subnets, which aren't enough. If you memorize the numbering used to convert binary to decimal format, you can simply look at those values, find the one greater than but closest to your requirement, and, based on which bit position the number lines up to, use that many bits of subnetting. We have determined how many bits to steal, so now we need to derive a subnet mask based on that number and then find the beginning and ending value of each segment.

We have 3 bits of subnetting, so our new subnet mask is 255.255.255.224 (11111111.11111111.11111111.11100000). You then apply that number to your router's interfaces as well as each host machine.

Now that we have derived our "custom" subnet mask, it's time to figure out the network addresses of our subnets and the available hosts addresses. There are shortcuts for accomplishing this task, but a shortcut leaves you not really seeing how subnetting works. Once you see what the subnet bits are doing, you can fully grasp subnetting and go on to be an excellent network engineer. The first step beyond allocating additional bits to your subnet mask is to write the classful network address in binary form, with the subnet mask directly below it. You then draw vertical lines around the subnet bits to mark the subnet space. Then you write every bit combination within this space, counting up from zero in binary (see Figure 2-3).

Figure 2-3 shows that the unchanged network bits are filled in to the left of the subnet space, while the host bits are filled in to the right of the subnet space. Converting the results to dotted-decimal notation gives you the six subnet addresses. Remember that

FIGURE 2-3	

Using every bit combination in our subnet space we can get all our valid subnet addresses

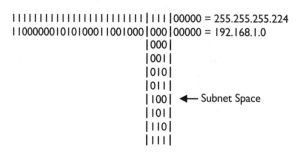

first and last addresses, which have the subnet bits 000 and 111, are not normally used. The final step is to write each subnet address in binary, starting with the host bits at 0 and counting up in binary from there until they are all 1s. The results are each host address. Bear in mind that when all host bits are 0s, you have reached the subnet address. When all host bits are set to 1, that is your broadcast address. Do not assign these addresses to hosts!

The benefit of subnetting should be apparent by now: it lets network administrators and engineers divide an address space between network segments, thus utilizing IP address space very effectively.

exam
ⓦatch

All you will have in the testing center is scrap paper and a writing implement. You will have no calculator to help you with all of this binary notation. It would be a good idea to memorize the eight bit positions and the numeric values associated with them so you can convert binary format to numeric, and vice versa, on scrap paper. The eight positions are in this chapter and are presented here as well for quick reference:

```
128 64 32 16 8 4 2 1
```

Because 11000000 has the left two bits set, we associate 128 and 64 with these bit positions and add them together to get 192.

FROM THE CLASSROOM

Binary Math Troubles

All of this binary discussion is hard to take in if the student does not have a background in it. It is a good idea to play around with binary notation and binary mathematics if you do not have any kind of previous binary experience. For example, learn how to count to 10 or 100 in binary. If you can learn how to count in binary from zero up, you can write IP addresses in binary format in a matter of seconds.

When you get time, write several numbers and IP addresses in binary and play with moving bit positions and logically ANDing two numbers. Learn how binary works. In doing so, all these subnetting and VLSM-style topics will be that much easier to understand. Besides, everything in computing relates back to binary.

—Richard Holland, CCNP, MCSE

Issues with IP Addressing

The explosion of the Internet has created several problems concerning IP addresses. At first, only 254 IP networks were allocated; then classes were designed to create more networks of varying sizes. As we discussed, even this isn't adequate. IP addresses are becoming scarce; ways to combat IP address exhaustion are needed.

Lack of Real Address Space: IP Address Exhaustion

If you have ever applied for a block of IP addresses, it is apparent that the Internet is running out of address space. Fewer and fewer large address spaces are being handed out, and strict rules on address utilization are being enforced. As a matter of fact, most Internet service providers (ISPs) are giving out only blocks of 16 addresses. That's 16 addresses, not 16 networks. You do not even get a whole Class C network unless you can provide very good justification for it, such as yours is an e-commerce business.

We now discuss the second major issue of IP addressing—the size of Internet routing tables—and then move on to discuss ways to combat these issues.

on the

ISPs apply for IP addresses from ARIN (www.arin.net). ARIN generally does not allocate CIDR blocks smaller than /20, giving you around 4,095 hosts, or 16/24 blocks. ARIN will go smaller than /20, but these are least likely to be globally routable. Check out www.arin.net and look at their other rules regarding IP address assignments.

Size of the Routing Table

Routers need a route to every destination in the Internet. You can only imagine the size of an Internet router's routing table. The more route entries a router has, the more RAM that is used and CPU utilization increases, taxing your pressure router in several ways.

The current size of the Internet routing table carried by the large ISPs contains over 70,000 summarized networks; the size of the full IP routing table is over 25MB. Without CIDR, a form of summarization, the number of entries in the routing table would be over 1 million networks. Imagine the time and process power required to search that table for the correct pathway for a packet going to network 200.100.50.0; your router might have to do this for 1 million packets per second. That is quite a load.

What Is Hierarchical Addressing?

Hierarchical addressing is a method for addressing your network devices in a logical tree fashion. The top of the tree is less specific in its addressing; as you move down the tree, the addressing gets more specific and is split up. The easiest way to understand this concept is to look at an illustration. As you can see from Figure 2-4, Router A advertises network 172.16.0.0 with a 16-bit mask to the Internet, making one route that encompasses the routes of Router B and Router C. Longer network masks reside on the bottom of the tree, whereas the top of the tree has a shorter mask.

FIGURE 2-4

A hierarchically addressed network

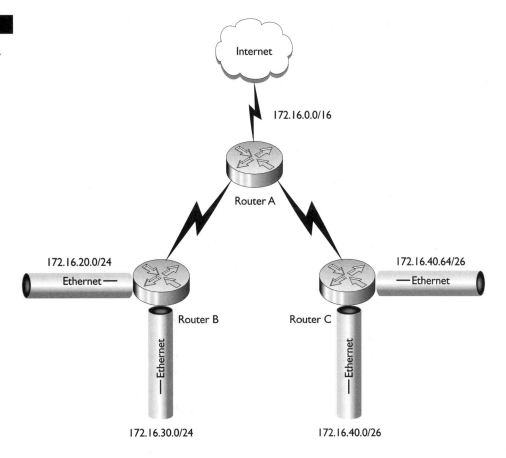

Benefits of Hierarchical Addressing

Addressing your network devices in a hierarchical fashion allows easy summarization of networks to upstream routers. Notice Router A in Figure 2-4 has to advertise only one route, 172.16.0.0/16, to all routers in the Internet. This keeps routing tables small and provides easier network administration. One of the keys to hierarchical network design is to keep your addressing contiguous. Notice that the networks attached to Router B are contiguous. If you had 172.16.20 .0 and 172.16.40.0, they would break the rule and require Router B to advertise the two separate networks to Router A rather than supernetting the two contiguous networks (discussed in detail later in the chapter).

IP Addressing Choices

When given an IP address space, you have several choices on managing the space. You might not even need to subnet, but it's a common practice. Subnetting on an octet boundary might suffice, or maybe we need a more complex setup such as the example in the preceding subnetting discussion. Maybe we need to use VLSM to divide our address space in a more efficient manor. It all depends on our needs and the kind of space we are assigned. Let's now look at an example of each.

Simple Subnetting

Simple subnetting occurs when your subnet mask ends on the boundary of an octet. For example, if you were given the network address of 172.16.0.0, you could use a 24-bit mask to create several Class C addresses. Your subnet mask would be 11111111.11111111.11111111.00000000. You can see that the mask ends on the boundary. The reason this concept is so simple is that you're basically breaking a given class of address space into smaller classes, just as the above example splits a full Class B address into several Class C addresses.

Both classful and classless routing protocols can use this addressing scheme. The key thing to remember is that classful routing protocols do not advertise a subnet mask with the subnet address, leaving the router with no way to determine the address space. RIP Version 1, for example, applies the subnet mask of the interface to the IP advertised. So, if you use VLSM, RIP V1 will possibly break, as will IGRP and so on.

Another thing to watch out for is discontiguous networks with classful routing protocols. For example, in Figure 2-5 you can see a three-router network that uses

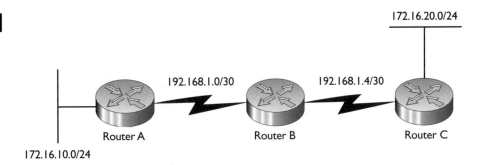

FIGURE 2-5

Discontiguous
subnets

172.16.20.0/24

192.168.1.0/30

192.168.1.4/30

Router A   Router B   Router C

172.16.10.0/24

the 172.16.0.0 network with 8 bits of subnetting. Most classful routing protocols autosummarize on network boundaries. Since Router A's serial interface is on the 192.168.1.0/30 network, classful routing protocols advertise 172.16.0.0/16, so the same thing will happen on Router C's serial link to Router B, causing Router B to get two routes to the network 172.16.0.0/16 and causing massive confusion.

One solution is to use the SECONDARY suffix on the IP ADDRESS IOS command. For example, on Router A you could go into interface configuration mode for the serial interface and type **ip address 172.16.20.1 255.255.255.0 secondary**, and do the same on Router B's serial link to Router A, changing it to 172.16.20.2 255.255.255.0, for example. This action causes Router B to remain a part of 172.16.0.0, making the network boundary summarization stop. The only problem with this solution is that updates for network 192.168.1.0 and 172.16.0.0 will be sent on that data link, using double the bandwidth. RIP Versions 1 and 2, IGRP, EIGRP, OSPF, IS-IS, and BGP can support simple subnetting. As mentioned previously, you must have the same subnet mask across the network for RIPv1 and IGRP to support this solution, so keep that in mind when implementing these protocols in your network.

Complex Subnetting

Complex subnetting was discussed in the subnetting section earlier this chapter. You extend the network portion of the subnet mask of a given class or IP address space, further dividing the address space equally. Let's run through another example to make sure you understand this concept.

Figure 2-6 shows the logical layout of a network. Router A has an Ethernet and Token Ring segment hanging off it as well as a serial link to Router B. Router B has a connection to the campus FDDI ring, an Ethernet segment, and the WAN link to Router A, making a total of five network segments. You were assigned the IP

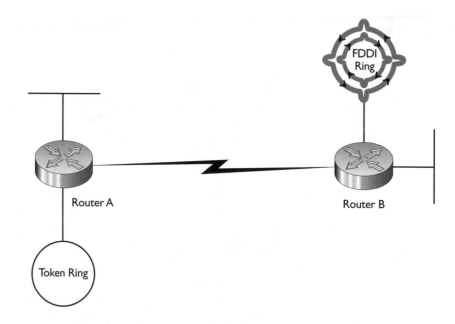

FIGURE 2-6

This network needs five subnets: one on each LAN segment and one for the point-to-point serial between the two routers

Router A

Router B

Token Ring

FDDI Ring

network address 192.168.1.0. This address provides you with 254 hosts but only one network. You need to subnet this space to create four subnets. Your company will add two more segments in the near future, so you need to account for seven total segments. Using 3 bits of subnetting (2 ^ 3 – 2) provides only six subnets, but using 4 bits (2 ^ 4 – 2) provides 14 subnets, easily meeting our requirements. Four bits of subnetting leave 4 bits left for host addresses; 2 ^ 4 – 2 leaves us with 14 hosts per subnet, and assuming this is satisfactory with the company, you've found your winner. Your new subnet mask is now 11111111.11111111.11111111.11110000, or 255.255.255.240 (192.168.1.0/28).

Earlier in this chapter we discussed how you find the start and end of each subnet and the host addresses for each address using binary notation. We now need to do this operation to find our subnet addresses and valid host addresses per subnet.

First, we write our network address and subnet mask in binary. Then we draw vertical lines around the subnet bits to mark our subnetted space. In this case, we draw our lines around the first and fourth bits of the final octet. We then count up from zero in binary format until all the bits between the vertical lines are 1s. This gives us all our subnets (see Figure 2-7). OSPF, IGRP, EIGRP, RIP Versions 1 and 2, IS-IS, and BGP support complex subnetting.

FIGURE 2-7

Counting up from
0 until all subnetted
bits are 1s gives us
all our possible
subnet addresses

```
255.255.255.224 = 11111111111111111111111|1111|0000
     192.168.1.0    = 11000000101010001100 1000|0000|0000
                                                    0000
                                                    0001
                                                    0010
                                                    0011
                                                    0100
                            Subnet Space - - - - ▶  0101
                                                    0110
                                                    0111
                                                    1000
                                                    1001
                                                    1010
                                                    1011
                                                    1100
                                                    1101
                                                    1110
                                                    1111
```

Therefore, writing each of these bits in binary, you can see we have 192.168.1.0, 192.168.1.16, and 192.168.1.32, all the way up to 192.168.1.240. So, we can give the WAN link in Figure 2-6 the 192.168.1.0/28 network, Router A's Token Ring segment the 192.168.1.16 network, Router A's Ethernet segment the 192.168.1.32 network, and so on.

Variable-Length Subnet Masking

Variable-length subnet masking (*VLSM* for short) is based on complex subnetting. The difference between VLSM and complex subnetting is that you use different masks throughout your network, splitting the network into different-sized subnets. Subnetting with fixed-length masks splits the network into equal chunks; VLSM allows you to allocate a large chunk to one network and then further divide your remaining space into smaller chunks. Let's look at a small example for now, moving on to discuss it in more detail in the next section. Figure 2-8 shows that Router A has a subnet mask of 255.255.0.0, whereas Routers B and C have longer masks. RIP Version 2, OSPF, EIGRP, IS-IS, and BGP support VLSM. RIP Version 1 and IGRP cannot use VLSM.

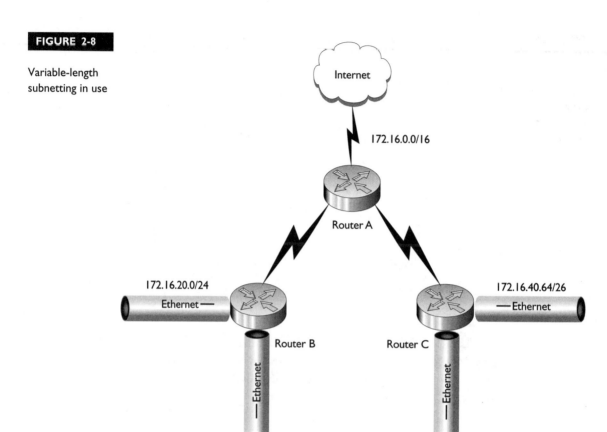

FIGURE 2-8

Variable-length
subnetting in use

EXERCISE 2-1

Subnetting

Your client has a network consisting of one Ethernet segment with a Cisco router
hooking the LAN to the Internet. The LAN has been assigned the Class C address
of 192.168.5.0. The client's director of technology wants to segment the LAN with
a router, confining the broadcast domain. Of the 100 hosts, he wants 50 on one
segment and 50 on the other. Your job is to subnet the 192.168.5.0 address space
into two subnets. The Internet side of the router uses the ISP's addressing and
needn't be dealt with in this exercise. Therefore, we need to split the address space of
192.168.5.0 in half.

1. The first step is to take a look at our needs, which is two subnets with 50 host addresses available in each. We also need to leave room to grow, so we'll shoot for more than 50.

2. Since the overall purpose of subnetting this network is to provide two network segments, we'll meet this requirement first, checking to make sure that both subnets have more than enough hosts.

3. Using our formula of $2 \wedge n - 2$, we look at using just 1 bit of subnetting. So, $2 \wedge 1 - 2$ gives us 0, which obviously does not work.

4. Using 2 bits yields two subnets, exactly what we're looking for. It is worth noting that if we could account for more than two subnets while still having more than 50 hosts each, we should do so to take into account future growth. For simplicity's sake, we'll stick with 2 bits of subnetting.

5. This creates 26 bits in the network portion, creating the subnet mask of 11111111.11111111.11111111.11000000 in binary, or 255.255.255.192.

6. We use the same formula to calculate how many hosts per subnet this address gives us. We have 6 bits for the host portion, so $2 \wedge 6 - 2$ gives us 62 host addresses. This gives us 12 extra addresses on each subnet, accounting for future growth.

CERTIFICATION OBJECTIVE 2.03

Maximizing IP Address Space Using Variable-Length Subnet Masking

VLSM provides network administrators the ability to create subnets of varying sizes by taking complex subnetting a bit further. Rather than apply one mask across the network, administrators apply several masks to the same address space, resulting in different-sized subnets. This allows us to give network segments the space they need, not wasting space. You'll recall from the preceding discussion that complex subnetting splits an address space up into *X* number of subnets of *equal* space.

Review of Complex Subnetting

Because VLSM is merely an extension of complex subnetting, let's review complex subnetting for a moment.

We stated before that complex subnetting involved using, or "stealing," host bits to extend the network portion, creating longer subnet masks. In this process, we extend the number of subnets we have while decreasing the host address space. Complex subnetting allows us to chop up a given IP address space among several network segments. Let's walk through an example of this process.

Figure 2-9 shows a network diagram of five serial links, one Token Ring, and one FDDI ring. These total seven network segments, each needing a network address. We were assigned the Class C network address of 192.168.5.0. We have seven segments, so 192.168.5.0 must be chopped into seven or more subnets.

Using the formula $2 \wedge n - 2$, we can see that replacing n with the number 4 gives us 14. Extending the network portion 4 bits will easily meet our requirements, giving each segment 14 hosts apiece. This results in the subnet mask of 11111111.11111111.11111111.**1111**0000, or 255.255.255.240.

In the last section we looked at an example in which we used 4 bits of subnetting to meet our requirements. Now we need to define each of our subnet addresses and the host addresses in each so we can assign them to our network. Figure 2-7 illustrates how we take the original network address in binary and, counting upward within the subnet space (4 bits in this example), we can derive our subnet addresses. Of course, our host addresses fall between these addresses. We have the following subnet addresses:

```
192.168.5.0
192.168.5.16
192.168.5.32
192.168.5.48
192.168.5.64
192.168.5.80
192.168.5.96
192.168.5.112
192.168.5.128
192.168.5.144
192.168.5.160
192.168.5.176
192.168.5.192
192.168.5.208
192.168.5.224
192.168.5.240
```

Therefore, the address 192.168.5.72 is part of the subnet 192.168.5.64/28.

There is a shortcut to all of this complexity. Once we figure out our new subnet mask, we add the number of hosts per subnet to our original network address. So, 16 + 0 gives us 16; add another 16 and we get 32. Do this for the number of subnets—in our case, 16 times. This gives you the subnet addresses of your network. Of course, your host address fall between them. This shortcut makes our lives much easier.

We can shorten this process even more by learning how to count in powers of 2. Counting up, we have 1, 2, 4, 8, 16, 32, 64, and 128. These numbers map to the

FIGURE 2-9

Because we were assigned one Class C address for this network, we definitely need to do complex subnetting

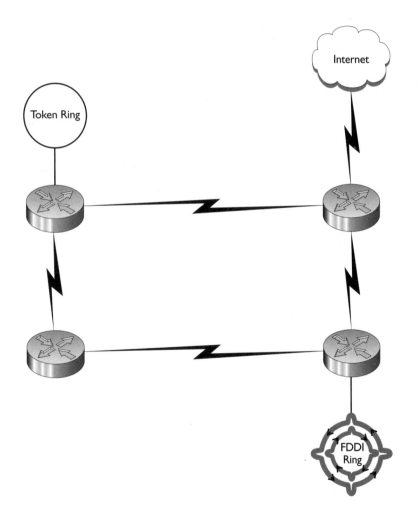

eight bit positions in an IP address octet, 128 being the eighth bit and 1 being the first bit. So, if you need 20 subnets, you can pick one of these that meets the requirements, account for the bit position it falls into, and that is how many subnet bits you need. In that case, 32 would do fine. (Keep in mind that you have to subtract the normal 2 for the subnet and broadcast addresses.) Figure 2-10 shows a possible addressing scheme for this example.

The same network as in Figure 2-9 with the devices addressed

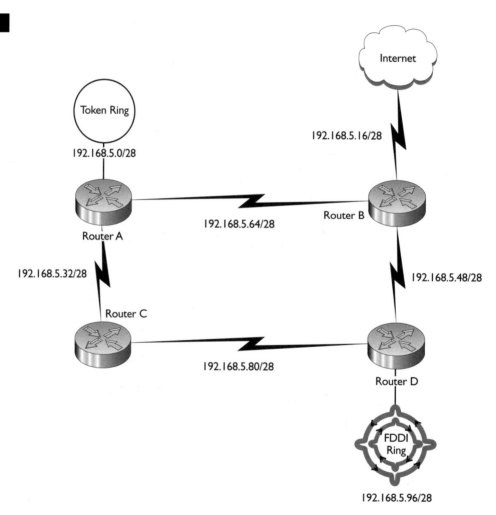

Now let's look at a few scenarios regarding complex and simple subnetting.

SCENARIO & SOLUTION

Can I simply subnet a Class C address?	No, a Class C address's octet boundary is the end of the address, so you have to do complex subnetting.
I have a Class C address and need to subnet it into 66 subnets. Can I do this?	No, you need to get more address space. Stealing 7 bits would do it, but it would leave you with only 1 bit for your host portion, which basically leaves you no hosts ($2 \wedge 1 - 2 = 0$).

Variable-Length Subnet Masking

VLSM was discussed briefly in the previous sections. It was defined earlier as simply an extension of complex subnetting, using variable-length subnets masked throughout the network. This practice provides more control in assigning subnets and maximizes your address space. VLSM allows us to chop a given address space into different-sized subnets, whereas complex subnetting only allows you to cut an address space into equal sections.

We accomplish VLSM by giving each subnet a different mask, which provides each subnet with a different amount of host space. You must be careful to make sure your subnets do not overlap, which is an easy mistake to make when you use VLSM.

Let's look at an example of VLSM in use. In Figure 2-11, you can see that we have five routers, each connected to several subnets. The core router at the top is connected to Router Hertell and Router Cover via serial links, and Routers Saunders and West Side are connected to Router Holland via serial links. Router Cover is connected to a 20-user Token Ring segment as well. Router Saunders is connected to a 20-user Ethernet segment. Point-to-point serial links are two-node subnets, so using normal subnetting, we could use 30 bits in our network portion, creating 64 subnets with four hosts on each. This provides us with just enough host addresses. However, this setup does not cover the 20-user Token Ring segments, and most real-world networks have more LAN segments with larger needs. Using VLSM, we can assign our 30-bit mask to only our serial subnets and use smaller masks that will give us larger subnets for our LAN segments, dividing our address space efficiently between networks.

FIGURE 2-11

A variably
subnetted
network

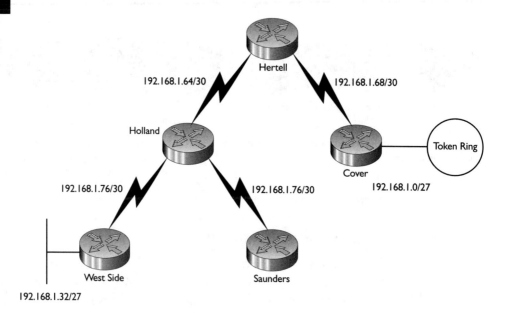

The first thing we want to do here is subnet for the segment containing the largest number of hosts. We have two LAN segments that need 20 users, so we subnet for those two first. Using the mask 255.255.255.224, we get five host bits; $2 \wedge 5 - 2$ is 30, so we get 30 hosts per subnet using this mask, meeting our requirement of 20 and giving us room for future expansion. We have three subnet bits, giving us eight subnetworks as follows:

```
192.168.1.0
192.168.1.32
192.168.1.64
192.168.1.96
192.168.1.128
192.168.1.160
192.168.1.192
192.168.1.224
```

We can use 192.168.1.0 for our Token Ring and 192.168.32.0 for our Ethernet segment, leaving us with six subnets left over to play with. Now that we have our large subnets taken care of, we need to provide for the rest. We have four serial links requiring their own subnet. We can take one of the leftover subnets—say, 192.168.1.64—and the mask of 255.255.255.252, which gives us 62 subnets with two hosts each, just enough for a point-to-point connection. Afterward we have split up 192.168.1.64 further into:

```
192.168.1.64
192.168.1.68
192.168.1.72
192.168.1.76
192.168.1.80
192.168.1.84
192.168.1.88
192.168.1.92
```

Remember, we don't want to go past 192.168.1.92; if we did, we would cross over into the 192.168.1.96 subnet we defined earlier. This would create severe routing problems. We can now apply any of those addresses to our serial connections, leaving plenty of address space for expansion.

You can see that implementing VLSM allows us to allocate enough host addresses to meet our segments' needs individually, maximizing our address space allocation.

Now that you've been presented several ways to subnet classful address space, let's take a look at some scenarios and solutions.

SCENARIO & SOLUTION

I'm using RIP Version 1. Can I still use VLSM?	No. VLSM will break classful routing protocols.
Can I turn autosummarization off for RIP Version 1 or IGRP?	No. These are classful routing protocols and do not advertise the mask.
Can I turn autosummarization off for IP classless protocols such as RIP Version 2 or EIGRP?	Yes. These protocols allow the use of the no autosummary command.

Applying VLSM

This exercise will further strengthen your understanding of VLSM.

You administer a small network consisting of three routers connected in a logical ring with point-to-point serial connections. Each router has a LAN segment with 20 users each. You need to utilize VLSM to assign each of the six network segments with the appropriate number of hosts. The network uses the address 192.168.1.0.

1. We need three subnets with two hosts per subnet for our point-to-point serial connections and three 20-host subnets for our LANs.

2. Starting with our point-to-point connections, we deduce that using 6 bits of subnetting will give us 62 subnets with two hosts each. We need only three of these, so we use the subnets of 192.168.1.0/30, 192.168.1.4/30, and 192.168.1.6/30. This brings us to 192.168.1.8.

3. We now need three additional subnets with 40 hosts each. Three bits of subnetting gives us six subnets with 30 hosts on each, so we now have 192.168.1.8/27, 192.168.1.40/27, and 192.168.1.62/27.

4. We set up our router's interfaces with these masks, and our host's addresses are assigned within their respective subnets, pointing to the correct default gateway address.

CERTIFICATION OBJECTIVE 2.04

Route Summarization

We can use *route summarization* as a way to combat the size of routing tables. As we discussed in previous sections, the size of a router's routing table can become a problem in large networks. Anything we can do to shrink our routing tables will make our lives easier and provide for better-functioning routers.

What Is Route Summarization?

Route summarization is a method of advertising a block of networks as a single network address and mask. For example, if you had the Class A network 10.0.0.0

using a subnet mask of 255.255.255.0, a person could advertise 10.0.0.0/8 to routers in other networks, summarizing a large number of networks into a single route advertisement. This practice is commonly referred to as *supernetting*. Supernetting involves taking several blocks of contiguous addresses and deriving one address with a network mask that will speak for them all.

You can perform summarization within an autonomous system (AS) and between ASs using CIDR.

Let's examine a few terms and look at their relationships to route summarization. Supernetting occurs when you use a subnet mask smaller than an address's natural mask—for example, 192.168.0.0/16. Supernetting, the direct opposite of subnetting, is used to group contiguous blocks of addresses together into one aggregate route. *Classless interdomain routing (CIDR)* occurs when you pay no attention to the high order bits of an address to determine its class. CIDR is in use when you present an IP address followed by the length of its network portion in a bit count—172.16.1.0/24, for example. CIDR was defined and implemented as an answer to classful IP addressing, so remember that with CIDR, there is no class of addressing, only the address and the length of its mask.

Performing Summarization Within an Autonomous System

Route summarization within an AS is closely related to hierarchical addressing. There are one or more core routers at the top of the "tree." The routers below the core hook to other networks and routers, advertising one route to the core router for all these networks. Figure 2-4, in the hierarchical addressing section, illustrates this concept. Routers B and C are both connected to a few networks, as well as connected with Router A. Router B and C can advertise one route, using supernetting (discussed in the route summarization walkthrough) to Router A.

Performing Summarization Between Autonomous Systems Using CIDR

Router summarization between autonomous systems works very similar to inter-AS summarization. The border routers in your AS advertise summarized routes to the other ASs. It is worth noting that CIDR basically involves advertising an IP address with its associated mask. In CIDR, we give no regard to classful network boundaries; we simply apply the mask to the IP address to obtain our network and host portions. So, a router advertises an address with a network portion length to the other routers in the next AS. The routers in the receiving AS can then add that address to their routing tables, routing all packets the other router advertised through the sending AS. An advertised CIDR block is commonly referred to as an *aggregate route*. Supernetting, mentioned earlier, involves shortening the bits of the network portion of an address to encompass more networks, creating an aggregate. So, you use supernetting to create an aggregate, which conforms to CIDR. These terms are a bit confusing, but just remember that supernetting is *not* CIDR; supernetting has to do with classful routing, as does subnetting. CIDR knows no super- or subnetting, only an address with the length of its mask.

Considerations for Summarization

You need to take several things into consideration when designing a network in which summarization will be used. We discuss these considerations in detail here.

Ensuring the Contiguous Block of Addresses

Route summarization and supernetting rely on *contiguous addressing blocks*. This means that blocks of addresses must not have other blocks of address spaces between them that you do not control. In other words, you can't summarize 172.16.20.0/24, 172.16.30.0/24, and 172.16.90.0/24, for example, because you do not own the address space between these three networks.

Ensuring the Same Highest-Order Bits for All Networks

Ensuring the same highest order of bits for all your networks will make sure your networks are all contiguous, for the most part. If you create your networks with this rule in mind, you'll inherently take care of the considerations we've discussed. For example, we stated that 172.16.30.0, 172.16.20.0, and 172.16.90.0 could not be summarized; let's take a look at these addresses in binary form to understand why your highest-order bits need to be the same:

```
10101100.00010000.00010100.00000000 = 172.16.20.0
10101100.00010000.00011110.00000000 = 172.16.30.0
10101100.00010000.01011010.00000000 = 172.16.90.0
```

You'll notice we've put the high-order bits these three addresses have in common in bold print. You'll also notice that .20 and .30 have 3 more bits passed that are in common. This leaves a huge gap, and if we supplied a summary of these three routes, it would not work. A router would think the advertising router (the router advertising a summary for the three networks) could get to the space between .30

and .90, so a packet destined to 172.16.72.4 would be sent to this router, even though this router has no knowledge of the network in which 172.16.72.4 lies. Furthermore, note that if we tried to summarize .20 and .30 with a 20-bit length, we'd oversummarize; we would speak for 172.16.16.0 through 172.16.31.0.

Ensuring the Block of Addresses Falls on a Power of 2, Bit Boundary

Your summarized addresses must fall on a power of 2, bit boundary. This means that if you have 10.1.4.0 through 10.1.7.255, all these addresses have 22 high-order bits in common, resulting in an aggregate of 10.1.4.0/22. On the other hand, if you have 10.1.6.0 through 10.1.9.0, this wouldn't work. In binary, 6 and 7 are 110 and 111, respectively, but 8 in binary is 1000, which moves us to the fourth bit position, crossing the bit boundary. We no longer have 22 common bits.

on the *Job*

We discuss black-holing routes by advertising summary routes that encompass more routes than you actually have, thus making some Internet routers think you have routes to networks you really do not have. This practice relates to Border Gateway Protocol (BGP) and can also happen with multihoming. Some networks advertise a block of addresses to one ISP and another block to a different ISP. Improper summary routes could cause packets for one network to go through the wrong ISP. Be aware of what you're advertising via BGP; it's a touchy situation, to say the least.

Rules for Summarization

There are a few rules to adhere to when using different styles of routing protocols. We mentioned discontiguous subnets and how classful routing protocols summarize falsely between them; we look at this subject more closely in the next section. In addition, we need to be aware of how classless routing protocols perform what is called *prefix-based routing* and how summarization affects this type of routing. We also discuss how routers and routing protocols use the longest match rule for route selection and how summarization intertwines with this concept.

exam *Watch*

You can bet large amounts of money that at least one question will crop up on your exam asking you to summarize some routes. All you'll have is your brain, scrap paper, and a means of writing, so you must get used to writing addresses in binary quickly. Luckily, the exam answers will be multiple choice, so if you make a big mistake, you can catch it more easily.

How Classful Routing Protocols Affect Network Boundary Summarization

Figure 2-12 shows a four-router network with three LAN segments and three serial connections. Router Holland is connected to an Ethernet segment with the network address of 172.16.20.0 and a 24-bit mask, breaking this Class B address into smaller Class Cs. The same situation is seen with Router Cover with its Ethernet segment of network 172.16.30.0 and Router North Side's Ethernet segment with the address 172.16.50.0. The point-to-point serial connection between Garn and North Side uses the network address of 192.168.20.0/24. This structure makes the network discontiguous.

Classful routing protocols perform route summarization between different networks classes, so Routers Cover and North Side will advertise the 172.16.0.0 to router Garn, creating a massive problem. Router Garn now has a route to 172.16.0.0 via Routers North Side and Cover.

FIGURE 2-12 Network boundary summarization will happen between Routers Cover and Garn

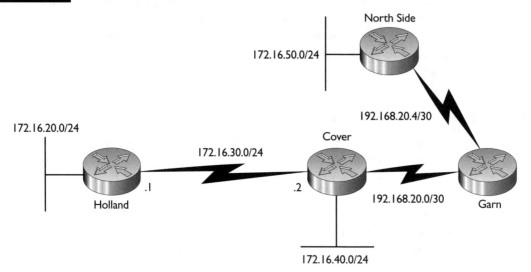

on the

Job

A very common situation in a job environment occurs when your company purchases another and both have their own routing protocols, addressing style, and network policy. Sometimes your well-designed OSPF network must integrate with a horribly designed RIP network, and, of course, you'll have to summarize between RIP and OSPF or whatever classless protocol you've chosen to implement. So, it's important that, even if you do not have classful protocols on your network, you understand how they handle summarization and discontiguous subnets. Be prepared: In today's volatile business world, there is no telling when your company could buy a large company that runs RIP or IGRP and whose network must be integrated with your well-designed and scaled environment.

Classless Routing Protocols Perform Prefix-Based Routing

Classless routing protocols advertise a prefix such as 192.168.0.0 and its associated subnet mask. This information is enough for classless routing protocols to define the network and host boundaries. CIDR is based on the same idea, but CIDR has no notion of the five classes of IP address.

Classless Routing Protocols Use Longest Match for Route Selection

The following code shows IP routing with routes to networks 192.168.1.0 and 10.0.0.0. Notice that network 10.0.0.0 is variably subnetted with three different masks. Route lookups are matched from the *longest match rule*, which means that the router will find the route that most closely matches the destination's bit count. For example, if a packet came in destined to 10.1.4.4, the router would match it to the route learned via Ethernet0 because it matches the first 26 bits with 10.1.4.0. On the other hand, if a packet came in destined to 10.1.5.2, the router would match it up with the route learned via Serial2 because it doesn't match the first 26 bits with 10.1.4.0, but it does match the first 16 bits of 10.1.0.0. If a packet came in destined for 10.2.2.2, it would be matched to the route on Serial0 because it doesn't match the first 26 or 16 bits of the other two routes, but it does match the first 8 bits of 10.0.0.0. This rule needs to be kept in mind when you are designing subnetted networks.

```
RouterA>show ip route
Codes: C - connected, S - static, I - IGRP, R - RIP, M - mobile, B - BGP
D - EIGRP, EX - EIGRP external, O - OSPF, IA - OSPF inter area
E1 - OSPF external type 1, E2 - OSPF external type 2, E - EGP
i - IS-IS, L1 - IS-IS level-1, L2 - IS-IS level-2, * - candidate default
U - per-user static route

Gateway of last resort is not set
C 192.168.1.0/30 is directly connected, Serial0
10.0.0.0 is variably subnetted, 3 subnets. 3 masks
R 10.0.0.0/8 [30/1] via 192.168.1.1, 00:00:26, Serial0
R 10.1.0.0/16 [30/2] via 172.16.20.4, 00:00:10, Serial2
R 10.1.4.0/26 [30/1] via 10.2.1.1, 00:00:04, Ethernet0
```

Route Summarization Walkthrough

Route summarization can make or break a network. Properly implemented, route summarization is an excellent tool, bringing route table sizes down. If mistakes are made, however, routing black holes and endless loops are sure to pop up.

Walkthrough Using a Binary Example

Let's look at an example of route summarization. Say that we administer a network consisting of 13 subnets, 10.1.22.0/24 through 10.1.34.0/24. We need to perform route summarization to lighten the routing updates BGP sends to our peer AS. Figure 2-13 shows these 13 subnets in binary format, starting at 10.1.22.0 down to 10.1.34. We must write these network addresses in binary format to view our high-order bits and determine a subnet mask to advertise with our summarizations.

You'll notice that networks 10.1.22.0 and 10.1.23.0 have the first 23 bits in common. In binary, 21 is 00010101, so summarizing 22 and 23 with their 23 common bits is safe, since any fewer would include 10.1.21.0, which isn't part of our block. It is always good to look at the next lower address in binary to be sure you're not advertising it as well. So, we know that 10.1.22/23 creates an aggregate for 10.1.22.0 and 10.1.23.0, and doing this with 22 bits would also put .21 and maybe a few more into our aggregate, which we do not want. So, now we look at .24 and beyond. If we look at the first 21 bits, we notice that .24 up to .31 are included in this group, and going up to 22 bits gets too specific. Therefore, we have 10.1.24.0/21. Next we look at our last three addresses and notice that they have the

FIGURE 2-13

Subnets for our example written in binary; notice the bits they have in common

```
00001010.00000001.00010110.00000000
00001010.00000001.00010111.00000000
00001010.00000001.00011000.00000000
00001010.00000001.00011001.00000000
00001010.00000001.00011010.00000000
00001010.00000001.00011011.00000000
00001010.00000001.00011100.00000000
00001010.00000001.00011101.00000000
00001010.00000001.00011110.00000000
00001010.00000001.00011111.00000000
00001010.00000001.00100000.00000000
00001010.00000001.00100001.00000000
00001010.00000001.00100010.00000000
```

first 23 bits in common. In binary, 10.1.25.0 is 00001010.00000001.00011001, which doesn't match its first 23 bits, so 10.1.32.0/23 creates our aggregate.

There are not really any shortcuts to summarization, and if there were, they would not be recommended for use. Creating bad summary routes is easy to do, and it makes nothing but trouble. When you summarize, remember to write down all your addresses and understand that you might have to create more than one aggregate, as we had to do previously. Write in binary the next lower address from your starting point, and make sure your length doesn't also include this address. If it does, you need to get more specific. Do the same for the ending address of your block. If you keep these things in mind and always deal with these concepts in binary, you'll have no problems at all.

Classless Interdomain Routing

Earlier, we briefly discussed CIDR. We defined the term as completely classless; you're given an IP address and network portion length (the address is commonly called the *prefix*, while the network portion length is referred to as the *length*). This makes network addresses such as 192.168.0.0/13 possible. Again, CIDR has no ties to the five classes of IP addresses.

CIDR was the next step after the five IP address classes, allowing us to have complete control of our network/host portions. What's the difference between CIDR and subnetting? Subnetting involves further dividing classful address spaces. CIDR knows no classes, so you can't further divide the space. CIDR blocks are assigned to ISPs and other organizations connected to the Internet.

CIDR Walkthrough

There is very little difference between CIDR and summarization. CIDR blocks normally have lengths less than what the lengths would be classfully. This means we can be assigned a CIDR of 198.24.0.0/13, giving us a range of 198.24.0.0 to 198.24.31.0.0. As you can tell, classfully we would have a bunch of Class C addresses used as a bunch of Class Bs.

Let's look at the above example in binary. Just as with summarization, writing all your addresses in binary format and looking at your highest-order bits are crucial steps. Writing 198.24.0.0 through 198.31.0.0 in binary looks like this:

```
11000110.00011000.00000000.00000000
11000110.00011001.00000000.00000000
11000110.00011010.00000000.00000000
11000110.00011011.00000000.00000000
11000110.00011100.00000000.00000000
11000110.00011101.00000000.00000000
11000110.00011110.00000000.00000000
11000110.00011111.00000000.00000000
```

Again, we have put the 13 high-order bits in bold, due to the fact that in our example, our CIDR block was 198.24.0.0/**13**. The first 13 bits match, of course, but because 198.23 and 198.32 don't match the first 13 bits, they can't be part of our CIDR block. It is important to write these addresses to make sure your aggregates that you advertise to other networks or ASs don't reference networks not on your network. So, double-checking your addresses in bit formation is a must, to make sure you fall on the correct boundaries. If we had 198.24.0.0/12, many more addresses would match the first 12 bits to 198.24.0.0.

CIDR is most commonly used in conjunction with BGP and is the way an ISP would assign network address space. If you were to apply for address space today, you would be assigned a CIDR block. Of course, you would probably get something like a /19 rather than a big /13.

When you deal with CIDR and route summarization, you must remember to make sure you're not advertising routes of which your network has no knowledge. There is nothing worse than an organization that gets a block of addresses, multihomes, uses BGP to advertise its networks, and advertises an aggregate describing networks not in their CIDR blocks. This creates "black holes" in the Internet, which occur when a router would route a packet to your AS, hoping to get to a destination your aggregate routers advertised to it, only to have the packet dropped by your routers because that network really isn't on your network. This occurrence tends to make most of us upset and want to jump out of windows high above the ground.

Remember, too, that routers and routing protocols alike use the longest match rule, which can affect routing. Look over your routing table, and make sure, if you have an aggregate and a more specific route or routes, that this is what is needed. Normally, aggregates are routed to Null0, stopping this madness.

Furthermore, we should clarify the terms *supernet, CIDR,* and *aggregate* once more. A *supernet* occurs when the mask of a given address is smaller than the address's natural mask. *CIDR* occurs when we use the *<prefix, length>* notation, and *aggregates* indicate a summary route. So, a CIDR block is not a supernet; CIDR doesn't deal with classes, but an aggregate could be a CIDR block or a supernet because aggregates are a form of route summarization, which can be accomplished using either a supernet or a CIDR notation.

exam
ⓦatch

It is very easy to confuse CIDR with summarization. Just remember that route summarization is a method of aggregating several routes into one, and CIDR is more a notation that does not refer to class. Therefore, CIDR does not have to be a form of summarization; it is actually how ARIN assigns IP address blocks. This allows address spaces smaller than Class B but larger than Class C to be assigned to an organization, and since they're mostly contiguous networks, summarization is inherent.

EXERCISE 2-3

Summarizing 192.168.1.0 through 192.168.10.0

Let's summarize 102.168.1.0 through 192.168.10.0 in this example.

1. First we need to write all 10 of our network addresses in binary:

```
11000000.10101000.00000001.00000000
11000000.10101000.00000010.00000000
11000000.10101000.00000011.00000000
11000000.10101000.00000100.00000000
11000000.10101000.00000101.00000000
11000000.10101000.00000110.00000000
11000000.10101000.00000111.00000000
11000000.10101000.00001000.00000000
```

```
11000000.10101000.00001001.00000000
11000000.10101000.00001010.00000000
```

2. We cannot summarize all these routes into one. However, 192.168.1.0 through 192.168.7.0 can be advertised by 192.168.1.0/21. We do not need to get more specific than 21 bits because 192.168.1.0 through 192.168.3.0, although they can be referenced by 23 and 22 bits, are included in our 21-bit mask.

3. 192.168.8 and .9 can be summarized as 192.168.8.0/23. Why can't we do 22 and include .10? Because that would also include 192.168.11.0 through 192.168.15.0.

4. The address 192.168.10.0 has to be advertised by itself.

5. You can see that the key to summarizing is writing the addresses in binary and figuring out whether or not your summary route would include addresses you do not want to speak for. We could easily create one summary that would speak for these addresses, but in doing so, we would be speaking for 192.168.1.0 through 192.168.15.0.

EXERCISE 2-4

Creating a CIDR Block

Here we create a CIDR block that will encompass 10.1.0.0 through 10.3.0.0.

1. First we need to write our three addresses in binary:

```
00001010.00000001.00000000.00000000
00001010.00000010.00000000.00000000
00001010.00000011.00000000.00000000
```

2. The first thing to notice is that we have a bit boundary problem here; 10.1.0.0 is on a different bit boundary than 10.2 and 10.3, so we cannot include 10.1.0.0 in our CIDR block.

3. The addresses 10.2.0.0 and 10.3.0.0 have the first 14 its in common, so 10.2.0.0/15 speaks for our two address blocks.

4. The address 10.4.0.0 crosses the bit boundary, so 10.2.0.0/15 speaks only for 10.2 and 10.3. This is perfect.

5. The address 10.1.0.0/16 has to be advertised separately.

CERTIFICATION OBJECTIVE 2.05

Related IP Addressing Commands

Now that we have the theory out of the way, let's look at some Cisco IOS commands relevant to what we've been talking about.

The IP UNNUMBERED Command

The IP UNNUMBERED command is commonly used in point-to-point environments to cut down on IP address usage. For any point-to-point serial link or point-to-point subinterface, IP UNNUMBERED lets you borrow the address of some LAN interface to use as a source address for routing updates and packets from that interface. No network is wasted, and precious address space is conserved. The syntax of IP UNNUMBERED is, in the interface's configuration mode. ROUTERA(CONFIG-IF)# IP UNNUMBERED ETHERNET0. This command gives the interface in question the same IP address as ETHERNET0. You can replace ETHERNET0 with any other active interface on the router that has an IP address.

You might be asking yourself, how are routing tables handled with this command? Normally, a router uses the source of a routing update as the next hop address. In the case of IP UNNUMBERED, the remote serial borrows its address from a LAN interface, ensuring that the source of routing updates won't be on a directly connected subnet. So, what happens is that the receiving router inserts the route as an interface route, bypassing the invalid next-hop address.

Figure 2-14 shows a two-router network, each with an Ethernet network with 172.16 subnetted. Both routers have the command IP UNNUMBERED ETHERNET0 on their serial interfaces. Both routers' Ethernet interfaces have the IP address of their network with a host address of 1. So, Router A has 172.16.2.1 on

FIGURE 2-14 The IP UNNUMBERED command is configured on the serial link between Routers A and B

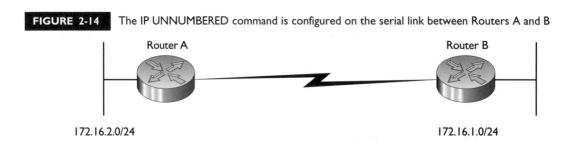

Router A   Router B

172.16.2.0/24   172.16.1.0/24

its Ethernet interface. Both routers are running IGRP. This means that Router A will advertise 172.16.2.0 via IGRP to Router B, with a source of 172.16.2.1. Router B will advertise 172.16.1.0 via IGRP to Router A, with a source of 172.16.1.1. Router A will insert the IGRP learned routes into the routing table with a next-hop address of its serial interface, and Router B will do the same. This saves us the address space we would have to use on the serial network. Please note that both sides of the link are not on the same subnet, and both sides need to use IP UNNUMBERED to be consistent. If one side did not use this command, the IP link would not set up.

The IP HELPER-ADDRESS Command

We learned early in our Cisco training that routers, by default, do not forward broadcast packets. Sometimes we need to forward them, however, so what do we do? The Cisco IOS, being as great as it is, offers us some commands to provide our routers in order to forward some broadcast packets to the right place. We'll get into these commands next.

The IP HELPER-ADDRESS and IP FORWARD-PROTOCOL Command Syntax

Two commands help us forward broadcasts in certain situations. The IP HELPER-ADDRESS *ADDRESS* command forwards certain UDP packets to *ADDRESS*. You can use the IP FORWARD-PROTOCOL {UDP [*PORT*] | ND | SDNS} address to pick and choose what you want forwarded. As you can see, you can specify UDP, with an optional port; ND (network disk, used in older diskless Sun workstations), and SDNS (Secure Data Network Services).

Default Broadcasts

When you issue the IP HELPER-ADDRESS *ADDRESS* command, eight protocols are sent to the address when they're broadcast:

- TFTP (69)
- DNS (53)
- Time (37)
- TACACS (49)
- BOOTP client (68)
- BOOTP server (67)
- NetBIOS name service (137)
- NetBIOS datagram service (138)

We can use the NO IP FORWARD-PROTOCOL command to specify that something should *not* be broadcast; otherwise, the eight protocols are always forwarded when we specify a helper address.

Walkthrough of a DHCP Exchange

Now, let's take a look at an example with DHCP. Say that you have a group of DHCP clients on an Ethernet segment, hooked to a router. The router hooks to your corporate headquarters via a Frame-Relay connection. The DHCP server lies on the corporate headquarters' Ethernet LAN, which is hanging off the router to which your router is logically hooked via the frame cloud. The address of the DHCP server is 10.1.2.1. It's important to realize that DHCP is a modified version of Bootp. With this in mind, we know that it uses the same ports as Bootp.

We need to get the clients' DHCP requests to the corporate LAN, where the DHCP server lives, so on your router, you do this:

```
conf t
ip helper-address 10.1.2.1
^Z
```

Now your router will take DHCP broadcasts, and set the destination address to a unicast of 10.1.2.1. Since 10.1.2.1 resides on another network, it does a route lookup, figures it needs to go to the corporate router over the frame cloud, and forwards it this way. The corporate router receives the unicast packet and gets it to the LAN segment, where the DHCP server picks it up. Since DHCP servers respond in unicast, we do not need a helper address set on the corporate router. Here is our configuration on our router:

```
ip helper-address 10.1.2.1
```

We can refine this command to forward only DHCP packets to the helper address by using this configuration:

```
ip helper-address 10.1.2.1
 ip forward-protocol udp 68
 no ip forward-protocol udp 69
 no ip forward-protocol udp 53
 no ip forward-protocol udp 37
 no ip forward-protocol udp 49
 no ip forward-protocol udp 68
 no ip forward-protocol udp 137
 no ip forward-protocol udp 138
```

exam
Watch

Cisco likes to include "fill in the blank" style questions on exams to test your knowledge of the IOS. It is very important that you memorize the syntax of the commands in this chapter as well as how to use the commands for various situations.

Figure 2-15 is basically the same example we just explored, but it provides a detailed network diagram so you can understand it better. You could also use a subnet broadcast address, such as 10.1.1.255, so you can throw the broadcast and hit an entire network segment, just in case you have multiple forwarded protocols with multiple servers.

Now imagine the same situation, but you have a TFTP server on another LAN segment — say, 10.2.1.0/8. The server's address is 10.2.1.5. By adding the command IP HELPER-ADDRESS 10.2.1.5, our TFTP broadcasts will be passed to the router on the top and then to the 10.2.0.0 LAN segment, where the TFTP server will pick up the packet. Figure 2-16 illustrates this procedure.

We could use the IP FORWARD-PROTOCOL command to pass only DHCP and TFTP packets, dropping all the rest. Our router's configuration would look something like this:

```
Ip helper-address 10.1.1.5
Ip helper-address 10.2.1.5
```

```
Ip forward-protocol udp 68 (dhcp)
Ip forward-protocol udp 69 (tftp)
no ip forward-protocol udp 53
no ip forward-protocol udp 37
no ip forward-protocol udp 49
no ip forward-protocol udp 137
no ip forward-protocol udp 138
```

In doing this, we limit the passing of broadcasts to include only DHCP and TFTP UDP packets. What if we wanted to keep the TFTP traffic from hitting the 10.1.0.0 LAN segment and keep DHCP traffic off the 10.2.0.0 LAN segment? We could create access lists on the outbound interfaces:

```
access-list 101 permit udp 192.168.1.0 0.0.0.255 10.1.0.0 0.
255.255.255 eq 68
```

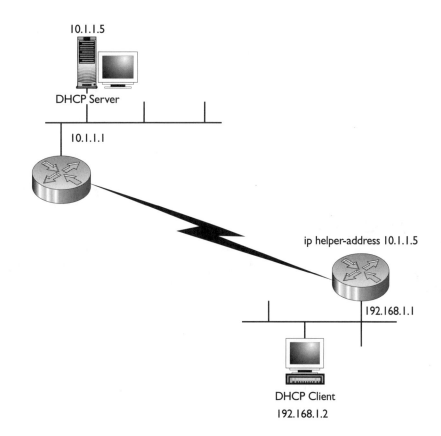

FIGURE 2-15

The router on the DHCP client side is configured to forward broadcasts to 10.1.1.5, the DHCP server across the WAN link

10.1.1.5

DHCP Server

10.1.1.1

ip helper-address 10.1.1.5

192.168.1.1

DHCP Client
192.168.1.2

The router serving the DHCP client now forwards broadcasts to both 10.2.1.5 and 10.1.1.5

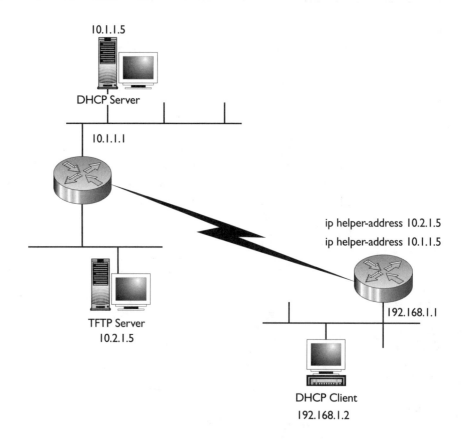

Apply this concept to the Ethernet segment of 10.1.0.0 outbound.

EXERCISE 2-5

Using the IP HELPER-ADDRESS and IP FORWARD-PROTOCOL Commands to Forward Broadcasts for DNS

1. Look back at Figure 2-16 for the network setup for this exercise. Notice that the DHCP server is a DNS server for the entire network. The TFTP server has no bearing on this exercise, so the host 192.168.1.1 must have DNS requests sent to the remote subnet. Therefore, on the router for the 192.168.1.0 subnet, we enter the command:

```
ip helper-address 10.1.1.1
```

2. We want to keep all broadcast traffic except the DNS requests from being forwarded, so we need to enter the command **ip forward-protocol udp 53**, in conjunction with NO IP FORWARD-PROTOCOL commands for the others you do not want to forward. The latter command will forward only UDP port 53, which is DNS, to 10.1.1.1.

```
access-list 101 permit udp 192.168.1.0 0.0.0.255 10.2.0.0 0.
255.255.255 eq 69
```

Apply this command to the Ethernet segment of 10.2.0.0 outbound.

Now that we have examined the IP HELPER and IP FORWARD-PROTOCOL commands, let's take a look at some possible scenarios and their solutions.

SCENARIO & SOLUTION

I need to direct all broadcasts to another host.	Use IP HELPER-ADDRESS IP_OF_HOST.
I need to direct all broadcasts to another subnet.	Use IP HELPER-ADDRESS SUBNET_IP.
I need to direct only DNS requests to a given address.	Use IP HELPER-ADDRESS in conjunction with IP FORWARD-PROTOCOL UDP 53 and no IP FORWARD-PROTOCOLS on the others for DNS only.

CERTIFICATION SUMMARY

IP addressing has several key parts and specific issues. Several requests for comment (RFCs) were created to specify why and how to use various IP addressing situations, such as the five classes, private IP addressing, and CIDR.

Subnetting involves dividing classful address space equally for network segments using bits in the host section for the network space of the address. Simple subnetting occurs when you take a class of address space — say, 172.16.0.0 — and divide it on an octet boundary, such as applying the mask 255.255.255.0 (which is for a Class C address) to create several Class C blocks out of our Class B address. Complex subnetting occurs when you take bits not on an octet boundary, such as applying the mask of 255.255.255.252 to 192.168.1.0 to create 64 subnets with four hosts each. VLSM is simply an extension of complex subnetting. You apply different masks to different segments to create different-sized subnets, maximizing address space. CIDR is a way of notating a block of addresses as one, using a prefix and length notation, such as 192.168.0.0/13.

A few commands in the Cisco IOS help you forward broadcasts between routed network segments. You can use IP HELPER-ADDRESS *ADDRESS* to specify a broadcast or unicast address to forward UDP broadcasts such as TFTP, NetBIOS, DNS, and DHCP. You can use the IP FORWARD-PROTOCOL UDP [PORT] | ND | SDNS command to refine your forwarding to whatever protocols or ports you want. You can define multiple helper addresses to point broadcasts to more than one subnet and apply access lists to confine your broadcasts to the correct segment.

Be sure you work through all examples you come across now and in the future in binary notation. If you do so, you'll soon be an expert on IP addressing and have a solid foundation for your CCIE, if you choose to pursue the pinnacle of all certification.

✓ TWO-MINUTE DRILL

Here are some of the key points from each certification objective in Chapter 2.

Request for Comments Dealing with IP Addressing Issues

❑ RFCs 1518, 1519, and 2050 discuss route summarization and CIDR.

❑ RFC 1918 defines private IP addressing standards.

❑ Internet RFCs were created to discuss various aspects of the Internet.

❑ RFC 1631 discusses Network Address Translation (NAT), which is a way to translate between private and public IP addresses.

❑ RFC 1812 discusses variable-length subnet masking (VLSM).

IP Addressing

❑ IP addresses are 32 bits long and, depending on the first octet value or the subnet mask, have a network portion and a host portion.

❑ There are five classes of IP address: A, B, C, D, and E. Each class has a different value for the first octet and network/host portion boundaries:

Class A = 1–126; the first 8 bits are used for the network portion.
Class B = 128–191; the first 16 bits are used for the network portion.
Class C = 192–223; the first 24 bits are used for the network portion.
Class D is for multicast operation.
Class E is experimental only.

❑ Subnetting involves dividing classful address space into equal subdivisions, unless you're utilizing VLSM.

There are three general ways to subnet an address space: basic (in which you subnet on the octet boundary), complex (in which you do not subnet on an octet boundary), and VLSM (in which you implement different complex subnetting masks on different network segments).

❑ Hierarchical addressing involves addressing your devices in a logical tree fashion, with more specific masks at the bottom and least specific routes and masks at the top.

Maximizing IP Address Space Using Variable-Length Subnet Masking

❑ VLSM is an extension of complex subnetting, simply applying different-sized masks to different subnets.

❑ VLSM allows more control over an address space.

❑ With VLSM, we can assign our point-to-point serial links a /30, providing four hosts per subnet, while utilizing the rest of our space for our LAN segments. This practice allows us not to waste valuable space on our point-to-point connections.

❑ It is important to look over your proposed VLSM addressing scheme to make sure you don't have overlaps due to improper subnet masks.

❑ Classful routing protocols such as RIP and IGRP do *not* support VLSM. Using VLSM with these protocols will yield very undesirable results.

Route Summarization

❑ Route summarization is a method of putting several routers together into one.

❑ A summarized route is often referred to as an *aggregate*.

❑ When performing route summarization, you must look at your addresses in binary form.

❑ When working in binary form, be sure to look at the next lower and next higher address blocks in binary, to make sure your aggregate doesn't speak for them as well. If it does, shorten your mask by 1 bit and try again.

❑ Route summarization is done by writing your addresses in binary format and counting the number of high-order bits that match, then advertising this number as your subnet mask.

❑ Summarized routes are commonly referred to as *supernets*, which occur when your subnet mask is shorter than the address's classful subnet mask.

Related IP Addressing Commands

❑ To forward broadcast for protocols such as DNS, TFTP, DHCP, BOOTP, TIME, TACACS, and some NetBIOS services, use the IP

HELPER-ADDRESS *ADDRESS* command, where *ADDRESS* is the IP of the remote server.

❑ Use the command IP FORWARD-PROTOCOL UDP [*PORT*] | ND | SDNS to further refine what you forward with the IP HELPER-ADDRESS command.

❑ Multiple instances of the HELPER-ADDRESS command can be used to account for multiple servers.

❑ Access lists can be used to limit traffic for one protocol from entering network segments the server(s) are not in.

❑ When you use the HELPER-ADDRESS command, broadcasts (only broadcasts defined in the preceding protocols or other situations with the FORWARD-PROTOCOL command are forwarded) are picked up by the router and re-encapsulated as unicast packets destined for the address or addresses specified.

❑ A unicast or broadcast address can be used as the address in the FORWARD-PROTOCOL command.

SELF TEST

The following questions will help you measure your understanding of the material presented in this chapter. Read all the choices carefully because there might be more than one correct answer. Choose all correct answers for each question.

Request for Comments Dealing with IP Addressing Issues

1. Which RFC defines the valid private IP address blocks?
   A. RFC 1920
   B. RFC 1918
   C. RFC 790
   D. RFC 1745

2. Which address range is *not* a valid address range for private use?
   A. 192.168.0.0 through 192.168.255.0
   B. 10.0.0.0 through 255.0.0.0
   C. 172.32.0.0 through 172.64.0.0
   D. 172.16.0.0 through 172.31.0.0

3. Which RFC defines Network Address Translation?
   A. RFC 1631
   B. RFC 1918
   C. RFC 791
   D. RFC 830

4. Which RFC defines CIDR?
   A. RFC 830
   B. RFC 2050
   C. RFC 790
   D. RFC 1934

IP Addressing

5. Your company has a small Ethernet LAN consisting of 20 users. Due to a recent expansion, 20 more users will be added from a different part of the building. You decide to put a router on your floor and on the new floor of the office to connect the networks. You hook the two routers together point to point with a serial cable and use PPP encapsulation. This creates three subnets, two for the LANs and one for the point-to-point between the routers. Your company has been assigned the class C network of 192.168.20.0. What subnet mask would meet the above requirements of three networks with around 20 hosts on each?

    A. 192.168.20.0/30 (255.255.255.252)

    B. 192.168.20.0/27 (255.255.255.224)

    C. 192.168.20.0/28 (255.255.255.240)

    D. 192.168.20.0/16 (255.255.0.0)

6. You administer a large network that has been assigned the Class B address of 172.16.0.0. You need to split this address into several Class C addresses for each of your branch offices. Which subnet mask will accomplish this task?

    A. 255.0.0.0

    B. 255.255.224.0

    C. 255.255.0.0

    D. 255.255.255.0

7. What is the purpose of the Class D address space?

    A. Multicast operation

    B. Experimental

    C. Video on demand

    D. On-demand routing

8. To what does the term *complex subnetting* refer?

    A. Using bits of the network portion for the host portion of the subnet mask

    B. Using bits from the host portion to extend the subnet mask

    C. Chopping address space into unequal portions

    D. Applying a different class's subnet mask to our network

Maximizing IP Address Space Using Variable Length Subnet Masking

9. You need to subnet a network containing four subnets, two point-to-point serials, and two 20-user LAN segments. You have a Class C network right now. Which address masks would *best* accomplish this goal?

A. Assign the point to points the mask of 255.255.255.252 and the LAN subnets 255.255.255.224.

B. Assign the point to points the mask of 255.255.255.240 and the LAN segments 255.255.255.224.

C. Assign the point to points the mask of 255.255.255.252 and the LAN segments 255.255.0.0.

D. None of the above.

10. Which routing protocols support VLSM? Choose all that apply.

A. RIP

B. OSPF

C. EIGRP

D. IGRP

11. Your manager wants you to apply VLSM to your network, which runs RIP Version 1. You develop a VLSM scheme, giving each network segment enough host addresses. You apply the changes to all your network devices. Upon doing so, you have reachability problems between some subnets. What is most likely the problem?

A. Your masks create address overlaps

B. RIP Version 1 does not support VLSM

C. You need to give the network time to converge

D. Some of your physical links are down

12. How does VLSM use address space more efficiently than complex subnetting?

A. Complex subnetting divides address space into equal sections, whereas VLSM allows us to divide address space into unequal portions, giving us the ability to assign each subnet exactly what we need.

B. Complex subnetting doesn't use bits in a way that we would like, and VLSM does.

C. VLSM allows for summarization, whereas complex subnetting does not.

D. They are both equally efficient in IP address utilization.

Route Summarization

13. What is route summarization?

    A. A type of OSPF LSA

    B. What BGP is used for

    C. Combining several network addresses into one

    D. Classless interdomain routing

14. How could 192.168.2.0 and 192.168.3.0 be summarized?

    A. 192.168.2.0/23

    B. 192.168.0.0/22

    C. 192.168.2.0/30

    D. 192.168.2.0/29

15. Your company has four subnets connected to the Internet via a Cisco router. The router advertises your routes via BGP. Your addresses are 10.0.2.0. (For this example, disregard that it is an RFC 1918 address space) through 10.0.15.0. How could you advertise this as a summary route?

    A. You can't summarize these with one route

    B. 10.0.2.0/20

    C. 10.0.0.0/20

    D. 10.0.2.0/21

16. Your company has been assigned the CIDR block 192.168.0.0/20. What is your address range?

    A. 192.168.0.0 through 192.168.255.0

    B. 192.168.0.0 through 192.168.15.0

    C. 192.168.0.0 through 192.168.16.0

    D. This isn't a valid CIDR block

Related IP Addressing Commands

17. Your network consists of two LAN subnets separated by a T1 between two routers. You need to forward only DNS requests from LAN1 to LAN2. You have already configured the correct IP HELPER-ADDRESS on LAN1's router. What is the next command you should execute?

A. IP CLASSLESS

B. IP ROUTING

C. IP FORWARD-PROTOCOL DNS

D. IP FORWARD-PROTOCOL UDP 53 with no IP FORWARD-PROTOCOL commands for the other UDP ports of the default eight you don't want to forward

18. You need to forward broadcast requests to the entire network 192.168.2.0 from 192.168.1.0. What command line would you enter on 192.168.1.0's router?

A. IP HELPER-ADDRESS 192.168.1.0

B. IP HELPER-ADDRESS 192.168.2.255

C. IP HELPER-ADDRESS SUBNET-BROADCAST 192.168.2.0

D. IP HELPER-ADDRESS will not do this; you can only give it unicast addresses

19. You have a point-to-point connection between two of your routers. To conserve IP addresses, you want to use your Token Ring 0 IP address as the address for your serial point-to-point connection. What command would accomplish this goal, entered on both routers under serial0's interface configuration mode?

A. IP UNNUMBERED

B. IP UNNUMBERED TO0

C. IP UNNUMBERED POINT-TO-POINT

D. This is not possible

20. Your network has a TFTP server and a DHCP server on subnet1 and a collection of hosts that need to use these services on subnet2. Subnet1 is hooked to Router A, which is hooked to Router B. Router B hooks to subnet2. What commands on Router B would only forward TFTP and DHCP to subnet1?

A. IP HELPER-ADDRESS SUBNET1'S IP and IP FORWARD-PROTOCOL UDP 68 and IP FORWARD-PROTOCOL UDP 69, with NO IP FORWARD-PROTOCOLS for the other UDP ports

B. This can't be done

C. IP FORWARD-PROTOCOL DNS and IP FORWARD-PROTOCOL TFTP

D. IP FORWARD-PROTOCOL 68 and IP FORWARD-PROTOCOL 69

LAB QUESTION

Figure 2-17 illustrates a three-router network. The top router has a WAN connection to the Internet. Each router is hooked to the others via a T1 with Frame Relay encapsulation. The bottom two routers have Ethernet segments with 20 users each. A TACACS server resides on one of the Ethernet segments. Using the Class C address of 192.168.20.0, subnet this with VLSM to provide for the two 20-user LAN segments and the three point-to-point networks. Set up the top router and the rightmost router to forward TACACS traffic to the subnet with the TACACS server. Make sure you can summarize this network to the Internet.

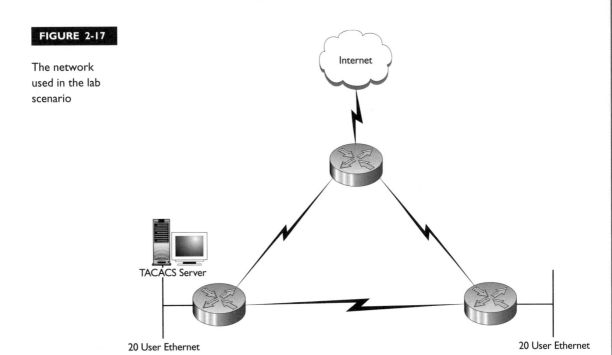

FIGURE 2-17

The network used in the lab scenario

SELF TEST ANSWERS

Request for Comments Dealing with IP Addressing Issues

1. ☑ **B.** RFC 1918 defines the classes of private IP addresses.
   ☒ **A, C,** and **D** are incorrect because RFCs 1920, 790, and 1745 discuss topics other than private IP address blocks.

2. ☑ **C.** The range 172.32.0.0 through 172.64.0.0 is not a valid RFC 1918 range.
   ☒ **A, B,** and **D** are incorrect because they are valid address ranges for private use.

3. ☑ **A.** RFC 1631 deals with NAT.
   ☒ **B, C,** and **D** are incorrect because they are RFCs that discuss other topics.

4. ☑ **B.** RFC 2050 outlines classless interdomain routing (CIDR).
   ☒ **A, C,** and **D** are incorrect because these RFCs do not discuss CIDR.

IP Addressing

5. ☑ **B.** 192.168.20.0/27 (255.255.255.224) gives us six subnets with 30 hosts on each ($2 \wedge 3 - 2 = 6$, $2 \wedge 5 - 2 = 30$).
   ☒ **A** is incorrect because 192.168.20.0/30 (255.255.255.252) gives us 62 subnets with two hosts on each. **C** is incorrect because 192.168.20.0/28 (255.255.255.240) gives us 14 subnets with 14 hosts on each. **D** is incorrect because 192.168.20.0/16 (255.255.0.0) is a supernet, speaking for additional Class Cs.

6. ☑ **D.** The address 255.255.255.0 is the natural address mask for a Class C, splitting the Class B up into several Class Cs.
   ☒ **A** is incorrect because 255.0.0.0 would supernet our address like a Class A. **B** is incorrect because 255.255.224.0 would complex subnet our Class B, giving us more subnets but not splitting it up into Class Cs. **C** is incorrect because 255.255.0.0 is the classful mask for a Class B and does not subnet our space at all.

7. ☑ **A.** Multicast operation is the purpose of the Class D address space.
   ☒ **B** is incorrect because "experimental" describes the purpose of the Class E address space. **C** and **D** are incorrect because video on demand and on-demand routing have nothing to do with the various classes of IP address.

8. ☑ **B.** Using bits from the host portion to extend the subnet mask describes complex subnetting, whereas simple subnetting is using bit boundary subnet masks, such as 255.255.0.0 and 255.255.255.0.

☒   **A** is incorrect because (in a roundabout way) it describes supernetting. **C** is incorrect because it describes VLSM. **D** is incorrect because subnetting has nothing to do with applying a different class's mask to our network.

Maximizing IP Address Space Using Variable Length Subnet Masking

9. ☑   **A.** Assign the point to points the mask of 255.255.255.252 and the LAN subnets 255.255.255.224. This answer meets the requirements more closely than the others. The mask of 255.255.255.224 or /27 gives us six subnets with 30 hosts on each. We would use four of them for our LANs and resubnet one for our serial interfaces with a 255.255.255.252 or /30 mask, which would give us eight /30 subnets for each /27 subnet.
    ☒   **B** is incorrect because it meets the LAN requirements, but the mask 255.255.255.240 gives us 14 subnets with 14 hosts each, too much for the point-to-point connection. **C** is incorrect because it gives us the two hosts per subnet mask of 255.255.255.252 on the point-to-point connection but gives us a bad mask for the LAN segments. **D** is incorrect because there is a correct answer.

10. ☑   **B and C.** Both OSPF and EIGRP provide masks with their packets, so VLSM is supported.
    ☒   **A and D** are incorrect because RIP and IGRP are classful protocols that don't have any knowledge of subnet masks, so it's impossible to tell what mask to apply to the learned routes.

11. ☑   **B.** RIP Version 1 does not support VLSM. RIP will apply the same subnet mask networkwide, based on one of the router's interfaces on that network. As a result, reachability problems will occur.
    ☒   **A, C, and D** are all possibilities, but RIP is a dead giveaway with VLSM.

12. ☑   **A.** Complex subnetting divides address space into equal sections, whereas VLSM allows us to divide address space into unequal portions, giving us the ability to assign each subnet exactly what we need.
    ☒   **B** is incorrect because the statement simply doesn't make any sense. **C** is incorrect because both VLSM and subnetting allow for summarization. **D** is incorrect because it is the opposite of the real answer.

Route Summarization

13. ☑   **C.** Route summarization is combining several network addresses into one "aggregate" address.
    ☒   **A** is incorrect because OSPF does have summary LSAs, but they aren't related to route summarization. **B** is incorrect because BGP will allow route summarization but is *not* route

summarization. **D** is incorrect because CIDR is classless notation for networks, somewhat related to summarization. CIDR is the method of referring to a network in a classless manner, talking about a prefix and mask length.

14. ☑ **A.** 192.168.2.0/23. This answer is correct because both addresses have the first 23 bits in common.

☒ **B** is incorrect because 192.168.0.0/22 has an incorrect prefix. **C** and **D** are incorrect because the subnet mask lengths of 192.168.2.0/30 and 192.168.2.0/29 go beyond what the networks have in common.

15. ☑ **B.** 10.0.2.0/20. All these addresses have the first 20 bits in common, and 10.0.16.0 and 10.0.0.0 are not included in these first 20 bits, so 10.0.2.0/20is a safe route summarization.

☒ **A** is incorrect because they can be summarized as one route. If you picked this answer, you were trying to match the bits too closely. Remember that we can find a common boundary for them all, and as long as other addresses don't fit into this boundary, we're safe. **C** is incorrect because our starting address is 10.0.2.0, so 10.0.0.0 speaks for addresses we don't have. **D** is incorrect because 10.0.2.0/21uses too many bits.

16. ☑ **B.** 192.168.0 through 192.168.15.0 have the first 20 bits in common.

☒ **A** is incorrect because only a /16 would speak for 192.168.0.0 through 192.168.255.0. **C** is incorrect because 16 in binary wouldn't match up to 15 in binary; only the fist 19 bits match in the case of192.168.0.0 through 192.168.16.0. **D** is incorrect because this is a completely valid CIDR block.

Related IP Addressing Commands

17. ☑ **D.** IP FORWARD-PROTOCOL UDP 53 with no IP FORWARD-PROTOCOL commands for the other UDP ports of the default eight you don't want to forward. This sequence will forward only UDP packets wanting to go to port 53 (DNS) to the address(s) specified in the IP HELPER-ADDRESS command.

☒ **A** is incorrect because IP CLASSLESS enables classless routing. **B** is incorrect because IP ROUTING enables routing. **C** is incorrect because IP FORWARD-PROTOCOL DNS is improper syntax.

18. ☑ **B.** IP HELPER-ADDRESS 192.168.2.255 will forward default helper-address broadcasts to 192.168.2.0.

☒ **A** is incorrect because IP HELPER-ADDRESS 192.168.1.0 is the network address for the originating subnet, so this would accomplish nothing. **C** is incorrect because IP HELPER-ADDRESS SUBNET-BROADCAST 192.168.2.0 is not a valid syntax. **D** is incorrect because you can specify subnet broadcast addresses or unicast addresses with IP HELPER-ADDRESS.

19. ☑ **B.** IP UNNUMBERED TO0 will have Serial0 use Tokenring0's IP address.
    ☒ **A** is incorrect because IP UNNUMBERED is incomplete. **C** is incorrect because IP UNNUMBERED POINT-TO-POINT is improper syntax. **D** is incorrect because it is possible.

20. ☑ **A.** IP HELPER-ADDRESS SUBNET1'S IP sets up Router B to forward the broadcasts to subnet1, and the FORWARD-PROTOCOL commands forward DHCP and TFTP requests; the NO IP FORWARD-PROTOCOLS tell it to forward only DHCP and TFTP.
    ☒ **B** is incorrect because it's easily accomplished. **C** is incorrect because IP FORWARD-PROTOCOL DNS and IP FORWARD-PROTOCOL TFTP is improper syntax and the HELPER-ADDRESS command has been left out. **D** is incorrect because the HELPER-ADDRESS command was left out.

LAB ANSWER

The serial connection from the left router to the top router gets the address of 192.168.20.0/30. The serial connection from the rightmost to the top router gets the address of 192.168.20.4/30, and the serial connection between the two LAN routers will take on 192.168.20.8/30. The leftmost LAN will take 192.168.20.32/27; the rightmost LAN will take 192.168.20.64/27. The TACACS server will be numbered 192.168.20.34, and the top and rightmost routers must have the command IP HELPER-ADDRESS 192.168.20.34. This scheme allows us to advertise 192.168.20.0/24 to the Internet.

3

OSPF Operation and Configuration for a Single OSPF Area

Open Shortest Path First (OSPF) is a link-state routing protocol that builds a complete picture of a network. The Internet Engineering Task Force (IETF) developed OSPF to provide support for Classless Interdomain Routing (CIDR) and a nonproprietary routing Internet Protocol (IP). OSPF is an open protocol that can run on many different platforms; no vendor owns it. OSPF was introduced to the world in RFC 1538; version 2 is currently defined in RFC 2328.

OSPF is classified as an interior gateway protocol, meaning it is designed to route within a single autonomous system. Recall that an autonomous system is a collection of networks under a single administrative control and governed by a common set of network policies. In the phrase *link-state routing protocol,* the word *link* refers to an interface on a router, and *state* is the status of that link (up or down, cost, etc.)

In this chapter, we compare OSPF with a distance vector protocol such as Routing Information Protocol (RIP). RIP bases its routing decisions on hop count and disregards any other factors that could help it select a better route.

on the job

As older distance vector protocols such as RIP become more ineffective at handling increased routing responsibilities, more and more organizations are migrating to routing protocols such as OSPF that offer greater flexibility and scalability.

There is really no such thing as a single "best" routing protocol. Your network circumstances will dictate the routing protocols you use. OSPF has a great advantage over RIP: scalability. It can be used on networks of all sizes, from a single router to an enterprise network.

OSPF does what its name implies: It finds the shortest path to a destination. Using the network shown in Figure 3-1, let's see how Router A builds its shortest paths. Particulars such as cost are discussed later in more detail. For now, we take a satellite view of this network. Keep in mind that each router sees itself at the top of the tree and will build its database accordingly.

The left side of Figure 3-1 shows the actual network topology; the right side shows Router A's view for the purposes of calculating the shortest path to E. In calculating costs, Router A, when it transits a router to each its destination, takes into its SPF calculation the costs of the neighbor's outgoing interface.

To reach Router E, Router A can traverse B and D; this path has a cost of 45. The alternative is for A to traverse C; this path has a cost of 65. OSPF routers can

FIGURE 3-1 OSPF SPF network topology versus SPF calculations

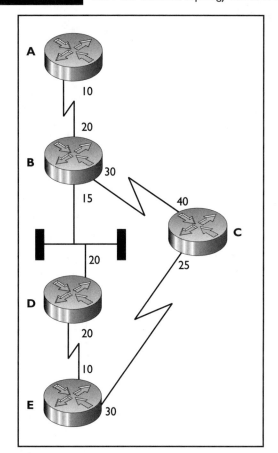
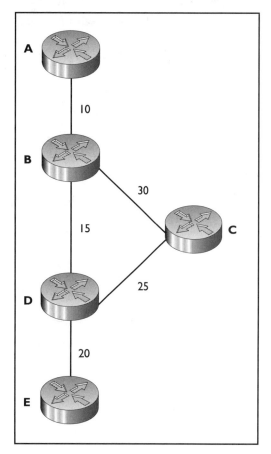

have up to six equal-cost alternate routes to the same destination in their routing tables. In the case shown here, the best path is the B–D path, and that will be added to the routing table to reach this network.

This chapter introduces you to OPSF and delves into its inner workings. For further information, refer to RFC 2538 OSPF Version 2 (April 1998), the primary RFC for OSPF. OSPF started life as an open standard with the IETF; today, it is widely implemented across a variety of vendor equipment and software. Cisco has embraced OSPF in its standard form and has also added nonstandard features such as totally stubby areas.

CERTIFICATION OBJECTIVE 3.01

Benefits of OSPF in Comparison to DV Protocols

OSPF has several advantages over a distance vector protocol such as RIP. One of the best features of OSPF is that it provides great flexibility in controlling routing updates and organizing the routing topology of a network.

Scalability

OSPF permits networks to grow or shrink, with a minimum of disruption. Areas can be added, deleted, or modified to accommodate any expansion or shrinkage. Consider a situation in which you need to add another 30 networks to your autonomous system. OSPF accommodates a large number of routers (hops)—over 1,000. Contrast that with the issues you would have if you tried to incorporate the same addition with the 15-hop limit of RIP.

Many OSPF updates can be exchanged using equal or less bandwidth than used by a few RIP updates. The area concept of OSPF enables the network engineer to accommodate networks of a few routers to networks of hundreds of routers.

Flexibility

OSPF allows networks to be logically grouped into a common area in a way that makes sense. For example, if you have a network address subnetted into 30 subnets, you can put them in a common area and summarize them at the area border into one advertisement. You can also organize your network into areas for easier control and comprehension of what you have.

Summarized Advertisements

OSPF supports classless (CIDR) routing, which can be used to summarize subnets into a single routing entry. Multiple routing table entries can be summarized into a single routing table entry.

VLSM

OSPF supports variable length subnet masks (VLSM). VLSM allows IP addresses to be subnetted according to your needs, rather than forcing you to work around a rigid classful structure. Within the same IP address, you can use various subnet masks such as /24 for a local area network (LAN) interface, /30 for point-to-point circuits, and /32 for loopback addresses. This feature maximizes IP address savings.

exam
ⓦatch

One area of OSPF that would make a good exam question is OSPF's support of VLSM. You might be presented with a network scenario, given a limited number of IP addresses, and be expected to choose a routing protocol that supports VLSM in order to achieve the optimal solution, which will most likely require that you use different subnet masks on the same network number.

Incremental Routing Updates

OSPF does not advertise its entire routing table at regular intervals. Instead, it builds its initial table and then exchanges small, incremental updates, as needed. Adjacencies are maintained by sending small hello packets every 10 or more seconds, depending on the interface type and speed. Contrast that with routing protocols, such as RIP, that send their entire tables, and the benefits of this approach become appreciable.

Faster Routing Convergence

OSPF rapidly converges when it detects a network change. Convergence is attained when the tables of the router represent the true state of the network. When RIP detects that a network is no longer reachable, it goes through several timers before the network gets flushed or replaced in order to ensure no loops will occur. When OSPF detects that a network is not reachable, it replaces that failed route with another route from its topology database (which is identical to all routers in its area). OSPF has no need for timers to prevent loops, since all OSPF routers have a complete picture of the network, and any alternate paths are learned during SPF calculations.

EXERCISE 3-1

OSPF Benefits

Question: What are the benefits of OSPF that make it a good candidate for conserving IP addresses and for reducing routing table sizes?

Answer: OSPF supports VLSM, which enables you to subnet IP addresses based on requirements rather than being locked into a classful structure and forced to use more IP addresses than necessary on a network. OSPF's support of CIDR enables you to summarize multiple subnets into a single entry, thus reducing the size of the routing table.

Other Benefits

OSPF has a *structured flow of packets*. Rather than broadcasting routing updates out of all its interfaces, OSPF sends updates out of only those interfaces that are actually participating in the OSPF routing process. OSPF also makes smart use of multicast addresses to send updates to only those routers participating in the OSPF process.

Decision Making

OSPF chooses the shortest path of all paths to a destination and puts that shortest path in its routing table. OSPF routers put themselves at the root of the tree and run the SPF algorithm to determine the shortest path to a destination. The OSPF router then selects the shortest path and adds it to its routing table as the path to the destination. If there are other paths (of equal or higher cost), OSPF keeps information about them in its topology database. In the event that the selected path fails, OSPF can replace it with one of these alternates. Cost, which can be modified by the network engineer, is a value assigned to a link; by default, it is calculated based on the bandwidth of the link. The faster the link, the lower the cost. We discuss the mechanics of cost calculation and manipulation later in this chapter.

The Complete Picture

All OSPF enables routers in the same autonomous system to have a complete picture of the networks in their area plus the summarized information of any external areas. All routers are the roots of the network, as far as the routers are concerned.

A router receives advertisements about other areas as a summary of all links and routers in that area rather than receiving information on every single link in that area. This feature results in a reduced database size. The OSPF topology database is maintained separately from the routing table and contains information about neighbors, cost links, designated routers, and so on.

CERTIFICATION OBJECTIVE 3.02

How OSPF Discovers, Chooses, and Maintains Routes

Before OSPF can build its tables, it must become adjacent with its neighbors. *Adjacency* is achieved when the router has successfully built its topology database and routing tables via link-state advertisements exchanged with its neighbors. In order to become adjacent, the router and its neighbors must agree and go through a structured process to become full neighbors. Unless this occurs, routers will not become neighbors and will not exchange routing updates.

OSPF Concepts

Before we go into our dissection of OSPF, we must become familiar with OSPF concepts and terms. Understanding and being able to apply these terms is critical to comprehending OSPF.

on the **!** Job

If you manage several routers jointly with other network engineers on a broadcast network, make it a policy that any changes to timers, priorities, or the like on a router are documented in a central database and on each router interface using the interface description command. This practice will ease troubleshooting and problem isolation.

Neighbor Relationships

Becoming neighbors is the first step that a router takes to achieve its eventual goal of building a topology database and routing table. Exchanging hello packets is the method used to become neighbors, which occurs when the router sees itself listed in a neighbor's hello packets.

exam
ⓦatch

Know the order in which OSPF routers operate, from power on to full adjacency. For example, routers must be neighbors before they can achieve adjacency.

Adjacency

Once routers become neighbors, they then continue on in the database exchange stage, known in OSPF parlance as *becoming adjacent*. During this stage, the routers go through several states until they have successfully completed their database exchange. (We discuss their states in a later section.) On multiaccess networks such as Ethernet or Frame Relay, the neighbors determine the designated routers for this segment.

Designated Router and Backup Designated Router

On networks that have more than two routers, OSPF has mechanisms to reduce the number of adjacencies formed. When OSPF is run on networks that are broadcast, such as Ethernet, or on nonbroadcast multiaccess (NBMA) networks such as frame relay, it elects a *designated router (DR)* and a *backup designated router (BDR)*. The DR reduces the link-state update (LSU, to be discussed later) propagation workload of non-DR (DROTHER) routers by forwarding and tracking acknowledgments.

OSPF can treat NMBA networks as point-to-point links (individual subnets are assigned to each links), a collection of point-to-point links (point to multipoint), or a simulated broadcast network (broadcast mode). The point is that special issues are involved in configuring OSPF on these NBMA networks. These issues are addressed in Chapter 4.

As is the nature of OSPF, all OSPF routers on the same network form neighbor relationships with each other. On broadcast-type networks of more than one router, this relationship building can cause significant overhead. OSPF reduces the number of adjacencies formed and the amount of traffic generated by electing a DR and a BDR.

All routers form adjacencies with the DR and BDR only and send their Link-State Advertisements (LSAs) to the DR and BDR. This reduces the number of adjacencies formed from $N(N-1)$ (where N is the number of routers on the network) to $N(2)$. For example, without the DR/BDR mechanism, a network with five OSPF routers would have to form $5(5-1) = 20$ adjacencies. When the DR/BDR is fielded, the same network has only $5(2) = 10$ adjacencies.

exam
Ⓦatch

All OSPF routers on a broadcast network will become neighbors with each other, but they will become adjacent with only the DR and the BDR.

The DR is responsible for sending the LSAs to all other routers that it receives on the network. The BDR does not send LSAs, although it does receive what the DR receives. In the event that the DR fails, the BDR takes over, and a new BDR is elected. All routers respond to the multicast IP address of 224.0.0.5; only the DR and the BDR get traffic going to the multicast IP address of 224.0.0.6. Should the original DR come back up, it will not be re-elected as DR or BDR. If the current DR fails, the BDR takes over, and the old DR can be elected as the new BDR and wait its turn to become the DR once again. This last statement is true as long as the original DR was elected because it had a higher router ID and/or priority than the other routers, not because it was the first active router on the network.

EXERCISE 3-2

OSPF Timers

Question: How do you change the wait timer on your point-to-point network so that it is set to 120 seconds?

Answer: There are no commands for changing the wait time directly. Remember that by default, dead time is four times the hello time, and wait time is always equal to dead time. Remember to make the same change to the other routers on the network. You therefore have two choices:

1. Change the hello time to 30 seconds:

   ip ospf hello-interval 30 (Dead time will then become 120 seconds; wait time will also become 120 seconds.)

2. Change the dead time to 120 seconds:

   ip ospf dead-interval 120 (Wait time is always equal to dead time.)

OSPF Tables

Even though OSPF maintains three databases, the table that you hear about most often is the routing table. OSPF maintains a picture of the network in its topology table; it tracks its neighbors in the neighbor databases and routes based on the contents of its routing table.

Neighbor Database   This database lists and details the neighbors of this router. The SHOW IP OSPF NEIGHBOR command can view it. This table keeps information on the neighbor's router ID, priority, state, dead time, address, and the interface through which this router connects to the neighbor.

Topology Database   This database contains information about router relationships and types, links, types of links (router or network), advertising routers, and links contained in particular areas (except for summary links). It also holds information about external links and summary links. The whole OSPF database, sorted by area, can be viewed with the SHOW IP OSPF DATABASE command. Sample output from this command is shown below:

```
         OSPF Router with ID (1.1.1.1) (Process ID 1)
                 Router Link States (Area 0)
Link ID          ADV Router      Age       Seq#          Checksum Link count
4.5.4.1          4.5.4.1         226       0x8000149E 0x7FF2      12
4.5.8.1          4.5.8.1         695       0x80007B0C 0xA266      10
4.5.21.129       4.5.21.129      1644      0x8000098B 0x4C15      17
```

Routing Table Entries   The routing table contains the actual routing entries. To view the entire routing table, use the SHOW IP ROUTE command. To view those routes learned specifically via OSPF, use the SHOW IP ROUTE OSPF command. OSPF routes are classified as intra-area, inter-area, or external. There are two types of external routers.

- **OSPF**   The *O* identifies intra-area routes. These are routes that are in the area(s) to which this router belongs.

- **OSPF Inter area (IA)**   *IA* identifies routes that are learned from other areas.

- **OSPF External Type 1 (E1)**   *E1* represents routes that come from outside this autonomous system or that were redistributed from another routing protocol such as RIP. An E1 route has two costs associated with it: the external cost, which comes from the source, plus an additional internal cost from the OSPF process that is advertising this route.

■ **OSPF External Type 2 (E2)** *E2 routes* are similar to E1 routes except that only the original external cost is factored in; there is no additional internal cost. E2 routes are always preferred over E1 routes, all else being equal.

exam
ⓦatch   *It is a good idea to learn the types of routes O, IA, E1, and E2 identify in a routing table.*

OSPF Neighbor Relationships

The formation of neighbor relationships is key to OSPF operations. Everything depends on becoming neighbors. In order to successfully navigate the adjacency process, OSPF routers must become neighbors before they can exchange databases initially and for incremental updates hereafter.

Building an OSPF Neighbor Relationship

The key to successful neighbor relationships is agreement. The routers have become neighbors when they see their router ID in a hello packet from the other router(s) on the network. We discuss what the routers must agree on in a later section.

If two neighbors do not agree, they will *not* become neighbors and will not exchange routing updates. The media type of each interface determines the OSPF timers for hellos, dead time, and wait time. The defaults are defined in the OSPF standards; however, if you must change the timer settings, ensure that you change them for all routers that share that common wire, including the neighbors of the router that you just changed. Only routers connecting to the interface you just changed must have their corresponding interfaces changed.

It is a good idea to document this change in the interface description field. For example, if you change the timers, you can edit the description field to describe or explain the change, as shown:

```
Interface serial 0
Description Frame-Relay Circuit Charged by packet OSPF Hellos:
@10 seconds, Dead: @40 seconds, Wait@ 40 seconds.
```

Behavior of Various Media Types

Various network types have specific default intervals for hello, dead, and wait times. These are configurable intervals, but you must take care that if you change them on one OSPF router on the network, you change it for all of them. If you do not make these changes, neighbor relationships will suffer and routing updates will not get exchanged. Note that wait time is always equal to dead time, and you cannot change the wait timer, although you can change the hello and dead timers. Table 3-1 shows default times for various network types.

DR and BDR elections occur on broadcast or in fully meshed NBMA networks operating as a broadcast network. On point-to-point or point-to-multipoint links, there is no need to elect a DR/BDR.

Each OSPF interface (with the exception of loop-back interfaces) has timers for the particular network to which it is attached. All timers are measured in seconds. The *hello timer* determines how often a router sends hellos to its neighbors. The *dead timer* shows how many seconds will elapse before a router is declared dead. The *wait time* (always equal to the dead interval) is the amount of time that the router waits after the dead timer has elapsed before it flushes information about the dead router out of its tables.

The default formula that OSPF uses to calculate dead and wait times is that dead is four times the hello interval, and wait is equal to dead. OSPF is highly configurable, and you can modify the hello and dead intervals to your liking. For example, you can set the hello interval to 20 seconds and the dead interval to 60 seconds; OSPF will automatically adjust the wait interval to equal dead.

You can change these timers, but it is recommended that you not do so unless there is a specific requirement for it. If you must, ensure that you change it for *all* routers on the segment. You should also document this change in such a way that it is obvious. Otherwise, you might add to your troubleshooting time.

TABLE 3-1	Network Type	Hello	Dead	Wait
OSPF Default Timers	Point to point	10	40	40
	Point to multipoint	30	120	120
	Broadcast	10	40	40
	Nonbroadcast multiaccess (NBMA)	30	120	120

For example, to adjust the hello interval on serial 0:

```
Interface serial 0
ip ospf hello-interval    <1-65535>  Seconds
```

To adjust the dead interval:

```
ip ospf dead-interval    <1-65535>  Seconds
```

Always make the same changes on the other routers on the network. If you do not, OSPF will not work between those routers!

Hello Packet Description and Important Fields

The hello packet is the workhorse of OSPF. Without it, OSPF could neither start its operations nor maintain its neighbor relations. The structure of the hello packet is shown in Figure 3-2.

The following points describe the fields of the hello packet:

- **Version** Indicates the version of OSPF being used; the current implementation defaults to version 2.

- **Packet Length** Length of the entire hello packet (in bytes).

SCENARIO & SOLUTION

How do I ensure that a particular router will always be the DR for a broadcast network?	Assuming all routers come up at the same time, set the priority of the router you want to be the DR higher than the other routers. Use the IP OSPF priority command. If you set OSPF priority to zero, that router is prohibited from becoming either a DR or a BDR. If all routers are not to be brought up at the same time, first configure the router that is to be the DR.
I want to see specific detail about my neighbor 1.1.1.1, including its priority.	Use the SHOW IP OSPF NEIGHBOR 1.1.1.1 command.
What is the default formula that OSPF uses to determine hello, dead, and wait time?	The hello timer depends on the interface type. The dead timer is four times the hello timer by default, and wait is equal to dead.

Version #	1	Packet Length	
Router ID			
Area ID			
Checksum	AuType		
Authentication			
Authentication			
Network Mask			
HelloInterval	Options	RTR	PRI
RouterDeadInterval			
Designated Router			
BackUp Designated Router			
Neighbor			

- **Router ID**   IP address used by this router to identify itself; comes from an active and operational interface. Loop-back interfaces are always preferred over physical interfaces, regardless of the IP address.

- **Area ID**   The area to which this router belongs. Neighbors must agree on this field.

- **CheckSum**   An error-detection mechanism; calculated based on contents of the hello packet. Discrepancies at the receiving end indicate a bad hello packet.

- **AuType**   The type of authentication used; typically none, plain text, or MD5. Neighbors must agree on this field.

- **Authentication**   If clear text, this field will be the password. If MD5 is used, this field will be the hashed sum. Neighbors must agree on this field.

- **Network Mask**   The subnet mask of this router's interface. Neighbors must agree on this field.

- **Hello Interval**   The frequency in seconds at which this router expects hellos for this interface. Neighbors must agree on this field, or they will not become adjacent.

- **Options**   Any TOS or QOS options specified by this router.

- **RTR PRI**   The priority of this router. A higher number increases the router's chances of becoming a DR or a BDR.

- **Router Dead Interval**   Time in seconds that will elapse before this router declares a neighbor dead. Neighbors must agree on this field.

- **Designated Router**   On broadcast networks, indicates what router this router knows as the DR.

- **Backup Designated Router**   On broadcast networks, indicates what router this router knows as the BDR.

- **Neighbor(s)**   The neighbor(s) of this router.

Elements That Must Match for a Neighbor Relationship to Happen

In order to become neighbors, routers must agree on the area ID (that is, agree that they are in the same area) and the authentication (plain text or message digest) that they will use to authenticate themselves to each other. They must also agree on the hello timer, which dictates how often they will exchange hello packets to maintain the neighbor relationship, and the dead timer, which tells how long a router will wait before declaring dead a neighbor that it hasn't heard from. Both timers are measured in seconds. Different interface types have different timer values; these timers can be adjusted (as we have discussed already). The final item that neighbors must agree on is the stub area flag. Having agreed and become neighbors, the routers will move on to the next stage, which is becoming adjacent.

DR and BDR Election

OSPF reduces the number of routing update advertisements on broadcast and NBMA networks by electing DRs. There is the DR for the network, which is active, and a BDR. These routers have an identical database and are the routers with which all other routers exchange updates. Without them, the network would have $N(N-1)$ relationships because all routers would have to send to their updates to all other routers; on large networks, this process can consume a significant amount of bandwidth.

Sending the updates to only the DR and the BDR can result in a significant savings in bandwidth and router CPU cycles. The election of a DR and a BDR is automatic, although a network engineer can influence the decision-making process. OPSF assumes that you will follow a consistent policy for a given network. If you want a certain router to be the DR and another certain router to be the BDR, set the priority of the DR higher than the defaults of the others, and set the priority of the BDR the second highest. If any election has already been held and the routers you want to be DR and BDR were not elected, you need to restart the routers to effect your changes. Restarting your routers is generally not recommended and should not be done on a production network. Instead, use the IP OSPF priority command as follows:

1. Set the router you want to be the DR with the highest priority and the one you want to be the BDR with the second highest priority. Set the priority of all other routers to 0. Set the priorities of the routers that were initially elected the DR and BDR to 0. The old DR and will become DROTHER routers, and based on the priorities you set, your DR and BDR of choice will be elected.

2. You can manipulate the priorities of each router until you have the routers you want as DR and BDR. When the election is done, you might want to consider restoring the priorities on the current DROTHER routers back to their defaults. If you do not, you run the risk of losing DR and BDR functionality should the two routers elected to the position fail. Remember that a priority of 0 means that the router will *never* become a DR or a BDR.

If the priorities for all routers are kept the same, the election of the DR and the BDR is determined by the highest router ID of all neighbors that share this network. The router ID is the highest loop-back address of a given router or, if no loop-back interfaces are configured, the highest IP address of an active interface. The router with the second highest router ID will be elected the BDR. Given a choice between using the IP address of a lower IP-addressed loop-back interface or a physical interface with a higher IP address, OSPF will use the loop-back interface because it provides more stability. If you have multiple loop-back interfaces on a router, OSPF will choose the loop-back interface with the highest IP address.

If you do not want a router to become either the DR or the BDR, set its priority to 0. You might want to do this in a situation such as on NMBA networks, where you want to prevent a router that does not have connectivity to all other routers on the network from becoming a DR or BDR. Another situation in which a priority of 0 might be used is in cases in which the DR or the BDR will be the last routers up on the network. Other than settings the IP address of a preferred router's loop-back interface as high as possible and the priorities of the routers you don't want to become a DR/BDR lower, you cannot force a particular router to become a DR or a BDR.

On broadcast and NMBA networks, routers on the medium (the network) hold elections at the beginning to determine which will be the DR/BDR for the network. The routers go through the election in the following stages until a DR/BDR is elected; then the exchange of routing updates occurs. Note that the election cannot occur until the neighbor relations are established, which is contingent on the routers agreeing on the timers, authentication, area ID, and the stub flag for the network.

After the neighbor formation is complete but before the database exchange, the election of a DR and a BDR on a multiaccess network must be settled. All else being equal, the first router up on a network will become the DR unless you set its priority to 0. If all routers come up at the same time, an election will occur, and the router's priority (if higher) will make it the DR and (if second highest) the BDR. If the priorities are all the same, the router with the highest router ID becomes the DR; second highest becomes the BDR. As previously discussed, OSPF prefers to use the loop-back IP addresses for its router ID. If there are no loop-back interfaces, it will use the highest IP address of an active physical interface, regardless of whether that interface is actually participating in the OSPF routing process.

A DR is elected for life. The only thing that can take away its DR status is if its interface into the network fails or it is restarted. The BDR then becomes the DR, and a new BDR is elected, as discussed. Should the original DR be restored, it will not regain status as the DR.

The IP OSPF PRIORITY Command

The IP OSPF PRIORITY command is an interface command used to influence, and if used in conjunction with a well-thought-out IP addressing scheme for loop-back interfaces, to determine what routers will be the DR and the BDR.

The command is used to set the priority of the router to increase (higher number) or lessen (smaller number) the router's chances of becoming a DR or a BDR. The default priority is 1. A priority of 0 means that the router will never become a DR or BDR and will always be listed as DROTHER.

OSPF States in Building a Neighbor Relationship

An OSPF router goes through several stages before it achieves full adjacency with its neighbors (the full state). *All* OSPF routers go through these states, with the exceptions noted previously.

There are unique events that occur during these different states, including what the routers will send and receive from each other.

In order to use the debug command and see the states on your SYSLOG server, you should enter the OSPF LOG-ADJ-CHANGES command in the router OSPF command mode. This command enables you to track and view the steps that occur; otherwise, you will see very little when the states do occur.

The DOWN State

The *DOWN state* is the beginning of the neighbor formation. No router has yet exchanged any packets to start the process.

The INIT State

In the *INIT state,* the router has sent a hello packet out its OSPF interfaces and is awaiting a response from its neighbor(s). The hello packet is sent to the multicast IP address of 224.0.0.5, which will be received by all OSPF-enabled routers on the network. The sending router puts out its area number, router ID, and source IP address.

The Two-way/Exstart State

In the *two-way/EXSTART state,* the router receives a response from other routers. It sees its RID in the hello packets that it receives (neighbor field), which indicates that the neighbor router has received the initial hello and is responding to it. The response is sent back to the originating router's source IP address—in other words, as a unicast packet.

It is during the EXSTART stage that the routers determine which will be the master and slave for the purposes of controlling the database exchange. If a router receives an empty packet that has the initialize (I), more (M), and master (MS) bits set to on, and the sending router's router ID is larger than this receiving router, the receiving router is now the slave. The slave responds by setting the MS bit to zero and uses the sequence number set by the master in its return packets.

If the router receives a packet with the I and MS bits set to Off, the packet sequence number is equal to its sequence number (indicating an acknowledgment, as discussed above), and the neighbor's router ID is smaller than this receiving router's router ID, this router is now the master. Sequence numbers increment as packets are exchanged.

The Two-way/EXCHANGE State

Routers send database description packets that describe their entire database in the *two-way/EXCHANGE state*. The receiving router uses these packets to see what LSAs it is missing or are out of date. This information will be used to generate *link state requests (LSRs)* that will be sent in the next step.

Two-way/LOADING State

At the *two-way/LOADING state* point, the router has a list of LSRs that will be sent to ensure it gets all the information needed from its neighbor. After the LSRs are sent, the router receives *link state update (LSU)* packets containing the missing or out-of-date information. Once the LSUs have been received from the router's neighbors' databases, they will be installed into its topology tables.

The FULL State

In the FULL state, the routers have become neighbors and have experienced a successful exchange of database. At this point, they are said to be adjacent.

OSPF Packet Types

OSPF uses several different packet types to maintain its topology and routing tables and its neighbor relations. These packets, starting with hellos, ensure that the OSPF routers have the complete information they need about the network to which they belong and enable the OSPF routers to maintain and modify information as needed. Figure 3-3 shows the common 24-byte header shared by all packets. To ensure that you follow the structure of the packets correctly, read them from left to right, then start on the next row and read from left to right. The fields are as follows:

■ **Version #** OSPF version number; RFC 2328 specifies version 2

FIGURE 3-3   A 24-byte OSPF packet header

Version #	Type	Packet Length	Router ID	Area ID	Checksum	AuType	Authentication	Authentication

- **Type**   The type of packet: 1 = hello, 2 = database description, 3 = link state request, 4 = link state update, 5 = link state acknowledgment
- **Packet Length**   Total packet size, including header length, in bytes

Hello (Type 1) Packets

Hello packets are critical to forming and maintaining neighbor relationships. Hello packets are used to initiate OSPF operations and routing information exchanges with neighboring routers. They also identify each router's settings as far as hello timers and other options are concerned. Hello packets are sent periodically; this is a configurable option, but the default setting set by the OSPF standards is 10 seconds for a multiaccess or point-to-point network. On networks with multicast or broadcast capabilities, hello packets are multicast. Routers on a common network, regardless of type, must agree on the hello, dead, area, authentication type, area type, and network mask; otherwise, there will be no agreement and thus no adjacency or exchange of routing information.

We have already discussed the header packet, so the only thing we need to mention here about the header is that the type field for hello packets is always 1. Now take a brief look at each field of a hello packet, as shown in Figure 3-4.

- **Network Mask**   The mask used by the interface that sent this packet.
- **Hello Interval**   The number of seconds between this router's hello packets.
- **RTR PRI**   The priority of this router on this network. Priority is used to determine which router will become the DR and which the BDR for this network. A priority of 0 means that this router will never become a DR or a

FIGURE 3-4   Hello packet format

Version #	Type	Packet Length	Router ID	Area ID	Checksum	AuType	Authentication	Authentication
Network Mask	HelloInterval	Options	RTR PRI	RouterDeadInterval	Designated Router BackUp	Designated Router

BDR. This field is applicable only on networks that require a DR or BDR, such as a broadcast network like Ethernet.

- **Designated Router** Identifies the DR that this router knows as the DR for this network.

- **Backup Designated Router** Identifies the BDR that this router knows as the BDR for this network.

- **Neighbor (additional field, not shown)** Router IDs of each neighbor known to this router on this network.

Database Description (Type 2) Packet

Database description (DD) packets are sent during the formation of the adjacency. DD packets summarize the contents of the link-state database of the sending router. The exchange of DD packets uses a poll-response model during which one router is the master and the other router is the slave. The master sends DD packets (polls) that are answered by the slave's DD packets (responses). DD sequence numbers link the polls to the responses.

The format of the DD packet is shown in Figure 3-5. The header is the same as that of the other packets except that the Type field is 2.

The following points describe each field:

- **Interface MTU** The largest IP packet size in bytes that this interface can receive.

- **Options** As supported and as required, additional capabilities that this router can support.

- **I-bit** When set to On, indicates that this is the first DD packet.

- **M-bit** When set to On, indicates that more DD packets will follow.

- **MS-bit** When set to On, indicates that this router is the master during the database exchange; if set to Off, this router is the slave.

FIGURE 3-5 A database description packet

Version #	2	Packet Length	Router ID	Area ID	Checksum	AuType	Authentication	Authentication

Interface MTU	Options	0	0	0	0	0	I	M	MS	DD Sequence Number	LSA Header

■ **DD Sequence Number** Sequences DD packets. The initial value is indicated by the I-bit, then it increments for later packets until the complete database has been sent by this router.

■ **LSA Header(s)** The contents of the rest of the packet consist of LSA for the networks known by this router.

Link-State Request (Type 3) Packets

Link-state request (LSR) packets are sent after a successful exchange of DD packets. After receiving another router's DD packets, the receiving router analyzes the contents of the DD packets and compares them to its link-state database. If there are unknown OSPF routers or updated database entries described by the DD packets it has received, the router generates LSR packets to request this new information. In other words, the router uses the DD packets to determine whether its information is out of date, and if it is, it sends the LSR packets necessary to bring itself up to date.

LSR packets contain precise requests; that is, these packets describe what information is outdated or missing. A sequence number, checksum, and age identify the requested information. A router receiving the LSR understands that the requesting router wants the newest and most updated version, not just the exact request.

The format of the LSR packet is shown in Figure 3-6. Notice that the header type is set to 3. The LS Type, Link State ID, and Advertising Router fields identify exactly what LSA this router is requesting. A specific instance (that is, a specific LSA at a specific time) is not requested, because it is understood by the OSPF routers that the request is for the most recent instance (the newest information requested).

Link-State Update (Type 4) Packets

Link-state update (LSU) packets are the "delivery boys" of OPSF. LSUs deliver link-state advertisements (LSAs) to the OSPF routers on the network. LSAs are the sections of the LSU containing the actual link information (the routing information).

On networks with multicasting and broadcasting capabilities, LSUs are multicast. Reliability is inherent in this process, because all LSAs are acknowledged. If

FIGURE 3-6 A link-state request packet

Version #	3	Packet Length	Router ID	Area ID	Checksum	AuType	Authentication	Authentication	LS Type	Link State ID	Advertising Router

FIGURE 3-7   A link-state update packet

Version #	4	Packet Length	Router ID	Area ID	Checksum	AuType	Authentication	Authentication	# LSA's	LSA's

retransmission is necessary, LSAs are sent directly to the neighbor needing it rather than reflooding throughout the network.

The format of the LSU packet is shown in Figure 3-7. Notice the Type field is set to 4. The packet format clearly shows the data-carrying nature of this packet, with the field for the number of LSAs contained in this packet (# LSAs) and the LSAs themselves.

Acknowledge (Type 5) Packets

Acknowledge (ACK) packets are sent by the receiving router of a LSA to let the sending router know that the LSA was received. More than one LSA can be acknowledged in a single ACK. The ACK packet format is similar to that of the DD packet. The ACK can be sent to a multicast address for all routers (224.0.0.5), to DRs (224.0.0.6), or unicast to the sender. How the ACK is sent depends on the state of the sending router's interface and the sending router.

Figure 3-8 shows the format of the ACK packet. Notice the Type field is 5. The LSA header fields identify LSAs that this router is acknowledging.

LSA Types

With the exception of the hello packet, there is an LSA section in each of the packets we've discussed. Depending on the packet type, this LSA contains link-state information relevant to the packet type and its purposes.

Five LSA types are used by OSPF to send and receive link-state routing updates. Table 3-2 shows the LSA types, the routers that generate them, and their contents.

FIGURE 3-8   An acknowledgment packet

Version #	5	Packet Length	Router ID	Area ID	Checksum	AuType	Authentication	Authentication	LSA Headers

TABLE 3-2 OSPF LSA Types

LS Type	Description	Generated By	Contents
1	Router links	Each router in an area	Describe the state and cost of the router's interfaces (those that are participating in the OSPF process for that area).
2	Network links	Designated router	Describe all routers attached to the broadcast or NBMA network in the area, including the DR itself. The LSID field contains the IP address of the DR.
3	Summary LSAs (IP)	Area border routers	Describe inter-area destinations. Type 3 is used when the destination is a IP Network.
4	Summary LSAs (ASBR)	Area border routers	Describe inter-area destinations. Type 4 is used when the destination is an ASBR.
5	AS-External LSA	AS boundary routers	Describe destinations external to the AS. Also describe a default route (LSIS is set to 0.0.0.0 with a mask of 0.0.0.0).

OSPF is very detailed and very specific, which can make it easy to lose sight of the big picture. Before you read on, remember that all OSPF communications occur using the OSPF packet types detailed earlier. The LSA types are an even more microscopic dissection of the OPSF packets. These LSAs are contained in the OSPF packets and vary depending on the information being sent or received by the OSPF.

Figure 3-9 gives the broadest view of the relationship between OSPF packet types and LSAs. Although this is a very simplistic picture, understanding it will help you keep the information about packet types and LSA types clear. The relationship of packets to LSAs is analogous to that of TCP segments being encapsulated into IP packets.

FIGURE 3-9

The OSPF packet and LSA relationship

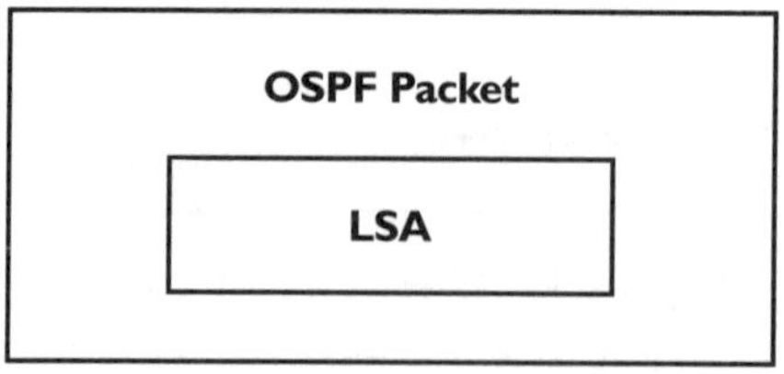

The LSA Header

All of the LSA types share a common 20-byte header (see Figure 3-10). The header identifies the LSA, including using the LS Age field to determine which LSA is newer, in case multiple instances of the same LSA are in the domain. OSPF routers always add the information of the newest LSA to their databases and disregard the older information.

The following points explain the fields of the LSA header shown in Figure 3-10:

- **LS Age**   Time in seconds since the LSA originated.

- **Options**   Optional capabilities that are supported by this part of the domain.

- **LS Type**   One of the five LSA types. This number varies depending on what is being advertised by this LSA. See Table 3-2.

- **Link State ID**   The IP address being advertised. In the case of a broadcast network, the IP address of the DR for the network described by this LSA.

- **Advertising Router**   The router ID of the router that sent this LSA. On broadcast networks in a network LSA, this would be the router ID of the DR.

- **LS Sequence Number**   Detects old or duplicate LSAs.

- **LS Checksum**   Error checking of the entire LSA contents except the LS Age field.

- **Length**   Total length in bytes, including the 20-byte header.

LSA Type 1: Router LSA

Router LSAs are generated by each router in an area for each interface (also called a *link*) participating in the OSPF routing process. This LSA describes the state (up or down) and cost of each of the router's interfaces to an area. *All* of the router's links must be described in a single router LSA.

Figure 3-11 shows the format and structure of the router LSA. Note that the Type field in the LSA header is set to 1 to identify it as a router LSA. The LSID field in the header is set the router's router ID. Router LSAs are flooded throughout a single area only; they do not leave the area in which they originated.

FIGURE 3-10   The LSA header

LS Age	Options	LS Type	Link State ID	Advertising Router	LS Sequence Number	LS Checksum	Length

FIGURE 3-11	A router LSA

LS Age	Options	I	Link State ID	Advertising Router	LS Sequence Number	LS Checksum	Length

O	V	E	B	# of Links	Link ID	Link Data	Type	# of TOS	Metric	TOS	0	TOS Metric	Link ID	Link Data

We have already discussed the LSA header; we now discuss the fields unique to the router LSA:

- **V** When this field is turned on, the router is the end point of a virtual link.

- **E** When this field is turned on, it identifies that the router is an autonomous system boundary router (ASBR).

- **B** When this field is turned on, it identifies that the router is an ABR.

- **# of Links** Shows the number of router links described in this LSA; this would be the total number of router links into this area.

The remaining fields describe the actual router links advertised by this router LSA:

- **Type** Description of the router link; can be point-to-point, connection to a transit or stub network, or a virtual link.

- **Link ID** What this router link is connecting to; could be another router or a network.

- **Link Data** Varies depending on the Type field; could be a network IP address, next hop, or the like.

- **# of TOS** Identifies the number of TOS given to this link.

- **Metric** The cost of this link.

The remaining TOS fields identify any additional TOS information about this link. Remember that TOS is optional and might not be implemented; OSPF is flexible enough to give you the option of providing information about TOS.

LSA Type 2: Network LSAs

The most important information you should understand and remember about *network LSAs* is that they are generated by a DR for broadcast and NBMA networks.

FIGURE 3-12   A network LSA

LS Age	Options	2	Link State ID	Advertising Router	LS Sequence Number	LS Checksum	Length	Network Mask	Attached Router

Given the nature of these types of networks, it will come as no surprise that network LSAs are generated by the DR of that particular network.

Compared to the router LSA, the network LSA advertises very little beyond the common header: just the network mask and the attached router. Figure 3-12 shows the structure of the network LSA. Notice the Type field is set to 2.

Because we have already discussed most of the fields in Figure 3-12, here we define only the two fields specific to the network LSA:

- **Network Mask**   The IP address mask for this network (could also be a subnet mask, as appropriate).

- **Attached Router**   Lists the router IDs of all routers attached to this network that are fully adjacent to the designated router. The DR is included in the listing.

LSA Type 3: Summary LSA and LSA Type 4: Summary LSA

LSA types 3 and 4 are both summary links and, except for the obvious difference in their Type fields, deliver the same information to different destinations. A *type 3 summary LSA* is destined for IP networks, while a *type 4 summary LSA* is destined for an ASBR. The information content they carry is the same; only the destination types differ.

Figure 3-13 shows the structure of the summary LSA. Since the TOS is rarely implemented in real-world OSPF, we do not discuss them. Summary LSAs can also be used to describe a default route.

For type 3, the network mask is that of the destination network IP address. The metric is the cost of the route.

FIGURE 3-13   A summary LSA (types 3 and 4)

LS Age	Options	3 or 4	Link State ID	Advertising Router	LS Sequence Number			
LS Checksum		Length	Network Mask	0	Metric	TOS	TOS Metric	

LSA Type 5: Autonomous System External LSA

Autonomous system (AS) external LSAs are originated by autonomous system boundary routers (ASBRs). Type 5 LSAs describe particular destinations external to the AS and are also used to describe a default route. When carrying information about a default route, the LSID is always set to a default destination of 0.0.0.0 with a mask of 0.0.0.0. Another way to think of AS external LSAs is that they pull information into the AS from foreign autonomous systems.

Figure 3-14 shows the format and structure of the AS external LSA. Notice that the Type field is set to 5. The TOS sections are not discussed.

The fields of the AS external LSA are defined as follows:

- **Network Mask**   IP mask for the advertised destination.

- **E**   If this field is not set, this is a type 1 external metric (costs will be the original external cost plus internal cost of this AS to reach it). If this field is set to On, this is a type 2 external metric (cost will be the original cost only). Obviously, type 2 are always lesser cost and preferred over type 1.

- **Metric**   The cost of reaching this route; this field will varying depending on whether the E bit is set.

- **Forwarding Address**   Traffic for this destination will be forwarded to this address. If this field is set to 0.0.0.0 (as for a default route), traffic will be forwarded to this ASBR.

- **External Route Tag**   This 32-bit field is not used by OSPF itself; rather, it might be used to communicate information between ASBRs.

Shortest Path First Algorithm and Route Selection

The *shortest path first(SPF) algorithm* (also known as the *Dijkstra's algorithm* after its creator) is the engine of OSPF. Basically, the algorithm states that all else being equal, you should choose the path with the lowest cost, regardless of the number of hops.

FIGURE 3-14   AS External LSA (Type 5)

Network Mask	E	0	Metric	Forwarding Address	External Route Tag	E	TOS	TOS Metric	Forwarding Address	External Route Tag

The SPF algorithm does route selection; network engineers can influence this decision by using map statements and the interface cost command. Recall from our introduction to SPF that an OSPF router puts itself at the root of the tree and calculates the costs to each destination. After that process is complete, it then puts the lowest cost into its routing table, and any alternatives are stored in the topology database against the advent of the chosen path's failure.

What Is the Shortest Path First Algorithm?

The SPF algorithm is a complex mathematical formula (fortunately calculated by the routers) that has each router viewing itself as the center of the network. From that center, it analyzes the topology information it has on hand and comes up with the shortest path to the destination. This path includes routes to the default destination (also known as the gateway of last resort or the default gateway).

The following discussion presents a simplified example of the OSPF decision-making process. The table in the middle of Figure 3-15 shows each router's lowest-cost path to a given network and what router it traverses to reach that network. Notice that each router considers the cost of a directly connected network

FIGURE 3-15   SPF calculations

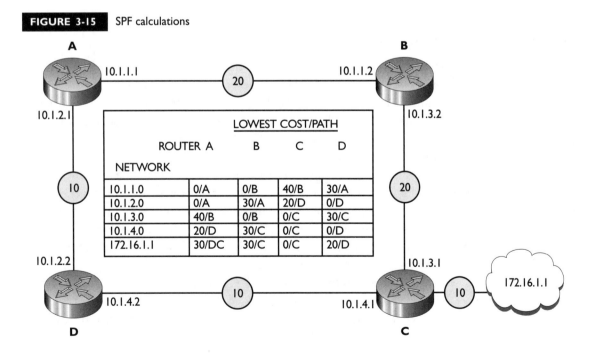

NETWORK	ROUTER A	B	C	D
10.1.1.0	0/A	0/B	40/B	30/A
10.1.2.0	0/A	30/A	20/D	0/D
10.1.3.0	40/B	0/B	0/C	30/C
10.1.4.0	20/D	30/C	0/C	0/D
172.16.1.1	30/DC	30/C	0/C	20/D

LOWEST COST/PATH

to be equal to 0. However, when the router must traverse a directly connected network to reach another work, it factors in its interface cost to that network plus the egress interface cost on other routers it must traverse. Given the network in Figure 3-15, we discuss how Router A will choose the shortest path to the 172.16.1.0 network behind Router C. The numbers in the circles represent the costs; for ease for discussion, all routers on the same network have the same cost, but in reality, each router can have a different cost to the same network.

All the routers have the same link-state database, with themselves as the root of the network. All routers have been built from the router out to the other networks.

Selection of the Best Route

Router A has two paths to reach 172.16.1.1. The path via ADC has a total cost of 30, and the path via ABC has a total cost of 50. The shortest path for Router A to reach 172.16.1.1 is via ADC; therefore, Router A's routing table will route traffic to 172.16.1.1 via Router B. The information on the ABC path will be maintained in the topology database and will be activated should the ADC path fail. From the table in the middle of Figure 3-15, you will see each router's lowest-cost path to each network and what neighbor it will list in its routing table to reach this network.

OSPF LSA Propagation

In order to understand what happens under the OSPF hood, let's configure our network as shown in Figure 3-16. Using packet captures and analysis, we can see what actually occurs during normal OSPF operations, including the failure of the DR and the elevation of BDR to DR. All the routers are in Area 0 because this chapter focuses on single area configuration. Addressing for the routers is given in the table on the right in the figure.

To get a good picture of the OSPF adjacency process, we use the network configured as in the following discussion. RTRC will be added after the fact. In other words, it will be a new router joining the OSPF cloud. Notice the process from INIT to FULL and what events occur. In order to see all these steps occurring from your SYSLOG server, use the ENABLE OSPF LOG-ADJ-CHANGES command under the OSPF routing process.

The following messages from DEBUG IP OSPF ADJ show the stages that an OSPF router goes through. Notes are sprinkled throughout to explain what is happening. We focus on the steps RTRC goes through to become adjacent with

FIGURE 3-16

LSA propagation

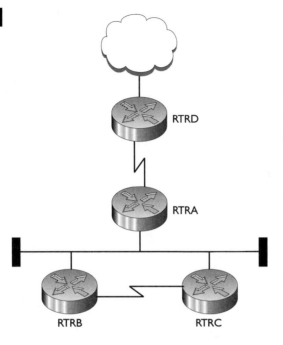

Router	Interface	IP Address/Mask
RTRA	Lo0	1.1.1.1/32
RTRA	Lo1	1.2.3.4/32
RTRA	S0	1.4.4.1/24
RTRA	E0	12.22.33.1/24
RTRB	Lo0	2.2.2.2/32
RTRB	E0	12.22.33.2/24
RTRB	S1	2.1.1.2/30
RTRC	Lo0	3.3.3.3/32
RTRC	E0	12.22.33.3/24
RTRC	S1	2.1.1.3/30
RTRD	Lo0	4.4.4.4/32
RTRD	S2	1.4.4.4/24

RTRA and RTRB (the BDR and the DR, respectively). We ignore the adjacency process on the serial link between RTRB and RTRC.

```
OSPF: Interface Loopback0 going Up
OSPF: Build router LSA for area 0, router ID 3.3.3.3
OSPF: Build router LSA for area 0, router ID 3.3.3.3
OSPF: Build router LSA for area 0, router ID 3.3.3.3
```

Comment: Here we see the OSPF preference for loop-back interfaces. RTRC has chosen 3.3.3.3 as its router ID. This is the IP address of the active loop-back interface.

```
OSPF: Interface Ethernet0 going Up
OSPF: Build router LSA for area 0, router ID 3.3.3.3
OSPF: Build router LSA for area 0, router ID 3.3.3.3
OSPF: Build router LSA for area 0, router ID 3.3.3.3
```

Comment: Ethernet 0 is participating in the OSPF routing process. Since this a broadcast network, the DR and BDR (in this case, RTRB and RTRA) have already been elected.

```
%OSPF-5-ADJCHG: Process 1, Nbr 1.2.3.4 on Ethernet0
from DOWN to INIT, Received Hello
```

Comment: The router is in the INIT state, it has sent a hello, and has received a hello from neighbor 1.2.3.4 (RTRA).

```
%OSPF-5-ADJCHG: Process 1, Nbr 1.2.3.4 on Ethernet0
from INIT to 2WAY, 2-Way Received
OSPF: 2 Way Communication to 1.2.3.4 on Ethernet0, state 2WAY
```

Comment: RTRC has received a hello from RTRA that contained its router ID.

```
%OSPF-5-ADJCHG: Process 1, Nbr 2.2.2.2 on Ethernet0
 from DOWN to INIT, Received Hello
%OSPF-5-ADJCHG: Process 1, Nbr 2.2.2.2 on Ethernet0
from INIT to 2WAY, 2-Way Received
OSPF: 2 Way Communication to 2.2.2.2 on Ethernet0, state 2WAY
```

Comment: Hellos have been sent and received with RTRB.

```
%OSPF-5-ADJCHG: Process 1, Nbr 2.2.2.2 on Serial1
from DOWN to INIT, Received Hello
%OSPF-5-ADJCHG: Process 1, Nbr 2.2.2.2 on Serial1
from INIT to 2WAY, 2-Way Received
OSPF: 2 Way Communication to 2.2.2.2 on Serial1, state 2WAY
```

Comment: RTRC has received a hello from RTRB containing its router ID.

```
%OSPF-5-ADJCHG: Process 1, Nbr 2.2.2.2 on Serial1
from 2WAY to EXSTART, AdjOK?
```

Comment: RTRC prepares to go to the database exchange state.

```
OSPF: Rcv DBD from 1.2.3.4 on Ethernet0 seq 0x1E6E opt 0x2
 flag 0x7 len 32 state 2WAY
OSPF: Nbr state is 2WAY
OSPF: Rcv DBD from 2.2.2.2 on Ethernet0 seq 0x1C89 opt 0x2
flag 0x7 len 32 state 2WAY
OSPF: Nbr state is 2WAY
OSPF: Backup seen Event before WAIT timer on Ethernet0
OSPF: DR/BDR election on Ethernet0
OSPF: Elect BDR 1.2.3.4
OSPF: Elect DR 2.2.2.2
        DR: 2.2.2.2 (Id)    BDR: 1.2.3.4 (Id)
```

Comment: This shows the identification of the DR and BDR. It says election, but since the DR and BDR were already in place before RTRC joined the OPSF cloud, no election took place again; instead, the DR and BDR were identified to RTRC.

```
%OSPF-5-ADJCHG: Process 1, Nbr 2.2.2.2 on Ethernet0
from 2WAY to EXSTART, AdjOK?
OSPF: Send DBD to 2.2.2.2 on Ethernet0 seq 0x235D opt
0x2 flag 0x7 len 32
%OSPF-5-ADJCHG: Process 1, Nbr 1.2.3.4 on Ethernet0
from 2WAY to EXSTART, AdjOK?
OSPF: Send DBD to 1.2.3.4 on Ethernet0 seq 0x12CA
opt 0x2 flag 0x7 len 32
OSPF: Build router LSA for area 0, router ID 3.3.3.3
```

Comment: RTRC, having identified the DR and BDR, sends its database to them.

```
OSPF: Rcv DBD from 2.2.2.2 on Ethernet0 seq 0x235D
opt 0x2 flag 0x2 len 132 state EXSTART
OSPF: NBR Negotiation Done. We are the MASTER
%OSPF-5-ADJCHG: Process 1,Nbr 2.2.2.2 on Ethernet0 from EXSTART
 to EXCHANGE,Negotiation Done
OSPF: Send DBD to 2.2.2.2 on Ethernet0 seq 0x235E opt 0x2 flag 0x3 len 132
```

Comment: During the database exchange with RTRB, RTRC is the master (it has the highest interface IP on this network).

```
OSPF: Database request to 2.2.2.2
OSPF: sent LS REQ packet to 12.22.33.2, length 12
```

Comment: RTRC sends an LS request to RTRB for the latest updates it has.

```
OSPF: Rcv DBD from 1.2.3.4 on Ethernet0 seq 0x12CA opt 0x2
flag 0x2 len 132 state EXSTART
OSPF: NBR Negotiation Done. We are the MASTER
%OSPF-5-ADJCHG: Process 1, Nbr 1.2.3.4 on Ethernet0
from EXSTART to EXCHANGE, Negotiation Done
OSPF: Send DBD to 1.2.3.4 on Ethernet0 seq 0x12CB opt 0x2 flag 0x3 len 132
OSPF: Database request to 1.2.3.4
OSPF: sent LS REQ packet to 12.22.33.1, length 12
```

Comment: In this section, we can see RTRC going through the exchange process with RTRA. Notice that RTRC sends an LS REQ and is the master for the database exchange process.

```
OSPF: Rcv DBD from 2.2.2.2 on Ethernet0 seq 0x235E
opt 0x2 flag 0x0 len 32 state EXCHANGE
```

> **Comment:** RTRC receives DD packets from RTRB. Notice that the slave (RTRB) sent back the packet with the same sequence number that the RTRC (master) sent initially.

```
OSPF: Send DBD to 2.2.2.2 on Ethernet0 seq 0x235F
opt 0x2 flag 0x1 len 32
```

> **Comment:** RTRC sends DD packets back to RTRB; the sequence number is incremented by RTRC because it is the master.

```
OSPF: Rcv DBD from 1.2.3.4 on Ethernet0 seq 0x12CB opt 0x2
flag 0x0 len 32 state EXCHANGE
OSPF: Send DBD to 1.2.3.4 on Ethernet0 seq 0x12CC opt 0x2 flag 0x1 len 32
```

> **Comment:** A similar exchange of DD packets with RTRA. Notice the incrementing of the sequence numbers.

```
OSPF: Rcv DBD from 2.2.2.2 on Ethernet0 seq 0x235F opt 0x2
 flag 0x0 len 32 state EXCHANGE
OSPF: Exchange Done with 2.2.2.2 on Ethernet0
%OSPF-5 ADJCHC: Process 1, Nbr 2.2.2.2 on Ethernet0
from EXCHANGE to LOADING, Exchange Done
OSPF: Synchronized with 2.2.2.2 on Ethernet0, state FULL
%OSPF-5-ADJCHG: Process 1, Nbr 2.2.2.2 on Ethernet0 from
LOADING to FULL, Loading Done
```

> **Comment:** Having received the DD packet back with its sequence number, RTRC knows that it has completed the process with RTRB. It then moves from LOADING to FULL and is now adjacent with RTRB. Hereafter, it sends only the necessary hellos, and updates/recalculates network changes.

```
OSPF: Rcv DBD from 1.2.3.4 on Ethernet0 seq 0x12CC opt 0x2
flag 0x0 len 32 state EXCHANGE
OSPF: Exchange Done with 1.2.3.4 on Ethernet0
%OSPF-5-ADJCHG: Process 1, Nbr 1.2.3.4 on Ethernet0
from EXCHANGE to LOADING, Exchange Done
OSPF: Synchronized with 1.2.3.4 on Ethernet0, state FULL
%OSPF-5-ADJCHG: Process 1, Nbr 1.2.3.4 on Ethernet0
from LOADING to FULL, Loading Done
```

Comment: As with RTRB, RTRC went through the same process with RTRA to reach the FULL state.

Regardless of what type of network to which OSPF routers connect, routers must go through this process in order to become adjacent. On certain networks such as point-to-point circuits, there will be no DR/BDR issues, but the routers will still take these steps to reach adjacency. During the DD packet exchange, one router will be elected the master to start the sequencing, and the other router will be the slave. This setup ensures that packets are tracked.

Walk-Through of an LSA Through a Designated Router

We next examine the behavior of OSPF when a network goes down on a router in the configuration shown in Figure 3-17. We delete loop-back interface 0 on RTRA,

FIGURE 3-17

Network 1.1.1.1
goes down

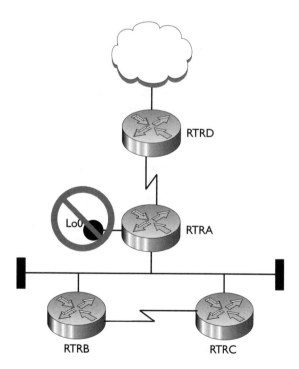

in essence deleting network 1.1.1.1. RTRA is neither a DR nor a BDR. We examine the packet exchange between RTRA and its DR/BDR.

```
rtrA(config)#no int lo 0
rtrA(config)#end
rtrA#sh
OSPF: Interface Loopback0 going Down
OSPF: 1.2.3.4 address 1.1.1.1 on Loopback0 is dead, state DOWN
%OSPF-5-ADJCHG: Process 1, Nbr 1.2.3.4 on Loopback0
from 2WAY to DOWN, Neighbor Down
```

> **Comment:** Network 1.1.1.1 on loop-back interface 0 went down when the interface was deleted.

```
OSPF: Stop timer (2) for Nbr 1.2.3.4 0x32CE6E4
OSPF: Build router LSA for area 0, router ID 1.2.3.4
OSPF: Build router LSA for area 0, router ID 1.2.3.4
OSPF: add router LSA seq 80000005 to flood queue
OSPF: Start timer for Nbr 3.3.3.3 after
adding 1.2.3.4 type 1 caller 0x32DF0B6
OSPF: Start timer for Nbr 2.2.2.2 after
adding 1.2.3.4 type 1 caller 0x32DF0B6
OSPF: Sending update on Ethernet0 to 224.0.0.6
```

> **Comment:** OSPF starts timer for its DR and BDR and sends them an update that network 1.1.1.1 is gone. There is an LSA ID assigned to this LSA.

```
OSPF: Send Type 1, LSID 1.2.3.4, Adv rtr 1.2.3.4, age 1, seq 0x80000005
```

> **Comment:** Sequence number for the DD packets.

```
OSPF: Start timer for Nbr 4.4.4.4 after
adding 1.2.3.4 type 1 caller 0x32DF0B6
OSPF: Sending update on Serial0 to 224.0.0.5
```

> **Comment:** RTRA also updates RTRD on the point-to-point circuit. Notice the all OSPF routers multicast used here.

```
OSPF: received update from 3.3.3.3, Ethernet0
OSPF: Rcv Update Type 1, LSID 1.2.3.4,
Adv rtr 1.2.3.4, age 2, seq 0x80000005 OSPF: Received same lsa
     Remove LSA from retransmission list
OSPF: Stop timer (1) for Nbr 3.3.3.3 after removing 1.2.3.4, type 1 0x32DE71C ip
```

Comment: RTRC received the update. Stop the timer for RTRC.

```
OSPF: Received ACK from 4.4.4.4
OSPF: Rcv Ack Type 1, LSID 1.2.3.4, Adv rtr 1.2.3.4, age 1, seq 0x80000005
    Remove LSA from retransmission list
OSPF: Stop timer (1) for Nbr 4.4.4.4 after removing 1.2.3.4, type 1 0x32DD8FE
OSPF: rcv. v:2 t:5 l:44 rid:2.2.2.2
    aid:0.0.0.0 chk:E662 aut:0 auk: from Ethernet0
OSPF: Received ACK from 2.2.2.2
OSPF: Rcv Ack Type 1, LSID 1.2.3.4, Adv rtr 1.2.3.4, age 2, seq 0x80000005
    Remove LSA from retransmission list
OSPF: Stop timer (1) for Nbr 2.2.2.2 after removing 1.2.3.4, type 1 0x32DD8FE
OSPF: rcv. v:2 t:1 l:48 rid:4.4.4.4 aid:0.0.0.0 chk:BC8A aut:
0 auk: from Serial0
OSPF: rcv. v:2 t:1 l:52 rid:2.2.2.2  aid:0.0.0.0 chk:9455 aut:
0 auk: from Ethernet0
```

Comment: These lines detail the sending, reception, and acknowledgment of the updates. Notice that RTRA updates only its DR/BDR on the Ethernet network; although not germane to our topic here, RTRA also sends an update to RTRD.

```
OSPF: running SPF for area 0
OSPF: Initializing to run spf
 It is a router LSA 1.2.3.4. Link Count 4
  Processing link 0, id 12.22.33.3, link data 12.22.33.1, type 2
   Add better path to LSA ID 12.22.33.3, gateway 12.22.33.1, dist 10
   Add path: next-hop 12.22.33.1, interface Ethernet0
  Processing link 1, id 4.4.4.4, link data 1.4.4.1, type 1
   Add better path to LSA ID 4.4.4.4, gateway 1.4.4.4, dist 64
   Add path: next-hop 1.4.4.4, interface Serial0
  Processing link 2, id 1.4.4.0, link data 255.255.255.0, type 3
   Add better path to LSA ID 1.4.4.255, gateway 1.4.4.0, dist 64
   Add path: next-hop 1.4.4.1, interface Serial0
  Processing link 3, id 1.2.3.4, link data 255.255.255.255, type 3
   Add better path to LSA ID 1.2.3.4, gateway 1.2.3.4, dist 1
   Add path: next-hop 1.2.3.4, interface Loopback1
OSPF: delete lsa id 12.22.33.3, type 2, adv rtr 3.3.3.3 from delete list
```

When all the updates are received, RTRA recalculates the SPF, with itself as the root, to determine the shortest paths to the networks in its area. When the process is done, we have a fully adjacent, fully updated RTRA. The other routers also have converged and know that 1.1.1.1 is no longer up.

Non-DR routers (called DROTHER in OSPF parlance) on a broadcast or NBMA network send their LSAs to both the DR and the BDR, and the DR then sends this LSA to the all other DROTHER routers in the network. The BDR does not generate any LSAs to the DROTHER routers in the network; it lets the DR handle that part of the workload. Should the DR go down, the BDR will become the DR and be responsible for keeping all the other routers updated.

The OSPF Decision Tree When Receiving an LSA

The sequence number is critical to the adjacency process and to ensuring that no mismatches occur during the database exchange process. Initially, the master sets the I bit to On and generates a sequence number to the slave. The slave in turn accepts the packet and sends it back to the master with the same sequence number, then sends its data to the master. If there is more data to follow, the M bit is set to 1. If there is no more data, the M bit is Off, and the slave sends back the packet to the master with the last sequence number unchanged.

Generally speaking, when the master receives an LSA with the sequence number the same as the last packet it sent, it does one of two things. If the more bit (M) is Off, it knows that there are no more packets coming. If the more bit is On, it knows that the slave has more data to send and it will increment the sequence number and send the packet back to the slave. If the slave receives a packet with the same sequence number as previously, and the bits are the same as before, it knows that this is a duplicate packet and will send the last packet it received to the master, in which case the master will generate a new packet because a problem has occurred.

If the sequence number is ever lower than what was originally sent, the actions taken depend on whether the router is the master or the slave. If it is the master, it restarts the process because an adjacency problem has occurred. Perhaps the router was restarted or its configuration was changed to where it thinks it is the master. For example, the slave IP address could now be higher, making it the master. If the slave receives a packet with a lower sequence number than previously, it generates sequence mismatch packets and forces the master to reinitialize the process.

When the slave receives a sequence number that is higher than a previous entry, it accepts the packet because the master increments the sequence number. If the master receives a packet with a higher sequence number, it knows it has a problem and goes through a process similar to the one outlined in the previous paragraph.

CERTIFICATION OBJECTIVE 3.03

Configuring OSPF in a Single Area

In this section, we talk about how you configure OSPF on Cisco routers. The commands listed here were taken from Cisco IOS 11.0 or later.

exam
ⓦatch

OSPF configuration starts with the ROUTER OSPF <PROCESS-ID> command.

on the
ⓙob

If you must configure OSPF with only a single area, ensure that it is area 0. Later, should your organization grow or split, adaptation of OSPF to fit the new configuration requirements will be easier.

The ROUTER OSPF <PROCESS-ID> Command

The first step in configuring OSPF is the ROUTER OSPF <PROCESS-ID> command. The PROCESS-ID is a number from 1 to 65,535 that uniquely identifies the OSPF process running on the router. You can have more than one OSPF process running at any given time. The PROCESS-ID is locally significant and can be different on each router in the autonomous system.

SCENARIO & SOLUTION

Given an IP address of 1.1.1.1 and a subnet mask of 255.128.0.0, what's the quickest way to add this network to the OSPF routing process (assuming area 0)?	Invert the 1s and 0s of the subnet mask to get the wildcard mask. You can also use 0.0.0.0 to make the interface hosting 1.1.1.1 participate in OSPF. In this case, the command is NETWORK 1.1.1.1 0.0.0.0 AREA 0.
How does OSPF select a router ID?	It prefers loop-back interfaces over anything else. If no loop-back interfaces are available, it selects an active interface with the highest IP address, regardless of whether it's participating in OSPF.
What's a disadvantage of using loop-back interfaces?	You must give it an IP address.

FROM THE CLASSROOM

Default Routes

OSPF can generate a *default route* for the entire autonomous system. Remember that a default route is essentially the route for all networks not explicitly learned via the OSPF or another dynamic routing process. Used wisely, a default route can ease the burdens of routing unknown traffic to its final destination.

A default route is a route not of your primary autonomous system. In many cases, it is the route to the Internet. Therefore, you should carefully choose the router that generates the default route. The ideal candidate is the autonomous system boundary router (ASBR)

that sits between your autonomous systems or between your AS and the Internet, if you like. Ensure that the router you choose for your ASBR has the processing power, memory, and connectivity necessary to route this potentially high volume of default traffic.

To generate a default route, execute DEFAULT-INFORMATION ORIGINATE and apply any options that you need.

Choose wisely. Make default routes a part of your overall OSPF design. A default route generated by the wrong router in the wrong place can play havoc with even the best OSPF configurations.

—*Charles Riley, MCSE, CCNP*

The NETWORK Command and the Wildcard Mask

On Cisco routers, the NETWORK command, with the exception of BGP, tells a routing process what interfaces to advertise out. It does not tell the routing process—in this case, OSPF—what networks and masks to advertise. It specifically identifies those interfaces that OSPF will advertise out. OSPF advertises out an interface with a source network address and a network mask of that interface. Until you enter at least one network statement under the OSPF process, the OSPF process will not start. The command syntax is:

```
router(config)# router ospf 1        (creates OSPF process 1)
```

After you press Enter, the command prompt changes to the routing protocol configuration mode:

```
router(config-router)#
router(config-router)# network 1.1.1.1 0.0.0.0 area 0
```

The preceding code is the minimum command needed to make an interface part of this OSPF process; that is, this network, as the source of the interface, will be advertised to neighbors via this OSPF process.

The IP address following *network* is the IP network that you want to advertise.

When calculating a wildcard mask for a particular network, replace 1 for 0, and vice versa, of the subnet mask used on the interface.

The 0.0.0.0 is the wildcard and tells OSPF what to match and advertise and what to disregard. In binary, the 0 means *must match*, and the 1 is *don't care*.

Translating the preceding code into binary:

```
1.1.1.1 becomes     0000 0001.0000 0001.0000 0001.0000 0001
0.0.0.0 becomes     0000 0000.0000 0000.0000 0000.0000 0000   (0=must match)
                    0000 0001.0000 0001.0000 0001.0000 0001
              (This is the subnet that this OSPF process will advertise.)
```

What if we change the wildcard mask to 0.0.255.255? Using the same IP address as before, we now get:

```
1.1.1.1             0000 0001.0000 0001.0000 0001.0000 0001
0.0.255.255         0000 0000.0000 0000.1111 1111.1111 1111
                    0000 0001.0000 0001.0000 0000.0000 0000
```

By changing our wildcard mask, we are telling the OSPF routing process that any interface with a network address of 1.1.0.0 and a wildcard mask of 0.0.255.255 is part of area 0 in OSPF process 1. Since OSPF advertises out those interfaces with source addresses matching the preceding ones, it also by default advertises the network address and subnet mask of these interfaces.

This demonstrates a shortcut in that the inverse of your subnet mask equals the wildcard mask you should use to advertise a specific network. For example, to advertise a network address of 192.34.56.0 that is subnetted using 255.255.255.0, your OSPF command would be NETWORK 192.34.56.0 0.0.0.255. The area option at the end of the network string is mandatory; an interface must be part of an area if it is to advertise via OSPF. If you only have one area, it must be area 0. All areas must connect to area 0, the backbone area. The area option is used to logically control and organize advertised routes.

OSPF Selection of a Router ID

The router ID is the OSPF version of an ID card: it identifies the router to its neighbors. The router ID is taken from an active interface, logical or physical, on the router—that is, from one of its interfaces that has an IP address assigned. OSPF has a definite hierarchical scheme to determine from which interface it selects its IP address; in order, it attempt to use the IP address of an active loop-back interface, if one is available. If there are no loop-back interfaces, it then uses the highest IP address of an active interface. The interfaces do not have to participate the OSPF routing process in order to be chosen as the OSPF router ID.

The IP address used as the router ID for OSPF does not have to be advertised by OSPF, although you might want to ensure that the neighbors can reach it for troubleshooting purposes.

It is recommended that you use loop-back interfaces because they are always active and never go down. The stability incurred when you use loop-back interfaces can make OSPF more reliable.

If you initially start out with a loop-back interface, then later remove it, OSPF picks a new router ID, following the appropriate order as stated previously.

EXERCISE 3-3

Adding Networks to the OSPF Process

Question: How would you add the networks 199.253.253.253/30 and 1.1.1.1/8 to the OSPF routing process 33? Assume only area 0.

Answer: As we discussed, you have two methods for adding these networks to the OSPF routing process.

1. Convert the subnet masks to the appropriate wildcard masks, as shown. A simple technique is to invert the 1s and 0s of the subnet mask to derive the wildcard mask. In other words, change subnet mask 1s to 0s, and vice versa.

   Router ospf 33
   Network 199.253.253.253 0.0.0.3 area 0
   Network 1.1.1.1 0.255.255.255 area 0

2. The 0.0.0.0 technique enables you to insert the interface hosting the network into the OSPF process as shown. The advantage of this ability is that it makes

troubleshooting easier, and you spend less time calculating the appropriate wildcard mask.

Router OSPF 33
Network 199.253.253.253 0.0.0.0 area 0
Network 1.1.1.1 0.0.0.0 area. 0

Trade-offs and the Loopback Address

Loop-back interfaces can introduce some measure of stability in OSPF operations, but they involve some tradeoffs. For starters, you must assign at least a /32 IP address to a loop-back interface (that is, an IP address with a 255.255.255.255 mask). Should you choose to advertise it, you must ensure that its contiguousness does not overlap or conflict with the addressing on other interfaces. The main argument against using loop-back interfaces might be insignificant if you cannot spare the addresses or your network is small enough that troubleshooting is not that much of an issue.

If you can spare the address and have a logical plan, use loop-back interfaces. It is recommended that you take a contiguous subnet, split it using at least a /32 mask, and assign it to the loop-back interface. To ease documentation and troubleshooting, advertise these interfaces; since OSPF supports VLSM, it can handle the fine-toothed subnetting that you do here. Using loop-back interfaces can be especially invaluable if you have an enterprise network; the practice can also perform double duty as an update source address for other protocols such as BGP.

The OSPF COST INTERFACE Command

Cost is the OSPF metric used to determine the preferred interface on a router. Cost can be likened to toll roads: if you have several toll roads between you and your destination, you will pick the one that minimizes your time on the road, the actual toll costs not withstanding. As in real life, you might pay a higher price for high-speed circuits because the cost (not monetary) to you is less.

The formula calculating cost is as follows. This formula is run by default and calculates based on the given speed of the interface.

```
COST = 100,000,000/Bandwidth in bits per second (bps)
```

With this formula, the default cost of a fast Ethernet running at 100 megabits per second (Mbps) is calculated as follows:

```
Fast Ethernet Interface Cost
100,000,000/100,000,000 = 1
```

This is a very low-cost link indeed. Contrast it with an interface with a T-1 connection:

```
T-1 Cost
100,000,000/1,544,000 = 64.7
```

As far as OSPF is concerned, the Fast Ethernet has the best cost of the two interfaces and will be the one used to route traffic to its destination.

These calculations are performed automatically and, by default, by the OSPF process. However, keeping our example, what if you wanted traffic to use the T-1 connection rather than the Fast Ethernet one? You can use the IP OSPF COST command to influence the selection of paths.

With the OSPF COST command, interfaces have an associated cost (a "toll"). Generally speaking (unlike in the real world), the wider and faster the road, the less it costs to use that road. There are default costs associated with various interfaces as shown in the table.

Harking back to our toll analogy, the network engineer can manually increase or decrease the cost of an interface to influence traffic flow or to load balance between interfaces (similar and dissimilar). Just as we can increase or decrease the tolls to decrease or increase traffic, we do the same with routed packets. By setting the cost high, we make an interface less preferred. The converse is also true.

There are several situations in which we want to modify an interface's cost. We might want to send more traffic over a faster circuit and less on the slow circuit. We might want to send more traffic over a slow but cheap circuit, as opposed to a faster but expensive circuit, to save monetary costs, especially on circuits for which we might be charged per packet. If one circuit functions as a backup circuit, we want to keep as much traffic off of it until it is needed.

Monitoring and Verifying OSPF Operations

exam
ⓦatch

In this section, we discuss commands that can be used to check the health of OSPF.

As you read this section, become familiar with the commands that show the routing tables, topology database, and neighbors of OSPF.

The SHOW IP PROTOCOLS Command

SHOW IP PROTOCOLS is the most basic and simple of routing commands; it merely shows what routing protocols are running on a router. It is best used to get a check summary of routing protocols on a router and to determine quickly whether OSPF is enabled. It also shows you what IP addresses are advertised via what protocol, what interfaces are participating in what protocol, and what redistribution, if any, is being performed.

The first two lines of this command list timer values (how often updates are sent, flush timer, invalid, and so on) and are set to 0. These timer values do not apply to OSPF because the SPF recalculates upon neighbor loss and shows the true current state of the networks.

The SHOW IP ROUTE Command

When entered with no options, the SHOW IP ROUTE command shows the current entries in the routing tables as learned from all IP routing protocols. The display is similar to what you see here:

```
Codes: C - connected, S - static, I - IGRP, R - RIP, M - mobile,
B - BGP        D - EIGRP, EX - EIGRP external, O - OSPF, IA - OSPF
inter area     E1 - OSPF external type 1, E2 - OSPF external type 2,
   E - EGP i - IS-IS, L1 - IS-IS level-1, L2 - IS-IS level-2, * -
candidate default   U - per-user static route
      Gateway of last resort is 199.123.111.1 to network 0.0.0.0
      1.1.0.0/16 is variably subnetted, 126 subnets, 9 masks
      O       1.1.1.0/24          [110/3] via 1.1.111.46, 00:43:40,
FastEthernet11/1/0 O       1.1.1.0/24
```

There are two significant options you can append to this command to narrow its output. One focuses on a particular host or network address; the other focuses on the routes learned via a particular routing protocol.

SHOW IP ROUTE 1.1.1.0 shows any and all networks, subnetted or not, that fall into this range.

```
        Routing entry for 1.1.0.0/16, 126 known subnets
            Attached (18 connections)
            Variably subnetted with 9 masks
            Redistributing via eigrp 99, ospf 1563, igrp 99
            Advertised by igrp 99
O   1.1.95.0/24    [110/3] via 199.123.111.46, 00:44:57, FastEthernet11/1/0
O   1.1.94.0/24    [110/3] via 199.123.111.46, 00:44:57, FastEthernet11/1/0
```

SHOW IP ROUTE 1.1.212.1 shows very specific information about a single link, including from where the link was learned and how it can be reached.

```
        Routing entry for 1.1.212.0/24
        Known via "eigrp 99", distance 90, metric 2195456, type internal
        Redistributing via eigrp 99, ospf 1563, igrp 99
        Advertised by ospf 1563 metric 10 metric-type 1 subnets  igrp 99
        Last update from 1.1.253.26 on Serial2/2, 03:40:09 ago
        Routing Descriptor Blocks:

        1.1.253.26, from 1.1.253.26, 03:40:09 ago, via Serial2/2
        Route metric is 2195456, traffic share count is 1
        Total delay is 21000 microseconds, minimum bandwidth is 1544 Kbit
        Reliability 255/255, minimum MTU 1500 bytes
        Loading 1/255, Hops 1
```

The SHOW IP OSPF INTERFACE Command

The SHOW IP OSPF INTERFACE command can be used to look at all OSPF interfaces. It shows you on what interfaces OSPF is operating. It also shows you the OSPF network type of this interface, which can be useful for troubleshooting OSPF failures.

If you type **SHOW IP OSPF INTERFACE** or **SHOW IP OSPF INTERFACE ETHERNET 1/1**, you will get the following output:

```
Ethernet1/1 is administratively down, line protocol is down
    OSPF not enabled on this interface
Ethernet1/2 is up, line protocol is up
```

```
Internet Address 1.1.1.1, Area 0
Process ID 1563, Router ID 1.1.1.1, Network Type BROADCAST, Cost: 10
Transmit Delay is 1 sec, State BDR, Priority 1
Designated Router (ID) 1.1.1.2, Interface address 1.1.1.2
Backup Designated router (ID) 1.1.1.3, Interface address 1.1.1.3
Timer intervals configured, Hello 10, Dead 40, Wait 40, Retransmit 5
  Hello due in 00:00:08
Neighbor Count is 1, Adjacent neighbor count is 1
  Adjacent with neighbor 1.1.252.1  (Designated Router)
```

The SHOW IP OSPF Command

The SHOW IP OSPF command shows what OSPF processes are running on this router, what areas this router is in, and how many interfaces are in this area. It also identifies whether the area has any authentication and how many times per area the SPF has been run.

```
Routing Process "ospf 1" with ID 1.1.1.1
Supports only single TOS(TOS0) routes
 It is an autonomous system boundary router
 External Link update interval is 00:30:00 and the update due in 00:26:16
 Redistributing External Routes from,
   eigrp 1 with metric mapped to 10, includes subnets in redistribution
 SPF schedule delay 5 secs, Hold time between two SPFs 10 secs
 Number of areas in this router is 1. 1 normal 0 stub
   Area 0
       Number of interfaces in this area is 30
       Area has no authentication
       SPF algorithm executed 11197 times
       Area ranges are
       Link State Update Interval is 00:30:00 and due in 00:26:13
       Link State Age Interval is 00:20:00 and due in 00:16:13
```

The SHOW IP OSPF NEIGHBOR Command

The SHOW IP OSPF NEIGHBOR command lists the contents of the neighbor table and the states of each neighbor. It also identifies the type of router.

```
Neighbor ID   Pri  State      Dead Time   Address       Interface
1.1.1.1       1    FULL/DR    00:00:33    1.1.1.1       Ethernet1/2
1.1.1.2       1    FULL/DR    00:00:31    1.1.1.2       FastEthernet11/0/0
1.1.1.3       1    FULL/DR    00:00:39    1.1.1.2       FastEthernet11/1/0
```

SCENARIO & SOLUTION

If OSPF, EIGRP, RIP, and IGRP all have a route to a specific network. Which routing protocol's route will be installed in the routing table?	EIGRP, because it has a lower administrative distance (90) than IGRP (100), OSPF (110), and RIP (120).
What command would show me how network 1.1.1.0 is being redistributed and by what protocols?	SHOW IP ROUTE 1.1.1.0.
I telneted to the router and entered the command DEBUG IP OSPF ADJ, but I am not seeing anything on my SYSLOG server.	You might need to execute the command TERMINAL MONITOR to log to the current session and possibly execute OSPF LOG-ADJ-CHANGES under the OSPF process you want to debug.

If you want specific details on a specific neighbor, narrow your command focus using the SHOW IP OSPF NEIGHBOR 1.1.1.2 command.

```
Neighbor 1.1.1.2, interface address 1.1.1.2
In the area 0 via interface Ethernet1/2
    Neighbor priority is 1, State is FULL
    Options 2
    Dead timer due in 00:00:36
```

The SHOW IP OSPF NEIGHBOR DETAIL Command

The SHOW IP OSPF NEIGHBOR DETAIL command provides a continuous listing of all neighbors. The output is the same as a specific SHOW IP OSPF NEIGHBOR 1.1.1.2 command, only it shows the same information for all neighbors.

```
Neighbor 1.1.1.2, interface address 1.1.1.2
In the area 0 via interface Ethernet1/2
    Neighbor priority is 1, State is FULL
    Options 2
    Dead timer due in 00:00:30
```

The DEBUG IP OSPF ADJ Command

When the SHOW commands cannot show you what is happening, you need to use DEBUG. This command shows you what is happening behind the OSPF scenes.

There are several DEBUG commands pertaining to OSPF, but we discuss only one, DEBUG IP OSPF ADJ, which shows the events relevant to adjacencies.

WARNING! Limit your use of debug commands in a production environment because they can place heavy loads on the router. If you must use them on a product router, use only the commands you need.

```
router#debug ip ospf ?
  adj              OSPF adjacency events
  database-timer   OSPF database timer
  events           OSPF events
  flood            OSPF flooding
  lsa-generation   OSPF lsa generation
  packet           OSPF packets
  retransmission   OSPF retransmission events
  spf              OSPF spf
  tree             OSPF database tree
```

The DEBUG IP OSPF ADJ command can be used to watch adjacencies being formed and to pinpoint problems when adjacencies cannot be formed successfully. This command can be useful in pinpointing adjacency formation failures that might be caused by network type mismatches, authentication conflicts, or hello parameter disagreements. In order to log OSPF adjacency events to a SYSLOG server, enter the OSPF LOG-ADJ-CHANGES command under the OSPF routing process. If you do not, you might not be able to see any debug information. The availability of this command varies, depending on your IOS.

EXERCISE 3-4

Listing the Contents of OSPF Databases

Question: Familiarization with the commands necessary to display the contents of OSPF databases is important for tracking routes and troubleshooting. What commands would you use to get a:

- List of neighbors
- List of interfaces participating in OSPF
- List of all routing protocols running on this router
- List of all OSPF processes running on this router
- Complete snapshot of the entire routing table

Answer:

- List of neighbors: SHOW IP OSPF NEIGHBOR
- List of interfaces participating in OSPF: SHOW IP OSPF INTERFACE
- List of all routing protocols running on this router: SHOW IP PROTOCOLS
- List of all OSPF processes running on this router: SHOW IP OSPF
- Complete snapshot of the entire routing table: SHOW IP ROUTE

CERTIFICATION SUMMARY

The chapter introduced you to OSPF and provided an overview of its structure. OSPF is a link-state routing protocol that uses the concept of areas to control and minimize routing information. It does not send out its entire routing table periodically; instead, it relies on LSAs and hellos to keep its routers synchronized.

Every OSPF router views itself as the root of the network and builds its topology database accordingly. Each router runs the SPF algorithm from this perspective to derive the shortest path to a destination.

The OSPF configuration process starts with the ROUTER OSPF <PROCESS-ID> command. From there, you add interfaces to the OSPF routing process with the NETWORK command and adjust parameters on the interfaces as needed.

There are a variety of SHOW and DEBUG commands that can be used to display OSPF for informational and troubleshooting purposes. DEBUG is best used to troubleshoot and should be used only to resolve a specific problem.

✓ TWO-MINUTE DRILL

Here are some of the key points from Chapter 3.

Benefits of OSPF in Comparison to DV Protocols

❑ OSPF benefits include scalability, flexibility, advertisement summarization, VLSM, incremental updates, fast convergence, and structure update exchange.

❑ OSPF routers have a complete picture of the network.

❑ OSPF chooses the shortest path and inserts it into its routing table.

How OSPF Discovers, Chooses, and Maintains Routes

❑ Becoming neighbors with the other routers on the network is the first step toward building its topology database and routing table.

❑ After the neighbor formation is complete, OSPF routers continue to the next phase: becoming adjacent.

❑ OSPF elects a DR and a BDR on broadcast networks or NBMA networks running in broadcast mode.

❑ On a broadcast network, adjacency is achieved only with the DR and the BDR.

❑ The neighbor database details the neighbors of a particular router, including neighbor router ID, priority, and so on. It can be viewed with the SHOW IP OSF NEIGHBOR command.

❑ The topology database can be viewed in its entirety with the SHOW IP OSPF DATABASE command.

❑ OSPF entries in the routing table are marked with O, IA, E1, and E2.

❑ Wait time is always equal to dead time, and dead time is, by default, four times the hello time.

❑ To become neighbors, routers must agree on the area ID, authentication method, hello timer, dead timer, and the stub area flag.

❑ The election of a DR and BDR cannot occur until after neighbor formation is complete.

❑ OSPF states in order of occurrence are DOWN, INIT, two-way/EXSTART, two-way/EXCHANGE, two-way/LOADING, and FULL.

❑ All OSPF packets have the same 24-byte header.

❑ The five LSA types we discussed are router links (1), network links (2), summary LSA (IP, 3), Summary LSA (ASBR, 4), and AS-External-LSA (5).

❑ Each router places itself at the root (center) of the network and runs the SPF algorithm accordingly.

Configuring OSPF in a Single Area

The first step in configuring OSPF is to enable it via the ROUTER OSPF <PROCESS-ID> command.

❑ To quickly calculate the wildcard mask and add networks to the OSPF process, change the 1s of the subnet mask to 0s, and vice versa. Alternatively, add the interface using a wildcard mask of 0.0.0.0.

❑ The router ID is taken from an active interface, regardless of whether it is participating in OSPF or not. Loop-back interfaces are always preferred over physical interfaces, and high IP addresses are preferred over lower ones.

❑ The formula for calculating the default interface cost is *100,000,000/bandwidth in bits*.

Monitoring and Verifying OSPF Operations

❑ SHOW IP PROTOCOLS displays all routing protocols running on the router.

❑ SHOW IP ROUTE lists the contents of the routing table.

❑ SHOW IP OSPF INTERFACES identifies interfaces participating in an OSPF process.

❑ SHOW IP OSPF shows what OPSF processes are running on a particular router.

❑ SHOW IP OSPF NEIGHBOR lists the OSPF neighbors of the router on which the command is executed.

❑ DEBUG IP OSPF ADJ displays real-time messages about adjacency events.

SELF TEST

The following questions will help you measure your understanding of the material presented in this chapter. Read all the choices carefully because there might be more than one correct answer. Choose all correct answers for each question.

Benefits of OSPF in Comparison to DV Protocols

1. What OSPF benefit permits networks to adapt to size changes?
   A. Scalability
   B. Flexibility
   C. Expandability
   D. Accountability

2. OSPF allows networks to be grouped to accommodate the needs of an organization. This is a demonstration of OSPF's:
   A. Expandability
   B. Flexibility
   C. Support for VLSM
   D. None of the above

3. Complete this sentence: OSPF supports _____, which enhances OSPF's ability to _____.
   A. Contiguous addressing, route packets
   B. Discontiguous addressing, reduce the number of routing entries
   C. VLSM, summarize advertisements
   D. Classful addressing, subnet on classful boundaries

4. OSPF's fast convergence is largely due to its:
   A. Topology database
   B. Routing table
   C. Neighbor table
   D. SPF algorithm

5. The OSPF router's complete picture of the network includes which of the following?

    A. The topology of the Internet

    B. Only those networks in its entire area

    C. All networks and all possible pathways to each network and any external routes

    D. All networks and only the best route to each network and any external routes

How OSPF Discovers, Chooses, and Maintains Routes

6. What is the first step an OSPF router takes toward building its topology database and routing tables?

    A. Becoming adjacent

    B. Becoming neighbors

    C. Agreeing on the link parameters

    D. Placing itself at the root of the network and calculating the SPF algorithm for all destinations

7. After becoming neighbors, OSPF routers then do which of the following?

    A. Negotiate the link parameters

    B. Calculate the SPF algorithm to all destinations

    C. Calculate the interface costs

    D. Start the database exchange process to become adjacent

8. The concept of designated routers and backup designated routers reduces the number of adjacencies and the amount of routing traffic generated. If OSPF did not have DRs and BDRs on a network, which of the following formulas shows the number of adjacencies that would have to be formed? (N is the number of routers on the network.)

    A. $N(2)$

    B. $N(N-2)$

    C. $N(N)$

    D. $N(N-1)$

9. In order to become neighbors, what must occur between routers?

    A. The link between the routers must have an IP address

    B. The routers must become adjacent to their network's designated router

    C. The routers must agree on the parameters for their common network

    D. The OSPF cost for the network must match on both routers

10. Elections occur when?

    A. Before the routers become neighbors

    B. After the routers become neighbors

    C. During neighbor formation

    D. None of the above

11. Router A was the DR until a power failure forced it off your network. Router B was the BDR and became the DR when Router A failed. Router C then won the election to be the BDR. Power has been restored to Router A, which has the highest priority and router ID of any router on the network. What will happen next?

    A. Nothing. Router A will accept its new role.

    B. A new election will occur, and Router A will become the BDR.

    C. A new election will occur, and Router A will become the DR again, with B and C going back to their old roles.

    D. No new election will occur, and Router A will not become neighbors with any other router.

12. You entered the DEBUG IP OSPF ADJ command and restarted the OSPF process, but nothing is displayed. You checked your OSPF process and interface; all is correct. What must you do now?

    A. In the OSPF process configuration mode, enter **OSPF LOG-ADJ-CHANGES**.

    B. Delete OSPF and start it again, this time using loop-back interfaces.

    C. Set the hello timers to 5 seconds to force more neighbor communications.

    D. Use the **CLEAR IP ROUTE OSPF** command to force adjacencies to recur.

13. In what order do the OSPF states occur?

    A. INIT, DOWN, two-way/EXSTART, two-way/FULL, two-way/LOADING

    B. DOWN, DROTHER, EXSTART, LOADING, FULL

    C. DOWN, INIT, two-way, EXSTART, EXCHANGE, LOADING, FULL

    D. DOWN, two-way, INIT, EXSTART, EXCHANGE, LOADING, FULL

14. To ensure routing data integrity and to control the process, OSPF routers enter into a master/slave relationship for purposes of database exchange. At what stage does this role assignment occur?

A. INIT

B. EXSTART

C. EXCHANGE

D. LOADING

15. An inter-area destination that is an IP address is described by a:

A. Router link (LSA type 1)

B. Network link (LSA type 2)

C. Summary LSAs (type 3)

D. Summary LSAs (type 4)

16. An inter-area destination that is an ASBR is described by a:

A. Router link (LSA type 1)

B. Network link (LSA type 2)

C. Summary LSAs (type 3)

D. Summary LSAs (type 4)

Configuring OSPF in a Single Area

17. What is the very first step in enabling OSPF on a router?

A. Router ospf <process-id>

B. IP ospf network (type) interface

C. No router eigrp (process-id)

D. None of the above

18. One of your interfaces is using IP address 1.1.1.1 with a subnet mask of 255.255.128.0. What is the command to put this interface into the OSPF process? Assume only an area 0.

A. IP ospf cost 64 (on the interface)

B. Network 1.1.1.1 0.0.127.255

C. Network 1.1.1.1 0.0.0.0 area 0

D. Network 1.1.0.0

19. Router A has a loop-back interface with an IP address of 1.1.1.1 and a physical interface with an IP address of 254.254.254.254. The loop-back interface is *not* participating in the OSPF routing process, but the physical interface is. Given that these are the only two active interfaces on this router, what will its router ID be?

    A. 254.254.254.254

    B. 1.1.1.1

    C. Both 254.254.254.254 and 1.1.1.1.

    D. None of the above

20. What is a valid reason for using loop-back interfaces as far as OSPF is concerned?

    A. To provide a stable router ID

    B. You should not use loop-back interfaces because they consume an IP address

    C. Loop-back can provide a stable interface address for unnumbered interfaces

    D. Loop-back interfaces enable testing via ICMP pings

21. You have a T-1 circuit. What is its default OSPF cost as calculated automatically by OSPF?

    A. 64

    B. 1,544

    C. 10

    D. 1

Monitoring and Verifying OSPF Operations

22. What command would you execute to find out how the router is learning to reach the host 1.1.1.1?

    A. SHOW IP ROUTE

    B. SHOW IP ROUTE 1.0.0.0

    C. SHOW IP HOST

    D. SHOW IP ROUTE 1.1.1.1

23. The command to show how many OSPF routing processes are enabled on the router and whether they are using authentication is:

    A. SHOW IP OSPF ROUTE

    B. SHOW IP OSPF NEIGHBOR

C. SHOW IP OSPF

D. SHOW IP PROTOCOLS

24. How would you find out the priority for the router's neighbor that is using IP address 1.1.1.1?

A. SHOW IP OSPF NEIGHBOR 1.1.1.1

B. SHOW IP OPSF NEIGHBOR

C. SHOW IP OSPF INTERFACE

D. SHOW IP OSPF

LAB QUESTION

You have been given responsibility for a network with three Cisco 2501 routers. You must ensure that the router ID for A is 1.1.1.1, B is 1.1.1.2, and C is 1.1.1.3. (These addresses will not participate in the OSPF process.)

Routers B and C connect to A via point-to-point circuits (default encapsulation). B is on A's interface serial 0, and C is on serial 1. Change the hello time on the link between A and B to 30 seconds; use IP address 192.87.34.0/30 for this link. Change the wait time on the link to A and C to 120 seconds; do not change the hello time; use IP address 192.87.34.4/30 for the link.

A, B, and C have a LAN attached to their Ethernet interfaces. The IP address on router A's LAN is 2.2.2.1/24, router B's LAN is 3.3.3.3/16, and router C's LAN is 200.129.17.253/28. Add A's and C's LAN to OSPF using wildcard masks not based on their subnet masks. Add the serial links and B's LAN to OSPF without using wildcard masks based on its subnet mask.

Diagram this network; show the links and addressing and the configurations necessary to achieve the stated goals. Verify the neighbor formation, and ensure that the routers can reach each other's LANs.

SELF TEST ANSWERS

Benefits of OSPF in Comparison to DV Protocols

1. ☑ A. Scalability is OSPF's ability to shrink or grow as needed.
   ☒ B is incorrect because flexibility refers to OSPF's ability to accommodate different topologies and network arrangements. C and D are incorrect because expandability and accountability are not a characteristic of OSPF.

2. ☑ B. Flexibility—OSPF's ability to accommodate different topologies and network arrangements.
   ☒ A is incorrect because expandability is not a characteristic of OSPF. C is incorrect because VLSM refers to OSPF's ability to handle different subnetting schemes. D is incorrect because there is a correct answer.

3. ☑ C. VLSM enables OSPF to support various subnetting schemes, which enhances its ability to summarize on classless boundaries if necessary.
   ☒ A, B, and D are incorrect because these are not benefits of OSPF.

4. ☑ A. Topology database. OSPF keeps a complete picture of the network in this database, including alternate paths to a destination.
   ☒ B and C are incorrect because the routing table gets its choices from the topology database and the neighbor table is just a listing of neighbors. D is incorrect because the SPF algorithm calculates the shortest path to a destination; it does not participate directly in convergence, although it helps build the topology database.

5. ☑ C. All networks and all possible pathways to each network and any external routes. This is by OSPF design.
   ☒ A is incorrect because it would mean a table of millions of entries. B is incorrect because it would exclude external routes to reach other areas. D is incorrect because it would be more information than the router needs.

How OSPF Discovers, Chooses, and Maintains Routes

6. ☑ B. Becoming neighbors.
   ☒ A is incorrect because becoming adjacent comes after becoming neighbors; C is incorrect because agreeing on the link parameters is part of the neighbor formation process. D is incorrect because placing itself at the root of the network occurs during the process of becoming neighbors.

7. ☑ **D.** Start the database exchange process to become adjacent. This is also known as becoming adjacent.

   ☒ **A** is incorrect because negotiating the link parameters occurs during the neighbor formation process. **B** is incorrect because calculating the SPF algorithm to all destinations occurs after the database exchange is successful. **C** is incorrect because calculating the interface costs is complete as soon as the interface participates in the OSPF process.

8. ☑ **D.** $N(N-1)$. With a DR and a BDR, all routers would become adjacent to each other and exchange the requisite amount of traffic. The $(N-1)$ part of the formula implies that a router will not become neighbors and adjacent with itself.

   ☒ **A** is incorrect because $N(2)$ shows the number of adjacencies necessary using DR/BDR. **B** and **C** are incorrect because $N(N-2)$ and $N(N)$ do not reflect either configuration.

9. ☑ **C.** The routers must agree on the parameters for their common network. This is correct because routers must agree in order to become neighbors.

   ☒ **A** is incorrect because OSPF supports the use of unnumbered links. **B** is incorrect because the statement is not true of all networks. **D** is incorrect because the cost of one router does not affect the cost of another router.

10. ☑ **B.** After the routers become neighbors.

    ☒ **A** is incorrect because the OSPF routers cannot talk OSPF until they become neighbors. **C** is incorrect because the only thing that occurs during neighbor formation is neighbor formation. **D** is incorrect because there is a correct answer.

11. ☑ **A.** The router will accept its lot in life.

    ☒ **B** and **C** are incorrect because no new elections occur once a DR and BDR are already elected. **D** is incorrect because the router will still become neighbors with the other routers.

12. ☑ **A.** In the OSPF process configuration mode, enter **OSPF LOG-ADJ-CHANGES.** This command ensures that the adjacency changes are logged.

    ☒ **B** is incorrect because it causes adjacency events to occur but that you will not be able to see them. **C** is incorrect because it causes neighbor relations to fail. **D** is incorrect because it clears the routing table but does not force a recalculation of the SPF algorithm.

13. ☑ **D.** DOWN, two-way, INIT, EXSTART, EXCHANGE, LOADING, FULL is the correct order in which the OSPF states occur.

    ☒ **A**, **B**, and **C** are incorrect because they are listed in the wrong order.

14. ☑ **B.** The roles are determined during the EXSTART stage.

    ☒ **A**, **C**, and **D** are incorrect because the role assignment occurs *only* during the EXSTART stage.

15. ☑ **C.** Summary LSAs (type 3). This is correct because the destination is an IP address.
    ☒ **A** is incorrect because it describes a router's interfaces. **B** is incorrect because it describes area routes. **D** is incorrect because the destination is not an ASBR. The formats of 3 and 4 are the same but have different purposes.

16. ☑ **D.** Summary LSAs (type 4). The format is the same as type 3, but the purpose is different.
    ☒ **A** is incorrect because it describes a router's interfaces. **B** is incorrect because it describes area routes. **C** is incorrect because the destination is not an IP network.

Configuring OSPF in a Single Area

17. ☑ **A.** OSPF activation starts with this command.
    ☒ **B** is incorrect because it does not enable OSPF on the router. **C** is incorrect because it has nothing to do with OSPF. **D** is incorrect because there is a correct answer.

18. ☑ **C.** Network 1.1.1.1 0.0.0.0. area 0. This answer makes the interface participate in OSPF.
    ☒ **A** is incorrect because it sets the interface cost. **B** is incorrect because it's missing the mandatory area argument. **D** is incorrect because it is incomplete.

19. ☑ **B.** 1.1.1.1. OSPF will always prefer a loop-back interface, whether or not it has the highest IP address and regardless of whether it is participating in OSPF.
    ☒ **A** is incorrect because OSPF prefers loop-back interfaces over physical interfaces. **C** is incorrect because a router can have only a single router ID. **D** is incorrect because there is a correct answer.

20. ☑ **A.** To provide a stable router ID. OSPF seeks to make its operations as stable as possible.
    ☒ **B** is incorrect because it lists a reason for not using a loop-back interface. **C** and **D** are incorrect because we are not discussing unnumbered interfaces or ICMP testing.

21. ☑ **A.** 64. This is incorrect because we use the OSPF formula of 100,000,000/1544000 = 64.
    ☒ **C, B**, and **D** are incorrect because they are not mathematically correct, using the cost formula.

Monitoring and Verifying OSPF Operations

22. ☑ **D.** SHOW IP ROUTE 1.1.1.1.
    ☒ **A** is incorrect because it shows all the routes. **B** is incorrect because it shows all routes in the 1.0.0.0 subnet. **C** is incorrect because it shows any named IP hosts on the router.

23. ☑ **C.** SHOW IP OSPF is the correct command to show how many OSPF routing processes are enabled on the router and whether authentication is used.
☒ **A** is incorrect because there is no such command as SHOW IP OSPF ROUTE. **B** is incorrect because SHOW IP OSPF NEIGHBOR shows OSPF neighbors. **D** is incorrect because SHOW IP PROTOCOLS shows all routing protocols.

24. ☑ **A.** SHOW IP OSPF NEIGHBOR 1.1.1.1 is the correct command.
☒ **B** is incorrect because SHOW IP OPSF NEIGHBOR shows a quick summary of all neighbors. **C** is incorrect because SHOW IP OSPF INTERFACE shows interfaces participating in OSPF. **D** is incorrect because SHOW IP OSPF shows OSPF processes running on the router.

LAB ANSWER

The student should come up with configurations for A, B, and C as shown in Figure 3-18. You should know to use the SHOW IP OSPF NEIGHBOR command to verify the neighbor formation and the SHOW IP ROUTE command to ensure the LAN networks are in each router's routing table.

The diagram and configurations should be similar to Figure 3-18.

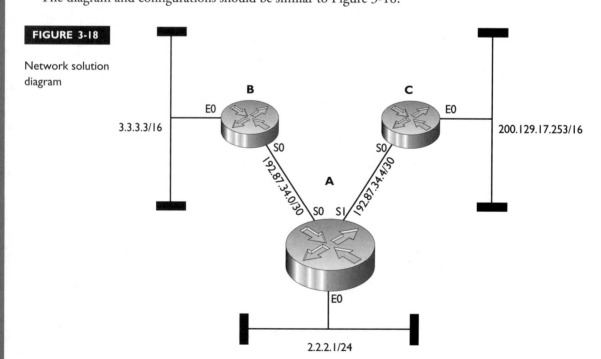

FIGURE 3-18

Network solution diagram

Router Configurations
<u>Router A</u>

```
Hostname Router_A
Interface serial 0
Description Link to Router B.  Hello Timer was changed to 30 seconds.
Ip address 192.87.34.1 255.255.255.252
Ip ospf hello-interval 30

Interface serial 1
Description Link to Router C.  Dead Timer was changed to 120 seconds.
Ip address 192.87.34.5 255.255.255.252
Ip ospf dead-interval 120

Interface loopback 0
Ip address 1.1.1.1 255.255.255.255

Interface Ethernet 0
Ip address 2.2.2.1 255.255.255.0

Router OSPF 33
Network 2.2.2.1 0.0.0.255 area 0
Network 192.87.34.5 0.0.0.0 area 0
Network 192.87.34.1 0.0.0.0 area 0
```

<u>Router B</u>

```
Hostname Router_B
Interface serial 0
Description Link to Router A.  Hello Timer was changed to 30 seconds.
Ip address 192.87.34.2 255.255.255.252
Ip ospf hello-interval 30

Interface loopback 0
Ip address 1.1.1.2 255.255.255.255

Interface Ethernet 0
Ip address 3.3.3.3 255.255.0.0

Router OSPF 33
Network 3.3.3.3 0.0.0.0 area 0
Network 192.87.34.2 0.0.0.0 area 0
```

Router C

```
Hostname Router_C
Interface serial 0
Description Link to Router A.  Dead Timer was changed to 120 seconds.
Ip address 192.87.34.6 255.255.255.252
Ip ospf dead-interval 120

Interface loopback 0
Ip address 1.1.1.3 255.255.255.255

Interface Ethernet 0
Ip address 200.129.17.253 255.255.255.240

Router OSPF 33
Network 200.129.17.240 0.0.0.15 area 0
Network 192.87.34.6 0.0.0.0 area 0
```

4

OSPF Behavior and Configuration for Wide Area Networks

CERTIFICATION OBJECTIVES

I n Chapter 3, you were introduced to and given a broad overview of Open Shortest Path First (OSPF). Chapter 3 introduced you to fundamental concepts and Cisco IOS commands relevant to OSPF. In this chapter we continue our study of OSPF by examining how OSPF operates on various types of networks, including nonbroadcast multiaccess (NBMA) networks such as Frame Relay.

Our discussions center on the idea that there are essentially four types of networks: broadcast, point-to-point, point-to-multipoint, and NBMA. We discuss the characteristics of these networks as they pertain to OSPF. Complicating our discussion is that OSPF can run as a network type that is different from the actual network. We explore and demonstrate the meaning of this aspect of OSPF.

You should take away from this chapter the ability to assess the network topology and determine what you must do in order to get OSPF working on the network. You must be able to understand and address concepts such as topology and partial versus fully meshed networks. Your job will be to implement a solution that optimizes the design of OSPF without unnecessarily consuming bandwidth. The nature of OSPF is such that it helps achieve these two goals.

One thing about OSPF that is worthy of note is its flexibility; but this adds to its complexity. We discuss the various network types and topologies in this chapter. OSPF can treat nonbroadcast networks as broadcast, and vice versa. For example, if you have two OSPF routers on a full-duplex Ethernet network (a broadcast network) and want it not to function as a broadcast network because you do not need the overhead of electing and maintaining designated router (DR) and backup designated router (BDR) relationships, you can configure the Ethernet as an OSPF nonbroadcast network type, and it will act accordingly. The merits of this practice are debatable; be aware that OSPF can treat a network as other than what it actually is.

CERTIFICATION OBJECTIVE 4.01

OSPF Behavior Over a WAN Link

We start with what must be the simplest OSPF configuration: a WAN point-to-point link. Later, we segue into broadcast networks and finish with

NBMA, which has characteristics of the point-to-point links and broadcast networks.

OSPF Behavior on an HDLC or PPP Link

Configuring OSPF on a point-to-point circuit (HDLC or PPP) is one of the easiest configurations of OSPF for the reasons outlined earlier. The configuration process is simple:

- Enable the OSPF routing process.
- Add the interfaces to the OSPF routing process.

Figure 4-1 shows a typical point-to-point configuration.

A point-to-point network requires the least amount of configuration. The only parameters you might need to configure are the Hello and Dead timers, and you might manually need to set the interface cost. As long as your interface types match, there is little need to adjust the timers other than to reduce an already insignificant amount of OSPF traffic.

exam
ⓦatch

Know which network types elect a DR, and which don't.

No Election of a DR

On point-to-point networks, there are only two routers. There is no need to elect a DR or BDR. The only two routers on the link will become adjacent with each other

FIGURE 4-1

OPSF over a point-to-point network

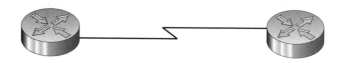

RTRA	RTRB
interface serial 0 ip address 1.1.1.1 255.255.255.252 router ospf 1 network 1.1.1.0 0.0.0.3 area 0	interface serial 0 ip address 1.1.1.2 255.255.255.252 router ospf 1 network 1.1.1.0 0.0.0.3 area 0

and exchange the necessary information to initiate and maintain this adjacency. This is one type of network in which the DR/BDR would result in no savings whatsoever; therefore, it is not used.

Only Two Neighbors on a Link

There are two and only two routers to configure on a point-to-point network. As long as the timers, network mask, area-ID, authentication, and the stub flag match, the two routers will become neighbors and achieve adjacency.

Split Horizon

Split horizon is a mechanism designed to prevent a router from advertising a route back out on the interface (network) from which it learned the route. It was designed to enhance distance vector routing protocols. Without split horizon, routing loops will occur. Referring back to Figure 4-1, if RTRA learned about 2.2.2.2 from RTRB, RTRA should not advertise back to RTRB that it knows how to reach 2.2.2.2, because it learned how to reach 2.2.2.2 from RTRB. If 2.2.2.2 on RTRB went down and split horizon was not being used, a routing loop between RTRA and RTRB could occur.

OSPF has an interesting relationship with split horizon: it does not need it or use it. Being a link-state routing protocol, OSPF builds a complete picture of the network by flooding LSAs to other routers in its area. OSPF learns about the links, networks, and routers in its area. The LSAs are specifically marked with the originating router ID and a sequence number to maintain data integrity. If a router were to receive one of its own advertisements back from a neighbor, it would know not to use it because of this rule.

Since all OSPF routers have a complete picture of the network, they know what links lie between them and a specific destination. Router A, in Figure 4-1, would know that 2.2.2.2 can be reached only via Router B and that it does not have an alternate route to 2.2.2.2.

If you are running OSPF in conjunction with a distance vector protocol such as RIP, split horizon is a concern. You need to make the adjustments necessary for the other routing protocol, not OSPF. Again, OSPF does not need or use split horizon on any network.

on the **Job**

Before you field OSPF, obtain documentation for the network on which you plan to field OSPF. Study it to determine the network topologies being used (point-to-point, multipoint, and so on), the network technologies being used (Ethernet, Frame Relay, or the like), and what would be the most appropriate OSPF network type for each network.

Unnumbered Interfaces

Unnumbered interfaces are a technique to avoid assigning IP addresses to a link in an effort to conserve IP addresses. They can also raise a number of interesting challenges. In Figure 4-2, the serial link between A and B does not have its own IP address. Instead, the serial interfaces linking the OSPF neighbors use the IP address of each respective router's Ethernet interface.

Figure 4-2 shows a potentially problematic configuration in that each end of the point-to-point circuit is "borrowing" a totally different IP address and network mask than its neighbor. There is no commonality or overlap in this scenario. Will this work? Let's discuss it further.

Earlier, we pointed out that in order to become neighbors, routers must agree on a variety of things, including the network mask. In Figure 4-2, we have differing IP addresses and network masks for the serial link.

FIGURE 4-2

A point-to-point network with unnumbered interfaces

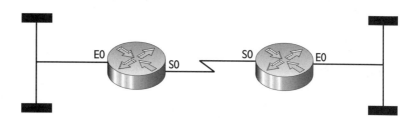

RTRA	RTRB
interface Ethernet 0	interface Ethernet 0
ip address 1.1.1.1 255.255.255.0	ip address 2.2.2.2 255.255.255.0
interface serial 0	interface serial 0
ip unnumbered Ethernet 0	ip unnumbered Ethernet 0
router ospf 1	router ospf 2
network 1.1.1.0 0.0.0.255 area 0	network 2.2.2.0 0.0.0.255 area 0

Unnumbered interfaces do offer an obvious saving in that IP addresses do not have to be "wasted" on a two-router point-to-point link. However, to ensure that you have no problems, you must ensure that unnumbered interfaces are configured according the guidelines that follow.

The common unnumbered link between the two routers must be in the same area (a requirement for becoming neighbors). Only point-to-point interfaces can be unnumbered. Addressing must be done under certain constraints. The addresses used by the unnumbered interfaces must be from the same network number (1.0.0.0 or 2.0.0.0) *and* must use the same subnet mask. In other words, the Ethernet interfaces in our example must use the same IP network address and the same mask.

If you want to use a different address for each Ethernet interface (in our example, 1.1.1.1 and 2.2.2.2, respectively, for A and B), you must use classful addressing with the natural mask. In this case, the 255.255.255.0 mask cannot be used. Instead, we must use 255.0.0.0 because it is a Class A network address. Therefore, the configuration given in Figure 4-2 will not work unless we use the natural mask for these IP network numbers. In the real world, you might not have the option to manipulate our address assignments and masks at will, so plan carefully!

Particular to X.25 and Frame Relay, you cannot use unnumbered interfaces if you are running them in other than point-to-point mode. In addition, be aware that address mappings will be more complicated; you must take greater care or resort to manual methods.

Although unnumbered interfaces can conserve address space, there is a caveat to using them. For one thing, you will lose some troubleshooting ability. For example, if you wanted to ping the serial interfaces of routers using unnumbered interfaces, you would not be able to do so. Furthermore, some network management packages might require an interface to be addressed before it can be monitored and supported.

exam
ⓦatch

What are the guidelines for using unnumbered interfaces with OSPF?

EXERCISE 4-1

Basic OSPF Configuration (Single Area)

You have been hired as a network engineer. One of your first tasks at your new job is to bring up a new T-1 link between Routers A and B. You must use PPP on the link; your address for the link is 123.4.5.0 and your subnet mask is

255.255.255.252 on each router's serial 0. Additionally, the ID of Router A must be 1.1.1.1 and the ID of Router B must be 2.2.2.2. Diagram this network, and show the configurations for Routers A and B. Put B's loop-back interface in the OSPF process, but not A's. Assume area 0 for all.

Solution:

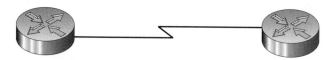

A
interface loopback 0 ip address 1.1.1.1 255.255.255.255 interface serial 0 encapsulation ppp ip address 123.4.5.1 255.255.255.252 router ospf 1 network 123.4.5.1 0.0.0.0 area 0

B
interface loopback 0 ip address 2.2.2.2 255.255.255.255 interface serial 0 encapsulation ppp ip address 123.4.5.2 255.255.255.252 router ospf 1 network 123.4.5.0 0.0.0.3 area 0 network 2.2.2.2 0.0.0.0 area 0

OSPF Configuration and Behavior on a X.25 Link

Here we do not discuss X.25 at any great length. Instead, we focus on configuring X.25 on a point-to-point link. The issues of configuring X.25 are similar to configuring Frame Relay. The concepts to which you will be exposed in the sections dealing with Frame Relay and OSPF are equally applicable to X.25.

X.25 is a packet-switching technology that uses X.121 addressing. IP addresses must be mapped to X.25 addresses, usually manually on Cisco routers using the X25 MAP IP *x.x.x.x yyyy* broadcast, where *x.x.x.x* is the IP address at the distant end and *yyyy* is the X.121 address for the distant router. You will need a similar configuration at the distant mapping toward this router.

Once the two routers on the point-to-point X.25 circuit can ping each other, you do not need to perform any special OSPF configurations on these interfaces. At that point, you can enable the OSPF process and add the networks needed.

Figure 4-3 shows a point-to-point network running OSPF using X.25. Notice the manual X.121 address to IP mappings. No special OSPF interface commands must be executed in order to get this network operating. In fact, except for the X.121 address mappings, the configuration is virtually identical to configuring a point-to-point circuit with encapsulation HDLC. Note that the broadcast parameter is necessary here to permit OSPF's multicasting.

OSPF Configuration and Behavior on Broadcast Networks

OSPF considers networks such as Ethernet, Fast Ethernet, FDDI, and Token Ring broadcast networks. A broadcast network is a multistation network on which all network devices receive the same data frame.

FIGURE 4-3

OSPF on an X.25
point-to-point
network

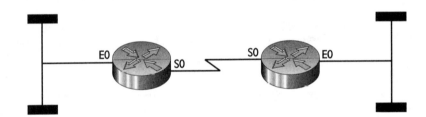

RTRA	RTRB
interface Ethernet 0	interface Ethernet 0
ip address 1.1.1.1 255.255.255.0	ip address 2.2.2.2 255.255.255.0
interface serial 0	interface serial 0
ip 1.2.3.1 255.255.255.252	ip 1.2.3.2 255.255.255.252
encapsulation x25	encapsulation x25
x25 address 1111	x25 address 2222
x25 map ip 1.2.3.2 2222 broadcast	x25 map ip 1.2.3.2 1111 broadcast
router ospf 1	router ospf 1
network 1.1.1.0 0.0.0.255 area 0	network 2.2.2.0 0.0.0.255 area 0
network 1.2.3.1 0.0.0.0 area 0	network 1.2.3.2 0.0.0.0 area 0

Configuring OSPF on broadcast networks requires an understanding of how OSPF works on broadcast networks. Ordinarily, OSPF routers on a network will become adjacent with all other OSPF routers on the same network. They will go through all the stages and exchange the packets necessary to achieve adjacency. On a broadcast network that can host numerous OSPF routers, this can result in an excessive amount of traffic.

On broadcast network, OSPF has a mechanism for limiting the amount of routing protocol-related traffic. In order to reduce the number of LSAs, OSPF elects a DR and a BDR with which all other routers form an adjacency. By doing so, the number of adjacencies formed is reduced from $N(N-1)$ to $N(2)$.

exam
ⓦatch

The command SHOW IP OSPF NEIGHBOR can show the states of your neighbors.

All routers on the OSPF broadcast network form neighbor relations with each other. However, all routers become adjacent (reach the full state) only with the DR and BDR. All routers on the network send their LSAs to the DR and the BDR. The DR (not the BDR) processes the received LSAs and sends them back out onto the network. DROTHER routers, which are all routers that are not the DR and the BDR, accept updates only from the DR. You will not see DROTHER routers updating each other. The BDR maintains an identical database to that of the DR and monitors the DR in preparation for becoming the DR should the DR fail.

When you view the states of all routers on the broadcast network using the SHOW IP OSPF NEIGHBOR command, you should see full states for the DR/BDR and two-way states with all DROTHER routers: DROTHER routers will never go past the two-way state with each other on a broadcast network. The only time this will change is if the DR or BDR is permanently removed and one of the DROTHER routers becomes the new BDR.

To configure OSPF on a broadcast network, enable the OSPF process and add the network(s) to it. If you change any timers on any of the router interfaces on this network, you must make the same change on them all; otherwise, they will not become neighbors. Figure 4-4 shows a typical broadcast network configuration. The OSPF defaults are not changed in this figure. Assuming all the routers come up simultaneously; RTRD will become the DR, and RTRC will become the BDR.

FIGURE 4-4

A typical broadcast configuration

RTRA	RTRC
interface Ethernet 0 ip address 1.1.1.1 255.255.255.0	interface Ethernet 0 ip address 1.1.1.3 255.255.255.0
RTRB	**RTRD**
interface Ethernet 0 ip address 1.1.1.2 255.255.255.0	interface Ethernet 0 ip address 1.1.1.4 255.255.255.0

RTRA/RTRB/RTRC/RTRD

router ospf 1
network 1.1.1.0 0.0.0.255 area 0

FROM THE CLASSROOM

Terminology: Topology, Type, and Mesh

Any discussion of OSPF can become quite complicated due to the phraseology involved. OSPF can mix and match between network topologies versus network types. This From the Classroom briefly discusses the meaning of these terms.

Network topology is the logical or physical structure of the network on which OSPF is running; that is, it is the geometry of the network. Topology is the arrangement of the network links and how the routers and switches on the network are interconnected to

FROM THE CLASSROOM

each other. As referenced by OSPF, the topology describes the actual structure and technology of the network.

Network technology (also called suites or protocols) identifies the type of media access, data structures, and contention methods running on the network. For example, *Ethernet* is a broadcast, multiaccess network technology in which each network device contends for access to the network medium. *Frame relay* is a packet-switching network technology that uses virtual circuits to transport data.

Network type is nothing more than how OSPF identifies the network on which it is running. The type does not necessarily have to match the underlying network topology or technology. OSPF has defaults for certain interfaces, such as automatically defaulting for broadcast for an Ethernet interface and defaulting to point-to-point for serial interfaces. These defaults are not set in stone; you can change them using the IP OSPF NETWORK command. For example, you can configure an Ethernet network (broadcast) as a nonbroadcast network. Once you have changed the identification of a network topology to OSPF, you must then configure OSPF as though it were running on that topology; in our example, you would need to

configure OSPF to run over a nonbroadcast network.

As far as OSPF is concerned, there are four network types: point-to-point, point-to-multipoint, broadcast, and nonbroadcast.

The terms *fully meshed* and *partially meshed* need not muddle things further. As used in networking circles, *mesh* refers to the amount of connectivity between all routers on a network. A network topology can be likened to a template for meshing: some network topologies have more mesh than others. A fully meshed network is one in which all the routers have connectivity to each other, whereas a partially meshed network is one in which some of the routers have connectivity to some of the other routers. How a network is meshed does not actually describe the network technology in use; the terms describe only the connectivity between routers on the same network.

When discussing networks in the context of OSPF, start with the network topology and determine how your routers are connected. From there, you'll be able to determine your network topology. A good rule of thumb by which to avoid confusion is to match the topology with the most appropriate OSPF network type. For example, it would not make sense to use the OSPF network type point-to-point for a broadcast topology such as Ethernet.

—*Charles Riley, CCNP, MSCE*

Topology Choices for an NBMA Network—Specifically, Frame Relay

Of all the network types, none is more challenging or problematic than an NBMA network such as Frame Relay or X.25. Throughout the remainder of this chapter, when discussing NBMA networks we focus on Frame Relay. The concepts of circuits and issues of configuring OSPF over Frame Relay apply equally well to X.25.

Frame relay is a packet-switching technology that utilizes both switched and permanent virtual circuits. Although Cisco can do Frame Relay SVC configurations very well, we confine ourselves to PVC configurations for ease of discussion in this chapter.

You as the network engineer must not only understand OSPF; you must also possess a thorough understanding of Frame Relay if you want to use the two together. You must be able to distinguish between point-to-point, point-to-multipoint, broadcast, and nonbroadcast networks because these terms are used by OSPF. The terms *fully meshed* and *partially meshed* add further complexity to the knowledge you must possess. When configuring OSPF, you must understand and be sensitive to the impact these configuration options will have. You also must know which mix is most appropriate for a given situation.

exam
ⓦatch

You should be able to answer these questions: what are the differences between the network types, and how does OSPF behave on them?

For the exam, ensure that the you understand how to start the OSPF configuration process. You should also know when a DR is used and on what network types. The following scenarios and solutions table highlights these and other important OSPF concepts.

SCENARIO & SOLUTION

What is the first command I should enter to start the OSPF configuration process?	ROUTER OSPF <PROCESS-ID>, where PROCESS ID is a number from 1 to 65535.
What command do I use to ensure that a particular router on a point-to-point link becomes the DR?	Point-to-point links do not elect a DR.
Does OSPF need split horizon turned on or off?	It doesn't matter, because OSPF does not use split horizon, which is designed to prevent loops in a distance vector routing protocol.

Fully Meshed Networks

When you use a fully meshed network, all routers have a connection to each other. Figure 4-5 shows a schematic view of a fully meshed network. The greatest advantage of a fully meshed network is that there is no single link of failure: should a link fail in a network of N links, there will still be $N-1$ links to use. In the real world, fully meshed networks can be expensive and difficult to troubleshoot. Such a network is most appropriate when you need to emulate a broadcast network or require redundant connections between remote sites. Designated router issues need to be addressed if you run fully meshed networks in broadcast mode (which is an ideal use of this network type).

Fully meshed topologies can be overly complex and difficult to troubleshoot for both Frame Relay and OSPF. This configuration does not work as well as partially meshed, which has fewer links and more applicability to a point-to-multipoint configuration. Controlling and identifying DR issues can be a major headache, too; good documentation on both the network topology and the OSPF configurations is essential, perhaps more so for fully meshed than for any of the other topology models.

Hub-and-Spoke Networks

In a hub-and-spoke configuration, one router is designated as the hub and all other routers are designated as spokes. All the spokes have a connection to the hub, which has a connection to all the spokes. The hub must be able to reach all the spokes. The hub ideally should be configured as a point-to-multipoint hub as far as OSPF is concerned, and the spokes should be configured as point-to-point spokes. Figure 4-6 shows a simplistic view of a hub-and-spoke topology.

FIGURE 4-5

A fully meshed topology

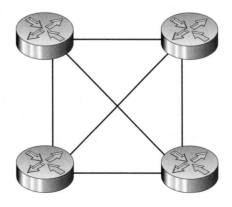

FIGURE 4-6

A hub-and-spoke
topology

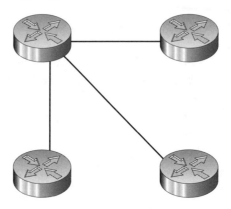

The hub-and-spoke topology can be considered a subset of the partially meshed network; one router has connectivity to all other routers. point-to-multipoint is the recommended network type for OSPF for this network topology because it avoids the DR/BDR issues. You could also use subinterface on the hub router and treat each of its links to the spokes as an independent IP subnet. In that case, the network type for the hub-and-spokes would be point-to-point. The third option is to set the Frame Relay network as OSPF network broadcast. *Use the broadcast type with caution: set the OSPF priority on the spokes to 0 so that they will never become the DR; because only the hub has connectivity to all other routers, it must become the DR for this network.*

Partially Meshed Networks

Partially meshed networks have some routers that have links to some of the other routers in the network. Figure 4-7 illustrates this concept. Notice that this configuration is almost the same physical layout as the hub-and-spoke topology, only it has two hubs: A and B. Since there are fewer links to maintain and support, a partially meshed network is easier to support. It also works better for OSPF than a fully meshed configuration, enabling the network engineer to reduce and control the flow of OSPF LSAs.

The hub-and-spoke configuration is a subset of the partially meshed topology. However, the hub-and-spoke configuration has a clear delineation between the hubs the spokes, which is not always true for partially meshed networks. A spoke for one network can be a hub for another network, and vice versa. In the partially meshed example in Figure 4-7, A and B are hubs, while C and D are purely spokes. In a

FIGURE 4-7

A partially
meshed topology

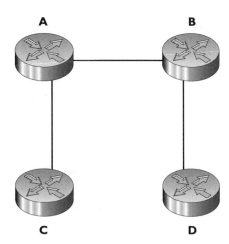

normal hub and spoke, there is a single hub and all others are spokes; in partially
meshed topologies, you can mix the number of hubs and spokes as you need.

The partially meshed topology enables the network engineer to arrange links as
needed, reducing the headaches and complexity associated with fully meshed
topologies. OSPF can treat partially meshed networks as separate point-to-point
links, point-to-multipoint circuits, broadcast, or NMBA. The most effective
network type is point-to-multipoint. Since not all routers are connected to each
other, this configuration carries the DR issues previously discussed. The NBMA
network type might not be appropriate for the same reason. Finally, making all links
point-to-point means greater consumption of IP addresses unless you use
unnumbered interfaces, and that is not a recommended option in this scenario.

Frame Relay and OSPF

We encounter several issues when running OSPF over Frame Relay. One of the
most important of these issues is understanding the various network types. Entire
books have been written on Frame Relay. Here we touch on those aspects of Frame
Relay that are most relevant to OSPF.

Frame Relay switches packets over *permanent virtual circuits (PVCs)* and *switched
virtual circuits (SVCs)*. A PVC is akin to a leased line and is always available. An
SVC is temporary in nature and is created as needed. *Data link circuit identifiers
(DLCIs)* identify Frame Relay circuits. These DLCIs must be mapped to the
network address of whatever router is at the distant end.

Cisco provides two methods to map network addresses to DLCIs. *Inverse ARP (INVARP)* automatically maps the IP address to the DLCI. The other method, more cumbersome, is to use Frame Relay map statements to accomplish the same thing. Unless you have a pressing reason not to use this method, such as a switch that does not support it, let the Cisco IOS do the address mappings using INVARP.

You can use a combination of the two methods on the same interface. However, *be warned!* When you do a manual map of an IP address to a specific interface DLCI, it disables INVARP for that particular protocol for that particular DLCI.

Frame Relay map statements can have an adverse impact on your INVARP mappings. When you use a Frame Relay map state on a particular DLCI for a particular network protocol, it will disable inverse ARP for that particular protocol on that particular DLCI. Further compounding the confusion is that fact that your INVARP mapping will remain in place after a map statement is entered. All routers will be able to reach each other and exchange routing updates until the next reload. When the reload happens, the mappings created by INVARP will be lost, and only your manual mappings will remain. This situation can cause no end of difficulties when you are troubleshooting.

In a hub-and-spoke configuration, if you are using a single DLCI on the hub to connect to two or more spokes and you use a map statement for one of the spokes, INVARP is disabled for that particular DLCI for that protocol, and the other spokes become unreachable.

OSPF Network Types and NBMA Networks

Four network types are used by OSPF to modify its behavior to reflect the network topology. Those types are point-to-point links, point-to-multipoint circuits, broadcast, and nonbroadcast. In this section we discuss each type in turn and point out in what network situations each is best used.

One thing that can complicate OSPF over Frame Relay configurations is that OSPF can treat the actual physical topology as something other than what it is. For example, although this is not recommended, you could configure a broadcast network as a point-to-point network. There are no DR/BDR elections on a point-to-point network; if the routers agree, they will become neighbors and exchange the necessary LSAs to build their databases.

The Cisco IOS command for setting network types is as follows:

```
ip ospf network ?
  broadcast          Specify OSPF broadcast multi-access network
  non-broadcast      Specify OSPF NBMA network
  point-to-multipoint Specify OSPF point-to-multipoint network
  point-to-point     Specify OSPF point-to-point network
```

Addressing and Network Types

The relationship between IP addresses (network addresses) and links must also be understood. Each point-to-point circuit (with the exception of unnumbered interfaces) consists of a single IP subnet. You could also have secondary IP addresses on a point-to-point interface, although the value of secondary addresses on a point-to-point link would be in doubt. On a point-to-multipoint interface, you can have either a single IP address (network) for the entire multipoint configurations or an IP network for each point; the multipoint would either need to use secondary addresses (not recommended) or have subinterfaces individually addressed.

Point-to-Point Links

Figure 4-8 shows a Frame Relay point-to-point circuit. With the exception of the ENCAPSULATION FRAME-RELAY command and the IP OSPF NETWORK POINT-TO-POINT command, the configuration is the same as that for any other point-to-point circuit. The IP OSPF NETWORK command identifies the network type to OSPF, enabling it to adjust its behavior accordingly. In this case, since OSPF now knows this is a point-to-point network, as opposed to a broadcast

FIGURE 4-8

A Frame Relay point-to-point network

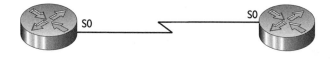

RTRA	RTRB
interface serial 0	interface serial 0
encapsulation frame-relay	encapsulation frame-relay
ip address 1.1.1.1 255.255.255.252	ip address 1.1.1.2 255.255.255.252
ip ospf network point-to-point	ip ospf network point-to-point
router ospf 1	router ospf 1
network 1.1.1.0 0.0.0.3 area 0	network 1.1.1.0 0.0.0.3 area 0

network, it will, for example, not hold DR/BDR elections. Use this command if a link contains only two routers in a point-to-point configuration.

Point-to-Multipoint Networks

A point-to-multipoint circuit consists of a link between a core router and two or more other routers. It is the design that works best with partially meshed NBMA networks. At least one router (the hub) in this configuration must have either physical or logical connectivity to all other routers (the spokes). This configuration is sometimes referred to as the *hub-and-spoke topology,* which we discussed earlier. Figure 4-9 shows the simplest point-to-multipoint configuration: a hub-and-spoke topology. Notice that we have mixed it up a little by using a subinterface on the hub and physical interfaces on the spokes. (We discuss subinterfaces later in the chapter.)

FIGURE 4-9

A point-to-multipoint configuration

RTRA

interface serial 0
encapsulation frame-relay
Interface serial 0.1 multipoint

ip address 1.1.1.1 255.255.255.248
Ip ospf network point-to-multipoint

router ospf 1
network 1.1.1.0 0.0.0.7 area 0

RTRA "Hub"

S0.1

RTRB "Spoke"

RTRC "Spoke"

S0

S0

RTRB

interface serial 0
encapsulation frame-relay
ip address 1.1.1.2 255.255.255.248
ip ospf network point-to-point

router ospf 1
network 1.1.1.0 0.0.0.7 area 0

RTRC

interface serial 0
encapsulation frame-relay
ip address 1.1.1.3 255.255.255.248
ip ospf network point-to-point

router ospf 1
network 1.1.1.0 0.0.0.7 area 0

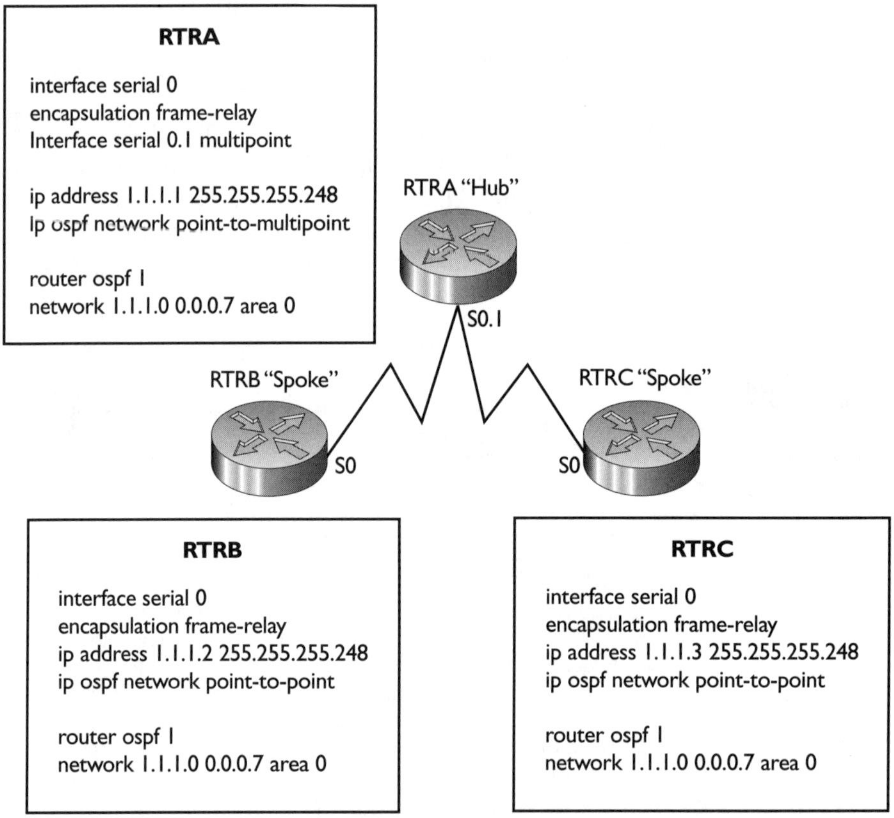

In a point-to-multipoint configuration, no DR/BDR is elected; the links are treated as a collection of point-to-point circuits. Issues involving manipulating loop-back interface IP addresses or router priorities are nonessential because they will not be used since there is no election. All routers on the network will become neighbors. Each router will have a collection of /32 entries in its routing tables describing connectivity to its remote neighbors. For spokes, the network will point to the hub to reach these neighbors; the hub points back to the interface on which the update came in.

Point-to-multipoint does have some extra overhead; each router will have 255.255.255.255 entries in its routing tables for each of its neighbors. On a network containing N routers, each router will have $N–1$ routes (to each of its neighbors). Contrast that with the same network running in broadcast mode, for which you would have a single routing entry for the subnet connecting the routers.

OSPF Requirements for Broadcast or Nonbroadcast Types

When you identify the network type as either broadcast or nonbroadcast, OSPF assumes that all the routers on the network have virtual or physical connections to each other or are fully meshed. Alternately, if the network topology is point-to-multipoint, you can set the network type to broadcast or nonbroadcast. If you set the type to broadcast, ensure that the hub becomes the DR. If you set the type to nonbroadcast, ensure that the hub has neighbor statements for each spoke, and vice versa.

Broadcast Networks

A broadcast network (Ethernet, Token Ring, FDDI) shares a common physical network medium such as a single cable or is connected via a common device such as a network switch. On a broadcast network, the network engineer can deploy the OSPF routers and, with little intervention from humans, the OSPF process on each router will take care of electing a DR/BDR and becoming adjacent with the other routers. Of all network types (with the exception of point-to-point), broadcast is one of the easiest to configure.

On an NBMA network, we can configure OSPF to run as though it were on a broadcast network. The caveat is that all the routers must be fully meshed to each other. If a full mesh is not possible, use either a more viable alternative such as point-to-multipoint or ensure that the router that has connectivity to all the other routers and becomes the DR. Alternately, if there is another router that also has connectivity to all other routers, you can configure it so that it becomes the BDR. For the most part, the spokes will have their priorities set to 0. A fully meshed network and the configuration for running as broadcast network type are shown in Figure 4-10.

Notice that the subinterface on RTRA is configured as a multipoint interface. The routers are connected with PVCs, and mapping is done via INVARP.

Nonbroadcast Multiaccess Networks

A nonbroadcast multiaccess (NBMA) network is similar to a broadcast network with the exception that there is no broadcast capability, although there are multiple stations on the same network. NBMA mode enables OSPF to recognize and treat NBMA networks as nonbroadcast networks.

This mode has the smallest link-state database and generates the least amount of protocol traffic. *All* routers must be able to communicate directly with each other. You can either implement a fully meshed topology or break the nonbroadcast

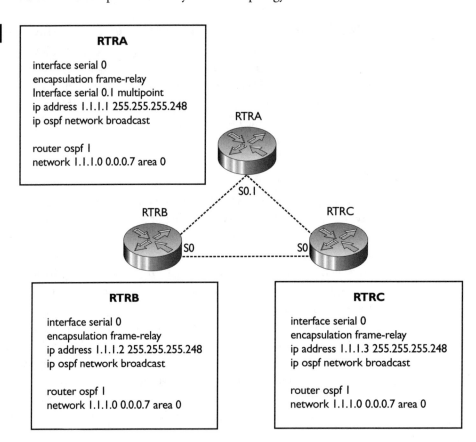

FIGURE 4-10

A fully meshed broadcast network

RTRA

interface serial 0
encapsulation frame-relay
Interface serial 0.1 multipoint
ip address 1.1.1.1 255.255.255.248
ip ospf network broadcast

router ospf 1
network 1.1.1.0 0.0.0.7 area 0

RTRB

interface serial 0
encapsulation frame-relay
ip address 1.1.1.2 255.255.255.248
ip ospf network broadcast

router ospf 1
network 1.1.1.0 0.0.0.7 area 0

RTRC

interface serial 0
encapsulation frame-relay
ip address 1.1.1.3 255.255.255.248
ip ospf network broadcast

router ospf 1
network 1.1.1.0 0.0.0.7 area 0

network into logical subnets. It is usually best to run a nonbroadcast network in point-to-multipoint mode.

Nonbroadcast networks will elect a DR and BDR as though they were broadcast networks. You must use more thought with this method than any other method because it has a combination of both broadcast characteristics and point-to-point characteristics. When you implement an NBMA network using a fully meshed topology, router configuration will look similar to the router configuration for OSPF running in broadcast mode.

OSPF on Frame Relay networks running as the OSPF NBMA type is configured similarly to OSPF running on Frame Relay network as OSPF broadcast type. The topology in Figure 4-11 shows an NBMA network running in the point-to-multipoint mode. Due to the requirement for a fully meshed topology and its complexity, most network engineers do not implement this mode.

FIGURE 4-11

OSPF running in NBMA mode using logical subnets and subinterfaces

RTRA

interface serial 0
encapsulation frame-relay

Interface serial 0.1 multipoint
description Logical Subnet with RTRB
ip address 1.1.1.1 255.255.255.248
ip ospf network non-broadcast

Interface serial 0.2 multipoint
description Logical Subnet with RTRC
ip address 2.2.2.2 255.255.255.248
ip ospf network non-broadcast

router ospf 1
network 1.1.1.0 0.0.0.7 area 0
network 2.2.2.0 0.0.0.7 area 0

RTRA "Hub"

S0.1   S0.2

RTRB "Spoke"   RTRC "Spoke"

S0   S0

RTRB

interface serial 0
ip address 1.1.1.2 255.255.255.248
ip ospf network non-broadcast

router ospf 1
network 1.1.1.0 0.0.0.7 area 0

RTRC

interface serial 0
ip address 2.2.2.2 255.255.255.248
ip ospf network non-broadcast

router ospf 1
network 2.2.2.0 0.0.0.7 area 0

In Figure 4-11, the only routers on the two separate networks are fully meshed to each other. Furthermore, the observant reader might wonder why the example is not configured as two separate point-to-point networks. The reason is that this network could experience growth in the future and become a true NBMA network. If we had configured the network type as point-to-point, we would have to undo and reconfigure it as point-to-multipoint to accommodate the growth. This highlights an interesting tenet of the network architect's job: configure for now *and* for the future.

Frame Relay Logical Interfaces vs. Physical Interfaces

Frame Relay interfaces can be classified as either logical or physical. A *physical interface* is an interface, such as a serial interface, that actually exists on the router. A *logical interface* is a logical division of the physical Frame Relay interface into one or more virtual interfaces, such as dividing serial 0 into serial 0.1, serial 0.2, and so on. Logical interfaces can be configured as though they were actually physical interfaces.

If the network to which your router is connected will always be a point-to-point connection with only two routers, use a physical interface. If the network to which your router is connected has more than two routers and is expected to grow, and you want a number of separate and logical subnets, use logical interfaces, or subinterfaces.

Subinterfaces offer great flexibility that might not be available with physical interfaces; this flexibility includes the ability to change the interface type from point-to-point-to-multipoint or to have multiple separate subnets off one interface and to route between them accordingly. For example, you could have a situation in which you need a point-to-point link for one network and a point-to-multipoint link to another network, all off the same physical interface.

You can specify whether a subinterface is point-to-point or multipoint only if you are using X.25 or Frame Relay on the physical interface. On interfaces using PPP or HDLC, the subinterfaces will be only point-to-point.

Assuming the encapsulation is either Frame Relay or X.25, you can create the subinterface using the following command. Notice that the physical interface is serial 1; to make the subinterface, we enter interface serial 1.# (where # is the number of the subinterface).

```
interface serial 1.5 ?
  multipoint Treat as a multipoint link
  point-to-point Treat as a point-to-point link
```

DR Elections Over NBMA Networks

DR elections occur on NMBA networks when the OPSF network type is set to nonbroadcast and broadcast. These network types indicate that there are more than two routers on a circuit, cueing OSPF's DR mechanism to step in to reduce the number of LSAs generated and the number of adjacencies formed.

There is no DR/BDR elected on a point-to-point link because there are only two routers on the link, and they will become adjacent. Point-to-multipoint requires a little more understanding since it is essentially treated as a point-to point link with more than two routers on the same subnet. It does not attempt to emulate a broadcast network and therefore does not elect a DR/BDR.

An NBMA is similar to a broadcast network, minus the support for broadcast. It elects a DR as a broadcast network does. And as you do with the broadcast network type, you must ensure that all routers on an NBMA are fully meshed or have virtual connectivity to each other. Additionally, you must manually configure neighbor statements to create neighbor relationships between the routers. The neighbor command will make each router on the network a neighbor, and from there, the DR elections will be held.

What Must Happen for DR Elections to Work?

As with OSPF on any network, the routers on an NBMA network must become neighbors. If they do not, they cannot hold elections to determine the DR. On point-to-point, point-to-multipoint, and broadcast networks, neighbor formation happens automatically, barring any other problems. On NBMA networks, you might need to manually set the neighbor relationships among the routers on the network.

On other than a true broadcast network, ensure the router that has logical or physical connectivity to all other routers is elected DR. Ensure that you choose the correct network type for your topology (nonbroadcast or broadcast) and that you choose the topology to support the network type you have chosen. Otherwise, you must manipulate the priorities to ensure that the correct router or routers get elected DR and BDR.

Determine your topology: hub-and-spoke, partially meshed, or fully meshed. If the topology is other than fully meshed, identify your hub. Set the priorities of the spokes to 0. You can leave the default priority of the hub alone; this is sufficient to ensure that the hub will become the DR. Remember that the hub is the router that has physical or logical connectivity to all other routers on the same subnet. If necessary, put neighbor statements on the spokes because they must become neighbors. Neighbor statements can become unwieldy as the network grows; for this reason, Cisco supports the point-to-multipoint network type.

A Fully Meshed NBMA Environment   Your job gets slightly easier when you use a fully meshed topology and the broadcast network type. If you set the OSPF network type to broadcast, OSPF will treat the NBMA network as though it were a LAN. DR and BDR elections will occur as though the network were a LAN. The network engineer has to do the same amount of work required a on a LAN. The caveat here is that this network type is most effective in a fully meshed topology; although it can be used on a partial mesh, it is not recommended, because you will have to ensure that the router that has connectivity to all other routers on the network becomes the DR.

A Partially Meshed NBMA Environment   The final network type, nonbroadcast, requires the most thought. You must not only intervene in neighbor formations; you must also beware of DR issues. If you want one specific router to always be the DR regardless of everything else and because of its ideal placement on the network, set the priorities of the non-DR routers to zero. Do this only if you are sure that this router must always be the DR. This will also prevent routers that do not have connectivity to all other routers but that come upon the network first from becoming the DR. For example, it does not make sense for a spoke to be elected DR, because a spoke does not have access to all the routers on the network and will not be able to exchange LSAs with them.

CERTIFICATION OBJECTIVE 4.02

Standard-Based (RFC-Based) Implementation and Operation of OSPF for an NBMA Network

The OSPF standard officially recognizes nonbroadcast and point-to-multipoint configurations for using OSPF. In other words, virtually any version and platform running OSPF supports these modes.

on the **job**

OSPF behaves differently on each network type. Before you deploy OSPF, know how each network type will cause OSPF to behave and whether you need to modify or adjust any parameters. For example, take the issue of DR: you should know which network types use it and whether you need to modify any parameters to ensure that the best router is chosen the DR for the network.

The Nonbroadcast Multiaccess Command Option

In Cisco parlance, the mode referred to nonbroadcast multiaccess, or NBMA, is called *nonbroadcast*. Recall that NBMA networks have many stations (routers) on the network but do not have the broadcast capabilities of networks such as Ethernet.

OSPF behaves as though it were a broadcast medium to the extent that a DR is elected. Unlike true broadcast networks, however, OSPF might require some manual intervention to ensure that the best router is elected the DR. This consideration is especially critical if you are implementing the nonbroadcast network type on a partially meshed topology. Regardless of the topology, whenever you use the NBMA type, ensure that you configure the neighbors. Otherwise, the most effective topology to be used for the NBMA network type is fully meshed, as shown in Figure 4-12. Notice that this network uses a single IP network; in other words, this is considered a single IP network. All IP-to-DLCI mappings are done automatically via INVARP.

```
rtrC#sh ip os nei
Neighbor ID Pri State Dead Time Address Interface
1.1.1.1 1 FULL/DROTHER 00:01:41 1.1.1.1 Serial 0
1.1.1.2 1 FULL/BDR 00:01:42 1.1.1.2 Serial 0
1.1.1.4 1 FULL/DR 00:00:32 1.1.1.4 Serial 0
```

When we do a SHOW IP OSPF NEIGHBOR command on RTRC, we obtain the display shown in the code. Notice that it is similar to what you would see on a broadcast network. The only difference is that the network engineer manually entered neighbor statements to achieve what happens automatically on a broadcast network. We made no priority changes to any of the routers. RTRD is the DR for this network because it has the highest router ID. Based on this fact, RTRC should have been the BDR; however, since RTRB was on the network first, it became the BDR instead.

FIGURE 4-12   A fully meshed Frame Relay network

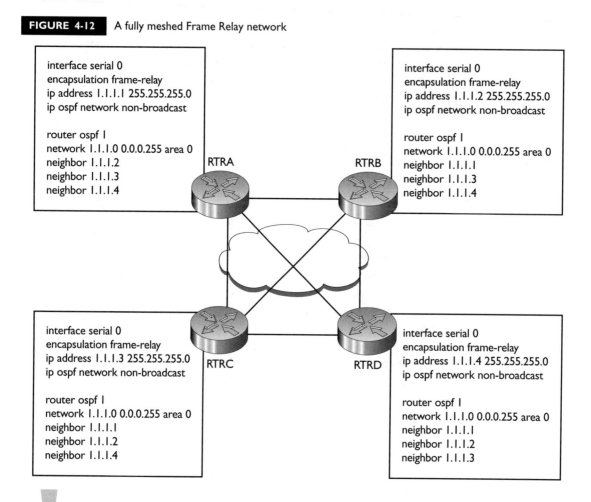

interface serial 0
encapsulation frame-relay
ip address 1.1.1.1 255.255.255.0
ip ospf network non-broadcast

router ospf 1
network 1.1.1.0 0.0.0.255 area 0
neighbor 1.1.1.2
neighbor 1.1.1.3
neighbor 1.1.1.4

RTRA

RTRB

interface serial 0
encapsulation frame-relay
ip address 1.1.1.2 255.255.255.0
ip ospf network non-broadcast

router ospf 1
network 1.1.1.0 0.0.0.255 area 0
neighbor 1.1.1.1
neighbor 1.1.1.3
neighbor 1.1.1.4

interface serial 0
encapsulation frame-relay
ip address 1.1.1.3 255.255.255.0
ip ospf network non-broadcast

router ospf 1
network 1.1.1.0 0.0.0.255 area 0
neighbor 1.1.1.1
neighbor 1.1.1.2
neighbor 1.1.1.4

RTRC

RTRD

interface serial 0
encapsulation frame-relay
ip address 1.1.1.4 255.255.255.0
ip ospf network non-broadcast

router ospf 1
network 1.1.1.0 0.0.0.255 area 0
neighbor 1.1.1.1
neighbor 1.1.1.2
neighbor 1.1.1.3

exam
ⓦatch   *What command should you use when you configure OSPF over a nonbroadcast network? Hint: this command can be used only for nonbroadcast and point-to-multipoint networks and helps achieve the first step toward adjacency.*

The Point-to-Multipoint Command Option

In a point-to-multipoint configuration, the router at the multipoint end of the circuit has multiple connections to the other routers, which have point-to-point links back to the multipoint router. Do not confuse the Frame Relay subinterface multipoint with the OSPF network type multipoint; the two can be exclusive of each other.

Point-to-multipoint works well with partially meshed topologies. The point-to-multipoint interfaces are treated as numbered point-to-point circuits on the same network (if desired) or as separate networks (using subinterfaces).

The point-to-multipoint network type frees you from having to use the NEIGHBOR command and is the Cisco-recommended alternative and replacement for using the nonbroadcast network type. Recall that a point-to-multipoint network is considered a point-to-point network with more than two routers. It acts like a point-to-point network; no DR is elected. When you implement a point-to-multipoint configuration, you remove the need for a DR as well as the need for the NEIGHBOR command (which can become quite onerous as your network expands.

The following Scenario and Solution questions highlight important OSPF concepts we have learned and discussed so far.

Figure 4-13 is the same network we used for the nonbroadcast configuration in Figure 4-11, only this time, we have converted our network to point-to-multipoint. Notice the differences and similarities in commands and the marked absence of neighbor statements. This configuration is much shorter and simpler than the configuration for the nonbroadcast network.

exam
ⓦatch

The point-to-multipoint network type generates host entries.

In point-to-multipoint networks, OSPF routers have multiple neighbor entries in their databases (host entries with a mask of 255.255.255.255); in absence of a DR, this is necessary. There will be one at least one 255.255.255.255 entry per neighbor.

SCENARIO & SOLUTION

What network types are recognized by the OSPF standard?	Point-to-point, point-to-multipoint, broadcast, and nonbroadcast.
When you configure a network as nonbroadcast, how do you ensure neighbor relationships occur despite the lack of broadcast capability?	Use the NEIGHBOR command to manually define your neighbors under the OSPF process configuration.
What are host entries?	Host entries are routing table entries generated by OSPF when it is run over a point-to-multipoint network. They are basically host addresses with a /32 mask (255.255.255.255) that point to a specific neighbor.

FIGURE 4-13 A point-to-multipoint configuration

interface serial 0
encapsulation frame-relay
ip address 1.1.1.1 255.255.255.0
ip ospf network point-to-multipoint

router ospf 1
network 1.1.1.0 0.0.0.255 area 0

interface serial 0
encapsulation frame-relay
ip address 1.1.1.2 255.255.255.0
ip ospf network point-to-multipoint

router ospf 1
network 1.1.1.0 0.0.0.255 area 0

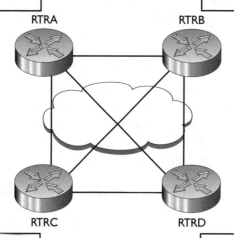

interface serial 0
encapsulation frame-relay
ip address 1.1.1.3 255.255.255.0
ip ospf network point-to-multipoint

router ospf 1
network 1.1.1.0 0.0.0.255 area 0

interface serial 0
encapsulation frame-relay
ip address 1.1.1.4 255.255.255.0
ip ospf network point-to-multipoint

router ospf 1
network 1.1.1.0 0.0.0.255 area 0

Notice that when we do SHOW IP ROUTE OSPF on RTRC (from our configuration in Figure 4-11), RTRC has host entries for its neighbors, RTRA and RTRB.

```
rtrC#show ip route ospf
 1.0.0.0/32 is subnetted, 2 subnets
O 1.1.1.2/32 [110/10] via 1.1.1.2, 00:01:33, Serial0
O 1.1.1.1/32 [110/10] via 1.1.1.1, 00:01:33, Serial0
```

Point-to-Multipoint Networks and OSPF

The point-to-point network you implemented before has grown to one more router, C. You need to modify your configuration to accommodate this new router, including changing the network type. Use a point-to-multipoint network type and change the encapsulation to Frame Relay. B and C will have a link to A but not to each other.

Use the same addressing scheme as before, 123.4.5.0, but expand your subnet mask to 255.255.255.248 on each router's serial 0. Recall that the router ID of A must be 1.1.1.1 and the router ID of B must be 2.2.2.2. Router C does not have a loop-back interface. Put B's loop-back interface in the OSPF process, but not A's. Assume area 0 for all. Diagram this network, and show the configuration for Routers A, B, and C.

Solution:

III 4-2

A

interface loopback 0
ip address 1.1.1.1 255.255.255.255

interface serial 0
encapsulation frame-relay
ip address 123.4.5.1 255.255.255.248
ip ospf network point-to-multipoint

router ospf 1
network 123.4.5.1 0.0.0.0 area 0

B

interface loopback 0
ip address 2.2.2.2 255.255.255.255

interface serial 0
encapsulation frame-relay
ip address 123.4.5.2 255.255.255.248
ip ospf network point-to-point

router ospf 1
network 123.4.5.0 0.0.0.7 area 0
network 2.2.2.2 0.0.0.0 area 0

C

interface serial 0
encapsulation frame-relay
ip address 123.4.5.3 255.255.255.248
ip ospf network point-to-multipoint

router ospf 1
network 123.4.5.0 0.0.0.7 area 0

CERTIFICATION OBJECTIVE 4.03

Cisco Proprietary Modes of Implementation and Operation of OSPF for an NBMA Network

As we have seen, OSPF can modify its behavior to run in different ways over an NBMA network. Cisco goes further and customizes OSPF to handle a variety of nonstandard configurations. In this section, we discuss some new commands and an even more complicated mix of topologies and network types.

on the
job

The nonbroadcast network type can be the most difficult to configure and deploy correctly. It requires more configuration than any of the other network types. With the NEIGHBOR command, OSPF cannot form proper neighbor relationships on a nonbroadcast network. Cisco advocates that engineers use the point-to-multipoint network type instead of the nonbroadcast type. Given the ease of configuration and troubleshooting that result, this is a sound recommendation.

The NEIGHBOR Command

Before we discuss the special features Cisco offers for configuring OSPF over NBMA, we need to discuss the NEIGHBOR command and its purpose. This command is entered under the OSPF configuration mode. With this command, the engineer manually identifies a router's OSPF neighbors. As a rule of thumb, you should let the OSPF process form the neighbor relationships to minimize configuration and ease troubleshooting. However, there may be networks or routers that do not support features of OSPF that are important to neighbor formation, such as multicasting.

The NEIGHBOR command was developed for use on networks lacking broadcast and multicast capabilities. Prior to IOS version 12.0, this command could be used only on NBMA networks. With version 12.0 or later, it can be used on NBMA and point-to-multipoint networks. It should not be used or required on a point-to-point or broadcast network (such as an Ethernet). The NEIGHBOR command can also be used to set the priority (not applicable to point-to-multipoint interfaces), the poll interval (which should be larger than the hello interval; not applicable to point-to-multipoint networks), and cost (applicable to point to-multipoint networks; not applicable to NBMA networks). The syntax of the command and its arguments are as follows:

```
[no] neighbor ip-address [priority number] [poll-interval
seconds] [cost number]
```

where:

- **IP-address** IP address of the neighbor.
- **Priority** Router priority of this neighbor. Default is 0. Does not apply to point-to-multipoint networks.
- **Poll-interval** How often this router should poll the neighbor. Default is 120 seconds, but should be larger than the hello interval.
- **Cost** Cost of this neighbor. If no cost is assigned, this router will use the cost of the interface (IP OSPF COST). Does not apply to NBMA network types.

The NEIGHBOR command is essential to forming neighbors when the neighbors in question can't or don't support multicasting.

The biggest advantage of the NEIGHBOR command is that a router can use it to become neighbors with those routers lacking multicast capability or without the means to become neighbors automatically. The biggest disadvantage of the NEIGHBOR command is that as your network grows, so does the list of NEIGHBOR statements on each router on the network. This can become quite cumbersome and make troubleshooting a nightmare. Point-to-multipoint is the recommended cure for NEIGHBOR statement ills.

The POINT-TO-MULTIPOINT NONBROADCAST Command

A point-to-multipoint network is essentially a point-to-point network in which each router has one or more neighbors. There is no DR on a Point-to-multipoint network, and all routers become neighbors via hellos (which are multicast). point-to-multipoint is the best network type for handling partially meshed topologies. The hub router has connectivity to all other routers, and all routing between the spokes goes through the hub router.

However, you could encounter situations in which the underlying network does not support any broadcast capabilities or you have routers that cannot support multicast capabilities. The POINT-TO-MULTIPOINT NONBROADCAST command is also recommended for situations in which you do not or cannot have either a fully meshed topology or connectivity between all routers—in other words, when you have a point-to-multipoint network that does not provide any type of broadcast support.

exam
ⓦatch

The POINT-TO-MULTIPOINT NONBROADCAST command is used for a point-to-multipoint topology in which the broadcast capabilities are not available.

For these situations, starting with IOS 11.3AA, Cisco developed the ip ospf network point-to-multipoint non-broadcast *command. This command identifies the network as point-to-multipoint, and the fact that there are no broadcast capabilities on this network. When you use this command, you must use the* neighbor *command to explicitly identify your neighbors on each router as shown in Figure 4-14.*

The output of the SHOW IP OSPF NEIGHBOR command shows that the neighbor states are all full; you force this state with the NEIGHBOR command. It is very important that you ensure that any Frame Relay mappings or INVARP mappings are consistent. Notice that there is no DR on this network.

```
rtrC#sh ip os nei
Neighbor ID Pri State Dead Time Address Interface
1.1.1.1 1 FULL/ 00:01:41 1.1.1.1 Serial 0
1.1.1.2 1 FULL/ 00:01:42 1.1.1.2 Serial 0
1.1.1.4 1 FULL/ 00:00:32 1.1.1.4 Serial 0
```

The BROADCAST Command

Cisco enables you to treat an NBMA network as a broadcast network. This is achieved via the IP OSPF NETWORK BROADCAST interface command. On Frame Relay and X.25 networks, ensure that you have enabled support for broadcasts appropriately enough; otherwise, OSPF multicasts will not function. In order to use this network type, you must ensure that the network is either fully meshed or that all routers on the network have connectivity to each other. Since this is a "broadcast network," the NEIGHBOR command is not necessary, because setting the network type to broadcast indicates that the network can and will provide broadcast capabilities. (You could not use the NEIGHBOR command anyway; it is used only for NBMA and point-to-multipoint networks).

FIGURE 4-14 A point-to-multipoint nonbroadcast topology

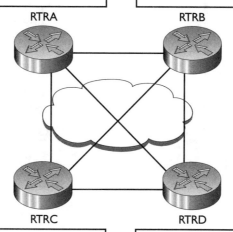

interface serial 0
encapsulation frame-relay
ip address 1.1.1.1 255.255.255.0
ip ospf network point-to-multipoint non-broadcast

router ospf 1
network 1.1.1.0 0.0.0.255 area 0
neighbor 1.1.1.2
neighbor 1.1.1.3
neighbor 1.1.1.4

RTRA

interface serial 0
encapsulation frame-relay
ip address 1.1.1.2 255.255.255.0
ip ospf network point-to-multipoint non-broadcast

router ospf 1
network 1.1.1.0 0.0.0.255 area 0
neighbor 1.1.1.1
neighbor 1.1.1.3
neighbor 1.1.1.4

RTRB

RTRC

RTRD

interface serial 0
encapsulation frame-relay
ip address 1.1.1.3 255.255.255.0
ip ospf network point-to-multipoint non-broadcast

router ospf 1
network 1.1.1.0 0.0.0.255 area 0
neighbor 1.1.1.1
neighbor 1.1.1.2
neighbor 1.1.1.4

interface serial 0
encapsulation frame-relay
ip address 1.1.1.4 255.255.255.0
ip ospf network point-to-multipoint non-broadcast

router ospf 1
network 1.1.1.0 0.0.0.255 area 0
neighbor 1.1.1.1
neighbor 1.1.1.2
neighbor 1.1.1.3

Since broadcast emulation by an NBMA might not have all the underlying characteristics of a true broadcast network, you might want to force a particular router to be the DR for the network. This step will ease troubleshooting and monitoring. To do so, use the IP OPSF PRIORITY 0 command on the non-DR routers to ensure that the router of your choosing becomes the DR, regardless of its or any other router's RID. The choice of a DR can be particularly critical if you have a partially meshed topology. Figure 4-15 illustrates a point-to-multipoint network operating as a broadcast type.

FIGURE 4-15   A broadcast network type used in a point-to-multipoint topology

interface serial 0
encapsulation frame-relay

interface serial 0.1 multipoint
ip address 1.1.1.1 255.255.255.0
ip ospf network broadcast

router ospf 1
network 1.1.1.0 0.0.0.255 area 0

interface serial 0
encapsulation frame-relay
ip address 1.1.1.2 255.255.255.0
ip ospf network broadcast
ip ospf priority 0

router ospf 1
network 1.1.1.0 0.0.0.255 area 0

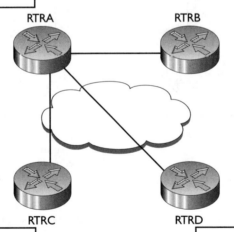

RTRA   RTRB

RTRC   RTRD

interface serial 0
encapsulation frame-relay
ip address 1.1.1.3 255.255.255.0
ip ospf network broadcast
ip ospf priority 0

router ospf 1
network 1.1.1.0 0.0.0.255 area 0

interface serial 0
encapsulation frame-relay
ip address 1.1.1.4 255.255.255.0
ip ospf network broadcast
ip ospf priority 0

router ospf 1
network 1.1.1.0 0.0.0.255 area 0

Executing the SHOW IP OSPF NEIGHBOR command on RTRC shows that the neighbor states are all full and that RTRC has become adjacent with RTRA. Notice that RTRA is the DR as we set the priority of all other routers to 0.

```
rtrC#sh ip os nei
Neighbor ID Pri State Dead Time Address Interface
1.1.1.1 1 FULL/DR 00:01:41 1.1.1.1 Serial 0
1.1.1.2 1 FULL/ 00:01:42 1.1.1.2 Serial 0
1.1.1.4 1 FULL/ 00:00:32 1.1.1.4 Serial 0
```

The POINT-TO-POINT Command

NBMA networks can be configured as point-to-point networks using a combination of Frame Relay (for example) and OSPF commands. The command IP OPSF NETWORK POINT-TO-POINT tells OPSF that the underlying NBMA is a point-to-point network. OSPF will then act accordingly: no DR is elected, and the two routers on the network will become neighbors (and adjacent). Frame Relay or X.25 mappings must be done accordingly to match what you actually have.

One thing we have not discussed is the relationship of the POINT-TO-POINT command to a point-to-multipoint configuration. In a hub-and-spoke configuration, set the network type to point-to-multipoint on the hub and to point-to-point on the spokes. The hub has connections to all the spokes; the spokes have a connection only to the hub (so to their "way of thinking," there are only two routers on the network).

Take a moment and review the following Scenario and Solution questions.

Regardless of whether you use physical interfaces or divide the physical interface into logical point-to-point subinterfaces, point-to-point interface operations remain

SCENARIO & SOLUTION

On what network types can the NEIGHBOR command be used?	It can be used *only* on point-to-multipoint and nonbroadcast networks.
You have a point-to-multipoint network on which there are routers that cannot process multicasts. What network type should you use?	Use the network type point-to-multipoint nonbroadcast in conjunction with the appropriate NEIGHBOR statements.
You want to view the states of your neighbors. What command do you use?	You use the SHOW IP OSPF NEIGHBOR command.

consistent. The routers become neighbors. There are no DR/BDR elections because there are only two routers on the network. An LSA is exchanged for the network. Figure 4-16 shows this configuration.

In the configuration shown in Figure 4-16, we have two uses of the POINT-TO-POINT command. On the link between RTRA and RTRB, we have configured a point-to-point subinterface on RTRA that connects to a physical interface on RTRB. OSPF identifies this network as a point-to-point network. We

FIGURE 4-16   A point-to-point network over Frame Relay using subinterfaces

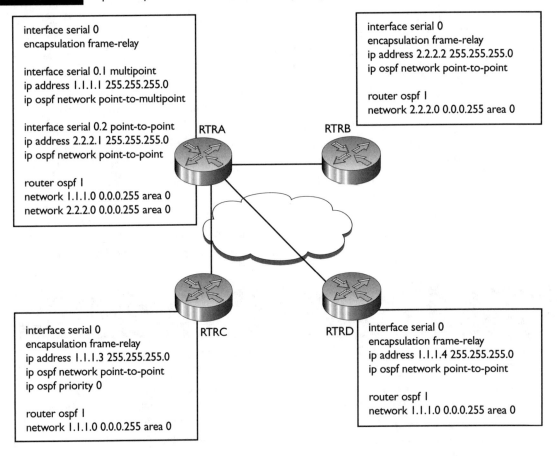

have also configured a multipoint subinterface on RTRA to connect to RTRC and RTRD, both of which are using IP OSPF NETWORK POINT-TO-POINT.

We can execute the SHOW IP OSPF NEIGHBOR command on RTRB to see the status of the neighbor relationships. As expected, RTRA has reached the full state with all its neighbors. Notice that there is no DR on any of these networks.

```
rtrA#sh ip os nei
Neighbor ID Pri State Dead Time Address Interface
1.1.1.3 1 FULL/ 00:01:41 1.1.1.3 Serial 0.1
1.1.1.4 1 FULL/ 00:01:42 1.1.1.4 Serial 0.1
2.2.2.2 1 FULL/ 00:00:32 2.2.2.2 Serial 0.2
```

If we execute the same command on RTRC, we see only one neighbor. This is to be expected because this is a point-to-point network as far as RTRC is concerned, and it has only one neighbor. We would get a similar result running the same command on RTRB.

```
rtrC#sh ip os nei
Neighbor ID Pri State Dead Time Address Interface
1.1.1.1 1 FULL/ 00:01:41 1.1.1.1 Serial 0
```

EXERCISE 4-3

A Point-to-Multipoint Network Without Broadcast Capabilities

You have been given the task of removing the broadcast capabilities of the point-to-multipoint network you designed in Exercise 4-2. There is also a virtual Frame Relay circuit between B and C. Nothing is to be changed, except the network type is now point-to-multipoint nonbroadcast. Change the network type, and add whatever commands you need to ensure that OSPF can work.

Keep your addressing, links, and loop-back interfaces among A,B, and C, as before. The network type is point-to-multipoint nonbroadcast. The encapsulation is Frame Relay. B and C will have a link to A but not to each other.

The address on the links among A, B, and C is the IP address 123.4.5.0/29 on each router's serial 0. The router ID of A must be 1.1.1.1, and the router ID of B must be 2.2.2.2. Router C does not have a loop-back interface. Put B's loop-back interface in the OSPF process, but not A's. Assume area 0 for all. Diagram this network, and show the configuration for Routers A, B, and C. The Frame Relay switch has been configured to add the new link between B and C on each router's serial 0. No subinterfaces are needed.

Solution:

III 4-3

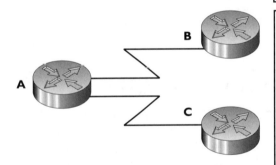

A

interface loopback 0
ip address 1.1.1.1 255.255.255.255

interface serial 0
encapsulation frame-relay
ip address 123.4.5.1 255.255.255.248
ip ospf network point-to-multipoint nonbroadcast

router ospf 1
network 123.4.5.1 0.0.0.0 area 0
neighbor 123.4.5.2
neighbor 123.4.5.3

B

interface loopback 0
ip address 2.2.2.2 255.255.255.255

interface serial 0
encapsulation frame-relay
ip address 123.4.5.2 255.255.255.248
ip ospf network point-to-multipoint non-broadcast

router ospf 1
network 123.4.5.0 0.0.0.7 area 0
network 2.2.2.2 0.0.0.0 area 0
neighbor 123.4.5.1
neighbor 123.4.5.3

C

interface serial 0
encapsulation frame-relay
ip address 123.4.5.3 255.255.255.248
ip ospf network point-to-multipoint non-broadcast

router ospf 1
network 123.4.5.0 0.0.0.7 area 0
neighbor 123.4.5.1
neighbor 123.4.5.2

CERTIFICATION SUMMARY

In this chapter, we discussed network topologies such as point-to-point and broadcast and what they mean to OSPF. We also learned what the term *mesh* means and how it relates to network topologies. The OSPF NETWORK command identifies the type of network, allowing OSPF to modify its behavior to suit the network on which it is running.

We learned that OSPF can treat one type of network topology as another network topology. For example, OSPF can run as a nonbroadcast network over a broadcast network as long as you correctly configure it and make liberal use of the NEIGHBOR command.

Cisco not only supports the OSPF standard; it also adds enhancements such as the point-to-multipoint nonbroadcast network type and the NEIGHBOR command. Cisco's implementation of OSPF is very flexible and can accommodate any type of network.

TWO-MINUTE DRILL

Here are some of the key points from each certification objective in Chapter 4.

OSPF Behavior Over a WAN Link

❑ The OSPF configuration process starts with the ROUTER OSPF <PROCESS-ID> and the NETWORK *x.x.x.x* commands.

❑ There are only two routers and no DR on a point-to-point network.

❑ Unnumbered interfaces must reference numbered interfaces that are using the same network number and mask. Alternately, different numbers can be used as long as only the natural mask for those network numbers is used (they must match).

❑ Designated routes are used to reduce the number of adjacencies formed on a broadcast network.

❑ Frame Relay is a packet-switching technology that uses switched and permanent virtual circuits.

❑ Fully meshed topologies can be expensive and difficult to troubleshoot.

❑ On a partially meshed network, some routers have connections to some other routers. The most effective type of partially meshed network is point-to-multipoint.

❑ A hub-and-spoke topology is a subset of the partially meshed network, with only one hub and multiple spokes. If appropriate, ensure that the hub is the DR.

❑ There are no DR/BDR elections on point-to-multipoint networks.

❑ To create a subinterface on serial 1, for example, enter INTERFACE SERIAL 1.1 <MULTIPOINT | POINT-TO-POINT>.

Standard-Based (RFC-Based) Implementation and Operation of OSPF for an NBMA Network

❑ A nonbroadcast network is similar to a broadcast network minus the broadcast abilities. You must use the NEIGHBOR command with a nonbroadcast network.

❑ Nonbroadcast networks elect a DR and a BDR, as broadcast networks do.

❑ Use SHOW IP OSPF NEIGHBOR to view the state of neighbor relations.

❑ Point-to-multipoint networks work well with partially meshed configurations.

❑ Point-to-multipoint networks generate host entries (mask is 255.255.255.255) in the routing table.

Cisco Proprietary Modes of Implementation and Operation of OSPF for an NBMA Network

❑ The NEIGHBOR command is used to manually define neighbor relationships on NBMA and point-to-multipoint networks (especially in nonbroadcast mode).

❑ If you have a router on a point-to-multipoint network that cannot support multicasting, use the IP OSPF NETWORK point-to-multipoint nonbroadcast network in conjunction with NEIGHBOR statements to make OSPF work.

❑ The command IP OSPF PRIORITY ensures that the router it is run on will never become a DR.

❑ For maximum efficiency in a hub-and-spoke configuration, set the hub network type to point-to-multipoint, and set the spokes as point-to-point.

SELF TEST

The following questions will help you measure your understanding of the material presented in this chapter. Read all the choices carefully because there might be more than one correct answer. Choose all correct answers for each question.

OSPF Behavior Over a WAN Link

1. What is the starting point for enabling OSPF on a router?

   A. Assign an IP address to an interface

   B. Create a loop-back interface and assign it an IP address

   C. Execute the command ROUTER OSPF # (where # is a number 1 to 65535)

   D. Run IP OSPF COST 1 on all interfaces participating in OSPF

2. What LSA field does OSPF use to implement split horizon?

   A. None; OSPF does not use split horizon

   B. The sequence number field in the LSA type 3

   C. The update field in LSU

   D. The I and MS bits set during the Exchange stage

3. The purpose of unnumbered interfaces is to:

   A. Reduce reliance on loop-back interfaces for router IDs

   B. Allow numbered interfaces to have secondary IP addresses

   C. Reduce the number of routing entries in the OSPF routing table

   D. Conserve IP address space by sharing the IP address of another interface

4. Which of the following is *not* a guideline for using unnumbered interfaces with OSPF?

   A. Unnumbered links must be in the same area.

   B. The common area between unnumbered links must be area 0

   C. Only point-to-point links can be unnumbered

   D. Addresses used by unnumbered links must be from the same network number and use the same mask

   E. Different network numbers can be used as long as the natural mask is used

5. On a point-to-point X.25 circuit, you entered x25 map *x.x.x.x y.y.y.y* at each end, and the routers can ping each other. However, the routers on this circuit have not become neighbors. What is the problem?

   A. You left off the broadcast argument at the end of the MAP statement.

   B. You did not enter a NEIGHBOR statement under OSPF.

   C. OSPF does not support X.25 over a point-to-point network; change the encapsulation to PPP or HDLC.

   D. None of the above.

6. On broadcast and nonbroadcast networks, OSPF uses the DR mechanism to:

   A. Reduce the number of neighbors formed on the network

   B. Reduce the amount of broadcast traffic

   C. Reduce the number of LSAs and adjacencies formed

   D. Reduce the number of intra-area updates

7. What command do you use to view states of your neighbors?

   A. SHOW IP OSPF DATABASE

   B. SHOW IP OSPF NEIGHBOR

   C. SHOW IP OSPF INTERFACE

   D. SHOW IP ROUTE OSPF

8. Only one router has connectivity to all other routers on the network. This is an example of what kind of configuration?

   A. Hub-and-spoke

   B. Partially meshed

   C. Fully meshed

   D. Point-to-point

9. The network type point-to-multipoint is considered the most effective for which of the following configurations?

   A. Hub-and-spoke

   B. Partially meshed

   C. Fully meshed

   D. point-to-point

10. You want to make serial 0 a multipoint Frame Relay interface, at both OSPF and Frame Relay levels. What configuration will do that?

    A. IP OSPF NETWORK POINT-TO-POINT

    B. ENCAPSULATION FRAME-RELAY

    C. INTERFACE SERIAL 0
       ENCAPSULATION FRAME-RELAY
       IP OSPF NETWORK POINT-TO-MULTIPOINT

    D. None of the above

11. You have a fully meshed topology on which you want to use Frame Relay and run OSPF in broadcast mode. What are the two minimum commands you must execute on all routers on this network?

    A. ENCAPSULATION FRAME-RELAY and IP OSPF NETWORK BROADCAST

    B. ENCAPSULATION FRAME-RELAY and NEIGHBOR statements

    C. ENCAPSULATION FRAME-RELAY and frame MAP statements

    D. IP OSPF NETWORK BROADCAST and NEIGHBOR statements

12. How is a nonbroadcast network similar to a broadcast network as far as OSPF is concerned?

    A. Both elect a DR

    B. Both require NEIGHBOR statements

    C. Both natively support OSPF's multicasting

    D. A and B

13. You have opted to set the network type as nonbroadcast on a Frame Relay network and have run the ENCAPSULATION FRAME-RELAY and the IP OSPF NETWORK NON-BROADCAST command on all routers. Are there any other OSPF commands you need to run?

    A. No, these are sufficient

    B. Yes: NEIGHBOR (IP address of neighbor) under OSPF configuration

    C. Yes: IP OSPF PRIORITY 0 on the non-DR routers

    D. None of the above

14. On serial 0 running Frame Relay, you want to create your first multipoint subinterface. What command do you execute?

   A. INTERFACE SERIAL 0.1 MULTIPOINT

   B. INTERFACE SERIAL 0.5 MULTIPOINT

   C. SUBINTERFACE SERIAL 0.1 MULTIPOINT

   D. A or B

15. You perform a SHOW IP ROUTE on your router and notice that you have many entries with /32 masks. What type of OSPF network is this?

   A. Broadcast

   B. Point-to-point

   C. Point-to-multipoint

   D. This is not enough information to determine the network type

Standard-Based (RFC-Based) Implementation and Operation of OSPF for an NBMA Network

16. You perform SHOW IP OSPF NEIGHBOR on your router and notice that you have a DR, a BDR, and several DROTHERs listed. What type of network(s) could this be?

   A. Broadcast

   B. Nonbroadcast

   C. Point-to-multipoint

   D. Both A and B

   E. Both A and C

17. You have a fully meshed topology over Frame Relay and have chosen to use the point-to-multipoint OSPF network type. Will there be any problems with this choice?

   A. No. The network type is suitable.

   B. Yes. The network type will not be able to identify the hub and spokes correctly.

   C. It depends. You will need to use NEIGHBOR statements to ensure the neighbor relationships are formed.

   D. None of the above.

18. You perform a SHOW IP ROUTE OSPF and notice that you have several /32 host entries. Which is of these entries identifies the hub on this point-to-multipoint network?

A. The highest IP address is the hub.

B. Locate the interface with the highest router ID, and the neighbor on that interface is the hub.

C. There is no hub on this network.

D. There is not enough information to answer this question.

Cisco Proprietary Modes of Implementation and Operation of OSPF for an NBMA Network

19. You have several neighbors on serial interface 0, one of which is 1.1.1.1. You want to set the cost of 1.1.1.1 to 120, but you do not want to change the costs of the other neighbors on this interface. What command do you use to accomplish this task?

A. NEIGHBOR 1.1.1.1 COST 120

B. IP OSPF COST 120

C. IP OSPF PRIORITY 40

D. Both B and C

20. What is an advantage and a disadvantage of using the NEIGHBOR command?

A. It reduces routing overhead; it consumes CPU cycles.

B. It allows neighbor formation on nonbroadcast networks; the number of NEIGHBOR statements can increase as the network grows.

C. It allows the engineer to identify neighbors on a X.25 point-to-point network; it must be done manually.

D. It overcomes the inability to locate a neighbor on any network type; the engineer must write NEIGHBOR statements.

21. On a Frame Relay network, you have opted to use the Cisco proprietary OSPF network type, point-to-multipoint nonbroadcast. The network is fully meshed; how do you make one of the routers the DR?

A. Set the spokes to a priority of 0.

B. Ensure that the DR router has the highest router ID.

C. This is still a point-to-multipoint network minus its broadcast support; it will not use a DR.

D. None of the above.

22. On a Frame Relay network, you have opted to use the Cisco proprietary OSPF network type, point-to-multipoint nonbroadcast. You have the encapsulation set to Frame Relay, you have the IP OSPF NETWORK POINT-TO-MULTIPOINT command on every interface, and the networks are all added to the OSPF process. Do you need to do anything else?

    A. No. The configuration is complete.

    B. Yes. Ensure that the hub can reach all other routers.

    C. Yes. Add NEIGHBOR statements to all routers.

    D. Both B and C.

23. You have chosen the OSPF network type broadcast for your point-to-multipoint network. The network has a hub-and-spoke topology. What command must you run at the spokes to ensure OSPF can function?

    A. IP OSPF PRIORITY 0

    B. IP OSPF COST 200

    C. No special commands need to be run at the spokes

    D. Both A and B

24. On a straight point-to-multipoint network, what should the IP OSPF NETWORK command be at the hub, and what should the command be at the spokes?

    A. IP OSPF NETWORK POINT-TO-MULTIPOINT at the hub, IP OSPF POINT-TO-POINT at the spokes

    B. IP OSPF NETWORK MULTIPOINT at the hub, IP OSPF NETWORK POINT at the spokes

    C. IP OSPF NETWORK POINT-TO-MULTIPOINT at the hub, IP OSPF POINT-TO-MULTIPOINT at the spokes

    D. None of the above

LAB QUESTION

Given the network diagram and table of IP addresses in Figure 4-17, configure your network as shown. Configure OSPF for all routing, and use a single area. Pay close attention to network types. Use Frame Relay on the network connecting A, B, and C. Note that the link between A and C is point-to-multipoint to accommodate the expected addition of more routers in the future.

FIGURE 4-17

Network diagram
and table of IP
addresses for Lab
Question

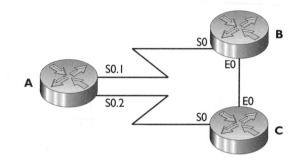

Router	Interface	IP Address	Network Type
A	S0.1	1.1.1.1/30	Point-to-Point
A	S0.2	2.2.2.1/29	Point-to-MultiPoint NonBroadcast
A	L0	4.4.4.1/32	Loopback Interface
B	S0	1.1.1.2/30	Point-to-Point
B	E0	3.3.3.1/24	Broadcast
B	L0	5.5.5.1/32	Loopback Interface
C	S0	2.2.2.2/29	Point-to-MultiPoint NonBroadcast
C	E0	3.3.3.2/24	Broadcast
C	L0	6.6.6.1/32	Loopback Interface

SELF TEST ANSWERS

OSPF Behavior Over a WAN Link

1. ☑ C. Execute the command ROUTER OSPF # (where # is a number 1 to 65535). This command enables OSPF.

   ☒ A is incorrect because it assigning an IP address to an interface has no impact on OSPF initialization. B is not correct because a loop-back interface does not affect OSPF until OSPF is started. D is incorrect because the IP OSPF COST 1 command will have no effect until OSPF is started.

2. ☑ A. None; OSPF does not use split horizon. Split horizon is a distance vector concept.

   ☒ B, C, and D are incorrect because OSPF does not use split horizon.

3. ☑ D. Conserve IP address space by sharing the IP address of another interface. This is correct because unnumbered interfaces do not require their own subnet.

   ☒ A is incorrect because loop-back interfaces can't be unnumbered. B is incorrect because numbered interfaces can have secondary addresses with or without unnumbered interfaces. C is incorrect because the reduced number of routing entries is an after-effect of unnumbered interfaces, not their purpose.

4. ☑ B. The common area between unnumbered links must be area 0. The interfaces only have to be in the same area, not necessarily area 0.

   ☒ A, C, D, and E are incorrect because these conditions must be met in order to use unnumbered interfaces.

5. ☑ A. You left off the broadcast argument at the end of the MAP statement. Multicasts are not reaching neighbors.

   ☒ B is incorrect because the NEIGHBOR statement is used only with nonbroadcast and point-to-multipoint networks. C is incorrect because OSPF does support X.25 over point-to-point networks. D is incorrect because there is a correct answer.

6. ☑ C. Reduce the number of LSAs and adjacencies formed. Adjacencies are formed only with the DR routers.

   ☒ A is incorrect because all routers on the network become neighbors. B is incorrect because reducing the amount of broadcast traffic is not a state goal of the DR. D is incorrect because the DR reduces the number of adjacencies formed, not the number of updates.

7. ☑ **B.** SHOW IP OSPF NEIGHBOR is correct because this command displays the state of a router's relationships with its neighbors.

    ☒ **A** is incorrect because SHOW IP OSPF DATABASE lists the contents of the OSPF databases. **C** is incorrect because SHOW IP OSPF INTERFACE lists interfaces running OSPF. **D** is incorrect because SHOW IP ROUTE OSPF shows routes learned via OSPF.

8. ☑ **A.** Hub-and-spoke. Only the hub has a link to all other routers.

    ☒ **B** and **C** are incorrect because partially and fully meshed networks have too much connectivity between the routers. **D** is incorrect because there are only two routers and they have connectivity to each other.

9. ☑ **B.** Partially meshed is correct because this network type adapts best to a point-to-multipoint network.

    ☒ **A, C,** and **D** are incorrect because they refer to other network types.

10. ☑ **D.** None of the above is correct because you must create a subinterface to make a multipoint interface for a Frame Relay network.

    ☒ **A, B,** and **C** are incorrect because the correct command is as follows:
    INTERFACE SERIAL 0
    ENCAPSULATION FRAME-RELAY
    INTERFACE SERIAL 0.1 MULTIPOINT
    IP OSPF NETWORK POINT-TO-MULTIPOINT

11. ☑ **A.** ENCAPSULATION FRAME-RELAY and IP OSPF NETWORK BROADCAST is correct because you need only set the encapsulation to Frame Relay and identify the network as broadcast.

    ☒ **B** and **C** are incorrect because neither NEIGHBOR nor Frame Relay MAP statements are required. **D** is incorrect because NEIGHBOR statements are not required for the broadcast network type.

12. ☑ **A.** Both elect a DR is correct because both broadcast and nonbroadcast use a DR.

    ☒ **B** is incorrect because only nonbroadcast requires NEIGHBOR statements. **C** is incorrect because only broadcast natively supports multicasting. **D** is incorrect because both A and B are not correct answers.

13. ☑ **B.** Yes: NEIGHBOR (IP address of neighbor) under OSPF configuration. Because there is no broadcast capability on a nonbroadcast network, you will need to manually intervene in the neighbor formation process.

    ☒ **A** is incorrect because you need the NEIGHBOR statements. **C** is incorrect because IP

OSPF PRIORITY 0 affects DR elections, which are not used on this network. **D** is incorrect because there is a correct answer.

14. ☑ **A, B,** and **D** are correct because either INTERFACE SERIAL 0.1 MULTIPOINT or INTERFACE SERIAL 0.5 MULTIPOINT demonstrates correct command syntax.
☒ **C** is incorrect because there is no such command as SUBINTERFACE SERIAL 0.1 MULTIPOINT.

15. ☑ **C.** Point-to-multipoint is correct because only the point-to-multipoint network type generates these types of entries for neighbors.
☒ **A** and **B** are incorrect because OSPF does not have to generate /32 entries for these two network types. **D** is incorrect because this is enough information to identify the network type.

Standard-Based (RFC-Based) Implementation and Operation of OSPF for an NBMA Network

16. ☑ **D.** Both A and B are correct because only broadcast and nonbroadcast networks have a DR.
☒ **C** is incorrect because a point-to-multipoint network does not have a DR. **E** is incorrect because only one of the network types has a DR.

17. ☑ **A.** No. The network type is suitable. This is correct because point-to-multipoint, although not optimal, is readily adaptable to the network topology.
☒ **B** is incorrect because all routers will become neighbors, which resolves this problem. **C** is incorrect because this network is fully meshed and supports broadcast capabilities.

18. ☑ **D.** There is not enough information to answer this question. You will need to execute the SHOW IP OSPF NEIGHBOR command to get this information.
☒ **A** and **B** are incorrect because the hub is identified by its placement in the network topology. **C** is incorrect because there is not enough information to determine whether or not there is a hub.

Cisco Proprietary Modes of Implementation and Operation of OSPF for an NBMA Network

19. ☑ **A.** NEIGHBOR 1.1.1.1 COST 120 is correct because this command sets the neighbor cost.
☒ **B** is incorrect because it sets the cost to all neighbors. **C** is incorrect because it changes the priority of only this router. **D** is incorrect because A and B are not both correct.

20. ☑ **B.** It allows neighbor formation on nonbroadcast networks; the number of NEIGHBOR statements can increase as the network grows.
☒ **A, C,** and **D** are incorrect because none of them lists an advantage or a disadvantage of the NEIGHBOR command.

21. ☑ **C.** This is still a point-to-multipoint network minus its broadcast support; it will not use a DR. This is correct because only broadcast and nonbroadcast networks have a DR.
☒ **A** and **B** are incorrect because this network type does not have a DR. **D** is incorrect because there is a correct answer.

22. ☑ **D.** Both B and C are correct because the hub must be able to reach all the routers, and the NEIGHBOR statements are necessary to help the routers become neighbors.
☒ **A** is incorrect because you still need to add NEIGHBOR statements.

23. ☑ **A.** IP OSPF PRIORITY 0 is correct because the spokes should not become the DR.
☒ **B** is incorrect because it only sets the cost of the interface; it does not ensure that the spokes do not become the DR. **C** is incorrect because you need to ensure the spokes never become the DR.

24. ☑ **A.** IP OSPF NETWORK POINT-TO-MULTIPOINT at the hub, IP OSPF POINT-TO-POINT at the spokes is correct because the hub is multipoint to the spokes, whereas the spokes are point-to-point to the hub.
☒ **B** is incorrect because there is no such command. **C** is incorrect because you want to ensure that spokes have a single connect on this interface. **D** is incorrect because there is a correct answer.

LAB ANSWER

<u>Router A</u>

```
interface Loopback0
 ip address 4.4.4.1 255.255.255.255

!
interface Serial0
 no ip address
 encapsulation frame-relay
!
interface Serial0.1 point-to-point
 ip address 1.1.1.1 255.255.255.252
```

```
 ip ospf network point-to-point
!
interface Serial0.2 multipoint
 ip address 2.2.2.1 255.255.255.248
 ip ospf network point-to-multipoint non-broadcast
!

router ospf 1
 network 1.1.1.0 0.0.0.3 area 0
 network 2.2.2.0 0.0.0.7 area 0
 network 4.4.4.1 0.0.0.0 area 0
 neighbor 2.2.2.2
```

<u>**Router B**</u>

```
 interface Loopback0
 ip address 5.5.5.1 255.255.255.255

!
interface Ethernet0 memory.
 ip address 3.3.3.1 255.255.255.0
! The below command is unnecessary as OSPF automatically defaults to this
! for Ethernet interfaces.
 ip ospf network broadcast

interface Serial0
 ip address 1.1.1.2 255.255.255.252
 encapsulation frame-relay
 ip ospf network point-to-point

!
router ospf 1
 network 1.1.1.0 0.0.0.3 area 0
 network 3.3.3.1 0.0.0.0 area 0
 network 5.5.5.1 0.0.0.0 area 0
```

<u>**Router C**</u>

```
interface Loopback0
 ip address 6.6.6.1 255.255.255.255

!
interface Ethernet0
```

```
 ip address 3.3.3.2 255.255.255.0

!
interface Serial0
 ip address 2.2.2.2 255.255.255.248
 encapsulation frame-relay
 ip ospf network point-to-multipoint non-broadcast

router ospf 1
 network 2.2.2.0 0.0.0.7 area 0
 network 3.3.3.2 0.0.0.0 area 0
 network 6.6.6.1 0.0.0.0 area 0
 neighbor 2.2.2.1
```

5

OSPF Operations in a Multiarea Network

CERTIFICATION OBJECTIVES

B y now you should know the features and operations of OSPF for a small number of routers within a single area. This chapter focuses on building and configuring large networks and the ways in which multiarea features affect the performance of an OSPF domain. Configuration examples are included and discussed in detail.

CERTIFICATION OBJECTIVE 5.01

Scalability Issues with a Single-Area OSPF Network

As the number of routers and networks in your organization grows larger, maintaining them becomes increasingly difficult. You can use multiple areas to create a hierarchical design that breaks down an OSPF domain into smaller, more manageable areas. These can be based on anything from departments (accounting, engineering, etc.) to geographic location, as shown in Figure 5-1.

In this example, the United States is configured as Area 1. Europe and Asia are Areas 2 and 3, respectively. The three are connected through Area 0, which is called the *backbone*; all areas must connect to the backbone area.

A multiarea design is also used to control the traffic generated by link-state advertisements (LSAs). Can you imagine 1000 routers flooding the network with routing updates? The large number of links increases the possibility of a link-state change, and every link-state change causes route computation on every router, creating a tremendous burden on the CPU. In a worst case scenario, a couple of faulty links could bring the entire network to a crawl.

With this in mind, refer back to Figure 5-1 and notice how the routers are divided into smaller groups. Is it really necessary for routers in the United States to know whether or not a link is up in the middle of Asia? Routers have to share their link-state database with only other routers within their area—not the entire internetwork. A smaller database, with a smaller number of links, means a reduced load on the processor and memory. This also prevents most of the LSAs from flooding across the OSPF domain.

The recommended number of routers to place in each area varies from source to source. Designers typically have different opinions based on experience and personal

FIGURE 5-1   Multiarea OSPF design by region

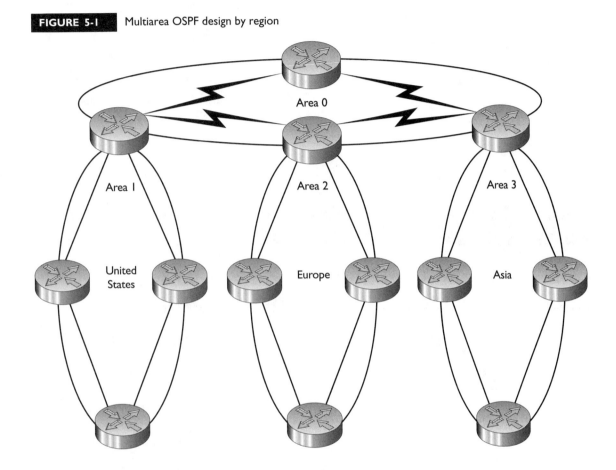

tastes. Some networks can get away with grouping 200 routers into a single area; others have so many links that 50 might be too many. It depends on the model of routers being used and whether or not other techniques (such as summarization) are implemented.

EXERCISE 5-1

Using a Multiarea Design to Control LSA Traffic

Scenario: One of your clients has a large (900-router) WAN infrastructure that spans five countries and three continents. They are using a single OSPF area design and are having problems with LSA traffic because of unstable links. They would like to implement newer technologies such as voice over IP (VOIP) and videoconferencing but need to improve their WAN performance first.

Solution: Separate the offices—by geographic region and function—and place them into a multiarea design. This will cut down on the number of LSAs flooding across the entire network and reduce the impact of bouncing links. Use summarization at area borders to further improve utilization across the backbone.

CERTIFICATION OBJECTIVE 5.02

Differentiating Among the Types of Areas, Routers, and LSAs in an OSPF Network

In order to configure a multiarea network, you first need to know the characteristics of various areas and how routers behave in or between them. Each router can also create multiple types of LSAs, which propagate differently through the network.

Functional Descriptions of Routers in an OSPF Network

OSPF routers are identified by where they are placed in different areas. The following four types of routers are supported and are displayed in Figure 5-2: internal routers, area border routers, backbone routers, and autonomous system boundary routers.

Internal Router

Internal routers have all interfaces located within a single area and require only one link-state database.

Area Border Router

Area border routers (ABRs) have interfaces in different, nonbackbone areas and at least one in the backbone area (area 0). These routers summarize connected areas

FIGURE 5-2 Types of routers in a multiarea OSPF model

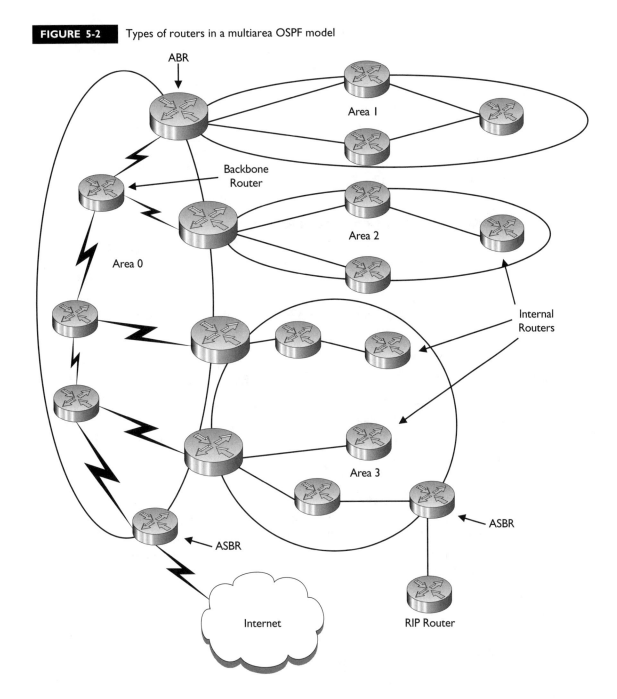

and advertise the networks to the backbone, where the summary routes are sent to each ABR. The ABR must run a separate copy of the SPF algorithm for each area to which it is connected; keep this requirement in mind when you purchase a router to go between multiple areas.

Backbone Router

A *backbone router* is a router that has at least one interface connected to area 0. ABRs qualify as backbone routers, but not all backbone routers are ABRs. When all interfaces are in area 0, the router is not an ABR.

Autonomous System Boundary Router

The *autonomous system boundary router (ASBR)* redistributes routes learned from other routing protocols (RIP, IGRP, EIGRP, and BGP) into the OSPF domain. ASBRs can be internal routers and do not have to be connected to the backbone. They are usually created to direct traffic to the Internet or for migrating from one routing protocol to another. An ASBR is also needed for routing between two different OSPF autonomous systems.

Types of OSPF Link-State Advertisements

All four types of OSPF router use LSAs to communicate, but different types of LSAs are used based on the kind of information passed. It is important to memorize the LSA types and their functions because this information is vital to understanding how each area functions.

LSA Type 1: Router LSA

Router LSAs are the most basic LSA and are generated by all routers. They list each of the router's interfaces as well as the state and cost of each link. Type 1 LSAs are flooded to only a single area. For example, a router in Area 2 would never receive a router LSA created in Area 1.

LSA Type 2: Network LSA

Network LSAs exist in multiaccess networks and originate from the DR. A network LSA contains a list of all attached routers and is flooded throughout a single area when there are two or more routers on the multiaccess network. If the DR is the only router, there is no need to send out a network LSA.

LSA Type 3: Network Summary LSA

Type 3 LSAs, called *network summary LSAs,* are produced by ABRs and advertise destinations outside the local area. When flooded to an attached area, they tell that area all the destinations it can reach within the OSPF domain. When sent to the backbone, a network summary LSA contains all networks that are attached to the ABR. Keep in mind that the router generates a network summary LSA for every router LSA received unless summarization is implemented.

LSA Type 5: External LSA

An ASBR produces *external LSAs.* They advertise routes to destinations outside the OSPF domain and are flooded to all areas of the network.

Other LSA Types

Other kinds of LSAs exist, but they are not covered on the test and are therefore outside the realm of this book. They are listed here for completeness:

- **LSA Type 4: ASBR Summary LSA**   Created by an ABR; contains the destination of the ASBR.

- **LSA Type 6: Group Membership LSA**   Describes multicast group members for multicast OSPF packets.

- **LSA Type 7: NSSA External LSA**   Generated by an ASBR to describe external routes. Type 7 LSAs are flooded into not-so-stubby areas (NSSAs).

Differentiating Between External Type 1 and External Type 2 OSPF LSAs

Routes to external destinations are redistributed into OSPF by the ASBR and flooded into the network with Type 5 LSAs. These LSAs are broken down into *External Type 1* (E1) and *External Type 2* (E2). In an E1, the ASBR assigns a cost to the external path, then adds the cost of the internal path to get to the ASBR. External Type 2 LSAs disregard the cost of the route to the ASBR and advertise only the cost of the external route. This is the default method on Cisco routers and can be changed by the administrator.

Figure 5-3 shows how using E1 or E2 type routes will affect a router's path selection. Router A can select two different paths to reach Router D. If E1 is used, the cost of path A-C-D is 215 (10 + 195 + 10 = 215) and will be chosen over path

FIGURE 5-3

Route selection
using E1 and E2
OSPF LSAs

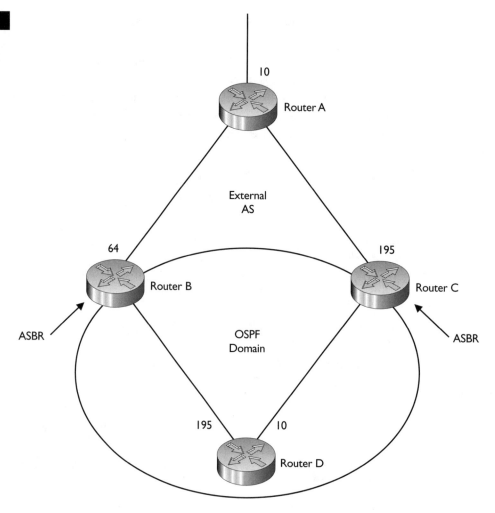

A-B-D, the cost of which is 269 (10 + 64 + 195 = 269). When E2 is used, the ASBR counts only the cost of the external route, and path A-B-D (10 + 64 = 74) is chosen over A-C-D (10 + 195 = 205).

Output of the SHOW IP OSPF DATABASE Command for LSA Types 1, 2, 3, and 5

The SHOW IP OSPF DATABASE command is used to display the contents of the link-state database. The database is divided into sections, reflecting the information processed from different types of LSAs, and it shows from which router the LSA was received:

- *Router Link States* is a listing of routers contained in Type 1 LSAs. The following code output has two of these sections, one for Area 0 and one for Area 1. This means the router is an ABR.
- *Net Link States* contains the LSAs received on a multiaccess network, or Type 2 LSAs.
- *Summary Net Link States* are the summary links injected by the ABRs and are propagated using Type 3 LSAs.
- *Summary ASB Link States* contain links from Type 4 LSAs and *AS External Link States* from Type 5.

```
Router#show ip ospf database

        OSPF Router with ID (192.168.20.100) (Process ID 10)

                Router Link States (Area 0)

Link ID          ADV Router       Age     Seq#          Checksum   Link Count
192.168.20.10    192.168.20.10    1084    0x80000048    0xB36A     3
192.168.20.20    192.168.20.20    964     0x80000003    0x65DD     3
192.168.20.30    192.168.20.30    1204    0x8000037F    0x1EAA     3
192.168.20.60    192.168.20.60    1007    0x800001F7    0xBAEB     3

                Net Link States (Area 0)

Link ID          ADV Router       Age     Seq#          Checksum
192.168.10.9     192.168.20.10    1231    0x800000CE    0xFD72
192.168.10.10    192.168.20.20    1003    0x80000523    0x3245
192.168.10.11    192.168.20.30    842     0x8000007F    0xB732
192.168.10.12    192.168.20.15    654     0x80000D24    0xA2FF

                Summary Net Link States (Area 0)

Link ID          ADV Router       Age     Seq#          Checksum
172.24.0.0       192.168.20.30    42      0x80000054    0x44DE
172.24.0.0       192.168.20.40    745     0x80000D75    0xB784
10.1.0.0         192.168.20.70    1243    0x80000B22    0xEEA2
10.1.0.0         192.168.20.90    1024    0x80001442    0x14AE
```

```
                     Summary ASB Link States (Area 0)

Link ID           ADV Router          Age    Seq#         Checksum
192.168.15.254    192.168.20.50       544    0x80000AED   0x32E0
192.168.15.254    192.168.20.60       602    0x80000052   0xB32A

                     Router Link States (Area 1)

Link ID           ADV Router          Age    Seq#         Checksum   Link Count
192.168.20.100    192.168.20.100      120    0x80000244   0xA2FE     4
192.168.20.110    192.168.20.110      1224   0x80000006   0xB36F     2
192.168.20.120    192.168.20.120      224    0x80000200   0xF722     2
192.168.20.130    192.168.20.130      568    0x80000620   0x2E4F     2

                   Summary Net Link States (Area 1)

Link ID           ADV Router          Age    Seq#         Checksum
172.24.0.0        192.168.20.100      28     0x80000242   0xB782
172.24.0.0        192.168.20.110      846    0x800000CD   0x8C4D
10.1.0.0          192.168.20.100      27     0x80000240   0xB8DD
10.1.0.0          192.168.20.110      847    0x80000052   0xC88A

                   Summary ASB Link States (Area 1)

Link ID           ADV Router          Age    Seq#         Checksum
192.168.15.254    192.168.20.100      34     0x800000FF   0xAD73
192.168.15.254    192.168.20.110      863    0x80000E46   0xB55B

                     AS External Link States

Link ID           ADV Router          Age    Seq#         Checksum
10.124.0.0        192.168.20.70       1240   0x80000D72   0xACD7
10.240.0.0        192.168.20.90       1030   0x80000003   0xBAD8
Router#
```

Relating the OSPF LSA Types to IP Routing Table Entries

In the following code listing, we see a sample output of the SHOW IP ROUTE command. Notice the codes listed in the beginning and how they fit into the routing table.

The second route in the table is a Type 5, E2, LSA. The *O* signifies a route learned from the OSPF routing protocol, and the *E2* describes the type of OSPF route. If the external type routing updates had been set to E1 at the ASBR, the routing table would have reflected this fact with *E1* in the routing entry.

Routes with an *IA* are entries for networks outside the local area—from network summary LSAs. The remaining entries were learned from Type 1 and Type 2 LSAs and originated from the local area.

```
Router#sh ip route

Codes: C - connected, S - static, I - IGRP, R - RIP, M - mobile, B - BGP
       D - EIGRP, EX - EIGRP external, O - OSPF, IA - OSPF inter area
       N1 - OSPF NSSA external type 1, N2 - OSPF NSSA external type 2
       E1 - OSPF external type 1, E2 - OSPF external type 2, E - EGP
       i - IS-IS, L1 - IS-IS level-1, L2 - IS-IS level-2, * - candidate default
       U - per-user static route, o - ODR
       T - traffic engineered route

Gateway of last resort is 10.16.20.2 to network 0.0.0.0

C    192.168.20.0/24 is directly connected, Loopback0
O E2 172.16.0.0/16 [110/75] via 192.168.20.2, 2d13h, Serial0
     10.0.0.0/12 is variably subnetted, 23 subnets, 3 masks
O IA    10.0.0.0/24 [110/65] via 192.168.20.2, 2d13h, Serial0
O IA    10.0.0.4/32 [110/65] via 192.168.20.2, 2d13h, Serial0
O       10.17.0.0/16 [110/130] via 192.168.20.2, 2d13h, Serial0
C       10.18.0.0 is directly connected, Serial0
C       10.19.0.0 is directly connected, Ethernet0
C       10.20.0.0 is directly connected, Ethernet1
O       10.21.10.0/24 [110/11] via 192.168.20.14, 2d10h, Ethernet1
O       10.22.10.0/24 [110/11] via 192.168.20.15, 2d11h, Ethernet0
O IA    10.32.0.0/12 [110/65] via 192.168.20.2, 2d13h, Serial0
O IA    10.48.0.0/12 [110/65] via 192.168.20.2, 2d13h, Serial0
O IA    10.64.0.0/12 [110/65] via 192.168.20.2, 2d13h, Serial0
O IA    10.80.0.0/12 [110/65] via 192.168.20.2, 2d13h, Serial0
--More--
```

exam
ⓦatch   *It is important to understand the purpose of each type of LSA and the information each contains—both for the exam and for general understanding of OSPF. Reread the previous section if these concepts are not clear.*

Types of OSPF Areas

Further control of LSA propagation is done with the configuration of different types of OSPF areas; see Figure 5-4. Each area serves a different function and allows specific types of LSAs to pass through.

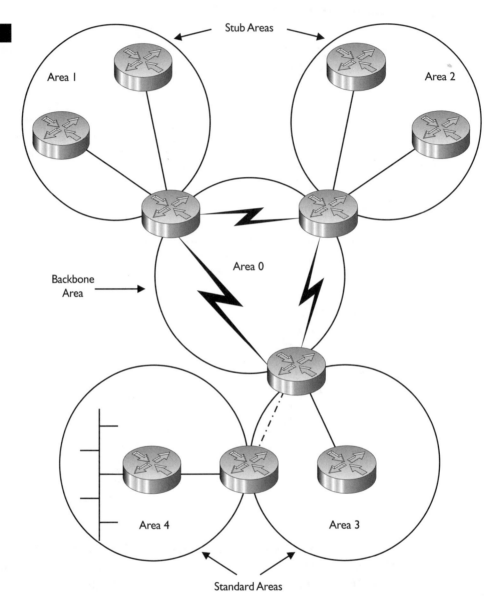

FIGURE 5-4

Types of OSPF
areas

Standard Area

By default, any area connected to the backbone becomes a standard area. All LSAs
are permitted, and propagation takes place normally.

Backbone Area

The backbone area is always designated as 0 or 0.0.0.0. All areas must be directly connected to the backbone or have a virtual link to this area. Area 0 characteristically contains high-speed routers and redundant links forming the core of a hierarchical network. Due to the nature of the backbone area, it is wise to keep all hosts off the backbone.

Stub Area

The stub area prevents ASBR External LSAs (Type 5) and ASBR Summary LSAs (Type 4) from flooding to the routers contained within. The ABR for a stub area inserts a default route (0.0.0.0) that all stub area routers use when no routes are found for a destination. In networks in which many external links are present, this causes a noticeable difference in performance by reducing the size of the routing table and database.

Totally Stubby Area

Cisco took the idea of a stub area one step further by eliminating Type 3 LSAs from flooding into totally stubby areas. The ABR inserts the default route again, and all routers within the area send inter-area and external traffic to the border router.

Requirements for a Stub and a Totally Stubby Area

In addition to the types of LSAs allowed into the area, there are a couple of other restrictions on stubs and totally stubby areas:

■ Virtual links cannot be configured or transit a stub or totally stubby area.

■ No ASBRs are allowed.

Take a look at the following Scenarios and Solutions for a breakdown of the different kinds of areas and the types of LSAs that are found in each.

exam
ⓦatch

Understanding the properties of each area is imperative to speed comprehension of multiarea OSPF scenario-based questions.

Now that you have seen the differences between LSAs, refer to the following Scenario & Solution.

SCENARIO & SOLUTION

In a stub area...	Type 5 LSAs will not be present.
In a totally stubby area...	Both Types 4 and 5 will not be present.
The backbone area...	All LSAs can be present.
On an Ethernet segment...	All types can be found, but only in a multiaccess network will Type 2 LSAs be present.
In a standard area...	All LSAs can be present.

on the **Ĵob**

It is not discussed here because it is not covered on the exam, but there is a way to configure an ASBR in a stub area, creating a new area called a not-so-stubby area, or NSSA. The ASBR floods the area with external links in the form of Type 7 LSAs, which are converted into Type 5 LSAs by the ABR and advertised to the rest of the network.

FROM THE CLASSROOM

Stub and Backbone Area Design Issues

Most large networks are not as simple as the previous sections might lead you to believe. There is more to stub areas and backbone design than simply knowing what types of LSAs are permitted in them.

First, stub areas sound so great, why not use them in every area that doesn't have virtual links or ASBRs? The answer is that suboptimal routing occurs when multiple exit points exist. When default routes are introduced, the internal routers don't know which ABRs have the best routes to ASBRs or other areas. This can cause a packet to bounce around the network to get to its destination instead of taking a shorter, more direct route.

Another issue is with backbone design. Something we have not mentioned is that once packets cross into the backbone, they cannot go into another area to reach another portion of the backbone. This condition can actually cause inefficient routing in certain situations.

For example, ABR1 needs to send a packet to the ASBR, which is attached to ABR6. ABR1 does not have a direct connection with ABR6, so it sends the packet to ABR5, which is in the same building as ABR6. The problem is that ABR5 has a direct connection to ABR6, but this connection is in another area; the packet cannot cross into the nonbackbone area to reach ABR6. This theoretical packet is then bounced around the backbone until it finds another router (possibly 10 hops away!) that has an Area 0 connection to ABR6.

One solution to this design issue is to simply make sure neighboring ABRs have direct connections in Area 0.

—*Tony Olzak, CCNP, MCSE*

LSA Propagation Across a Standard-Area OSPF Network

All the routers are configured. Every link is up. Adjacencies have been established. We know about LSAs, areas, and routers, but how does it all come together? How does it work?

Figure 5-5 shows a model OSPF network with standard areas, a backbone area, and an ASBR. Here we specifically analyze how networks 10.31.0.0 and 172.16.0.0 are propagated throughout the internetwork and compare that to stub areas and totally stubby areas.

R1 is an internal router within a standard area. It floods Area 1 with router LSAs containing its connections to 10.17.0.0 and 10.31.0.0. R2, which is an ABR, records these links in its database. The ABR generates network summary LSAs containing entries for networks 10.16.0.0 and 10.31.0.0, and sends it to R4 and R5. R4 generates its own Type 3 LSA and notifies Area 2 of both networks.

172.16.0.0 is learned by R5 (ASBR) through the EIGRP routing protocol. This network is redistributed into OSPF and flooded through the backbone as a Type 5 LSA. Routers R2 and R4 both take this LSA and flood it into their respective areas via Type 5 LSAs.

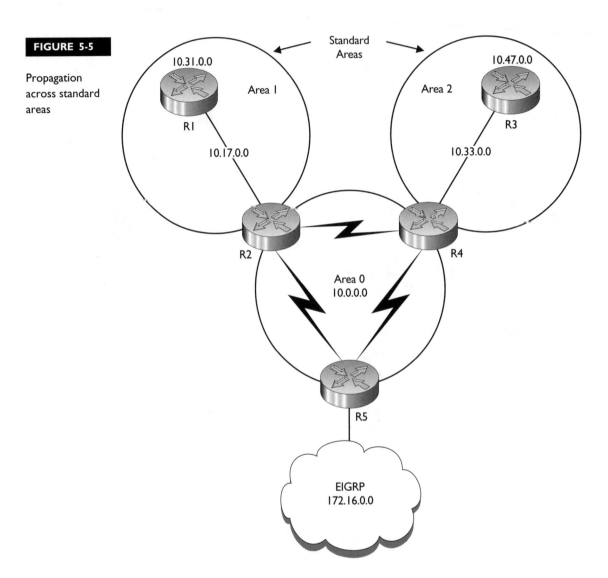

FIGURE 5-5

Propagation across standard areas

LSA Propagation Across a Stub Area and Standard-Area OSPF Network

Figure 5-6 takes the previous network and modifies Area 2 from a standard area to a stub area. With this configuration, 10.31.0.0 is advertised to Area 2 using the same method as in Figure 5-5. R1 floods Area 1 with Type 1 LSAs, which are received by R2 and sent to R4 in a Type 3 LSA. R4 generates its own Type 3 LSA containing 10.31.0.0 and sends it to Area 2.

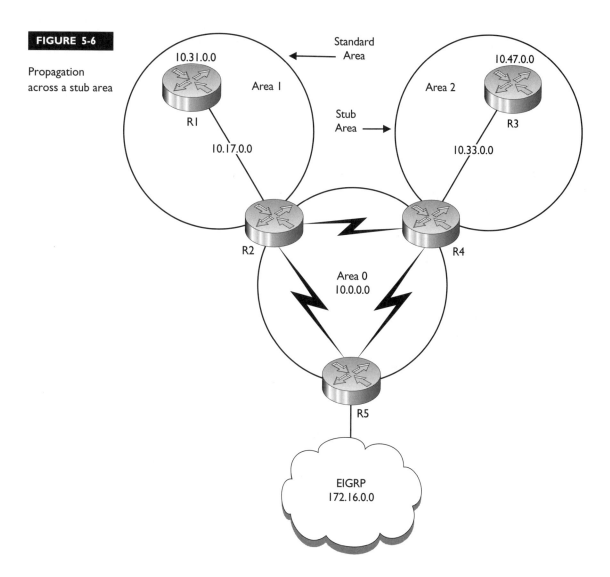

FIGURE 5-6

Propagation across a stub area

In looking at how the 172.16.0.0 network is advertised, we see some change. It is still advertised with Type 5 LSAs and passed into Area 1, but this time R4 does not send the advertisement into Area 2. Because Area 2 is a stub area, no Type 4 or 5 LSAs are allowed.

R4 creates a default route (0.0.0.0) and sends it to R3. Now R3 will send any packets not destined for the OSPF domain to the ABR (R4), unless static routes are used.

LSA Propagation Across a Totally Stubby Area and Standard-Area OSPF Network

The model in Figure 5-7, again, makes a modification to Area 2. This time we have a totally stubby area, one standard area, and a backbone area with an ASBR.

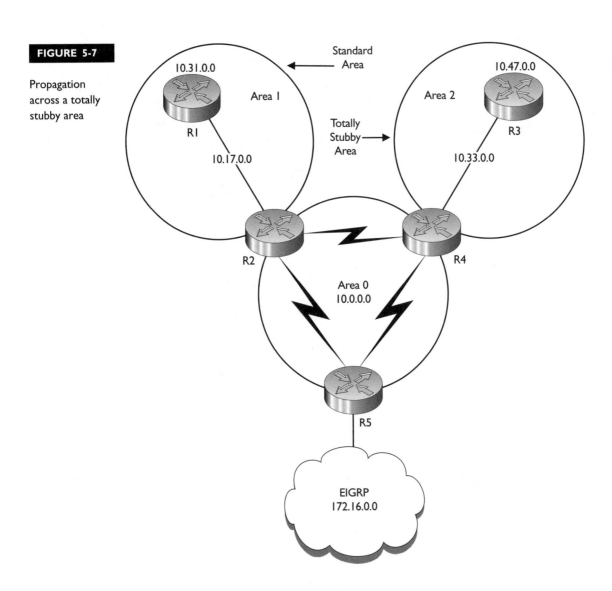

FIGURE 5-7

Propagation across a totally stubby area

R1 sends Type 1 LSAs to R2, which in turn packages these advertisements into a Type 3 LSA. This network summary LSA is flooded into the backbone and received by R4 and R5.

Now that Area 2 is a totally stubby area, Types 3, 4, and 5 LSAs are not allowed. The ABR (R4) adds the Type 3 LSA from R2 to its database and floods a default route to R3 for all inter-area and external destinations. Whenever R3 needs to send anything outside Area 2, it uses the default route to send the packet to R4.

There is no change in the way network 172.16.0.0 is handled.

Benefits of OSPF Summarization

Summarization is an important configuration technique that provides many benefits to an OSPF domain. It allows a router to use *variable-length subnet masks (VLSMs)* and one route entry to symbolize a series of contiguous networks.

For example, in the previous section we discussed how the network 10.31.0.0 was advertised to the rest of the OSPF domain. The area also contained the network 10.17.0.0. In this example, we'll say it also contained 10.18.0.0–10.30.0.0, all with the subnet mask 255.255.0.0. By default, the ABR has to advertise every one of these networks, and other routers will have a single routing table entry for every network.

Using the AREA <AREA ID> RANGE <NETWORK ADDRESS> <SUBNET MASK> command, the ABR can be configured to advertise a single network that covers all previously mentioned networks. This command, as well as how an ASBR summarizes external links, is mentioned in more detail in the configuration portion of this chapter.

By moving the subnet mask to the left—specifically, to 255.240.0.0—the ABR can generate one LSA that contains the network 10.16.0.0/12. This subnet mask tells other routers that the ABR can reach networks 10.16.0.0–10.31.0.0. That's much more efficient than advertising all 16 networks individually.

Using one entry instead of 16 also reduces the size of the routing table. Route lookup is quicker, and less memory is required for normal operation.

Another benefit of summarization lies in reducing the number of times the SPF algorithm must be run by hiding the specifics of an area. In the previous example, if the link for network 10.18.0.0 goes down, routers in another area won't have to make any changes. The ABR still advertises 10.16.0.0/12, as normal. This is especially beneficial if the link is bouncing—continuously going up and down.

The Effects of Addressing and Summarization in an OSPF Environment

Good addressing schemes are critical to efficient summarization. The networks must be contiguous for summarization to work. During the planning phase of a design, make sure to keep summarization in mind. Allot a set of addresses that are contiguous and fall on a "bit border." Our previous example would not have been as effective if Area 1 had contained networks 10.13.0.0–10.35.0.0. Keep addresses in sets of 2, 4, 8, 16, 32, 64, 128, and 256.

EXERCISE 5-2

Troubleshooting Poor Backbone Performance

Scenario: You are the administrator of a new multiarea OSPF network. Users have been complaining of poor performance from the office just down the road from a mainframe.

You check the link and everything seems to be fine. Utilization is low, and there are no resets and no errors. You do a ping and are surprised when the Time to Live (TTL) comes back with more hops than you expected. The resources to which the users are connecting should be only three hops away, but the TTL indicates a distance of six hops. You do a traceroute and confirm the number of routers traversed—it is six.

The remote facility is in Area 5 and has an ABR that connects to an ABR at your facility. Your department is in Area 2. The mainframe is in your building in Area 4, which has an ABR that connects to other offices and your ABR through an Ethernet segment in Area 2.

When packets leave the ABR at the remote office, they exit Area 5 and enter the backbone. They reach your ABR but don't use the Ethernet segment to get to Area 4's ABR and the mainframe. The packets go through two other remote offices to reach the ABR attached to Area 4 in your building.

Solution: Connect your ABR and the mainframe's ABR to each other over an Ethernet segment and place it in the backbone area. The problem is that even though the two routers have a connection to each other over Area 2, once packets enter the backbone, they cannot leave until they reach their destination area.

CERTIFICATION OBJECTIVE 5.03

Configuring a Multiarea OSPF Network

Now that we have formed a foundation in theory, it is time to put it to use. The following section contains many commands used for configuring routers in a multiarea OSPF design.

exam
ⓦatch

Be sure to practice all commands until you know them cold. The exam is not forgiving; you must know the exact syntax and where to use each command.

The OSPF NETWORK Statement

The NETWORK command tells the OSPF process which interfaces should be included in OSPF routing and to which area they belong. The syntax for the command is as follows:

```
Router(config-router)#network <network address> <wildcard mask>
area <area ID>
```

It is important to remember that the NETWORK statement uses a wildcard mask, not a standard subnet mask.

Configuration Example of an Internal Router and an ABR

The following configurations show how some of the routers from Figure 5-5 would be configured:

```
R1(config)#router ospf 100
R1(config-router)#network 10.17.0.0 0.0.255.255 area 1
R1(config-router)#network 10.31.0.0 0.0.255.255 area 1

R2(config)#router ospf 100
R2(config-router)#network 10.0.0.0 0.0.255.255 area 0
R2(config-router)#network 10.17.0.0 0.0.255.255 area 1
```

The wildcard mask in the last NETWORK statement tells the router that 10.17 must match exactly, but the last two octets, 0.0, can be anything. The way this kind of mask works is that every 0 bit must match, and every 1 bit can be 1 or 0.

For example, the wildcard mask 0.0.255.255, for network 10.17.0.0, breaks down into binary as follows:

```
0.0.255.255 = 00000000.00000000.11111111.11111111
```

All those zero bits tell the router that the first two octets must be 10 and 17. If the network was 10.16.0.0/12, it would break down as follows:

```
10.16.0.0    = 00001010.00010000.00000000.00000000
0.15.255.255 = 00000000.00001111.11111111.11111111
```

This tells the router that 10 must match exactly, but the second octet can be 16-31. The first 4 bits (0001) make the number 16; any combination of the next 4 bits can be used to make the number anything between 16 and 31.

on the **Job**

NETWORK statements can be used like access lists in that the router will go through each line until one matches. You can specify a small range of addresses (for example, 10.16.0.0–0.15.255.255) that need to go into a certain area and follow it with a NETWORK statement that throws everything else into another range (10.0.0.0–0.255.255.255, for instance). The router will match all addresses in the 10.16.0.0/12 range, then match everything else to the 10.0.0.0/8 network.

The OSPF STUB Command

After using the NETWORK command to tell the router which networks are in each area, use the AREA <AREA ID> STUB [NO-SUMMARY] command to make it a stub area.

```
R4(config-router)#network 10.33.0.0 0.0.255.255 area 1
R4(config-router)#area 1 stub

R3(config-router)#network 10.33.0.0 0.0.255.255 area 1
R3(config-router)#area 1 stub
```

All the routers in the area must have the same stub configuration or they will not be able to create adjacencies. When the STUB command is configured, a special bit (an E bit) is set to zero in the hello packet. All routers must agree on this setting or they will not become neighbors.

The OSPF STUB Command with a NO-SUMMARY Modifier

The NO-SUMMARY modifier at the end of a STUB command turns a stub area into a totally stubby area. This command is needed only at the ABR, since it does not affect the hello packet, as the STUB command does.

```
R4(config-router)#network 10.33.0.0 0.0.255.255 area 1
R4(config-router)#area 1 stub no-summary
```

The OSPF DEFAULT-COST Command

The DEFAULT-COST command is used in stub areas that have multiple exit points. It changes the cost of the default route generated by an ABR. The default cost is 1; use the command to raise the cost of the ABR you do not want to use.

```
R4(config-router)#network 10.33.0.0 0.0.255.255 area 1
R4(config-router)#area 1 stub
R4(config-router)#area 1 default-cost 64
```

The OSPF ABR SUMMARIZATION Command

The syntax for the ABR SUMMARIZATION command is:

```
Router(config-router)#area <area ID> range <network address> <subnet mask>
```

This command takes a range of contiguous addresses within an area and creates one summary LSA for the rest of the network. If we wanted R4 to make only one advertisement for Area 1, we would configure it as follows:

```
R4(config-router)#area 1 range 10.32.0.0 255.240.0.0
```

Other routers know that R4 can reach networks 32–47 because it will advertise the route as 10.32.0.0/12. Only the networks that fall within this range will be suppressed; all others will still be advertised normally. You can also use multiple instances of this command to summarize multiple blocks of addresses.

Be aware that an ABR may only summarize Type 3 LSAs that are in its area. An ABR that is attached to Areas 1 and 2 might receive Type 3 LSAs from an ABR in Area 3 but will not be able to summarize them.

exam
ⓦatch

Note that the ABR SUMMARIZATION command uses a standard subnet mask, not a wildcard mask, as the NETWORK statement does.

The **OSPF ASBR SUMMARY-ADDRESS** Command

The SUMMARY-ADDRESS <SUMMARY ADDRESS> <SUMMARY MASK> command is used on the ASBR to summarize external networks. This cuts down on the number of Type 5 LSAs that are flooded into the network:

```
R5(router-config)#summary-address 172.16.0.0 255.240.0.0
```

This command tells the rest of the network that R5 can reach the external networks 172.16.0.0 through 172.31.0.0.

Note: This command summarizes only Type 5 LSAs and can be done only by the ASBR. An ABR, receiving Type 5 LSAs, cannot summarize before flooding them into its area.

OSPF Virtual Link

A *virtual link* allows an area that is not connected to the backbone to communicate with the rest of the network. As illustrated in Figure 5-8, ABR2 creates a virtual link to ABR1 to reach the backbone. The routers on both sides of the link must be configured using the router IDs.

FIGURE 5-8   Virtual links

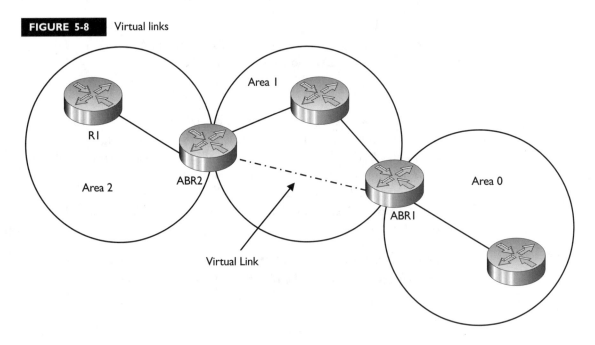

```
ABR2(config-router)#area 1 virtual-link ?
A.B.C.D  ID (IP addr) associated with virtual link neighbor

ABR2(config-router)#area 1 virtual-link 192.168.20.10

ABR1(config-router)#area 1 virtual-link 192.168.20.20
```

Any custom attributes of Area 1 (such as the hello interval, authentication) must also be set with the VIRTUAL-LINK command. Area 1 is the *transit* area, or the area through which the virtual link travels. The IP address in the command is the router ID, not the IP address of the interface.

on the

Ｊob

Virtual links should be used only to reconnect a segmented backbone, connect backbones when two companies merge, or as a temporary fix to a detached area. Using virtual links as a permanent fix to any situation will downgrade the performance of both the area using the link and the area through which it transits. It will also complicate troubleshooting.

Now that you have a better understanding of some of the configuration commands, refer to the following Scenario & Solution.

SCENARIO & SOLUTION

The backbone is segmented…	Repair with a virtual link.
Too many Type 5 LSAs are coming from the ASBR…	Use the SUMMARY-ADDRESS command to summarize external links.
There is a large number of continuous networks in an area…	Use the AREA RANGE command to summarize networks attached to the ABR.
Restrict Type 5 LSAs from entering a specific area…	Create a stub area to prevent Type 5 LSAs from entering.
Make an interface belong to a specific area…	Use the NETWORK command to make an interface participate in OSPF and join a specific area.

EXERCISE 5-3

Troubleshooting the NETWORK Command

Scenario: You have configured your router with the following OSPF configuration:

```
interface e0
ip address 10.0.0.1 255.255.0.0
!
interface e1
ip address 10.16.0.1 255.255.0.0
!
router ospf 100
network 10.0.0.0 0.255.255.255 area 2
network 10.16.0.0 0.15.255.255 area 3
```

When you enter the second NETWORK command, you get the following error:

```
% OSPF: "network 10.16.0.0 0.15.255.255 area 3" is ignored. It
is a subset of a previous entry.
```

Solution: Change the first NETWORK statement to:

```
network 10.0.0.0 0.0.255.255 area 2
```

The original statement caused both interfaces to join Area 2. Therefore, the next NETWORK command had no effect.

CERTIFICATION OBJECTIVE 5.04

Monitoring and Verifying OSPF Operations

After the configurations are complete, the operation of the network needs verification. The following discussions constitute a select group of SHOW commands to help you monitor the operation of an OSPF network.

e x a m
ⓦa t c h *The SHOW commands can be confusing when you are trying to remember which protocols use which variables. Be sure to practice all the commands and understand their outputs. A good way to do this is to change the configurations of your lab setup and see how the outputs of different SHOW commands are affected.*

The SHOW IP OSPF DATABASE Command

This command displays the contents of the link-state database. It is useful in monitoring proper LSA propagation and troubleshooting DR issues. For example, the Net Link States section can be used to verify that the router is receiving updates from the designated router (DR). This command can also use variables to filter the output to just one type of LSA.

```
Router#show ip ospf database

        OSPF Router with ID (192.168.20.100) (Process ID 10)

                Router Link States (Area 0)

Link ID           ADV Router        Age      Seq#         Checksum   Link Count
192.168.20.10     192.168.20.10     1084     0x80000048   0xB36A     3
192.168.20.20     192.168.20.20     964      0x80000003   0x65DD     3
192.168.20.30     192.168.20.30     1204     0x8000037F   0x1EAA     3
192.168.20.60     192.168.20.60     1007     0x800001F7   0xBAEB     3

                Net Link States (Area 0)

Link ID           ADV Router        Age      Seq#         Checksum
192.168.10.9      192.168.20.10     1231     0x800000CE   0xFD72
192.168.10.10     192.168.20.20     1003     0x80000523   0x3245
192.168.10.11     192.168.20.30     842      0x8000007F   0xB732
192.168.10.12     192.168.20.15     654      0x80000D24   0xA2FF

                Summary Net Link States (Area 0)

Link ID           ADV Router        Age      Seq#         Checksum
172.24.0.0        192.168.20.30     42       0x80000054   0x44DE
172.24.0.0        192.168.20.40     745      0x80000D75   0xB784
10.1.0.0          192.168.20.70     1243     0x80000B22   0xEEA2
10.1.0.0          192.168.20.90     1024     0x80001442   0x14AE
```

```
                    Summary ASB Link States (Area 0)

Link ID          ADV Router        Age    Seq#         Checksum
192.168.15.254   192.168.20.50     544    0x80000AED   0x32E0
192.168.15.254   192.168.20.60     602    0x80000052   0xB32A

                    Router Link States (Area 1)

Link ID          ADV Router        Age    Seq#         Checksum   Link Count
192.168.20.100   192.168.20.100    120    0x80000244   0xA2FE     4
192.168.20.110   192.168.20.110    1224   0x80000006   0xB36F     2
192.168.20.120   192.168.20.120    224    0x80000200   0xF722     2
192.168.20.130   192.168.20.130    568    0x80000620   0x2E4F     2

                    Summary Net Link States (Area 1)

Link ID          ADV Router        Age    Seq#         Checksum
172.24.0.0       192.168.20.100    28     0x80000242   0xB782
172.24.0.0       192.168.20.110    846    0x800000CD   0x8C4D
10.1.0.0         192.168.20.100    27     0x80000240   0xB8DD
10.1.0.0         192.168.20.110    847    0x80000052   0xC88A

                    Summary ASB Link States (Area 1)

Link ID          ADV Router        Age    Seq#         Checksum
192.168.15.254   192.168.20.100    34     0x800000FF   0xAD73
192.168.15.254   192.168.20.110    863    0x80000E46   0xB55B

                    AS External Link States

Link ID          ADV Router        Age    Seq#         Checksum
10.124.0.0       192.168.20.70     1240   0x80000D72   0xACD7
10.240.0.0       192.168.20.90     1030   0x80000003   0xBAD8Router#
```

The following is a description of each field header:

- **Link ID**   The IP address of the interface on which OSPF is active. In the case of ABRs and ASBRs, it can also be a network number that summarizes the various contiguous networks contained within an area or external system.

- **ADV router**   The advertising router's ID.

- **Age**   Link-state age in seconds. When the LSA reaches an age of 1800 seconds (30 minutes), the originating router resends the LSA with an incremented sequence number. If the entry reaches an age of 3600 seconds (1 hour), it is flushed from the database.

- **Seq#**   Link-state sequence number. Basically, this number serves as a version number.

- **Checksum**   Checksum of the LSA's contents.

- **Link count**   Number of interfaces advertised on each router. A link will come up repeatedly to describe point-to-point links, virtual links, stub areas, and transit networks. For example, if a point-to-point link also describes a stub area, it will appear twice in the link count.

The SHOW IP OSPF BORDER-ROUTERS Command

The SHOW IP OSPF BORDER-ROUTERS command displays the internal routes to area border routers and autonomous system boundary routers. The following is a sample output from the command:

```
Router# show ip ospf border-routers

OSPF Process 10 internal Routing Table

Destination        Next Hop        Cost    Type    Rte Type Area        SPF No

172.16.57.23       172.17.10.52    10      ABR     INTRA    0.0.0.1     3
172.16.223.64      172.18.92.50    10      ABR     INTRA    0.0.0.1     3
160.89.103.52      172.17.10.52    20      ASBR    INTER    0.0.0.1     3
160.89.103.52      172.18.92.50    65      ASBR    INTER    0.0.0.1     3
```

The following is a description of the field headers:

- **Destination**   The destination's router ID.

- **Next Hop**   Router ID of the next hop toward the destination.

- **Cost**   Cost of using this route based on bandwidth.

- **Type**   The router type of the destination; it is an ABR, ASBR, or both.

- **Rte Type**   The kind of route. This can be intra-area or inter-area.

- **Area**   The number of the area from which this route was learned.

- **SPF No**   The SPF calculation number that inserted the route.

The SHOW IP OSPF VIRTUAL-LINKS Command

The SHOW IP OSPF VIRTUAL-LINKS command displays virtual links and detailed information about each connection. The output describes to which router

ID the virtual link is connected, the interface used, and all OSPF timer intervals configured:

```
Router# show ip ospf virtual-links

Virtual Link to router 192.168.100.68 is up
Transit area 0.0.0.3, via interface Ethernet0/1, Cost of using 1
Transmit Delay is 1 sec, State POINT_TO_POINT
Timer intervals configured, Hello 10, Dead 40, Wait 40,
Retransmit 5
Hello due in 0:00:02
Adjacency State FULL
```

The following is a description of the information in each line:

- **Virtual Link to router 192.168.100.68 is up**   Specifies the OSPF router to which the link is formed and its state.

- **Transit area 0.0.0.3**   The area that the virtual link crosses.

- **Via interface Ethernet0/1**   The interface through which the virtual link is formed.

- **Cost of using 1**   The cost of reaching the OSPF neighbor through the virtual link.

- **Transmit Delay is 1 sec**   The transmit delay on the virtual link.

- **State POINT_TO_POINT**   The state of the OSPF neighbor.

- **Timer intervals**   The timer intervals configured for the link.

- **Hello due in 0:00:02**   When the next hello is expected from the neighbor.

- **Adjacency State FULL**   The adjacency state between the neighbors.

The SHOW IP OSPF <PROCESS-ID> Command

The SHOW IP OSPF < PROCESS-ID> command shows a generic summary of all OSPF characteristics of the router. These include the process ID, router ID, type of router, redistributed protocols, and area information.

```
Router# show ip ospf 100

Routing Process "ospf 100" with ID 192.168.100.254
Supports only single TOS(TOS0) route
```

```
It is an area border and autonomous system boundary router
Redistributing External Routes from,
        rip with metric mapped to 100
Number of areas in this router is 2
Area 0.0.0.3
        Number of interfaces in this area is 4
        Area has simple password authentication
        SPF algorithm executed 12 times
```

The following points describe some of the lines from the preceding output:

■ **Routing process "ospf 100" with ID 192.168.100.254** Process ID and OSPF router ID.

■ **Supports...TOS(TOS0)** Number of Types of service supported (Type 0 only).

■ **It is an area border and autonomous system boundary router** The types are internal, area border, or autonomous system boundary.

■ **Redistributing External Routes from** Lists of redistributed routes, by protocol.

■ **Number of areas** Number of areas in router, area addresses, and so on.

Now that you have a better understanding of how to monitor an OSPF network, refer to the following Scenario & Solution.

SCENARIO & SOLUTION

See the status of a virtual link...	Use the SHOW IP OSPF VIRTUAL-LINKS command.
See all border routers within an area...	Use the SHOW IP OSPF BORDER-ROUTERS command.
Look at the OSPF database...	Use the SHOW IP OSPF DATABASE command.
Display statistics for a specific instance of the OSPF routing process...	Use the SHOW IP OSPF <PROCESS ID> command to specify which routing process you want to view.

EXERCISE 5-4

Troubleshooting Virtual Links

Scenario: You and another engineer have configured two routers with a virtual link between. After you bring both routers up, you notice that the virtual link is not functioning properly. You can't contact the other engineer and don't know the enable password of the other router. How do you check to see whether or not the other side was configured properly without doing a SHOW RUNNING-CONFIG?

Solution: Telnet to the other router and type the SHOW IP OSPF VIRTUAL-LINKS command from user mode. It will show you the status of the virtual link, the router ID entered, and all the various OSPF timers (such as hello).

CERTIFICATION SUMMARY

In this chapter, you have learned how to scale a single OSPF area into a multiarea, hierarchical network model. With a better understanding of areas, LSA propagation, and the kinds of routers available, you've formed an excellent foundation for comprehending exam questions and responding to real-world situations.

We have also covered most commands needed to actually configure a multiarea OSPF network, including how to summarize areas and create virtual links. The SHOW commands are invaluable for monitoring and verifying proper operation.

Use the information here to get started, but make sure to actually get hands-on experience in order to solidify the concepts covered in this chapter.

✔ TWO-MINUTE DRILL

Here are some of the key points from each certification objective in Chapter 5.

Scalability Issues with a Single-Area OSPF Network

❑ Using multiple areas reduces traffic caused by the flooding of LSAs.

❑ Hiding the details of a group of networks decreases the number of times the SPF algorithm must be run.

❑ A hierarchical design based on geographic region or departments enables the OSPF domain to scale easily to future demands.

Differentiating Among the Types of Areas, Routers, and LSAs

❑ The backbone is a high-speed transit area for inter-area traffic.

❑ All areas must connect to the backbone, either directly or through a virtual link.

❑ Stub areas prevent the propagation of Types 4 and 5 LSAs.

❑ Totally stubby areas prevent Types 3–5 LSAs.

❑ Area border routers (ABRs) connect one or more areas to the backbone.

❑ Autonomous system border routers (ASBRs) connect the OSPF network to another routing protocol.

❑ Type 2 LSAs are created only by designated routers (DRs).

Configuring a Multiarea OSPF Network

❑ All routers in a stub area must be configured with the "stub" attribute.

❑ The NETWORK command uses a wildcard mask.

❑ Standard masks are used by the AREA RANGE and SUMMARY-ADDRESS commands.

Monitoring and Verifying OSPF Operation

❑ Use the SHOW IP OSPF BORDER-ROUTERS command to view routes to ABRs and ASBRs.

❑ LSA propagation can be observed with the SHOW IP OSPF DATABASE command.

SELF TEST

The following questions will help you measure your understanding of the material presented in this chapter. Read all the choices carefully because there might be more than one correct answer. Choose all correct answers for each question.

Scalability Issues with a Single-Area OSPF Network

1. What are some issues with maintaining a large number of routers in a single OSPF area? Choose all that apply.

    A. Frequent OSPF recalculations

    B. Large routing tables are exchanged periodically

    C. Large routing tables are maintained

    D. Continuous flooding of LSAs

2. You manage a network that uses a single-area design. Lately, unstable links have caused LSA flooding to become a problem with your WAN performance. What is the best way to improve WAN performance?

    A. Use static routes.

    B. Create virtual links to spoof the bouncing link.

    C. Break up the single area into a multiarea design.

    D. Use a different routing protocol.

3. The CPU utilization on an ABR in your organization is consistently above 90 percent. Eight areas are connected to this router. What can you do to improve performance? Choose all that apply.

    A. Upgrade the router.

    B. Move some of the areas to another router.

    C. Use HSRP to take some of the load off the ABR.

    D. Configure virtual links to connect to the areas.

4. How does a bouncing link wreak havoc in a single-area design? Choose all that apply.

    A. They cause frequent OSPF recalculations.

    B. They bring excessive LSA traffic.

C. You must reboot the router after every interface reset.

D. It doesn't.

5. What are some ways to divide a single-area into a multiarea OSPF network?

A. By department

B. By IP range

C. By geographic region

D. All the above

Differentiating Among the Types of Areas, Routers, and LSAs

6. What is the difference between stub areas and totally stubby areas?

A. Stub areas allow an ASBR.

B. Totally stubby areas also prevent Type 3 LSAs.

C. Stub areas can have virtual links.

D. Totally stubby areas do not allow Type 1 LSAs.

7. For what is an area border router responsible?

A. It connects the area to other routing protocols.

B. It is the border between LAN and WAN communication.

C. It connects an IP area to an IPX area.

D. It connects one or more areas to the backbone.

8. How are an ABR and an ASBR different?

A. An ABR is the border router between two or more areas, and the ASBR is a border router between an OSPF area and an external autonomous system.

B. An ASBR is the border router between two or more areas, and the ABR is a border router between an OSPF area and an external autonomous system.

C. An ABR connects two different backbones together, and an ASBR connects a backbone to an OSPF area.

D. An ABR connects a stub area to a totally stubby area, and an ASBR connects a stub area to the backbone.

9. Where are Type 2 LSAs found?

  A. They are used to forward inter-area summary routes to internal routers.

  B. They are used on point-to-point links.

  C. The DR creates them in a multiaccess, broadcast network.

  D. They describe the route to the ASBR.

10. What's the difference between External Type 1 and External Type 2 LSAs?

  A. In an External Type 1, the ASBR adds the internal cost of the route to itself to the external route, and in an External Type 2, only the cost of the external route is included.

  B. External Type 1 is a Type 1 LSA, and External Type 2 is a Type 2 LSA.

  C. External Type 1 is from an ABR, and External Type 2 is from an ASBR.

  D. External Type 2 is for link-state external protocols, and External Type 1 is for distance-vector external protocols.

Configuring a Multiarea OSPF Network

11. A router located in Area 0 goes down and segregates the backbone. Communication can take place within each area, but certain areas cannot route inter-area traffic. Area 1 has no connection to Area 0, but it can connect to Area 2. Area 2 has a connection to the backbone. How do you fix this situation with the least amount of administration?

  A. Configure the separated areas as single-area OSPF domains to eliminate the backbone.

  B. Configure the entire OSPF domain as a single area.

  C. Configure a virtual link to connect the separated areas.

  D. Do nothing. Area 1 can simply route traffic through Area 2.

12. What is wrong with the following configuration? Choose all that apply.

```
Router ospf 100
network 10.16.0.0 255.240.0.0 area 0
network 10.17.0.0 255.255.0.0 area 1
```

  A. The 100 should not be there.

  B. The NETWORK command uses wildcard masks.

  C. Network 10.17.0.0/16 will be in Area 0.

  D. Nothing is wrong.

13. On your OSPF network, you would like an ABR to summarize networks 192.168.32.0–192.168.39.0 in Area 2. What command would you use to accomplish this task?

    A. ROUTER(CONFIG)#SUMMARY-ADDRESS 192.168.32.0 255.255.248.0

    B. ROUTER(CONFIG-INT)#AREA 2 RANGE 192.168.32.0 255.255.248.0

    C. ROUTER(CONFIG-ROUTER)#AREA 2 RANGE 192.168.32.0 255.255.248.0

    D. ROUTER(CONFIG-AREA)#SUMMARY-ADDRESS 192.168.32.0 255.255.248.0

14. How many Class C networks can be summarized by the following command?

```
Router(config-router)#summary-address 204.156.64.0 255.255.192.0
```

    A. 192

    B. 32

    C. 252

    D. 64

15. You've created a stub area with multiple exit points. How do you tell the area which border router to use?

    A. Create static routes on each internal router to point to the border router.

    B. Do nothing. The internal routers will automatically pick the best border router.

    C. Use the DEFAULT-COST command to change the cost of the default routes.

    D. Install a Layer 2 switch to switch the traffic to the right router.

16. You have a small number of routers in an area that is being flooded with Type 5 LSAs. How do you keep this traffic from propagating into the area?

    A. Create a separate OSPF autonomous system with a static default route to the other OSPF autonomous system.

    B. Configure the area as stub.

    C. Use an access list to stop OSPF traffic from coming into the area.

    D. Configure a virtual link between the ABR and the ASBR.

Monitoring and Verifying OSPF Operation

17. What command would you use to display the contents of the link-state database?

    A. ROUTER#SHOW IP OSPF DATABASE

B.   ROUTER(CONFIG)#SHOW IP OSPF DATABASE

C.   ROUTER#SHOW IP OSPF LINK-STATE

D.   ROUTER#SHOW OSPF DATABASE

18.   You are receiving misconfigured packets from a router configured with a virtual link. What command will you use to check the status of the virtual link?

A.   ROUTER#SHOW OSPF VIRTUAL LINKS

B.   ROUTER>SHOW OSPF VIRTUAL-LINKS

C.   ROUTER(CONFIG-ROUTER)#SHOW IP OSPF VIRTUAL-LINKS

D.   ROUTER#SHOW IP OSPF VIRTUAL-LINKS

19.   What is wrong with the following configuration?

```
Router ospf 100
network 176.16.24.0 0.0.0.255 area 0
network 192.168.20.0 0.0.0.255 area 1
summary-address 192.224.0.0 0.7.255.255
```

A.   "Area" should not be included in the NETWORK statement.

B.   The summary address should use a standard mask.

C.   The NETWORK statement should use a standard mask.

D.   Nothing is wrong.

20.   One of your routers went down, and you believe it to be an ABR. What command allows you to quickly see all border routers attached to an area?

A.   ROUTER(CONFIG)#SHOW OSPF BORDER-ROUTERS

B.   ROUTER#SHOW IP OSPF BORDER-ROUTERS

C.   ROUTER>SHOW BORDER ROUTERS

D.   ROUTER#SHOW IP OSPF ABR

LAB QUESTION

The following diagram in Figure 5-9 displays a complex OSPF network. How would you configure each router?

FIGURE 5-9

A diagram for the
multiarea OSPF
lab

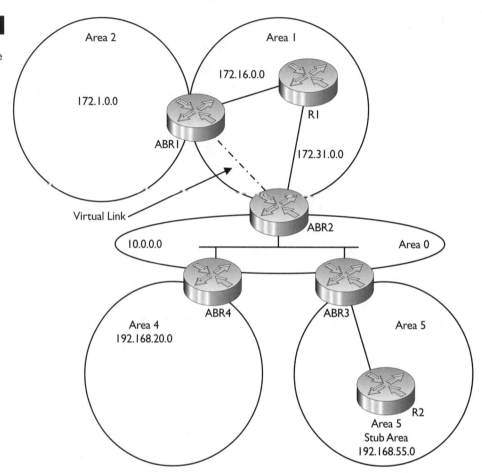

SELF TEST ANSWERS

Scalability Issues with a Single-Area OSPF Network

1. ☑ **A and D. A**, frequent OSPF recalculations, is correct because any changes within a single area cause all routers to run the SPF algorithm. As the number of routers increases, the chances of this event occurring rise. **D**, continuous flooding of LSAs, is an effect of routing table changes when too many routers are within a single area. Using multiple areas reduces the propagation of LSAs.
   ☒ **C**, large routing tables, is incorrect because these are not the result of having many routers in a single area; they are the result of having many networks. **B** is incorrect because large routing tables are not exchanged in OSPF. OSPF uses LSAs to exchange routing information.

2. ☑ **A**. Use static routes. This answer is correct because it will limit the routing updates affected by the bouncing link to a single area. That traffic won't have to flood the entire network.
   ☒ **C and D** are incorrect because they discontinue use of the OSPF routing protocol. **B** is incorrect because a virtual link will not make OSPF think a link is up all the time.

3. ☑ **A and B. A** is correct because a higher-series router will be able to better handle the workload. However, this is not the recommended solution. **B** is correct because you are moving some of the areas off the ABR and therefore reducing its workload. Remember that an ABR has to keep a separate copy of the OSPF database for every area to which it is connected.
   ☒ **C** is incorrect because HSRP creates a standby router; that won't help this situation. **D** is incorrect because virtual links are not used for this purpose and would not decrease CPU utilization.

4. ☑ **A and B. A** is correct because every time a link goes down, OSPF recalculation is triggered. The same happens when the link comes back up. **B** is correct because every time the database changes, routing updates are flooded to the network. In a single-area design, this affects the entire network.
   ☒ **C** is incorrect because you don't have to reboot a router every time one of its interfaces goes down and comes back up. **D** is incorrect because bouncing links do cause problems.

5. ☑ **D**. All the above is correct because all three are good ways to split a single area into multiple areas.
   ☒ There are no incorrect choices.

Differentiating Among the Types of Areas, Routers, and LSAs

6. ☑ **B.** ABRs attached to a totally stubby area keep Types 3, 4, and 5 LSAs from propagating to the area. Stub areas prevent only Types 4 and 5.
   ☒ **A** is incorrect because ASBRs are not allowed in stub or totally stubby areas. This is a pretty logical conclusion, since ASBRs flood the network with Type 5 LSAs. Virtual links are not allowed in either area, making **C** incorrect. If totally stubby areas did not allow Type 1 LSAs, they would not know which networks are connected to adjacent internal routers. Therefore, **D** is incorrect.

7. ☑ **D.** It connects one or more areas to the backbone.
   ☒ **A** is incorrect because it describes an ASBR, not an ABR. **B** is incorrect because an ABR can connect multiple areas that are on any kind of physical interface. **C** is incorrect because IPX is not supported in OSPF.

8. ☑ **A.** An ABR connects two or more areas, and an ASBR connects the OSPF area to an external autonomous system.
   ☒ **B** is incorrect because the definitions are reversed. Although two backbones from merging companies can connect through ABRs, **C** is incorrect because an ASBR does not connect the backbone to an OSPF area. **D** is incorrect because an ASBR is not allowed in a stub area.

9. ☑ **C.** The DR creates them in a multiaccess, broadcast network. Type 2 LSAs are present on multiaccess networks such as Ethernet. The DR uses them to send routing information to other routers on the segment. All routers within an area will flood Type 2 LSAs to all other routers in the area. A DR will create the LSA and flood it to all adjacencies.
   ☒ **A** is incorrect because it describes a Type 3 LSA. **B** is incorrect because point-to-point links do not qualify as multiaccess networks. **D** is incorrect because it describes a Type 4 LSA.

10. ☑ **A.** This answer is correct because both External Types 1 and 2 are Type 5 LSAs and are created by an ASBR. The ASBR adds the internal cost to an External Type 1 and uses only the external cost in an External Type 2.
    ☒ **B** is incorrect because External Types 1 and 2 LSAs are both a kind of Type 5 LSA. **C** is incorrect because both are created by the ASBR. **D** is incorrect because OSPF does not use different kinds of LSAs when redistributing particular routing protocols; they all become Type 5 LSAs.

Configuring a Multiarea OSPF Network

11. ☑   C. Configure a virtual link to connect the separated areas. This answer is correct because a virtual link will connect a separated area to the backbone through a virtual connection that transits another area.

    ☒   A will eliminate the backbone, but this solution will not allow for inter-area routing.
    B will fix the problem, but it will take too much work and could cause other problems (such as scalability issues with single-area designs). D is incorrect because all inter-area traffic must pass through the backbone.

12. ☑   B and C. B is correct because OSPF NETWORK statements use a wildcard mask. C is correct because the first NETWORK command will force 10.17.0.0/16 to join Area 0. The second command will not be accepted.

    ☒   A is incorrect because the process ID is indeed shown in the configuration. D is incorrect because there are multiple errors in the configuration.

13. ☑   C. ROUTER(CONFIG-ROUTER)#AREA 2 RANGE 192.168.32.0 255.255.248.0 tells the router that Area 2 has a range of addresses from 192.168.32.0 to 192.168.39.0. This command is given at the router configuration level.

    ☒   A and D are incorrect because the SUMMARY-ADDRESS command is used on ASBRs to summarize external networks. This command is also used at the (CONFIG-ROUTER) prompt. There is no such config prompt as (CONFIG-AREA). B is incorrect because it is not used at the right configuration mode.

14. ☑   D. Sixty-four is correct because 192 uses 2 bits for the network portion of the address. This leaves 6 bits ($2 \wedge 6$, or 64) for multiple Class C networks to fit within the range (64–127).

    ☒   A and C are incorrect because that many Class C networks would have to use a mask of 255.255.0.0. B is incorrect because it describes a mask of 255.255.224.0.

15. ☑   C. The AREA <AREA ID> DEFAULT-COST <COST> command is used to change the cost of the default routes inserted into an area by the ABR.

    ☒   A would work, but it requires too much work and will complicate troubleshooting and changes in the future. B is incorrect because the internal routers will pick the default route with the lowest cost. D is incorrect because a Layer 2 switch cannot route Layer 3 traffic to other routers.

16. ☑   B. By configuring the area as stub, you will prevent Type 5 LSAs from flooding the area.

    ☒   A will work, but it requires too much work and your network will no longer be a single administrative domain. Routing efficiency could also be affected. C will stop OSPF from communicating altogether, and **D** will not solve the problem. A virtual link is simply used to make a virtual connection to the backbone.

Monitoring and Verifying OSPF Operation

17. ☑ **A.** This is the correct answer because the output from the ROUTER#SHOW IP OSPF DATABASE command displays the router's link-state database.
☒ **B** is incorrect because it is the right syntax but not at the right prompt. **C** and **D** are incorrect because they are not valid commands.

18. ☑ **D.** ROUTER#SHOW IP OSPF VIRTUAL-LINKS is the only command that will actually work in the Cisco IOS.
☒ **A, B,** and **C** are all incorrect because they are invalid commands.

19. ☑ **B.** The SUMMARY-ADDRESS command always uses a standard mask. The line should read SUMMARY-ADDRESS 192.224.0.0 255.248.0.0.
☒ **A** is incorrect because "area" does belong at the end of a NETWORK statement. **C** is incorrect because the NETWORK statement does use a wildcard mask. **D** is incorrect because there was an error in the configuration.

20. ☑ **B.** ROUTER#SHOW IP OSPF BORDER-ROUTERS is the correct answer because it will show you every border router attached to the area.
☒ **A, C,** and **D** are incorrect because they are not valid commands.

LAB ANSWER

```
ABR1
!
interface e0
ip address 172.16.0.1 255.255.0.0
!
interface e1
ip address 172.1.0.1 255.255.0.0
!
router ospf 100
network 172.1.0.0 0.0.255.255 area 2
network 172.16.0.0 0.0.255.255 area 1
area 2 virtual-link 172.31.0.2

ABR2
!
```

```
interface e0
ip address 172.31.0.2 255.255.0.0
!
interface e1
ip address 10.0.0.1 255.0.0.0
!
router ospf 100
network 10.0.0.0 0.255.255.255 area 0
network 172.31.0.0 0.0.255.255 area 1
area 2 virtual-link 172.16.0.1
area 2 range 172.16.0.0 255.224.0.0

ABR3
!
interface e0
ip address 10.0.0.3 255.0.0.0
!
interface s0
ip address 192.168.48.1 255.255.255.0
!
router ospf 100
network 10.0.0.0 0.255.255.255 area 0
network 192.168.48.0 0.0.0.255 area 5
area 5 stub
area 5 range 192.168.48.0 255.255.248.0

ABR4
!
interface e0
ip address 10.0.0.2 255.0.0.0
!
interface e1
ip address 192.168.20.1 255.255.255.0
!
router ospf 100
network 10.0.0.0 0.255.255.255 area 0
network 192.168.20.0 0.0.0.255 area 4

R1
!
interface e0
ip address 172.16.0.2 255.255.0.0
!
interface e1
ip address 172.31.0.1 255.255.0.0
```

```
!
router ospf 100
network 172.16.0.0 0.0.255.255 area 1
network 172.31.0.0 0.0.255.255 area 1

R2
!
interface e0
ip address 192.168.55.1 255.255.255.0
!
interface s0
ip address 192.168.48.2 255.255.255.0
!
router ospf 100
network 192.168.48.0 0.0.0.255 area 5
network 192.168.55.0 0.0.0.255 area 5
area 5 stub
```

The interface specifics could have been configured in many different ways. The configuration above is just one example. Double-check your virtual-link commands to verify you used the router ID and not the IP address. Also, make sure all routers in area 5 contain the command "area 5 stub". All routers in a stub area must have this command or they will not reach the full state.

CISCO® CERTIFIED NETWORK PROFESSIONAL

6

EIGRP Operations and Configuration

I n Chapter 1, "IP Routing Fundamentals," we looked briefly at routing protocols and their characteristics. The Enhanced Interior Gateway Routing Protocol (EIGRP), a proprietary routing protocol developed by Cisco, first appeared in IOS 9.21 to overcome many of the limitations of IGRP, notably its inability to handle variable-length subnets, slow time to convergence, and nonsupport for other Layer 3 protocols such as IPX or AppleTalk. EIGRP is, like its predecessor IGRP, a distance-vector protocol and uses a similar composite metric. Beyond this, the two protocols share very little in common.

EIGRP is a highly efficient routing protocol consisting of two primary components: the Protocol Engine and the Protocol-Dependent Modules. Figure 6-1 shows the modular structure of EIGRP.

FIGURE 6-1   The modular components of EIGRP

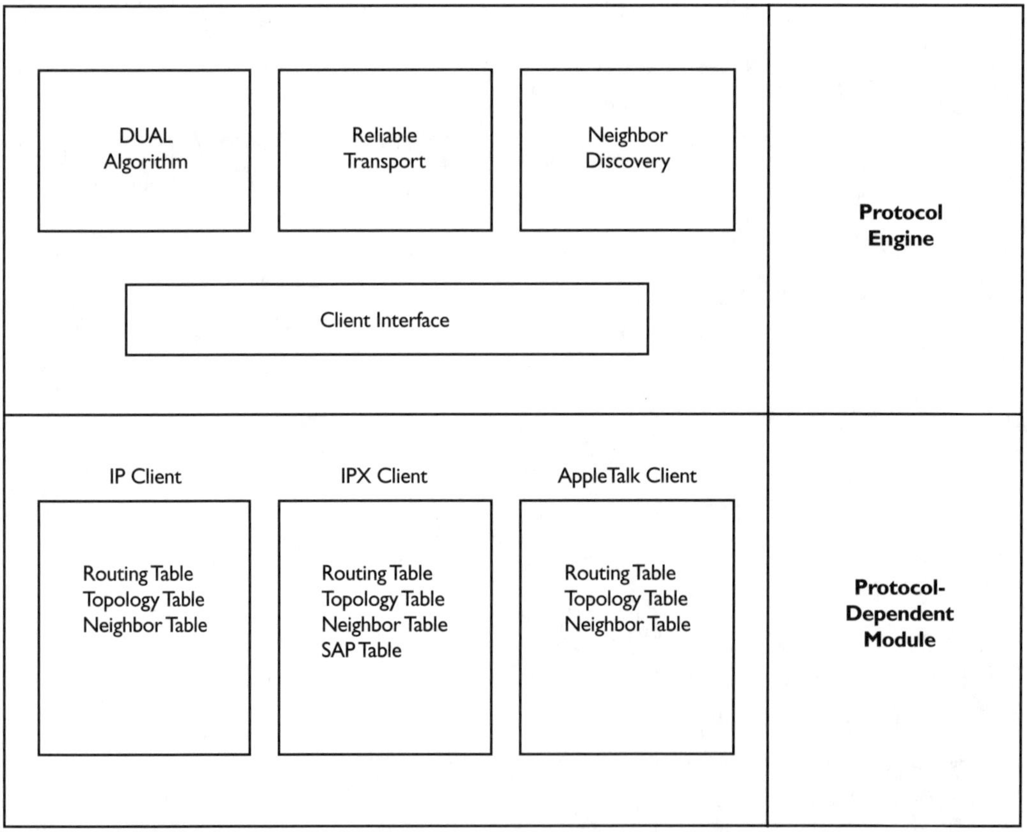

The workhorse of EIGRP is the *Protocol Engine*, which provides processing of the Diffusing Update Algorithm (DUAL), neighbor discovery, and reliable transport for the exchange of routing information among neighbors, as well as the interface with the router's main processing functions and routing table. The Protocol-Dependent Modules (PDMs) provide interfaces to multiple network protocols, namely IP, IPX, and AppleTalk, allowing for a modular and efficient approach to multiprotocol routing, without the necessity to run several different routing protocols on the router. EIGRP, however, maintains separate routing tables and uses separate hello packets for neighbor discovery for each network protocol configured. For this reason, EIGRP is considered a "ships-in-the-night" (SIN) protocol. Route redistribution is, nevertheless, automatic between similar protocols. For example, EIGRP automatically redistributes into IGRP, and vice versa, when both are configured on the same router and with the same autonomous system. Likewise, EIGRP automatically redistributes *Routing Table Maintenance Protocol* (RTMP) and Service Advertisement Protocol (SAP) tables for AppleTalk and IPX.

CERTIFICATION OBJECTIVE 6.01

Enhanced IGRP Features and Operations

We have now looked at the background behind EIGRP, so let us take a look at how it actually works. As we already stated, EIGRP was developed as an enhancement to IGRP, primarily to overcome many of its shortcomings. Remember that EIGRP uses the same metric calculation formula as EIGRP but scales this metric by a factor of 256. This scaling allows for much finer granularity, thus allowing more precise distance and path calculations. Apart from the basic similarities, there is little else which EIGRP shares with IGRP. EIGRP is considered to offer the best aspects of both distance-vector and link-state routing protocols, bundled into one protocol. A large number of features of EIGRP, including more advanced configuration options, are beyond the scope of this chapter or indeed this book. Let's begin with a list of some of the more prominent features, which we will expand on as we progress through this chapter:

■ It is relatively simple to configure.

■ It is virtually free of routing loops and has a fast convergence time as a result of DUAL.

■ It consumes considerably less bandwidth and router internal resources than other protocols.

■ It supports variable-length subnet mask (VLSM) and automatic route aggregation.

■ It uses a system of neighbor discovery and management, enabling a router running EIGRP to automatically detect and exchange routing updates with other EIGRP routers on the network as well as detecting when a neighbor becomes unavailable.

■ It employs a reliable transport protocol (RTP) to ensure that routing updates are successfully exchanged between neighbors.

■ EIGRP supports multiple network protocols, maintaining separate neighbor, topology, and routing tables for each protocol, and allows for automatic route redistribution between IGRP, IPX SAP, and RTMP.

■ It allows for routing of discontiguous subnets without confusing or overlapping route aggregation.

We now take a look at these operational features as well as the key aspects of operation of EIGRP, including comparison with other routing protocols, in closer detail. We also take an in-depth look at how EIGRP calculates metrics for making path determination decisions as well as the various tables that EIGRP maintains concerning neighbors, routing tables, and network topology. As we progress, we also include configuration scenarios, which you are encouraged to perform in your routing lab, so that you will be able to view these operational parameters and features beyond their "textbook" or theoretical meanings.

EIGRP and Its Major Features

It is important to note that *EIGRP is a distance-vector routing protocol*, despite several features it exhibits that are inherent to link-state protocols. Do not be confused when we mention features such as partial or bounded updates, which can often be seen when speaking of link-state protocols. EIGRP is sometimes called a *hybrid protocol* due to its use of features found in link-state protocols. For the purposes of this chapter, however, it is sufficient to understand that EIGRP is an *enhanced* distance-vector protocol, as the name itself implies.

Benefits of EIGRP in Comparison to Other IP Routing Protocols

Let us begin by looking at the operation of a typical distance-vector protocol such as RIP. With such a protocol, the router examines the path to a destination network from the information it receives from its neighbors. With RIP, the number of hops to the destination network is directly used to determine the metric. If the router sees multiple paths to the destination, it will select the shortest path and discard the rest.

Figure 6-2 depicts the typical operation of a distance-vector protocol. The router R1 receives route updates from R2 and R3, both of which contain routes to Network A. Since the path through R2 contains one less hop than through R3, the router R1 will select R2 as the next-hop path and discard the update received from R3. In other words, R1 selects the shortest path to reach the destination Network A.

This method of path determination, although simple, gives rise to certain problems. Let us assume, for a moment, that the traffic to be passed between R1 and Network A is critical and time-sensitive information and consumes considerable

FIGURE 6-2   Typical distance-vector protocols make path selection based on distance to the destination

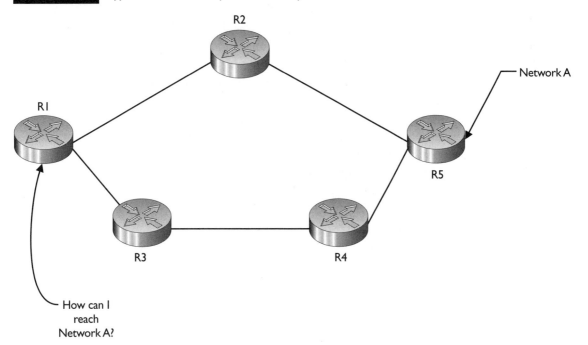

bandwidth. Let's also imagine that the bandwidth available on the links from R1 to Network A, via R3, are all at T1 speed, but the connection from R1 to R2 is only 56k over a Frame Relay connection. With this additional information concerning the internetwork, there is now a very strong possibility that the path that the router determined to be the best (via R2) could become saturated, causing severe degradation or even data loss. Obviously, this is not an ideal situation.

EIGRP overcomes this problem by using a composite metric, which includes factors such as minimum bandwidth on the link, delay across the link, and link loading. The exact manner in which EIGRP calculates the best path will be discussed shortly, but for now remember that EIGRP takes these other factors into consideration when selecting the best path to a destination network.

Another problem with the network in Figure 6-2 is the convergence time in case of failure of the path to R2. Bearing in mind the operation of a typical distance-vector protocol, the routing table of a router is passed on to a neighboring router at regular intervals. In the case of the network shown in Figure 6-2, assume R2 becomes unavailable. R1 maintains the route until it expires from the routing table, which is typically three times the update period. For RIP, this makes a delay of 90 seconds before the route is dropped from the routing table. After dropping the route, R1 no longer has a path to Network A because it had previously calculated R2 as the best path and discarded the update from R3. The router now must wait for the next periodic update from R3 before it can update its own routing table with the new path, which could take up to an additional 30 seconds. As a result, it would take 90 to 120 seconds for R1 to finally select the path through R3 as its path to Network A.

EIGRP, on the other hand, maintains a *topology table* in which it keeps a record of all the paths available to the given destination, including all metric information as well as flags to indicate which path is actually installed into the routing table as the best path. In this case, if R2 becomes unavailable, R1 already has the route information from R3 and simply has to remove the old path from the routing table and install the new information. This can be done immediately and without waiting for further updates from neighboring routers. As a result, the delay due to convergence is dramatically decreased or, in some cases, eliminated.

EIGRP further increases computation and convergence time by only sending updates when there is a change to the network topology or metric. If the network is completely stable and without change, no updates need be sent. This saves considerable bandwidth usage by the routing protocol. You will remember that RIP, by comparison, includes its entire routing table in every periodic update. This can consume an enormous amount of resources on larger networks.

Distance-vector protocols are also prone to the formation of routing loops within the internetwork. Since most distance-vector protocols use some variant of the Bellman-Ford algorithm for determining the best path to a given destination by selecting the path with the shortest distance, it is possible for two routers to receive conflicting path information, especially during a topology change before all routers on the network have successfully converged their routing tables. Additionally, there is a likelihood that such a loop could cause the routers to increment their hop counts to infinity.

In Figure 6-3, the link between Network A and router R3 failed. With a typical distance-vector protocol, such as RIP, Router R3 will send its update to R2 and R4, indicating that the route is unavailable. Router R2 now marks the route as unreachable, but R1 is still advertising it three hops away, so R2 then selects R1 as the path to the network. R2 then sends an update to R3, indicating that it now has a path to Network A. R3 then inserts this information into its routing table and updates R4, indicating that the destination is available four hops away. R4 tells R1 that the network is five hops away, and R1 tells R2 that it is six hops away. Router R2 notices that R1's path to the network has increased, but since it is the only path

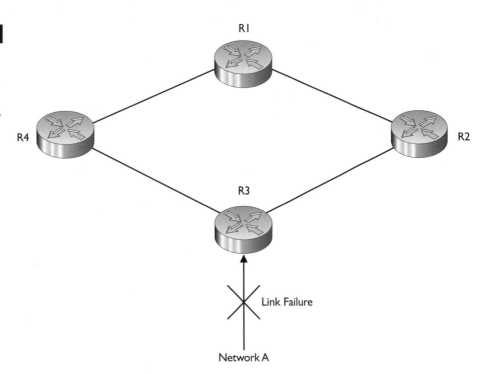

in the table, it uses it anyway and updates R3. The loop continues in this fashion until the metric reaches infinity, which, in the case of RIP, is 16, at which time all routers finally mark the network as unreachable. This could continue for as long as 7 minutes due to convergence times.

To combat this problem, most distance-vector protocols employ additional loop-avoidance measures, such as split horizon. Recall from what you learned about RIP that split horizon prohibits a router from advertising a route back to the router on the same interface from which it learned about the path initially. This method of split –horizon, called *simple split horizon*, works by the suppression of route information during an update advertisement. The other form of split horizon works by allowing the advertisement to be made, but when the advertisement is sent from a specific interface, any routes learned from that interface are flagged as unreachable. This is called *split horizon with poisoned reverse*, and although it is somewhat more robust than simple split horizon, it still could present some problems in complex or large internetworks. Additionally, these methods of loop avoidance require additional calculations and resources internal to the router.

EIGRP, on the other hand, does not require the use of split horizons or poisoned reverse updates, since DUAL provides a more rigid form of path determination based on calculated distances to a destination network and comparison of those distances among the various neighbors. DUAL is discussed in detail later in this chapter.

Finally, EIGRP provides the capability to support multiple network protocols, namely IP, IPX, and AppleTalk, since it contains its PDMs, which were discussed earlier. This permits EIGRP perform routing calculations for these protocols in a modular fashion. Each plug-in module handles the network protocol for which it was designed, and that module then works with the Protocol Engine via the client interface. For example, although there is a form of RIP for IPX called IPX RIP, it uses a slightly different method of metric calculation than IP RIP. As you will recall, IP RIP uses hop count as its metric, whereas IPX RIP uses a delay expressed as ticks. Other protocols, such as IGRP, support only IP, so for these it is necessary to run multiple protocol-specific routing protocols on a router to enable routing for IP, IPX, and AppleTalk at the same time. EIGRP provides the support for multiple network layer protocols, allowing them to be run concurrently.

Now that you have a general overview of EIGRP, let's consider a few concepts, described in the following Scenario & Solution.

SCENARIO & SOLUTION

Why does EIGRP not require loop-avoidance measures, such as split horizon?	EIGRP makes use of DUAL, so it has all the necessary information concerning metrics and paths. It can therefore avoid paths that might lead to routing loops.
Why should I use EIGRP on my network rather than IGRP?	Since available IP space is becoming more and more scarce, many networks now use subnets to conserve space. EIGRP supports variable-length subnets, whereas IGRP does not. Additionally, networks incorporate multiple protocols, such as IPX or AppleTalk. Since IGRP is designed for IP only, additional protocols would have to be used. EIGRP, on the other hand, will work with all these protocols, so they might coexist happily.
I am already running IGRP on my network. Can I change to EIGRP without completely reconfiguring everything?	Yes. EIGRP is configured in exactly the same way as IGRP. It does, however, have additional features that can be enabled, but for basic default operation, its configuration is identical. EIGRP and IGRP also automatically redistribute their routing information between each other as long as both routing processes are configured in the same AS.

EIGRP Terminology

A key to understanding the operation of EIGRP is the understanding the various terms used to reference aspects of its operation. We now examine these topics in more detail.

Neighbor Table

A router configured for EIGRP maintains a table of neighbors with which it exchanges routing information. This table also includes other details, such as on which interface or interfaces the neighbor is seen, hold-timers, the address of that neighbor, time of activity, and update sequence numbers. The neighbor table can be viewed using the SHOW IP EIGRP NEIGHBORS EXEC command, which we examine later in this chapter.

Topology Table

As routing updates are received from neighbors, the router includes information concerning these routes, including metrics advertised by the neighboring router, and inserts this information into the topology table. The router can then use this topology table to keep track of alternative paths to the destination. After calculation of metrics, the router can build an overall "view" of the network paths advertised by its neighbors, so in the event of failure of one of those neighbors, the router can select an alternative path without waiting for updates. This can greatly reduce network convergence as well as help avoid loops, since any router will know the metrics advertised by its neighbors for a given destination.

Successor

When the topology table is built, a listing of possible feasible successors to the destination network is also built. The feasible successor whose path yields the lowest cost, and thus the lowest metric, becomes the successor. The successor can be defined as the selected next-hop router in the path to the destination.

Feasible Successor

Any neighbor that has an *advertised distance* that is less than the router's *feasible distance* can become a feasible successor (FS). That is to say, it meets the criteria necessary to possibly be selected as a next-hop router in the path to the destination network. The concepts of feasible distance and advertised distance will be discussed in more detail shortly, when we examine the operations of the DUAL.

Building EIGRP Neighbor Relationships

As previously discussed, EIGRP maintains a method of neighbor discovery and maintenance, enabling it to easily locate and exchange routing information with other routers within the same routing domain. The method in which this neighbor discovery works depends on the media type of the link between neighbors, but the basic concept is the sending of a hello packet at regular intervals.

When two neighbors can see each other's hello packets, they can then exchange routing information between them and thus are considered neighbors, as depicted in Figure 6-4. The neighboring routers then pass information using EIGRP's RTP, confirming their establishment as neighbors or peers. Note that unlike OSPF, the

FIGURE 6-4

Neighbor relationships are established when two routers can see each other's hello packets

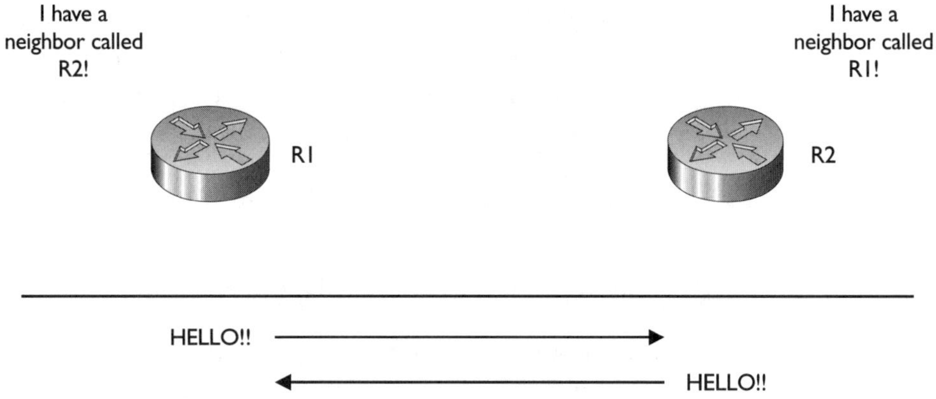

I have a neighbor called R2!

R1

I have a neighbor called R1!

R2

HELLO!! ⟶

⟵ HELLO!!

hello intervals in EIGRP do not have to be the same on all routers in order for them to become working neighbors, although it is recommended.

Routing updates, in EIGRP, are sent only as a link or topology change occurs, not at regular intervals of time, as in RIP. At first thought, this might appear to present problems with determining whether or not a given route to a destination is no longer available. However, EIGRP uses its neighbor maintenance features to overcome this stumbling block.

Behavior of Different Media Types

The most prominent behavioral differences between neighbors can be seen, depending on the network media between them. The default hello interval depends on the type of media and speed of the link, although this may be manually adjusted by the use of the IP EIGRP HELLO-INTERVAL command.

The second interval, which can be seen in the neighbor table, is called the *hold-time*. This is the maximum period that a neighbor may be considered to be alive without receiving a hello packet from it. This parameter may also be manually adjusted per interface, using the IP EIGRP HOLD-TIME interface command.

on the *job*

Note that if you manually change the hello interval, the hold-time is not automatically updated. Therefore, you must manually configure the hold-time accordingly. Remember that if a router does not see a hello packet from a neighbor before the hold-time expires, the neighbor is declared dead, preventing the routers from becoming neighbors.

Frequency of EIGRP Neighbor Relationships by Media Type

On broadcast and high-speed links, the default hello interval is 5 seconds. (In reality, it is 5 seconds plus a small random delay to avoid synchronization or collision of hello packets among all neighbors.) Examples of such media are the following:

- Broadcast media, such as Ethernet, FDDI, and Token Ring
- Point-to-point serial links using PPP or HDLC encapsulation
- Point-to-point Frame Relay and ATM subinterfaces

On other, slower or nonbroadcast, media types, the default hello period is 60 seconds. Examples of such interfaces include these:

- ISDN BRI
- Serial links at T1/E1 speed and slower
- Frame Relay and ATM point-to-multipoint subinterfaces
- Frame Relay and ATM switched virtual circuits

Again, these hello intervals may be manually adjusted, as previously described.

Declaring a Neighbor Dead

Note that one of the timers, when dealing with EIGRP neighbor relationships, is the hold-time. If a hello packet is not seen from a given neighbor before expiration of the hold-time, the neighbor is then declared dead. At this time, any routes in use, which reflect this neighbor as a successor, are dropped. The router then looks for an alternative successor in its topology table and selects another path, if one is available. If no alternative path is available, the router enters active mode and queries its neighbors in an attempt to find a path to the destination.

The other scenario in which a neighbor is declared dead is when it fails to acknowledge an EIGRP packet sent using the reliable multicast protocol. If the ACK is not received from the neighbor after the multicast, the transmission is resent using unicast to that neighbor. If an ACK is still not received after 16 unicast messages, the neighbor is declared dead. The reliable multicast protocol is explained in more detail in the next section.

On recovery, a previously dead neighbor will re-establish its neighbor relationship again, following the same manner as previously outlined.

The Default Hold-Time

Like the hello interval, the hold-time may be manually adjusted. By default, however, the general rule of thumb is that the hold-time is three times the hello interval. So for broadcast and high-speed links in default operation, where the hello interval is 5 seconds, the hold-time is 15 seconds. On slower and nonbroadcast media, with a 60-second hello interval, the hold-time will be 180 seconds.

Forming Neighbor Relationships in EIGRP

It is vital to note that EIGRP will form neighbor relationships only on primary addresses. If an interface is configured with secondary addresses, a neighbor relationship cannot be established between these addresses.

On the other hand, unlike OSPF, neighbor relationships may be formed between routers, even though the hello and hold-times are configured differently, provided that the configured hello interval on the local router does not exceed the hold-time of the neighbor.

exam
ⓦatch

Do not confuse the hold-time in EIGRP with the hold-down timer in RIP. The hold-time in EIGRP is the maximum time that a router waits for a neighbor to send its hello packet. If the neighbor does not send a hello before the hold-timer expires, that neighbor is declared dead.

EIGRP Packet Types

As indicated previously, EIGRP uses an RTP for neighbor discovery and management as well as routing updates. The RTP ensures that routing and neighbor discovery packets are delivered and that they are received in order. In order to assure delivery of these packets, a protocol proprietary to Cisco called *reliable multicast*, is used. To ensure delivery in order, the packet includes two sequence numbers. These two sequence numbers are a number incremented by the sending router with each packet and the sequence number of the last packet received from the destination router. The multicast packets are sent on the reserved Class D address of 224.0.0.10, where the acknowledgments are sent using unicast.

In this section, we examine the various types of EIGRP packets, their purposes, and when they are used.

Hello Packets

EIGRP *hello packets* are sent by each router at regular intervals. These intervals depend on the default hello intervals outlined in the previous section, but they can also be manually configured. They serve as a sort of heartbeat, allowing all routers within the same media domain to know that there is another EIGRP router alive on the network with which it can share routing information. The hello packet is vital for both establishing a neighbor relationship between routers and determining whether or not a neighbor has died or is no longer available. Remember that if a hello packet is not received from a neighbor before its hold-time expires, that neighbor is declared dead.

Hello packets are multicast and expect no reply; therefore, do not use the reliable delivery method.

Update Packets

Update packets are used to send information concerning routes. These packets are sent only when there is a change to the network topology, such as a route becoming unavailable. They contain only the essential information concerning the route in question and are sent only to neighbors that are affected by the change. In other words, they are bounded updates, sent only to neighbors that need the information. If this update information is required by several neighbors, a multicast packet is sent. If the change affects only one router, however, a unicast packet is sent.

Update packets always use reliable delivery and expect acknowledgments.

Query Packets

Query packets are used by the DUAL to manage diffusing metric calculations. Remember that EIGRP uses a topology table in which it maintains a listing of successors, feasible distance, and the feasible successors to the destination network. If the successor becomes unavailable, EIGRP then looks in the topology table for an alternative feasible successor. If none is available, the router sends a query to attempt to find a path to the destination.

Queries may be sent via either unicast or multicast and always use reliable delivery.

Reply Packets

When a router sends a query packet in an attempt to find a path to a given destination, the other routers with which the router has a neighbor relationship send a *reply packet* indicating their route information for the queried path.

Reply packets are always unicast and use reliable delivery.

ACK Packets

ACK packets are simply acknowledgments sent as a result of a packet sent by the reliable delivery method. As mentioned in the previous section, a neighbor is declared dead if it fails to acknowledge 16 consecutive unicast packets using the reliable delivery method.

The router expecting an ACK from a neighbor waits for a specified period of time before switching to unicast to attempt to send the data again. The multicast flow timer defines this period. After switching to unicast, the time between unicast attempts is determined by the *retransmission timeout (RTO)*. The RTO is calculated on a per-neighbor basis and is derived from the *smooth round-trip time (SRTT)*. The SRTT is an average time, measured in milliseconds, between sending a packet and receiving an acknowledgment. The calculated RTO and SRTT for any given neighbor can be seen in the EIGRP neighbor table using the SHOW IP EIGRP NEIGHBORS command.

The Neighbor Table

On several occasions, we have mentioned the SHOW IP EIGRP NEIGHBORS command. This command can be typed from EXEC or privilege EXEC modes of the command-line interface of a Cisco router. The code listing that follows shows the output of the SHOW IP EIGRP NEIGHBORS command and is followed by a discussion of each element shown.

```
Router>sho ip eigrp neighbors
IP-EIGRP neighbors for process 1
H   Address           Interface   Hold Uptime    SRTT    RTO   Q     Seq
                                  (sec)          (ms)          Cnt   Num
1   192.168.2.15      Et0/0        14 2d12h         4     200   0     109
0   192.168.1.13      Se0/0        10 5d01h       976    5000   0     554
Router>
```

The first line shows the EIGRP process, which is identified by the ASN used in the router EIGRP CONFIGURATION command.

The leftmost column, headed by the letter H, is left over from initial testing by Cisco and bears no significance to the end user other than for informational purposes. It refers to the order in which the neighbors were learned by the router.

The next two columns contain the IP address of the neighbor followed by the interface on which the hello packets are received from that neighbor.

The hold-time shows the number of seconds remaining for the neighbor's hold-time, as defined earlier in this chapter. Remember that if no hello packets are received from a neighbor before the hold-timer expires, the neighbor is declared dead.

Uptime refers to the total time that this neighbor relationship has been established.

The SRTT is the smooth round-trip time, which we have already mentioned briefly. This figure refers to the average time between the transmission of a packet to the neighbor and the ACK received from the neighbor following that transmission. The SRTT is also used by the router to calculate the next field, the RTO, which is the interval between unicast transmission attempts after switching to unicast mode following failure of the multicast method of transmission.

The next field shows the number of packets waiting in the queue to be sent to the neighbor.

Finally, the last field contains the sequence number of the last query, reply, or update packet. The reliable transport protocol uses this number to ensure delivery of packets in order.

EIGRP Reliability

When discussing the neighbor discovery properties of EIGRP, we mentioned that EIGRP uses a system of reliable multicast to ensure packet delivery and sequencing. The system of reliable multicast used with EIGRP was developed by and is proprietary to Cisco. Its basic theory of operation is relatively simple in that if a router sends a routing information packet, it should be received by neighboring routers. The packets must also be received in the order in which they were sent.

Depending on the type of packet and the intended recipient, the packet can be sent either via multicast, using the reserved Class D address 224.0.0.10, or by unicast directly to a given neighbor. Certain packet types, as discussed in the previous chapter, are sent only in unicast; others are sent only as multicast. The rest may be sent using either method. The concept of reliable delivery implies that a sender must have a means of knowing if the recipient has received the message. In EIGRP, this concept is no different. An example of typical EIGRP packet exchanges can be seen in Figure 6-5.

EIGRP and Packet Acknowledgment

As discussed previously, in regard to neighbor relationships and EIGRP packet types, EIGRP uses an RTP to ensure that the recipients receive EIGRP routing

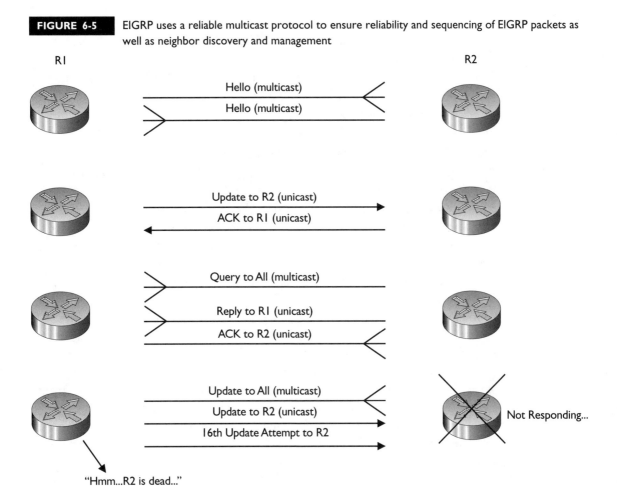

FIGURE 6-5 EIGRP uses a reliable multicast protocol to ensure reliability and sequencing of EIGRP packets as well as neighbor discovery and management

information and that this information is received in order. Using the Cisco-proprietary Reliable Multicast Protocol, EIGRP uses a combination of multicast packets to the reserved Class D address 224.0.0.10 and unicast packets.

When an update is sent to a neighbor, the router then expects a response, indicating that the update was received. The update can be in the form of either unicast or multicast, depending on the target recipient. The response to this update, called an *acknowledgment (ACK),* is always unicast. If the neighbor fails to respond to the update, the router makes further attempts; by default, this effort occurs 16 times. If the neighbor still fails to respond with an ACK, it then declares the neighbor dead.

Hello packets, on the other hand, do not require an ACK to be returned. A query packet can be sent using either multicast or unicast and the router then expects a response packet. Remember that a query is sent when a router loses a route to a destination and has no other successors available to choose from in the topology table. As a result, it then polls the other routers in an attempt to find a new successor. The response packet is then acknowledged with an ACK.

Updating Retransmissions and Timeouts

In the event of a change of topology or metric of a router, a router notifies its neighbors of the change using an update packet. Remember that update packets require acknowledgments from the recipient. If a neighbor fails to respond, the router then tries again to send the update to the neighbor and continues to do so until either the neighbor finally responds or it determines that the neighbor is dead, whichever occurs first.

To understand how a router determines how long to wait for a response, refer back to the listing of the SHOW IP EIGRP NEIGHBORS command output. The column marked SRTT indicates the average time, in milliseconds, from the time an update is sent to the time that an ACK is received from that neighbor. The router waits for a generic period of time, determined by the multicast flow timer, to receive an ACK from the neighbor. If the neighbor fails to respond before expiry of this timer, the router then sends the packet as a unicast directed to that neighbor. At this time, the router begins to use the RTO. The RTO is calculated based on the SRTT using a proprietary algorithm. After switching to unicast mode to attempt to send the update to the neighbor, the router waits for the period of time indicated in the RTO. If the neighbor still fails to respond, a counter is incremented and the router attempts to transmit the update again. Once the counter reaches 16, the neighbor is declared dead. If the neighbor finally sends a valid ACK before the expiration of these counters, operation continues as normal.

Initial Exchange of Packets

Let's now walk through what happens when two routers form a neighbor association and exchange their routing information. Figure 6-6 shows the establishment of a simple neighbor relationship, routing update exchanges, and subsequent calculations of metrics leading to insertion of the advertised routes into the routing tables.

FIGURE 6-6 Routes appear in the router's routing table after neighbor associations have been formed, route updates exchanged, and metrics calculated

R1   R2

Hello (multicast)

Hello (multicast)

We Are Neighbors

Network A   Network B

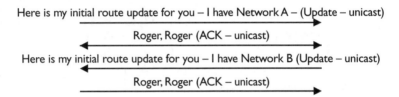

Here is my initial route update for you – I have Network A – (Update – unicast)

Roger, Roger (ACK – unicast)

Here is my initial route update for you – I have Network B (Update – unicast)

Roger, Roger (ACK – unicast)

I have performed my metric calculations based on your update information, and inserted the information into my topology table. You are my feasible successor to Network B.

My routing table now shows the path to Network B via R2

I have performed my metric calculations based on your update information, and inserted the information into my topology table. You are my feasible successor to Network A.

My routing table now shows the path to Network B via R1

As you can see from Figure 6-6, once the routers see each other's hello packets, they know that they can form an association and exchange routing information. Consequently, Router R1 sends its routing information in the form of an update to R2, which in turn responds with an ACK. R2 then reciprocates, sending its update to R1, which also responds with an ACK. Both routers perform their metric and DUAL calculations on the updates. Let's assume that the updates in this example are new routes and that metric calculations are simple. As a result, the routers form their topology tables, select their feasible successors for the advertised networks, and insert those feasible successors into the topology tables with the successor shown as the next-hop router to reach the destination. The successor is then entered into the routing table.

The overall operation in this example is quite straightforward and simple to comprehend. In reality, however, many more events, such as calculation of metrics and DUAL calculations, take place before the route is inserted into the routing table.

EIGRP Route Selection and Metric Calculation

Since EIGRP is still a distance-vector protocol, it is logical that it should select as the best path the route with the shortest distance to the destination. However, remember that since EIGRP is a hybrid protocol, its "definition" of distance might not necessarily be as clear as the logic behind it. You will recall that RIP uses the hop count as its metric to indicate distance to a destination network. EIGRP, on the other hand, uses a composite metric rather than a hop count. A *composite metric* is one that is formed from the combination of multiple factors or variables. In the case of EIGRP, the following variables can all be used in the calculation of the metric value:

- Bandwidth
- Load
- Delay
- Reliability
- MTU

In the default operation of EIGRP, however, only bandwidth and delay are used for metric calculation. These five metric components are signified by constants used in the EIGRP metric calculation formula. These constants, known as *K values*, are named K1 through K5. Modification of these values tells the router to include that element, as well as the magnitude of its inclusion, in its metric calculation. Table 6-1 shows the K values and their default values.

The default values may be modified by use of the METRIC WEIGHTS router configuration command in the EIGRP router configuration mode, which enables EIGRP to include the K values' corresponding constants in its metric calculations. However, it is strongly recommended that you keep the default settings for these values. The actual use of the METRIC WEIGHTS command is beyond the scope of this book and is not discussed further.

on the ᴊob

Although the K values can be modified, it is highly recommended that you leave them at their default settings unless you are aware of the consequences and know how changing them affects the metric calculation.

TABLE 6-1	K Value	Default Value
	K1	1
K-Value Constants and Their Default Values	K2	0
	K3	1
	K4	0
	K5	0

After the router receives an update from its neighbor, it performs metric calculations based on the metric passed to it from that neighbor, and it compares the result to the metrics calculated by its other neighbors, as well as its own self-calculated metric. The metric, to all intents and purposes, can be considered the cost of the given path or, if you want to think in terms of distance (since we are talking about a distance-vector protocol), the distance to the destination. The shortest distance (or lowest cost) is then chosen, subject to criteria required by the operation of DUAL, which will be discussed shortly.

EIGRP Metric Calculation Formula

EIGRP uses a formula based on the components we just discussed to arrive at a metric value. This formula is shown in Figure 6-7.

This is approximately the same formula used for IGRP. However, remember that EIGRP scales the metric by a factor of 256. Specifically, we scale bandwidth and delay before applying it to the formula, as follows:

Bandwidth = (10000000/Bandwidth) x 256
Delay = Delay x 256

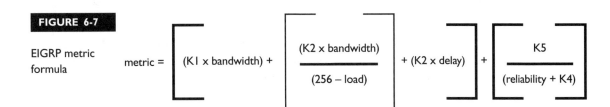

FIGURE 6-7

EIGRP metric formula

$$\text{metric} = \left[(K1 \times \text{bandwidth}) + \frac{(K2 \times \text{bandwidth})}{(256 - \text{load})} + (K2 \times \text{delay}) \right] + \left[\frac{K5}{(\text{reliability} + K4)} \right]$$

For EIGRP default operation, however, only K1 and K3 are used, so this formula can be very much simplified as follows:

= [(1 x Bandwidth) + [(0 x Bandwidth) / (256 – Load)] + (1 x Delay)]
    + [0 / (Reliability + 0)]
= [(Bandwidth) + [0] + (Delay)]   +   [0]
= Bandwidth + Delay

Metric = Bandwidth + Delay

Here, bandwidth and delay are already scaled as they were previously. Note that the delay specified in the formula is the sum of all delays to the destination, not just the direct delay to the next hop. The bandwidth is the minimum bandwidth configured along the path to the destination. When a router advertises its route information, it includes its metric and calculated total delay in the update. The receiving router then adds its local delay to the total received for use in its metric calculation.

Let's now take a practical look at the metric calculation to view how each router in a network calculates its metric and determines its best path to the destination. We begin with router R5 in Figure 6-8, since it is the closest to the destination network and, in practical terms, will be the router advertising the network to its neighbors. Network A is connected to R5 on its Ethernet interface, with a bandwidth of 10 Mbps (10,000 kbps) and a delay of 10 microseconds. First, we scale the bandwidth and delay components:

Delay = Delay x 256 = 10 x 256 = **2560**

Bandwidth = (10000000/Bandwidth) x 256 = (10000000/10000) x 256
= 1000 x 256 = **256000**

Next we plug the scaled components into the default formula:

Metric = Bandwidth + Delay = 256000 + 2560 = **258560**

exam
ⓦatch   *Remember that the delay component is the sum of all delays across the given path, not simply the local delay to the next-hop router. Bandwidth is the minimum bandwidth configured along the path.*

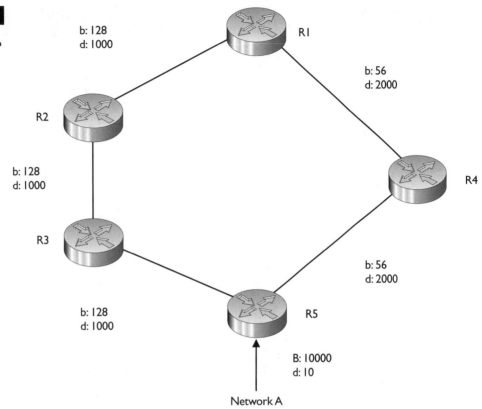

FIGURE 6-8

By default, EIGRP uses bandwidth and total path delay when calculating metrics to a destination

b: 128
d: 1000

b: 56
d: 2000

R1

R2

b: 128
d: 1000

R4

R3

b: 56
d: 2000

b: 128
d: 1000

R5

B: 10000
d: 10

Network A

Now that you have seen how EIGRP performs metric calculations in default operation, the following exercise will allow you to deepen your understanding of the EIGRP metric calculation formula and its application in a typical network scenario.

EXERCISE 6-1

EIGRP Metric Calculation

Refer to the diagram in Figure 6-8 when performing this exercise.

1. Using the default EIGRP metric formula, calculate the metrics for R4, R3, R2, and R1 in the network depicted in Figure 6-8.

TABLE 6-2	Router	Bandwidth	Delay	Metric	Via
Calculated Metrics from Exercise 6-1	R4	44912281	514560	45426840	R5
	R3	20000000	258560	20258560	R5
	R2	20000000	514560	20514560	R3
	R1	20000000	770560	20770560	R2
	R1	44912281	1026560	45938841	R4

2. Once you have calculated the metrics for the routers in the network, identify which path will be taken from R1 to reach Network A.

Solution:

We have already calculated R5's metric to Network A as 258560. There are two connections from R5, one to R4 and one to R3. Table 6-2 shows the calculated metrics to Network A for all the routers in the scenario.

Remember that in all cases, the delay is the sum of all delays through the path, then scaled by 256. As you can see, Router R1 is showing two possible paths to Network A—one via R2 with a metric of 20770560 and the other via R4 with a metric of 45938841. Since the path with the lowest metric or cost is preferred, Router R1 will choose R2 as its best route to Network A.

CERTIFICATION OBJECTIVE 6.02

The Diffusing Update Algorithm

We have now seen the overall features of EIGRP, its neighbor discovery and management, and the method in which it performs metric calculations. We can now proceed onto the basic algorithm of EIGRP's operation, the *Diffusing Update Algorithm (DUAL)*.

Recall that the basic functions of DUAL include loop avoidance, path selection, and metric calculation among all routers in the network. The word *diffusing* in the name of the algorithm is very appropriate in that these calculations spread across the network in a distributed fashion, allowing each router to arrive at metric values while taking into consideration the metric values of its neighbors and without recalculating all the paths in its routing table.

The DUAL Algorithm

As you will recall from the first section in this chapter, EIGRP uses DUAL, sometimes referred to as the *DUAL finite-state machine*. The term *finite state* refers to the concept that DUAL calculations will be only either active or passive.

To be in a *passive state* means that the algorithm performs its calculations based on information received from its neighbors and does not need to search for a given path. In other words, the algorithm is given the information with which it needs to work. If, for example, a neighbor carrying the best or only path to a destination is declared dead, the router must attempt to find another path from its topology table. However, if it has no other information to work with, it must attempt to acquire new information from its neighbors. To do this, it enters an *active state* and requests information on a path to the destination network from its neighbors. Once it receives new information, it returns to passive state, relying on inbound updates from that neighbor if necessary. If it does not receive a response, it remains in the active state and continues to obtain the required information until it receives the information or its response indicates that the destination is unreachable. A router also enters the active state if it needs to send an update to a neighbor. In this case, it switches to active state, sends the update, and then returns to passive state after it has received the ACK from that neighbor.

Let's look again at the network we used for our metric calculations. This time we show the metrics in the diagram to aid explanation. Each router in the network passes its own calculated metric along to its neighbors. If a router calculates that it has multiple paths to the destination, it advertises its lowest calculated metric. The lowest calculated metric on any given router for a specified destination is called the *feasible distance (FD)*. The FD serves two purposes: first, it identifies the lowest-cost path to the destination; second, it becomes the *advertised distance (AD)* for the next neighbor downstream. To better understand this relationship, refer to Figure 6-9, which shows the network we have just seen. R5 calculated its own metric of 258560. Network A is directly connected to R5, so its routing table contains an implicit static route indicating that the network is directly connected. Next, R5 advertises the existence of Network A to R4 and R3, along with its calculated metric.

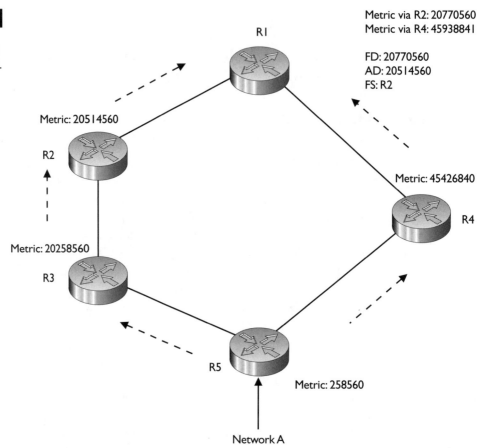

FIGURE 6-9

Metric calculations
are used by DUAL
to determine FD,
AD, and FSs

Metric via R2: 20770560
Metric via R4: 45938841

FD: 20770560
AD: 20514560
FS: R2

R1

Metric: 20514560

R2

Metric: 45426840

R4

Metric: 20258560

R3

R5

Metric: 258560

Network A

This process continues all the way to R1. Now, let's look at the information R1 has concerning Network A. We know that it received a metric of 20514560 from R2 and a metric of 45426840 from R4. From these metrics, R1 calculates its own possible metrics—20770560 through R2 and 45938841 via R4. Of the two metrics received from R1's neighbors, R2's metric is lower. R1 must then find which of its own calculated metrics is smaller. The metric via R2, 20770560, is smaller, so this metric becomes the FD, and we have received an AD of 20514560 from R2, which is smaller than our FD of 20770560. Therefore, R2 may become a *feasible successor (FS)* to Network A. R4's AD is 45938841, which is not smaller than R1's calculated FD, so it cannot become a feasible successor for R1 to use to get to Network A. Finally, the DUAL looks at all available FSs to the destination it has built into its topology table. The FS that has the least cost, or metric, becomes the successor, or next hop, and is installed in the routing table. In the case of our example, R1 has only one FS, so it logically becomes the successor.

Feasible Distance

As we have just seen, the lowest metric calculated by a router to a given destination becomes that router's FD. This metric also takes into consideration the path delay between the router and the next-hop router, since we are forming this metric based on cumulative delay, as discussed previously.

Advertised Distance

Since each router passes its lowest calculated metric, or its feasible distance, to its direct neighbors, this metric becomes the AD for the neighbors. That is to say, in our sample network, the AD is the metric it received from R2, or R2's *own* FD.

exam
Ⓦatch

The FD is the lowest calculated metric to a destination network and is locally calculated. The FD is then used as the AD to neighbors downstream.

Feasibility Condition

If the AD from a given neighbor is less than the locally calculated FD, that neighbor meets the criteria to become the FS. That is to say, it has met the *feasibility condition (FC)*. If multiple neighbors meet the feasibility condition, the path with the lowest metric becomes the successor.

exam
Ⓦatch

A neighbor must meet the FC in order to become a FS.

Loop Avoidance

DUAL maintains a loop-free routing environment by ensuring that the metric of a closer hop to the destination is never higher than the locally calculated metric. During periods of network stability, metric values are constant; route updates are not required, since there is no change to the network topology. Since the router already knows the topology of the network, which is stored in its topology table, it can very easily avoid paths that could lead to routing loops. In other words, the router will not choose a path that leads back to itself, since the metric calculated for that path will be higher than its own FD.

Now that you have a basic understanding of DUAL, Exercise 6-2 will allow you to apply to a typical scenario this understanding as well as your understanding of EIGRP metric calculations.

EXERCISE 6-2

A DUAL Scenario

Use the network shown in Figure 6-10 and what you have learned about EIGRP metric calculations and DUAL to solve the scenario. For the purposes of this exercise, assume that EIGRP is running in the default mode.

FIGURE 6-10

Scenario network for Exercise 6-2

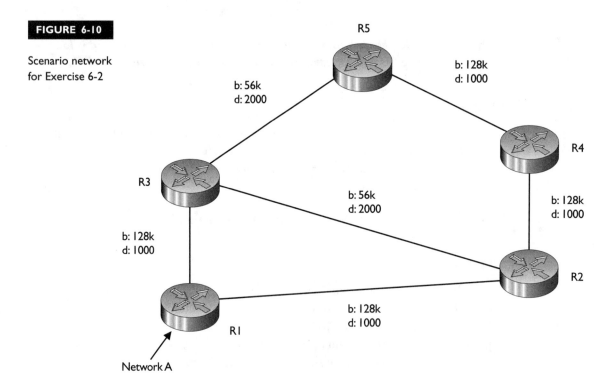

Assume that the metric calculated by R1 is 25600 and the delay from R1 to network A is 10us. Then:

1. Calculate the feasible distance from R5 to the destination Network A.
2. Identify the FS or FSs from R5.
3. Identify which router will become the successor and be installed in the routing table as the next hop.

Solution: First, we know that the metric at R1 is 25600, as was already given. Next, we calculate the first metric at R2 for the route via R1. We have a delay of 10us at R1, plus 1000us across the link. This gives us a total delay of 1010us. Using our scaling formula gives us a magnitude of 258560. Next we calculate our bandwidth component. The minimum bandwidth between R2 and R1 is 128K, so (1000000/128) x 256 = 20000000. Add these two components to get the metric of 20258560. We know that the properties of R3 are the same, so we can already tell that the metric from R3 to R1 will also be 20258560. This leaves another path between R2 and R3. Apply the same calculations, including the sum of all delays, and this yields a metric of 46484846 for both R2 and R3 via each other. Since the FD is the lowest calculated metric, which is 20258560 for both R2 and R3, we know that the logical FS to each will be R1, since it has the lowest AD of 25600.

As a result of these calculations, the metrics shown in Table 6-3 (on the following page) can be derived from the network in our exercise.

From the information we now have, R5 has two possible metrics—20770560 via R4 and 46484846 via R3. Since the path via R4 has the lower metric, this one becomes the FD. Now, R5 looks for the FS by looking at the ADs via both paths. These are showing as 20258560 via R3 and 20514560 via R4. Note that in this case, both R3 and R4 meet the FC, so *both* become FSs. Next we look at the locally calculated metrics for the two FSs. Since the metric via R4 is lower, it will be selected as the successor, and this route is installed in the routing table.

---

exam

⚠ atch

Remember that after the FD has been calculated, any neighbor with an advertised distance smaller than the FD will meet the FC and can be selected as an FS.

	Router	Metric(s)	Via (FS in Boldface Type)	Feasible Distance	Successor (Next Hop)
TABLE 6-3 Table of Metrics from Exercise 6-2	R1	25600	Connected	25600	–
	R2	20258560	**R1** AD: 25600	20258560	R1
		46484846	R3 AD: 20258560		
	R3	20258560	**R1** AD: 25600	20258560	R1
		46484846	R2 AD: 20258560		
	R4	20514560	**R2** AD: 20258560	20514560	R2
	R5	20770560	**R4** AD: 20514560	20770560	R4 (since its metric is lower)
		46484846	R3 AD: 20258560		

Let's now consider a few scenarios and solutions that could come in handy when we are working with EIGRP. Please refer to the following Scenario & Solution.

CERTIFICATION OBJECTIVE 6.03

Basic EIGRP Configuration

Now that you have an understanding of the operation of EIGRP, we will start applying this theory by looking at its configuration. As has already been mentioned, one of EIGRP's features is that it is fairly simple to configure, requiring only an EIGRP routing process to be configured and at least one network to advertise. Many classroom instructors, when asked how to configure EIGRP, will simply say "Just configure IGRP, but add an E." For the basic operations of EIGRP, this is exactly correct in that configuration of EIGRP is exactly the same as for IGRP. Most of the

SCENARIO & SOLUTION

I have changed the EIGRP hello interval on the Ethernet interface of my router to 30 seconds, since my network doesn't change much. Since I did so, my routers will no longer form neighbor associations, so routing updates are no longer exchanged. My network is now broken. How do I fix it?	Remember that a router uses the hold-time to determine whether or not a neighbor is still active. By default, the hold-time is three times the hello interval for the given media type. However, if you change the hello interval, you must remember to also change the hold-time to take this into account. With your change, the hold interval is still 15 seconds, so the neighbor is always declared dead. Use the IP EIGRP HOLD-TIME interface configuration command to change this setting.
In my network, why is R2 selected as a Feasible Successor but not the chosen as the successor, even though it has fewer hops than my path through R3?	Remember that EIGRP uses a composite metric and takes bandwidth and delay into account as well as hop count. It is likely that although the ADs from both R2 and R3 are lower than your FD, the metric through R2 is higher than through R3. Therefore, the path through R3 will still be preferred.

enhanced features of EIGRP will be immediately available. Those that are not can be easily added as necessary with simple additional commands.

The **ROUTER EIGRP** Command

The first required element of a basic EIGRP configuration is the actual EIGRP process. This is performed using the ROUTER EIGRP command in the global configuration mode of the IOS command line of a Cisco router. Into this line is also put the ASN to be used for the EIGRP process. Here is an example, using 33 as our ASN:

```
Router# configure terminal
Router(config)# router eigrp 33
Router(config-router)#
```

The ASN is common to all routers within the same routing domain—that is, all routers with which we form neighbor associations. You may have as many EIGRP processes on a router as you want, each with its own ASN. Each process will not exchange route information outside its own routing domain unless the routes are *redistributed* between EIGRP processes. (Route redistribution is discussed in a later chapter.)

This ASN is also referred to by the router as an *ID*, as in the output of the SHOW IP EIGRP NEIGHBORS command. However, this ID should not be confused with the process ID used for OSPF, which is only locally significant. In OSPF, multiple routers within the same routing domain could have the same or different process IDs, whereas in EIGRP, all routers in the same routing domain must share the same ASN. While we are on the subject of ASNs, the EIGRP ASN should not be confused with the ASN used in Border Gateway Protocol (BGP). These ASNs serve totally different purposes and have completely different practical applications.

The NETWORK Statement

The next basic required configuration directive for EIGRP is the NETWORK statement. This statement identifies the locally connected network that should be advertised to EIGRP neighbors. The statement takes one argument, which is the network address:

```
Router(config)# router eigrp 33
Router(config-router)# network 192.168.16.0
Router(config-router)#
```

In EIGRP, as in IGRP, the NETWORK statement is classful. That is, although you may enter specific networks into the configuration, such as NETWORK 10.32.10.0 and NETWORK 10.32.11.0, EIGRP consolidates all such entries into one classful statement of NETWORK 10.0.0.0. The NETWORK statement identifies the interfaces on which to advertise networks. EIGRP, as with IGRP and RIP, finds all interfaces that match the NETWORK statement and uses the IP address and netmask configured on the interface to determine how to advertise that subnet to its neighbors.

In default operation, EIGRP is classful, just as IGRP and RIP (versions 1 and 2) are; therefore, it performs network summarization at the classful network boundary. For example, if the router found four subnets for network 10.0.0.0 and the advertisement were going out of an interface with a subnet within that network, the router would advertise each of the 10.0.0.0 subnets. However, if the route advertisement were going out of an interface that is not part of the network 10.0.0.0

but rather 192.168.131.0, the router would advertise only the classful summary 10.0.0.0/8, since that interface is the boundary of network 10.0.0.0. This automatic summarization can be disabled in EIGRP as well as in RIP v2 to allow *variable-length subnet masks (VLSM),* which is discussed in Chapter 7, "Advanced EIGRP Behavior and Configuration."

The two elements we just discussed are the two basic elements required to enable EIGRP on a Cisco router and enable it to exchange routing information with neighbors. Figure 6-11 is an example of a very simple network using EIGRP and the routing configurations of the two routers involved.

The network in Figure 6-11 is a simple point-to-point network, each point with its own local networks connected to it. The two routers are linked by a 56 kbps connection to their respective serial interfaces. In this scenario, each network, A and B, needs to be able to communicate with the other. To accomplish this goal, the

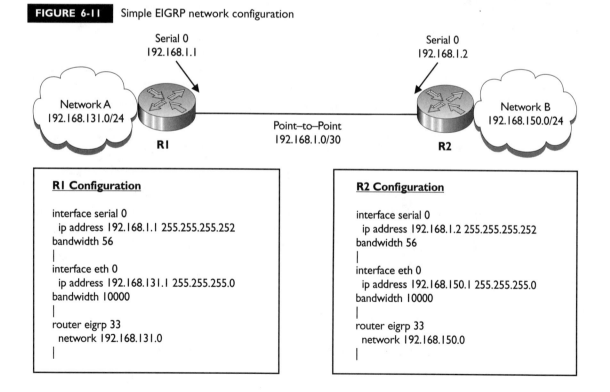

FIGURE 6-11   Simple EIGRP network configuration

Serial 0
192.168.1.1

Serial 0
192.168.1.2

Network A
192.168.131.0/24

Network B
192.168.150.0/24

Point–to–Point
192.168.1.0/30

R1

R2

R1 Configuration

interface serial 0
  ip address 192.168.1.1 255.255.255.252
bandwidth 56
|
interface eth 0
  ip address 192.168.131.1 255.255.255.0
bandwidth 10000
|
router eigrp 33
  network 192.168.131.0
|

R2 Configuration

interface serial 0
  ip address 192.168.1.2 255.255.255.252
bandwidth 56
|
interface eth 0
  ip address 192.168.150.1 255.255.255.0
bandwidth 10000
|
router eigrp 33
  network 192.168.150.0
|

configuration in R1 contains the NETWORK 192.168.131.0 statement. This statement corresponds to the directly connected network on its Ethernet interface. Similarly, R2 has NETWORK 192.168.150.0 in its configuration.

When the two routers have their EIGRP processes enabled, they exchange their routing information. R1 sees a route to Network B via R2, and inversely, R2 sees a route to Network A via R1. In this simple case, there is no need to include the point-to-point network of 192.168.1.0/30 in the EIGRP configuration, since this network is directly connected so will already be present in their respective routing tables.

Now that you have an understanding of how to configure simple EIGRP operation on Cisco routers, Exercise 6-3 gives you the chance to apply what you have learned.

EXERCISE 6-3

Basic EIGRP Configuration

You have already built the network shown in Figure 6-12 and until now all routing configuration has been statically entered routes. Your management has decided that since the network will grow rapidly over the next few months to include redundant connectivity; dynamic routing should be implemented now, to reduce the transition period when it comes to expanding the network. You have decided that since the network is expected to grow considerably, RIP would not be a suitable routing protocol to use due to its vulnerability to routing loops and relatively long convergence time. Since the company also wants to implement VLSM at some point, IGRP is not a feasible option. Additionally, management has announced the acquisition of another company whose network is based on Novell NetWare (IPX). For these reasons, you have decided that EIGRP will satisfy the requirements for the transition to a dynamic routing protocol.

You must take the following factors into consideration when implementing your EIGRP configuration:

- R1 will be considered the main aggregation router for the network. All point-to-point networks on the serial connections should be advertised from this router only, rather than from the access Routers R2 and R3.

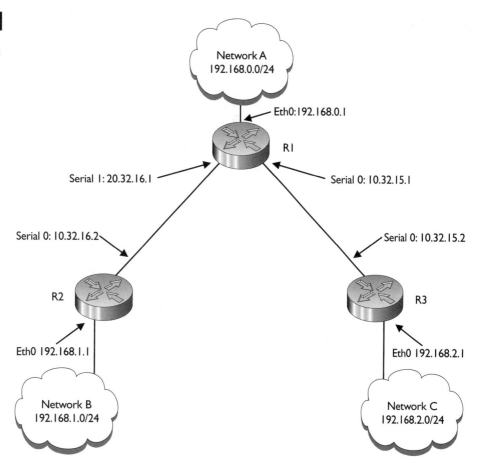

FIGURE 6-12

Network diagram
for Exercise 6-3

- The ASN for all routers in your routing domain is 5.
- All networks in the routing domain must be able to access all other networks, including the point-to-point networks.

The routers in the network are currently configured with only the interface addresses. You must complete the configuration for all three routers to enable the EIGRP processes. The current configurations are shown in Figure 6-13.

FIGURE 6-13

Current router
configurations for
Exercise 6-3

R1 Configuration:
```
interface serial 0
  ip address 10.32.15.1 255.255.255.252
  bandwidth 64
!
interface serial 1
  ip address 10.32.16.1 255.255.255.252
  bandwidth 128
!
interface ethernet 0
  ip address 192.168.0.1 255.255.255.0
  bandwidth 10000
!
```

R2 Configuration:
```
interface serial 0
  ip address 10.32.16.2 255.255.255.252
  bandwidth 128
!
interface ethernet 0
  ip address 192.168.1.1 255.255.255.0
  bandwidth 10000
!
```

R3 Configuration:
```
interface serial 0
  ip address 10.32.15.2 255.255.255.252
  bandwidth 64
!
interface ethernet 0
  ip address 192.168.2.1 255.255.255.0
  bandwidth 10000
!
```

Solution:

1. Enable the EIGRP routing process on each router.

2. Add NETWORK statements as appropriate, corresponding to the networks that the given router should advertise to its neighbors.

Since router R1 will be the central router, it should advertise its point-to-point networks. Therefore, R1 has three NETWORK statements in its EIGRP configuration; one for each point-to-point network and one for Network A. The remaining Routers R2 and R3 have network statements for their own locally connected networks.

The resulting completed configurations appear in Figure 6-14. Check the configurations you performed against the answers provided. You will notice that the NETWORK statements for R1 are classful. Remember that you can insert the individual subnets, but the router will automatically combine them into a single classful NETWORK statement. If you are still unsure of any configuration steps, be sure to review this configuration section before proceeding with the next section, "Monitoring and Verifying EIGRP Operation."

As you can see, basic configuration of EIGRP is fairly straightforward. The more advanced issues of EIGRP configuration are discussed in Chapter 7. With the basic

FIGURE 6-14

Completed
router
configurations
from Exercise 6-3

```
R1 Configuration:
interface serial 0
  ip address 10.32.15.1 255.255.255.252
  bandwidth 64
!
interface serial 1
  ip address 10.32.16.1 255.255.255.252
  bandwidth 128
!
interface ethernet 0
  ip address 192.168.0.1 255.255.255.0
  bandwidth 10000
!
router eigrp 5
network 192.168.0.0
!

R2 Configuration:

interface serial 0
  ip address 10.32.16.2 255.255.255.252
  bandwidth 128
!
interface ethernet 0
  ip address 192.168.1.1 255.255.255.0
  bandwidth 10000
!
router eigrp 5
network 192.168.1.0
!
```

```
R3 Configuration:
interface serial 0
   ip address 10.32.15.2 255.255.255.252
   bandwidth 64
!
interface ethernet 0
   ip address 192.168.2.1 255.255.255.0
   bandwidth 10000
!
router eigrp 5
   network 192.168.2.0
!
```

understanding that you now have, let's look briefly at a few simple scenarios concerning the topics we have discussed to this point.

SCENARIO & SOLUTION

Can I use a different ASN on neighboring routers?	If the neighbors are all to share routing information, the answer is no. The ASN is unique to the routing domain, and all routers within that routing domain must have the same number configured.
I have two totally separate networks, sharing a common router in the middle. The networks themselves do not talk to each other. Can I use more than one EIGRP process on the router in the middle, one for each network?	Yes. You can have as many EIGRP processes as you want on the router, each with its own ASN. Each EIGRP process will be independent and not route to the other one unless you configure route redistribution.
I have noticed that my Cisco router allows a NEIGHBOR statement to be entered for EIGRP configurations. Do I need this statement to define neighbors?	No. EIGRP uses multicast hello packets to acquire and maintain neighbor relationships. The NEIGHBOR statement, which is available in EIGRP, serves no functional purpose so is not needed. It is present in EIGRP because EIGRP was developed as an enhancement of IGRP. With IGRP, this command was used to define a unicast neighbor, usually on a nonbroadcast multiple access network, with which to form a neighbor adjacency. In EIGRP, this function is obsolete because of the neighbor discovery and maintenance mechanism.

Monitoring and Verifying EIGRP Operations

Now that we have learned how EIGRP operates and how to configure it for use on our network, the next step is to look at ways to verify its operation. Occasionally, you might encounter problems in your network due to misconfiguration or broken links. Cisco routers have a series of commands that enable you to view how the protocol is performing, simplifying any troubleshooting tasks.

Show IP Protocols Command

The SHOW IP PROTOCOLS command is used to display information about the currently running IP routing protocols on the router. Figure 6-15 shows a typical output of the SHOW IP PROTOCOLS command. Let's examine the relevant fields in detail.

First, you will see information about the running process, including the ASN. The next two lines, are not used for EIGRP operation. These lines describe the update interval, which is the time interval between periodic routing updates, such as for RIP, as well as the values of the various timers to prevent routing loops in other

| **FIGURE 6-15**<br><br>The SHOW IP PROTOCOLS command shows information about the router's running IP routing protocols | ```
vin-1>show ip protocols
Routing Protocol is "eigrp 33"
  Outgoing update filter list for all interfaces is
  Incoming update filter list for all interfaces is
  Default networks flagged in outgoing updates
  Default networks accepted from incoming updates
  EIGRP metric weight K1=1, K2=0, K3=1, K4=0, K5=0
  EIGRP maximum hopcount 100
  EIGRP maximum metric variance 1
  Redistributing: eigrp 33

  Automatic network summarization is in effect
  Routing for Networks:
    192.168.15.0
  Routing Information Sources:
    Gateway         Distance      Last Update
    192.168.33.1      90           2d12h
  Distance: internal 90 external 170
``` |
```

distance-vector protocols, such as hold-down and flush timers. The next few lines identify inbound and outbound update filters.

The next line, indicated in bold, contains the metric weights, or K values. You will notice that the values are set to default in this case. Below this line, we are told that automatic route summarization is in effect. This means that the router will automatically send a single classful summary route for all advertised networks.

Finally, we have information on what local networks are configured for advertisement to neighbors and a listing of neighbors from which we are receiving routing updates. The Distance field here refers to the administrative distance of the routing protocol, not the FD or AD used in DUAL calculations. We also see here the time since the last route update from that neighbor.

Show IP Route Command

You can verify that the route to a given destination is installed in the routing table using the SHOW IP ROUTE command. This command takes an optional argument of the destination host or network. If this argument is omitted, the command returns the entire routing table. Let's look at both versions now.

As you can see from the output shown in Figure 6-16, we can see the whole routing table. You can skip past the legend at the top, which gives the definitions of the codes used to identify the source of the routes in the table.

FIGURE 6-16   The SHOW IP ROUTE command used without an argument shows the router's entire routing table

```
vin-1>sho ip route
Codes: C - connected, S - static, I - IGRP, R - RIP, M - mobile, B - BGP
       D - EIGRP, EX - EIGRP external, O - OSPF, IA - OSPF inter area
       N1 - OSPF NSSA external type 1, N2 - OSPF NSSA external type 2
       E1 - OSPF external type 1, E2 - OSPF external type 2, E - EGP
       i - IS-IS, L1 - IS-IS level-1, L2 - IS-IS level-2, * - candidate default
       U - per-user static route, o - ODR

Gateway of last resort is 192.168.1.13 to network 192.168.0.0

D*   192.168.0.0/24 [90/1764352] via 192.168.1.13, 5d01h, Serial0/0
C        192.168.1.3/32 is directly connected, Loopback0
C        192.168.1.12/30 is directly connected, Serial0/0
C        192.168.2.0/24 is directly connected, Ethernet0/0

vin-1>
```

The first line, flagged with a D, is a route received via EIGRP. This line contains the following information, in order: address of the target network, AD from the routing protocol in use (the first number in square brackets), actual metric calculated for the route (second number in square brackets), next-hop address, age of the route, and interface on which the route is found.

You can also use the routing protocol on the command line to show only the routes learned from that protocol—for example, SHOW IP ROUTE EIGRP. This command is invaluable in determining whether or not a route exists in the routing table to a given network and can be the first step in troubleshooting EIGRP operations.

The other method of using the SHOW IP ROUTE command is by specifying a destination address or network as the command argument, as shown in Figure 6-17. This version of the command shows more specific detail concerning the route requested. We can see from this output that the route was learned via EIGRP in the ASN 33. The routing protocol has an administrative distance of 90, and the calculated metric by the router is 1789952. The route was learned from an internal source—that is, it was originated within the routing domain.

The routing descriptor blocks show details of the path selected—in this case, the next-hop address of 192.168.2.1, which was advertised by that same router 6 hours, 50 minutes, and 18 seconds ago. Other information included is the interface for the route and the metric component details, such as bandwidth, delay, reliability, MTU, load, and hop count.

FIGURE 6-17   The SHOW IP ROUTE command can also take an argument of a destination address or network

```
vin-2>sho ip route 192.168.0.32
Routing entry for 192.168.0.0/24
  Known via "eigrp 33", distance 90, metric 1789952, type internal
  Redistributing via eigrp 33
  Last update from 192.168.2.1 on Ethernet0/0, 06:50:18 ago
  Routing Descriptor Blocks:
  * 192.168.2.1, from 192.168.2.1, 06:50:18 ago, via Ethernet0/0
      Route metric is 1789952, traffic share count is 1
      Total delay is 21100 microseconds, minimum bandwidth is 2048 Kbit
      Reliability 255/255, minimum MTU 1500 bytes
      Loading 1/255, Hops 2

vin-2>
```

This version of the command provides more detailed information than only the summarized routes shown in the first version and is used to gather more specific information about the metric components used to select the route.

SHOW IP EIGRP NEIGHBORS Command

The SHOW IP EIGRP NEIGHBORS command was discussed in detail earlier in this chapter. It is used for displaying the status of the neighbor discovery and management features of EIGRP.

SHOW IP EIGRP TOPOLOGY Command

Remember that EIGRP stores a topology table of routes received from EIGRP updates. Figure 6-18 shows an example of a typical output from the SHOW IP EIGRP TOPOLOGY command.

In this command, we can see the status of the route, followed by the number of successors to the destination. Next we have the FD (lowest calculated metric from all available paths) and the address of the FS. The numbers in parentheses are the local metric via that FS and the advertised distance for that successor. Again, the interface is shown.

Consider the situation found in Exercise 6-3 when the selected successor to Network A was not necessarily the one we were expecting, yet both routes met the *feasibility condition (FC)*. By looking at the metric and advertised distances and

FIGURE 6-18   The SHOW IP EIGRP TOPOLOGY command is used to show information used by DUAL concerning the route information used by EIGRP

```
vin-1>show ip eigrp topology
IP-EIGRP Topology Table for process 33

Codes: P - Passive, A - Active, U - Update, Q - Query, R - Reply,
       r - Reply status

P 192.168.0.0/24, 1 successors, FD is 1764352
        via 192.168.1.13 (1764352/28160), Serial0/0
P 192.168.2.0/24, 1 successors, FD is 281600
        via Connected, Ethernet0/0
P 192.168.1.12/30, 1 successors, FD is 1761792
        via Connected, Serial0/0
```

comparing it to the FD, you can use this command to review the reason that the successors were chosen.

exam
ⓦatch

The metrics given in the SHOW IP EIGRP TOPOLOGY command after the next-hop router are the locally calculated metric and the advertised metric from the indicated neighbor.

SHOW IP EIGRP TRAFFIC Command

In order to gather general statistics on the overall EIGRP routing traffic, you can use the command SHOW IP EIGRP TRAFFIC. An example of this command is shown in Figure 6-19.

The output from this command is fairly clear and does not require further explanation. Remember, however, the various EIGRP messages that can be sent.

The SHOW IP EIGRP EVENTS Command

In order to show fairly detailed information about how a route learned from EIGRP is eventually entered into the topology table and routing table, use the SHOW IP EIGRP EVENTS command. This command displays the last 500 events in reverse chronological order (most recent to oldest). The output from this command is considerably more complex than the other SHOW commands, as indicated in Figure 6-20, so we will look at the information step by step.

Remember that this display is in reverse order, so if we start from Line 6, we can see that the router is attempting to find the FS to the network 192.168.1.12/30 with an FD of 1787392. As we progress to Line 5, we see that the FC has been satisfied by the next-hop router of 192.168.2.1 for the metric/feasible distance from Line 6. In Line 4, we continue to satisfy the FC with our local routing table metric, which in this case is also the feasible distance, and the advertised metric received from the

FIGURE 6-19

General EIGRP traffic information can be seen using the SHOW IP EIGRP TRAFFIC command

```
vin-1>sho ip eigrp traffic
IP-EIGRP Traffic Statistics for process 33
   Hellos sent/received: 7921886/7586709
   Updates sent/received: 304/268
   Queries sent/received: 113/37
   Replies sent/received: 37/108
   Acks sent/received: 343/368
   Input queue high water mark 2, 0 drops
```

FIGURE 6-20

Detailed operation
of routing
information learned
from EIGRP can be
derived from
SHOW IP EIGRP
EVENTS

```
vin-2>show ip eigrp events
Event information for AS 33:
1     11:40:07.047 Change queue emptied, entries: 1
2     11:40:07.047 Metric set: 192.168.1.12/30 1787392
3     11:40:07.047 Route install: 192.168.1.12/30 192.168.2.1
4     11:40:07.047 FC sat rdbmet/succmet: 1787392 1761792
5     11:40:07.047 FC sat nh/ndbmet: 192.168.2.1 1787392
6     11:40:07.047 Find FS: 192.168.1.12/30 1787392
```

next-hop router, which is 1761792. Since the advertised metric is less than the feasible distance, this meets the FC. Finally, the route is installed into the routing table, and the metric for the route is set.

The SHOW IP EIGRP INTERFACE Command

By using SHOW IP EIGRP INTERFACE command, as shown in Figure 6-21, we determine all the interfaces on which the EIGRP process is running. This command also shows the average SRTT, delay, and the multicast flow timer, which we briefly mentioned earlier when discussing EIGRP's reliable multicast protocol.

The fields shown from this command are as follows:

1. Interface

2. Number of EIGRP neighbors on the interface

3. Status of the transmit queue, including reliability information

4. Average SRTT

FIGURE 6-21 Summary information concerning EIGRP operation on all interfaces

```
vin-1>show ip eigrp interface
IP-EIGRP interfaces for process 33
```

Interface	Peers	Xmit Queue Un/Reliable	Mean SRTT	Pacing Time Un/Reliable	Multicast Flow Timer	Pending Routes
Se0/0	1	0/0	976	0/11	4891	0
Lo0	0	0/0	0	0/10	0	0
Et0/0	1	0/0	4	0/10	50	0

5. Pacing time on the interface; pacing is used to inject a small random period of time to prevent packets from being sent by all neighbors at the same time, causing possible collisions and loss of hello packets, which, if the situation is severe, could lead to a neighbor being declared dead

6. The value of the multicast flow timer

7. The number of route updates waiting to be sent on the interface

The DEBUG EIGRP PACKET Command

In case of problems in the network, which cannot be resolved by the information in the normal SHOW commands, there are also several debugging-level commands that yield even more detail on the operation of EIGRP. One such command is DEBUG EIGRP PACKET, as shown in Figure 6-22.

As you can see, the data returned from this command is very detailed and includes components of the actual packets sent and received by the EIGRP process on the router's interfaces. The packets you can see in Figure 6-22 depict typical hello packets being sent and received.

on the

o b

Due to the amount of information and additional processor overhead required by the router, it is recommended that you use debugging commands only in a laboratory and not on a live network; otherwise, you risk overloading the router, causing downtime.

FIGURE 6-22 Detailed information concerning EIGRP packets can be seen using DEBUG EIGRP PACKETS

```
13w3d: EIGRP: Received HELLO on Ethernet0/0 nbr 192.168.2.1
13w3d:    AS 33, Flags 0x0, Seq 0/0 idbQ 0/0 iidbQ un/rely 0/0 peerQ un/rely 0/0
13w3d: EIGRP: Sending HELLO on Ethernet0/0
13w3d:    AS 33, Flags 0x0, Seq 0/0 idbQ 0/0 iidbQ un/rely 0/0
13w3d: EIGRP: Sending HELLO on Loopback0
13w3d:    AS 33, Flags 0x0, Seq 0/0 idbQ 0/0 iidbQ un/rely 0/0
13w3d: EIGRP: Received HELLO on Loopback0 nbr 192.168.1.4
13w3d:    AS 33, Flags 0x0, Seq 0/0 idbQ 0/0
13w3d: EIGRP: Packet from ourselves ignored
13w3d: EIGRP: Received HELLO on Ethernet0/0 nbr 192.168.2.1
13w3d:    AS 33, Flags 0x0, Seq 0/0 idbQ 0/0 iidbQ un/rely 0/0 peerQ un/rely 0/0
13w3d: EIGRP: Sending HELLO on Ethernet0/0
13w3d:    AS 33, Flags 0x0, Seq 0/0 idbQ 0/0 iidbQ un/rely 0/0
```

FIGURE 6-23 Neighbor discovery and management anomalies can be seen with neighbor debugging enabled

```
vin-2#debug eigrp neighbors
EIGRP Neighbors debugging is on
vin-2#
13w3d: EIGRP: Holdtime expired
13w3d: EIGRP: Neighbor 192.168.2.1 went down on Ethernet0/0
13w3d: EIGRP: Packet from ourselves ignored
13w3d: EIGRP: New peer 192.168.2.1
```

The DEBUG EIGRP NEIGHBOR Command

Recall from our discussion about neighbor discovery and management the issues concerning hello interval and hold-time. Remember also that if the hello interval is manually changed, the hold-time is not automatically updated, so it too should be manually configured. The DEBUG EIGRP NEIGHBOR command helps identify this and similar situations, as shown in Figure 6-23.

As you can see from the sample output, the neighbor 192.168.2.1 was declared dead on Ethernet 0/0. Shortly after, we received a new hello packet, and the neighbor relationship was re-established.

The DEBUG EIGRP FSM Command

One of the more complex debugging commands available for EIGRP operations allows you to view the activity of the DUAL finite-state machine. Viewing this activity will enable you to trace routes that are dropped due to loss of a successor or discover why a router cannot find a path to a destination. Figure 6-24 shows the typical output from the DEBUG EIGRP FSM command, where FSM is the abbreviation for *finite-state machine*.

FIGURE 6-24 Routes being dropped may be verified and debugged by looking at the activity of DUAL

```
vin-2#debug eigrp fsm
EIGRP FSM Events/Actions debugging is on
vin-2#
13w3d: DUAL: linkdown(): start - 192.168.2.1 via Ethernet0/0
13w3d: DUAL: Destination 192.168.2.16/32
13w3d: DUAL: Find FS for dest 192.168.2.16/32. FD is 286720, RD is 286720
13w3d: DUAL:    192.168.2.1 metric 4294967295/4294967295 not found Dmin is 4294967295
13w3d: DUAL: Dest 192.168.2.16/32 not entering active state.
13w3d: DUAL: Removing dest 192.168.2.16/32, nexthop 192.168.2.1
13w3d: DUAL: No routes.  Flushing dest 192.168.2.16/32
```

In the case of Figure 6-24, we can see that we lost a neighbor; as a result, the route we had to 192.168.2.16/32 was no longer valid. Using the last-known feasible distance and calculated metric, both of which were 286720, we are not able to find another path. On this router, 192.168.2.1 was the only neighbor, so we cannot send a query to find an alternative path. As a result, we now raise our metric, FD, and minimum distance found to infinity to indicate that the route is unavailable. We do not switch to active mode, since there are no other neighbors to query; as a result, we remove the route from the routing table.

Now that we have covered some of the commands used to verify and troubleshoot EIGRP operation, let's apply what you have learned.

EXERCISE 6-4

Troubleshooting EIGRP Operation

You have just upgraded one of the links to a remote network from 56k to 128k. Even though the path to the network is now all 128k and EIGRP should prefer the path via the new upgraded connection, it is still passing the traffic via a longer, slower route. From the output of your SHOW IP ROUTE command, you notice that the minimum bandwidth on the link is still showing as 56k, as shown here:

```
Router> show ip route 192.168.121.0
Routing entry for 192.168.121.0/24
   Known via "eigrp 50", distance 90, metric 1789952, type internal
   Redistributing via eigrp 50
   Last update from 192.168.1.1 on Ethernet0, 00:32:18 ago
   Routing Descriptor Blocks:
   * 192.168.1.1 from 192.168.1.1, 00:32:18 ago, via Ethernet0
       Route metric is 1789952, traffic share count is 1
       Total delay is 1023000 microseconds, minimum bandwidth is 56 kbit
       Reliability 255/255, minimum MTU 1500 bytes
       Loading 1/255, Hops 4
```

As a result, you double-check your interface configuration, which is as follows:

```
Interface serial0
   ip address 192.168.15.31 255.255.255.252
   description serial connection to network A
   ip eigrp hello-interval 1200
   ip eigrp hold-time 180
   bandwidth 56
   no ip directed-broadcast
```

1. Identify the configuration errors from the above output.

2. Explain what corrections you should make.

Solution: First, note that the link was upgraded to 128k. Therefore, the bandwidth statement in the interface configuration should be modified to reflect this upgrade. However, other problems in the configuration cause this router to not even form a neighbor association across the serial connection. This problem, in and of itself, would not necessarily eliminate this route, since the minimum bandwidth found on the other path is also 56k.

The hello interval is manually set to 1200 seconds. By default on this kind of connection, it would be 60 seconds. The hold-time is set to 180 seconds, which can be considered default for the media type, being three times the default hello interval. However, since the actual hello interval is set to 1200, the hold-time will always expire, thus preventing establishment of a neighbor association. You should, therefore, either change the hello interval back to the default setting of 60 seconds or increase the hold-time to higher than the hello interval, preferably three times the value, or 3600.

FROM THE CLASSROOM

Troubleshooting and Verification Methodology

Every engineer has a different approach to verification and troubleshooting, especially when it comes to routing protocols such as EIGRP. Here are a few hints that help to reduce the overall time needed to verify correct operation as well as to identify and fix problems:

■ **Walk before you run (start with the simplest first)** Check your physical connections. Then check your basic configuration. If you have a complex configuration, remove items one by one until you reach the bare minimum required for the protocol. Then check the operation again. Continue to add the other commands one at a time, performing the checks at each step.

■ **Don't use a hammer for a screw (use the right tool for the job)** Every aspect of verification and debugging serves a certain purpose. It is vital that you use the right command or debugging tool to show you the information you are seek. For example, it is useless to employ the SHOW IP EIGRP TOPOLOGY command if you are attempting to verify that neighbor relationships are being correctly established, since not every neighbor will necessarily be shown in the topology table. For this task, it is better to use SHOW IP EIGRP NEIGHBORS.

■ **Don't bite off more than you can chew** Try to limit the amount of information you are trying to read to exactly the information you need. For example, if you are debugging neighbor discovery, the DEBUG EIGRP NEIGHBOR command gives you precisely the information you need concerning neighbor discovery. A command such as DEBUG EIGRP PACKET will also show you neighbor discovery information, such as hello packets, but it is filled with information concerning every other form of packet used by EIGRP, giving you much more information than you need.

■ **Don't destroy when you can simply maim** Many students, as well as colleagues, get a giggle out of this point before they know what I mean by it. In the simplest sense, this rule means to take an action that as closely as possible affects only the operation with which you are concerned, not all operations on the equipment—for example, using the RELOAD command when all you want to do is clear your EIGRP neighbor relationships to watch them form again, or when migrating from, say, RIP to EIGRP, removing the entire RIP configuration before the EIGRP configuration is completed. This rule sounds like simple common sense, but you would be surprised to learn how many engineers don't follow this rule. What's worse is what could happen if you don't follow this rule while you are performing remote management of a router on the other side of town. Imagine that you are migrating from RIP to EIGRP and you remove the RIP advertisements for the routes to the router before you finish configuring EIGRP. You then lose connection to a now half-configured router. As some would say, this is "not a good thing."

—Leland Vandervort, CCNP, CCDA, CNE

CERTIFICATION SUMMARY

We have discussed the features and operation of the Enhanced Interior Gateway Routing Protocol in considerable detail. EIGRP is an enhanced distance-vector routing protocol that exhibits some of the properties of link-state protocols. Unlike other distance-vector protocols, however, in EIGRP, routing updates are sent only when there is a change to a route, topology, or metric. Additionally, unlike its predecessor IGRP, EIGRP supports IP as well as IPX and AppleTalk, and route redistribution is automatic to and from IGRP for IP, SAP for IPX, and RTMP for AppleTalk.

EIGRP uses a system of neighbor discovery and management to allow routers within the same routing domain, or AS, to exchange routing information. At the same time, neighbors that disappear might also be detected using this method, thus avoiding the possibility of routes remaining, even if a neighbor dies.

The fundamental metric calculation algorithm used by EIGRP is essentially the same as for IGRP except that the bandwidth and delay components are scaled by a factor of 256 to allow more control over path selection. These metrics are also used by the Diffusing Update Algorithm (DUAL), as well as loop avoidance, to further refine the path selection process. The essential principle relies on the concept that the lowest calculated metric is called the feasible distance (FD). In order to choose a path, the router compares the advertised distance (AD), which is the metric (or FD) calculated by the neighbor, to determine if it is smaller than the FD. If it is, the route meets the feasibility condition (FC), and that neighbor is determined to be a feasible successor (FS). If the router finds multiple FSs for a given destination, the one that yields the lowest route metric becomes the successor, or the next-hop router.

In its simplest and default form of operation, configuration of EIGRP is identical to that of IGRP. The minimum required configuration commands to enable EIGRP are the ROUTER EIGRP statement with the ASN, which must be common among all routers that will exchange routing information, and the NETWORK statement, which identifies the interfaces out of which to advertise EIGRP routing updates. Other aspects of EIGRP operation can be configured according to specific requirements. Verification of EIGRP operation can be performed by SHOW commands, such as SHOW IP EIGRP TOPOLOGY, to allow you to confirm the correct behavior and configuration of the EIGRP process.

In case of problems, troubleshooting can be performed in an attempt to pinpoint the actual cause. For example, one might use the command DEBUG EIGRP FSM to determine why a route is inexplicably being dropped, even though the neighbor from which it was learned is stable.

More advanced configuration concepts and fine-tuning of EIGRP's behavior are discussed in Chapter 7, "Advanced EIGRP Behavior and Configuration."

TWO-MINUTE DRILL

Here are some of the key points from each certification objective in Chapter 6.

Enhanced IGRP Features and Operation

❑ EIGRP is an enhanced distance-vector protocol.

❑ For default operation, the EIGRP Metric = Bandwidth + Delay.

❑ EIGRP supports IP as well as IPX and AppleTalk.

❑ Metrics in EIGRP are used not only for path determination; they are also used by DUAL to form a view of the network topology.

The Diffusing Update Algorithm

❑ The lowest calculated metric to a destination is the feasible distance (FD).

❑ Advertised distance (AD) is the metric received from a neighboring router for a given path and corresponding to that neighbor's own FD.

❑ Any neighbor with an AD less than the router's FD meets the feasibility condition (FC) and becomes a feasible successor (FS).

❑ Among multiple FSs, the one that bears the lowest locally calculated metric to the destination becomes the successor, or next-hop router.

Basic EIGRP Configuration

❑ Basic configuration of EIGRP on a Cisco router is identical to that of IGRP.

❑ The ROUTER EIGRP statement contains the ASN, which must be common among all routers in the same routing domain.

❑ The NETWORK statement identifies the interfaces out of which EIGRP will advertise routing information. For each interface EIGRP advertises out, EIGRP includes the network/subnet for that interface in its advertisements. The statement itself uses a classful network address, so a netmask is not allowed.

Monitoring and Verifying EIGRP Operations

❑ Basic status information for the running EIGRP process can be acquired using the SHOW IP PROTOCOLS command.

❑ The SHOW IP EIGRP NEIGHBORS command gives more detailed information about neighbors within the same routing domain, including hold-time, retransmission timeout, smooth round-trip time (SRTT), and address of the peer.

❑ You can use SHOW IP EIGRP EVENTS to give a chronological listing of the last 500 updates, calculations, metric changes, and the like, sent or received.

❑ Real-time information on all updates, queries, responses, hellos, and acknowledgments for IP, IPX, and AppleTalk can be viewed using the DEBUG EIGRP PACKET command.

SELF TEST

The following questions will help you measure your understanding of the material presented in this chapter. Read all the choices carefully because there might be more than one correct answer. Choose all correct answers for each question.

Enhanced IGRP Features and Operation

1. What is the default action of a router when a neighbor fails to send a hello after 5 seconds using broadcast media?

   A. The neighbor is declared dead.

   B. The metrics for all associated routes are increased.

   C. The router will not send any more updates to that neighbor until it becomes active again.

   D. The router will wait for another 10 seconds to receive a hello packet.

2. Your manager has asked you to use a dynamic routing protocol for your network, in view of the company's planned expansion. The protocol must have fast convergence, loop avoidance, support for VLSM, and support for AppleTalk so that the graphics department can exchange information with a remote location. You have chosen EIGRP for this purpose. From the following list, select the best reasons for your decision; choose all that apply.

   A. Because EIGRP supports multiple network protocols and has faster convergence than RIP.

   B. Because some author in a book told me to.

   C. Because IGRP does not support variable-length subnet masks.

   D. Because EIGRP is a link-state protocol, so it better meets these requirements.

3. What are the four primary functions of the EIGRP Protocol Engine?

   A. AppleTalk, IPX, IP, and DECNet

   B. DUAL, reliable transport, neighbor discovery, and client interface

   C. Routing table, topology table, neighbor table, and SAP table

   D. Metric calculation, interface rate limiting, access-list matching, and storage of the entire routing table

4. Which two metric components are used for calculation of EIGRP metrics in default operation?

   A. Load and MTU

   B. Hop count and interface status

C. Delay to the next-hop router and bandwidth

D. Bandwidth and cumulative delay to the destination

5. Why is EIGRP considered a "ships-in-the-night" protocol?

A. Because EIGRP cannot exchange routing information with any other protocol

B. Because each router running EIGRP in a network can be considered a "ship at night" that cannot see any other router

C. Because EIGRP maintains completely separate and independent tables for each supported network protocol (IP, IPX, and AppleTalk)

D. Because EIGRP cannot run during the daytime

6. The inclusion or exclusion of components, as well as their magnitude or weighting, in EIGRP metric calculations is determined by which of the following?

A. Bandwidth

B. K values

C. MTU

D. Delay

7. If a neighbor fails to send an acknowledgment to a multicast update, the sending router then takes what course of action?

A. The neighbor is declared dead.

B. The router attempts to send the update to that neighbor using unicast.

C. The routes associated with that neighbor are dropped.

D. The router sends a hello packet via a unicast packet to that neighbor.

The Diffusing Update Algorithm

8. When a neighbor is declared dead, the router attempts to find an alternative route for networks for which that neighbor was the successor. If there are no other feasible successors, what is the next action taken by the router?

A. The router increases the metric for that network to infinity.

B. The router queries its remaining neighbors to find a path to the network.

C. The router drops the route completely and sends an update indicating that the network is unreachable.

D. The router waits until the hold-down timer has expired before removing the route from its routing table.

9. The lowest calculated metric to a given destination among all available paths is known as which of the following?

A. Feasible successor

B. Feasibility condition

C. Administrative distance

D. Feasible distance

10. Refer to Figure 6-25 for the following question. Based on the information provided, which router will be installed as the successor from Router R1 to destination Network A?

A. R2

B. R4

C. R2 and R4 using EIGRP load balancing

D. No successor will be found

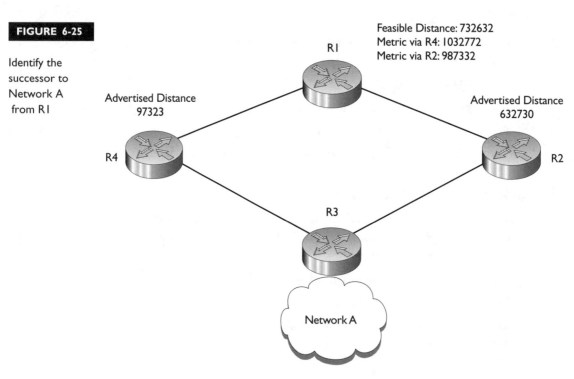

FIGURE 6-25

Identify the successor to Network A from R1

Feasible Distance: 732632
Metric via R4: 1032772
Metric via R2: 987332

R1

Advertised Distance
97323

Advertised Distance
632730

R4

R2

R3

Network A

11. When the advertised distance for a given destination network is less than the feasible distance, this is known as which of the following?

    A. Feasible successor

    B. Hold-time

    C. Active update

    D. Feasibility condition

12. What does it mean when an EIGRP route becomes "active"?

    A. The router is attempting to locate another path to the destination network by sending queries to its neighbors.

    B. The route has been entered into the routing table and is now in use.

    C. DUAL has failed to operate, so all routes are now being recalculated.

    D. The router is sending its entire routing table in its update message to neighbors.

Basic EIGRP Configuration

13. You have just added another network on 192.168.121.0/24 and you need to turn on the routing to that network. The network is connected on the Eth1 interface of your Cisco 2511 router, and you can ping hosts in that network from the router. How would you now tell EIGRP to include that network in routing updates to neighbors, assuming you have already entered router configuration mode using ROUTER EIGRP 33?

    A. ROUTER(CONFIG)# IP ROUTE 192.168.121.0 255.255.255.0 ETH1

    B. ROUTER> NETWORK 192.168.121.0

    C. ROUTER(CONFIG-ROUTER)# NETWORK 192.168.121.0

    D. ROUTER(CONFIG-IF)# IP EIGRP ANNOUNCE 192.168.121.0

14. When configuring EIGRP, what is the significance of the autonomous system number?

    A. It must be the same on all routers in the network.

    B. It is only locally significant.

    C. It identifies the number of routers to be found in the network.

    D. It is an identifier for the EIGRP process and must be the same on all routers that are expected to share routing updates.

15. Other than the ROUTER EIGRP statement, what other configuration statement is required for default EIGRP operation?

    A. The NEIGHBOR statement

    B. The NETWORK statement

    C. The AREA 0 RANGE statement

    D. The IP AS-PATH ACCESS-LIST statement

Monitoring and Verifying EIGRP Operations

16. You have noticed that one of your EIGRP neighbors fails to maintain its neighbor relationship. Which command might you use on the router to determine the reason for this failure?

    A. WRITE ERASE

    B. SHOW IP EIGRP TOPOLOGY

    C. DEBUG EIGRP NEIGHBORS

    D. IP EIGRP HOLD-TIME 360

17. How would you verify that your router has a path to a destination network?

    A. By looking at the routing table using the SHOW IP ROUTE command

    B. By monitoring the DUAL calculations with DEBUG EIGRP FSM

    C. By using the RELOAD command

    D. By changing the hello interval on the interface that leads to that network

18. You want to verify the K values in your EIGRP configuration. Which command allows you to view the current settings?

    A. SHOW IP PROTOCOLS

    B. SHOW IP EIGRP INTERFACE

    C. DEBUG EIGRP FSM

    D. SHOW IP EIGRP EVENTS

19. You have noticed that the path to one of your remote networks keeps being removed from the routing table. Which of the following commands might help you discover why this is occurring? Choose all that apply.

    A. SHOW IP ROUTE

    B. SHOW IP EIGRP EVENTS

C. DEBUG EIGRP FSM

D. SHOW IP PROTOCOLS

20. You have just added another router to your network that will be participating in routing updates using EIGRP. You want to verify that this router is seen by the other routers and forms neighbor relationships. What is the first command you would issue to verify the neighbor relationships?

A. SHOW IP EIGRP TOPOLOGY

B. DEBUG EIGRP PACKET

C. SHOW IP EIGRP NEIGHBORS

D. DEBUG EIGRP DUAL

LAB QUESTION

You are the network engineer for Books-R-Us Publishing. Currently, your network consists of three segments. One segment, at a remote location, contains the administrative departments. The largest segment, the editorial department, is at the central site; the third department, production, is located at another remote site so that the production staff can interact directly with the printers and binders next door. The administrative network is connected via a 56k leased line to the central office. The production department is connected via a 128k leased line, also to the central office. Due to lack of IP space, you plan to use subnetting in the near future to conserve IP space.

Currently, you are using RIP to perform routing updates, but you are finding that the RIP updates are consuming a large portion of bandwidth on both links to remote networks. Additionally, due to the volume of traffic between the editorial and production departments, the 128k line is becoming saturated, causing some of the RIP updates to be dropped. This results in periods during which there is no routing between the editorial department and the production department. Management has decided to add a second line to the production department, with a bandwidth of 512k, but keeping the 128k as a backup connection. You must therefore choose a routing protocol that will take these aspects of bandwidth into consideration when making path selection as well as only sending routing updates when required, rather than periodically, as is the case with the current protocol. To achieve this goal, you have chosen EIGRP.

Given the proposed network diagram, shown in Figure 6-26, configure the three routers for EIGRP, ensuring that the traffic between production and editorial will be preferred across the new 512k connection and will revert to the 128k line if the primary link goes down. Highlight any observations you might have as you perform this task. The central router will advertise the point-to-point networks. The ASN you have chosen for your routing domain is 33.

FIGURE 6-26   Books-R-Us Publishing proposed network

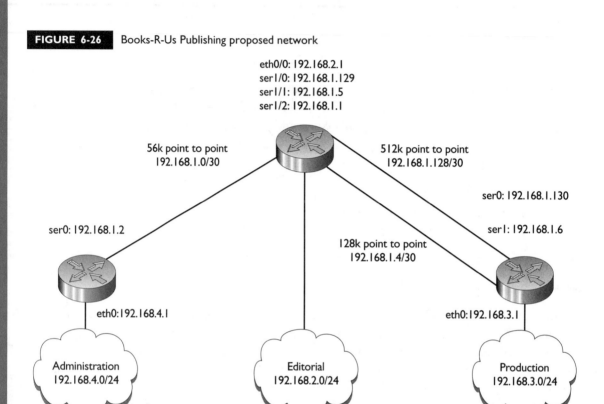

SELF TEST ANSWERS

Enhanced IGRP Features and Operation

1. ☑ **D.** By default, the router will wait until the hold-time, which is three times the hello interval, expires before declaring the neighbor dead.
    ☒ **A** is incorrect because after only 5 seconds the hold-time will not have expired. **B** is incorrect since metrics are recalculated only when there is a change in topology or loss of the only successor. **C** is incorrect because although the neighbor has missed the hello, the hold-time has not expired; therefore, the neighbor is still considered alive.

2. ☑ **A** and **C**. EIGRP supports IP, IPX, and AppleTalk through the use of its protocol-dependent modules, or PDMs. It also supports VLSM, whereas IGRP does not.
    ☒ **B** is incorrect because relying solely on information in a book does not allow you to demonstrate the reason for the answer. You should test the theories for yourself in a lab environment. **D** is incorrect because first, EIGRP is a distance-vector protocol, not a link-state protocol, and second, the type of protocol in this scenario doesn't really make a difference in fulfilling the objectives.

3. ☑ **B.** DUAL, reliable transport, neighbor discovery, and client interface. The Protocol Engine is the workhorse of EIGRP. It maintains all calculations of metrics and DUAL processing, controls the reliable multicast protocol used for reliable transport of EIGRP traffic, handles neighbor discovery and maintenance, and provides an interface to the specific clients contained in the PDM.
    ☒ **A** is incorrect because AppleTalk, IPX, IP, and DECNet are network protocols. **C** is incorrect because the EIGRP routing table, topology table, neighbor table, and SAP table are maintained by the IPX client within the PDM. **D** is incorrect because these functions are performed by the router's processor and are not necessarily related to EIGRP operations.

4. ☑ **D.** Bandwidth and cumulative delay to the destination. In default operation, EIGRP metrics are calculated using the formula *Metric = Bandwidth + Delay,* where bandwidth is (10000000/Bandwidth) x 256 and the delay is the sum of all delays in the path times 256.
    ☒ **A** is incorrect since load and MTU are not considered for default operations. They may be included, however, by manipulation of K values. **B** is incorrect since interface status is not a metric component. Hop count is the metric used for RIP. **C** is incorrect since the delay is cumulative across all hops to the destination, not just to the next-hop router.

5. ☑ C. Because EIGRP maintains completely separate and independent tables for each supported network protocol (IP, IPX, and AppleTalk). The ships-in-the-night concept refers to the fact that EIGRP maintains separate, distinct information for each network protocol in use. These protocols can exist on the same network, completely independent from each other.

☒ A is incorrect because EIGRP does automatically redistribute routing information between like protocols. For example, routing information is exchanged with RTMP for AppleTalk or with IGRP for IP. **B** is also incorrect, despite the metaphor, since EIGRP uses a system of neighbor discovery and maintenance so that routers will "see" each other. **D** is incorrect because time of day has no bearing on EIGRP's ability to function.

6. ☑ B. K values. K values are values assigned to the components of the metric; the setting of K values determines whether or not and to what extent that component is included.

☒ A, C, and D are incorrect since these are actual components referenced by K values.

7. ☑ B. The router attempts to send the update to that neighbor using unicast. When a neighbor fails to acknowledge an update, the sending router attempts to resend the update by unicast. It makes 16 such attempts, at intervals defined by the retransmission timeout (RTO). If a response is still not received, the neighbor is declared dead.

☒ A, C, and D are incorrect because routes associated with the neighbor are not dropped until the neighbor is declared dead and no other alternative paths can be found. Furthermore, hello packets are always multicast.

The Diffusing Update Algorithm

8. ☑ B. The router queries its remaining neighbors to find a path to the network. If a neighbor disappears, it first looks in its topology table for an alternative FS. If there is none, it then sends a query to its peers to attempt to find another path.

☒ A is incorrect because the router increases the metric to infinity, thus marking the route as unreachable, only after it has exhausted all methods of finding a new successor. **C** is incorrect since the router attempts to find an alternative path first. **D** is incorrect because RIP uses a hold-down timer to set an expiration time on the route, whereas EIGRP does not.

9. ☑ D. Feasible distance. As discussed, the lowest calculated metric is called the feasible distance.

☒ A, B, and C are incorrect because the FC is satisfied when the advertised distance of a neighbor is lower than the FD to the network. In that case, the neighbor may be a feasible successor. The administrative distance is a weighting mechanism used to allow a router to prioritize routes based on the routing protocol from which it was learned and has nothing to do with normal EIGRP operations. It is, however, taken into consideration when performing route redistribution.

10. ☑ **A.** R2. Although both R2 and R4 satisfy the FC, the locally calculated metric through R2 is lower than that for R4. Both R2 and R4 become FSs, but R2 is installed as the successor, or next-hop router.

☒ **B** is incorrect since although it also satisfies the FC, the path cost, or metric, from R1 is higher than via R2. **C** is incorrect since the metrics via each path are not equal; therefore, EIGRP will not automatically load balance the two paths. **D** is incorrect since the successor is found to be R2.

11. ☑ **D.** Feasibility condition. The FC is satisfied when the AD to a network is less than the FD. A neighbor that meets the FC becomes an FS.

☒ **A, B,** and **C** are incorrect. The hold-time is the maximum time that can elapse between receipt of a neighbor's hello packets before that neighbor is declared dead.

12. ☑ **A.** The router is attempting to locate another path to the destination network by sending queries to its neighbors. Under normal operations, all routes are stable and the routes are considered "passive." When the router must attempt to find a new path due to loss of a neighbor, it switches to active status and queries its neighbors to find a route. It then remains active until a response is received.

☒ **B** is incorrect since, if the route is in the routing table, the route is passive. **C** is incorrect since route calculations are performed using DUAL, so if DUAL were to fail, the route calculations would fail as well, although it is not likely that this would ever happen. **D** is incorrect since EIGRP sends only information that changes, such as loss of a connection or change of metric, rather than the entire routing table.

Basic EIGRP Configuration

13. ☑ **C.** ROUTER(CONFIG-ROUTER)# NETWORK 192.168.121.0. The (CONFIG-ROUTER)# prompt tells you that you are in router configuration mode. The NETWORK statement is used to indicate what network to advertise in updates.

☒ **A** is incorrect since this is the command to enter a static route in the routing table. This command is not needed anyway, since the network is directly connected to interface eth1. **B** is incorrect because the Router> prompt indicates that you are in user exec mode, not router configuration mode, so the command will not work. **D** is incorrect because the command IP EIGRP ANNOUNCE in interface configuration mode does not exist.

14. ☑ **D.** It is an identifier for the EIGRP process and must be the same on all routers that are expected to share routing updates. The EIGRP autonomous system identifies the EIGRP process on the router as well as being a unique identifier for the routing domain. All routers within a routing domain must be configured with the same ASN. However, a router may participate in more than one routing domain and thus may run multiple EIGRP processes, each with its own ASN.

☒ **A** is incorrect because all routers in a given network are not necessarily members of the same routing domain. **B** is incorrect since the ASN is unique to a routing domain, so all routers within the same routing domain must share the same number. Therefore, it is not locally significant. **C** is incorrect since the number of routers in an internetwork is insignificant.

15. ☑ **B.** The NETWORK statement identifies the local network to advertise to EIGRP neighbors.

☒ **A** is incorrect because some routing protocols do use a NEIGHBOR statement, which is used to configure neighbors on nonbroadcast media or to adjust parameters for specific neighbors. However, since EIGRP uses reliable multicast for neighbor discovery and maintenance, it is not required. The command itself is supported by EIGRP but has no effect on operation. **C** is incorrect since the AREA 0 RANGE command is used to identify an address range for an OSPF area. **D** is incorrect because the IP AS-PATH ACCESS-LIST statement is used to define a BGP AS-Path filter that can be applied to BGP inbound and outbound routing advertisements. This command has nothing to do with EIGRP operation.

Monitoring and Verifying EIGRP Operations

16. ☑ **C.** DEBUG EIGRP NEIGHBORS. Neighbor discovery and maintenance issues can be viewed using DEBUG EIGRP NEIGHBORS. If a neighbor disappears due to hold-time expiration, you will notice it in the debug trace. You can then check other configuration parameters and correct any anomalies you find.

☒ **A** is incorrect because the command WRITE ERASE is used to erase the startup configuration. **B** is incorrect because, if the neighbor is declared dead, nothing will be listed for that neighbor in the topology table. **D** is incorrect because the task here is to determine why the neighbor is dropping. The IP EIGRP HOLD-TIME command can be used on the interface configuration to fix the problem by increasing the neighbor hold-time.

17. ☑ **A.** By looking at the routing table using the SHOW IP ROUTE command. The SHOW IP ROUTE command determines whether or not a route to the destination has been installed in the router's routing table.

☒ **B** is incorrect since the DEBUG EIGRP FSM command is used to troubleshoot the DUAL calculations. **C** is incorrect because the RELOAD command is used reboot the router. **D** is incorrect because modification of the hello interval affects neighbor discovery and shows no information concerning the routing table.

18. ☑ **A.** SHOW IP PROTOCOLS. The SHOW IP PROTOCOLS command gives pertinent information concerning the configured IP routing protocols running on the router. In the case of EIGRP, the command displays the values to which K1–K5 are set in the line marked "EIGRP metric weight."

    ☒ **B, C,** and **D** are incorrect because these commands show no information concerning the metric weights configured.

19. ☑ **B** and **C.** SHOW IP EIGRP EVENTS and DEBUG EIGRP FSM. Remember that the SHOW IP EIGRP EVENTS command lists the last 500 EIGRP events in reverse chronological order and shows information on metric calculation, updates received and sent, and installation of routes into the routing table. The DEBUG EIGRP FSM command provides additional information concerning metric calculations and DUAL operations, including feasible distance, feasible successors, and path queries.

    ☒ **A** is incorrect since SHOW IP ROUTE is used merely to show what information is already installed in the routing table. **D** is incorrect because SHOW IP PROTOCOLS gives overall information concerning the currently running IP routing protocols.

20. ☑ **C.** The SHOW IP EIGRP NEIGHBORS command is used to display the EIGRP neighbors of a router as well as other information such as hold-time and RTO.

    ☒ **A** is incorrect because the topology table does not necessary contain all neighbors, especially if no neighbors carry routes to a given destination. **B** is incorrect because DEBUG EIGRP PACKET can be used to determine why a neighbor association might not be behaving correctly, rather than to simply verify that a neighbor association has been formed. **D** is incorrect because the command DEBUG EIGRP DUAL does not exist.

LAB ANSWER

Do not be confused by the fact that there are redundant connections to the production network. After configuration of EIGRP, each router will view these as two different neighbors, one on each interface, with the IP address of the remote end of the point-to-point link shown as the neighbor's address.

Since the editorial router is the central router, it requires two network statements, one for the editorial network itself and the other for the point-to-point networks. Therefore, look at the configuration of the central router first; it is shown in Figure 6-27.

It is important that the bandwidth statements be set correctly on the interfaces, since this is where EIGRP gets the bandwidth information for metric calculations. Next, since this is the central router, we advertise the editorial network (192.168.2.0/24) as well as the point-to-point networks (192.168.1.0).

```
Editorial (central) Router:

interface eth0/0
  description editorial lan
  ip address 192.168.2.1 255.255.255.0
bandwidth 10000
!
interface ser1/0
  description 512k to production
  ip address 192.168.1.129 255.255.255.252
bandwidth 512
!
interface ser1/1
  description 128k backup to production
  ip address 192.168.1.5 255.255.255.252
bandwidth 128
!
interface ser1/2
  description 56k to admin
  ip address 192.168.1.1 255.255.255.252
bandwidth 56
!
router eigrp 33
  network 192.168.1.0
  network 192.168.2.0
!
```

Next we look at the configuration for the production department, which is shown in Figure 6-28. Notice that in this case, although we are advertising only the production network of 192.168.3.0/24, we must also include 192.168.1.0 in our NETWORK statement to form a neighbor adjacency across that interface. Since the local point-to-point networks are directly connected to the router, the connected route gets entered into the routing table.

Let's now look at the situation with the redundant connections. You might wonder if the central router might see only one neighbor and thus potentially see the incorrect one. The quick and simple answer to this question is no. With this configuration active, the central router will see two distinct neighbors, 192.168.1.130 on its ser1/0 interface and 192.168.1.6 on its ser1/1 interface. Even though both of these neighbors (the production router) are advertising the production network, EIGRP will perform its metric calculations nevertheless and prefer the link across the 512k connection. Since the other neighbor, across the 128k link, is still advertising the network, if the 512k line goes down, there will still be a path to the production network.

FIGURE 6-28

Production
department
router
configuration

```
Production Router:

interface eth0
  description production lan
  ip address 192.168.3.1 255.255.255.0
  bandwidth 10000
!
interface ser0
  description 512k to central
  ip address 192.168.1.130 255.255.255.252
  bandwidth 512
!
interface ser1
  description 128k backup to central
  ip address 192.168.1.6 255.255.255.252
  bandwidth 128
!
router eigrp 33
  network 192.168.1.0
  network 192.168.3.0
!
```

Last, the administrative router's configuration is very straightforward and is no different from the exercise we performed earlier in Chapter 6. This configuration is shown in Figure 6-29.

FIGURE 6-29

Administrative
router
configuration

```
Administrative Router:

interface eth0
  description admin lan
  ip address 192.168.4.1 255.255.255.0
bandwidth 10000
!
interface ser0
  description 56k to central
  ip address 192.168.1.2 255.255.255.252
  bandwidth 56
!
router eigrp 33
  network 192.168.1.0
  network 192.168.4.0
!
```

Notice that all three routers are in the same routing domain, so they all use the same ASN. You can confirm the neighbor associations with SHOW IP EIGRP NEIGHBORS, which will resemble the result shown in Figure 6-30.

The central router has NETWORK statements configured for the editorial network as well as the point-to-point networks and advertises these to its neighbors. The remote networks advertise only their local networks back to the central router. Thus this configuration satisfies the requirements of Books-R-Us Publishing.

FIGURE 6-30   Neighbor relationships can be confirmed at the central site with SHOW IP EIGRP NEIGHBORS

```
editorial>show ip eigrp neighbors
IP-EIGRP neighbors for process 33
H   Address              Interface    Hold Uptime    SRTT    RTO   Q  Seq
                                      (sec)          (ms)          Cnt Num
2   192.168.1.2          Se1/2        132 0d01h      1032    5000  0   201
1   192.168.1.6          Se1/1        142 0d01h       993    5000  0   109
0   192.168.1.130        Se1/0        151 0d01h       512    5000  0   554
editorial>
```

7

Advanced EIGRP Behavior and Configuration

CERTIFICATION OBJECTIVES

Enhanced Interior Gateway Routing Protocol (EIGRP) is an updated version of Cisco's IGRP. Enhanced IGRP arrived to meet the demand of today's changing large-scale networks by providing a diverse protocol. In this chapter you will discover the features that make EIGRP a dependable protocol to be considered for all IP, IPX, and AppleTalk networks. You will also learn about EIGRP IP address summarization and manual summarization and the benefits they provide.

This chapter not only provides you with the knowledge to prepare for the exam, but it will also give you advanced knowledge of how EIGRP works and an understanding of what to expect of EIGRP in networks of any size.

CERTIFICATION OBJECTIVE 7.01

Considerations for a Large-Scale Network Using EIGRP

Enhanced Interior Gateway Routing Protocol was designed to handle the stress of today's large-scale network environments. Based on fast convergence, the protocol's ability to consume very little bandwidth, support growing networks, and consume very little CPU utilization make EIGRP a very scalable protocol.

Fast convergence is an important factor in a large-scale network. The ability of routing protocols to quickly adapt and provide updates of the routes in response to changes that occur is very critical. Slow convergence can induce routing loops and possibly even cause a network outage. The fast convergence of EIGRP is due to the use of the Diffusing Update Algorithm (DUAL). As discussed in Chapter 6, DUAL provides EIGRP with the ability to keep backup routes within the routing table. EIGRP recalculates and updates only the few affected routers in the topology. This provides a timely response to link outages, enhancing the network's stability.

Another notable attribute of EIGRP is its ability to handle large networks while consuming less bandwidth than the distance-vector and link-state protocols. As with OSPF, EIGRP sends partial updates only when there is a change in the metric or route availability to the destination network. This helps cut down the amount of bandwidth consumed by periodic updates of large routing tables. In today's networks, which are continually growing in size, routing protocols that can scale a network consisting of many routers are in great demand. EIGRP provides network administrators with the ability to achieve very large network configurations. Many have found that using RIP as a routing protocol can result in many limitations. One such limitation is the 15-hop limit, whereas EIGRP's 255 hop limit allows networks to grow in size with virtually no limit.

EIGRP's ability to minimize CPU usage occurs through the use of DUAL. Partial updates sent using EIGRP's routing algorithm result in less bandwidth and CPU usage. The load on the CPU depends highly on the size of the network's routing updates and its stability.

Today's networks need a routing protocol that is diverse in nature. EIGRP supports Novell IPX, IP, and AppleTalk protocols. Many of today's large-scale networks support more than one protocol, which makes diversity a major issue when you are deciding on a suitable routing protocol. OSPF, a link-state protocol, provides support for IP-only environments.

Using the Proper Bandwidth for the WAN Interfaces

EIGRP routing metrics are computed by the total delay and the minimum bandwidth on the path to a destination network. It is not recommended that you configure other metrics, because doing so can cause routing loops in your network. Using EIGRP, the bandwidth and delay metrics are determined by the values configured on the interfaces used to reach the destination network. EIGRP calculates the total metric using the bandwidth and delay metrics via the following formula:

Bandwidth = (10000000/Bandwidth) x 256
Delay = Delay x 256
Metric = Bandwidth + Delay

exam
ⓦatch

The exam will expect you to know how EIGRP calculates its metrics to determine the best path.

EXERCISE 7-1

How Metrics Dictate Traffic Paths Using Eigrp

You are a network engineer for a major law firm. Your firm would like an additional circuit connecting to the Chicago branch office for redundancy purposes. The company would like you to find out to which path all traffic would default, without you having to alter any statements in the router. Using Figure 7-1, calculate which path to Site B possesses the highest metric.

Solution:

Path A:

> Bandwidth/56k   Delay/2000
> Formula: Bandwidth = (10000000/56) x 256
> Delay = 2000 x 256
> Metric = Bandwidth + Delay = 46226285.71

Path B:

> Bandwidth/128k   Delay/1000
> Formula: Bandwidth = (10000000/128) x 256
> Delay = 1000 x 256
> Metric = Bandwidth + Delay = 20256000

Path A, which is the original circuit, contains the better metric. EIGRP will continue to advertise Route A as the preferred path.

FIGURE 7-1

Law firm's topology

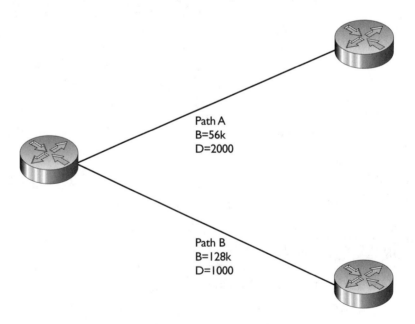

Good Addressing

Support of manageable IP addressing is another feature of EIGRP. Defining an address space for use by EIGRP is important when you are developing the routing architecture. EIGRP's support for route summarization and variable-length subnet masks (VLSM) makes it possible to save address space and provide an appropriate address scheme for future growth. Route summarization reduces router overhead, routing table sizes, and the bandwidth required for EIGRP to send routing updates.

Hierarchical Network Design

In networking, tasks such as addressing and managing devices are made simple using a hierarchical design. The following points describe the three-layer internetworking model:

- **Core layer** The central backbone of the network. Provides stability and reliability to an internetwork.
- **Distribution layer** Provides access to services. Most commonly relates to the campus backbone.
- **Access layer** Provides access to the network from remote segments.

Network topologies can be viewed in two ways: flat or hierarchical. EIGRP is a flat topology by default. Flat routing topologies use network addressing to divide large networks into smaller, interconnected networks. Even though EIGRP can be used in a flat topology design, using the summarization features of EIGRP, you can make it into a hierarchical network. As an example, you can have a network with 25 routers in every state. In Ohio, every remote site flows up to the two main sites, Columbus and Dayton. Ohio has been given the block of 10.3.0.0 /16 address space and has decided to use /24 for all of its Ethernets and /30 subnets for the serial links. At the main sites leading back to the other sites, we can use EIGRP summarization techniques to announce 10.3.0.0 /16 and suppress all the more specific 10.3.0.0 subnets.

Other flat routing protocols are RIP, RIP2, and IGRP. OSPF and IS-IS are considered hierarchical designs, meaning that routers are placed in areas as opposed to segregating with network addressing. Using a hierarchical approach to addressing provides your network with the ability to expand without having to reassign a new addressing structure.

exam
ⓦatch
You should be able to determine the difference between a flat network and a hierarchical network.

on the
Ⓙob
Having a network with a hierarchical structure and using proper addressing aids in properly documenting and troubleshooting a network. Many network troubleshooting software packages on the market can aid you in supporting your network, but these network aids rely on a structured network environment using proper network addressing.

Sufficient Memory on the Router

This section describes why EIGRP is more "memory friendly" than other routing protocols. EIGRP is a hybrid protocol. It uses distance-vector metrics but emphasizes more accurate metrics than conventional distance-vector protocols. This

---

FROM THE CLASSROOM

Hierarchical Network Schemes

When designing or restructuring a network, you must know the importance of a hierarchical scheme and what it brings to a large-scale network. Without hierarchy, proper route summarization cannot exist. Your means of defining your network are limited. You and your fellow engineers' ability to read your network through routing tables, determine problems, and benchmark your network's convergence is also affected. Through proper hierarchical addressing schemes, you should be able to identify your core routers and also

detect missing routes that would not be so easy to recognize in flat topologies.

Hierarchical addressing also aids in providing a stable network, limiting your routers' adjacency responsibilities by cutting down on query and update traffic. In a hierarchical scheme, you are also cutting down your chances of links that become stuck in active (SIA). Due to the fact that your traffic is either flowing up or down your hierarchical tree, providing a limited but stable pattern for traffic and packet flow results in timely delivery and network query response.

—Derek Winchester, CCNP, CCNA, MCSE

balanced hybrid protocol is exclusively a proprietary creation of Cisco Systems, designed to decrease the load placed by distance-vector and link-state protocols and delivering a much more stable routing protocol. EIGRP converges faster than distance-vector protocols but avoids the overheads of link-state updates. EIGRP obtains the partial routing tables from topology databases that are exchanged between peer routers on the network. This is different from distance-vector protocols, which process entire updated routing tables, consuming more CPU cycles and more memory than EIGRP. Due to EIGRP's algorithm, CPU computation is made more efficient, resulting in improved memory utilization. On a large network containing more than 500 routers without a hierarchical design, EIGRP can consume 4MB in size.

Sufficient Bandwidth on WAN Interfaces to Handle Update Traffic

Using sufficient bandwidth on WAN interfaces is very important. When you design a network, you want to make sure that all your paths are able to withstand the amount of traffic a network can deliver on average during a working day.

Compare a network to using our streets and highways in society. If your morning commute consists of driving on a major interstate, your trip would be hampered if the interstate were controlled by a speed limit of 30mph. In fact, so would your nerves. Congestion on the highway would be considerably high, rendering that highway commute just about useless. You would probably have to leave for work hours before you normally would if you typically drive 60mph and higher and providing you have an 8-to-5 job like most of us.

Designing networks works the same way. Your high-speed links as well as your low-speed links must be able to provide users with enough bandwidth to survive bursts of traffic and prevent congestion, just as interstate highways do. To the other extreme, too much bandwidth should be avoided also. In communications today, bandwidth is expensive, so you should properly rate your network to ensure that you are not over- or under-using your links.

Limiting the Update and Query Range

Another way of optimizing EIGRP to perform in a large-scale network is by limiting updates and queries. Updates and queries are used to establish adjacencies within a

SCENARIO & SOLUTION

How can I check to see if EIGRP is correctly summarizing routes?	Using the SHOW IP ROUTE EIGRP command, you can display all IP addresses and the entries for EIGRP. This command displays the IP subnet and the bits used to summarize the network portion of the address.
How do I verify the load placed on an interface to see whether or not my router is dropping packets and/or traffic?	You can verify several different ways. SHOW INTERFACE SHOW FRAME-RELAY PVC
How do I change the hello time intervals on my router for EIGRP?	Use this command: IP HELLO-INTERVAL EIGRP *AS NUMBER SECONDS*

network. They are also used to tell a router when an adjacency is no longer valid. Providing limitations on updates and queries provides the router with smaller tables, making it less responsible for routes or links that the router deems unimportant to its network. Updates and queries can be limited by physical design of a network or by the use of bit boundaries, established by using route summarization and VLSM. We will discuss these topics in greater detail later in this chapter.

CERTIFICATION OBJECTIVE 7.02

EIGRP IP Address Summarization

In a typical large-scale network using EIGRP, maximizing the address space assists in reducing resource utilization and maximizes route summarization. As mentioned previously in this chapter, the default IP address summarization technique for EIGRP is a classful boundary summarization. Classful boundary summarizations, usually known as *bit boundaries,* use the first 3 bits in an IP address to differentiate Class A, B, and C networks. Classful boundary summarization works only on networks that utilize a contiguous IP addressing scheme and will not work in a discontiguous environment.

The most efficient design of an EIGRP network is achieved by utilizing a hierarchical addressing scheme. EIGRP supports VLSM. We must disable the automatic classful boundary summarization feature to do use hierarchical addressing. Using VLSM, route summarization is maximized at the backbone area. The use of VLSM and route summarization in a hierarchical scheme designs a network to which you can add new routers in the future. Route summarization increases the stability of an EIGRP network and keeps routing changes within a network. Classful route summarization is enabled by default using EIGRP but can be disabled for manual summarization.

Let's now discus how to configure route summarization and its various characteristics.

Disabling Automatic Summarization

Disabling automatic summarization displays information on all routes regardless of subnet masks. This information could be useful in determining specific routes that could provide information needed for troubleshooting. Although the router would use more memory to hold such a large table without summarization, it could make it much easier to troubleshoot a route issue in a network. The following example is how you disable automatic summarization:

```
Router#(config) Router EIGPR 1
Router#(config) No auto-summary
```

EIGRP Manual Summarization

EIGRP allows you to summarize internal and external routes using any bit boundary. Manual summarization (discussed in more detail in a moment) gives added control to the way your network routes will be summarized. You can provide summarization to only those subnets in your network that consume a great deal of your routing tables or for which you simply don't need to see details.

The EIGRP Interface Command for Summarization

EIGRP can summarize routes on any router in the network. This is different when using OSPF. In OSPF, internal routes are summarized on *area border routers,* and external routes are summarized on *autonomous system border routers.* This limitation can prove unhelpful in discontiguous networks. You can summarize the whole network using EIGRP, or you can summarize subnets on a per-interface basis.

The following command is used by EIGRP when it announces an update out of an EIGRP interface. Using this command suppresses the more specific entries that fall in the range of summarization. If a network is not a subset of summarization, it will be announced as a standard entry in the EIGRP router's routing table. The interface command for summarization using EIGRP is as follows:

`IP summary-address EIGRP` `autonomous-system-number address mask`

AUTONOMOUS-SYSTEM-NUMBER specifies the EIGRP AS number used by the network. ADDRESS MASK specifies the IP address and the mask that is to be summarized.

Benefits of the EIGRP Summarization Method

The benefits of EIGRP summarization as discussed in this section are its ability to support future growth in networks and its ability to preserve bandwidth and CPU utilization. In addition, compared with OSPF, EIGRP offers more flexibility as to where you can use summarization.

Examination of the IP Routing Table with EIGRP Summarization

The following is an example of an output of a network router running EIGRP:

```
Router#sho ip rou
Codes: C - connected, S - static, I - IGRP, R - RIP, M - mobile, B - BGP
       D - EIGRP, EX - EIGRP external, O - OSPF, IA - OSPF inter area
       N1 - OSPF NSSA external type 1, N2 - OSPF NSSA external type 2
       E1 - OSPF external type 1, E2 - OSPF external type 2, E - EGP
       i - IS-IS, L1 - IS-IS level-1, L2 - IS-IS level-2, * - candidate default
       U - per-user static route, o - ODR

 Gateway of last resort is not set

      172.16.0.0/24 is subnetted, 1 subnets
C        172.16.3.0 is directly connected, Ethernet0
      10.0.0.0/8 is variably subnetted, 16 subnets, 2 masks
D        10.1.11.0/24 [90/409600] via 172.16.3.101, 00:01:40, Ethernet0
D        10.1.10.0/24 [90/409600] via 172.16.3.101, 00:01:40, Ethernet0
D        10.1.9.0/24 [90/409600] via 172.16.3.101, 00:01:40, Ethernet0
D        10.1.8.0/24 [90/409600] via 172.16.3.101, 00:01:40, Ethernet0
D        10.1.15.0/24 [90/409600] via 172.16.3.101, 00:01:40, Ethernet0
D        10.1.14.0/24 [90/409600] via 172.16.3.101, 00:01:40, Ethernet0
```

```
D        10.1.13.0/24 [90/409600] via 172.16.3.101, 00:01:40, Ethernet0
D        10.1.12.0/24 [90/409600] via 172.16.3.101, 00:01:41, Ethernet0
D        10.1.3.0/24 [90/409600] via 172.16.3.101, 00:01:41, Ethernet0
D        10.1.2.0/24 [90/409600] via 172.16.3.101, 00:01:41, Ethernet0
D        10.1.1.0/24 [90/409600] via 172.16.3.101, 00:01:41, Ethernet0
D        10.1.7.0/24 [90/409600] via 172.16.3.101, 00:01:42, Ethernet0
D        10.1.6.0/24 [90/409600] via 172.16.3.101, 00:01:42, Ethernet0
D        10.1.5.0/24 [90/409600] via 172.16.3.101, 00:01:42, Ethernet0
D        10.1.4.0/24 [90/409600] via 172.16.3.101, 00:01:43, Ethernet0
D        10.1.0.0/16 is a summary, 00:01:42, Null0
```

From this example, notice that the current network uses route summarization. If autosummary were on for Ethernet 0 (network 172.16.3.0), only network 10.0.0.0/8 would be announced out of that interface. You would have problems if there were other routers out E0, which had network 10.0.0.0 subnets. If the IP SUMMARY-ADDRESS EIGRP 100 10.1.0.0 255.255.0.0 command is applied to Ethernet 0, this router will only advertise the summarization. Any route in the routing table, which falls between 10.1.0.0 and 10.1.255.255, would be suppressed. All other routes including 172.16.3.0/24 would be announced. This router is basically saying to the rest of the internetwork that it has all of network 10.1.0.0 /16 behind it. Hopefully, this is true, or you can have routing problems.

If someone else owns 10.1.200.0/24 and is also announcing 10.1.0.0/16 with a summarization command, a router in the middle of these two routers will not know where to go for a specific route such as 10.1.12.0/24. If the router with 10.1.200.0/24 announces it correctly as a specific route, this router and all other routers will have two entries concerning these networks—10.1.200.0/24 and 10.1.0.0/16—and will use the longest match to figure out how to get to the subnets of 10.1.0.0. Notice the Null0 entry. All traffic not specifically destined for the network is sent to the Null0 interface, which is essentially a bit bucket.

Null0 Route Removal

EIGRP is a classless protocol, which means that it looks for the longest match when selecting a route from the routing table. The null route is generated automatically by the EIGRP summarization command and will not be removed from the routing table unless the EIGRP summarization command is removed.

EIGRP announces only the summarized route, which hides changes of more specific networks, such as in the example concerning the summarization of 10.1.0.0 /16. If 10.1.12.0 goes down, Router A—the router summarizing with 10.1.0.0 /16—knows about the problem and goes into active state to find another pathway to 10.1.12.0 (if one exists). Other routers out Ethernet 0 never learned that this network is down because the details of it are suppressed with the summarization. The other routers will continue to forward traffic to the summarizing router for network 10.1.12.0 /24. If Router A had a default route to another router (potentially out Ethernet 0) and did not have the null 0 statement in the routing table and network 10.1.12.0 /24 was down, a routing loop could occur.

When EIGRP creates the summarization, it places the null route in the routing table so that it can hide from its neighbors changes to suppressed routes. Once network 10.1.12.0 goes down, Router A removes it from its routing table. A router out Ethernet 0 will forward traffic to Router A, destined for network 10.1.12.0. Router A would discard these packets because of the match against 10.1.0.0 /16 going to the Null0 interface instead of the 0.0.0.0 /0 interface.

exam
Ⓦatch

For the exam, you will be expected to be able to identify the elements of a routing table. In the preceding example, a null route is depicted and explained.

EIGRP Load Balancing

If you are like most of us when you drive to work in that morning traffic, you wonder why do so many people use the same route you do. You think, "Where does my hard-earned tax money go? It's not going toward developing alternate routes, that's for sure." But just think: if everyone had four or more routes to choose from, you wouldn't have so much time to think about what you'll be having for dinner.

This example can be extended to load balancing. *Load balancing* involves spreading traffic through four or more paths, all reaching the destination in a timely manner. Load balancing breaks down congestion and, in return, adds stability to a fast-paced, high-traffic network. Let's look at the components of load balancing.

Load Balancing with EIGRP

Load balancing allows a router to take advantage of multiple paths to a given destination. The paths stem from either static routes or routing protocols such as OSPF, RIP, IGRP, and EIGRP.

Maximum Number of Equal-Cost Routes in the Routing Table

Load balancing can occur in up to six equal-cost paths. Some routing protocols have different limits; EIGRP's default setting is four paths. You can change the maximum number of paths EIGRP uses by executing the command MAX-PATHS under the EIGRP process. The following is the syntax for this command:

```
Router eigrp 1
Maximum-paths maximum
```

Default Number of Equal-Cost Routes Allowed

The default number of equal cost routes is four paths. Although this value can be changed, EIGRP recommends that four paths is sufficient for proper load balancing.

Unequal-Cost Load Balancing with EIGRP

Unequal-cost load balancing provides load balancing in up to four paths of varied metrics. Only feasible paths are used for load balancing and are contained in the routing table. This limits the number of situations in which unequal-cost load balancing can be used.

Considerations for Using VARIANCE

The VARIANCE command is used to define how much worse an alternate path can be before it is disallowed. VARIANCE, by default, is set to one (in equal-cost load balancing). Using the variance feature in load balancing, traffic can be balanced across all feasible paths and immediately converge to another path if one of the paths fail. Variance controls load balancing in an EIGRP network.

The VARIANCE Command

The VARIANCE command is as follows:

```
Variance multiplier
Multiplier- default value is one (equal cost load balancing)
value can be from 1-28.
Defines metric value.
To disable metric use:
No variance
```

Load Balancing Unequal CIR (Committed Information Rate)

You are a network engineer working for a major consulting group. Your client would like you to implement load balancing on his network. Load balancing will be done over four links of unequal metrics:

- S0: 1000
- S1: 1000
- S2: 2000
- S3: 2200

Solution: Using the VARIANCE command, you will be able to alter the multiplier to make all four of these links appear to the router as equal.

1. VARIANCE, by default, uses a multiplier of 1, which states that all the links are equal. In this scenario, all links must use a metric of 1000, because 1 x 1000 equals 1000. We see that Serial 0 and Serial 1 use the same metric, but we are trying to incorporate Serial 2 and Serial 3 using load balancing. If we use a multiplier of 2, that would place Serial 2 in the loop. We would then have three links used for load balancing, so the multiplier we end up using is 3.

2. To activate load balancing on this particular router, we use the following command:

```
Router(config)# variance 3
```

This command will enable load balancing using the default four links, providing that the links fall within the multiplier of 3.

SCENARIO & SOLUTION

How do I monitor EIGRP Neighbor Adjacency changes?	The SHOW EIGRP NEIGHBOR command lists all the adjacency information that pertains to EIGRP.
What is the best way to document and keep track of adjacency changes in my network?	Adjacency changes are normally not logged by Cisco IOS software. Logging is enabled using the command LOG-NEIGHBOR-CHANGES.
I am seeing error messages on my router, stating "%DUAL-5-NBRCHANGE." What does this message mean?	This message is an identifier that indicates the EIGRP process ID (mentioned after the message) has recognized a change in the neighbor status. Basically, it identifies an adjacency change.

CERTIFICATION OBJECTIVE 7.03

EIGRP WAN Optimization

EIGRP is suited for many different topologies. EIGRP scales well and provides extremely fast convergence in a properly designed network. Complete EIGRP WAN optimization is achieved when the proper bandwidth allotted on links coincides with the amount of traffic routed in the network. This optimization is needed to support the overall workload of any organization.

Using Bandwidth Statement

In this section, you will learn why the BANDWIDTH command is a very valuable command in link-state and hybrid routing protocols. EIGRP as well as OSPF use the BANDWIDTH statement to calculate the best path to use to reach a routing destination. You will also see why altering the BANDWIDTH statement in order to force a protocol to be the best path is not recommended. EIGRP, as a default setting, uses only 50 percent of the bandwidth setting for sending updates, which ensures that routing overhead will not monopolize the slow-speed links.

As a network engineer, documentation can be your best friend. Lack of it could be your worst nightmare. All changes to routers must be documented as much as possible. In numerous cases, changed hello timers have caused many large networks to completely shut down. In 90 percent of those cases, the result was that the engineer who changed the timers didn't document it. When convergence stopped on a dime, engineers were still looking for answers.

Default Bandwidth Setting for a Serial Interface

Serial interfaces on a router use the default bandwidth parameter of 1.5 mbps. This value should be changed to reflect the actual bandwidth of the link connected to the serial interfaces. Failure to reflect the actual bandwidth could result in network degradation caused by regular traffic as well as EIGRP packets.

NBMA Bandwidth Settings

Frame Relay, X.25, and ATM are nonbroadcast multiaccess (NBMA) interfaces and should be configured properly to prevent loss of EIGRP packets in a switched network. Three rules to remember when configuring NBMA interfaces are as follows:

- EIGRP traffic cannot exceed the specified capacity of the virtual circuit.
- Total EIGRP traffic for all virtual circuits cannot exceed the total actual bandwidth of the interface.
- Bandwidth for EIGRP on all virtual circuits must be configured the same way in each direction.

Let's look at each of these rules in more detail. Rule 1 specifies that EIGRP traffic cannot exceed the specified capacity of the virtual circuit. This means that altering the BANDWIDTH statement to give a particular interface higher preference for metric reasons should be seriously considered before you take action. You are risking sending more traffic over a link than the interface can handle, which will result in slow convergence caused by a loss of EIGRP packets and traffic loss due to congestion.

Rule 2 relates to this issue as well. You must pay close attention to the bandwidth specified for each virtual circuit and make sure that the interface accurately represents the total bandwidth of the link. Failure to do so could result in congestion of the link and slow convergence.

Rule 3 states that the BANDWIDTH statement defined for one end of a virtual circuit must reflect what is defined for the same virtual circuit at the other end. Accurate representation of the actual bandwidth at both ends balances your network's traffic flow and helps you accurately troubleshoot any convergence issue your network experiences.

BANDWIDTH Statement Per Subinterfaces   Each subinterface should be configured using its own BANDWIDTH statement. In this case, all the subinterfaces should equal the amount of bandwidth allotted for the overall interface. The following sections discuss the "how and why" of configuring point-to-point subinterfaces and multipoint subinterfaces.

Limiting the Percentage of Bandwidth EIGRP Uses

Accurate bandwidth should be configured for WAN interfaces using the BANDWIDTH statement. By default, EIGRP will use no more than half (50 percent) of the actual bandwidth. Configuring higher or lower than the actual bandwidth will slow convergence and degrade the network considerably. If configured higher than the actual bandwidth, a loss of EIGRP packets could occur. The retransmission of these packets will actually slow the convergence of the network.

Configuring a WAN interface lower than the actual bandwidth, depending on the size of the routing tables, could cause convergence to be so slow that SIA detection will be triggered. This could prevent the network from converging further. SIA is occurring when the following message is displayed:

```
%DUAL-3-SIA: Route XXX stuck-in-active state in IP-EIGRP YY. Cleaning up
```

The IP BANDWIDTH-PERCENT EIGRP Command

The BANDWIDTH-PERCENT command dictates the percentage of the configured bandwidth EIGRP will use. The following is the command syntax:

```
Ip bandwidth-percent EIGRP <AS-number> <percentage>
```

Point-to-Point Subinterfaces with CIR Per Subinterface

Point-to-point configuration allows for more control over virtual circuits. Interfaces can be divided into subinterfaces, thus allowing bandwidth to be configured separately for each virtual circuit. Each interface should have the bandwidth configured with a value no greater than the actual available bandwidth. If the interface is oversubscribed, bandwidth must be divided among the subinterfaces, not to exceed the overall bandwidth associated with the interface.

Using subinterfaces provides more control over how much bandwidth a virtual circuit is committed to use. The benefit of giving each subinterface its own bandwidth statement is that EIGRP can differentiate per virtual circuit on the amount of routing traffic each circuit can handle.

Multipoint Circuit with Equal CIR Per Neighbor

When using a multipoint circuit, the BANDWIDTH statement is given for the interface. On a multipoint circuit, all PVCs are mapped to the interface; therefore, they are controlled at the interface level. Since there are no subinterfaces, you must specify bandwidth for the overall link. The bandwidth should equal the sum of all the PVCs' bandwidth. For example, if you have four PVCs on a Frame Relay T1 and the PVCs are all 56 kbps CIR, your interface bandwidth should be set at 224 kbps. The command should look like this:

```
Router(config-if) bandwidth 224
```

In this scenario, as opposed to subinterfaces, EIGRP divides your BANDWIDTH statement by the number of virtual circuits to determine the rate of EIGRP routing update packets to transmit. This is fine if all virtual circuits have the same CIR, but it can cause problems if this interface has unequal CIR for some virtual circuits.

Multipoint Circuit with Unequal CIR Per Neighbor (Not Recommended)

If you are using a multipoint circuit and all the virtual circuits have unequal CIR, it is *not* recommended that you add each value for the overall bandwidth. The bandwidth should be evenly configured with the lowest common denominator. For example, a T1 access line has four virtual circuits—three at 56k and one at 256k—so the lowest denominator would be 56k. Therefore, EIGRP traffic will not overload each virtual circuit. The formula for setting the bandwith for unequal CIR using a multipoint circuit is as follows:

```
(Lowest CIR * number of PVCs)
```

Each virtual circuit can have up to 32k of EIGRP traffic at any time, but this formula can slow convergence on the circuit that has a 256k CIR because, if configured correctly, it could use up 128k of the circuit for EIGRP routing updates.

Multipoint Circuit with Unequal CIR Per Neighbor (Recommended)

The method of configuring a multipoint circuit that utilizes virtual circuits that differ in CIR involves putting the virtual circuits that are different onto their own point-to-point subinterface, then configuring the multipoint circuit with the remaining virtual circuits that have equal CIR. This method is highly recommended.

EXERCISE 7-3

Configuring Frame Relay

You are a network engineer for a major advertising firm. Your manager has just given you a project. He would like you to configure a router for a Frame Relay circuit that needs to be turned up. The circuit will connect to four different locations. The line is subscribed at 256k. One of the sites subscribes to a 56k CIR; the other three are to be given a 32k CIR each. Configure the appropriate EIGRP and Frame Relay statements for the core site that has these four virtual circuits.
Solution:
The solution is to create subinterfaces for Frame Relay, as shown in Figure 7-2. The first subinterface could be the multipoint with the three virtual circuits that have a 32k CIR each. The correct BANDWIDTH statement would be BANDWIDTH 96. EIGRP takes the BANDWIDTH statement for the interface/subinterface and divides it equally among all three virtual circuits. The second subinterface would be the point-to-point configuration with a bandwidth of 56 because it has only one virtual circuit.

EIGRP will now send only up to 16k per second of EIGRP update traffic over each of the three virtual circuits associated with the multipoint subinterface and will send up to 28k per second of update traffic over the point-to-point subinterface.

Core A

```
Hostname CoreA

Interface serial 0
No ip address
Encapsulation frame-relay
Interface s0.1 multipoint
Bandwidth 96
Ip address 10.1.1.1 255.255.255.0
frame-relay interface-dlci 731
frame-relay interface-dlci 732
frame-relay interface-dlci 733
Interface s0.2 point-to-point
Bandwidth 56
Ip address 10.1.2.1 255.255.255.0
frame-relay interface-dlci 734
Router EIGRP 1
Network 10.0.0.0
```

FIGURE 7-2

Subinterfaces for
Frame Relay

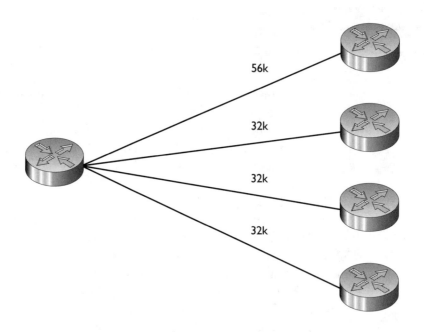

SCENARIO & SOLUTION

How do I summarize a route for advertisements out specific interfaces?	Further summarization of routes is possible through the use of the following interface configuration command: IP summary-address EIGRP *as-number address mask*
When supporting IPX traffic, what is the command to only display IPX routes?	Show IPX Route EIGRP
When troubleshooting IPX you will arrive at a lot of situations in which you will troubleshoot server SAP's on your network; what is the command used to view all SAPs that are received by your router?	Show IPX Server

exam
ⓦatch

It is important to know how to configure bandwidth on a given interface as well as the result it will have on the network.

CERTIFICATION OBJECTIVE 7.04

EIGRP Query Issues

In this section, you will develop an understanding of how a router running EIGRP is able to maintain accurate routing tables in a network. Let's begin by defining the term *query*. A query is a message used to inquire about routes that exist or do not exist in a routing environment. For the exam, you need to know the reason that a routing table is important and how not having accurate routing tables can greatly affect a network.

The EIGRP Query Process

A *path* consists of a source router and a destination router. To maintain adjacency, a router sends hello packets to its neighboring routers. Hello packets are sent out at a default of 60 seconds on low-bandwidth connections and at 5 seconds for high-speed connections. To determine a path, the router uses metrics. The path with the highest metric becomes the successor; the path with the second highest becomes the feasible successor. If the successor goes down, it is unable to send hello packets at its specified interval to its neighboring routers.

When a neighboring router realizes that it has no response from the successor, it then recognizes that the path to the destination is down. The router then sends a query to the successor. Of course, if the successor is down, that query is not answered. Then the source router sends a query through the feasible router asking for a route to the destination. If the route exists, the feasible successor responds with a message called an *update packet.* If the route doesn't exist, it marks the destination as unreachable and sends the packet back so that the source can update its table to reflect that fact.

In a hierarchical design, summarization limits the way one router recognizes another router due to subnet mask limitation. Another factor that limits query and update packets is distribution lists. Both of these factors are discussed in detail in this section.

The "Stuck in Active" State

Have you ever heard the phrase "A network is only as strong as its weakest link"? You haven't? That's because I just thought of it—but it's true. Slow convergence is usually the cause of network problems. In fact, slow convergence is usually the reason it takes a very long time for a query to be answered. The result is that the router that issued the query gives up and simply clears the adjacency to the router that isn't answering, forcing a restart of the neighbor session. This state is known as *stuck in active (SIA).*

A basic example of an SIA route occurs when a query is delayed traveling to the opposite end of the network, therefore delaying a route traveling back. You can use the following command to change the time that a router waits after sending a query before declaring it an SIA:

```
Router(config)# router eigrp <ASN>
        Router(config-router)#Timers active-time
```

exam
⑩atch

The default percentage of bandwidth that EIGRP uses for EIGRP packets is 50 percent. Changing this value could cause more harm than good for your network. Before you change default values on your network, fully research the alternatives.

exam

ⓦatch

SIA is a very common error on large networks. Knowing what causes SIA and how to avoid SIA will be covered on the exam.

EIGRP Query Range

This section explains the range of a query in a network and reviews methods of preventing routing loops in an EIGRP network. Table 7-1 details the rules a router must follow when responding to queries and how various actions regulate the queries' range.

TABLE 7-1   Router's Query Responsibilities

Query From	Neighbor (not the current successor)	Successor	Any neighbor	Any neighbor	Neighbor (not the current successor)	Successor
Route State	Passive	Passive	No path through this neighbor before query	Not known before query	Active	Active
Action	Reply with current successor information	Attempt to find new successor. If successful, reply with new information. If not successful, mark destination unreachable and query all neighbors except the previous successor	Reply with best path currently known	Reply that the destination is unreachable	If there is no current successor to this destination, reply with an unreachable	Attempt to find new successor; if successful, reply with new information; if not successful, mark destination unreachable and query all neighbors except the previous successor
					If there is a good successor, reply with the current path information	

In an EIGRP network, routing loops can be very dangerous. Routing loops can cause links to become SIA, or it can slow convergence to a halt. Split horizon prevents routing loops. EIGRP uses the feasible distance and the reported distance to determine whether or not a route is a possible loop. When a router sends queries and update packets to the network, split horizon's job is to make sure that it never advertises a route out of the same interface from which it has received the information.

exam
ⓦatch

The key to EIGRP's fast convergence revolves around queries and updates. To know thoroughly how EIGRP operates in a network, you must know how queries and updates are propagated.

Limiting the Scope of Updates and Query Propagation

This section discusses how to limit query and update packets. It is very important to place boundaries on query and update packets in your network. Boundaries lower the entries in your routing tables and, as a result, reduce the overhead large routing tables impose on a network.

How Summarization Can Help

Updates and query propagation can be controlled when using EIGRP. With the help of a proper hierarchical design, the summarization feature can limit the range of update and query packets.

For example, let's suppose we have four routers connected to the backbone router. Each router represents four different networks. All the routers summarize a 10.1.0.0/16 network. Because all the routers are doing route summarization for the 10.1.0.0/16 network, they do not announce the more specific routes. When network 10.1.1.0/24 goes down, a query goes out telling all routers of the down subnet. The routers respond to all queries searching for network 10.1.1.0/24 with the message "Destination unreachable" because that route was not listed in the tables due to summarization. If route summarization were not used on each of the routers, the routers would have a more detailed routing table and thus respond to all queries with an accurate route. This would limit all queries to the router responsible for the subnet and, due to summarization, the router will not forward the queries to outside routers.

How Filters Can Help

Distribution lists can be an effective way of limiting updates and queries. A distribution list reacts the same way access list does; when it receives a query for a network in its list, it sends a reply of "Unreachable," even if it does contain a proper route to the source destination. Distribution lists are considered the most reliable method for limiting the query range and update packets.

A Nonscalable EIGRP Network with Bad Addressing

A problem that lies in most poorly designed legacy networks and networks is bad network addressing. To use all the benefits of a scalable routing protocol, you must have a properly designed hierarchical network, which is achieved by using a hierarchical network-addressing scheme. Without a hierarchical foundation, poor addressing can cause routing loops and incomplete routing tables, not to mention poor convergence. With bad addressing, the queries are even further limited, but instead of properly advertising routes, your queries would propagate throughout your network, ignorant of any boundaries that summarization would impose.

A Scalable EIGRP Network with Good Addressing

A properly designed hierarchical addressing scheme gives you many benefits. It gives you many of the advantages of EIGRP, such as route summarization, query boundaries, and VLSM. It also decreases the overhead of large routing tables. Good addressing prevents routing loops and allows your routing protocol to work as it was designed to work. As discussed earlier in this section, proper addressing limits your query propagation to the border routers of your subnets.

CERTIFICATION SUMMARY

This chapter covered the most advanced EIGRP features. You learned that when you are using a routing protocol for a large-scale network, one of the most important features is convergence. The ability to provide fast convergence is only one of the many features that EIGRP provides. Large-scale networks benefit from EIGRP's consumption of minimal bandwidth, and because of the low overhead, routers consume very little CPU. EIGRP was designed to handle the stress of today's large-scale networks and, because it's a hybrid routing protocol, it carries benefits of both link-state and distance-vector protocols.

Also covered in this chapter was EIGRP's support of IP address summarization. Route summarization is best used in a hierarchical addressing scheme; it provides the benefits of preserving address space, limits query and update propagation, aids in support of using VLSMs, and increases the stability in an EIGRP network by easing the load of the CPU when propagating routing changes. EIGRP uses autosummarization by default.

This chapter discussed the correct way to configure BANDWIDTH statements on a router's interface. We learned that changing the values can have an effect on how much bandwidth is actually used by EIGRP. We also learned how to configure the percentage value that controls EIGRP's usage of the links. The default value that EIGRP uses on a link is 50 percent. This chapter also mentioned the correct way and the not-so-correct way to configure a multilink interface. We also learned the value of load balancing. In a large environment, load balancing becomes a necessity when dealing with solutions to high-volume traffic situations.

Finally, we examined query and update packets and their place in an EIGRP network. We discussed the importance of query and update packets to keeping your routing tables updated, as well as how these packets are used to provide adjacencies between routers. You also learned about stuck in active (SIA) mode and learned what causes an SIA error.

EIGRP provides the user a number of advantages. This chapter discussed only some of these benefits. If you want to find more information on EIGRP, please visit the Cisco Web site at www.cisco.com.

TWO-MINUTE DRILL

Here are some of the key points from each certification objective in Chapter 7.

Considerations for a Large-Scale Network Using EIGRP

❑ EIGRP recalculates and updates only the few affected routers in the topology.

❑ EIGRP sends partial updates only when there is a change in metric or route availability to the destination network.

❑ EIGRP supports Novell IPX, IP, and AppleTalk.

❑ Partial updates sent using EIGRP's routing algorithm result in less bandwidth and CPU usage.

EIGRP IP Address Summarization

❑ Maximizing the address space assists in reducing resource utilization and maximizes route summarization.

❑ Route summarization is enabled by default using EIGRP.

❑ Disabling route summarization will display information of all routes, regardless of subnet masks.

❑ EIGRP can summarize routes on any router in the network.

EIGRP WAN Optimization

❑ Complete EIGRP WAN optimization is achieved when the proper bandwidth allotted on links coincides with the amount of traffic routed over the network.

❑ Failure to reflect the actual bandwidth could result in network degradation.

❑ A point-to-point configuration allows for more control over virtual circuits.

EIGRP Query Issues

❑ A *query* is a message used to inquire about routes that exist or do not exist in a routing environment.

❑ Hello packets are sent out at a default of 60 seconds on low-bandwidth connections and 5 seconds on high-speed connections.

❑ In a hierarchical design, summarization limits the way one router recognizes another router due to subnet mask limitation.

❑ Slow convergence is usually the cause of network problems.

SELF TEST

The following questions will help you measure your understanding of the material presented in this chapter. Read all the choices carefully because there might be more than one correct answer. Choose all correct answers for each question.

Considerations for a Large-Scale Network Using EIGRP

1. EIGRP stands out because of its ability to do which of the following? Choose all that apply.

    A. Converge quickly

    B. Minimize CPU usage

    C. Support only Novell IPX and AppleTalk

    D. Have routing loops

2. EIGRP's hop limit can exceed which of the following?

    A. 225

    B. 15

    C. 255

    D. All of the above

3. EIGRP calculates the total metrics using which of the following formulas?

    A. Bandwidth = (10000000/Bandwidth) x 250
       Delay = Delay x 250
       Metric = Bandwidth + Delay

    B. Bandwidth = (100000000/Bandwidth) x 256
       Metric = Delay x 256
       Delay = Bandwidth + Metric

    C. Bandwidth = (100000000/Bandwidth) $\pm$ 256
       Delay = Delay x 256
       Metric = Delay + Bandwidth

    D. Bandwidth = (10000000/Bandwidth) x 256
       Delay = Delay x 256
       Metric = Bandwidth + Delay

4. Which of the following are flat topologies? Choose all that apply.

A. EIGRP

B. IGRP

C. OSPF

D. RIP and RIP2

5. What is EIGRP? Choose all that apply.

A. A protocol developed by Cisco

B. The successor of IGRP

C. A scalable protocol

D. All of the above

EIGRP IP Address Summarization

6. In load balancing with EIGRP, paths to a given destination stem from which of the following? Choose all that apply.

A. VLSM

B. Static routes

C. Routing protocols

D. Being SIA

7. Load balancing can occur in up to how many equal-cost paths?

A. Four

B. Fifteen

C. One

D. Six

8. The VARIANCE setting, by default, is set to which of the following values?

A. Four

B. Fifteen

C. One

D. Six

9. Removing the null route from the routing table will have which of the following effects?

A. Increase the amount of traffic received by the network for which it was not destined

B. Increase the amount of traffic received by the network that it was destined to reach

C. Make all the components of the summarized entry available

D. You cannot remove the null route

EIGRP WAN Optimization

10. "Stuck in active" (SIA) mode can be triggered by which of the following? Choose all that apply.

A. Bandwidth is configured higher than the actual bandwidth

B. The WAN interface is configured lower than the actual bandwidth

C. None of the above

D. All of the above

11. Which of the following apply when configuring NBMA interfaces? Choose all that apply.

A. Bandwidth for EIGRP and all virtual circuits must be configured the same way in each direction

B. Total EIGRP traffic for all virtual circuits can exceed the total actual bandwidth of the interface

C. EIGRP traffic should not exceed the specified capacity of the virtual circuit

D. All of the above

12. When proper bandwidth allotted on links coincides with the amount of traffic routed in the network, which of the following is complete?

A. Route summarization

B. WAN optimization

C. Load balancing

D. Address summarization

13. Network degradation can result from which of the following? Choose all that apply.

A. Too many routers

B. Failure to reflect actual bandwidth

C. EIGRP packets

D. No variance

14. On a multipoint circuit, if you have four PVCs and your interface bandwidth is set at 224 kbps, what is the CIR of each PVC?

    A. CIR = 64 kbps

    B. CIR = 56 kbps

    C. CIR = 224 kbps

    D. CIR = 256 kbps

15. *Lowest CIR * number of PVCs* is the formula for which of the following?

    A. Setting the bandwidth for unequal CIR

    B. Setting the bandwidth for equal CIR

    C. Setting the CIR

    D. Counting the number of PVCs

16. Point-to-point configuration allows which of the following?

    A. Messages to be sent

    B. More control over virtual circuits

    C. Networks to coincide

    D. None of the above

EIGRP Query Issues

17. A query is which of the following?

    A. Packets used by a router to discover and recover its neighbors

    B. Packets used to indicate that a client is still operating on a network

    C. An ordered list of elements waiting to be processed

    D. None of the above

18. Hello packets are sent out at a default rate of which of the following? Choose all that apply.

    A. Two seconds

    B. Five seconds

    C. Sixty seconds

    D. Twelve seconds

19. During the query process, if a successor is down, which of the following occurs?

    A. Hello packets will be returned from the successor

    B. A update packet will be sent to the successor

    C. Your network will shut down

    D. A query will not be answered by the successor

20. If a router receives a query from a successor, it will do which of the following?

    A. Reply with the best path currently known

    B. Reply with current successor information

    C. Attempt to find a new successor, and if successful, reply with new information; if not successful, it will mark the destination unreachable and query all neighbors except the previous successor

    D. Reply "Destination unreachable"

21. Routing loops can be dangerous in an EIGRP network because it they can do which of the following?

    A. Shut the entire network down

    B. Cause links to be SIA

    C. Slow convergence to a halt

    D. All of the above

LAB QUESTION

You have been given responsibility for a network with two Cisco 3640 backbone routers. You must ensure that each of these routers are designed for redundancy and load balance of traffic between core sites. Core A has four links connected to Core B. There are four paths to Core B, and the metrics for these paths are as follows:

- Path 1: 1100
- Path 2: 1100
- Path 3: 2000
- Path 4: 4000

How would you handle this task?

SELF TEST ANSWERS

Considerations for a Large-Scale Network Using EIGRP

1. ☑ **A** and **B.** EIGRP is a hybrid routing protocol that provides fast convergence compared with distance-vector routing protocols. Its ability to consume less processor utilization makes it a sound protocol.

   ☒ **C** is incorrect because EIGRP not only supports Novell IPX and AppleTalk; it also supports IP. **D** is incorrect because routing loops stem from slow convergence and, because of EIGRP's ability to converge quickly, routing loops are not common.

2. ☑ **D.** All of the above. EIGRP's hop limit can exceed 255, which is choice **C.** Because **A** and **B** are less than this amount, EIGRP can exceed them, too.

   ☒ **A, B,** and **C** are incorrect because they do not fully answer the question.

3. ☑ **D.** This answer is correct because it is the proper formula.

   ☒ **A** is incorrect because 250 should be 256. **B** is incorrect because the second and third parts of the formula are reversed. **C** is incorrect because it should read Bandwidth + (10000000/Bandwidth) x 256 and Metric = Bandwidth + Delay, not Bandwidth = (100000000/Bandwidth) $\pm$ 256 or Metric = Delay + Bandwidth.

4. ☑ **A, B,** and **D.** EIGRP, IGRP, and RIP/RIP2 are flat topologies because they use network addressing to divide large networks into interconnected networks.

   ☒ **C,** OSPF, is incorrect because it is hierarchical.

5. ☑ **D.** All of the above. EIGRP was developed by Cisco to enhance IGRP. By enhancing IGRP, Cisco was able to create a scalable protocol that is more diverse than its predecessor.

   ☒ **A, B,** and **C** are incorrect because they do not answer the question fully.

EIGRP IP Address Summarization

6. ☑ **B** and **C.** Paths stem from either static routes or routing protocols such as OSPF, RIP, IGRP, or EIGRP.

   ☒ **A** and **D** are incorrect because VLSM is a variable-link subnet mask that has nothing to do with routes, and SIA (stuck in active) is a condition caused by slow convergence.

7. ☑ **D.** Load balancing can occur in up to six equal-cost paths.

   ☒ **A** is incorrect because four is EIGRP's limit only by default. **B** and **C** are incorrect because they specify incorrect values.

8. ☑ **C.** One is the VARIANCE setting value by default.
   ☒ **A, B,** and **D** are incorrect because they specify incorrect values.

9. ☑ **D.** You cannot remove the null route. Using the EIGRP SUMMARIZATION command automatically creates the null 0 route.
   ☒ **A, B,** and **C** are incorrect because to remove the null route would be to remove the summarization.

EIGRP WAN Optimization

10. ☑ **A** and **B.** Bandwidth is configured higher than the actual bandwidth, and the WAN interface is configured lower than the actual bandwidth. Both of these situations can trigger SIA.
    ☒ **C** and **D** are incorrect because there are two correct choices.

11. ☑ **A** and **C. A** is correct because if traffic exceeds specified capacity, the link might not be able to handle the traffic, resulting in slow convergence, loss of packets, and traffic due to congestion. **C** is correct because it allows you to balance network traffic flow, enabling you to accurately troubleshoot any convergence issue your network experiences.
    ☒ **B** is incorrect because virtual circuits cannot exceed the total actual bandwidth of the interface. **D** is incorrect because there is an incorrect choice.

12. ☑ **B.** WAN optimization is complete.
    ☒ **A** is incorrect because route summarization occurs when routing tables' IP addresses are summarized. **C** is incorrect because load balancing allows routers to use multiple paths to a given destination. **D** is incorrect because address summarization is the same as route summarization.

13. ☑ **B** and **C.** Failure to reflect the actual bandwidth can cause congestion in the network if the settings are advertised to low. By default, EIGRP knows to use only 50 percent of the bandwidth.
    ☒ **A** is incorrect because "Too many routers" does not impose a threat on network performance if the network is designed properly. **D** is incorrect because "No variance" is not an issue in network performance.

14. ☑ **B.** CIR = 56 kbps. To figure out the missing number of the formula, divide 224 kbps by 4 PVCs and you get 56 kbps.
    ☒ **A, C,** and **D** are incorrect because when 224 kbps is divided by 4, 56 is the product.

15. ☑ **A.** This is the standard formula for setting the bandwidth for unequal CIR.
    ☒ **B, C,** and **D** are incorrect because they do not have a formula.

16. ☑ **B.** Point-to-point configuration allows for more control because it allows interfaces to be divided into subinterfaces, thus allowing bandwidth to be configured separately for each virtual circuit.
    ☒ **A** and **C** are incorrect because point-to-point configuration does not allow messages to be sent or networks to coincide. **D** is incorrect because there is a correct choice.

EIGRP Query Issues

17. ☑ **D.** None of the above. A query is a message used to inquire about the value of some variables or set of variables.
    ☒ **A** is incorrect because it describes CDP. **B** is incorrect because it describes hello packets. **C** is incorrect because it describes a queue.

18. ☑ **B** and **C.** Hello packets are sent out at a default rate of 60 seconds on low-bandwidth connections and 5 seconds on high-speed connections.
    ☒ **A** and **D** are incorrect because the defaults are 60 and 5 seconds.

19. ☑ **D.** A query will not be answered by the successor. If a successor were down, there would be no way for it to receive the query, so it would not know to answer it.
    ☒ **A** is incorrect because the successor is down and hello packets are not sent in response. **B** is incorrect because the successor is down and will not be able to respond with an update. **C** is incorrect because a successor being down is not an extreme enough situation to shut down an entire network.

20. ☑ **C.** Attempt to find a new successor, and if successful, reply with new information; if not successful, it will mark the destination unreachable and query all neighbors except the previous successor. A router must first attempt to find a new successor. Once a new successor is found, it then replies with updated information. If a new successor is not found, it responds with "Destination unreachable."
    ☒ **A** is incorrect because it must first find a new successor to determine the best path known. **B** is incorrect because current successor information is not available, since the successor is down. **D** is incorrect because it must first follow the steps to determine whether or not the destination is unreachable.

21. ☑ **D.** All of the above. Routing loops can cause all these situations to occur.
    ☒ **A, B,** and **C** are incorrect because they do not answer the question fully.

FIGURE 7-3

Metric values of
Core A and B

Core A

metric—1100

metric—1100

metric—2000

metric—4000

Core B

LAB ANSWER

The student should come up with configurations for Core A and B, as shown in Figure 7-3. The student should use the SHOW IP ROUTE command to verify that the configuration is correct and that the routers are load balancing traffic across these links.

Router Configurations
<u>Core A</u>

```
Hostname CoreA

Interface loopback 0
Shutdown

Interface Ethernet 0
Ip address 192.1.1.1 255.255.255.0

Interface serial 0
Ip address 10.1.1.1 255.255.255.0

Interface serial 1
Ip address 10.1.1.3 255.255.255.0

Interface Serial 2
Ip address 10.1.1.5 255.255.255.0

Interface Serial 3
Ip address 10.1.1.7 255.255.255.0

Router EIGRP 1
Network 10.0.0.0
Network 192.1.1.0 Variance 4
```

<u>Core B</u>

```
Hostname CoreB

Interface loopback 0
Shutdown

Interface Ethernet 0
Ip address 192.2.2.1 255.255.255.0

Interface serial 0
Ip address 10.1.1.2 255.255.255.0

Interface serial 1
Ip address 10.1.1.4 255.255.255.0

Interface Serial 2
Ip address 10.1.1.6 255.255.255.0

Interface Serial 3
Ip address 10.1.1.8 255.255.255.0

Router EIGRP 1
Network 10.0.0.0
Network 192.1.1.0
Variance 4
```

8

BGP Basic Operations and Configuration

I n this chapter, we introduce you to the Border Gateway Protocol (BGP). BGP is the routing protocol of choice for Internet routing. It is no small statement to say that without BGP, the Internet would not be the success it is today. BGP is the glue that ties together the heterogeneous networks connected to the Internet.

BGP is classified as an exterior gateway protocol, not to be confused with the Exterior Gateway Protocol (EGP) that BGP replaced. As an exterior gateway protocol, BGP is responsible for routing traffic between different autonomous systems (ASs). Recall that an AS is a collection of networks operating under the same set of routing policies and under a single administrative technical control. Contrast that with interior gateway protocols such as RIP and OSPF, which route traffic within the same autonomous system. It could be argued that a modern protocol such as OSPF could route between ASs, but that would not be as efficient as BGP in handling the voluminous number of routes typically associated with Internet class routing. BGP can also do intra-AS routing.

exam
⓪atch
*BGP is classified as a path vector routing protocol. **Ensure that you understand how this differs from a distance vector and a link-state routing protocol.***

Just as we classify RIP as a distance vector and OSPF as a link-state protocol, so we can classify BGP as a path vector protocol. BGP routes traffic based on the AS, not by link or hop count. The rationale behind this makes sense when you consider the quantity of networks on the Internet. A single AS could contain thousands of routers and networks; if BGP routed similarly to RIP and OSPF, the routing tables of Internet routers would become unmanageable.

BGP uses TCP port 179. If there is an error, BGP does not handle retransmission; TCP does. Before routing updates can be exchanged, the peer relationships between the routers in the ASs must be defined by the network engineer. If the peer relationship is not established or if it breaks, updates will not be exchanged. BGP peers initially exchange their full routing tables and then incremental updates as the network changes. The health of the peering is maintained and monitored via the use of KEEPALIVE packets (essentially, the 19-byte header of the BGP packet with no data).

We discuss BGP in depth in this chapter. As we do, remember that BGP is a path vector routing protocol and that it was designed to route between ASs.

CERTIFICATION OBJECTIVE 8.01

Alternatives to BGP

BGP does a great job of handling amounts of routing that would overwhelm most IGPs. If your AS must connect to the Internet, at whatever level, chances are you will use BGP; it is the standard for most providers. There are reasons for using BGP, and there are also situations when it might not be appropriate to use BGP.

When It Is Appropriate to Use BGP

A short and quick reason for using BGP is if you have a large number of networks consisting of hundreds and thousands of routers, and understand BGP well and thoroughly. If your AS is used to pass traffic between other ASs, use BGP. If you want to tightly filter and control routing updates between ASs, use BGP to keep the routing tables manageable.

When an Autonomous System Is a Transit AS

You should use BGP if your AS is a transit AS—that is, if traffic for other ASs pass through it. Another way of phrasing it is to say that a transit AS has traffic that has a source and a destination outside of it. In Figure 8-1, traffic for AS2, AS3, and AS4 passes through AS1 to reach these destinations. AS1 is the transit AS in Figure 8-1.

The network engineer or provider determines whether an AS is transit or nontransit. If an AS is nontransit, it passes traffic only from its own AS. All traffic passed in a nontransit AS has its origin within the AS, although destinations can be anywhere.

When Multiple Exit Points and Traffic Must Be Manipulated

When an AS has multiple exit points, it is said to be *multihomed*. Figure 8-2 is the same diagram we saw in Figure 8-1, only we are looking at it from the viewpoint of AS1. AS1 is multihomed in that it has multiple exit points via AS2, AS3, and AS4.

As the network engineer, you can manipulate BGP parameters to control the flow of traffic entering and exiting via these multiple exit points. For example, you may configure BGP so that traffic to Network 1 always transits AS2 and traffic for

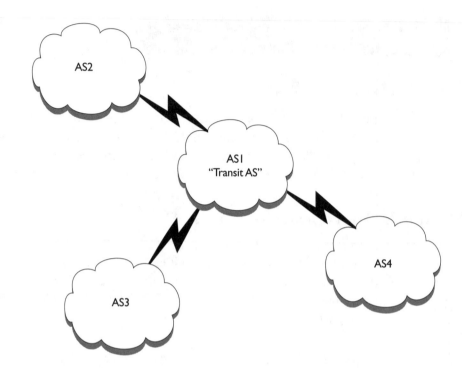

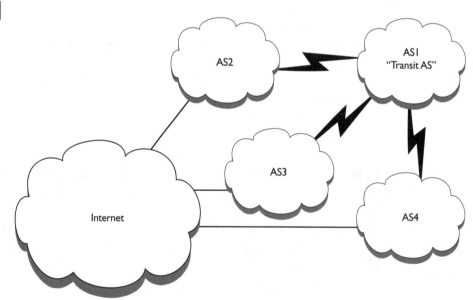

Network 2 always goes out via AS1's link to AS4. BGP gives you the flexibility and control to determine how traffic transits your AS.

When discussing BGP, it is common to put the terms *multihomed, transit,* and *nontransit* together to describe the BGP configuration being discussed. Without diverting our discussion of BGP into a paragraph on semantics, we should mention that a *multihomed transit AS* is an AS that has more than one exit point and passes traffic from other ASs. A *multihomed nontransit AS* is one that has multiple exit points but does not pass traffic from other ASs.

When the Effects of BGP Are Well Understood

BGP is a deceptively simple path-vector exterior gateway protocol and can be configured with a few simple commands. It routes by AS. The network engineer needs to know and understand that *all* relationships between peers must be manually established (there is no automatic peer discovery), and the peers must be able to reach other. If you change the IP address of a peer, you must ensure that the change is reflected in each peer configuration. If you have numerous networks and a complex configuration, you must know how to control the updates and how to aggregate to reduce the size of BGP's tables (reducing the number of routing entries). Filtering and aggregation have consequences; ensure that you know how your networks will be affected.

exam
ⓦatch

You should use BGP if you are connecting to the Internet and other autonomous systems via multiple points and/or if your AS is a transit AS.

When It Is Not Appropriate to Use BGP

At times, as robust and powerful as it is, BGP use would be akin to hunting fleas with an elephant gun. The axiom "The right tool for the right job" is very much applicable when you are considering BGP—in fact, when you are considering any routing protocol. We now discuss when *not* to use BGP. Keep in mind that this discussion contains recommendations and lessons learned about BGP; there is no law that says you must follow them, but you would be wise to keep them in mind.

A Single Entry/Exit Point to an Autonomous System

If your AS connects to the Internet via a single link, running BGP in partnership with your ISP does not make much sense. In fact, your AS could potentially be flooded with thousands of routes for which it has no need. An AS with a single exit point is called a *stub AS;* obviously, it can never be a transit AS.

Routing Policy or Path Selection Manipulation Is Not Required

If your AS is multihomed but you do not need to manipulate traffic such that traffic to Network 1 goes out via AS2 and traffic to Network 2 goes out via AS2, don't use BGP. If your requirements do not necessitate that you specify a particular AS for particular traffic to transit, you can let traffic choose its own best path at the time. This situation would render moot the usefulness of BGP.

Lack of Memory or CPU Resources on BGP Routers

BGP routers on the Internet handle routing updates numbering in the thousands and tens of thousands. If your router does not have the requisite memory or processing power to handle such high volumes, it is not a good candidate on which to run BGP.

Limited Understanding of Route Filtering and BGP

Knowledge is power and, in the case of BGP, stability. There are no half measures when it comes to knowing BGP; you must know all aspects and behavior of BGP in order to successfully deploy it. Most providers are inflexible in not allowing AS administrators with a limited understanding of BGP to peer with them. This is good policy because BGP is the Internet routing protocol, and a single misconfiguration can and will knock out thousands of networks. Unless you have a BGP expert on your staff or have a contract with a networking organization such as Sprint Paranet or Cisco, do not attempt to deploy BGP on a wide scale. The potential for disaster is far greater than for an IGP.

Low Bandwidth Between Autonomous Systems

Ensure that each link between the ASs can handle the traffic loads of BGP. If there is insufficient bandwidth, routing updates might not be exchanged successfully or in a timely way, or the links might become so congested that the peering between ASs is destroyed; the KEEPALIVE packets might not be delivered in time to maintain the peering.

on the
Øob

Your first step in implementing BGP successfully is to have a complete, comprehensive, and coherent routing policy. Analyze and plan every aspect of your BGP implementation and test it on nonproduction systems before fielding it.

Static and Default Routes

Static routes are routes entered by an engineer that point to a destination. Static routes remain in the routing table as long as the interface referenced remains up or the next-hop network remains reachable. If you configure a static route with the permanent option, it will not be removed from the routing table. This is a very important point to remember when configuring any routing, as is that fact that static routes have, by default, an administrative distance of 1. This is lower than the administrative distance of BGP and most routing protocols and ensures that the static route will be the route placed in the routing table, even if a dynamic routing protocol offers a better route.

Static routes can be useful in stub ASs. (Recall that a stub AS has a single exit point.) In the case of a stub AS, it would not make sense to have all numerous BGP-injected routes from the Internet, because you can enter a static route in your AS and point to this single exit point as the gateway of last resort. Static routes make sense when you need to connect to the Internet but lack the processing power to field BGP or have low-bandwidth links that could become congested if BGP is used.

Default routes can be static or dynamic. A default route is one in which all unknown traffic is sent, which is typical of a router connected to the Internet. Most routing protocols have the ability to originate and propagate a default route within their ASs. You can also enter a static route and use it as a default route. We discuss the command syntax of this concept shortly. A default route pointing to a router connected to the Internet can be substituted for a full-scale BGP implementation throughout your AS. The only caveat is that you ensure that the link to the Internet is reliable and robust; otherwise, traffic could make an unnecessary trip, only to find out the link is down.

Static and Default Route Commands

A default route created using a static route can be controlled and simple to troubleshoot. The network administrator explicitly identifies the interface or next-hop address to be used as a route of last resort to reach destinations for which there is no entry in the routing table. Note that the commands for creating static and default routes have many options and arguments; we focus only on a minimal configuration here.

The command syntax for entering a static route is as follows:

```
ip route network [mask] {address | interface} [distance] [permanent]
```

You can either specify the IP address of the next-hop router to be traversed to reach this network, or you can specify the outgoing interface to reach this network. In our example, we specify the outgoing interface. Distance allows you to adjust the default administrative distance of the static route from the default of 1. You can create what's called a *floating static route* by setting the administrative distance higher than that of any routing protocol you are running; if that routing protocol loses the route, the static route will be injected into the routing table.

exam
ⓦatch

A default can be created via a static route or be dynamically learned. Whichever way you use, ensure that the default network is reachable.

The command syntax for entering a default route is as follows:

```
ip default-network network-number
```

For example, to create a static default route via network 1.1.1.1, you would execute the following series of commands. Do not change the administrative distance:

```
ip route 1.1.1.1 255.255.255.255 serial 0 # Creates the static route.
ip default-network 1.1.1.1 # Creates the default route.
```

on the
Ⓙob

A static route can be a very good substitute for BGP if your AS only has one exit point and does not need to receive the routes of other ASs. The other advantage of static routes is that you can always replace or supplement them with BGP as your enterprise network grows and changes.

Redistribution of Default Routes and RIP

We discussed how to create a static route and then use that route as a default route. Next we discuss how to create a default route using RIP and pass that default route to all the RIP speakers in the AS. To achieve this goal, we create a static route and use it as the default route and have RIP originate and propagate the default route itself. Ensure that the router you want to use as the gateway of last resort does have a default route; otherwise, it will not be able to service the traffic sent its way due to its propagating the default route.

To create and use a static route as your default route, perform the following. The steps are the same as outlined in the previous discussion:

```
ip route network [mask] {address | interface} [distance]
[permanent]
ip default-network network-number
```

Configure RIP on the router, as shown in the example:

```
router rip
version 2
network x.x.x.x
default-information originate
```

DEFAULT-INFORMATION ORIGINATE is not really necessary for RIP or other distance-vector protocols to propagate a default route. You can create a default route by entering IP ROUTE 0.0.0.0 0.0.0.0 SERIAL 0, for example, and RIP will automatically advertise this default route to the other RIP speakers in the AS. The command is shown here to make you aware of it.

On the other hand, if you use the IP DEFAULT-NETWORK X.X.X.X command to point to a network you reach via a static route of IP ROUTE X.X.X.X 255.255.255.0 SERIAL 0, using the DEFAULT-INFORMATION ORIGINATE command will ensure that this router advertises itself as a gateway of last resort and that it has a default route of its own.

What you are doing in the preceding configuration is creating the default route via static means—in other words, you are giving this router the means to route traffic toward unknown destinations. The DEFAULT-INFORMATION ORIGINATE command entered under RIP means that this router will be considered the gateway of last resort for all RIP speakers in the AS. The default route will appear as 0.0.0.0/0 in the routing tables of the other routers that receive the update from the default router.

Redistribution of Default Routes and OSPF

The process for propagating a default route in OSPF is similar to the process for RIP. Create the default route, and configure OSPF on the default route to originate the default route. OSPF has more options than RIP regarding the default route. For example, it can originate a default route, whether it actually has one or not; routing will become erratic if a router originates a default route but does not actually have one.

The syntax for the OSPF command to originate a default route follows. Since this command is more complex than RIP, we discuss some of the more relevant arguments in more detail:

```
default-information originate [always] [metric metric-value]
[metric-type type-value] [route-map map-name]
```

- **ORIGINATE** Generates a default route into an OSPF domain if the router already has one. Will propagate to other routers.

- **ALWAYS** Optional. Always generate a default route whether or not the router has one.

- **METRIC METRIC-VALUE** Optional. Metric for the default route. Default is 10.

- **METRIC-TYPE TYPE-VALUE** Optional. Type 1 or 2 external route associated with the default route advertised into the OSPF routing domain. Default is Type 2.

- **ROUTE-MAP MAP-NAME** Default route is generated only if the route map is matched.

The default router advertises the default route as 0.0.0.0 to the routers in the OSPF domain. With OSPF, you can either create a static route and use it as a default route and have OSPF originate a default route, or you can forgo static routes altogether and use a combination of the default network command and OSPF originate to propagate the default route. Either way, the other routers in the domain will receive the default route as 0.0.0.0. You must run the DEFAULT-INFORMATION ORIGINATE command under OSPF or it will not propagate an advertisement for the default network 0.0.0.0.

We start by using a static route to see what steps we take using this method. As before, create the static route, and use it as the default route:

```
ip route network [mask] {address | interface} [distance]
ip default-network network-number
```

Next, under OSPF (notice that we are *not* using the ALWAYS keyword), have the default router originate a route:

```
Router ospf 44
Network x.x.x.x y.y.y.y area 0
default-information originate
```

We can also forgo static routes altogether. Assuming that OSPF has a route to network z.z.z.z, we can simply execute the following command. Notice that we have not created a static route and that the z.z.z.z network is not participating directly in the OSPF routing process. By not creating a static route and not including z.z.z.z in the OSPF routing process, the z.z.z.z network is a directly connected network.

```
Ip default-network z.z.z.z
```

Then, under the OSPF process:

```
Router ospf 44
Network x.x.x.x y.y.y.y area 0
Default-information originate.
```

The DEFAULT-INFORMATION ORIGINATE Command   We have discussed and used the DEFAULT-INFORMATION ORIGINATE command in the previous paragraphs. This command allows a routing protocol to generate a default route and pass it throughout the routing domain. This command is part of various routing protocols, including RIP, OSPF, IGR, EIGRP, and, of course, BGP. The structure of the command is used similarly in each routing protocol. Only the arguments change to reflect the unique workings of the protocol under which the command is being run. The end result of this command is the propagation of a special routing table entry with the network address 0.0.0.0 that indicates a default route.

There are some special issues with the command as implemented by various protocols. For example, OSPF has an ALWAYS argument that enables OSPF to propagate a default route, regardless of whether it actually has a default route. With BGP, DEFAULT-INFORMATION ORIGINATE redistributes 0.0.0.0 into BGP; it is functionally equivalent to entering network 0.0.0.0 under BGP.

EXERCISE 8-1

Reasons for Using and Not Using BGP, and Using a Default Route with BGP

1. List at least three reasons or situations in which BGP should be used. List at least three reasons or situations in which BGP should *not* be used.

2. Create a default route 12.12.192.3, referencing serial 0, and configure BGP 4444 to propagate this route to its peers.

Solution:
Reasons to Use BGP

1. Your AS is a transit AS.

2. Your AS has multiple exit points.

3. Traffic entering and exiting the AS needs to be manipulated.

4. Your AS is connecting to the Internet and will exchange routes with Internet routers.

5. Skilled BGP talent and support is available to configure and maintain BGP implementations.

Reasons for *Not* Using BGP

1. Your AS has a single connection to the outside world. (Use a static route.)

2. A routing policy or traffic manipulation is not required or present.

3. There are no routers available that have the memory or CPU resources to support BGP.

4. *No* skilled BGP talent or support is available.

5. There is low bandwidth between ASs.

Configuring a Default Route

```
ip route 12.12.192.3 255.255.255.255 serial 0
ip default-network 12.12.192.3

router bgp 4444
default-information originate
```

CERTIFICATION OBJECTIVE 8.02

Understanding the Border Gateway Protocol

A thorough understanding of BGP is critical to its successful configuration and implementation. This includes being able to distinguish and comprehend what an exterior gateway protocol is, how BGP operates, and how it populates the routing table. This section discusses all these topics and more.

What Is an Exterior Routing Protocol?

BGP is classified as an exterior gateway protocol—again, not be confused with the Exterior Gateway Protocol (EGP) that BGP replaced. The purpose of BGP is to provide inter-AS routing information exchange. In other words, BGP facilitates the exchange of routing information between autonomous systems. By contrast, an interior gateway protocol (IGP) provides intra-AS routing information exchange. An IGP is designed to allow the exchange of routing information within a single autonomous system.

Figure 8-3 shows a simplified view of where EGPs and IGPs should be run. Generally speaking, BGP is typically run by Internet service providers (ISPs), network access providers, and large organizations that have such voluminous networks that an IGP cannot handle the routing information effectively, so these networks must communicate over the Internet. BGP is the standard for Internet class routing because it is designed to handle the large volume of routing information.

BGP differs from most routing protocols in that it routes by AS and enables routing policies to be implemented. The focus of BGP is not routing Network A to Network B (although it does achieve that) over the best path possible (it might need manual intervention to achieve this), but rather, routing traffic on an AS-to-AS basis. Looking at it another way, an AS could potentially contain thousands of links; processing each one individually could take too long. A network engineer can determine that traffic belonging to a certain AS will traverse a certain link or a certain AS.

Most IGPs use metrics to determine the best route to a destination, whether hop count like that of RIP or link cost like that of OSPF. BGP uses *attributes*, which provide the requisite information about a route to allow BGP to select the best one.

FIGURE 8-3

Possible IGP
and EBP
implementation
points

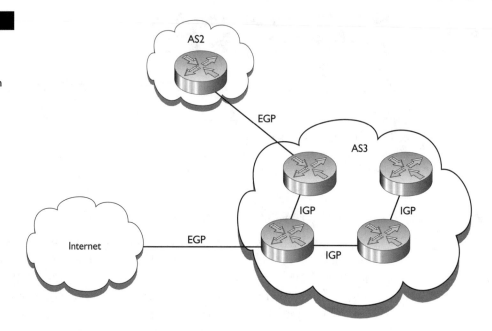

We will come back to attributes in a later section of this chapter. Like most IGPs, BGP can do summarization to reduce routing table sizes; likewise, the restrictions and caveats of using summarizations with IGPs apply to BGP.

Recall that a distance-vector routing protocol routes based on hop count; examples of these protocols are RIP and IGRP. Link-state protocols build a complete picture of the network and select the best path to be injected in the routing table; examples of link-state protocols include OSPF and IS-IS. BGP is classified as a path-vector protocol; its routing information has a sequence of ASs that has been transited. This sequence of ASs (rather than a specific IP address) is the path to reach a destination.

BGP also advertises networks that are not directly connected to the router on which BGP is running. It is important that BGP be able to reach any networks that it is advertising, regardless of whether it learns about the route statically or dynamically.

Border Gateway Protocol Version 4 and How It Differs from Its Predecessors

Version 4 is the most current version of BGP. It enhances and improves on previous versions by offering new features discussed in this section. BGP4 is backward compatible with BGP3 and can exchange routing information with a BGP3 speaker.

BGP Version 4 Compared With Version 3

Several improvements were made to BGP with Version 4. It adds new features and resolves issues that were apparent in Version 3.

Classless Interdomain Routing The most significant enhancement to BGP Version 4 was the incorporation of *classless interdomain routing (CIDR)* support. CIDR removes the concepts of class from IP addresses, enabling them to be subnetted and supernetted on other than classful boundaries. In other words, CIDR enables engineers to disregard the natural masks for IP addresses and create their own. Engineers are not limited to 255.0.0.0 for Class A addresses, 255.255.0 for Class B, and 255.255.255.0 for Class C. From the subnetting perspective, CIDR enables engineers to allocate only the necessary IP addresses.

Aggregation A benefit of BGP4 support of CIDR is *aggregation*, which is the ability to condense several networks into one advertisement. This reduces CPU cycles, memory, and table size; it is possible because CIDR enables the advertisement of an IP prefix (really several IP network addresses summarized into one network address with the correct mask). For example, the following networks use a subnet mask of 255.255.255.0:

```
x.x.0.x
x.x.1.x
x.x.2.x
x.x.3.x
```

With CIDR, these four networks can be condensed into one routing entry x.x.0.x using a mask of 255.255.252.0.

The LOCAL_PREF Attribute BGP4 also added the LOCAL_PREF attribute, which facilitates the selection of routes for the BGP routing table. A BGP router generates LOCAL_PREF for its internal peers; it tells the peers the degree of preference for external routes (routes outside the AS). In earlier versions, a BGP router did not have a simple way to pass this information along.

One indirect advantage of aggregation is that if a subset of a summarized route experiences problems, it will not be noticeable to external BGP speakers, thus resulting in a more stable network.

exam
Ⓦatch

The most significant enhancement in Version 4 of BGP was adding CIDR support.

Major RFCs for BGP

BGP has been and is a nonproprietary, open standard. It was first proposed in RFC 1105 Border Gateway Protocol (BGP) (K. Lougheed and Y. Rekhter, June 1, 1989). Since then, it has been modified extensively to achieve Version 4, which is used today. At the time of this writing, there were 37 RFCs pertaining to BGP. Some of the more interesting and relevant for study purposes are the following:

■ RFC 1267: Border Gateway Protocol 3 (BGP-3)

■ RFC 1403: BGP OSPF Interaction

■ RFC 1771: A Border Gateway Protocol 4 (BGP-4) (March 1995)

■ RFC 1930: Guidelines for Creation, Selection, and Registration of an Autonomous System (AS)

■ RFC 1966: BGP Route Reflection: an Alternative to Full-Mesh IBGP

■ RFC 2439: BGP Route Flap Damping

These RFCs can be downloaded from www.ietf.org. RFC 1771 is the fundamental RFC for BGP Version 4. It describes BGP fully and is worth reading if you are to master BGP.

on the
Ⓙob

The RFCs found at www.ietf.org are an excellent source of information, not only for BGP but for many other routing protocols, including IGPs such as RIP and OSPF. Although the RFCs can sometimes be dry and intimidating, the successful network engineer will make them required reading.

Packet Manipulation

BGP can control routing only within its own AS; it cannot manipulate or control packets once they leave its AS. Through the use of attributes, BGP can influence route selection intra-AS. For example, LOCAL_PREF can be used by an originating router to indicate its preference for particular advertised external routes to the other BGP speakers in the AS. LOCAL_PREF is concerned with traffic leaving the AS.

Another attribute, MULTI_EXIT_DISC (MED), provides hints to external neighbors about the entry and exit points of the AS. This is an attempt by one AS to influence the decision of another AS. The AS receiving the MED is not required to factor it into its routing decisions. The MED is exchanged between ASs, and when it enters an AS, it does not get propagated out of that AS; it is a one-shot arrangement from one AS to another.

The AS_PATH attribute can also be used to influence routing decisions, both internally and externally. A network engineer can pad this attribute with dummy AS numbers to make a path seem longer and therefore less preferable. Recall that BGP routes on a hop-by-hop basis (or AS by AS, if you will) and prefers the path with fewest hops, regardless of any other factors.

It is important to understand that BGP has no direct control over routing decisions after a packet leaves its own AS. It can make recommendations to other ASs or attempt to make a path seem longer. This is the extent of BGP's ability to manipulate the routing of another AS.

BGP Uses Attributes to Make Policy Decisions

Attributes, which are nothing more than the description of a route (also called a *prefix*), are used by BGP to make its decisions regarding what gets injected into its routing table. An attribute describes the preference of the route, how many hops the route has, and any other aspects of the route that BGP can and will use to make its decisions. We will return to attributes in a later section to discuss the types of attributes and highlight a few of the better-known ones.

The Hop-by-Hop (AS-by-AS) Routing Paradigm

In an earlier section, IGPs and EGPs were briefly mentioned. To help keep the differences in perspective, think of an IGP as being detail oriented in that it is concerned with getting through an AS, including links it must transit to reach its final destination. An EGP, on the other hand, is concerned with the "big picture": it is concerned about only the autonomous systems it must transit to reach a

SCENARIO & SOLUTION

What does *path vector* mean?	*Path vector* means that the routing protocol does not route link by link (or hop by hop). Instead, it routes AS by AS.
Can BGP be used to replace RIP or OSPF?	Yes and no. BGP can perform intra-AS routing; however, it is designed to route between ASs or between an AS and the Internet. The design of BGP is such that it needs to reach any route it advertises via default, static, or dynamic methods (IGP). The configuration overhead to use BGP as an IGP replacement does not make it an attractive replacement, but it can be done.
Does BGP use metrics like RIP or OSPF?	BGP "metrics" are called *attributes* and are used to identify the route to include in the routing table.

destination network, and once it is in that destination AS, the intra-AS routing could then be turned over to an IGP.

In a way, BGP is similar to RIP, only at a higher level. Recall that RIP routes on the basis of hop count—that is, the fewer links traversed, the better. BGP routes on the basis of AS count (a sequence of AS numbers is the path), and the fewer ASs traversed, the more preferred the route. Unlike a link-state protocol such as OSPF, BGP does not put itself at the center of the network and build a complete picture. If this were case, given the size of the Internet, the initial startup would be enough to saturate the Internet!

An Autonomous System in Relation to BGP

First and foremost, in order to route successfully and reliably, have a coherent routing policy in place before you even start to type your Cisco IOS commands. Entire books have been written on routing policy. To put it very succinctly, *routing policy* is how all routers and networks in an AS reach a particular destination and exchange the information necessary so that each router has a consistent and reliable view of the network. This policy includes using the most appropriate IGPs and fielding an EGP such as BGP to reach non-AS destinations.

BGP handles the inter-AS aspects of the routing policy, channeling traffic in and out of the AS. It is not concerned with the internal routing of an AS; it is concerned only with reaching an AS, where it can hand off the responsibility to the routing mechanism that is handling the internal routing for the AS.

Unless the network engineer crafts the routing policy and enforces it, routing will be problematic. All routers in the AS must operate under the same policy. If you have one router using BGP for its external routing and another router using EGP and still another router relying on a static route and yet another router using an IGP, control will be nonexistent at best and troubleshooting will be a nightmare. The most important thing you can do for your routing policy is keep it simple and consistent.

How to Get an Official Autonomous System Number

Autonomous system numbers (ASNs) are tightly controlled by the IANA (Internet Assigned Numbers Authority) because only about 65,000 ASNs are available. An organization can obtain a unique AS number for itself only if it can satisfy two conditions. First, the organization must have a unique routing policy; in other words, its routing policy must differ from that of its peers in a neighboring AS. Second, the organization must be multihomed or will immediately become multihomed. There is a one-time registration fee and an annual fee to maintain the registration. At the time of this writing, there were three regional registries: ARIN (North America, South America, the Caribbean, and sub-Saharan Africa), RIPE-NCC (Europe, the Middle East, and parts of Africa), and the AP-NIC (Asia/Pacific). For more information, see the ARIN Web page at www.arin.net.

Autonomous System Numbers Found in RFC 1930 If you do not meet any of the above criteria but still want to run BGP in your enterprise, use the private ASNs 64512 through 65535. Like the reserved private IP addresses, these ASNs can be used by any organization. They are *not* to be advertised to the Internet! In fact, BGP has a feature to strip off the private ASN on updates leaving the autonomous system. Again, even if you are using only these private ASNs, ensure that your routing policy is consistent and that you have a plan for propagating them. Your routing policy should also address how you connect to the Internet if you are using private ASNs.

exam
ⓦatch

If you use private ASNs on Cisco products, Cisco IOS software provides a feature to strip them off before propagation.

The Internet and Routing

The Internet will never get smaller; in fact, it is growing daily as more and more individuals and organizations discover what it can do for them and new uses are found for it. In 1999, ARIN issued 1,685 ASNs. For 2000, at the time of this writing, ARIN had issued 1,145 ASNs, and the year is not even half over!

The Internet is a collection of autonomous systems all running their own routing policies but that agree to share routing information with each other. The common protocol via which these autonomous systems share information is BGP.

Over 70,000 Summarized Routes

At the time of this writing, the "Internet routing table" contained over 70,000 *summarized* routes! Without aggregation, the number would be significantly higher.

30 Megabyte Routing Table

As of this writing, the "Internet routing table" was 30 megabytes (MB) and growing. Without the aggregation and CIDR support of BGP, the table would be significantly larger.

BGP Terminology and Characteristics

In this section, we define and clarify the terminology associated with BGP. We also discuss some relevant characteristics of BGP.

Terminology

Mastery of BGP requires mastery of its unique and sometimes blurred vocabulary. BGP has associated with it terms that are very specific in their meanings but that everyday use has muddied. This section exposes you to BGP phraseology and hopefully provides you with working definitions you can use to achieve success with BGP.

Prefix   Many network professionals use the terms *prefix, route, network,* and *CIDR block* interchangeably, albeit slightly inaccurately, to refer to the information that BGP collects in its tables. RFC 1771 defines a *route* as "a unit of information that pairs a destination with the attributes of a path to that destination"—in other words, information that tells a router what path to take to reach a particular destination.

Some quick and correct definitions for each of these loosely used terms follow, all defined within the context of routing:

- A *route* is either the complete path (in the case of BGP) to take to reach a destination or the next hop (in the case of RIP) to take to reach a destination.

- A *network* is a destination that is advertised within a routing update; it is the final goal of routing.

- A *CIDR block* typically refers to IP addresses that have been summarized into a single or small number of routing entries. It involves the manipulation of the wildcard masks to achieve the best summarization and results in smaller routing tables and fewer updates.

- A *prefix* is the summarized address that is derived as the result of summarizing address. The term *prefix* is also sometimes used to refer to the network part of an IP address.

Despite these specific meanings, the terms will still be used interchangeably. When you encounter these terms on your exam, remember their exact meanings.

Incremental Updates   Once neighbor negotiation has completed successfully, BGP peers initially exchange their entire databases. After that, they perform incremental updates on any network changes rather than resending the entire database. Incremental updates conserve bandwidth and CPU cycles.

Reliable Updates   BGP neighbors communicate over TCP port 179. TCP, a reliable transport layer protocol, is responsible for segmentation, reassembly, error detection, and error correction. BGP relies on TCP to ensure that the data arrives at its destination.

Multiple Metrics/Attributes   BGP does not use metrics. Instead, it relies on attributes to make its decisions. The 10-step decision process that BGP goes through to select the single best path for injection into the BGP routing table will be discussed later in this chapter.

Complex Path Selection Process   If BGP receives an advertisement with more than one route to the same destination, it goes through a 10-step process to select the best route. It does not necessarily go through the entire 10 steps; it stops once it has determined the best route.

Characteristics

Some characteristics of BGP demonstrate why it is not grouped with most other routing protocols. Its behavior and purpose clearly indicate that BGP was designed to accomplish a specific task.

Does Not Look for the Fastest Pathway   BGP has no concept of link cost or speed. Instead, it uses a hop-count (path-vector) mechanism to select the best path.

Designed to Scale to Huge Networks   BGP scales very well to large, Internet-sized networks. This is due to the fact that BGP routes AS by AS rather than link by link. Recall that a single AS can have a multitude of links.

Has a Forwarding Database Containing Known Pathways to All Known Networks   The *forwarding database* of BGP contains those networks that BGP has learned and the paths to reach them. The forwarding database contains routes that have been selected after passing through any filters but that have not necessarily been chosen as the best route. In other words, the forwarding database is a database of alternate routes.

Submits Best Routes from Forwarding Database to Routing Table
BGP executes its 10-step decision process on entries to the forwarding database to select the best route for its routing table. We will go over this process in a later section.

exam
Watch

BGP peers initially exchange their entire tables, then incremental updates thereafter if there are any network changes. KEEPALIVES maintain the peer connection.

BGP Peering

Peering is the act of forming a relationship with another BGP speaker in either the same AS system or an external AS. Until they peer (that is, become neighbors), BGP routers will not become neighbors and will not exchange routing updates.

What Are BGP Neighbors, BGP Speakers, and BGP Peers?

As used by BGP, the terms *neighbor* and *peer* mean the same thing: two or more BGP routers that have formed a TCP connection between themselves and exchanged the messages necessary to form a relationship that enables them to send and receive updates between themselves. A *BGP speaker* is any router that runs BGP, although it might not necessarily be a direct peer.

Internal BGP Neighbors

BGP speakers in the same AS can become neighbors with the other BGP speakers in the AS. This is called an *Internal BGP (IBGP) peer connection* and is used to ensure that all BGP speakers in the same AS have the same BGP database. IBGP neighbors must already be reachable via an IGP route (or static). IBGP peers do not have to be directly connected to each other. IBGP neighbors must be fully meshed with each other because, although an IBGP neighbor will propagate any information it receives over its EBGP links, it will not propagate any information it receives over its IBGP links to other IBGP peers. In addition, an IBGP peer will propagate any information it receives over its IBGP peer connections to its EBGP peers. Some alternatives to the full mesh requirement are route reflectors and confederations.

exam
ⓦatch

IBGP peers should be fully meshed.

External BGP Neighbors

Neighbors in other ASs are called External BGP (EBGP) neighbors. EBGP neighbors, by default, must be directly connected to each other. Cisco provides a command called EBGP_MULTIHOP to compensate for situations in which the EBGP peers cannot be directly connected.

What Is a BGP Attribute?

As we previously discussed, an *attribute* is a description of a route. It contains information describing the path to a destination. There are several categories of attribute, and the categories are usually grouped together to describe the class of attribute and its nature. The type of attribute present is identified by the first 3 bits in the flag field of the UPDATE message. The first 8 bits are the attribute flag field, and the last 8 bits are the attribute type field. The type code actually identifies the attribute, as illustrated in Figure 8-4 and outlined below:

- **O** Optional if 1 or well known if 0
- **T** Transitive if 1 or nontransitive if 0
- **P** Partial if 1 or complete if 0
- **L** Length of the attribute: if 1, it is 2 bytes long; if 0, it is 1 byte long

Well Known vs. Optional

A *well-known attribute* must be recognized by all implementations of BGP across all platforms. Well-known attributes constitute the core of BGP attributes. Well-known attributes are always transitive. *Optional attributes* do not have to be recognized or part of the BGP implementation.

Mandatory vs. Discretionary

Mandatory attributes must exist and must be used by all BGP implementations. *Discretionary attributes* do not have to be used by all BGP implementations and do not have to be sent in the UPDATE message.

Transitive vs. Nontransitive

Attributes classified as *transitive* must be passed along to BGP peers. *Nontransitive attributes* do not get passed along to BGP peers.

Partial vs. Complete

An attribute with the P bit turned on to indicate it is *partial* means that at least one BGP peer in the path did not recognize an optional attribute. When turned off, it

FIGURE 8-4					
Attribute fields in the UPDATE message	O	T	P	L	Type Code

means that all BGP peers in the path were able to recognize all optional attributes. This is typically used with transitive attributes.

exam
Watch

Be able to differentiate among optional, well-known, transitive, nontransitive, partial, and complete attributes.

BGP Attributes

Several important attributes need to be highlighted because they are particularly important or are mandatory attributes that are critical to understanding BGP. This is not a comprehensive list; see RFC 1771 for more attributes. Some BGP implantations can have their own optional attributes that might not be supported by Cisco.

AS_PATH Type Code 2

AS_PATH Type Code 2 is a well-known mandatory attribute that identifies the ASs that this UPDATE message has passed through to reach this point. It contains the sequence of ASs, with the first AS being last in the list. It can be modified directly by the network engineer using route maps and regular expressions to change its length.

NEXT_HOP Type Code 3

NEXT_HOP is a well-known mandatory attribute that identifies the border router (by IP address) that is the next hop to the destination listed in the UPDATE message. The NEXT_HOP attribute identifies the router that should be used to reach the destination. What is identified as the "border router" depends on what router is receiving the UPDATE message from what peer.

An IBGP router receiving the UPDATE message will see its IBGP peer as the next hop if the route originated in its AS. An EBGP router receiving the UPDATE message from an EBGP peer will see that EBGP peer as the next hop. If the route is external to the AS, an IBGP router receiving the update from an IBGP peer will see the EBGP router that originated the message, rather than the IBGP peer from which it received the update, as the next hop.

On multiaccess networks with the peers on the same subnet, the NEXT_HOP will be passed along unaltered, regardless of whether the network is broadcast or nonbroadcast. On nonbroadcast multiaccess (NBMA) networks running in point-to-multipoint mode, the spoke router will be responsible for disseminating the next-hop information, with its IBGP peer from which it learned the route as the next hop or passing the EBGP peer along as the next hop.

IBGP peers, by default, are fully meshed; therefore, when an IBGP peer receives an update from one of its IBGP peers, it will not advertise that route to any of its other IBGP peers. On the other hand, an IBGP peer will advertise any routes it receives from an EBGP peer to all its IBGP peers because there is no full-mesh assumption about EBGP peerings. Conversely, an IGBP peer will forward updates from its IBGP peers to all its EBGP peers; the assumption here is that the other IBGP peers do not peer with this EBGP peer.

Having said all that, how does BGP decide what the next hop to a particular destination is? The answer is, as with many things in life: it depends. Knowing how the next hop is derived is important for you to understand BGP as used on production networks—and for passing the exam.

Probably the most ambiguous next-hop calculations come from updates exchanged between IBGP peers. If the network advertised is owned by the AS and is advertised by an IBGP peer into BGP, that peer will be the next hop, even if it is several hops away. This is radically different from the way most IGPs operate; their next hop is always a directly connected neighbor. The configuration in Figure 8-5 illustrates this behavior.

In Figure 8-5, A and B have network statements for 198.101.24.0/24 and announce this fact to all their peers via IBGP and EBGP. C must traverse A to reach B. An IGP running on C would select A as the next hop to reach B; BGP on C would select B as the next hop, since it has the lowest RID, which creates a problem for C: how does it reach B, which is not directly connected? The answer is that C must do a lookup and find a route to B via a static route, an IGP, or an EGP. In our figure, C would most likely end up using A as the next hop for B. Both A and B are advertising the network 198.101.24.0/24; we again run into a similar problem if C selects B as the next hop (on the basis of having the lowest RID, for example): even though A also has a path to this network, C will select B and must transit B (as previously described) to reach this network. The network would be reachable, but tracing the path and understanding the rationale of the path selection process could become troublesome in a large network. For internal networks, Cisco routers, by default, prefer IGP routes (all with an administrative distance of less than 200) over IBGP routes with an administrative distance of 200.

Determining the next hop for an external network can be just as confusing as determining the next hop for an internal network. Figure 8-6 shows an EBGP peering between AS1 and AS2.

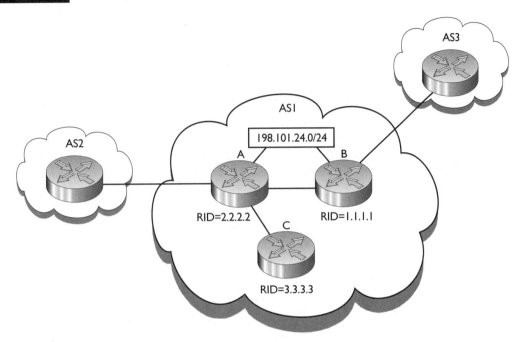

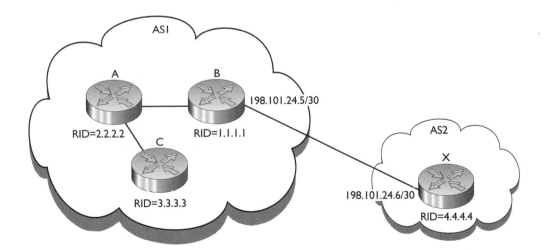

Routers B and X have a point-to-point link with the network address of 198.101.24.0/30 and are neighbors. All the AS1 routers (A and C) would see prefixes learned from Router X as having the next-hop address of 198.101.24.6 because the next-hop address of external networks will be injected into the AS unaltered. A and C need to perform a lookup to determined how to get to X; unless B is announcing this address via a routing protocol to A and C, or A and C have a static route to X, they will not be able to reach any networks in AS2. Remember that BGP routes AS by AS, not network by network, as most IGPs do.

BGP behaves the same on NBMA networks such as Frame Relay, but you must take care that routers can reach the next hop as needed or that a hub router acts as the next hop for routers that the spokes cannot reach. Figure 8-7 illustrates BGP running over a partially meshed hub-and-spoke network. B (the hub) has connectivity to A and X (spokes); A and X have no connectivity to each other except via B, even though A and X are on the same network. A configuration of this sort can cause problems for BGP—in fact, for other routing protocols, too.

There are three approaches to resolving this situation: a full mesh (not done in Figure 8-7), subinterfaces, or a NEXT-HOP-SELF statement on the hub router (B). A full mesh might be cost and resource prohibitive, but it will resolve the problem and enable all the routers on the same network to reach each other. You can use subinterfaces to connect A to B and B to X; this would result in two separate networks and consume address space, however. B would route between A and X; A

FIGURE 8-7   A next hop over a point-to-multipoint partially meshed network

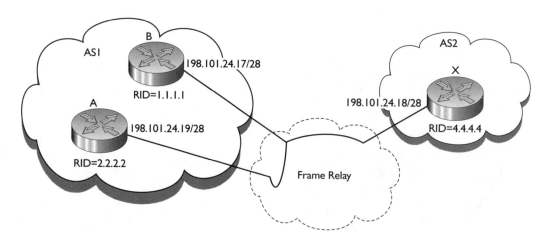

and X would not peer with each other, because EBGP peers must be directly connected. The final option requires the least amount of change: insert a NEXT-HOP-SELF statement on the hub router. The NEXT-HOP-SELF enables B to insert its IP address as the next hop for X and A when advertising to A and X, respectively.

The NEXT-HOP-SELF command can be important, not only in the situation described in the previous paragraph but especially for large ISPs connected to the Internet and exchanging updates with other large ISPs. Keep in mind that the original purpose of BGP was to exchange updates between ISPs at public connection points using (at the time) high-speed media such as FDDI or Ethernet. As of this writing, over 500 ISPs are exchanging updates; a single router for a single ISP is no longer sufficient to process all these updates. The workload must be distributed.

An ISP can accomplish this workload distribution by having several routers connected to the connection point and creatively using the NEXT-HOP-SELF command to "load balance" the traffic between several routers. For example, ISP1 could have routers 1, 2, 3, and 4 handle traffic from ISPA, ISPB, ISPC, and ISPD, respectively, by having 1,2, 3, and 4 identify themselves as the next hops for A, B, C, and D, respectively, when advertising into that ISP's AS. When a router in the ISP's AS wants to reach A, B, C, or D, that router will send to the most appropriate router as the next hop. This method can muddle troubleshooting, but it is a most effective and simple way to handle large volumes of routing traffic. In addition, the single point of failure is removed.

LOCAL_PREF Type Code 5

LOCAL_PREF is a mandatory discretionary attribute that is included in all UPDATE messages that a BGP speaker sends to all BGP speakers in its own AS. It will *not* be sent to EBGP peers. This attribute is restricted to the AS of the BGP router.

MULTI_EXIT_DISC Type Code 4

MULTI_EXIT_DISCRIMINATOR (MED) is an optional nontransitive attribute that provides a hint to the receiving EBGP router as to what route it should take to reach the destination. It is exchanged between ASs but does not leave the AS that it enters. It is used to make a decision within the AS that it enters. When passed to another AS, the MED, since it is nontransitive, is reset to 0.

ORIGIN Type Code 1

ORIGIN is a well-known mandatory attribute. It is generated by the AS that originated the route(s) in the UPDATE message. The ORIGIN information is propagated to BGP speakers. Values can be 0 if the route was learned via an IGP, 1 if the route was learned via an EGP such as BGP, and 2 for INCOMPLETE if the route was learned by means other than an IGP or EGP. The ORIGIN attribute is used by the BGP route selection process to pick the best route. The order preference, from most to least, is IGP, EGP, INCOMPLETE.

COMMUNITY Type Code 8

COMMUNITY is a variable-length optional nontransitive attribute. A community consists of logically grouped destinations that share a common set of attributes or characteristics. Of particular interest are two well-known communities used to control updates. NO_EXPORT COMMUNITY (0xFFFFFF01) means that this route should be advertised only within the AS; it should not be advertised to any other AS. NO_ADVERTISE COMMUNITY (0xFFFFFF02) indicates that the route should not be advertised to any BGP router within the receiving AS.

The COMMUNITY attribute is designed to simplify routing policy and enhance control over how routes should be handled when passed to another AS. One well-known community is INTERNET, which indicates that a route can be advertised by anyone.

WEIGHT (Proprietary to Cisco)

WEIGHT is an optional nontransitive attribute that is proprietary to Cisco products. A higher weight is more preferred and can range from 0 to 65535; the default is 32768. It is used to help a BGP router select the best route out of several routes to the same destination.

exam
ⓦatch

WEIGHT is a proprietary attribute found only on Cisco products.

BGP Synchronization

Synchronization is a BGP feature whereby BGP will not advertise a route to other autonomous systems until the IGP has advertised the route to all other IGP speakers in the AS. This prevents BGP from advertising a route to other ASs unless the route is reachable via an IGP. With synchronization, BGP will check with the IGP and ensure that it has the route before BGP advertises the route to its EBGP peers. Synchronization is enabled by default or can be enabled if turned off by entering the SYNCHRONIZATION command under the BGP routing configuration.

What BGP Synchronization Does When It Is Turned On (Default Setting)

By default, synchronization is turned on. The result is BGP will not advertise a route until the IGP has injected it into the routing table.

What Happens When BGP Synchronization Is Turned Off

When synchronization is turned off, BGP will advertise its routes to its EBGP peers, regardless of whether the IGP has the route in its table or not. There is no wait period when synchronization is disabled, because BGP will start advertising the route as soon as it gets it.

When and Why Synchronization Might Be Disabled

There are times when you might need to turn off synchronization to avoid delays in getting the route propagated to EBGP peers. Use the NO SYNCHRONIZATION command under the BGP routing process if BGP needs to advertise the route as soon as it gets it, without waiting for the IGP to acquire the route. You can safely turn off synchronization if the AS is not a transit AS—that is, it will not pass traffic from other ASs. If your AS is a transit AS and you turn off synchronization, connectivity could become a problem if traffic arrives for a destination before you have a route.

You may also disable synchronization if all transit routers in the AS are fully meshed IBGP peers. All these routers have the same routing information; therefore, the impact from turning off synchronization will be nil.

You can also turn off synchronization if BGP is acting solely as a border router to the Internet and is merely propagating a default route into the AS itself while sending routing information from its AS to the Internet. In other words, this border router's only purpose in life is to connect your AS to the Internet; your other routers see it as the gateway of last resort. Whether or not it can reach your AS is immaterial to its purpose.

When you turn off synchronization, you are guarantceing that the BGP process has a BGP path between this router and the next-hop address of the destination.

If updates are not propagating, check your synchronization settings.

BGP Message Types

BGP peers become neighbors and exchange routing information using *messages*. There are four message types, and all of them have the same 19-byte header.

HEADER

All messages have the same fixed 19-byte header, as shown in Figure 8-8.

- **Marker**   A 16-byte value that the receiver of the message can predict. Used to detect loss of synchronization or to authenticate incoming messages. If this is an OPEN message or if the OPEN message has no authentication, this field will be set to all 1s. Otherwise, it will have a calculated value based on the authentication information.

- **Length**   Length must be at least 19 bytes but no more than 4096 bytes. Indicates the total length of the message.

- **Type**   Indicates whether this is an OPEN, UPDATE, NOTIFICATION, or KEEPALIVE message.

OPEN

Each side sends an OPEN message after the TCP connection is established between the peers. A KEEPALIVE is sent if the OPEN message is deemed acceptable. The OPEN message starts and completes the neighbor negotiations. The format of the OPEN message is shown in Figure 8-9. The minimum length of an OPEN message is 29 bytes.

- **Version**   One byte. BGP version. Current BGP version number is 4.

- **My Autonomous System**   Two bytes. Identifies the sender's ASN.

FIGURE 8-8   BGP message header structure

Marker (16–bytes)	Length (2–bytes)	Type (1–byte)

FIGURE 8-9	OPEN message format

Version (1–byte)	My Autonomous System (2–bytes)	Hold Time (2–bytes)	BGP Identifier (4–bytes)	Optional Parameters Length (1–byte)	Optional Parameters		
					Type	Length	Value

- **Hold Time**   Indicates the maximum amount of time in seconds that may elapse between KEEPALIVE or UPDATE messages. When a BGP speaker receives an OPEN message, it *must* calculate the Hold Time by using either its Hold Time or the Hold Time received in the OPEN message. The Hold Time *must* be either 0 or greater than 3 seconds. If it is 0, the other side must be configured with a Hold Time. Three seconds is the minimum because Hold Time is three times the KEEPALIVE interval. The minimum for the KEEPALIVE interval is 1 second.

- **BGP Identifier**   Four bytes. BGP Identifier of the sender (sender's router ID).

- **Optional Parameters Length**   One byte. Total length of the Optional Parameters field in bytes. A value of 0 means there are no optional parameters.

- **Optional Parameters**   <Parameter Type, Parameter Length, Parameter Value>.

- **Parameter Type**   One byte. Identifies individual parameters. For example: Authentication is Type 1.

- **Parameter Length**   One byte. Length of the Parameter Value field in bytes.

- **Parameter Value**   Variable length. Depends on value of Parameter Type.

UPDATE

UPDATE messages carry the routing information between neighbors. They advertise routes and identify invalid routes for removal from the database. The format of the UPDATE message is shown in Figure 8-10.

- **Unfeasible Routes Length**   Two bytes. Total length of Withdrawn Routes in bytes. 0 means no routes are being withdraw with this message (the Withdrawn Routes field is not present).

- **Withdrawn Routes**   Variable length. Lists IP prefixes (<length, prefix>) being withdrawn.

FIGURE 8-10 UPDATE message format

Unfeasible Routes Length (2–bytes)	Withdrawn Routes (variable)		Total Path Attribute Length (2–bytes)	Path Attributes (variable)		Network Layer Reachability Information (variable)	
	Length	Prefix		Flags	Type Code	Length	Prefix

- **Length**   Length in bits of the IP prefix; 0 matches all IP addresses.

- **Prefix**   IP prefixes with sufficient trailing bits to end on a byte boundary.

- **Total Path Attribute Length**   Two bytes. Total length of the Path Attributes field in bytes. 0 means no Network Layer Reachability Information (NLRI).

- **Path Attributes**   Variable length. Path attribute is a triple <attribute type, attribute length, attribute value>.

- **Attribute Type**   Two bytes. Field is divided into an Attribute Flags byte and an Attribute Type Code byte.

- **Attribute Flags**

- **High-order bit (bit 0)**   Optional bit. Defines whether the attribute is optional (1) or well known (0).

- **Second high-order bit (bit 1)**   Transitive bit. Defines whether an optional attribute is transitive (1) or nontransitive (0). Must be set to 1 for well-known attributes.

- **Third high-order bit (bit 2)**   Partial bit. Defines whether the information contained in the optional transitive attribute is partial (1) or complete (0). Must be set to 0 for well known and optional nontransitive attributes.

- **Fourth high-order bit (bit 3)**   Extended Length bit. Defines whether the Attribute Length is one octet (0) or two octets (1). Two octets are used if the size of the attribute is greater than 255 bytes; otherwise, this field is set to 0.

- **Lower-order four bits (bit 4-7)**   Unused. Must be 0 and be ignored when received.

- **Attribute Type Code**   Identifies attributes associated with this route. For example: Code 1 is Origin, Code 2 is AS_PATH.

NOTIFICATION

NOTIFICATION messages are sent immediately upon an error, and the peer connection is terminated after sending it. The ability to decipher the error codes contained in NOTIFICATION messages can expedite troubleshooting and aid in resolving problems with BGP. It has the same fixed 19-byte header as the other messages, and its minimum length it 21 bytes. Figure 8-11 shows the format of the NOTIFICATION message.

- **Error Code**   One byte. Identifies the nature of the error: 1 = Message Header; 2 = OPEN Message; 3 = UPDATE; 4 = Hold Timer Expired; 5 = Finite State Machine; 6 = Cease.

- **Error Subcode**   One byte. Contains more specific information about the error; 0 is used if no specific error subcode is defined for the error message.

- **Data**   Variable length. Identifies the reason for the NOTIFICATION. Depends on Error Code and Error Subcode fields.

exam
ⓦatch

All message types share the same 19-byte header format.

KEEPALIVE

The KEEPALIVE message is nothing more than the 19-byte header. It is sent between peers at regular intervals to maintain their connection. BGP does not use TCP KEEPALIVES to maintain its peer connections. KEEPALIVES cannot be sent at a rate of more than one a second. Instead, just enough are sent so that the Hold Timer will not expire; typically, one-third of the Hold Timer is sufficient. The format of the KEEPALIVE message (which is also the HEADER format for all BGP messages) is shown in Figure 8-12.

- **Marker**   Sixteen bytes. Predictable value. Will be all 1s if an OPEN message; otherwise, will be the computed value. Used to detect loss of synchronization and to authenticate incoming messages.

FIGURE 8-11   NOTIFICATION message format

Error Code (1–byte)	Error Subcode (1–byte)	Data (variable)

FIGURE 8-12 KEEPALIVE message format

Marker (16–bytes)	Length (2–bytes)	Type (1–byte)

- **Length**   Two bytes. Shows total length of the entire message, including header, in bytes. Enables the next message in the stream to be located. Values must be at least 19 bytes but no more than 4096. No padding allowed.

- **Type**   One byte. Indicates the type of message: 1 = OPEN, 2 = UPDATE, 3 = NOTIFICATION, 4 = KEEPALIVE.

on the job

Half the battle of mastering BGP is mastering its very specific terminology! Start with the RFCs to master BGP terms, and every other BGP book you read will become much easier to understand. Be sure you understand the different attribute and message types.

FROM THE CLASSROOM

Comprehensive and Wide Ranging Routing Policies

In many networking periodicals, books, and manuals, the term *routing policy* is often quickly and classically defined as "how routing is controlled and managed." In discussions of a routing protocol such as BGP, the definition is modified slightly to "the BGP decision-making process, or what BGP does with a route as the route gets run through various filters and route maps."

There is nothing wrong with any of these definitions. In fact, they constitute a good starting point for creating an organizationwide, comprehensive routing policy that covers the whole routing spectrum, from internal routing protocol decision making to routing emergency

recovery. In other words, let's take the word *policy* literally!

The first phase in creating this enterprise routing policy is to identify *all* networks that *all* your routing protocols should be advertising. Determine to which destinations these networks should be advertised and via what routing protocols. Diagram the routing protocols you are running on what routers and networks and, in the case of legacy routing protocols such as RIP, why you are running them when there are better alternatives. Redistribution among protocols should be minimized and very tightly managed; in fact, avoid redistribution altogether if possible. Identify all route maps, distribution lists, and access lists through which all routes must be passed. Document and explain the purpose of each. This part of the routing policy will create a complete routing picture of your enterprise; it takes care of the mechanical details.

In the second phase, centralize your routing decision-making authority. Democracy and freedom of choice are great for humans, but they can be horrendous for routing! The organization that lets any network engineer arbitrarily make decisions on the elements outlined in the previous paragraph will soon be an ill organization as far as routing is concerned. An organization should strive for a benevolent dictatorship—regardless of whether it's a dictatorship of one or a dictatorship by committee. The point is that decisions about routing protocols to use, processing ASN registrations, enabling access on routers, IP addressing schemes, and other issues related to routing should be decided by a central authority for the organization. These decisions must be open to and accept input from all network personnel in the organization to forestall decisions being made in a vacuum. By centralizing routing policy decision making, an organization can ensure that its networks remain consistent and easy to maintain and troubleshoot. Many organizations implement this policy already in the form of a network operations center (NOC).

People are the single most important nontechnical element when crafting your routing policy, so you should address them. Your routing policy should address the level of skills and knowledge required to work with the various routing protocols your organization uses. Do the personnel who work on the network have the skills and knowledge necessary to support and troubleshoot it? Your routing policy should incorporate a training plan to keep your personnel updated to work with any changes or updates that occur. No one person can know everything, so ensure that access to support is available; examples of such support include access to the Cisco TAC (Technical Assistance Center) and on-call experts. Finally, your routing policy should ensure that *all* personnel understand the need to protect and secure all aspects of the network, especially routing.

Make Murphy's Law ("If anything can go wrong, it will") a part of your routing policy. Identify as many show-stoppers as you can, and determine what the organization will do to overcome them. This includes addressing actions to take if routing becomes unstable, links go out, the service provider goes bankrupt, or even if disgruntled personnel wreak havoc.

Put all these pieces together, and you will have a comprehensive routing policy that not only addresses internal routing protocol decision making but covers many other aspects of routing not typically addressed. To ensure the success of your routing policy, always send it out for comments, and incorporate any good comments or suggestions you receive. By doing so, you make the routing policy everyone's, not just yours.

—*Charles Riley, CCNP, MCSE*

BGP Route Selection Process

BGP evaluates routes against preset criteria to determine the best route to submit to the routing table. BGP selects only the best route, and only one. If it has several routes to the same destination, it will go through the following criteria to pick the best route. BGP evaluates each route against each criterion, as shown in Figure 8-13. If there are still multiple routes after evaluating against the criterion, BGP moves to

FIGURE 8-13 The BGP decision process

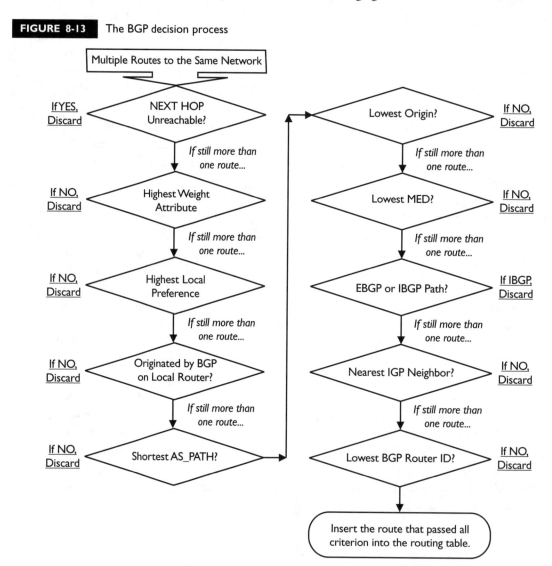

SCENARIO & SOLUTION

Why is CIDR so important?	It enables any routing protocol that supports it to advertise networks that are using subnet masks of varying lengths. It also enables wiser use of IP addresses by allowing the network engineer to allocate per need rather than following a rigid class structure, thus conserving IP addresses and enabling them to still be advertised.
Can BGP Version 4 exchange routing information with BGP Version 3?	Yes, although there might be some extra configuration involved. For example, you might need to configure a NEIGHBOR statement to have BGP4 send out updates to that neighbor in a Version 3-compatible format.
Can BGP advertise directly connected networks?	Yes, as well as networks that are not directly connected. Contrast this with most IGPs, which can advertise only directly connected networks.

the next evaluation criterion. The process continues until BGP has identified a single best route.

Next-best routes are stored in the BGP routing table as alternates, to be used if the best route fails or is removed. If the BGP multipath and load-balancing features are enabled, BGP can select more than one BGP route for inclusion in the routing table.

EXERCISE 8-2

Identifying Message Formats and Purposes

For each message in Table 8-1, match it with its purpose and format from the lists that follows.

TABLE 8-1	Message	Purpose	Format
Message Formats and Purposes	KEEPALIVE		
	UPDATE		
	NOTIFICATION		
	OPEN		

Purpose

Place the correct letter from the following list in the box in the Purpose column of Table 8-1 to describe the purpose of each message.

A. Sent immediately upon an error; shortly after it is sent, the peer connection is reset.

B. Sent after the TCP connection is established on port 179 to start and complete the neighbor negotiation process.

C. Carries the routing information between neighbors; also used to withdraw routes.

D. Consists of only a 19-byte header; maintains the connection between peers.

Format

Place the correct letter from the following list in the box in the Format column of Table 8-2 to describe the structure of each message.

A.

Error Code (1-byte)	Error Subcode (1-byte)	Data (Variable)

B.

Marker (16-bytes)	Length (2-bytes)	Type (1-byte)

C.

Version (1-byte)	My Autonomous System (2-bytes)	Hold Time (2-bytes)	BGP Identifier (4-bytes)	Optional Parameters Length (1-byte)	Optional Parameters Type Length Value

D.

Unfeasible Routes Length (2-bytes)	Withdrawn Routes (Variable) Length Prefix	Total Path Attribute Length (2-bytes)	Path Attributes (Variable) Flags Type Code	Network Layer Reachability Information (Variable) Length Prefix

Solution:

TABLE 8-2			
	Message	**Purpose**	**Format**
Solution to Exercise 8-2	KEEPALIVE	D	B
	UPDATE	C	D
	NOTIFICATION	A	A
	OPEN	B	C

CERTIFICATION OBJECTIVE 8.03

Configuring Basic BGP

Configuring BGP on Cisco routers and switches starts with a simple command. From there, BGP is configured to meet the needs of the AS. As with all other routing protocols, you perform your BGP configurations in Configuration mode and add the networks that you want BGP to advertise to its peers.

The ROUTER BGP AUTONOMOUS-SYSTEM Command

BGP is started on Cisco products with the ROUTER BGP AUTONOMOUS-SYSTEM command. Notice how similar this command is to the commands you execute to start IGPs such as RIP or OSPF. One major difference is that the process ID for the BGP routing process is tied to the ASN and is globally significant.

```
router bgp <autonomous-system>
<Your autonomous-system that is a number from 1-65535>.
```

This command creates a BGP routing process for the AS identified. You are limited to one BGP process per router (in essence, one BGP AS per router).

If you cannot obtain your own ASN from ARIN or you will not be connecting to the Internet, or if will be using Cisco's advanced features to strip ASNs before propagating to the Internet, you can use a private ASN for your AS. Those reserved numbers are 64512 through 65535.

exam
Ⓦatch   *The range of numbers reserved for private ASNs is 64512 through 65535.*

The NETWORK Statement Under Router BGP

You need to configure BGP to let it know what networks to advertise to its peers. This is done by entering the NETWORK command under the BGP routing process configuration. Certain IGPs, such as OSPF, use this command to indicate the interfaces that are participating in the OSPF process and to which interfaces to send updates. BGP uses the NETWORK command to identify those networks belonging to a particular AS and to put the networks into its table.

The syntax of the command follows. We discuss what each of the options and arguments does in this section. At the time of this writing, there is a limit of 200 NETWORK statements.

```
network network-number [mask network-mask] [route-map route-map-name]
  [backdoor] [weight]
```

- **NETWORK-NUMBER**   IP prefix to be advertised to peers.

- **MASK**   The network mask associated with the IP prefix. Defaults to classful mask if none is specified. Enables subnetting and supernetting. Also injects IGP routes into the BGP table.

- **ROUTE-MAP**   Identifies the route map to be applied to this route before it gets advertised.

- **BACKDOOR**   Makes a route learned via an IGP the preferred route rather than the same route learned via an EBGP. Use when it is not advisable to change the route's distance.
- **WEIGHT**   Cisco proprietary option. 0 to 65535; the default is 32768. Helps the receiving router to select the best route from several routes to the same destination.

Pay close attention to how you use the deceptively simple NETWORK command! The behavior of BGP can become quite odd if you do not specify the correct network address and subnet mask. For example, if you enter NETWORK 132.56.1.0, BGP will search the routing table for 132.56.1.0/16 (the exact network number you entered, plus the natural mask); it would not look for 132.56.0.0/16 or 132.56.1.0/24. Since this is an odd pairing, it will not be found; therefore, BGP would not announce it, regardless of whether synchronization is turned off. If you entered the command NETWORK 132.56.0.0, BGP still needs to see at least one address of this network, such as 132.56.1.0, before it will advertise 132.56.0.0/16.

The NEIGHBOR Command

The NEIGHBOR command is used to establish peering with neighboring routers. Note that unlike certain IGPs such as OSPF, there is no automatic neighbor acquisition. If the network engineer does not execute the NEIGHBOR command manually, BGP will *not* form neighbor relations with any other routers.

The syntax for the NEIGHBOR command follows. The most relevant options and arguments are explained. This information is taken directly from the Cisco IOS Help listing for the command. Notice that almost all aspects of communications with a neighbor can be modified on a neighbor-by-neighbor basis.

```
router1(config-router)#neighbor x.x.x.x
 advertise-map specify route-map for conditional advertisement
 advertisement-interval Minimum interval between sending BGP routing updates
 default-originate Originate default route to this neighbor
 description Neighbor specific description
 distribute-list Filter updates to/from this neighbor
 ebgp-multihop Allow EBGP neighbors not on directly connected networks
 filter-list Establish BGP filters
```

```
maximum-prefix Maximum number of prefix accept from this peer
next-hop-self Disable the next hop calculation for this neighbor
password Set a password
peer-group Member of the peer-group
remote-as Specify a BGP neighbor
remove-private-AS Remove private AS number from outbound updates
route-map Apply route map to neighbor
route-reflector-client Configure a neighbor as Route Reflector client
send-community Send Community attribute to this neighbor
soft-reconfiguration Per neighbor soft reconfiguration
timers BGP per neighbor timers
unsuppress-map Route-map to selectively unsuppress suppressed routes
update-source Source of routing updates
version Set the BGP version to match a neighbor
weight Set default weight for routes from this neighbor
```

The minimal NEIGHBOR command necessary to establish peering with a neighbor is to provide the IP address and ASN of the neighbor. The syntax for this is as follows:

```
neighbor ip-address remote-as ASN
```

Routers will not become peers unless they are directly connected (on the same segment—a must for EBGP) or can reach each other via an IGP (works for IBGP). Generally speaking, and especially when establishing an EBGP peering, you should use the IP address from the segment that contains the remote router with which you want to peer. What about using loop-back addresses that have been recommended for fault tolerance and stability in IGPs? If EBGP peers are on the same physical segment that has its own IP address, a loop-back will not help matters much. If the link between EBGP peers is prone to failure, the peering will fail anyway. Loop-back interfaces are best used for establishing IBGP peerings. If a loop-back address is used for EBGP peers, it must be reachable via an dynamic protocol or a static route. You also need to use the UPDATE SOURCE command to specify the loop-back address as the source address for a peering.

Internal or External Neighbors

Internal neighbors in the same AS are established as an IBGP peering. External neighbors are in a remote AS and are established as an EBGP peering. The router is able to distinguish between the two by comparing its ASN with the ASN of the neighbors. The same command is used to establish internal and external peer relationships. BGP is able to distinguish between an internal peer (the peer's ASN is the same as its ASN) and an external peer (the peer's ASN is different from its ASN) by comparing its ASN with the ASN of its peer. The command syntax is the same; different peerings will be established based on the ASN.

BGP Basic Configuration

Figure 8-14 shows a very basic BGP configuration. Routers 1 and 5 have both EBGP and IBGP peers. Unlike most IGPs, BGP does not have an automatic neighbor discovery feature; the network engineer must identify to BGP who its neighbors are.

BGP can communicate only with directly connected EBGP peers—that is, the EBGP peers must reside on the same segment as the local router. IBGP peers do not have to be directly connected. All neighbors must be reachable. Notice that each router is advertising networks that are not directly connected to it; this is a marked difference between BGP and IGPs. BGP can advertise networks that are not directly connected. A NEIGHBOR statement must be entered for IBGP peers in your AS because IBGP requires a fully meshed network. A BGP router needs NEIGHBOR statements only for directly connected peers; it will learn about external peers from its IBGP peers.

The **NEIGHBOR NEXT-HOP-SELF** Command

On NBMA networks such as Frame Relay or X.25, not all routers on the same segment have connectivity to each other. This is especially true in partially meshed topologies and point-to-multipoint configurations. Typically, you will have one router (the hub) that has connectivity to all other routers (the spokes). The spokes will be able to reach the hub, and vice versa, but not each other. As a result, BGP peerings must be established with the hub routers, and when the hub router passes information gleaned from a spoke to other spokes, it may use the NEIGHBOR NEXT-HOP-SELF command. This command will identify the hub as the source for the routing information from each spoke. On point-to-point, broadcast, or fully meshed networks, the NEXT-HOP-SELF option will not help; in fact, it could hinder by adding an unnecessary hop to process.

FIGURE 8-14 A basic BGP configuration

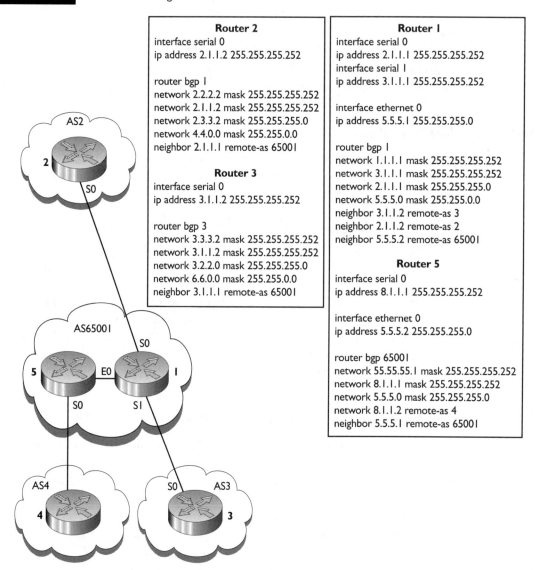

Router 2
interface serial 0
ip address 2.1.1.2 255.255.255.252

router bgp 1
network 2.2.2.2 mask 255.255.255.252
network 2.1.1.2 mask 255.255.255.252
network 2.3.3.2 mask 255.255.255.0
network 4.4.0.0 mask 255.255.0.0
neighbor 2.1.1.1 remote-as 65001

Router 3
interface serial 0
ip address 3.1.1.2 255.255.255.252

router bgp 3
network 3.3.3.2 mask 255.255.255.252
network 3.1.1.2 mask 255.255.255.252
network 3.2.2.0 mask 255.255.255.0
network 6.6.0.0 mask 255.255.0.0
neighbor 3.1.1.1 remote-as 65001

Router 1
interface serial 0
ip address 2.1.1.1 255.255.255.252
interface serial 1
ip address 3.1.1.1 255.255.255.252

interface ethernet 0
ip address 5.5.5.1 255.255.255.0

router bgp 1
network 1.1.1.1 mask 255.255.255.252
network 3.1.1.1 mask 255.255.255.252
network 2.1.1.1 mask 255.255.255.0
network 5.5.5.0 mask 255.255.0.0
neighbor 3.1.1.2 remote-as 3
neighbor 2.1.1.2 remote-as 2
neighbor 5.5.5.2 remote-as 65001

Router 5
interface serial 0
ip address 8.1.1.1 255.255.255.252

interface ethernet 0
ip address 5.5.5.2 255.255.255.0

router bgp 65001
network 55.55.55.1 mask 255.255.255.252
network 8.1.1.1 mask 255.255.255.252
network 5.5.5.0 mask 255.255.255.0
network 8.1.1.2 remote-as 4
neighbor 5.5.5.1 remote-as 65001

Figure 8-15 shows a situation that the NEXT-HOP-SELF command was designed to resolve. This is a point-to-multipoint (hub and spoke) network in which B is the hub and A and C are spokes Neither A nor C can directly communicate

FIGURE 8-15

The
NEXT-HOP-SELF
command

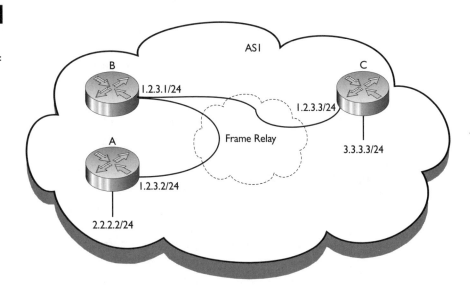

with the other, although they are on the same subnet. A and C will peer with and exchange updates to B, and B in turn will pass the updates to the spokes. Since A and C cannot communicate with each other, A will not be able to reach 3.3.3.3 and C will not be able to reach 2.2.2.2, even though both will have a routing entry for these routes in their tables. On B, entering the following commands will make B act as the next hop for A and C; this will make all networks reachable to the spokes. As far as they are concerned, B is the next hop.

```
Router 1 (on Router B)
neighbor 1.2.3.2 next-hop-self
neighbor 1.2.3.3 next-hop-self
```

The **NO SYNCHRONIZATION** Command

Recall from our previous discussions that BGP will not advertise a route unless it can reach it. Synchronization is a feature of BGP by which BGP will wait until the IGP responsible for the route has inserted the route into the routing table and advertised it throughout the AS via the IGP. BGP checks the IGP to see whether or not it contains an entry for the route before it advertises. Even if BGP has learned about the route via an IBGP peer, it will still wait until the IGP has propagated it.

This can sometimes be a long wait, especially if you are running an older IGP such as RIP; turning off synchronization can get a route advertised faster with BGP. However, *be warned!* If you turn off synchronization and a network gets advertised to a EBGP peer, that EBGP will send traffic to that network, regardless of whether BGP can actually reach the route or not. At a minimum, ensure that BGP can reach the route via IBGP.

The syntax for turning off synchronization is simple:

```
no synchronization
```

The AGGREGATE ADDRESS Command

Aggregation is the process of combining several IP addresses into a single IP prefix—that is, enabling the routing to use a single network number to advertise several networks. BGP supports aggregation as part of its CIDR features. Aggregation is also sometimes referred to as *summarization* or *supernetting*.

Unlike certain IGPs such as OSPF, address aggregation does not occur automatically in BGP. The network engineer must determine what networks can be summarized into a single advertisement and turn on aggregation. The law of the Internet (per NANOG [North American Network Operator's Group] and ARIN [American Registry for Internet Numbers]) is that you can summarize network addresses if you own at least 51 percent of the address block; owners of the remaining 49 percent must specifically announce them. This enables the size of the routing table to be reduced in those circumstances in which the addresses might not have been allocated in a summarization-friendly fashion.

The syntax for the aggregation command follows, along with its various options. As needed, some of the options have explanatory text that should be read carefully:

```
ROUTER(config-router)#aggregate-address x.x.x.x y.y.y.y ?
  advertise-map Set condition to advertise attribute

  as-set Generate AS set path information
```

This option is very important, especially if you are aggregating routes learned from another AS. This option combines the AS path of the original and more specific route with the AS path of its aggregation. This incorporates the complete path and ensures that the originating AS is clearly identified. Without this option, the aggregating AS will be seen as the source AS for the route, which could cause routing loops.

```
attribute-map Set attributes of aggregate
```

Use a route map to set the attributes of the routes meeting the criteria:

```
route-map Set parameters of aggregate
summary-only Filter more specific routes from updates.
```

Advertise the prefix of the route only, such as 1.0.0.0, rather than 1.1.1.0:

```
suppress-map Conditionally filter more specific routes from
updates
```

BGP will not advertise those specific routes identified. This is useful if you want to exclude networks from the range that do not belong to the AS.

The AS-SET and SUMMARY-ONLY options are handy when doing aggregation. We discuss only those aspects of the network in Figure 8-16 that actually pertain to aggregation; we will not rehash basic BGP configuration.

FIGURE 8-16 An aggregation example

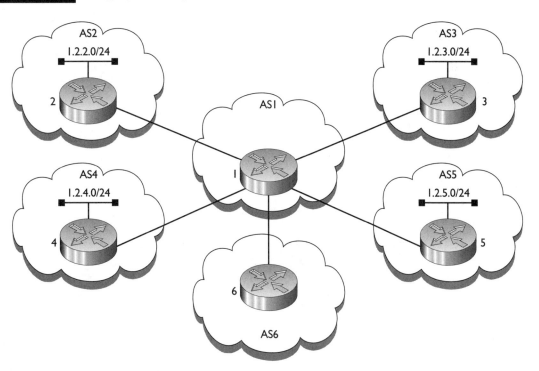

Router 1 is learning about the network 1.2.2.0 from Router 2, 1.2.3.0 from Router 3, 1.2.4.0 from Router 4, and 1.2.5.0 from Router 5; it is advertising those routes to Router 6 in AS 6. With no aggregation, when you perform a SHOW IP BGP on Router 6, the output is similar to the display given here. Notice that there is no summarization; Router 6 sees Router 1's address of 1.1.1.1 as the next hop.

```
Router 6# show ip bgp
BGP Table Version is 3, local router ID is 6.6.6.6.
Status codes: s suppressed, d damped, h history, * valid, > best, I - internal
Origin codes: I - IGP, e - EGP, ? - incomplete
 Network Next Hop Metric LocPrf Weight Path
*> 1.2.2.0/24 1.1.1.1 0 20 1 2 I
*> 1.2.3.0/24 1.1.1.1 0 20 1 3 I
*> 1.2.4.0/24 1.1.1.1 0 20 1 4 I
*> 1.2.5.0/24 1.1.1.1 0 20 1 5 i
```

On Router 1, we enter the following command to aggregate the network previously outlined. Notice that since we did not use the AS-SET option, the original AS information is stripped off the aggregated address and only AS1 is displayed as the path:

```
Router BGP 1
Aggregate-address 1.2.0.0 255.255.0.0

Router 6# show ip bgp
BGP Table Version is 4, local router ID is 6.6.6.6.
Status codes: s suppressed, d damped, h history, * valid, > best, I - internal
Origin codes: I - IGP, e - EGP, ? - incomplete
 Network Next Hop Metric LocPrf Weight Path
*> 1.2.0.0/16 1.1.1.1 0 0 1 i
*> 1.2.2.0/24 1.1.1.1 0 20 1 2 i
*> 1.2.3.0/24 1.1.1.1 0 20 1 3 i
*> 1.2.4.0/24 1.1.1.1 0 20 1 4 i
*> 1.2.5.0/24 1.1.1.1 0 20 1 5 i
```

Now we do the same thing again, only this time we use the AS-SET option. This time, we see the originating ASN listed with the aggregated address:

```
Router BGP 1
Aggregate-address 1.2.0.0 255.255.0.0 as-set
```

```
Router 6# show ip bgp
BGP Table Version is 4, local router ID is 6.6.6.6.
Status codes: s suppressed, d damped, h history, * valid, > best, I - internal
Origin codes: I - IGP, e - EGP, ? - incomplete
 Network Next Hop Metric LocPrf Weight Path
*> 1.2.0.0/16 1.1.1.1 0 0 1 {2,3,4,5} i
*> 1.2.2.0/24 1.1.1.1 0 20 1 2 i
*> 1.2.3.0/24 1.1.1.1 0 20 1 3 i
*> 1.2.4.0/24 1.1.1.1 0 20 1 4 i
*> 1.2.5.0/24 1.1.1.1 0 20 1 5 i
```

If we had used the SUMMARY-ONLY option on Router 1 in our aggregation efforts, network 1.2.2.0, 1.2.3.0, 1.2.4.0, and 1.2.5.0 would have appeared as 1.0.0.0; SUMMARY-ONLY aggregates to the natural prefix of the address only.

The **CLEAR IP BGP** Command

BGP provides sufficient mechanisms to report and recover from problems with neighbors, such as error notifications and automatic resets. There are times, however, when the network engineer needs to intervene directly and manually reset or clear the neighbor peerings. Cisco provides the CLEAR IP BGP command to do this and more.

Purpose of CLEAR IP BGP

The purpose of CLEAR IP BGP is to reset a BGP connection. When you reset a BGP connection, you clear entries obtained via that connection and restart the BGP peering process all over, from neighbor negotiations to routing information exchange (including full table updates).

Why You Should Never Use the * Option

CLEAR IP BGP * clears *all* and *every single* BGP connection established on a router! This is equivalent to total restart of BGP! You should *never* perform this command on a production router—especially not on a production router with multiple neighbors. The load placed on the router and the bandwidth will be very resource intensive. However, if you are absolutely sure that the command will solve your problems, contact the Cisco TAC first and get your assumptions verified. There might be another way to resolve your problem. Even then, use the command only if the situation is so bad that nothing else is working. In a lab environment, as part of a prescribed training program, you could use this command with impunity.

What Is Soft Reconfiguration?

Soft reconfiguration allows you to request and resend routing updates with your neighbors *without* resetting the entire connection to the neighbors. There are two approaches. Regardless of which of the two approaches you use, software reconfiguration has significantly lower overhead than a total reset of the sessions between the neighbors.

You can perform an outbound software configuration that will request fresh information from a neighbor and install it into the table. Essentially, your router sends out a request for the "latest and greatest" version of the neighbor's table and provides the remote router with its latest information. The caveat here is that unless you own or control both routers in question, you can not force a remote router to send you its routing table. You would have to perform a soft reconfiguration on both routers to have them send each other their routing tables.

The other approach is configuring the BGP routing process to store (not process) inbound soft reconfiguration requests and then execute the inbound version of the command to inject these updates into the table. This approach is to be used when you don't have control over the remote router. The changes will not be done on your router until you execute the CLEAR IP BGP X.X.X.X IN command. In other words, your router stores its inbound updates until you execute the CLEAR IP BGP X.X.X.X IN command. The major downside to this approach is that it could consume copious amounts of memory, depending on the table size, until you execute the CLEAR command. This approach accomplishes the same result as the remote router executing CLEAR IP BGP X.X.X.X SOFT OUT toward your router.

exam
ⓦatch

Soft reconfiguration of peers refreshes routing information with resetting the peer connection.

The syntax for both commands follows. Only the inbound option needs to have a NEIGHBOR statement under the BGP process:

```
clear ip bgp x.x.x.x soft {in|out}
neighbor 1.1.1.1 soft-reconfiguration in
```

What Is the Difference Between Soft Reconfiguration In and Out

Soft reconfiguration has two directions. In refers to those soft reconfiguration requests coming from a neighbor. The BGP router receiving them will store them in memory until the CLEAR command is executed. Soft reconfiguration out provides the remote peer with the latest version of the local router's table.

BGP Configuration

Figure 8-17 gives a more complex configuration. The configuration is basically the same as that in Figure 8-14 except that the link between Routers 1 and 5 is now a Frame Relay point-to-multipoint link, with Router 1 as the hub. (Frame Relay commands are not shown, for the sake of brevity.)

Since Router 1 is the hub and Router 5 is the spoke, Router 1 will act as the next hope for Router 5 because spokes cannot directly communicate with each other. Notice that the 19.x.x.x network was aggregated into a single prefix; instead of four, BGP now advertises only one. Synchronization has been turned off; BGP will not wait for the IGP to acquire and verify the route.

<hr>

EXERCISE 8-3

<hr>

Resetting Peer Connections

You are on a job interview and are being tested on your knowledge of BGP commands. You have been asked to reset BGP. The questions that you have been asked are as follows:

1. What is the command to reset the entire peer connection with the peer at IP address 1.2.3.4?

2. What is the command to refresh routing information from peer 1.2.3.4?

3. BGP is not working right. Should you use the CLEAR IP BGP * command?

Solution:

This exercise is designed to test your understanding of what the CLEAR IP BGP command does and whether you understand the difference between the hard and soft versions of this command. Generally speaking, the hard version resets all aspects

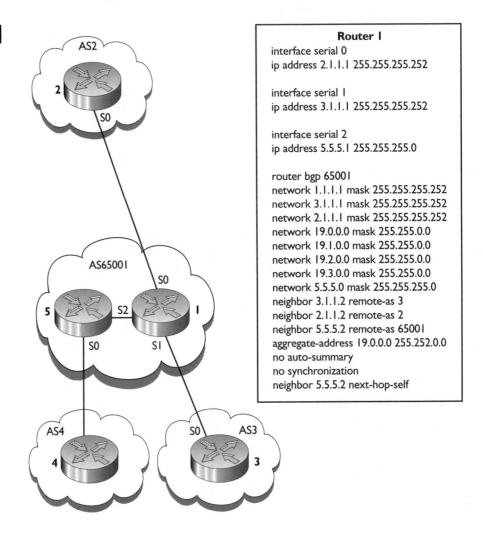

FIGURE 8-17

A BGP configuration using enhanced commands

Router 1
interface serial 0
ip address 2.1.1.1 255.255.255.252

interface serial 1
ip address 3.1.1.1 255.255.255.252

interface serial 2
ip address 5.5.5.1 255.255.255.0

router bgp 65001
network 1.1.1.1 mask 255.255.255.252
network 3.1.1.1 mask 255.255.255.252
network 2.1.1.1 mask 255.255.255.252
network 19.0.0.0 mask 255.255.0.0
network 19.1.0.0 mask 255.255.0.0
network 19.2.0.0 mask 255.255.0.0
network 19.3.0.0 mask 255.255.0.0
network 5.5.5.0 mask 255.255.255.0
neighbor 3.1.1.2 remote-as 3
neighbor 2.1.1.2 remote-as 2
neighbor 5.5.5.2 remote-as 65001
aggregate-address 19.0.0.0 255.252.0.0
no auto-summary
no synchronization
neighbor 5.5.5.2 next-hop-self

of peering with the neighbor, and the soft version seeks only to get refreshed routing information.

1. CLEAR IP BGP 1.2.3.4 (this command resets the entire peer connection with 1.2.3.4 and gets refreshed information from this peer).

2. CLEAR IP BGP 1.2.3.4 SOFT IN; the local router merely requests new routing information to replace what is in the table.

3. Not enough information; BGP not working right could be due to a number of factors. See the section in this chapter about using the CLEAR IP BGP * command and what effects it will have.

CERTIFICATION OBJECTIVE 8.04

Monitoring BGP Operations

Just as important as configuring BGP is the ability to monitor it and to find information related to routing and BGP. Cisco provides many commands for this purpose. We discuss several BGP-relevant commands in this section.

The SHOW IP PROTOCOLS Command

This command displays information about the various routing protocols running on the router, both IGPs and EGPs. It provides a quick snapshot of high-level detail about each protocol, such as what networks are participating in the routing process. The following is output from this command. Notice that for BGP, it identifies the routing process and AS and lists filters and route maps that have been applied to certain networks. It also lists the peers of this router. You can see that IGP synchronization, by default, is turned on.

```
Router#sh ip pro
Routing Protocol is "bgp 44"
 Sending updates every 60 seconds, next due in 0 seconds
 Outgoing update filter list for all interfaces is not set
 Incoming update filter list for all interfaces is not set
 IGP synchronization is enabled
 Automatic route summarization is enabled
 Neighbor(s):
 Address FiltIn FiltOut DistIn DistOut Weight RouteMap
 2.2.2.2
 Routing for Networks:
 1.1.1.1
```

```
Routing Information Sources:
Gateway Distance Last Update
3.3.3.3 20 00:00:00
Distance: external 20 internal 200 local 200
```

The SHOW IP ROUTE Command

This command displays the IP routing table. It lists all routes, including routes from IGPs, EGPs, static routes, and default routes. The syntax of the command follows. You can narrow the output down to a particular network or routing protocol:

```
show ip route [address [mask]] | [protocol [process-id]]
Router# show ip route
Codes: I - IGRP derived, R - RIP derived, O - OSPF derived
 C - connected, S - static, E - EGP derived, B - BGP derived
 * - candidate default route, IA - OSPF inter area route
 E1 - OSPF external type 1 route, E2 - OSPF external type 2 route
Gateway of last resort is 11.11.24.40 to network 29.10.0.0
O E2 15.10.0.0 [160/5] via 131.119.254.6, 0:01:00, Ethernet2
B 29.6.11.0 [200/128] via 131.119.254.244, 0:02:22
O IA 10.13.0.0 [160/5] via 131.119.254.6, 0:00:59, Ethernet2
```

The output of this command identifies the source of the router by protocol. Notice that unlike the IGP entries previously, BGP does not reference a router interface. You will never see a BGP entry in the routing table that references an interface; this is partly due to the fact that BGP does advertise networks that are not directly connected. The routing entry for 29.66.11.0 came from an IBGP peer (administrative distance of 200). The next hop for this entry might not be the router from which this update was received; rather, it is probably the next-hop address of a router in another autonomous system.

The SHOW IP BGP NEIGHBORS Command

The SHOW IP BGP NEIGHBORS command displays very detailed information about a particular neighbor. You can focus the output of this command by using the argument that follows. This command shows how many connections have been established, any routes or filtering being performed, and the number of messages that have been exchanged with this neighbor:

```
Router#show ip bgp neighbors 1.1.1.1 ?
advertised-routes Display the routes advertised to an EBGP neighbor
dampened-routes Display the dampened routes received from neighbor
flap-statistics Display flap statistics of the routes learned from neighbor
paths Display AS paths learned from neighbor
received-routes Display the received routes from neighbor
```

Output from the SHOW IP BGP NEIGHBOR command is as follows:

```
Router2 # show ip bgp neigbor

BGP neighbor is 1.1.1.1, remote AS 1, external link
BGP version 3, remote router ID 1.1.1.1
BGP state = Established, table version = 7, up for 0:05:23
Last read 0:05:22, hold time is 180, keepalive interval is 60 seconds
Received 12 messages, 0 notifications
Sent 13 messages, 2 notifications
Connections established 1; dropped 0
Connection state is ESTAB, I/O status: 1, unread input bytes: 0
Local host: 2.2.2.2, 12007 Foreign host: 1.1.1.1, 179

Enqueued packets for retransmit: 0, input: 0, saved: 0

Event Timers (current time is 835828):
Timer: Retrans TimeWait AckHold SendWnd KeepAlive
Starts: 12 0 10 0 0
Wakeups: 1 0 1 0 0
Next: 0 0 0 0 0

iss: 44331 snduna: 44409 sndnxt: 44409 sndwnd: 1872
irs: 94278043 rcvnxt: 94279011 rcvwnd: 2023 delrcvwnd: 162

SRTT: 253 ms, RTTO: 1582 ms, RTV: 472 ms, KRTT: 0 ms
minRTT: 3 ms, maxRTT: 300 ms, ACK hold: 300 ms
Flags: higher precedence
Datagrams (max data segment is 1450 bytes):
Rcvd: 12 (out of order: 0), with data: 9, total data bytes: 1801
Sent: 32 (retransmit: 2), with data: 28, total data bytes: 1712
```

We could write a book on the output of this command. Some particular parts can alert you to problems with BGP. BGP Version indicates the version being used to communicate with this peer. A rapidly incrementing Table Version shows a communications problem (link dropping) or a problem with the BGP configuration (perhaps mismatched NEIGHBOR statements). A high number of Connections Established versus Dropped can highlight a network problem.

The SHOW IP BGP Command

You can view the contents of the BGP routing table using SHOW IP BGP. Each network address in the BGP routing table is shown with its associated network hop address, metric, local preference, weight, and the AS path it has traversed. The following shows the output for this command; explanatory text follows the listing:

```
Router2#sh ip bgp
BGP table version is 6, local router ID is 222.222.222.222
Status codes: s suppressed, d damped, h history, * valid, > best, i - internal
Origin codes: i - IGP, e - EGP, ? - incomplete

 Network Next Hop Metric LocPrf Weight Path
*>i5.5.5.0/25 199.88.7.1 0 100 0 12 5 4 3 2 i
*>i7.0.0.0 199.88.7.1 0 100 0 12 5 4 3 i
*> 8.0.0.0 0.0.0.0 0 32768 i
*>i11.11.11.11/32 199.88.7.1 0 100 0 i
*> 22.22.22.22/32 0.0.0.0 0 32768 i
Router2#
```

- **BGP TABLE VERSION** This router's table number; it is incremented whenever the table changes. A rapidly incrementing table version could indicate network instability.

- **LOCAL ROUTER ID** The router ID of this router.

- **Status of the table entry** Identifies the status of each table entry. It can be any of the following:

    - **s** Table entry is suppressed (alternate, not active)

    - ***** Reachable and valid

    - **>** Best route for this network; the active route to the network

    - **i** Route was learned from an IBGP peer.

■ **Origin codes**   Indicate the type of source for the route.

- **i**   IGP; advertised via a network command

- **e**   EGP

  ?   Unknown, possibly redistributed into BGP from an IGP

Entries with a next-hop address of 0.0.0.0 are local interfaces participating in BGP and are advertised to the neighbors. Notice that the default value for local preference is 100. The MED for this route (shown as Metric in the display) is 0.

The PATH column displays the autonomous systems that must be transited to reach this destination network. Notice that the routes local to this AS do not have the ASN listed; instead, *i* (for internal) is shown, indicating that the network is internal to this router's AS. Networks 5.5.5.0 and 7.0.0.0, on the other hand, involve the crossing of several ASs to reach them. The rightmost number in the PATH column is this AS, followed by the AS to be transited; the leftmost number, before the *i*, is the originating AS for this network.

BGP has a feature to handle flapping routes called *dampening*. Referring back to our display, suppose a network in AS2 went down. The EBGP peer in AS would send a withdrawal to its peer in and so on until it reached the end of AS path. As soon as that withdrawal completes, the network suddenly comes back up; AS2 sends an update message that gets passed along as previously described. If the network in AS2 is constantly going up and down (flapping), this can generate a lot of routing traffic.

Enter dampening. When a route is withdrawn, it gets a penalty (the default is a 1000) applied to it. It will still be advertised to the peers the first time it happens, but it will have the penalty attached to it. The route will be placed in the history state, which will indicate that this router does not have the best path. The more the network flaps, the more the penalties will accumulate until the suppression level (default is 2000) is reached. The route will not be advertised until the penalty is reduced to the reuse level (750). All of these are configurable options.

The **SHOW IP BGP SUMMARY** Command

Cisco provides a way to view snapshot statistics on all of a router's connections to its neighbor via the SHOW IP BGP SUMMARY command. This command shows how many messages have been exchanged with a particular neighbor and how long the peer connection has been up. It also shows the state of the connection. Some of the statistics with less obvious meanings are explained in the list following this output:

```
Router1# show ip bgp summary
BGP table version is 71, main routing table version 71
100 network entries (196 paths) using 18575 bytes of memory
91 BGP path attribute entries using 200 bytes of memory

Neighbor V AS MsgRcvd MsgSent TblVer InQ OutQ Up/Down State/PfxRcd
3.0.96.1 4 5 326 297 71 0 0 0:37:41 Active
```

- **V**   Version of BGP used to communicate with the neighbor—in this case, BGP4.

- **AS**   The AS system of the neighbor.

- **MSGRCVD/MSGSENT**   Number of messages received from/sent to this neighbor.

- **TBLVER**   Last version of this router's BGP table sent to this neighbor.

- **INQ**   Number of messages received from the neighbor that are queued to be processed.

- **OUTQ**   Numbers of messages queued to be sent to this neighbor.

- **UP/DOWN**   Amount of time in hours:minutes:seconds that the router has been in the current state with this neighbor.

- **STATE/PFXRCD**   Current state of the connection with the neighbor; also can show number of prefixes received from the neighbor. If ADMIN is listed, it means that the connection was shut down using the neighbor shutdown command. ACTIVE means that BGP is in the process of establishing the peer relationship. IDLE shows that the BGP peer has not started the peer relationship process; that is, BGP is waiting for the session to start (maybe the network engineer to configure the remote router for BGP). A number in this field indicates that the peering has been successfully established.

The DEBUG IP BGP UPDATES Command

When you are experiencing problems with BGP, Cisco provides a comprehensive DEBUG facility that enables you to monitor and analyze BGP events as they occur.

SCENARIO & SOLUTION

I want to see what routes in the routing table were learned via BGP 345. How do I do that?	Use a modified form of the SHOW IP ROUTE command: SHOW IP ROUTE BGP 345.
Most authors warn you repeatedly about using the DEBUG command with extreme caution. If it is such a problem, why do we use it?	The blessing of DEBUG is also the curse of DEBUG. DEBUG enables the real-time capture and display of events as they occur. The SHOW command displays either static events or the results of events that have already occurred; DEBUG actually displays either part or all of the events as they occur. This can be a potential resource drain (CPU and memory); hence all the warnings you receive about using it.
How do I see what neighbor relationships have been formed by my router?	Use the command SHOW IP BGP SUMMARY or SHOW IP BGP NEIGHBORS.

When you run DEBUG, the output is sent to your screen; the output can be fast and voluminous, so turn on the text-logging feature of what software you are using to connect to the router.

Be warned! DEBUG can generate copious amounts of output and can consume many CPU cycles. Use it sparingly on a production network *only* to resolve specific problems; be sure that DEBUG is the correct tool for problem analysis before you use it.

The syntax for the DEBUG commands relevant to BGP are as follows. We discuss each option briefly and then show output from the DEBUG IP BGP UPDATES command:

```
debug ip bgp[A.B.C.D.| dampening| events| in | keepalives | out |
 updates | vpnv4]
```

- **A.B.C.D** IP address of the neighbor; displays information sent to/from this neighbor.

- **DAMPENING** Displays dampening events (penalizing of unstable routes).

- **EVENTS** Generic display of BGP events, such as neighbor negotiations, state changes, etc.

- **IN**   Lists summary of incoming messages and also identifies to/from the messages.
- **KEEPALIVES**   Shows KEEPALIVES being sent and received.
- **OUR**   Same as IN, only outward bound.
- **Updates**   Shows routing information updates being exchanged between peers.

When you execute DEBUG IP BGP UPDATES, you will see a listing similar to the following:

```
BGP: 1.2.3.4 send UPDATE 4.3.2.1/24, next 1.2.3.5, metric 1000, path 3
BGP: 1.2.3.4 send UPDATE 5.3.2.1/24, next 1.2.3.5, metric 1000, path (65111)
BGP: 1.2.3.4 send UPDATE 5.3.2.1/24, next 1.2.3.5, metric 1000, path 3 4 5
```

Comment: This router, 1.2.3.4, is sending routing updates about the networks (includes CIDR mask information) to its neighbors. Notice the metric and the paths. NEXT identifies the next hop for this update. METRIC is actually the MED. PATH is the sequence of ASs that must be traversed to reach this network.

```
BGP: 1.2.3.4 rcv UPDATE about 12.13.14.0/24, next hop 4.3.2.1,
metric 1000, path 11 12 metric
```

Comment: This router has received an update for the network 12.13.14.0 from its peer at 4.3.2.1.

```
BGP: 1.2.3.4 rcv UPDATE about 11.11.11.0/24 - withdrawn.
```

Comment: This router has received an UPDATE message with routes to be withdrawn.

```
BGP: 1.2.3.4 update run completed, ran for 31ms, neighbor version 0,
 start version 1, throttled to 1, check point net 0.0.0.0
```

Comment: The initial update has been completed (version 0). After this, you will see only incremental updates.

EXERCISE 8-4

Monitoring BGP

The following scenario will probably never happen, because you have many ways you could automate the manual process proposed here. For purposes of this exercise, assume that you have no way to automate any of this and must use this assistant as described.

Your boss has called you in; he has hired an assistant for you who will manually check certain aspects of BGP every hour. The assistant is a network novice. Your boss wants you to provide this assistant with a list of commands and tell her what to look for in those commands. Basically, your assistant will be responsible for verifying the routing information and will ensure that the routing information stays correct.

Here's what you know and require to be verified:

1. There should be 10 and only 10 BGP routes inserted in the routing table.

2. The gateway of last resort is 1.2.3.4.

3. Your local router should have five peers.

4. The table version number is needed to see if it is incrementing unnecessarily.

As you prepare to depart, your boss requests that you provide enough information necessary that the assistant can capture statistics on KEEPALIVE traffic every two hours.

Solution:

Give the assistant the following list of commands and point out what to look for.

1. SHOW IP ROUTE BGP (the assistant can count the routes)

2. SHOW IP ROUTE (show the assistant where to find the gateway of last resort information in this display).

3. SHOW IP BGP NEIGHBORS.

4. SHOW IP BGP or SHOW IP BGP SUMMARY (tell the assistant to record the table version every hour).

5. DEBUG IP BGP KEEPALIVES (explain to the assistant that she is to run this command *only* and should *not* run this command with any other

arguments); ensure the assistant runs UNDEBUG after all the desired information is obtained.

CERTIFICATION SUMMARY

This chapter introduced you to the path-vector protocol known as Border Gateway Protocol (BGP). BGP was designed to connect ASs and to connect ASs to the Internet. In a fashion similar to RIP, BGP routes AS by AS: it does not know or care about the internal details of a particular AS.

BGP is an open standard crafted by the IETF and documented in several RFCs. It uses TCP; in fact, it relies on TCP for error detection and correction. Version 4 is the most current version of BGP, and one of its most significant enhancements was the addition of support for CIDR. CIDR enables several advertisements to be aggregated into one, thus reducing the number of messages needed to advertise multiple networks.

All BGP configuration starts with the ROUTER BGP <1-65535> command. BGP is configured like most IGPs: start the routing process and add those networks that you want BGP to advertise. Several SHOW and DEBUG commands enable you to monitor and verify your BGP configuration. One notable command is the SHOW IP BGP command, which displays the BGP routing table.

✓ TWO-MINUTE DRILL

Here are some of the key points from each certification objective in Chapter 8.

Alternatives to BGP

❑ Use BGP if your AS is a transit AS or if you want to control and filter traffic to and from ASs.

❑ Use BGP if your AS is multihomed.

❑ Do not use BGP if you have a single connection to the Internet.

❑ Do not use BGP if you do not have a coherent routing policy.

❑ Static and default routes can be acceptable substitutes for BGP in some situations.

Understanding the Border Gateway Protocol

❑ BGP is a path-vector EGP.

❑ BGP Version 4 introduced CIDR support, which enabled aggregation.

❑ BGP Version 4 introduced the LOCAL_PREF attribute.

❑ Refer to the RFCs at www.ietf.org for more information about BGP.

❑ BGP uses attributes for making policy decisions.

❑ BGP routes hop by hop; each AS is considered a hop.

❑ Attributes describe the route and enable BGP to select the best route.

❑ All BGP messages have the same header.

❑ The BGP message types are OPEN, UPDATE, NOTIFICATION, and KEEPALIVE.

Configuring Basic BGP

❑ All BGP operations start with the router bgp <1-65535> command.

❑ The BGP NETWORK command identifies networks that BGP will advertise to its peers.

❑ The BGP NEIGHBOR command establishes peering with neighbor routers.

❑ External neighbors must be directly connected; internal neighbors do not have to be directly connected.

❑ The NEIGHBOR NEXT-HOP-SELF command enables a local router to act as the next hop for a particular neighbor; this can be useful on those networks where not all neighbors can reach each other.

Monitoring BGP Operations

❑ SHOW IP PROTOCOLS shows all IP routing protocols running on a router.

❑ SHOW IP ROUTE displays the contents of the routing table.

❑ SHOW IP BGP NEIGHBORS lists the BGP peers of the local router.

❑ SHOW IP BGP displays the contents of the BGP routing table, as opposed to the main routing table.

❑ DEBUG IP BGP provides real-time viewing of BGP events and messages as they occur. Use this command with caution on a production router.

SELF TEST

The following questions will help you measure your understanding of the material presented in this chapter. Read all the choices carefully because there might be more than one correct answer. Choose all correct answers for each question.

Alternatives to BGP

1. Which of the following is *not* an appropriate situation or time to use BGP?

    A. When the autonomous system is a transit autonomous system

    B. When there are multiple exit points

    C. When there is a single exit point

    D. When the network engineer has sufficient knowledge and understanding of BGP

2. When should you *not* use BGP?

    A. When you have no routing policy

    B. When the processing power and memory of your routers is not adequate

    C. When there is a single exit and a single entry point to your autonomous system

    D. All of the above

3. What is the default administrative distance of a static route with a next-hop address?

    A. One hundred

    B. Two hundred

    C. One

    D. None of the above

4. You want to create a static route for network 1.1.0.0/16, referencing serial 0. What is the command string to accomplish this task?

    A. Use OSPF's or BGP's default route to generate a static route

    B. IP ROUTE 1.1.0.0 255.255.0.0 SERIAL 0

    C. IP ROUTE 1.1.0.0 INTERFACE SERIAL 0

    D. IP DEFAULT-NETWORK 1.1.0.0

5. Your gateway of last resort needs to be 1.2.3.4, which will be out your serial 0. What static command do you enter to achieve this goal?

    A. IP DEFAULT-NETWORK 1.2.3.4

    B. IP DEFAULT-NETWORK 1.2.3.4 SERIAL 0

    C. IP ROUTE 1.2.3.4 255.255.255.255. SERIAL 0

    D. None of the above

Understanding the Border Gateway Protocol

6. According to the classical definition, an EGP provides _____ routing, while an IGP provides _____ routing.

    A. Internet; autonomous system

    B. Path-vector; distance-vector

    C. Network; intranetwork

    D. Interautonomous system; intraautonomous system

7. Assuming that BGP's defaults have not been changed, which of the following is true about BGP's routing abilities?

    A. BGP can route based on speed

    B. BGP can advertise networks that are not directly connected

    C. BGP does not need to reach a network to advertise it

    D. BGP's support of CIDR enables it to advertise more networks

8. Which of the following is *not* an addition or enhancement made by BGP Version 4?

    A. Version 4 added the MED attribute.

    B. Version 4 added CIDR support.

    C. Version 4 added aggregation abilities.

    D. Version 4 added the LOCAL_PREF attribute.

9. After the initial routing exchange, BGP peers will make _____ updates, and they will be _____ updates.

    A. Periodic (every 5 minutes); unacknowledged

    B. Full; reliable

    C. Incremental; reliable

    D. Incremental; unacknowledged

10. Which of the following describes a BGP attribute?

    A. A positive characteristic that enhances the quality of BGP packet transfers

    B. A description of a route

    C. A well-known aspect of a route used to make routing decisions

    D. Contained in the header of all BGP messages

11. Which of the following attribute types is a hint to neighbors as to what route to take to reach the destination?

    A. AS-PATH

    B. MULTI_EXIT_DISC

    C. NEXT_HOP

    D. LOCAL_WEIGHT

12. When can synchronization be turned off? Choose all that apply.

    A. You are using BGP for all your intra-AS routing (fully meshed IBGP peers).

    B. Your autonomous system is not a transit AS.

    C. You are not connected to the Internet.

    D. Your IGP supports redistribution.

13. BGP encounters an error; before it resets the peer connection, it will do which of the following?

    A. Log the reset event to the console.

    B. Remove all routes associated with that peer.

    C. Inform its IBGP peers of the error.

    D. Send a notification message to the peer with the error.

Configuring Basic BGP

14. What is the first command you enter to start the BGP routing process?

    A. ROUTER BGP <1-65535>

    B. IP ROUTING

    C. IP SUBNET ZERO

    D. NEIGHBOR X.X.X.X REMOTE-AS <1-65535>

15. After you have started BGP, you need to configure it to advertise networks. What command is used to do this?

- **A.** The NEIGHBOR command
- **B.** The IP ROUTE command
- **C.** The NETWORK command
- **D.** None of the above

16. You want to establish peering with a neighboring router (1.1.1.1) in AS 5678. Your IP address is 2.2.2.2, and your AS is 34. What command would you enter to establish the neighbor relationship? Assume that BGP has already been started.

- **A.** NETWORK 1.1.1.1 255.255.255.255
     NETWORK 1.1.1.2 255.255.255.255
- **B.** NEIGHBOR 1.1.1.1 REMOTE-AS 5678
- **C.** NETWORK 1.1.1.1 255.255.255.255
     NEIGHBOR 1.1.1.2 REMOTE-AS 5678
- **D.** NEIGHBOR 1.1.1.2 REMOTE-AS 5678

17. Routers A, B, and C are connected via a point-to-multipoint Frame Relay network and are on the same subnet. B and C are spokes, and A is the hub. What command needs to be entered to ensure that BGP routing is successful, and where should it be entered?

- **A.** EBGP-MULTIHOP; on all routers
- **B.** EBGP-MULTIHOP; on Router A
- **C.** NEIGHBOR X.X.X.X NEXT-HOP-SELF; on Routers B and C
- **D.** NEIGHBOR X.X.X.X NEXT-HOP-SELF; on Router A

18. You are running OSPF and BGP. Routes learned via OSPF are also being advertised out from the AS via BGP. Your EBGP peers are not getting any of these routes. Assuming that the network statements of both OSPF and BGP are correct, what command can you use to fix the problem?

- **A.** NO SYNCHRONIZATION
- **B.** REDISTRIBUTE OSPF {PROCESS-ID}
- **C.** Both **A** and **B**
- **D.** ADD A DEFAULT ROUTE

19. You are experiencing problems with your neighbor at 1.1.1.1. What command can you use to reset the connection with this peer?

    A. CLEAR IP BGP *

    B. Perform a shut/no shut on the interface connected to the peer.

    C. Delete and reinstall the BGP routing process.

    D. CLEAR IP BGP 1.1.1.1 SOFT

Monitoring BGP Operations

20. You enter the command SHOW IP ROUTE. What will be displayed?

    A. The current IP routing table

    B. All IP routes learned via an IGP

    C. All directly connected networks

    D. None of the above

21. You want to view details about your neighbor, and only that neighbor, at IP address 1.1.1.1. What command will help you accomplish this feat?

    A. SHOW IP ROUTE 1.1.1.1

    B. SHOW IP BGP NEIGHBOR 1.1.1.1

    C. SHOW IP BGP NEIGHBORS

    D. B and C

22. The SHOW IP BGP SUMMARY command will do which of the following?

    A. Provide a summary of all BGP events that have occurred

    B. Provide a quick snapshot of all BGP routes in the IP routing table

    C. Provide statistics on the local router's connections to its neighbors

    D. Display attributes associated with BGP routes

23. You want to monitor the KEEPALIVE packet exchange. What command will accomplish this goal? Assume the neighbor is 1.1.1.1.

    A. DEBUG IP BGP 1.1.1.1 KEEPALIVES

    B. DEBUG IP BGP KEEPALIVES

    C. SHOW IP BGP SUMMARY

    D. None of the above

24. You telneted to your router and started debugging BGP packets. Assuming that your command syntax is correct, you still see nothing. You even reset BGP, to no avail. What could solve the problem?

    A. Nothing. BGP cannot be monitored

    B. Enter the TERMINAL MONITOR command

    C. Identify your SYSLOG server and verify its reachability

    D. None of the above

LAB QUESTION

Given the network in Figure 8-18, configure all routers except for Router 5 (assume that Router 5 is configured correctly) such that:

- Addressing and loop-back interfaces must be configured as shown in the address table in Figure 8-13.

- All Frame Relay networks use inverse ARP, so manual map statements are not necessary.

- Router 5's serial 0 is the gateway of last resort, and this fact must be learned by all routers in AS65535.

- RIP is used within AS65535 to advertise the 171.3.x.x on Routers 1–4; this route must be advertised via BGP to Router 5, regardless of whether it can reach the network or not.

- Routers 1, 2, and 3 are connected via a Frame Relay network, where 1 is the hub and 2 and 3 are spokes. Ensure that BGP works between 1, 2, and 3.

- Router 4 is not running BGP.

- Aggregate the 93.x.x.x and the 191.73.88.x networks on Router 3 such that there are only two prefixes to advertise them out via BGP.

- All routers must be able to reach the interfaces of all other routers.

FIGURE 8-18 A diagram for the lab exercise

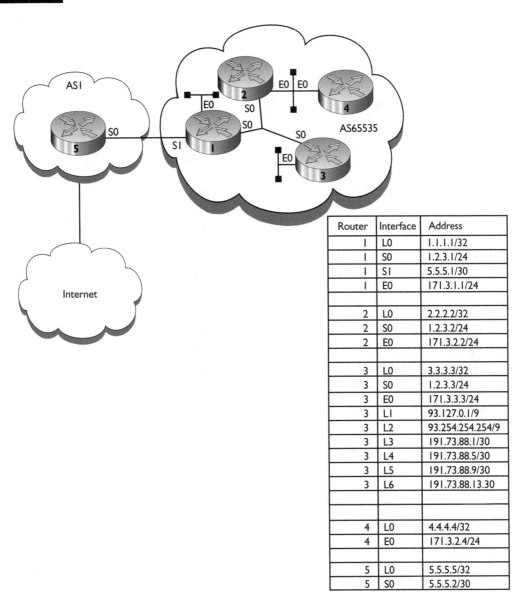

Router	Interface	Address
I	L0	1.1.1.1/32
I	S0	1.2.3.1/24
I	S1	5.5.5.1/30
I	E0	171.3.1.1/24
2	L0	2.2.2.2/32
2	S0	1.2.3.2/24
2	E0	171.3.2.2/24
3	L0	3.3.3.3/32
3	S0	1.2.3.3/24
3	E0	171.3.3.3/24
3	L1	93.127.0.1/9
3	L2	93.254.254.254/9
3	L3	191.73.88.1/30
3	L4	191.73.88.5/30
3	L5	191.73.88.9/30
3	L6	191.73.88.13.30
4	L0	4.4.4.4/32
4	E0	171.3.2.4/24
5	L0	5.5.5.5/32
5	S0	5.5.5.2/30

SELF TEST ANSWERS

Alternatives to BGP

1. ☑ C. When there is a single exit point is correct because a single exit point does not require the use of BGP.
    ☒ A, B, and D are incorrect because these are factors that recommend the use of BGP for successful routing.

2. ☑ D. All of the above is correct; these are all reasons not to use BGP.
    ☒ A, B, and C are incorrect because they do not include all the correct answers.

3. ☑ C. One is correct because it is the *default* administrative distance of any static route; this is why a static route is preferred over any dynamically learned routes.
    ☒ A and B are incorrect because 100 and 200 are not the default distance of a static route. D is incorrect because there is a correct answer.

4. ☑ B. IP ROUTE 1.1.0.0 255.255.0.0 SERIAL 0 is correct because this is the command you use to create a static route that can be redistributed by BGP.
    ☒ A is incorrect because OSPF and BGP cannot generate static routes. C is incorrect because the command syntax of IP ROUTE 1.1.0.0 INTERFACE SERIAL 0 is wrong. D is incorrect because DEFAULT-NETWORK 1.1.0.0 identifies the default network, not a static route.

5. ☑ A. IP DEFAULT-NETWORK 1.2.3.4 is correct because it is the correct command syntax to identify the default network. You'll still need a route to the default network to make this work as the gateway of last resort; the route can either be static or dynamic.
    ☒ B is incorrect because the command syntax of IP DEFAULT-NETWORK 1.2.3.4 SERIAL 0 is wrong. C is incorrect because IP ROUTE 1.2.3.4 255.255.255.255. SERIAL 0 creates a static route, not a default route. D is incorrect because there is a correct answer.

Understanding the Border Gateway Protocol

6. ☑ D. Interautonomous system; intraautonomous system is correct because EGPs are designed to route between autonomous systems, whereas IGPs are designed to handle the more detailed intra-AS routing.
    ☒ A, B, and C are incorrect because they either describe part or none of the types of routing that an EGP and IGP do.

7. ☑ **B.** BGP can advertise networks that are not directly connected. When a BGP router receives an update from its IBGP peers, it can advertise those networks to its EBGP peers with itself as the next hop, which usually is not the case.

☒ **A** is incorrect because BGP uses attributes, not speed. **C** is incorrect because synchronization is turned on by default and therefore prevents BGP from advertising a network it cannot reach. **D** is incorrect because CIDR enables BGP to advertise more networks using a single advertisement; it does not increase the number of networks that BGP can advertise.

8. ☑ **A.** Version 4 added the MED attribute. This answer is correct because Version 4 did not add the MED attribute; it was already in Version 3.

☒ **B, C,** and **D** are incorrect because these are all new additions made by Version 4.

9. ☑ **C.** Incremental; reliable. Updates will be triggered thereafter and will be reliable since BGP uses TCP.

☒ **A, B,** and **D** are incorrect because BGP peers initially exchange their entire tables, then incremental updates as changes occur, and the transfer is reliable due to use of TCP.

10. ☑ **B.** A description of a route is correct; an attribute contains information about the route's characteristics.

☒ **A** is incorrect because an attribute is neither positive nor negative; it merely describes. **C** is incorrect in that attributes can be well-known or optional. **D** is incorrect because attributes are used only in UPDATE messages.

11. ☑ **B.** MULTI_EXIT_DISC.

☒ **A** is incorrect because this attribute lists ASs that have been traversed. **C** is incorrect because it is a fact, not a hint. **D** is incorrect because there is no such attribute as LOCAL_WEIGHT.

12. ☑ **A** and **B.** You are using BGP for all your intra-AS routing (fully meshed IBGP peers), and your autonomous system is not a transit AS. These answers are correct because your IBGP peers will not miss an update, and since your AS is not being used as a transit AS, no coordination issues are involved with passing external routes through.

☒ **C** is incorrect because not being connected to the Internet does not automatically resolve the synchronization issue. **D** is incorrect because redistribution has nothing to do with synchronization.

13. ☑ **D.** Send a notification message to the peer with the error. BGP attempts to notify the remote peer of the impending reset; this aids in keeping the peers in sync.

☒ **A** and **B** are incorrect because they occur after the reset. **C** is incorrect because the reset is a matter between the peers affected, not all peers.

Configuring Basic BGP

14. ☑ **A.** ROUTER BGP <1-65535> is correct; all other BGP commands either can't be used or will have no impact until this is done.
    ☒ **B** and **C** are incorrect because they do not start BGP. **D** is incorrect because this command does not start BGP and cannot be executed until BGP is started.

15. ☑ **C.** The NETWORK command indicates what networks to advertise and to what peer.
    ☒ **A** is incorrect because the NEIGHBOR command is used to establishing peering. **B** is incorrect because the IP ROUTE command is used to create static routes. **D** is incorrect because there is a correct answer.

16. ☑ **B.** NEIGHBOR 1.1.1.1 REMOTE-AS 5678 is correct because this command will establish peering with 1.1.1.1.
    ☒ **A** is incorrect because these commands identify what network to advertise. **C** is incorrect because it correctly identifies what network to advertise but has the wrong IP address for the neighbor. **D** is incorrect because it has the correct syntax and wrong IP address for the neighbor.

17. ☑ **D.** NEIGHBOR X.X.X.X NEXT-HOP-SELF; on Router A is correct because Routers B and C cannot directly communicate; they will get each other's updates (passed on by A), but they will not be able to reach other.
    ☒ **A** and **B** are incorrect because the EBGP-MULTIHOP command is used to establish peering between nondirectly connected EBGP peers. **C** is incorrect because Routers B and C are spokes and cannot communicate directly with each other; therefore, this command will make little difference.

18. ☑ **A.** NO SYNCHRONIZATION is correct because it will configure BGP to advertise routes immediately without checking to see if the route is reachable via an IGP.
    ☒ **B** is incorrect because it is the wrong solution to a problem that is caused by BGP's inability to reach the networks learned via OSPF. **C** is incorrect because only **A** is correct. **D** is incorrect because the routes will still not be advertised.

19. ☑ **D.** CLEAR IP BGP 1.1.1.1 SOFT is correct because it will only reset the connection with peer 1.1.1.1.
    ☒ **A** is incorrect because it resets all peer connections and causes a temporary network and router outage. **B** is incorrect because it resets everything, not just BGP processes. **C** is incorrect because it is too extreme and affects all BGP peers.

Monitoring BGP Operations

20. ☑ **A.** The current IP routing table.
☒ **B** is incorrect because the SHOW IP ROUTE command shows all routes, both from EGPs and IGPs. **C** is incorrect because directly connected routes might be only a small subset of the routing table. **D** is incorrect because there is a correct answer.

21. ☑ **B.** SHOW IP BGP NEIGHBOR 1.1.1.1 is correct because you want to view information about only a particular neighbor.
☒ **A** is incorrect because HOW IP ROUTE 1.1.1.1 shows how to reach that neighbor. **C** is incorrect because SHOW IP BGP NEIGHBORS shows information on all neighbors. **D** is incorrect because only **B** is correct.

22. ☑ **C.** Provide statistics on the local router's connections to its neighbors. This answer is correct because SHOW IP BGP summary provides statistics on the neighbors.
☒ **A** is incorrect because there is no summary log kept on BGP events. **B** is incorrect because this is a function of the SHOW IP ROUTE command. **D** is incorrect because you must use the SHOW IP BGP X.X.X.X to get this information.

23. ☑ **A.** DEBUG IP BGP 1.1.1.1 KEEPALIVES is the correct command.
☒ **B** is incorrect because the syntax is wrong. **C** is incorrect because it shows information on peer connections.

24. ☑ **B.** Enter the TERMINAL MONITOR command. This will direct output of the debug to the current terminal session that you are using.
☒ **A** is incorrect because BGP can be monitored. **C** is incorrect because we want to view the data during an active TELNET session. **D** is incorrect because there is a correct answer.

LAB ANSWER

Router 1

```
!
version 11.2
no service password-encryption
no service udp-small-servers
no service tcp-small-servers
!
hostname Router1
!
```

```
interface Loopback0
 ip address 1.1.1.1 255.255.255.255
!
interface Ethernet0
 ip address 171.3.1.1 255.255.255.0
!
interface Serial0
 ip address 1.2.3.1 255.255.255.0
 encapsulation frame-relay
!
interface Serial1
 ip address 5.5.5.1 255.255.255.0
!
router rip
 redistribute bgp 65535 metric 1
 network 171.3.0.0
!
router bgp 65535
 network 1.1.1.1 mask 255.255.255.255
 network 1.2.3.1 mask 255.255.255.0
 network 5.5.5.1 mask 255.255.255.252
 network 171.3.1.0 mask 255.255.255.0
 no synchronization
 neighbor 1.2.3.2 remote-as 65535
 neighbor 1.2.3.2 next-hop-self
 neighbor 1.2.3.3 remote-as 65535
 neighbor 1.2.3.3 next-hop-self
 neighbor 5.5.5.2 remote-as 1
 default-information originate
!
ip default-network 5.5.5.2
ip route 5.5.5.2 255.255.255.255 Serial1 253
!
line con 0
line aux 0
line vty 0 4
 login
```

Router 2

```
!
version 11.2
no service password-encryption
no service udp-small-servers
no service tcp-small-servers
```

```
!
hostname Router2
!
interface Loopback0
 ip address 2.2.2.2 255.255.255.255
!
interface Ethernet0
 ip address 171.3.2.2 255.255.255.0
!
interface Serial0
 ip address 1.2.3.2 255.255.255.0
 encapsulation frame-relay
!
router rip
 network 171.3.0.0
!
router bgp 65535
 network 2.2.2.2 mask 255.255.255.255
 network 1.2.3.2 mask 255.255.255.0
 network 171.3.2.0 mask 255.255.255.0
 no synchronization
 neighbor 1.2.3.1 remote-as 65535
!
line con 0
line aux 0
line vty 0 4
 login
!
end
```

Router 3

```
!
version 11.2
no service password-encryption
no service udp-small-servers
no service tcp-small-servers
!
hostname Router3
!
ip subnet-zero
!
interface Loopback0
 ip address 3.3.3.3 255.255.255.255
!
```

```
interface Loopback1
 ip address 93.127.0.1 255.128.0.0
!
interface Loopback2
 ip address 93.254.254.254 255.128.0.0
!
interface Loopback3
 ip address 191.73.88.1 255.255.255.252
!
interface Loopback4
 ip address 191.73.88.5 255.255.255.252
!
interface Loopback5
 ip address 191.73.88.9 255.255.255.252
!
interface Loopback6
 ip address 191.73.88.13 255.255.255.252
!
interface Ethernet0
 ip address 171.3.3.3 255.255.255.0
!
interface Serial0
 ip address 1.2.3.3 255.255.255.0
 encapsulation frame-relay
!
router rip
 network 171.3.0.0
!
router bgp 65535
 network 3.3.3.3 mask 255.255.255.255
 network 1.2.3.0 mask 255.255.255.0
 network 171.3.3.0 mask 255.255.255.0
 network 93.127.0.1 mask 255.128.0.0
 network 93.254.0.0 mask 255.128.0.0
 network 191.73.88.1 mask 255.255.255.252
 network 191.73.88.5 mask 255.255.255.252
 network 191.73.88.9 mask 255.255.255.252
 network 191.73.88.13 mask 255.255.255.252
 aggregate-address 93.0.0.0 255.0.0.0
 aggregate-address 191.73.88.0 255.255.255.240
Neighbor 1.2.3.1 remote-as 65535
!
line con 0
line aux 0
line vty 0 4
 login
```

Router 4

```
version 11.2
no service password-encryption
no service udp-small-servers
no service tcp-small-servers
!
hostname Router4
!
interface Loopback0
 ip address 4.4.4.4 255.255.255.255
!
interface Ethernet0
 ip address 171.3.2.4 255.255.255.0
!
router rip
 network 171.3.0.0
 network 4.0.0.0
!
line con 0
line aux 0
line vty 0 4
 login
!
end
```

9

BGP Scalability
Issues

CERTIFICATION OBJECTIVES

T he Border Gateway Protocol (BGP) Version 4 was first defined in RFC 1771 in March 1995. The purpose of BGP was to provide routing between different autonomous systems (ASs) and define routing policy. At the time BGP was defined, networks were much smaller in scale than the networks of today. The exponential growth of ISP networks quickly brought to light inherent scaling issues with Internal BGP (iBGP) and the requirements for a full mesh between all iBGP neighbors within an AS.

Networks and Internet connectivity have reached the point of being mission critical in today's marketplace. The requirements for continued service in the event of an Internet provider experiencing a catastrophic failure have increased the need for connectivity to multiple service providers, or *multihoming*. A network that is multihomed is able to provide redundant connectivity in the case of failure and optimize routing during normal operation through the application of routing policy.

The use of BGP requires an Interior Gateway Protocol (IGP) to run underneath it, providing reachability to BGP next-hop addresses and between BGP speakers. This raises the question of which prefixes should be carried in BGP and which should be carried in IGP. The purpose of BGP to advertise the prefixes outside the local AS implies the need for passing information between BGP and the IGP. The methods to perform this exchange of routing information are examined in this chapter.

This chapter entails an examination of the scalability issues that are involved in a full iBGP mesh and the solutions that are available. Concentration is given to route reflectors as defined in RFC 1966 and updated in RFC 2796. The operation of route reflectors is presented in conjunction with the configuration required to utilize them.

The practice of multihoming is discussed in detail in this chapter, and the various methods available are presented, along with their respective benefits and drawbacks. The use of local preference, as defined in RFC 1771, is examined, in addition to the Cisco-specific WEIGHT parameter, in regard to defining policy for the determination of preferred egress path. Defining ingress policy is examined through the use of filtering routing updates that use Cisco's Prefix List route-filtering feature in conjunction with route summarization.

The final section of this chapter addresses how routing information is injected into BGP. The topics of redistributing the IGP routing table into BGP and vice versa are presented, along with the issues that each entails. The architectures that service provider networks use are examined and compared with those in the enterprise.

CERTIFICATION OBJECTIVE 9.01

Scalability Issues and Solutions with iBGP

BGP was designed to exchange routing information from one AS with other ASs, making it an Exterior Gateway Protocol. The original design was done with the intention that BGP would reside at the edge of the AS, where connections to other ASs would reside. This decision was based on the topology of the Internet, which at that time involved a small number of public peering points. The use of multiple peering points brought with it the need for a way to exchange information between BGP speakers within an AS. This resulted in the definition of two types of BGP session: external and internal. As explained in the previous chapter, an External BGP (eBGP) session is between two different ASs, whereas an iBGP session is between two BGP speakers in the same AS.

Peering with iBGP Neighbors

The topic being addressed is that of scalability issues with iBGP, so the first questions that arise are, how are iBGP sessions different from eBGP sessions, and why don't the same scalability issues exist with eBGP? Two major points must be examined to identify the key differences. The first is that all routers in the path between two eBGP speakers that are connected via iBGP must also run iBGP, as shown in Figure 9-1.

This example uses the assumption that RTRA and RTRD both have eBGP sessions to different ISPs. These two routers have an iBGP session between them, with the physical path between them through RTRB and RTRC. Both routers RTRB and RTRC are not running BGP and are receiving a default route. RTRB prefers the default route to RTRA, and RTRC prefers the default route to RTRD. The prefix 10.1.1.0/24 is received by both RTRA and RTRD. RTRA has an AS_PATH of 2; RTRD has an AS_PATH of 3. This results in a preference for the path through RTRA. The path of the packet is as follows:

1. A packet arrives at RTRC with the destination of 10.1.1.1 and is forwarded using the default route to RTRD.

FIGURE 9-1

Internal BGP
requirements

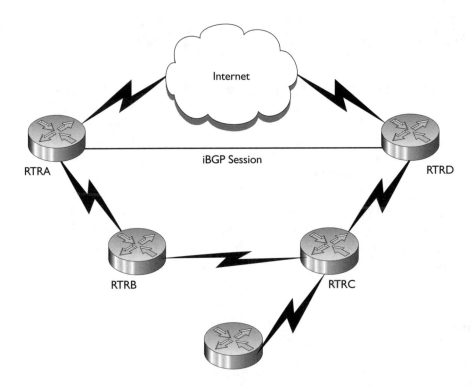

2. When the packet arrives at RTRD, the route lookup identifies the
   NEXTHOP to be through the ISP connected to RTRA.

3. RTRD forwards the packet back to RTRC as its IGP routing table identifies
   this as the path to the NEXT-HOP IP address.

4. RTRC, which is not running BGP, utilizes the default route again, creating a
   routing loop.

The preceding example indicates why it is essential that iBGP exist on all routers
in the path between eBGP speakers connected via iBGP. This results in an increased
number of routers that must run BGP, many of which utilize only iBGP. The number
of routers that are required to run iBGP increases very quickly to encompass all
routers within the network when eBGP speakers are distributed throughout the AS.

The need to run iBGP on all routers within the AS has been established for
networks with even a small number of diverse eBGP-based egress points. At the
least, it should be run across the routers that provide transit between the BGP

routers with external peerings. The next aspect of BGP that needs to be examined is why a full mesh is required. If it were possible to simply peer with each directly connected BGP speaker, the scaling issue would be drastically reduced, except in the case of a network that is fully meshed physically. The simple answer to our question is, "Because an iBGP speaker can't propagate updates learned via iBGP to another BGP speaker via iBGP." That answer won't quite work here, however, because it is the reason for that rule that is being determined. The actual answer is found when we examine the loop detection mechanism.

The primary reason that the AS_PATH attribute was developed was to prevent an AS from accepting routing updates that it has already advertised. Figure 9-2 displays how a prefix could be advertised back to the AS that generated it.

For this example, assume that AS1 is a customer of both AS 2 and AS3. AS1 is advertising prefix X out AS2 and prefix Y out AS 3. AS2 will advertise prefix X to AS3, and AS3 will advertise prefix Y to AS2. If AS_PATH based loop detection did not exist, the only thing to stop AS2 from advertising prefix Y back to AS1 or AS3 from advertising prefix X back to AS2 is route filtering. Human error is common enough that it is certainly worthwhile to build in automatic loop prevention, so if

FIGURE 9-2

Routing advertisements back to originating AS

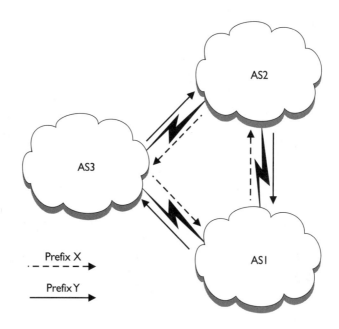

Prefix X

Prefix Y

AS2 receives an UPDATE with a prefix containing its own AS in the AS_PATH, it will not consider that path in the decision process.

The loop detection mechanism has been examined. Now the question is, how does this relate to iBGP and the propagation of routing information? The AS number for all routers within an AS is the same, which results in the inability to use the AS_PATH for loop prevention. There are no other provisions for providing loop prevention, which would lead to iBGP routing information being propagated continuously throughout the network, creating an infinite routing information loop.

Contrasting iBGP Behavior to an IGP Method of Propagating Changes

The method that iBGP uses to provide routing information is an important piece of the picture that will provide a better understanding of the issues that exist in attempting to scale the iBGP network. The iBGP network is being utilized to provide routing internally, taking on some of the responsibilities of the IGP, in a sense. With this in mind, it is useful to compare the behavior of iBGP with that of standard IGPs.

OSPF and IS-IS are examples of link-state protocols that will automatically form adjacencies with all directly connected routers that are part of the IGP domain. Link-state updates are then flooded over these adjacencies to all routers participating in the routing domain, providing each router with full knowledge of the topology. This excludes any router that is not part of the IGP domain from becoming involved in the forwarding path for packets, which helps prevent routing loops within the IGP by routers not having consistent information.

RIP and IGRP are examples of distance-vector protocols that are also capable of excluding routers not involved in the IGP from being present in the forwarding path. They utilize a broadcast, or *multicast*, propagation method but do not rely on the actual formation of adjacencies. They simply flood out all ports except the port on which the update was received, utilizing split horizon for faster convergence. Only those routers that are involved in the IGP propagate the updates, constraining the forwarding path to only those routers that have adequate information to make intelligent routing decisions. The convergence capabilities and comparison with link-state protocols are outside the scope of this chapter and are not covered in more depth here.

EIGRP is a bit of a special case, although it does not differ significantly. It forms adjacencies with other EIGRP speaking routers in the same AS and floods information over these adjacencies. This allows it to also exclude routers not participating in the IGP routing domain from existing in the forwarding path.

BGP was not designed to act as an IGP and does not automatically form neighbors with all directly connected systems. This creates a situation in which BGP cannot guarantee that all routers in the forwarding path are running BGP. The lack of assurance that all BGP speakers are contiguous leaves us with the requirement to manually ensure that all BGP speakers are directly able to propagate any external changes to all other BGP speakers. An important reason that this becomes an issue is how the actual routing lookup is done. The NEXTHOP attribute is not updated for prefixes sent via iBGP. When a packet arrives at a BGP router, the NEXTHOP is examined for the matching prefix. If the NEXTHOP is not directly connected, a *recursive route lookup* is performed, which identifies the path to the NEXTHOP. The path to the NEXTHOP is based on IGP information and results in a disconnect in the forwarding decision. Part of the decision is made based on the BGP information and part on the IGP information, requiring that BGP be running on all routers in the forwarding path.

Scalability Issues with iBGP Neighbors

The last couple of sections concentrated on the reason that so many routers must speak BGP within the AS and why those routers must be configured as a full mesh. It's now time to look at the reason why those constraints are undesirable and to what the result of those constraints actually amounts.

Before examining the downside of the full mesh, there is actually an upside that warrants addressing. The only router that has to actually create UPDATE packets is the router on which the change occurred or the eBGP speaker that received the UPDATE notification. The full mesh enables this router to send the UPDATE to all iBGP speakers and, using TCP's reliable transport mechanism, ensure it has been received, maintaining consistent information in all BGP speakers. This covers only the propagation to the iBGP speakers; any eBGP sessions on other routers are likely to have to issue an UPDATE of their own for each eBGP session.

To understand the scaling issues that exist, it is important to understand the end result for a full mesh. The number of iBGP sessions required to fully mesh an AS with n routers is $n(n-1)/2$. If we consider an AS with 500 routers, which is not uncommon for a large Tier 1 ISP, this results in 499 iBGP sessions per router and a total of 124,750 total iBGP sessions for the AS. This number is unmanageable from an administrative point of view and presents a serious issue for the actual routers to handle. Figure 9-3 shows the growth rate of iBGP sessions as the number of routers increases.

Consider a network with 101 routers in a full iBGP mesh, which results in 100 iBGP sessions per router and a total of 5050 for the network. Because routing information is constantly changing across the Internet, routing updates are almost always being sent. One estimate states that on an average eBGP session, there is a 4000-byte change every minute. On the 101 router network, this translates to 400,000 bytes worth of routing updates that must be sent—4000 bytes to each iBGP neighbor. If the router receiving the UPDATE has 10 eBGP neighbors in addition to the iBGP sessions, it could potentially have to send up to 4,000,000 bytes in UPDATE information to its iBGP neighbors, at 40,000 bytes each. Applying this concept to our example of a 500-router network results in 20,000,000 bytes of routing information every minute!

In light of this new information, re-examination of what was termed an upside earlier does not appear to be so beneficial now. In small networks, it is in fact an upside, but as the network grows, it can develop into a serious scaling issue. The scaling issues that come to light are the administrative issues of managing the configurations, the packet replication for sending updates to all iBGP peers, and the amount of state that must be maintained on each router.

This scaling issue was quickly met after the BGP4 was standardized. Two methods to deal with scaling were developed. The first is BGP confederations, which is defined in RFC 1965, published in June 1996. The second is route reflectors, a

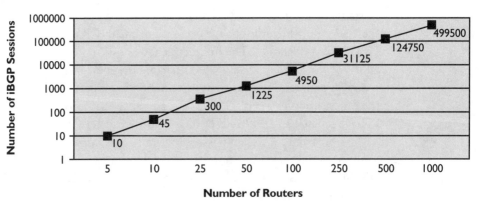

FIGURE 9-3

Internal BGP session scalability

method defined in RFC 1966, also published in June 1996. This chapter examines route reflectors in depth.

Route Reflectors as a Scalability Solution

There are typically two methods for resolving scaling issues; the first is divide and conquer, and the second involves introducing a hierarchy. The BGP confederation is the divide-and-conquer method. The route reflector method utilizes hierarchy. This section discusses the route reflector method, which is the most common method for scaling iBGP.

The Purpose of Route Reflectors

The basic idea behind route reflectors is to designate certain routers to act as reflectors and have the rest of the routers act as clients. The reflectors are all connected in a full mesh, with each client peering to one or more route reflectors. The reflector is responsible for receiving the update from the client and "reflecting" it out to all its other clients and the other reflectors. A route reflector uses only the following rules to determine how to reflect a route:

- If the prefix was received from a client, reflect it to all other clients and regular iBGP peers.
- If the prefix was received from a regular iBGP peer, reflect it to all local clients.

These rules prevent a routing update from being reflected around indefinitely. There are provisions for having clients connect to multiple route reflectors for redundancy. This feature is covered later in the chapter.

The Benefits of Route Reflectors

Route reflectors, a proven solution to the full-mesh scalability problem, have seen significant deployment across the Internet. The deployment of this feature is transparent to the route reflector clients. The ability to have redundancy through the use of multiple route reflectors was built into the feature because it avoids a single point of failure with a wide scope in a failure scenario.

Solves the Full-Mesh Problem   Route reflectors provide a significant improvement over the iBGP full mesh through the application of a hierarchy. Route reflector clients in a nonredundant design are required to have only one iBGP session to the route reflector. A network with n route reflectors with m total route reflector clients will have only $(n(n-1)/2) + m$ iBGP sessions. In the next section, we will see an example of reducing the number of iBGP sessions required if we migrate our 101-router network to utilizing 10 route reflectors with 9 clients each. The 101st router will act as a normal BGP speaker, oblivious to the use of route reflectors. For our network, n will equal 10 and m will equal 90, so $(10(9)/2) + 90 = 135$ iBGP sessions, plus an additional 10 sessions for the 101st router, which will peer with the 10 route reflectors for a total of 145 iBGP sessions instead of 5050. This is assuming that route reflector redundancy is not being used, allowing each client to only have one iBGP session.

Packet Forwarding Is Not Affected   The use of route reflectors does not affect the forwarding path for packets. Remember that the path a packet will traverse is defined by the NEXTHOP attribute in an UPDATE and the IGP path to reach the NEXTHOP address. Route reflectors are specifically required not to modify the NEXTHOP information in UPDATEs that are reflected, leaving this information intact as though it were directly received from the router that originated it.

Multiple Route Reflectors for Redundancy   A client is allowed to utilize multiple route reflectors for redundancy. Special attributes were developed to support loop prevention. This feature is discussed in more depth later in the chapter.

Works with Normal BGP Peers   Route reflectors are able to peer with both eBGP and iBGP routers that are not involved in the route reflection. This is possible because the normal BGP speakers ignore the route reflector-specific attributes, making this feature invisible to them. Route reflector clients are not even required to know that they are in fact peering with a route reflector but are allowed to think they are part of an iBGP network consisting of only themselves and one other router.

Easy Migration Path   The migration path to a route reflector topology is very easy because of the seamless interoperability with BGP speakers that are not involved in the route reflection. The use of route reflection is also invisible to the router reflector clients.

Typically, route reflectors are found only in environments that utilize pervasive BGP. This means most deployments of route reflectors are ISPs. A general rule of thumb is: if there are over 100 iBGP sessions per router, route reflectors are in order.

Route Reflector Terminology

The discussion of route reflection brings with it some new terminology. Before examining the inner workings of route reflection, it is important that the terms used are clearly defined to remove any ambiguity.

Route Reflector

A *route reflector* is a BGP speaker that reflects or readvertises iBGP updates received from its clients to other iBGP neighbors. The route reflector also reflects to its clients iBGP routing information that it received from other route reflectors and regular iBGP neighbors.

Route Reflector Client

A *route reflector client* is a regular BGP speaker that depends on a route reflector to simulate the effect of a full iBGP mesh and ensure that its routing information is propagated through the rest of the autonomous system.

Route Reflector Cluster

The combined set of route reflectors and route reflector clients make up the *route reflector cluster*. In designs utilizing logical redundancy, this cluster could consist of multiple route reflectors.

Nonclient Peer

A *nonclient peer* is any BGP speaker that is a part of the iBGP network and that is not a route reflector client. This includes route reflectors and regular iBGP peers that are fully meshed with the route reflectors.

Originator ID

The *Originator ID*, an optional and nontransitive BGP attribute, is a 4-byte value that is used to identify the BGP speaker that originated the prefix. The route reflector applies the originator ID to prefixes it receives from its route reflector clients. The value the route reflector uses is the router ID of the client that advertised the prefix.

Cluster ID

The *cluster ID* is a 4-byte value that is appended to a CLUSTER-LIST by route reflectors. If a cluster contains a single route reflector, the router ID is used as the cluster ID. If multiple route reflectors exist in a cluster, they all share the same cluster ID, which must be manually configured.

Cluster List

The *cluster list*, an optional and nontransitive BGP attribute, is a variable length field that identifies the route reflectors through which this prefix has passed. The purpose of this attribute is to prevent routing information loops when multiple levels of hierarchy are used for route reflection.

exam
ⓦatch

The cluster ID is based on the route reflector, and the originator ID is based on the actual client's router ID.

Route Reflector Design and Migration Tips

The effects of route reflection on the iBGP mesh can be demonstrated by taking a look back at our previous example of a network with 101 BGP speakers. In that network there was a total of 5050 iBGP sessions. To understand the effects of route reflection, we will create 10 route reflectors, with 9 route reflector clients each. One of the routers will act as a regular iBGP speaker and be included in the full mesh between the route reflectors. Table 9-1 demonstrates a comparison of the number of sessions for our lone regular iBGP speaker, the route reflectors, and the route reflector clients.

TABLE 9-1	A Sample Route Reflector Design

	Regular iBGP Speakers	Route Reflectors	Route Reflector Clients	Total Sessions
Full iBGP mesh	100	NA	NA	5050
Route reflection	10	19	1	145

As we can see, utilizing route reflection has reduced the total number of iBGP sessions in our network to just under 3 percent of the number used for a full iBGP mesh. A quick synopsis of how these numbers were developed is in order for the sake of completeness.

The full iBGP mesh number was explained previously and is defined using the formula $n(n-1)/2$, where n is the number of iBGP speakers.

The route reflection scenario is as follows: Using $(n(n-1)/2) + m$, where n equals 10 and m equals 90, or $(10(9)/2) + 90$, which equals 135 plus 10 sessions for the regular iBGP speaker peering with the 10 route reflectors for a total of 145.

The lone regular iBGP speaker is fully meshed with the 10 route reflectors, using the preceding formula, amounting to a total of 55 iBGP sessions used for the required full mesh of regular iBGP speakers and route reflectors. This leaves us with the iBGP sessions to each of the clients. There are 90 route reflector clients, each with one iBGP session to its route reflector, because we are not utilizing route reflector redundancy. This combines for a total of 145 iBGP sessions. In developing the numbers, it is important not to double-count sessions, which would happen if we simply added up the sessions on all routers.

The effects of route reflection are quite pronounced on all of the routers, with 19 on each route reflector being the maximum number of sessions on any router. The route reflector clients, however, have the most impressive improvement, requiring only a single iBGP session instead of 100.

The design of our network has a very serious flaw in that the failure of any route reflector amounts to the total loss of connectivity for nine of our other routers. The solution to this design issue is the use of multiple route reflectors for each client, which increases the number of failure points from a route reflector standpoint.

The demonstration of multiple route reflectors within a single cluster is best observed in a scenario a bit smaller than 101 routers. The new scenario consists of only six routers: four route reflector clients, and two route reflectors acting as a single cluster.

The first scenario we will examine entails logical redundancy of iBGP sessions from each of the route reflector clients to both route reflectors. Each route reflector is singly homed to the core of the network, where the route reflectors reside. Figure 9-4 depicts the network topology.

This design provides logical redundancy but has a fatal flaw. The illusion of redundancy is provided in that we are peering with two route reflectors, so in theory, if one were to go down, the other would still provide routing information. The

FIGURE 9-4

Internal BGP
without physical
redundancy

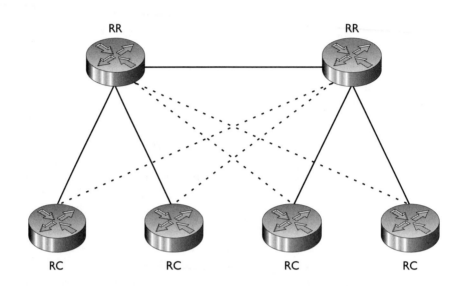

RR   RR

RC   RC   RC   RC

iBGP Sessions follow physical links

- - - - - - - Logical iBGP Session Only

problem here is that no physical redundancy exists, so in the event of a route reflector failing, there is no physical path to the other route reflector. It is very important that the logical topology also follow the physical topology. The result of logical redundancy in this design is an increase in resource utilization but no added functionality or resiliency. Figure 9-5 is the correct design, which provides both logical and physical redundancy.

The migration path to route reflectors is very simple because of the configuration requirements. A route reflector client requires no configuration and acts just like a regular iBGP speaker. The only configuration required is on the route reflector itself, where the iBGP session to the client is specified as a route reflector client session. Once the iBGP neighbor session to the client has been defined as a route reflector client, the iBGP sessions on the client to all other routers can be removed one at a time. The configuration for those sessions on the other routers within the network should also be removed.

The originator ID and the cluster list are used to prevent routing information loops. Routing information loops usually occur when there is a misconfiguration—in other words, the following is not a good design and should be avoided.

FIGURE 9-5

Internal BGP with physical redundancy

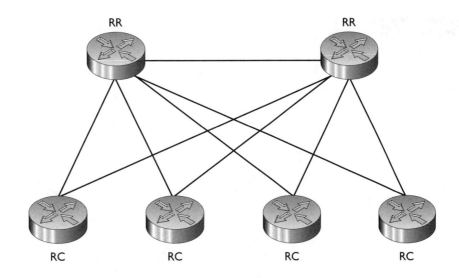

iBGP Sessions follow physical links

As we can see, the route reflector client is participating in two separate clusters. The prefixes sent into Cluster 1 are reflected to the route reflector of Cluster 2 and then reflected back down to the originating client. This same behavior is seen with the same prefixes as they are advertised to the route reflector for Cluster 2 and reflected first to the route reflector for Cluster 1 and back down to the client. The client sees the originator ID with its own router ID and drops the updates.

Figure 9-6 illustrates how an incorrect configuration can result in the cluster list being utilized to drop updates that would otherwise loop endlessly.

The route reflectors are all configured as clients of each other, which causes them to reflect the updates back and forth to each other endlessly, in addition to constantly bombarding the true route reflector clients with the "new" routing updates. The update from RCB would flow to RRB, which would reflect the update to RRA and RRC. RRA would then reflect the update to RCA and RRC. RRC would reflect the update from RRB to RRA and RCC. RRC would then reflect the update from RRA to RRB and RCC. If the cluster-list attribute were not being used, the cycle would begin again, with RRB advertising the update out to RRA and back to the originator RCB! The use of a cluster list, however, would cause RRA to drop the update and the loop would break. RRA would drop the update because it has already passed through router RRA and the cluster ID for RRA was appended to the

FIGURE 9-6

Routing
information loop:
cluster ID

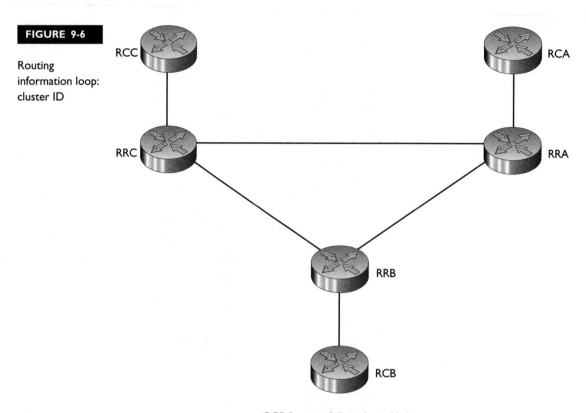

iBGP Sessions follow physical links

cluster list. When RRA sees its own cluster ID in the cluster list, it knows this update is looping and will drop it.

Route Reflector Operations

The BGP extension for route reflection has specific rules that have been defined for handling BGP updates during the reflection process. There are also very specific rules that must be followed for which updates are reflected and to whom they are reflected. The rules that are defined in RFC 2796 are as follows:

- Routing updates received from a route reflector client will be reflected to nonclient peers and all other route reflector clients for that route reflector, except the originating client.

■ Routing updates received from a nonclient will be reflected only to route reflector clients for that route reflector.

A key requirement of route reflection is that the resulting forwarding path be identical to the path if a full iBGP mesh were used. This requirement is intended to prevent routing loops. It is important to remember that the forwarding path used is identified by the IGP path to the NEXT-HOP. The result is that the NEXT-HOP attribute must not be modified in the route reflection process. The NEXT-HOP attribute must be preserved through the entire iBGP network, from the point the prefix entered the routing domain all the way down to the route reflector clients.

The use of the cluster ID was described in our discussion of how routing information loops can be prevented in a misconfiguration. The cluster ID is also utilized in the scenario in which multiple route reflectors are configured within the same cluster. Figure 9-7 shows the network topology with two route reflectors and four route reflector clients.

The routing updates sent from RC1 to RRA have the cluster ID of 1000 (as configured) appended into the cluster list. The update is then sent to all other iBGP peers. When RRB, which is also configured with a cluster ID of 1000, receives the update, it disregards it. The reason for this is that RC1 is supposed to have an iBGP

FIGURE 9-7

Redundant route
reflectors

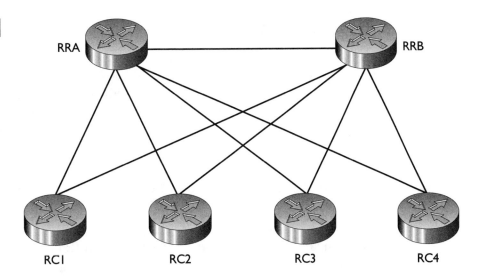

iBGP Sessions follow physical links

session with both RRA and RRB. This session provides both route reflectors with the information directly from RC1. If RRB had accepted the update, it would have reflected it back to RC1, where the originator ID would have caused RC1 to disregard the update.

Route Reflector Configuration

The configuration for route reflectors is fairly straightforward. The route reflector-specific configuration takes place on the actual route reflectors. The route reflector clients require no special configuration except to set up the correct number of iBGP sessions with the correct routers.

The Route-Reflector-Client Configuration Option

The *route-reflector-client configuration option* to the NEIGHBOR command is all that is needed on the route reflector to identify an iBGP neighbor as a route reflector client. The following example provides the necessary configuration to create an iBGP neighbor on the router reflector and to identify that neighbor as a route reflector client:

```
neighbor 10.10.10.1 remote-as 1
neighbor 10.10.10.1 route-reflector-client
```

The BGP CLUSTER-ID <X> Command

The BGP CLUSTER-ID command is used to identify the cluster ID when multiple route reflectors are utilized in a cluster. If a single route reflector is used, the router ID is used as the cluster ID. The BGP CLUSTER-ID command is configured under the BGP protocol configuration and should be configured only on the route reflectors, not the route reflector clients:

```
bgp cluster-id 1000
```

This command needs to be configured identically on all route reflectors within the cluster.

Configuration Using Redundant Route Reflectors

The following example demonstrates the full BGP configuration for a single cluster containing two router reflectors and three route reflector clients. Each of the clients

FIGURE 9-8

Sample redundant
route reflectors
topology

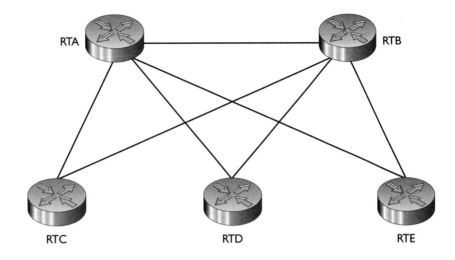

iBGP Sessions follow physical links

is dual homed to the route reflectors to provide physical redundancy in addition to
logical redundancy. Figure 9-8 identifies the physical topology in addition to the
BGP peering sessions that will exist.

The RTRA configuration is as follows:

```
router bgp 1
 no synchronization
 neighbor 10.1.1.10 remote-as 1
 neighbor 10.1.1.5 remote-as 1
 neighbor 10.1.1.5 route-reflector-client
 neighbor 10.1.1.26 remote-as 1
 neighbor 10.1.1.26 route-reflector-client
 neighbor 10.1.1.14 remote-as 1
 neighbor 10.1.1.14 route-reflector-client
 bgp cluster-id 1000
```

The RTRB configuration:

```
bgp router 1
 no synchronization
 neighbor 10.1.1.9 remote-as 1
 neighbor 10.1.1.1 remote-as 1
 neighbor 10.1.1.1 route-reflector-client
 neighbor 10.1.1.21 remote-as 1
```

```
neighbor 10.1.1.21 route-reflector-client
neighbor 10.1.1.18 remote-as 1
neighbor 10.1.1.18 route-reflector-client
bgp cluster-id 1000
```

The RTRC configuration:

```
bgp router 1
 no synchronization
network 172.30.0.0
neighbor 10.1.1.6 remote-as 1
neighbor 10.1.1.2 remote-as 1
```

The RTRD configuration:

```
bgp router 1
 no synchronization
network 172.20.0.0
neighbor 10.1.1.25 remote-as 1
neighbor 10.1.1.22 remote-as 1
```

The RTRE configuration:

```
bgp router 1
 no synchronization
network 172.19.0.0
neighbor 10.1.1.14 remote-as 1
neighbor 10.1.1.17 remote-as 1
```

This configuration example shows that only the route reflectors themselves needed special directives. The configuration for the router reflector clients contains no special configuration. The need for special configuration on the route reflectors only makes the transition to route reflection a fairly easy process. The route reflection process is transparent to the clients in addition to the regular iBGP peers that are included in a full mesh with route reflectors.

EXERCISE 9-1

Route Reflector Redundancy

Solution: If redundant route reflectors are used but a client peers with only one of them, what routes advertised by the client will the route reflector, in that cluster that is not peered with the client, see? Why?

Scenario: That route reflector would not see any of the routes advertised by the client. The client would advertise them up to the route reflector with which it is peered, but those routes would not be propagated to the other route reflector in the cluster due to the matching cluster ID.

Verifying Route Reflectors

The configuration of our route reflector is complete. Now it is important to verify the operation of our route reflection environment. In order to do this, we must first confirm that our route reflectors have correctly identified the clients as being clients. We can do so with the SHOW IP BGP NEIGHBOR command in Exec mode. The following output is from RTRA in the previous example for the route reflector client RTRC.

```
BGP neighbor is 10.1.1.5, remote AS 1, internal link
 BGP version 4, remote router ID 10.4.1.2
 BGP state = Established, up for 00:27:26
 Last read 00:00:27, hold time is 180, keepalive interval is 60
seconds
 Neighbor capabilities:
  Route refresh: advertised and received
  Address family IPv4 Unicast: advertised and received
 Received 31 messages, 0 notifications, 0 in queue
 Sent 31 messages, 0 notifications, 0 in queue
 Route refresh request: received 0, sent 0
 Minimum time between advertisement runs is 5 seconds

 For address family: IPv4 Unicast
 BGP table version 3, neighbor version 3
 Index 3, Offset 0, Mask 0x8
 Route-Reflector Client
 1 accepted prefixes consume 36 bytes
 Prefix advertised 1, suppressed 0, withdrawn 0
```

The boldfaced line of this output identifies the neighbor as a route reflector client; this output was truncated. It is important to check both route reflectors for all three clients to ensure that all neighbor sessions are operational and identified as clients. To verify that routing information is being propagated correctly, examine the SHOW IP BGP output for the prefix advertised by RTRC on the RTRE router:

```
BGP routing table entry for 172.30.0.0/16, version 8
Paths: (2 available, best #1)
 Not advertised to any peer
 Local
   10.1.1.1 (metric 74) from 10.1.1.17 (10.4.1.2)
    Origin IGP, metric 0, localpref 100, valid, internal, best,
ref 2
     Originator: 10.4.1.2, Cluster list: 0.0.3.232
 Local
   10.1.1.5 (metric 128) from 10.1.1.13 (10.4.1.2)
    Origin IGP, metric 0, localpref 100, valid, internal, ref 2
     Originator: 10.4.1.2, Cluster list: 0.0.3.232
```

The bottom line of the output contains the route reflection information. The originator is set to the router ID for the router that originated the prefix, and the cluster list contains cluster ID 1000, in a slightly different notation, which was configured. After verifying that all clients contain the routes for the other clients with the correct originator and cluster list values, our verification of the route reflection environment is complete.

SCENARIO & SOLUTION

How do I look at all the path information for a given prefix and identify which path was chosen and why?	Use the SHOW IP BGP <PREFIX> command.
How many route reflectors can a client peer with?	There is no limit; however, iBGP sessions should follow physical links.
Can a route reflector be a client of another route reflector?	Yes, this is how extremely large networks are able to scale using a route reflector hierarchy.
Can a client peer with a route reflector in another cluster?	Yes, this is acceptable. Any looping routing information will be stopped with the cluster ID and the originator ID.

Policy Control

The BGP routing protocol is typically used to exchange routing information between different ASs. ASs can be multihomed or connected to multiple other ASs. This diversity introduces the need to define routing policy, which allows administrators greater control over the flow of data in and out of their networks.

The first criterion for path selection when you are routing a packet is finding the routes that match the destination IP address in the data packet to be routed. This is the point at which the longest match rule is applied. The *longest match rule* states that a packet follows the most specific route to a destination, or that route that has the most number of bits set to 1 in the network mask. This rule provides for one of the most common methods of policy definition in use today.

To gain a better understanding of how this concept works in practice, consider this example: a network that uses the address space 10.1.0.0/16 subnetted across the network could be broken into two /17 subnets. This autonomous system is multihomed to two autonomous systems to provide transit. If AS1 (the example AS) is connected to AS2 and AS3, the following prefixes could be announced:

AS2:
10.1.0.0/17
10.1.0.0/16

AS3:
10.1.128.0/17
10.1.0.0/16

When the network is fully operational with both connections active, it causes all traffic to 10.1.0.0/17 to enter the network through AS2 and all traffic destined to 10.1.128.0/17 to enter the network through AS3. The prefix 10.1.0.0/16 is advertised out both links to allow traffic to fall over to the other connection in a failure scenario, ensuring that there is always a prefix in the global routing table for the entire network. The longest match rule, however, ensures that during normal operation, the routes for the /17s are used, leaving the /16 to be used only in the absence of one of the /17s.

In the past, a modification of extended access lists was used to provide route-filtering capabilities. The distribute lists needed for our scenario are as follows. Distribute list out to AS2:

```
access-list 102 permit ip host 10.1.0.0 host 255.255.128.0
access-list 102 permit ip host 10.1.0.0 host 255.255.0.0
```

Distribute list out to AS3:

```
access-list 103 permit ip host 10.1.128.0 host 255.255.128.0
access-list 103 permit ip host 10.1.0.0 host 255.255.0.0
```

The source portion of the extended access list is used to match exactly on the network number in the prefix, and the destination portion is used to match exactly on the netmask of the route. For matching specific routing prefixes, this system is not terribly difficult, but at peering points, ISPs often want to define the size of prefixes they will accept from other ISPs in certain address ranges. As an example, if an ISP (AS1) wanted to accept only prefixes that are /19s or shorter in the whole Class B address space (128.0.0.0/2), the following entry on a distribute list would be used:

```
access-list 101 permit ip 128.0.0.0 63.255.255.255 0.0.0.0 255.255.224.0
```

This access list is not very intuitive! This nonintuitiveness leads to the need to create a new way to define route filtering that is much easier for humans to understand. The result was the creation of prefix lists. Prefix lists carry other benefits besides ease of use; they are covered later in this section.

Defining Prefix Lists

A *prefix list* is a feature that provides route prefix-filtering capabilities. This feature was introduced into Cisco IOS in 11.1CC, 11.3 and is in 12.0 and later IOS code. This feature is only to filter routing updates and is not supported for filtering data packets. Prefix lists can be used with BGP to filter routing information inbound and outbound and for distribute lists with distance vector IGPs (RIP, IGRP, or EIGRP).

Benefits of Prefix Lists

When prefix lists were created, the functionality was defined for specifically filtering routing updates. Narrowing the scope of a feature often allows for greater performance optimizations. This is the case with prefix lists, which have the following benefits over access lists for route filtering: increased performance, incremental updates, and a user-friendly command-line interface.

Increased Performance

The implementation of prefix lists was optimized to provide for faster loading of very large lists in addition to providing increased performance of the actual route-filtering function. This is especially important to ISPs that can have very long route-filtering policies defined. In addition, current Internet routing tables contain approximately 80,000 prefixes. This amounts to quite a lot of work for a router with several eBGP sessions on the same router!

Incremental Updates

The order in which access control elements are placed within an access control list (ACL) is very important. This is because packets are compared sequentially through the list until there is a match; the search function then breaks out. There can be overlapping elements within a list, but as soon as the first match is found, that is the element that is used. Standard and extended ACLs do not provide a method to incrementally update entries; to add or remove an entry in an ACL, the whole ACL is removed and the new ACL is entered. Prefix lists have the capability for each entry to be assigned a sequence number, allowing for entries to be added in the middle of the list.

A User-Friendly Command-Line Interface

The first part of this section demonstrated how configuring complex policies can be very unintuitive. A key requirement for prefix lists was to improve this system by providing an easy-to-understand method for defining complex routing policy. The actual configuration of prefix lists is examined in the following sections.

Prefix List Operations

The operation of prefix lists is very similar to that of ACLs. Several of the key features of ACLs were preserved in the design of prefix lists. These features are as follows:

■ Allowing each element to be either Permit or Deny

■ Using an ordered list, in that the first match wins using a sequential search

■ The ability to use both an exact match and a range match

■ An empty list is essentially a Permit All list

■ Every prefix list contains an implicit Deny All at its end

The processing in a prefix list is the same as in an ACL. A routing update is compared against each entry in the list until a match is found. The Permit or Deny is executed, and the search function breaks out of the list. A key difference with ACLs and prefix lists is that noncontiguous masks are not supported in prefix lists because of how entries are defined in a prefix list. Prefix lists also allow the use of a name instead of a number to define a list, along with the ability to provide a description line.

Prefix lists are used only for filtering routing information. They cannot be used to filter general data traffic.

Configuring Prefix Lists

The configuration of prefix lists is a bit different from ACLs. The following commands are used to define and apply prefix lists.

IP PREFIX-LIST

IP PREFIX-LIST is the base command used to define entries in the prefix list and has several options.

```
no ip prefix-list <list-name>
```

This command is used to delete the entire prefix list.

```
[no] ip prefix-list <list-name> description <text>
```

This command allows a description to be given to a prefix list, which helps administrators quickly identify the purpose of a list. Prepending a "no" will remove only this line from the configuration.

```
[no] ip prefix-list <list-name> [seq <seq-number>] deny|permit
<network>/<len> [ge <ge-value>] [le <le-value>]
```

This command is used to define entries in a prefix list. Prepending a "no" will remove only this line from the prefix list.

<LIST-NAME> A mandatory command used to specify the list that is being modified.

SEQ <SEQ-NUMBER> An optional command that specifies the placement of the entry in the list. This is significant because prefix lists are ordered lists. By default, if no sequence number is specified, the entry is placed at the end of the list and is assigned a sequence number of the last sequence number plus five. When you are deconfiguring an entry, you do not need to specify the sequence number.

DENY|PERMIT A mandatory command that defines the action to take when a routing update matches this entry.

<NETWORK>\<LEN> A mandatory command that defines the actual prefix to match. <NETWORK> is the network number; <LEN> is the number of contiguous bits set to one in the network mask. This is why noncontiguous masks are not supported.

GE <GE-VALUE> and LE <LE-VALUE> Both of these are optional and are used to specify a range of prefixes. If neither of these is used, an exact match will be made. The specified <GE-VALUE> and <LE-VALUE> must satisfy the following rule:

```
len < ge-value < le-value <= 32
```

Configuration Examples Permit 10.1.0.0/17 and 10.1.0.0/16 require an exact match on network and mask:

```
ip prefix-list test permit 10.1.0.0/17
ip prefix-list test permit 10.1.0.0/16
```

Permit only prefixes with a network mask of /19 or shorter for all Class B space:

```
ip prefix-list test permit 128.0.0.0/2 le 19
```

Let's take a moment to examine this entry in a bit more detail. The LE and GE options are the most confusing aspects of prefix lists. The 128.0.0.0/2 indicates that the first two bits of the prefix must match 01. This allows only the Class B space because Class A space would be 00 and Class C space would be 11. If the LE option were not specified, an exact match would be required on the network mask, permitting only a single route that represents the entire Class B space. The LE option has been configured, however. This option means less than or equal to and matches against the network mask. The LE option refers to the length of the vector of contiguous bits in the network mask. This means a /8 is less than a /16. This rule applies to our example in that any network that has the first 2 bits of 01 with a network mask of /2 through /19 will be permitted. If GE had been used instead, any network with the first 2 bits of 01 and a network mask of /19 through /32 would be permitted.

Deny the default route, permit everything else:

```
ip prefix-list test deny 0.0.0.0/0
ip prefix-list test permit 0.0.0.0/0 le 32
```

This example can be a bit confusing. Both entries have the 0.0.0.0/0 in them, but one denies and the other permits. The use of the /0 means that when you are matching against this entry, the actual network does not matter; none of the bits are compared and all networks are an automatic match. The difference between the two is that the first one is an exact match for the route that has a 0.0.0.0 network mask or represents the entire IPv4 address space. The first entry will not match any route other than the default route because that is the only route with a 0.0.0.0 network mask. The second entry will match every possible route, including the default route. This is because all the bits in the network are not compared again, so all networks match and the range that has been defined to match for the network mask is /0 through /32, which constitutes the entire IPv4 table.

Allow only prefixes that are a /8 or longer and a /24 or shorter:

```
ip prefix-list test permit 0.0.0.0/0 ge 8 le 24
```

NEIGHBOR X.X.X.X PREFIX-LIST

The NEIGHBOR X.X.X.X PREFIX-LIST configuration command allows a prefix list to be applied to a BGP neighbor. The format of this command is as follows:

```
bgp router y
  neighbor x.x.x.x prefix-list <name> in|out
```

It is required that the application of the prefix list be defined as incoming or outgoing for the direction of the route filtering.

Prefix List Sequence Numbering

A key requirement for prefix lists, as mentioned above, was to provide the ability to do incremental changes. This feature allows new lines to be inserted into the middle of the prefix list without removing and reapplying the entire list, as is the case with ACLs. In order to accomplish this task, each entry in a prefix list is given a sequence number. If a sequence number is not specified when the entry is added, a sequence number is assigned. The number that is assigned is the current maximum sequence number in the list plus five.

exam
ⓦatch

Prefix list autosequencing is in increments of five. Adding an entry to a list takes the last sequence number and adds five; it does not use the next largest multiple of five.

EXERCISE 9-2

Prefix List Configuration

Create a prefix list that satisfies the following conditions:

- Blocks all RFC 1918 routes (10.0.0.0/8, 172.16.0.0/12, 192.168.0.0/16)
- Allows any routes in the Class A space with a network mask of /8 or shorter
- Allows any routes in the Class B space with a network mask of /16 or shorter
- Allows any routes in the Class C space with a network mask of /24 or shorter
- Denies the default route and all other routes not matching these criteria

Solution:

```
ip prefix-list EXAMPLE deny 10.0.0.0/8
ip prefix-list EXAMPLE deny 172.16.0.0/12
ip prefix-list EXAMPLE deny 192.168.0.0/16
ip prefix-list EXAMPLE deny 0.0.0.0/0
ip prefix-list EXAMPLE permit 0.0.0.0/1 le 8
ip prefix-list EXAMPLE permit 128.0.0.0/2 le 16
ip prefix-list EXAMPLE permit 192.0.0.0/3 le 24
```

Prefix List Example

We have discussed the configuration commands; now it is time to put it all into action. The scenario for this example is a company with a single Internet router that is multihomed to two ISPs. They use a /16 network internally and want to have the traffic for half of that space enter through ISPA and traffic for the other half of the address space enter through ISPB. It is very important that they have redundancy in case a circuit goes down. However, due to budgetary constraints, router redundancy is not being used. Figure 9-9 displays the topology for this example.

The Internet router configuration is as follows:

```
router bgp 1
 no synchronization
 redistribute static
 neighbor 10.1.1.2 remote-as 2
 neighbor 10.1.1.2 prefix-list ISPA out
 neighbor 10.1.2.2 remote-as 3
 neighbor 10.1.2.2 prefix-list ISPB out

ip prefix-list ISPA permit 172.16.0.0/16
ip prefix-list ISPA permit 172.16.0.0/17
ip prefix-list ISPB permit 172.16.0.0/16
ip prefix-list ISPB permit 172.16.128.0/17
ip route 172.16.0.0 255.255.0.0 null0
ip route 172.16.0.0 255.255.128.0 null0
ip route 172.16.128.0 255.255.128.0 null0
```

FIGURE 9-9

Sample prefix list configuration topology

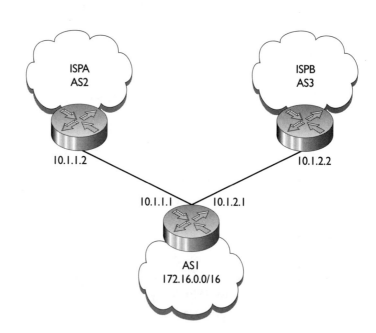

SCENARIO & SOLUTION

What purpose does the sequence number serve?	The sequence number provides the ability to do incremental updates to a prefix list.
What version of IOS first supported prefix lists?	Prefix lists were first supported in 11.1CC, 11.3T, and 12.0.
Are noncontiguous masks supported by prefix lists?	No, the very notation of prefix lists does not allow for noncontiguous masks, because the number of contiguous bits is used to specify prefix length.

Verifying Prefix Lists

After configuring a prefix list, it is useful to know how many matches there have been for each entry, especially when troubleshooting.

The SHOW IP PREFIX-LIST Command

The SHOW IP PREFIX-LIST command identifies the entries in the prefix list and provides general statistics on the list. The following is the output from the SHOW IP PREFIX-LIST DETAIL command on the router from the preceding example:

```
Prefix-list with the last deletion/insertion: ISPB
ip prefix-list ISPA:
   count: 2, range entries: 0, sequences: 5 - 10, refcount: 1
   seq 5 permit 172.16.0.0/16 (hit count: 1, refcount: 1)
   seq 10 permit 172.16.0.0/17 (hit count: 1, refcount: 1)
ip prefix-list ISPB:
   count: 2, range entries: 0, sequences: 5 - 10, refcount: 2
   seq 5 permit 172.16.0.0/16 (hit count: 1, refcount: 1)
   seq 10 permit 172.16.128.0/17 (hit count: 1, refcount: 1)
```

The first line of this output indicates that the last prefix list modified was the prefix list ISPB. An examination of the prefix list ISPB tells us that this list has two entries and that none of the entries matches a range of prefixes but that they are all exact matches. The hit counters are all 0, which means that either no prefixes matched the entry or there have been no routing updates processed through this list.

The CLEAR IP PREFIX-LIST Command

This command clears the hit count field in the SHOW IP PREFIX-LIST output.

on the !job *Prefix lists can be used with other protocols besides BGP. If prefix lists are supported on the IOS version you are using, it is a good idea to use them. They can be applied to distance-vector protocols such as RIP and EIGRP on a per-interface basis or at redistribution points. Using them will make your configurations easier to create, read, and troubleshoot.*

CERTIFICATION OBJECTIVE 9.03

Multihoming

Throughout this chapter, the term *multihoming* has been used, but it has not been explained in any real depth. This section examines multihoming in greater detail, along with the various methods to implement designs that incorporate multihoming. In short, multihoming with respect to BGP requires connecting to multiple ASs to provide redundant connectivity. Multihoming is also used to provide more optimal routing.

The features of BGP that are used to define policy are brought into play in a multihomed environment. In environments in which there is only a single path out of the network or a single-homed environment, defining preference in route selection is largely meaningless, because there is ultimately only one path to enter or leave the network.

Types of Multihoming

A BGP environment features multiple methods to implement multihoming. The method used can have a significant impact on traffic patterns and resource utilization. The primary difference between the various methods is the amount of information that is lost, resulting in a loss of granularity available in defining policies. The three methods used for BGP are default routes only, partial routing tables plus default, and full BGP tables.

Default Routes from All Providers

The default routes method involves accepting only the default route from all your providers. This method works best when a primary link is used for all traffic, with secondary links used only for backup connectivity. This method provides no insight into the best path to reach a given destination over the Internet and often results in suboptimal routing from a high-level view.

Benefits of Using Default Routes Alone

The main benefit of this method of multihoming is the number of resources it uses. Only a single prefix needs to be advertised and held in the routing information base on the routers, which requires very little memory. In addition, general instabilities in the Internet are masked, much the same way that applying summarization can mask instabilities within your IGP.

Disadvantages of Using Default Routes Alone

The reduction in complexity and resource utilization has a price, however. Using this method of multihoming can lead to suboptimal routing. If you prefer the route to one ISP (ISPA), even traffic destined to another ISP (ISPB) to which you are directly connected will still go through the first ISP (ISPA) to reach its destination (ISPB). The use of default routes only removes the ability to apply policy with any granularity.

Example of Default Routes Alone for Multihoming

Configuring this method of multihoming can be done on either the customer side or the ISP side. It makes more sense to have the ISP block all routes but originate only the default route, because sending all the routes is a waste of bandwidth and CPU cycles if the updates will be denied inbound on your router.

If the ISP is sending all routes and the default route, adding a prefix list inbound will allow you to accept only the default route. This allows migrating to full routing tables by simply removing the prefix list if your policy requirements change without having to contact your ISP. Building off the prefix list example, the following configuration allows the use of a default route for BGP only. The topology is shown in Figure 9-10.

```
router bgp 1
 no synchronization
 redistribute static
 neighbor 10.1.1.2 remote-as 2
 neighbor 10.1.1.2 prefix-list ISPA out
 neighbor 10.1.1.2 prefix-list DEFAULTONLY in
 neighbor 10.1.2.2 remote-as 3
 neighbor 10.1.2.2 prefix-list ISPB out
 neighbor 10.1.2.2 prefix-list DEFAULTONLY in
 ip prefix-list ISPA permit 172.16.0.0/16
ip prefix-list ISPA permit 172.16.0.0/17
ip prefix-list ISPB permit 172.16.0.0/16
ip prefix-list ISPB permit 172.16.128.0/17

ip prefix-list DEFAULTONLY permit 0.0.0.0/0

ip route 172.16.0.0 255.255.0.0 null0
ip route 172.16.0.0 255.255.128.0 null0
ip route 172.16.128.0 255.255.128.0 null0
```

FIGURE 9-10

Sample
default-only
topology

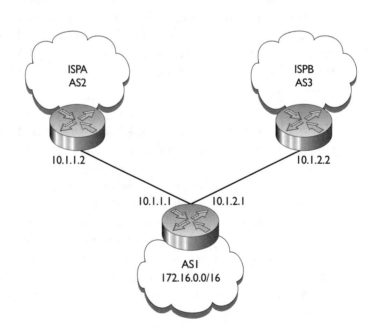

Limited BGP Table and Default Route from Each Provider

The limited BGP table with default routes is a very popular method for multihoming. The resource requirements are less than that of carrying a full table, but greater granularity is available. This method involves having your ISP advertise all its local networks and usually those of its customers in addition to the default route. This method is also referred to as *partial routes* and requires configuration on the ISP side to implement.

Benefits of Receiving a Limited BGP Table

This method allows for increased granularity, which improves some of the issues that default only has with suboptimal routing. Partial tables are significantly smaller than full BGP tables, allowing for reduced resource requirements. The use of partial routing tables provides specific routes to destinations located inside the ASs of your direct upstream providers, removing the need to traverse peering points to reach those destinations. This allows better use of bandwidth on egress links from your network.

Drawbacks of Using Limited BGP Table

The granularity of routing information in this design is limited to only those networks that are your direct upstream providers. This setup introduces situations of suboptimal routing because the default route could be followed to one of your providers that is two ASs away from the destination while one of your other providers is only a single AS away.

Example of Receiving a Limited BGP Table

The configuration required to use the limited BGP design is identical to that for using full BGP routing tables. All route filtering is handled by the upstream ISP, where typically all routes that are received by peers and noncustomer eBGP peers are blocked. To implement a limited BGP table with default routes, the example configuration for default only needs a small modification: the inbound prefix list DEFAULTONLY should be removed.

Full BGP Table from All Providers

This method is the most common and involves accepting full Internet routing tables from all your upstream providers. The resource requirements for this method are significant. At this time, the full Internet routing table contains approximately 80,000 routes. This means that any router accepting full Internet routes should have at least 128MB of RAM. Accepting full routes does not require a default route, because any destination that exists on the Internet should have a specific entry in the table. This method also provides the most optimal routing of any method for multihoming because it has the most granularity available, allowing for complex policy to be defined. Policy is often defined based on incoming routing updates using the Cisco-specific WEIGHT attribute and the RFC-defined Local Preference attribute, which is discussed in the next section.

Benefits of Receiving the Full BGP Table

The benefit to receiving full BGP tables is the minimal loss of information incurred. Some loss to summarization might exist, but the full AS_PATH is delivered intact for all routes, allowing data to traverse the least number of ASs possible to reach the destination. This also allows policy information that was originated by the destination AS to be used in defining your own policy. The policy information that is originated from the destination AS consists of AS_PATH prepends and prefix length information.

Drawbacks of Receiving the Full BGP Table

The primary drawback of accepting the full BGP table is the sheer size of the table and the resources required to process and hold the table. Another drawback of receiving a full BGP table is that instabilities in the Internet become visible in your own routing table, which—in the case of serious instability—can cause significant churn and CPU utilization.

Example of Receiving the Full BGP Table

The configuration required for receiving the full BGP table is straightforward. The neighbor sessions need to be configured along with outbound filtering to ensure that your network does not become a transit network for traffic between the ISPs you are using. Figure 9-11 shows the topology for this example.

The configuration of the Internet router in AS1 is as follows:

```
router bgp 1
 no synchronization

 redistribute static
 neighbor 10.2.1.1 remote-as 2
```

```
neighbor 10.2.1.1 prefix-list AS2OUT out
neighbor 10.3.1.1 remote-as 3
neighbor 10.3.1.1 prefix-list AS3OUT out
no auto-summary
!
ip prefix-list AS2OUT seq 5 permit 172.16.0.0/16
ip prefix-list AS2OUT seq 10 permit 172.16.128.0/17
!
ip prefix-list AS3OUT seq 5 permit 172.16.0.0/16
ip prefix-list AS3OUT seq 10 permit 172.16.0.0/17

ip route 172.16.0.0 255.255.0.0 null0
ip route 172.16.0.0 255.255.128.0 null0
ip route 172.16.128.0 255.255.128.0 null0
```

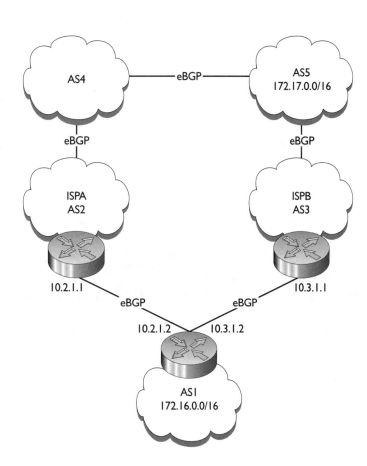

FIGURE 9-11

Sample full-BGP
tables topology

The prefix 172.17.0.0/16 is being originated out of AS5. A quick look at our BGP tables on our customer-edge router in AS1, which is multihomed to AS3 and AS2, shows us the multiple entries in the routing table using the command SHOW IP BGP 172.17.0.0.

```
BGP routing table entry for 172.17.0.0/16, version 3
Paths: (2 available, best #1)
 Not advertised to any peer
 3 5
   10.3.1.1 from 10.3.1.1 (10.3.2.2)
    Origin incomplete, localpref 100, valid, external, best, ref 2
 2 4 5
   10.2.1.1 from 10.2.1.1 (10.205.100.100)
    Origin incomplete, localpref 100, valid, external, ref 2
```

This output shows us the prefix entering the network from both AS3 and AS2. The route preferred is that received from AS3 because there are only two AS hops in the AS_PATH. The reason AS_PATH length was used is because the WEIGHT is not set, and LOCAL PREFERENCE is equal for both routes. The prefix list provides protection from becoming a transit AS or providing routing for external traffic between AS2 and AS3.

on the **job**

Often, a combination of these methods is used. It is possible to have two providers, one providing the full BGP table and the other providing partial routes plus the default.

SCENARIO & SOLUTION

Who typically applies the filters to the BGP session when the partial routes and default method is used?	The ISP, because it has knowledge of which routes are from peers and which are customer and internal routes.
Does a company that is not multihomed need to accept full tables?	No, because there is only one path out of the network. Accepting full tables would be a waste of resources.
Does a company that is multihomed need to accept full tables?	This depends on the routing policy that is required. This is a design decision with no hard-and-fast rule.

BGP Metric Commands

The ability to apply policy has been mentioned throughout the chapter and is covered in this section. We have discussed the topic of applying policy for ingress to the network through the use of multiple prefixes with differing lengths. The next step is to define policy concerning egress from the network. To accomplish this task, two BGP attributes, the Cisco-specific WEIGHT attribute and the standards-based LOCAL PREFERENCE attribute, are used.

The Cisco-specific WEIGHT attribute is applied to incoming BGP updates. The WEIGHT attribute is at the very top of the list in the decision process as long as the next-hop address is reachable. This attribute is local to the device on which it is applied and is not included in iBGP or eBGP updates. The highest WEIGHT attribute is preferred in the decision process.

The standards-based LOCAL PREFERENCE attribute can be applied to routes inbound or outbound through the use of an access list. This method allows significant granularity in applying preference values. LOCAL PREFERENCE can also be applied to all iBGP updates from a single BGP speaker. LOCAL PREFERENCE is local to the autonomous system and is included in iBGP updates but not eBGP updates. The highest value of LOCAL PREFERENCE is preferred, and LOCAL PREFERENCE is immediately after WEIGHT in the BGP decision process.

exam
ⓦatch

Make sure you have a very solid understanding of the BGP decision process. This process was covered in the previous chapter. It is essential that you memorize this process.

The NEIGHBOR X.X.X.X WEIGHT <VALUE> Command

The WEIGHT attribute can be applied on a per-session basis. This configuration command applies the weight specified to all incoming route prefixes. The weight value applied here is not included in any eBGP or iBGP updates and is local to the BGP speaker on which it is configured.

The BGP DEFAULT LOCAL-PREFERENCE <VALUE> Command

This command sets the LOCAL PREFERENCE attribute for all route prefixes advertised through iBGP to all other internal neighbors. The LOCAL

PREFERENCE attribute is carried through the entire AS. In order to apply LOCAL PREFERENCE with greater granularity, a route map must be used on a per-neighbor basis. It is important to remember that the default LOCAL PREFERENCE is 100.

EXERCISE 9-3

Combining Multihoming Methods

Scenario: In a network that is multihomed to two ISPs, using a subrate DS3 to ISPA and a T1 to ISPB, what combination of multihoming methods will provide the best combination of best-path routing and balancing the load over both links?

Solution: Many other factors could contribute to this situation, but in general, running full tables with ISPA and partial routes with ISPB provides the best results for the outlined criteria. The effectiveness of this solution is highly dependent on traffic patterns. As with many aspects of networking, many factors can make a solution that works well in one environment work poorly in another.

A Multihoming BGP Configuration Example

The same network that was used in the example with multihoming and using full BGP tables is used in this example. The goal here is to prefer AS2 for everything, with AS3 as backup. Provided that the next-hop IP address is reachable for all prefixes received, only two attributes provide us with a way to override the AS_PATH length: the WEIGHT attribute and the LOCAL PREFERENCE attribute. This network uses only a single BGP router, so the local attribute of WEIGHT provides a simple method for shifting traffic. The 172.17.0.0/16 prefix is used again to verify that our policy has been applied.

The router configuration is as follows:

```
router bgp 1
 no synchronization
 aggregate-address 172.16.0.0 255.255.0.0
 redistribute static
 neighbor 10.2.1.1 remote-as 2
 neighbor 10.2.1.1 weight 40000
```

```
neighbor 10.2.1.1 prefix-list AS2OUT out
neighbor 10.3.1.1 remote-as 3
neighbor 10.3.1.1 prefix-list AS3OUT out
no auto-summary
```

Now the SHOW IP BGP 172.17.0.0 command contains the updated prefix information, with the preferred path through AS2:

```
BGP routing table entry for 172.17.0.0/16, version 5
Paths: (2 available, best #2)
 Not advertised to any peer
 3 5
  10.3.1.1 from 10.3.1.1 (10.3.2.2)
   Origin incomplete, localpref 100, valid, external, ref 2
 2 4 5
  10.2.1.1 from 10.2.1.1 (10.205.100.100)
   Origin incomplete, localpref 100, weight 40000, valid,
external, best, ref 2
```

exam
ⓦatch

The WEIGHT attribute is Cisco specific and is not propagated but has local scope. The LOCAL PREFERENCE attribute is propagated via iBGP only, not eBGP, and is significant throughout the AS in which it was applied.

CERTIFICATION OBJECTIVE 9.04

Redistribution with IGPs

The BGP and the IGP do not automatically exchange routing information. There are multiple methods in which the two can interact, and the method used can have a significant impact on the scalability and stability of the network. The previous section mentioned that the BGP table contains approximately 80,000 routes, which is considered far beyond the limits of all current IGPs. Since BGP routes in this type of environment cannot be injected into the IGP routing process, there must be another way for that information to be utilized.

The BGP routing information base (RIB) is separate from the IP routing table. There are multiple BGP RIBs; the two with which we are concerned are the RIB-In and the RIB-Loc. The BGP RIB-In is all the BGP routing information that has been received by this router. This information is then injected into the decision process, which finds the best-path routes for each prefix. This distilled set of prefixes is what makes up the RIB-Loc, or the local RIB. The RIB-Loc is then compared against the IP routing table in the router, and the best routes are entered into the IP routing table, where actual route lookups are handled.

It is important to note that although BGP forwarding information is inserted into the routing table, it is not automatically injected into the IGP. The same is also true for IGP information—it is not automatically injected into BGP. In order for BGP to advertise a prefix, it must be told to do so. The methods for defining the interaction between BGP and the IGP are covered through the rest of this section.

Notifying BGP of Which Networks to Advertise

There are four common ways that routing information enters the BGP RIB on a router. Three of these methods involve injecting the routing information from the IGP or static routes; the fourth is information received from other BGP speakers.

The NETWORK Command

The NETWORK command is used to specifically define prefixes to inject into the BGP process. The NETWORK command allows you to specify a network and, optionally, a network mask. For that prefix to be injected into BGP, there must be a route in the IGP that matches the network and mask exactly. Routes that are injected into BGP using the NETWORK command have their ORIGIN attribute set to IGP.

exam
ⓦatch

The value of the ORIGIN attribute is significant. It is used in the BGP decision process. A network injected via the NETWORK command is preferred over the same prefix that has been redistributed if the BGP decision process is not satisfied prior to that step.

Redistribution of Static Routes

Static routes can be configured and then redistributed into BGP. Often, the static routes are configured as summaries, which are pointed to Null0 and then redistributed into BGP. This masks instabilities within the AS from being made visible to the rest of the Internet and prevents unstable prefixes from being dampened or suppressed.

Redistribution of Dynamic Routing Protocols

The IGP can be redistributed directly into BGP. This method reflects any instabilities in the IGP out to the rest of the Internet because the flapping routes will be inserted and removed from the BGP table repeatedly as they flap. This method requires route filtering at the redistribution point to ensure that only the correct information is advertised. Prefixes injected into BGP using this method will have their ORIGIN attribute set to Incomplete.

Learned from Another BGP Speaker

BGP information learned from another iBGP speaker is the final way to advertise BGP information to the rest of the Internet. However, in order for information to have been advertised via BGP, it must have used one of the first three methods initially.

Using the NETWORK Command

The use of the NETWORK command in conjunction with enabling synchronization is the preferred method for injecting routing information into BGP. When this method is used, if a route goes down within the network, the IGP removes it from the table and BGP ceases to advertise this prefix. This method also allows the administrator to specifically define which networks should be allowed into the BGP process and identifies them as having an ORIGIN of IGP, which plays a role in the BGP decision process. The use of this command and an explanation of synchronization were given in the previous chapter.

Redistributing Static Routes into BGP

The redistribution of static routes into BGP is another common method for injecting routing information into BGP. This method allows BGP to run on the border of the network. Static routes, which typically are summaries of IGP routing information, are configured pointing to Null0. This process is known as *nailing up a route*. Nailing up a route hides instability within the IGP from the rest of the Internet. When a packet destined to a prefix contained within the summary enters the network, the route lookup checks for the most specific route. If there is a route, it is followed; if there is not, the static to Null0 causes the packet to be discarded at the edge of the network. This method can cause traffic to be black-holed, which should be taken into consideration when you use this method. The example in Figure 9-12 identifies how redistributing static supernets can cause traffic to be black-holed.

This situation involves a network that is connected or located behind RTC. The only path to the border is via RTC. Both RTA and RTB have aggregated static routes nailed up to Null0 and redistributed into BGP. If the link between RTC and RTA were to go down, the static route would still exist and the announcement would not be withdrawn. This scenario would allow traffic to continue to enter the network via RTA, at which point it would all be routed to Null0 or thrown away, even though there is a valid path through RTB.

Redistributing Dynamic Routing Protocols into BGP

The routing information in the IGP can be directly redistributed into BGP. This method causes instabilities within the network to be reflected to the Internet as flapping routes. Instabilities can result in having routing information dampened or suppressed, which causes black-hole traffic until the route has stabilized. When you

FIGURE 9-12

A sample
black-hole
topology

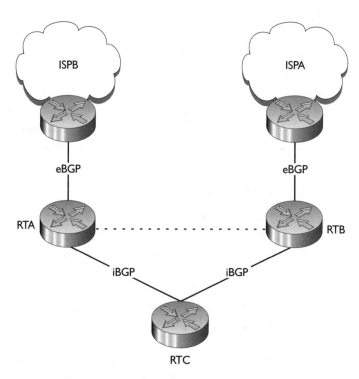

- - - - - - - Logical iBGP Session only

are redistributing directly from the IGP into BGP, it is essential that you place filters on the redistribution to ensure that private networks, such as those defined in RFC 1918, are not advertised. This method is typically not recommended.

Redistribution of BGP into a Local Routing Protocol

We have covered the topic of injecting routing information into BGP; now let's examine the other side of the coin. It is entirely possible to redistribute BGP into your IGP. Any redistribution from BGP into the IGP should be done with very careful route filtering and in general is not suggested. The BGP table carries far too many routes for all current IGPs to support and remain stable.

The Internet routing table also has approximately 4000 bytes of routing updates every minute, which would be detrimental to the stability of the IGP. If routing information is redistributed from BGP into the IGP, it should be sent via the default route. It should also be noted that when BGP information is redistributed into the IGP, all path information is lost. This fact, coupled with misconfiguration, could result in black-holing traffic to other ASs and inconsistent BGP entries.

EXERCISE 9-4

Redistribution of BGP into IGP

Scenario: When BGP is redistributed into the IGP, all path information is lost, which can result in traffic being black-holed. What do we mean by "path information being lost," and how can this event result in traffic being black-holed if the routes are redistributed back into BGP?

Solution: The path information is the AS_PATH, which identifies the autonomous system that generated this prefix and the autonomous systems that the prefix has traversed. If these routes were redistributed back into BGP, they could be advertised back out to the Internet with the wrong source, causing traffic destined to these prefixes to be forwarded to the wrong AS. The entries would show up in remote routes as having an inconsistent AS, or the same prefix originated from multiple autonomous systems.

If you find yourself redistributing BGP into the local IGP, step back and think about it again. In general, this redistribution is not considered a good practice, so make sure there isn't a better option. If you must redistribute BGP into your IGP, don't redistribute it back into BGP, and do make sure you have filters on your redistribution.

ISP Policy on Redistribution

The typical architecture used by ISPs does not involve redistribution of BGP and IGP in either direction. ISPs keep their BGP and IGP separate, with each serving a different function. The IGP is used to provide reachability for BGP speakers and routing information to next-hop addresses. BGP is run on all routers, a technique called *pervasive BGP*. The IGP carries only internal networks, so the customer networks are injected either via eBGP or as static routes that are redistributed at the customer aggregation routers. This system allows the bulk of the information to be carried in BGP, which is able to handle significant churn in routing information more gracefully, using the reliable transport of TCP. The IGP is then used only to maintain reachability through the AS itself, which is where the fast convergence is most needed to provide rerouting around failures and a loop-free topology.

End Autonomous Systems Policy on Redistribution

The architecture used by most end ASs is different from that used by the ISPs. Most end ASs do not want to run BGP and carry full tables on all routers in their networks, because the cost of supplying the required resources can be significant. In this scenario, BGP is typically run on the border routers that are directly connected to the Internet. Routing information is injected into BGP through the use of the NETWORK command.

Running a BGP core in an enterprise network is usually not necessary unless there are a few thousand routes. However, networks with fewer prefixes can utilize BGP between different administrative domains within a single company's network, such as between U.S. operations and European operations.

FROM THE CLASSROOM

BGP Deployment in Enterprise Networks

As corporate networks continue to expand, it has become common practice to create a BGP core. This is done because legacy address assignment does not allow for efficient summarization and the size of the IGP routing tables is causing instabilities. This BGP core is often separate from the BGP peering used for Internet connectivity and utilizes private AS numbers. IGP routing information is redistributed directly into BGP; however, BGP routes are usually not redistributed back into the IGP unless default routes only would cause significantly suboptimal routing. The BGP core injects a default route into the IGP. This allows multiple IGP domains to be used, reducing the resources required on the routers and bringing the IGP routing tables back to a manageable size.

—*Micah Bartell, CCIE #5069*

CERTIFICATION SUMMARY

The original design of BGP created inherent scalability issues within Internal BGP. The most prominent scalability issue is the number of iBGP peering sessions required in large autonomous systems running Pervasive BGP. This issue has been addressed through the creation of route reflection, which enables a hierarchy to be added into the BGP domain. The use of route reflection does not change the forwarding path of the packets by preserving the next-hop attribute in the iBGP updates.

Route filtering through the use of access control lists can be difficult when you are creating complex route filters. Cisco has provided the prefix list feature to improve route-filtering performance, ease of use through a more intuitive command structure, and incremental changes for easier administration. The availability of prefix lists is in 11.1CC, 11.3T, and 12.0. It is highly recommended that you utilize the 12.0 release of Cisco IOS if prefix list functionality is desired.

BGP is not only used for advertising routing information to other ASs; it is also used as a policy definition tool. The protocol was designed to be very flexible, allowing significant variety in the design of BGP networks. Although BGP is used to improve the scalability of enterprise networks, its primary purpose is to connect networks under different administrative controls.

TWO-MINUTE DRILL

Here are some key points from each certification objective in Chapter 9.

Scalability Issues and Solutions with iBGP

❑ A full iBGP mesh does not scale well due to the number of sessions increasing at an exponential rate as more iBGP speakers are added to the network.

❑ Route reflection deals with the scalability issues in iBGP through the introduction of a hierarchy.

❑ Routing updates received by a route reflector from a client are reflected to all other clients and normal iBGP peers.

❑ Routing updates received by a route reflector from a normal iBGP peer are only reflected to route reflector clients in the same cluster.

❑ The cluster ID and the originator ID are used to prevent routing information loops.

Policy Control

❑ Prefix lists provide incremental updates to existing lists.

❑ Prefix lists provide improved route-filtering performance.

❑ Prefix lists provide a more intuitive command-line interface for route filtering.

❑ Prefix lists can be used only for filtering routing information, not for filtering data traffic.

❑ Prefix lists are not exclusively for BGP but can be used through distribute lists and route maps with other protocols.

Multihoming

❑ Multihoming with respect to BGP is connecting to multiple autonomous systems to provide redundant connectivity.

❑ Default only is a method of multihoming that has small resource requirements but can result in suboptimal traffic patterns due to lack of routing information granularity.

❑ The method of limited routes with the default route, also called partial routes, provides increased granularity and improves the optimality of traffic flow at the cost of increased resource requirements.

❑ The full BGP table method provides the most granularity and allows the most potential for optimal traffic flow but requires significant resources due to the sheer amount of routing information.

❑ The WEIGHT attribute is a BGP attribute that is Cisco specific and is local to the router to which it is applied.

❑ The LOCAL PREFERENCE attribute is standards based and is propagated through iBGP but not eBGP; it is local to the autonomous system in which it is applied.

Redistribution with IGPs

❑ Routing information can be redistributed directly into BGP from the static routing entries or a dynamic routing protocol.

❑ The NETWORK command is the preferred method for injecting prefixes into BGP to be advertised to the Internet.

❑ BGP can be redistributed into the local IGP, but this is not recommended due to the loss of BGP path information and the instability this can inject into the IGP.

❑ Large enterprise networks have begun to use BGP in the core to improve the stability and scalability of the network.

SELF TEST

The following questions will help you measure your understanding of the material presented in this chapter. Read all choices carefully because there might be more than one correct answer. Choose all correct answers for each question.

Scalability Issues and Solutions with iBGP

1. What BGP attribute prevents routing updates from being advertised back to a route reflector client?

   A. LOCAL PREFERENCE

   B. Originator ID

   C. WEIGHT

   D. Cluster ID

2. You design your network with a single cluster using two route reflectors. You decide to peer each client to only one of the route reflectors in the cluster. All the clients are able to see the routes from the other clients peering to the same reflector, but they can see none of the routes from the other reflector. How can this problem be fixed? Choose all that apply.

   A. Break the cluster into two separate clusters.

   B. Set the WEIGHT attribute on each route reflector for the routes learned from the other route reflector.

   C. Configure all the clients so that they think they are also route reflectors and with their route reflectors being their clients.

   D. Peer all the clients to both route reflectors.

3. If 10 routers have an iBGP full mesh between them, how many total iBGP sessions are in the network?

   A. 10

   B. 100

   C. 45

   D. 90

4. What command is used to configure route reflection?

   A. On the client, BGP REFLECTOR CLIENT; on the reflector, BGP ROUTE REFLECTOR

B. On the client, NEIGHBOR X.X.X.X ROUTE-REFLECTOR

C. On the reflector, NEIGHBOR X.X.X.X ROUTE-REFLECTOR-CLIENT

D. On the reflector, BGP ROUTE REFLECTOR

5. You have two Internet routers, each taking full BGP routes. They are connected by a router that does not have enough memory to run BGP, so you have only iBGP running between the two Internet routers. What will happen to traffic that reaches an Internet router and realizes the other Internet router is its preferred path?

A. The traffic will be forwarded to the other router and sent out.

B. Delivery of traffic will be inconsistent; some traffic could loop extensively and be dropped.

C. The traffic will be forwarded directly out, even though the other path is better.

D. The traffic will be dropped immediately at the Internet router.

Policy Control

6. In order to take advantage of the command structure provided by prefix lists, you have configured several to do traffic filtering on your interfaces. How do you apply them to your interfaces?

A. Prefix lists are not supported for traffic filtering.

B. Use the ACCESS-CLASS command.

C. Use the ACCESS-GROUP command.

D. Use the PREFIX-GROUP command.

7. If the sequence number on the last entry in a prefix list is 82, what will be the next one if you add an entry without specifying one?

A. 85

B. 83

C. 92

D. 87

8. Which of the following entries will permit the default route using a prefix list?

A. IP PREFIX-LIST TEST PERMIT DEFAULT

B. IP PREFIX-LIST TEST PERMIT 0.0.0.0/32

C. IP PREFIX-LIST TEST PERMIT 0.0.0.0/0

D. IP PREFIX-LIST TEST PERMIT DEFAULT-ONLY

9. Which of the following are benefits of using prefix lists?

   A. Improved route-filtering performance

   B. Improved traffic-filtering performance

   C. Incremental changes

   D. Support for noncontiguous network masks

10. You want to apply policy to the inbound path of packets on your network to help spread the load over multiple connections. Which attribute will provide the best solution?

   A. LOCAL PREFERENCE

   B. WEIGHT

   C. Advertising longer prefixes in addition to summaries

   D. Cluster ID

Multihoming

11. The network has a single Internet router with 64MB of RAM and connections to two ISPs, each one a DS3. Which multihoming method will be best?

   A. Default route only

   B. Limited routes and default route

   C. Full Internet tables

   D. Static routing

12. The network has a single Internet router with two Internet connections. One connection is a DS3; the other is a T1. BGP runs only on this one router, with no iBGP peers internally. The router is accepting default only and traffic is all exiting the network over the T1, using the router ID as its decision point for path selection. What would be the best way to prefer the DS3?

   A. Advertise longer prefixes on the DS3.

   B. AS_PATH prepend over the T1.

   C. Set the WEIGHT attribute on all updates over the DS3.

   D. Set the WEIGHT attribute on the T1.

13. Which attribute is first relative to the others in the decision path?

   A. LOCAL PREFERENCE

B. AS_PATH LENGTH

C. ORIGIN

D. WEIGHT

14. Your network is multihomed to two ISPs, each coming into a different router. Both routers are directly connected, and iBGP is running between them. The connection on RTRA is a DS3; the connection on RTRB is a T1. You are running full tables. What should you do to ensure all traffic exits the network via RTRA?

A. Configure BGP DEFAULT LOCAL-PREFERENCE 110 on RTRB.

B. Configure BGP DEFAULT LOCAL-PREFERENCE 90 on RTRA.

C. Configure BGP DEFAULT LOCAL-PREFERENCE 110 on RTRA.

D. Configure BGP DEFAULT LOCAL-PREFERENCE 100 on RTRB.

15. Your network is multihomed to four ISPs. You accept full routing tables. How do you best protect from becoming a transit AS?

A. Set LOCAL PREFERENCE to 120 on all incoming routes.

B. Set the WEIGHT for each neighbor to a different number.

C. Apply inbound prefix lists to each BGP peer

D. Apply outbound prefix lists to each BGP peer.

Redistribution with IGPs

16. Prefixes that are inserted into BGP using the network statement have their ORIGIN set to what value by default?

A. Incomplete

B. EGP

C. IGP

D. Unknown

17. Which is a drawback of redistributing directly from the IGP into BGP?

A. The ORIGIN is set to IGP.

B. Internal route instability is reflected externally to the AS.

C. External route instability is reflected internally.

D. None of the above.

18. Why is redistributing BGP into the IGP not a good practice? Choose all that apply.

    A. The IGP cannot handle full Internet tables.

    B. Constant BGP churn will destabilize the IGP.

    C. It causes loss of BGP path information.

    D. It is not possible to redistribute BGP into the IGP.

19. The typical ISP architectures involves:

    A. Running BGP on just the edge routers in the autonomous system

    B. Running BGP on all routers in the autonomous system

    C. Redistributing BGP into the IGP

    D. Redistributing the IGP directly into BGP at the edge

20. Redistributing BGP into the IGP and back into BGP can cause which of the following? Choose all that apply.

    A. Black-holing traffic and inconsistent updates

    B. Faster convergence

    C. Higher optimization in path selection

    D. A complete network meltdown

LAB QUESTION

You have been given the task of setting up external connectivity for your company. The company has chosen four ISPs and will have two Internet routers for redundancy. Two of the connections are OC3 and two are DS3. Your manager has stated that the DS3 connections should be used only if OC3 on the same router fails for outbound traffic. For inbound traffic, the DS3s should be used only if both OC3s are down. ISPA and ISPC are on OC3 connections; ISPB and ISPD are the DS3 connections. The best path should be taken between ISPA and ISPC. The AS number for your company is AS 10, and the IGP for your network is EIGRP, using the same autonomous system number as BGP. The network internal to your company is 10.0.0.0/8.

Your manager has requested that you develop the BGP configurations for this design. The diagram of the network topology is shown in Figure 9-13.

Note: For this example, we assume that 10.0.0.0/8 is not RFC 1918 space and is globally routable.

FIGURE 9-13 Lab topology

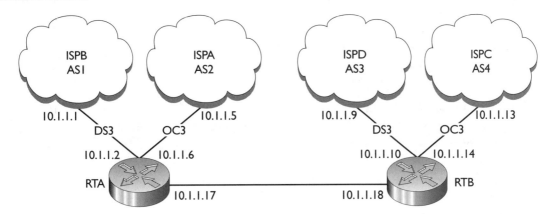

SELF TEST ANSWERS

1. ☑ **B.** The originator ID identifies the source of the update.
   ☒ **C** is incorrect because the WEIGHT attribute identifies route reflectors the update has passed through. **A** and **D** are incorrect because the LOCAL PREFERENCE attribute and the cluster ID are policy attributes used in path selection.

2. ☑ **A and D.** The CLUSTER-LIST attribute is causing the route reflectors to drop the updates. Peering the clients with both route reflectors will cause each to be updated, or using different cluster IDs will allow the reflectors to accept updates concerning their clients from each other.
   ☒ **B** is incorrect because the weight would never be applied to routing updates that are not accepted. **C** is incorrect because it does not have any effect on the communication between the two route reflectors with which all the clients are talking.

3. ☑ **C.** 45. The formula is $n(n-1)/2$, where n is the number of routers in the mesh.
   ☒ **A, B,** and **D** are incorrect because they are simply random numbers.

4. ☑ **C.** On the reflector, NEIGHBOR X.X.X.X ROUTE-REFLECTOR-CLIENT. Only the route reflectors must know reflection is happening and be configured to support it.
   ☒ **A, B,** and **D** are incorrect because they are all invalid commands.

5. ☑ **B.** Delivery of traffic will be inconsistent; some traffic could loop extensively and be dropped. All routers in the forwarding path between iBGP speakers must have BGP forwarding information.
   ☒ **A** is incorrect because the router in the middle will not necessarily be able to forward the packets to the other router due to inconsistent routing information. **C** is incorrect because traffic will always take the path that is most preferred in the table. **D** is incorrect because there is a route, so there is no reason to drop the traffic.

Policy Control

6. ☑ **A.** Prefix lists are not supported for traffic filtering. Prefix lists are only for route filtering.
   ☒ **B** and **C** are incorrect because ACCESS-CLASS and ACCESS-GROUP are for access control lists. **D** is incorrect because the PREFIX-GROUP command does not exist.

7. ☑ **D.** 87. Five is added to the current maximum, which in the question is 82.
   ☒ **A, B,** and **C** are incorrect sequence numbers.

8. ☑ **C.** IP PREFIX-LIST TEST PERMIT 0.0.0.0/0. The default route has a 0-bit network mask.
   ☒ **A** and **D** are incorrect because they are not valid commands. **B** is incorrect because it has the wrong mask.

9. ☑ **A** and **C.** Improved route-filtering performance and incremental changes are benefits of using prefix lists.
   ☒ **B** is incorrect because prefix lists do not support traffic filtering. **D** is incorrect because prefix lists do not support noncontiguous network masks, as ACLs do.

10. ☑ **C.** Advertising longer prefixes in addition to summaries. This provides longest match externally to direct traffic in specific interfaces, with summaries providing redundancy.
    ☒ **A** and **B** are incorrect because they are for policy outbound. **D** is incorrect because it does not affect path selection.

Multihoming

11. ☑ **B** is correct because the router has sufficient RAM to hold partial tables and will utilize both links.
    ☒ **A** is incorrect because it would waste an entire DS3. **C** is incorrect because you do not have enough RAM to hold the full routing table. **D** is incorrect because static routing will not allow you to advertise your routes to both ISPs.

12. ☑ **C.** Set the WEIGHT attribute on all updates over the DS3. This will prefer the default route over the DS3.
    ☒ **A** and **B** are incorrect because they are for controlling traffic inbound to the network. **D** is incorrect because the router would still prefer the T1.

13. ☑ **D.** WEIGHT is first in the decision path.
    ☒ **A, B,** and **C** are incorrect because they all come after WEIGHT in that order relative to each other.

14. ☑ **C.** Configure BGP DEFAULT LOCAL-PREFERENCE 110 on RTRA. Highest local preference wins in the decision process.
    ☒ **A** and **B** are incorrect because they would prefer the T1. **D** is incorrect because it would have no effect since 100 is the default for LOCAL PREFERENCE already.

15. ☑ **D.** Apply outbound prefix lists to each BGP peer. You must block the routing updates learned from other providers from being sent to the rest of the providers.
    ☒ **A** and **B** are incorrect and will not block routes from being sent to other providers but could influence which routes are sent. **C** is incorrect and would require blocking all routes to stop from acting as a transit AS entirely.

Redistribution with IGPs

16. ☑ **C.** IGP.
    ☒ **A** is incorrect because incomplete is for routes that are redistributed. **B** is incorrect because

EGP is for routes redistributed specifically from EGP. **D** is incorrect because unknown is not a valid setting.

17. ☑ **B.** Internal route instability is reflected externally to the AS. Route flapping can affect updates externally; however, summarization can reduce this effect substantially.
    ☒ **A** is incorrect because it sets ORIGIN to incomplete. **C** is incorrect because it is in the wrong direction. **D** is incorrect because there is a correct answer.

18. ☑ **A, B,** and **C** are all correct. IGPs cannot handle 80,000 routes, and BGP has enough routing table churn the IGP can destabilize. The loss of AS_PATH information can also cause problems, especially if the IGP is redistributed back into BGP.
    ☒ **D** is incorrect because it is possible to redistribute BGP into the IGP.

19. ☑ **B.** Running BGP on all routers in the autonomous system. Most ISPs run Pervasive BGP.
    ☒ **A** is incorrect because it is typically used by enterprises. **C** is incorrect because it is seldom done by anyone and definitely not ISPs. **D** is incorrect because it is done by some enterprises, but ISPs often do not carry customer routes in the IGP.

20. ☑ **A** and **D.** Traffic can be black-holed for traffic sourced from external locations that is destined to other locations in addition to melting down the network through increased instability in the IGP.
    ☒ **B** and **C** are incorrect because convergence of the IGP would suffer from the amount of flooding required and the path selection information would be lost when BGP was redistributed into the IGP.

LAB ANSWER

The solution to this lab has two parts, one for incoming traffic and one for outbound.

The solution to the outbound traffic policy issue is to prefer the advertisements from the ISPs with the OC3 connections on each. Remember that iBGP advertises only those routes that are selected via the decision process. Setting the weight on the advertisements from the peers via the OC3s ensures those are the routes sent via iBGP. The WEIGHT attribute is also set equally for incoming updates via iBGP, so the routes via both OC3 connections will be compared. If the OC3 goes down, the DS3 routes from that router are sent to the other router and the WEIGHT attribute is applied to those, allowing comparison for best path.

The solution to the inbound traffic is to advertise longer prefixes out each of the OC3 connections, with a shorter prefix out the DS3 connections. If both OC3s are down, traffic will enter the network via the DS3s due to the 10.0.0.0/8 prefix.

RTA Configuration:

```
router eigrp 10
 network 10.0.0.0

router bgp 10
 no synchronization
 redistribute eigrp 10
 aggregate-address 10.0.0.0 255.128.0.0
 aggregate-address 10.128.0.0 255.128.0.0
 aggregate-address 10.0.0.0 255.0.0.0
 neighbor 10.1.1.1 remote-as 1
 neighbor 10.1.1.1 prefix-list DS3OUT out
 neighbor 10.1.1.5 remote-as 2
 neighbor 10.1.1.5 prefix-list OC3OUT out
 neighbor 10.1.1.5 weight 1000
 neighbor 10.1.1.17 remote-as 10
 neighbor 10.1.1.17 weight 1000

ip prefix-list DS3OUT permit 10.0.0.0/8

ip prefix-list OC3OUT permit 10.0.0.0/8 ge 8 le 9
```

RTB Configuration:

```
router eigrp 10
 network 10.0.0.0

router bgp 10
 no synchronization
 redistribute eigrp 10
 aggregate-address 10.0.0.0 255.128.0.0
 aggregate-address 10.128.0.0 255.128.0.0
 aggregate-address 10.0.0.0 255.0.0.0
 neighbor 10.1.1.9 remote-as 3
 neighbor 10.1.1.9 prefix-list DS3OUT out
 neighbor 10.1.1.13 remote-as 4
 neighbor 10.1.1.13 prefix-list OC3OUT out
 neighbor 10.1.1.13 weight 1000
 neighbor 10.1.1.18 remote-as 10
 neighbor 10.1.1.18 weight 1000

ip prefix-list DS3OUT permit 10.0.0.0/8

ip prefix-list OC3OUT permit 10.0.0.0/8 ge 8 le 9
```

CCNP
CISCO® CERTIFIED NETWORK PROFESSIONAL

10

Route Filtering and Redistribution

CERTIFICATION OBJECTIVES

We have seen in previous chapters how routing protocols are used in large environments to propagate information about the various networks known by the routers within the topology. Each routing protocol has its strengths and weaknesses. As internetworks expand and companies merge, situations occur in which different network protocols must be accommodated within the same topology. In order to propagate the information known by one protocol to another, routing protocols must *redistribute* their information into other protocols. These situations are common.

The Internet, for example, is based exclusively on a protocol called Border Gateway Protocol (BGP). Organizations connecting to the Internet must therefore have an edge router that can speak BGP with the rest of the world. Internally, however, very few organizations run BGP as their internal routing protocols. Simpler protocols such as RIP or IGRP are more commonly used for this task. The information shared among the IGRP-speaking routers must somehow be propagated throughout the Internet in order for remote machines to be able to communicate with these systems. Redistribution from IGRP into BGP is required in this case.

A similar situation occurs when companies merge. Let's say that Company A, which developed its network using non-Cisco products, is using OSPF as its routing protocol. Company B, a purely Cisco shop, adopted EIGRP as its routing protocol a long time ago. When these two companies merge, one of two things must happen: Company B must transition its entire network to OSPF since non-Cisco products do not understand EIGRP, or redistribution between EIGRP and OSPF must be configured between the two networks. In normal circumstances, redistribution is adopted as the immediate solution, whereas a longer-term migration can be planned to standardize the architecture.

Redistribution does not come without its challenges. Many factors must be taken into account when inserting routes from another routing protocol. Not all protocols use the same information to determine the best path. EIGRP, for example, has no concept of the "hop count" used by RIP. IGRP doesn't understand the metrics used by OSPF. A solid understanding of the routing protocols and their operation is necessary for successful redistribution. Finally, in this chapter, we will see that more information is not always better. Indeed, in many situations, routers do not need to be told about every last route in the internetwork. This chapter covers how to filter routing updates and how to inject default information into other routing protocols to resolve these situations.

FROM THE CLASSROOM

Key Points to Remember

The following are key points to remember when reviewing this chapter. It contains essential topics that you must thoroughly understand in order to successfully attain the CCNP and CCIE certifications. As you review these topics, take the time to carefully read and understand the concepts that surround the subject:

VLSM/FLSM Variable- and fixed-length subnet mask (FLSM) issues must be understood to successfully configure redistribution between routing protocols. Be aware of which protocol does or does not support VLSM and the impact of redistributing between VLSM and FLSM routing protocols.

Administrative distance Understanding a protocol's administrative distance helps you

control and troubleshoot the flow of traffic within your internetwork.

Distribute lists The use of distribute lists provides network administrators with a filtering mechanism to decide which routes are sent to other routers and which routes are accepted from other routers. Distribute lists can be used within a singular routing protocol or to filter the routes redistributed in from another routing protocol.

Access lists Although this subject is a prerequisite for this book, it is important to know how to construct access lists for entire networks all the way down to a single IP address. Access lists will be used extensively throughout your certification process.

—*Ron Panus, CCIE 5823, CCNP, CCDA, MCSE, CCNA*

CERTIFICATION OBJECTIVE 10.01

Selecting and Configuring Ways to Control Route Update Traffic

In dealing with routing update issues, the most important tasks are to recognize what is happening in your network and understand what is required in order for the network to operate properly. The routing update control options at our disposal are redistribution, route filtering, and passive interfaces. Redistribution and route

FIGURE 10-1 The R2 route table without filtering

```
r2#sir
Codes: C - connected, S - static, I - IGRP, R - RIP, M - mobile, B
       D - EIGRP, EX - EIGRP external, O - OSPF, IA - OSPF inter ar
       N1 - OSPF NSSA external type 1, N2 - OSPF NSSA external type
       E1 - OSPF external type 1, E2 - OSPF external type 2, E - EG
       i - IS-IS, L1 - IS-IS level-1, L2 - IS-IS level-2, * - candi
       U - per-user static route, o - ODR
Gateway of last resort is not set
     172.16.0.0/24 is subnetted, 1 subnets
C       172.16.1.0 is directly connected, Serial1
D    192.168.1.0/24 [90/2195456] via 172.16.1.1, 00:00:01, Serial1
D    192.168.2.0/24 [90/2297856] via 172.16.1.1, 00:00:01, Serial1
D    192.168.3.0/24 [90/2297856] via 172.16.1.1, 00:00:01, Serial1
r2#
```

filtering use distribute lists in tandem with access lists to define the traffic that must be filtered. We cover each of these topics at length in this chapter. The following is an introductory example of using an access list to define the filtering requirements for a distribute list. Figure 10-1 shows the routing table of Router r2 without any filtering. Notice the three EIGRP routes that were received from Router r1 via interface Serial1.

Figure 10-2 illustrates the configuration of Router r2 for a route filter that permits only inbound route update traffic on interface Serial1 for network 192.168.1.0. All other EIGRP route updates will be dropped since the updates do not meet the requirements defined in the access list. The configuration command NO AUTO-SUMMARY shown in the configuration turns off EIGRP's automatic

FIGURE 10-2

The route filtering configuration of Router r2

```
interface Serial1
 ip address 172.16.1.2 255.255.255.0
 no ip directed-broadcast
!
router eigrp 1
 network 172.16.0.0
 distribute-list 1 in Serial1
 no auto-summary
!
ip classless
!
access-list 1 permit 192.168.1.0
```

boundary summarization feature and gives EIGRP the ability to handle both classful and classless routing updates.

Once the access list has been applied to r2, we see in Figure 10-3 that the EIGRP process on r2 has successfully filtered all incoming routing updates except for the permitted network 192.168.1.0.

exam
ⓦatch

You must fully understand the classful and classless nature of each routing protocol. Commands such as IP CLASSLESS and NO AUTO-SUMMARY are sometimes necessary in order for routing protocols to operate properly, depending on the IP architecture of your network.

When to Use Redistribution

In working with multiple routing protocols, it is important to understand when and where redistribution is required and how it should be performed. Most people think that redistribution is the simple process of sending routing update information from one protocol to another. This is only partially correct. Route redistribution can also be used to *selectively* advertise dynamically learned or static routes in addition to manipulating the redistribution metrics in order to affect the overall path selection. In some situations, only specific routes might be required to be passed along to other routers.

Redistribution is also used when a router needs to exchange routing information between two different routing protocols. When two protocols are configured to redistribute their known routes to each other, the process is called *mutual*

FIGURE 10-3 Resulting routing table of Router r2

```
r2#show ip route
Codes: C - connected, S - static, I - IGRP, R - RIP, M - mobile, B - BGP
       D - EIGRP, EX - EIGRP external, O - OSPF, IA - OSPF inter area
       N1 - OSPF NSSA external type 1, N2 - OSPF NSSA external type 2
       E1 - OSPF external type 1, E2 - OSPF external type 2, E - EGP
       i - IS-IS, L1 - IS-IS level-1, L2 - IS-IS level-2, * - candidate default
       U - per-user static route, o - ODR
Gateway of last resort is not set
     172.16.0.0/24 is subnetted, 1 subnets
C       172.16.1.0 is directly connected, Serial1
D    192.168.1.0/24 [90/2195456] via 172.16.1.1, 00:00:20, Serial1
r2#
```

redistribution. Special consideration must be given to a router configured to mutually redistribute two protocols. (This topic is covered in detail later in this chapter.) Additionally, distribution lists can be used to eliminate route feedback when you are mutually redistributing route information between a classful and classless routing protocol.

exam

ⓦatch

Route feedback is a potential problem with routers performing mutual redistribution. The term refers to a situation in which a routing protocol feeds information received from another routing protocol back into that protocol. In certain circumstances, this feedback can create routing loops within an internetwork and cause certain networks to be unreachable. We cover these circumstances later in this chapter.

Defining Redistribution

Redistribution is the process of advertising the routes learned by one routing protocol into another routing protocol or between similar protocols running as different processes on the same router. Normally, different routing protocols do not exchange route advertisements without the help of route redistribution. In certain instances, mutual redistribution occurs automatically between protocols. These cases are explained in further detail later in this chapter.

Redistribution Considerations

Redistribution is a very powerful tool and should be used with careful consideration. Some of these considerations are as follows:

- **Convergence times**   Each protocol utilizes unique convergence characteristics that are different from those of other protocols. It is imperative to understand the convergence parameters of routing protocols and their impact on the overall stability of a large internetwork.

- **Route feedback**   Route feedback is a serious issue when configuring redistribution. When redistributing a network from one protocol to another, it is important to ensure that the receiving protocol will not advertise that route back into the sending protocol. For example, if RIP receives routing updates from OSPF through redistribution, these updates must not be passed back into OSFP at some other redistribution point. A native pathway through OSPF for that network is probably better than the pathway from OSPF to RIP to OSPF. The pathway through OSPF would be free of any routing loops and use consistent metrics for the path determination. This situation could not be guaranteed for the OSPF-to-RIP-to-OSPF pathway.

■ **Metrics used**   Routing protocols use different methods for determining the best path to be used. When you are redistributing between dissimilar protocols, information about metrics must often be added to the redistributed routes in order for the receiving protocol to successfully insert those routes in its routing table and correctly calculate a path for them. For example, when you redistribute EIGRP into OSPF, EIGRP tries to tell OSPF about a certain network with attributes covering bandwidth, MTU, reliability, load, and delay. OSPF, which uses none of these parameters to determine path selection, does not understand these parameters when they are redistributed from EIGRP. Instead, OSPF is looking for information about path cost, which is not a function of EIGRP. Metric information specific to the receiving protocol must therefore manually be included in the redistribution of the routing updates in order for that protocol to successfully insert that routing update within its own routing table.

■ **Classful nature**   Some routing protocols understand the concept of VLSM; others do not. When you redistribute a VLSM protocol such as OSPF into a classful, or FLSM, protocol such as RIP, routing updates that do not fall on a classful boundary are lost. It is important to understand that fact and to know when default routes need to be injected in the FLSM routing protocol in order to provide connectivity to the VLSM networks that were dropped during the redistribution.

Selecting the Best Routing Protocol

Selecting the best routing protocol for redistribution depends on several factors. First, what routing protocol is already in service? Is there a need to apply an additional routing protocol to the configuration? Are there classful/classless routing protocol issues? Is the current routing protocol configured with a required security feature, such as MD5 authentication, that cannot be removed? How large is the network? If your network spans a large number of routers, RIP might be a poor choice due to its limited hop count. A large network with some unstable links can cause a flat OSPF topology to consume a good deal of time recomputing its shortest path first (SPF) algorithm. Before thinking of redistribution, the selection of an appropriate routing protocol is essential to the proper operation of a network. The following discussions cover some factors that impact the selection of one protocol over another.

Administrative Distance

The administrative distance of a protocol represents its "believability" when it is compared with another protocol. When a router has identical routes from two different routing protocols, the administrative distance is used to determine which route to install in the routing table. Remember that the longest-match rule applies before the administrative distance. This means that a more granular routing update is always preferred over a less accurate routing update, even if the less accurate route comes from a more believable protocol. In case two different routing protocols receive updates for the same network, the protocol with the lowest administrative distance prevails. Table 10-1 shows a list of routing protocols and their associated administrative distances.

The following Scenario & Solution tests your understanding of the administrative distance parameter with respect to route selection. From the routing updates received, determine which route will be inserted into the routing table, and explain why.

Administrative distances can also be manipulated or changed in order to make one routing update preferred over another route. The most common use of this technique is to increase the administrative distance of static routes above the distance of a dynamic routing protocol for backup purposes. The following example

TABLE 10-1	Protocol	Administrative Distance
Selected Protocols' Administrative Distances	Connected interface	0
	Static	1
	BGP (external)	20
	EIGRP (internal)	90
	IGRP	100
	OSPF	110
	RIP	120
	EIGRP (external)	170
	BGP (internal)	200

SCENARIO & SOLUTION

RIP: 10.0.0.0/8 OSPF: 10.0.0.0/8	In this case, the two networks are identical. The administrative distance is used to determine which update is more believable. OSPF, with a distance of 110, will prevail over RIP, which has a higher distance of 120.
OSPF: 172.20.0.0/24 EIGRP (internal): 172.20.0.0/16	In this case, the advertisements are clearly different. The network received via OSPF is more granular with its /24 mask than the update received via EIGRP. In this case, both updates are entered into the routing table. When the router makes its routing decision, it applies the longest-match rule against each update.

shows the proper manipulation of the administrative distance so that one route is preferred over another. In the following code output, router Concord is configured with two static routes:

```
concord(config)#interface Ethernet 0
concord(config-if)#ip address 10.1.1.2 255.255.255.0
concord(config-if)#interface ethernet 1
concord(config-if)#ip address 10.1.2.2 255.255.255.0
concord(config)#exit
concord(config)#ip route 20.1.1.0 255.255.255.0 10.1.1.1
concord(config)#ip route 20.1.1.0 255.255.255.0 10.1.2.1 200
```

Notice how the static route for network 20.1.1.0 declares a nondefault administrative distance of 200 for that particular entry. This forces router Concord to use the route through 10.1.1.1, since it uses the default administrative distance of 1 assigned to static routes.

This type of configuration is usually performed in situations in which one route is used to back up a primary route. In this example, the primary route goes through Concord's Ethernet 0 interface. If Concord's Ethernet 0 interface goes down, the router immediately removes from the routing table all routes associated with that interface. Since there is no more competition for the route to network 20.1.1.0, the second static route with the higher administrative distance comes into action to reroute the traffic through a different path.

Here is a similar example using a dynamic routing protocol: imagine a wide area network with the capability of using Integrated Services Digital Network (ISDN) as a backup means of communication. A static route with a high administrative distance is configured to reach the remote network through the ISDN link. Although the WAN is operational, the router receives from the remote site dynamic routing updates that include information about the same network. Since the dynamic routing protocol was made to be more believable than the static route, the router uses the learned route in its routing table. Should the WAN link go down, the router will cease receiving updates from its remote peer. After the timers for the dynamic routing protocol have elapsed, the dynamic route is removed from the routing table and the static route through the backup ISDN link is now used to reroute the traffic through the backup path. Changing the default administrative distance for a particular protocol should be done for specific purposes only. Any change to the default administrative distance of a routing protocol must be consistent throughout all the routers that use the same protocol.

exam
ⓦatch

It is important to remember the administrative distance value of each protocol. You might be presented with routing updates from various routing protocols and asked to determine which update will make it into the routing table.

Seed Metric

Each protocol uses its own defined set of metrics for path selection. Normally, the lower the metric, the more preferred the path. When one protocol is redistributed into another protocol, the redistributed protocol's metric must be interpreted to fit the receiving protocol's needs. For example, if EIGRP is redistributed into RIP, RIP cannot understand the metrics used by EIGRP to describe that route. When configuring the redistribution process, a translated metric—hop count, in the case of RIP—must be manually configured so that RIP can attach a value to the route received from EIGRP. The *seed metric* is the value that RIP understands and uses as the metric for the routes learned from EIGRP.

Automatic Redistribution

Automatic redistribution is the process by which two different routing protocols mutually redistribute routing updates, with no redistribution configurations required. This happens in a few different situations. A router running both Cisco's

IGRP and EIGRP under the same autonomous system number (ASN) will see these protocols exchanging routes with no redistribution configuration necessary. In non-IP environments, IPX EIGRP with IPX RIP and RTMP with AppleTalk EIGRP, will also see automatic redistribution happening between these protocols. It is important to remember these facts when you configure network topologies that include a combination of these protocols. Unwanted redistribution can occur if these features are forgotten.

The following example shows the automatic mutual redistribution between IGRP and EIGRP running under the same ASN—in this case, process number 1. The protocols automatically redistribute routing updates between each other. Figure 10-4 shows a network diagram representing the described network.

Router r1 is strictly running EIGRP with an ASN of 1 out of all its interfaces. Router r2 is running IGRP 1 on its Ethernet 0 segment and EIGRP 1 on its serial connection to r1. Since the IGRP and EIGRP processes on r2 both use ASN 1, the two routing protocols mutually redistribute information about their known networks. Figure 10-5 shows the output of the command SHOW IP PROTOCOL on r2. Notice how the two protocols show that they are redistributing with each other.

Figure 10-6 shows the configuration of the routing protocols on Router r2. Notice that there are no redistribution commands for either IGRP or EIGRP. Automatic redistribution occurs because the EIGRP and IGRP processes use the same ASN.

The resulting routing table of r1 is shown in Figure 10-7. We clearly see that r1 has learned the route for network 200.200.1.0 via EIGRP from Router r2. This indicates that r2 successfully redistributed its IGRP 1 network 200.200.1.0 into its EIGRP 1 process and then advertised that network to r1 through EIGRP.

The EIGRP process on r1 also shows that the route was learned through a process external to EIGRP 1 because the administrative distance is 170 (EIGRP external

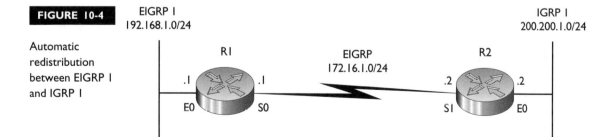

FIGURE 10-4

Automatic redistribution between EIGRP 1 and IGRP 1

EIGRP 1
192.168.1.0/24

IGRP 1
200.200.1.0/24

R1

EIGRP
172.16.1.0/24

R2

.1   .1

.2   .2

E0   S0

S1   E0

```
r2#sh ip protocol
Routing Protocol is "eigrp 1"
  Outgoing update filter list for all interfaces is
  Incoming update filter list for all interfaces is
  Default networks flagged in outgoing updates
  Default networks accepted from incoming updates
  EIGRP metric weight K1=1, K2=0, K3=1, K4=0, K5=0
  EIGRP maximum hopcount 100
  EIGRP maximum metric variance 1
  Redistributing: eigrp 1, igrp 1
  Automatic network summarization is not in effect
  Routing for Networks:
    172.16.0.0
  Routing Information Sources:
    Gateway         Distance      Last Update
    172.16.1.1            90      01:20:07
  Distance: internal 90 external 170
Routing Protocol is "igrp 1"
  Sending updates every 90 seconds, next due in 61 seconds
  Invalid after 270 seconds, hold down 280, flushed after 630
  Outgoing update filter list for all interfaces is
  Incoming update filter list for all interfaces is
  Default networks flagged in outgoing updates
  Default networks accepted from incoming updates
  IGRP metric weight K1=1, K2=0, K3=1, K4=0, K5=0
  IGRP maximum hopcount 100
  IGRP maximum metric variance 1
  Redistributing: eigrp 1, igrp 1
  Routing for Networks:
    200.200.1.0
  Routing Information Sources:
    Gateway         Distance      Last Update
  Distance: <default is 100>
r2#
```

```
router eigrp 1
 network 172.16.0.0
 no auto-summary
!
router igrp 1
 network 200.200.1.0
!
```

FIGURE 10-7   Route table of Router r1

```
r1#show ip route
Codes: C - connected, S - static, I - IGRP, R - RIP, M - mobile, B - BGP
       D - EIGRP, EX - EIGRP external, O - OSPF, IA - OSPF inter area
       N1 - OSPF NSSA external type 1, N2 - OSPF NSSA external type 2
       E1 - OSPF external type 1, E2 - OSPF external type 2, E - EGP
       i - IS-IS, L1 - IS-IS level-1, L2 - IS-IS level-2, * - candidate default
       U - per-user static route, o - ODR
Gateway of last resort is not set
D EX 200.200.1.0/24 [170/2169856] via 172.16.1.2, 01:07:54, Serial0
     172.16.0.0/24 is subnetted, 1 subnets
C        172.16.1.0 is directly connected, Serial0
C    192.168.1.0/24 is directly connected, Ethernet0
```

administrative distance). This is because the route was redistributed from IGRP. If the route had originated from an EIGRP-only environment, the administrative distance associated with this route would have been 90, which is the internal administrative distance of EIGRP. This means that should identical network advertisements be received through EIGRP, the selection process will prefer native EIGRP routes (lower administrative value) to routes that have been redistributed into EIGRP somewhere along the way.

Hierarchical Routing Protocols

In large, flat network topologies, even advanced routing protocols such as OSPF or EIGRP can fail miserably. Consider, for example, an OSPF network with a single area 0 and a dial-up access server in California that connects small ISDN routers on demand. Whenever a remote ISDN router connects, a route to the remote network is inserted into the entire OSPF topology. All the routers participating in this OSPF area must recompute the SPF algorithm every time an ISDN router connects or disconnects. This constant recomputing across the entire WAN can wreak havoc with the CPU budget of the routers.

Hierarchical routing protocols such as OSPF can alleviate this problem by creating multiple areas within the network, which are then interconnected through border area routers. Should the routing topology within an area change, only the routers within that area must recompute the SPF. Routers in remote areas do not care about the internal structure of that area. All they worry about is which border router to send packets to in order for them to reach their destination.

Multiple processes of EIGRP can also be used to create a core process over the WAN and local processes controlling the LANs. By judiciously redistributing summarized information into the WAN EIGRP process, we can minimize the number of routes required within a network topology and alleviate the impact of route recalculation within the LAN process.

EXERCISE 10-1

The Case of the Missing Routes

Your company recently acquired its biggest competitor and is in the process of merging all the departments into a new, stronger company. The two corporate networks also need to be merged in order to provide connectivity across the entire new company. Your company uses EIGRP; the acquired competitor uses IGRP. Both companies use ASN 100 for their routing protocol. As the acquiring company, management decided that your router would be configured to use IGRP as well as EIGRP in order to communicate with the acquired company's router and redistribute from one routing protocol to another. You are aware of the automatic redistribution nature of IGRP and EIGRP and wonder if this will become a factor. The following are the configurations of your router, R1, and the remote router, R2:

Router R1:

```
R1(config)#interface Ethernet 0
R1(config-if)#ip address 10.1.1.1 255.255.255.0
R1(config-if)#interface Ethernet 0
R1(config-if)#ip address 10.2.2.0 255.255.255.0
R1(config-if)#interface serial 0
R1(config-if)#ip address 20.1.1.1 255.255.0.0
R1(config-if)#router eigrp 100
R1(config-rtr)#no auto-summary
R1(config-rtr)#network 10.0.0.0
R1(config-rtr)#router igrp 100
R1(config-rtr)#network 20.0.0.0
```

Router R2:

```
R2(config)#interface Ethernet 0
R2(config-if)#ip address 192.168.10.1 255.255.255.0
R2(config-if)#interface Ethernet 0
R2(config-if)#ip address 192.168.20.1 255.255.255.0
```

```
R2(config-if)#interface serial 0
R2(config-if)#ip address 20.1.1.2 255.255.0.0
R2(config-rtr)#router igrp 100
R2(config-rtr)#network 20.0.0.0
R2(config-rtr)#network 192.168.10.0
R2(config-rtr)#network 192.168.20.0
```

After looking at your routing table on R1, you see that networks 192.168.10.0 and 192.168.20.0 are properly received from R2. However, after discussing it with the network administrator at the remote site, you find out that R2 does not have any entries for network 10.1.1.0/24 and 10.2.2.0/24 from your site. It only has an entry for 10.0.0.0/8. What is the cause of this? The following code listing shows the resulting routing table on Router R2:

```
R2>show ip route
Codes: C - connected, S - static, I - IGRP, R - RIP, M - mobile, B - BGP
       D - EIGRP, EX - EIGRP external, O - OSPF, IA - OSPF inter area
       N1 - OSPF NSSA external type 1, N2 - OSPF NSSA external type 2
       E1 - OSPF external type 1, E2 - OSPF external type 2, E - EGP
       i - IS-IS, L1 - IS-IS level-1, L2 - IS-IS level-2, ia - IS-IS inter area
       * - candidate default, U - per-user static route, o - ODR
       P - periodic downloaded static route

Gateway of last resort is not set

     20.0.0.0/24 is subnetted, 1 subnets
C       20.1.1.0 is directly connected, Serial 0
C    192.168.10.0/24 is directly connected, Ethernet0
C    192.168.20.0/24 is directly connected, Ethernet1
I    10.0.0.0/8 [100/8610] via 20.1.1.1, 00:00:07, Serial0:0
R2>
```

Solution: Even though IGRP and EIGRP automatically redistribute routing updates, the nature of the routing protocols themselves must be remembered. IGRP is a classful routing protocol. As such, it does not understand how network 10.0.0.0 is subnetted on R2. R1 therefore summarizes the route to its classful boundary when redistributing it into IGRP. Had the networks on R2 been classful—for example, 10.0.0.0/8 or 172.20.0.0/16—IGRP would have had no difficulties entering these networks in its routing table.

Configuring Route Redistribution with a Single Redistribution Gateway

Identifying a need for redistribution is normally not an issue. Situations, such as company mergers, arise, requiring that two different routing protocols interact with each other. Recognizing that redistribution is necessary between these two protocols is the first step. The more interesting step is to accurately determine how and where in your network redistribution should take place.

This section describes a situation in which a single redistribution point is used to exchange routing information between all the routing protocols in an internetwork. This practice is common in merger situations as well as in hierarchical network designs. Large internetworks often have a core routing protocol running over the WAN segment, which redistributes information from edge routing protocols that control the routing process of the LAN connecting to the WAN. In this section, we discuss these scenarios and the process for exchanging information through a single redistribution point.

Selecting the Core and Edge Routing Protocols

Selecting the appropriate routing protocols can depend on several factors. Some of these factors are as follows:

- Are existing protocols in place, and if so, are they adequate for current and future environments?

- What type of protocol—distance-vector or link-state—will best suit the needs of the infrastructure?

- What is the present stability of the network, and what mechanisms are available to maximize network availability?

- Can a proprietary protocol such as EIGRP be implemented?

Defining the Core Routing Protocol

The core protocol is usually used in the backbone of a corporate infrastructure. It is responsible for linking all the major sites that comprise the WAN. In a hierarchical network design, the edge routing protocols redistribute the local routing information into the core protocol for dissemination throughout the entire WAN. There are no hard rules as to which protocol to use in the core, but normally, one of the following protocols is used due to its features and scalability:

- EIGRP
- OSPF
- BGP

Each of these protocols is a good candidate to operate as a core protocol due to its ability to function well in large environments. OSPF could very well be used throughout the entire internetwork topology. In this case, the core protocol and the edge protocol would be the same. If a core OSPF protocol needs to communicate with a non-OSPF edge protocol, that router is defined as an autonomous system boundary router (ASBR) and redistribution is required between the two protocols.

exam
ⓦatch

The selection of a core router is critical to the proper performance of a large internetwork. If a poor selection is made originally, the core protocol could eventually become ill suited to handle the growth and expansion of the network. RIP, for example, might seem to suit your needs today, but as your network grows, performance will likely suffer from your initial choice for core protocol.

Defining the Edge Routing Protocol

The edge protocol represents the routing protocol used at the edge of the core boundary. Edge areas can be thought of as plant leaves attaching to a single core stem. The edge protocol controls all the routing updates contained within its area. At the border point using redistribution, the core routing protocol will advertise the edge protocol's routes out to the rest of the internetwork. If a routing change occurs within the area, the core does not usually need to be informed, since the border point for these networks will not change. This hierarchical approach minimizes the impact on the core protocol and limits the need to exchange routing information.

Imagine, for instance, an edge internetwork consisting of multiple subnets based on network 10.0.0.0. For example:

- 10.1.1.0 /24
- 10.1.2.0 /24
- 10.2.0.0 /16

If network 10.0.0.0 based addresses are only contained within that edge internetwork, the entire edge could be properly summarized by advertising only the aggregate 10.0.0.0/8 within the core. This way, should network 10.1.2.0/24 go down, the routing updates would be propagated within the edge internetwork but not to the core. In this case, the core does not need to know about the internal structure of the edge network. If we decided to redistribute the edge protocol into the core protocol, any change within the edge internetwork will have to be propagated by the edge protocol into the core protocol. This can have significant impact on the entire network should the edge internetwork have unstable links. The same rule applies for redistribution from the core protocol into the edge protocol. Very often, edge internetworks have a single exit point to the core network. Why then inform the edge of every network when there is but a single path to take? In these cases, the injection of a single default route into the edge protocol may be a more judicious choice.

An edge protocol, as in the core, can be any routing protocol. The most common scenarios, however, involve using one of following protocols:

- RIP
- IGRP
- Static routes

Redistributing the Edge Routing Protocol and Sending a Default Route

The need for redistribution varies from situation to situation. In some circumstances, mutual redistribution is the required solution between edge and core; in others, injecting a default route into the edge protocol is all that is required. What situations would call for this type of scenario? What concerns should you be aware of? Why not redistribute in both directions so that all routes are learned dynamically? These are all questions that need to be addressed to help us better understand this requirement. Take, for example, the network topology depicted in Figure 10-8.

The two remote locations R4 and R5 are both running RIP. Each router is in turn peering with a corporate router running RIP and EIGRP (R1 and R2). Routers R1 and R2 are configured to redistribute the RIP route advertisements that are received from R4 and R5, respectively. The RIP routes are redistributed into EIGRP throughout the corporate backbone so that all core routers dynamically learn about all networks advertised by the edge routers.

Should routers R4 and R5 be made aware of all the routes known by EIGRP? Depending on the needs of your internetwork, this is a possibility. If that were the case, redistribution from EIGRP back into RIP would be a requirement. However, Figure 10-8 shows that the only direction in which Routers R4 and R5 can go is to Routers R1 and R2, respectively. Knowing about all the known networks is therefore not a necessity, since there is only one path to select from anyway. In this

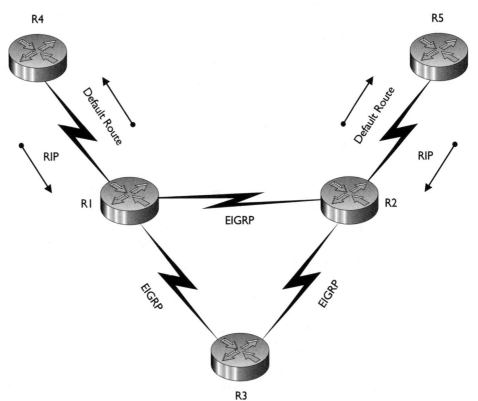

FIGURE 10-8

Typical corporate backbone

case, injecting a default route into the edge protocol will save memory on the edge routers and avoid using costly WAN bandwidth for network advertisements, especially if you are using a verbose routing protocol such as RIP. In this situation, Routers R1 and R2 are advertising no routes through RIP back to edge Routers R4 or R5. Instead, R4 and R5 can both have static route entries pointing to the core routers or have Routers R1 and R2 inject a default route back into the edges.

This configuration has several advantages over mutual redistribution. First, a lot less traffic is traversing the infrastructure, since the edge routers receive no advertisements from the corporate backbone. Additionally, each edge router receives no advertisements from other edge routers. If traffic needs to get from one edge network to another, the traffic path uses the default route, which forwards all traffic through the core.

Security is another good reason for such a configuration. The edge routers might not have a requirement to learn the internal structure of the core. Service providers, for example, might not want their clients to know the internal topology of their networks. By having the edge router use a static route, no advertisement information is required to be passed on to the edge protocol. Finally, configuring a router for mutual redistribution is more prone to problems stemming from an incorrect configuration than is a router configured for one-way redistribution.

Understanding the project requirements as well as your network topology enhances your ability to choose the correct solution for a situation. Finally, in-depth knowledge of IP protocols and their characteristics is essential to their successful implementation of mutual redistribution.

Mutually Redistributing the Routing Protocol and Preventing Routing Loops

As previously mentioned, mutual redistribution of routing protocols can allow two individual routing environments to exchange route advertisements with each other. In this situation, however, issues can arise from the fact that not all information exchanged is of a useful nature. Due to the administrative distance of routing protocols, routing information that is fed back into a routing protocol could incorrectly show a better path to a network through the redistributed protocol. Figure 10-9 shows a typical example, in which route feedback leads to problems with the routing topology.

In this scenario, Router R2 mutually redistributes routes received from RIP and EIGRP. In order for RIP to understand the routes received from EIGRP, R2 uses a

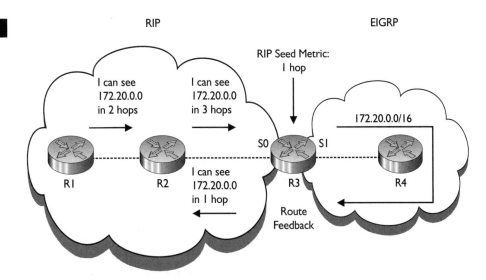

FIGURE 10-9

Route feedback
problems

default metric of 1 hop for all redistributed routes that it injects into RIP. Notice
the routing update received from R1. By the time it reaches R3, R3 knows that it
can reach network 172.20.0.0 through R2 in 3 hops. R2 redistributes the route into
EIGRP and passes the route along to R4. If that route were to return to R3 from R4
through EIGRP, because of the lower administrative distance of EIGRP, R2 would
replace the previous route to show network 172.20.0.0 as being accessible through
Router R4. R4 therefore points to the wrong router to reach network 172.20.0.0.

The problem compounds when R3 redistributes that EIGRP route into RIP.
Because R3 uses a default metric of 1 for redistributed routes, it announces network
172.20.0.0 back to Router R2 with a hop count of 1. R2 compares the route it
originally received from R1 with this new route from R3 and concludes that the
lower hop count of R3 makes that route a better path. Router R2 now points to the
wrong router in order to reach network 172.20.0.0.

How do we solve this problem? The key is to understand the flow of information
and to know the topology of your network. Looking at the IP topology of the
network, you see that there is no reason for R3 to learn the route for 172.20.0.0
through EIGRP. We therefore apply a filter on R3 to prevent the route from being
received back through EIGRP from R4. This is done through the use of a
distribution list. Distribution lists use access lists to define which traffic update to
accept and which to receive. The following code shows the configuration of R2, in

which a filter is applied to reject network 172.20.0.0 from inbound EIGRP updates on Interface S1:

```
!
router eigrp 100
 network 10.0.0.0
 redistribute rip metric 1500 1 255 1 1500
 distribute-list 10 in
 no auto-summary
!
access-list 10 deny   172.20.0.0 0.0.255.255
access-list 10 permit any
!
```

Filtering is essential when you are mutually redistributing between two routing protocols. The filter should allow only those network paths that require advertising to be redistributed. All other routes should be filtered. In the preceding example, applying a distribute list to EIGRP prevents a routing loop from occurring for network 172.20.0.0.

Mutually Redistributing Protocols and Preventing Routing Loops

At times, a router might need help deciding which route is the best route. When facing two identical routes received from two different routing protocols, the router normally chooses a path based on a protocol's administrative distance. Remember that the administrative distance defines the trustworthiness of a routing protocol. The lower the distance, the more trustworthy the protocol. This makes sense. But what if you needed to influence the router's decision so that packets follow a specific path?

An easy option is to manipulate the administrative distance of the routing protocols. Take the example we used previously, in Figure 10-9. If EIGRP had a higher administrative distance than RIP, when Router R3 received the feedback advertisement for network 172.20.0.0 through EIGRP, it would compare the administrative distance of RIP and EIGRP and select the RIP route as the more believable route. Since the feedback routing update never made it to the routing table as an EIGRP-based route, it does not get redistributed into RIP, avoiding the same pitfalls discussed in that scenario. The following code shows the manipulation of the administrative distance of EIGRP on Router R3:

```
!
router eigrp 100
 network 10.0.0.0
 redistribute rip metric 1500 1 255 1 1500
 distance eigrp 180 180
 no auto-summary
!
```

In this scenario, changing the default administrative distance of internal and external EIGRP to 180 makes the RIP advertisements more believable, since RIP's default administrative distance is 120, which is the lower of the two. The feedback route for network 172.20.0.0 will therefore not be entered in the routing table of R3 and will not be redistributed back into RIP, either.

Let's break for a quick knowledge check to make sure we are on track. Take a look at the following Scenario & Solution.

SCENARIO & SOLUTION

The _____ routing protocol makes up the backbone of a corporate network.	Core
What is the name of the process that allows two protocols to share route advertisements?	Mutual redistribution
What defines a router readvertising a network that it learned through mutual redistribution?	Route feedback

Configuring Redistribution into RIP

RIP is a *classful* routing protocol. Care must be given when you are redistributing information into a classful routing protocol due to the fact that the protocol does not understand the concept of subnet masks. The protocol therefore accepts only advertisements that fall on a classful network boundary. Since RIP is most often used as an edge protocol, the insertion of a default route at the edge's boundary can usually compensate for the information lost in the redistribution.

When you redistribute from a different routing protocol, RIP must be told how to handle the redistributed routes. The foreign routing protocol does not provide RIP with the hop-count information that RIP uses to make its routing decisions.

There are two ways of helping RIP with this process. First, you can declare a default hop count for the entire RIP process. This means that all the routes received through redistribution will adopt the default metric when they are received. This is a general approach that covers all the routes received through redistribution. The following code output shows the successful configuration of a default metric of 3 hops for RIP to use with redistributed routes:

```
router rip
 redistribute eigrp 100
 network 192.168.10.0
 default-metric 3
 !
```

If the router redistributes from multiple foreign routing protocols, you might not want RIP to interpret all these routes in the same manner. The REDISTRIBUTE command provides the capability of adjusting the default, or *seed* metric, used by RIP for each redistributed protocol. The following code output shows the redistribution of IGRP and OSPF routes into a RIP process using different seed metrics. OSPF routes are assigned a seed metric of 2 hops; IGRP routes are assigned a seed metric of 4 hops:

```
 !
router rip
 redistribute igrp 100 metric 4
 redistribute ospf 100 metric 2
 network 192.168.10.0
 !
```

When VLSM routes are lost at the edge boundary, the edge router might be required to inject a default route into the RIP cloud. There are two ways of doing this:

- **Configuring a default static route on the edge router**   When there is a static route entry of 0.0.0.0 on the edge router, the RIP process picks up that route and forwards it to all its RIP-speaking neighbors within the edge cloud.

- **The DEFAULT-INFORMATION ORIGINATE command**   Specifying the command DEFAULT-INFORMATION ORIGINATE within the configuration of the RIP process forces RIP to advertise a default route within the RIP cloud without the need of a static 0.0.0.0 route entry.

Configuring Redistribution into OSPF

OSPF gives us several options when configuring redistribution. Table 10-2 shows the parameters available with redistribution into OSPF.

The PROTOCOL parameter is straightforward. It is the protocol that is redistributed into OSPF. The METRIC parameter represents the default cost information that OSPF should associate with the incoming routes. Like other protocols, OSPF must be told how to interpret the routes it receives by manually specifying a metric value for the received routes.

The METRIC-TYPE parameter is also an important one to remember. OSPF classifies routes into two different types. Type 1 routes add the actual cost of the path from source to destination. This means that the cost of the route increases as the update is passed from router to router. You can specify the use of the Type 1 parameter when redistributing routes into OSPF. Conversely, Type 2 routes keep the same metric throughout the OSPF network. This is the default metric type used by OSPF when redistributing incoming routes.

The SUBNETS option is also a very important one that we can use during redistribution. As shown in the redistribution options, OSPF redistributes only classful networks by default. The SUBNETS keyword instructs OSPF to maintain the VLSM attributes of redistributed routes. Consider the network shown in Figure 10-10. Router R2 is configured with both EIGRP and OSFP and is redistributing EIGRP into the OSPF environment.

Router R2 receives an EIGRP advertisement for network 10.1.1.0/24 from Router R3. The route is inserted into the routing table of R2 as an EIGRP learned route.

TABLE 10-2   OSPF Redistribution Command Options

Option	Description
PROTOCOL	The IP protocol you are redistributing into OSPF.
METRIC	The seed metric that you define as the metric the redistributed protocol will use. You can also specify the DEFAULT-METRIC command and omit this option.
METRIC-TYPE	This option allows you to specify whether the route will be advertised as an External Type 1 or External Type 2 (default)
SUBNET	Routes redistributed into OSPF are advertised as an OSPF Update Type 5 External LSA. The Type 5 LSA is classful by default, so if RIP is announcing subnets for network 10.0.0.0, such as 10.1.1.0, OSPF, without this command, advertises to other OSPF routers a Type 5 LSA for network 10.0.0.0 /8. With this command, OSPF advertises a Type 5 LSA for each network 10.0.0.0 subnet such as 10.1.1.0 /24.

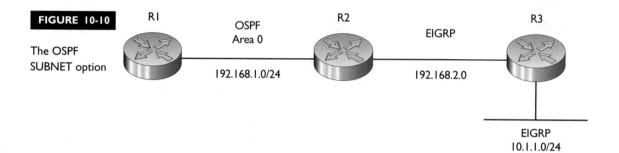

FIGURE 10-10

The OSPF
SUBNET option

When R2 redistributes the EIGRP route into OSPF and the keyword SUBNETS is not specified, R2 advertises the route into OSPF on the classful boundary of the network. In this case, R2 advertises the route 10.0.0.0/8 to Router R1. By configuring the keyword SUBNETS, OSPF advertises the route as 10.1.1.0/24, breaking the classful boundary of the network. The resulting configuration for R2 is shown in the following code output. In this scenario, the router redistributes routes from EIGRP 100 and tags these routes as Type 1 routes. It also assigns a metric value of 10 to these routes. The SUBNETS keyword ensures that classless subnets are properly interpreted and processed by OSPF.

```
!
router ospf 100
 redistribute eigrp 100 metric 10 metric-type 1 subnets
 network 192.168.1.0 0.0.0.255 area 0
!
```

As with RIP, OSPF can configure a global default metric for the entire OSPF process. This is done with the same router configuration DEFAULT-METRIC command shown in the RIP redistribution chapter. OSPF is also capable of inserting a default route into an area when it is used as an edge protocol. This is accomplished using the command DEFAULT-INFORMATION ORIGINATE. The following code output shows the configuration of a default metric for an OSPF process that is also advertising a default route:

```
!
router ospf 100
 redistribute eigrp 100 metric 10 metric-type 1 subnets
 network 192.168.1.0 0.0.0.255 area 0
 default-information originate always
 default-metric 10
!
```

Configuring Redistribution into EIGRP

The process of redistributing routes into EIGRP follows the same rules as the other protocols. EIGRP, however, uses a composite metric to calculate the best path. The metric is composed of five different parameters:

- Bandwidth
- Delay
- Reliability
- Load
- MTU

When you specify a metric for routes redistributed into EIGRP, you must specify each of these parameters. The following code output shows the configuration of redistribution of OSPF 100 into EIGRP by specifying a default bandwidth of 1500 kbps, a reliability of 100 percent, a load of approximately 1 percent, a delay of 10 ms, and an MTU value of 1500 bytes:

```
R2(config)#
R2(config)#router eigrp 100
R2(config-router)#network 192.168.10.0
R2(config-router)#no auto-summary
R2(config-router)#redistribute ospf 100 metric ?
  <1-4294967295>  Bandwidth metric in Kbits per second

R2(config-router)#redistribute ospf 100 metric 1500 ?
  <0-4294967295>  IGRP delay metric, in 10 microsecond units

R2(config-router)#redistribute ospf 100 metric 1500 1 ?
  <0-255>  IGRP reliability metric where 255 is 100% reliable

R2(config-router)#redistribute ospf 100 metric 1500 1 255 ?
  <1-255>  IGRP Effective bandwidth metric (Loading) where 255 is 100% loaded

R2(config-router)#redistribute ospf 100 metric 1500 1 255 1 ?
  <1-4294967295>  IGRP MTU of the path

R2(config-router)#redistribute ospf 100 metric 1500 1 255 1 1500
R2(config-router)#end
R2#
```

e x a m
ⓦ a t c h

Note how the load and reliability parameters range from 1 to 255. When you are asked to configure a load metric of 50 percent, the proper value to be entered is 128, not 50. This is a common certification question, and you must recognize this issue when it is presented to you.

EIGRP and OSPF Redistribution Example

Figure 10-11 shows a complex network with a single redistribution point between EIGRP and OSPF. The previous sections explained the mechanisms used to perform successful redistribution between protocols. Try to write down the proper configuration of Router R1 in order to perform this task, then look at the proposed configuration that follows. Make sure that OSPF and EIGRP mutually redistribute information, and ensure that no feedback routes can occur in the network.

The proposed configuration is as follows.

```
!
router eigrp 100
 redistribute ospf 10 metric 1500 1 255 1 1500
 network 20.0.0.0
 distribute-list 10 in
 no auto-summary
!
router ospf 10
 redistribute eigrp 100 metric 10 subnets
 network 10.5.5.0 0.0.0.255 area 0
 distribute-list 20 in
!
access-list 10 deny   10.0.0.0 0.255.255.255
access-list 10 permit any
access-list 20 deny   20.0.0.0 0.255.255.255
access-list 20 permit any
!
```

Configuring the DEFAULT-METRIC Command

We have discussed the seed metric in regard to redistribution and its importance. We know that we can define the seed metric during the configuration of the REDISTRIBUTION command. But what if you are redistributing several protocols or have special requirements for the seed metric? We can set the seed metric to a default value that eliminates the need to include the metric in our REDISTRIBUTION command line. First, let's take a look at an example of how to use the

FIGURE 10-11 EIGRP and OSPF redistribution

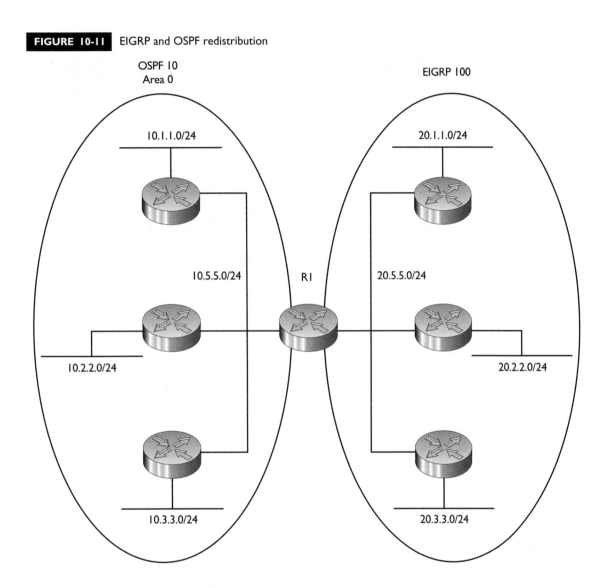

DEFAULT-METRIC command and its proper syntax. Table 10-3 follows the example and defines each option.

To configure the default metric for IGRP or EIGRP, use the following syntax:

```
router(config-router)#default-metric bandwidth delay reliability loading mtu
```

| **TABLE 10-3** | IGRP and EIGRP Redistribution Metric Parameters. |

DEFAULT-METRIC Option	**Description**
BANDWIDTH	Sets the minimum bandwidth that the protocol will use (kbps)
DELAY	Specifies the delay
RELIABILITY	How reliable or successful the packet transfer will be. Value is 0 to 255 (255 is most reliable).
LOADING	The effectiveness of the bandwidth for this route. Value is 0 to 255 (1 is most effective).
MTU	Specifies the maximum transfer unit size for the route (in bytes).

To configure RIP, OSPF, or BGP, use the following syntax:

```
router(config-router)#default-metric number
```

Configuring the metric parameters for RIP, OSPF, and BGP is straightforward, since the only parameter required is a single value to reference the cost of the path.

Configuring the PASSIVE-INTERFACE Command

Sometimes, not every interface of a router needs to participate in the advertisement of routing updates. Take, for example, the network in Figure 10-12, in which Router R2 is configured for EIGRP.

Let's assume that in order to conserve costly WAN bandwidth on interface S0, we want R1 *not* to advertise EIGRP routes over that interface. The configuration of EIGRP, however, uses a classful declaration for the supported network. The

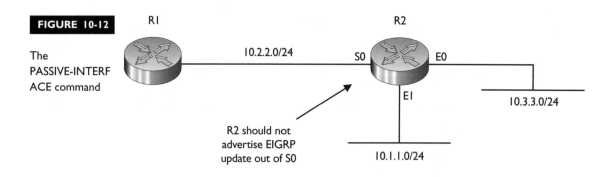

FIGURE 10-12

The PASSIVE-INTERFACE command

R2 should not advertise EIGRP update out of S0

command on R2 would therefore be NETWORK 10.0.0.0. This, unfortunately, covers the IP subnet running on interface S0, which means that if not told otherwise, R2 will advertise EIGRP routes over interface S0. The router configuration command PASSIVE-INTERFACE allows network administrators to declare specific interfaces that will participate in the advertisement of routes. These interfaces still listen to the routing process but do not advertise routes. That interface is in passive mode. The following shows the configuration of R2 declaring interface S0 as a passive interface:

```
!
router eigrp 100
 passive-interface Serial0
 network 10.0.0.0
 no auto-summary
!
```

Configuring Static Routes

Static routes can play a very important role in the routing process. They are manually entered static entries in a router's routing table. The following are some of the benefits of static routes:

- They have lower traffic overhead, since static routes do not send advertisements (unless they are redistributed into a routing protocol).

- Static routes have an administrative distance of 1, so are preferred over dynamically learned routes. This gives network administrators better control over the normal path selection process.

- Static routes allow for better security because hackers will see no network advertisements.

- Static routes allow two individual routing domains to communicate without having to configure redistribution or enable a common routing protocol.

As we mentioned before, static routes can be configured as "floating static routes"; here the administrative distance of the static routes is increased beyond the distance of a routing protocol operating on the router. The static route will not be used unless the existing route, defined with a lower distance than the floating static route, goes down. At that point, the floating static route will be applied to the routing table, since it has a distance lower than any other route available. The floating static route will become dormant if another route with a lower cost becomes available.

As we have seen, floating static routes are often used in dial-on-demand scenarios. There are basically two different methods to configure a static route. They differ in the way the next-hop system is defined. The first method uses the IP address of the next-hop router in order to reach a specific segment. The second method simply declares the outbound interface on which to place the routed packets. This method is especially useful on unnumbered serial links, since no IP address is declared for the next-hop router.

Static Route Example

Figure 10-13 shows the network topology used in this example. In this case, we want to configure a static route on Router r1 for network 192.169.2.0. The following code output shows the configuration of two static routes for that network on Router r1, each using a different method of declaring the next-hop system. Static routes show up in the routing table as a Type S route.

```
!
ip route 192.168.3.0 255.255.255.0 192.168.3.2
ip route 192.168.3.0 255.255.255.0 Serial0
!
```

When we configure static routes using the outbound interface instead of the next-hop IP address, the static route appears in the router as "directly connected." The route is still classified as an S-type route but does not show a next-hop IP address for that route.

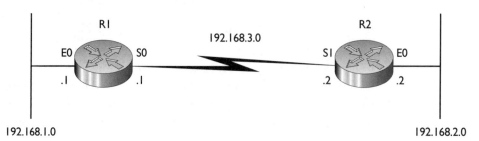

FIGURE 10-13

Simple static route scenario

Configuring a Default Route and the DEFAULT-NETWORK Command

One topic that can be confusing is the definition of a default route compared with a default network. The terms sound alike, and both provide a default path for packets that do not have a matching entry in the routing table. So what is the difference between them? Is it advantageous to use one over the other? Does each IP protocol recognize and understand both default commands?

Let's start answering these questions by first looking at Table 10-4 to see some of the characteristics of each command.

The syntax for the default ROUTE command follows. In this example, we declare the next-hop router 192.168.1.1 as the default route for the router:

```
ip route 0.0.0.0 0.0.0.0 192.168.1.1
```

The syntax for the DEFAULT-NETWORK command is as follows:

```
iP default-network 192.168.1.0
```

It declares the classful network 192.168.1.0 as the network to send packets to when these packets do not have a matching entry in the routing table: the IP ROUTE 0.0.0.0 command is straightforward. The IP DEFAULT-NETWORK command, however, is more complicated and needs further explanation. It is important to remember that the network that you specify as the default network *must* belong to a major network class other than the one currently being advertised on the router that you are configuring. Let's take a look at a scenario in which the IP DEFAULT-NETWORK configuration must be applied.

Figure 10-14 displays a network with two active protocols, IGRP and OSPF. You can see that IGRP is set up using a full Class C (24-bit) mask. OSPF, on the other hand, is a little more complicated, with 20 bits of subnetting within area 0. Area 1 is configured using 24 bits for subnetting, like IGRP, but is using a Class C IP address.

TABLE 10-4	Characteristics of the DEFAULT-NETWORK Commands

ip route 0.0.0.0 0.0.0.0 *next-hop*	ip default-network *classful-network*
Recognized by BGP, OSPF, RIP	Recognized by EIGRP, IGRP, RIP, and BGP
Advertises an address of 0.0.0.0	Advertises the network only

FIGURE 10-14 An advanced redistribution scenario

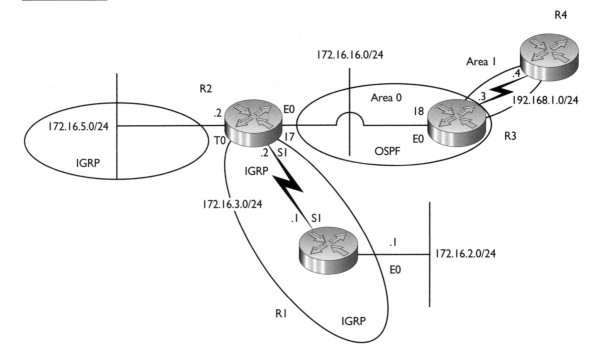

The goal is to end up with every router able to ping every other router. Let's assume that static routes cannot be used in this environment. Furthermore, we cannot use the redistributed connected command. IGRP will be redistributed into OSPF, whereas a default network will be injected into IGRP in order for the IGRP-speaking routers to reach networks in the OSPF environment. Our focal point is Router r2, for two reasons. First, we will have to some sort of redistribution to allow the IGRP packets to traverse the OSPF portion of the 20-bit network. Second, r2 is configured with multiple subnets. This is not a problem for OSPF, but IGRP will have some issues.

The best method for configuring a scenario such as this is to first configure each protocol separately. Make sure that all OSPF-enabled routers can ping each other. Next, do the same for the IGRP-enabled routers. Looking at the route table of r2 in Figure 10-15, we see that everything looks good so far. OSPF routers can see and communicate with each other and IGRP routers can communicate between each other.

FIGURE 10-15 Route table of r2 prior to redistribution

```
r2#show ip route
Codes: C - connected, S - static, I - IGRP, R - RIP, M - mobile, B - BGP
       D - EIGRP, EX - EIGRP external, O - OSPF, IA - OSPF inter area
       E1 - OSPF external type 1, E2 - OSPF external type 2, E - EGP
       i - IS-IS, L1 - IS-IS level-1, L2 - IS-IS level-2, * - candidate default
Gateway of last resort is not set
O IA 192.168.1.0 [110/74] via 172.16.18.0, 00:01:47, Ethernet0
     172.16.0.0 is variably subnetted, 4 subnets, 2 masks
C       172.16.16.0 255.255.240.0 is directly connected, Ethernet0
C       172.16.5.0 255.255.255.0 is directly connected, TokenRing0
I       172.16.2.0 255.255.255.0 [100/8576] via 172.16.3.1, 00:00:58, Serial1
C       172.16.3.0 255.255.255.0 is directly connected, Serial1
r2#
```

The next step is also straightforward: we will redistribute IGRP into OSPF. Since OSPF is a classless routing protocol, it is able to handle anything that IGRP has to offer with regard to subnetting, as long as the SUBNETS keyword is specified. OSPF can easily understand IGRP's 24-bit mask or any other mask that we might have used. So far we can communicate from IGRP to OSPF but not back the other way.

Now we use the DEFAULT-NETWORK command in order to inject a default route into the IGRP process. We also have to use a DISTRIBUTE-LIST command for redistribution in order to ensure that r2 sends to r1 only the network specified in the IP DEFAULT-NETWORK command. Again, we must specify a classful network that the IGRP process is not directly using. Doing so marks the network defined as the default network as an exterior network, which is required. This is an easy rule to forget. The following code output shows the configuration of Router r2 with the DEFAULT-NETWORK command:

```
router ospf 1
 redistribute igrp 1 metric 100 subnets
 passive-interface Serial1
 network 172.16.16.0 0.0.15.255 area 0
!
router igrp 1
 redistribute ospf 1 metric 1500 1 255 1 1500
distribute-list 2 out ospf 1
 passive-interface Ethernet0
 network 172.16.0.0
```

```
!
ip default-network 192.168.1.0
!
access-list 2 permit 192.168.1.0 0.0.0.255
access-list 2 deny any
!
```

We see that we are mutually redistributing IGRP and OSPF on Router r2. On the redistribute line, we have properly defined the seed metrics and used the SUBNET option to redistribute IGRP into OSPF. Figure 10-16 shows the DEBUG output for r2 after we apply the IP DEFAULT-NETWORK 192.168.1.0 command. Notice that the network 192.168.1.0 is marked as an exterior network. Remember that our default network must be an exterior network in order to function correctly.

Now let's take a look at the routing table on r2 in Figure 10-17 and see what the network 192.168.1.0 looks like. Note the "Gateway of last resort" entry in the routing table, which points to the classful network entered with the DEFAULT-NETWORK command.

In addition, notice the asterisk next to the 192.168.1.0 network, marking the network as the candidate default network. So far, everything looks good. As long as our REDISTRIBUTE command is working, Router r1 should also have a candidate default network of 192.168.1.0. Figure 10-18 shows us the route table on r1.

The candidate default network on r1 was advertised from r2 via the REDISTRIBUTE command.

exam
Ⓦatch

Remember that the command IP DEFAULT-NETWORK <NETWORK> uses a classful network entry in declaring the default network to be used.

FIGURE 10-16

Default network is marked as an exterior route

```
r2#
RT: 192.168.1.0 is now exterior
RT: default path is now 192.168.1.0 via 172.16.18.0
RT: new default network 192.168.1.0
r2#
```

FIGURE 10-17 Router r2's route table

```
r2#show ip route
Codes: C - connected, S - static, I - IGRP, R - RIP, M - mobile, B - BGP
       D - EIGRP, EX - EIGRP external, O - OSPF, IA - OSPF inter area
       E1 - OSPF external type 1, E2 - OSPF external type 2, E - EGP
       i - IS-IS, L1 - IS-IS level-1, L2 - IS-IS level-2, * - candidate default
Gateway of last resort is 172.16.18.0 to network 192.168.1.0
O*IA 192.168.1.0 [110/74] via 172.16.18.0 00:07:36, Ethernet0
     172.16.0.0 is variably subnetted, 4 subnets, 2 masks
C       172.16.16.0 255.255.240.0 is directly connected, Ethernet0
C       172.16.5.0 255.255.255.0 is directly connected, TokenRing0
I       172.16.2.0 255.255.255.0 [100/8576] via 172.16.3.1, 00:00:06, Serial1
C       172.16.3.0 255.255.255.0 is directly connected, Serial1
r2#
```

Configuring a Redistribution Using the IP DEFAULT-NETWORK Command

Some scenarios require one-way redistribution from the edge router into the core router. The core routers learn routes from the edge, but the edge learns no routes from the core routers. The question then becomes, how will the traffic know how to get back to the edge routers if we redistribute in only one direction? Table 10-5 displays the router configurations for r1 and r2.

FIGURE 10-18 Route table of r1 with default route

```
r1#show ip route
Codes: C - connected, S - static, I - IGRP, R - RIP, M - mobile, B - BGP
       D - EIGRP, EX - EIGRP external, O - OSPF, IA - OSPF inter area
       N1 - OSPF NSSA external type 1, N2 - OSPF NSSA external type 2
       E1 - OSPF external type 1, E2 - OSPF external type 2, E - EGP
       i - IS-IS, L1 - IS-IS level-1, L2 - IS-IS level-2, * - candidate default
       U - per-user static route, o - ODR
Gateway of last resort is 172.16.3.2 to network 192.168.1.0
     172.16.0.0/24 is subnetted, 3 subnets
I       172.16.5.0 [100/8539] via 172.16.3.2, 00:00:31, Serial1
C       172.16.2.0 is directly connected, Ethernet0
C       172.16.3.0 is directly connected, Serial1
I*   192.168.1.0/24 [100/8576] via 172.16.3.2, 00:00:31, Serial1
r1#
```

TABLE 10-5 Router Configuration Examples of the IP DEFAULT-NETWORK and REDISTRIBUTION Commands

r1	r2
interface serial 1 ip address 20.1.1.1 255.255.255.0 router rip network 20.0.0.0 ip classless	interface serial 2 ip address 192.168.2.1 255.255.255.0 interface serial 1 ip address 20.1.1.2 255.255.255.0 router rip network 20.0.0.0 router ospf 65 network 192.160.2.0 0.0.0.255 area 0 ip default-network 192.168.3.0

Notice how Router R2 is not connected to the classful network 192.168.3.0, which it declares the default network. In order for r2 to advertise a default route into RIP, r2 must dynamically learn of network 192.168.3.0 through OSPF advertisements. Had 192.168.3.0 been somehow directly connected to r2, it would not inject a default route into RIP.

We have covered a lot of material so far, so let's see what we have learned by answering a few questions in the following Scenario & Solution.

SCENARIO & SOLUTION

_____ protocols could do not differentiate whether a protocol is subnetted or is defined on a classful boundary.	Classless
OSPF's External Type _ metric adds the cost of the seed metric and the cost of the data path to define the numeric value of the metric.	1
Defining a _____ _____ eliminates the need to define the seed metric value during redistribution.	Default metric
What type of static route is defined with a high distance value at the end of the command line?	Floating static route
A route is marked as an _____ route when defined with the IP DEFAULT-NETWORK command.	Exterior

EXERCISE 10-2

The Correct Filter

You are the network administrator of a company that recently merged with another. Your network and the acquired company must merge in order for the newly formed company to start operating as a team. It was decided, however, that the development subnets would not be propagated to the new company until the new employees have had a background check done for security purposes. The development group is working on top-secret stuff for the government. You must therefore filter the outbound advertisements for the networks used by the development group. The network allocation is shown in Table 10-6.

The production networks must be redistributed from OSPF 10 into EIGRP 100. The development subnets, however, must not be advertised. Construct a filter with the least number of entries possible in the access list controlling the filtering process and show the resulting configuration.

Solution: An obvious method of constructing the access list for this scenario would be to list all the networks that need filtering. This would make for a tedious and long access list that could even impact the performance of the router. Instead, an in-depth understanding of how the reverse mask of access lists operates allows us to filter all the development networks with a single access-list entry. Note how the third octet of the development networks is always an even number, whereas production networks are odd numbers. Using the last bit of the reverse mask, we can construct a statement that covers only even-numbered entries:

```
access-list 10 deny 172.20.0.0 0.0.254.255
access-list 10 permit any
```

TABLE 10-6	Production	Development
Network Allocation for the Production and Development Groups	172.20.1.0	172.20.2.0
	172.20.3.0	172.20.4.0
	172.20.5.0	172.20.6.0
	...	...
	172.20.253.0	172.20.254.0

If you take a look at the third octet of the reverse mask, the binary mapping looks like this: 254 = 11111110. This means that only the last bit of the reverse mask *must* match. In this case, the third octet value of the network, 0 = 00000000, has a must-match value of 0 as its last bit placement. The resulting possibilities are therefore as follows:

```
00000000 = 0
00000010 = 2
00000100 = 4
00000110 = 6
...
11111110 = 254
```

The resulting configuration is therefore as follows:

```
router eigrp 100
  network 172.20.0.0
  no auto-summary
  redistribute ospf 10 metric 1500 1 255 1 1500
  distribute-list 20 out ospf 10
!
access-list 20 deny 172.20.0.0 0.0.254.255
access-list 20 permit any
!
```

CERTIFICATION OBJECTIVE 10.03

Configuring Route Redistribution with Multiple Redistribution Gateways

Multiple route redistribution gateways involve a higher degree of planning and configuration than a scenario involving a single redistribution point. It is very important to understand distribute lists and their proper usage. Understanding the tools that allow a network engineer to stop route feedback and to force packets to follow the optimal data path is also essential.

Resolving Path Selection Problems Resulting from Redistribution

A single router performing mutual redistribution allows two different protocols to advertise route information to each other. We have covered this scenario in detail and are familiar with many of the issues that might arise. Let's now consider two routing domains. Each domain communicates with the other via a network connection. Each domain also uses a different routing protocol than the other. Figure 10-19 shows a network using multiple redistribution points.

Network with multiple redistribution points

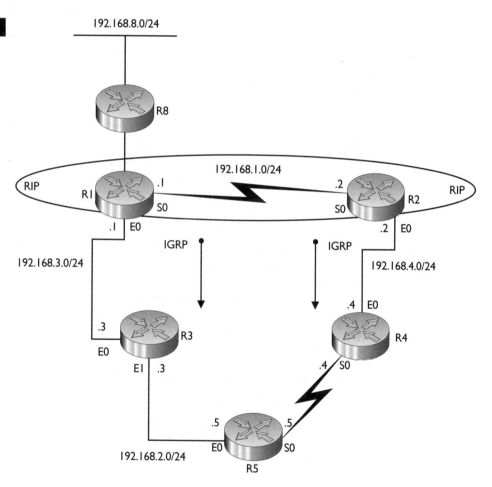

What are some of the possible issues that we might face in this type of environment? Let's take a look at a couple in the following list:

- Routing loops
- Suboptimal paths

These are common issues that a network engineer often faces. Say, for instance, that r4 wants to send data to r1. Even though r4 is connected to a router that is directly connected to r1, it sends the packets through the suboptimal route via r5, r3, and finally to r1. This happens because IGRP has a better administrative distance than RIP (110 versus 120). r4 checks its route table as to which path to send the data. It all seems to make sense, but as you can tell, this scenario can create a big problem.

Routing loops are another problem in these types of scenarios. Essentially, each router has two paths to any one given destination. In the network diagram, Router r8 advertises network 192.168.8.0 through RIP to Router r1. Router r1, in turn, advertises that network to r2 via RIP and to r3 by redistributing the route into IGRP. r2 also redistributes the route into IGRP and starts advertising the route to r4. With two routing updates going in both directions on IGRP, it is likely that Routers r1 and r2 will find the route through IGRP more appealing than the route learned through RIP. At that point, any packet destined for network 192.168.8.0 starts bouncing back and forth between routers in the IGRP cloud, resulting in dropped packets when the TTL field reaches 0.

on the job *Building a network from the ground up presents many issues that you must overcome. Walking in cold and troubleshooting an existing network is tougher yet. When dealing with issues such as routing loops and suboptimal routing, make sure you fully understand the network topology and each protocol that is advertising routes. Remember that a customer does not always tell you everything that you need to know.*

Solutions for Path Selection Problems

Manipulating the routing path is a necessary skill that all CCNP candidates need to master. More important, your customers or employers will expect you to know path manipulation filtering. The following text will help you better understand when, where, and how to use some of the filtering options available to you.

Filters

Filters are one method that you can use to correct path selection problems. With the aid of a distribute list, you can force the router to choose the path rather than depend on the routing protocol. Access lists are used to define the filter criteria for each distribute list. These tools allow network administrators to select the routes that can be entered in a routing table in accordance with specific routing policies that were deemed necessary. (Distribute-list examples are discussed later in this chapter.)

Administrative Distance Control

Administrative distance control is another tool to force the router to favor one path over another. Modifying the administrative distance is an alternative to filtering, in some instances. Adding a higher administrative distance to a static route creates a floating static route entry. Remember that floating static routes are often used in dial backup situations with regard to analog or ISDN environments.

Using Route Filtering

So far we have discussed suboptimal routing, distribute lists, and general route filtering. Now let's put all this knowledge together and create more efficient network environments as well as enhance our troubleshooting skills.

Configuring Route Filtering

Route filtering is one method of filtering unwanted route advertisements from either entering or leaving a router. Each distribute list is defined under the routing process that requires filtering. The filtered network advertisements are defined in an access list that is then associated with a distribute list. The following configuration syntax defines a distribute list and demonstrates filtering for inbound and outbound advertisements.

Distribute list for *outbound* update advertisements:

```
Distribute-list access-list # out interface # routing-process AS #
```

Distribute list for *inbound* update advertisements:

```
Distribute-list access-list # in interface #
```

As you can tell, distribute lists are pretty straightforward regarding their configuration. Let's examine the options available for distribute lists, and then we will look at a few examples. First, the options:

1. The first step is to create an access list that defines the network updates requiring a filter.

2. The second step is to decide whether or not the network updates require filtering for inbound or outbound advertisements.

3. Finally, you assign the access list number to the distribute list.

You must carefully analyze each situation to determine which interfaces will or will not receive updates.

Basic Example of Route Filtering

In Figure 10-19, there was no need for Router r1 to accept routing updates about network 192.168.8.0 via EIGRP. The only path to that network is through Router r8, which is directly connected to r1 via RIP. We can therefore safely filter inbound IGRP updates to deny network 192.168.8.0 from entering Router r1 via IGRP. The configuration is as follows:

```
!
router igrp 100
 network 192.168.3.0
 distribute-list 10 in
!
ip classless
ip default-network 192.168.1.0
ip route 0.0.0.0 0.0.0.0 172.21.1.254
!
access-list 10 deny   192.168.8.0 0.0.0.255
access-list 10 permit any
!
```

This configuration prevents r1 from learning an incorrect path through IGRP coming from the redistribution of the RIP route via r2.

Outbound filtering of redistributed routes can be a valuable tool. Take for example the topology shown in Figure 10-20.

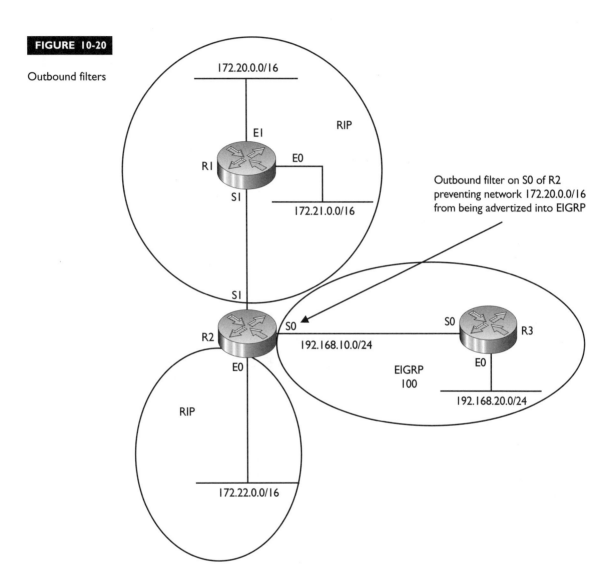

FIGURE 10-20

Outbound filters

Let us assume that subnet 172.20.0.0 on interface E1 of Router R1 carries sensitive information, and as such, must not be redistributed to R3 via EIGRP. R3 still needs to know about the other routes learned by R2 via RIP. In this case, an outbound EIGRP filter on R2 could be used to filter out the route advertisement for network 172.20.0.0. The distribution list configuration of Router R2 would be as follows:

```
!
router eigrp 100
 network 192.168.10.0
 no auto-summary
 redistribute rip metric 1500 1 255 1 1500
 distribute-list 11 out rip
!
router rip
 network 172.21.0.0
 network 172.22.0.0
 redistribute eigrp 100 metric 5
!
access-list 11 deny   172.20.0.0 0.0.255.255
access-list 11 permit any
!
```

Notice the syntax of the command "distribute-list 11 out rip" in the code output above. The keyword "rip" at the end of the command makes it confusing to understand. The distribute-list does not filter EIGRP routes going "out" into "rip," but filters routes that were redistributed into EIGRP from a "rip" source, going "out" to adjacent EIGRP neighbors.

Using Administrative Distance

Using the ADMINISTRATIVE DISTANCE command can also be beneficial. Changing the distance, or believability, of a routing protocol forces a router to choose one path over another. This tool is pertinent to environments in which multiple protocols are enabled but a suboptimal path is being advertised. You have the option of using a distribute list that would completely block the suboptimal path advertisement, but some situations might void this method because, if the best pathway goes down, a distribute-list command that filters the suboptimal path will prevent the network from rerouting traffic to its destination. Keep in mind, however, that changing the administrative distance of a protocol requires a greater analysis of the network. If you are mutually redistributing protocols, changing the distance for one protocol might have an adverse effect on the rest of the network. Each scenario must be analyzed on a case-by-case basis.

Configuring Administrative Distance Control

You can configure a new distance value for all updates advertised by a routing protocol. You can also configure only specific advertisements to be manipulated by the distance parameter. The following examples show how to change a protocol's administrative distance during redistribution:

```
Router Router-process
Distance Value 0.0.0.0 255.255.255.255 1
Access-list 1 permit 192.168.1.0
```

The configuration shown here is accomplished under the routing process that the administrative distance is to be manipulated. The value for the new administrative distance is entered, followed by the wildcard mask, followed by the access-list number. The access list contains the actual network numbers to which the new distance value will be applied. If you needed a RIP route to be preferred over an OSPF route, you would enter a value lower then OSPF's administrative distance (110) for the *value* parameter. Doing so forces the RIP networks defined in the access list to be preferred over the OSPF network path.

Complex Example of Administrative Distance Control

Figure 10-21 displays a small network in which r3 is receiving OSPF- and RIP-advertised gateways for network 192.168.1.0.

In this example, the preferred path to network 192.168.1.0 from r3 is through Router r1. This is so because the administrative distance for OSPF is 110 and is lower than RIP's administrative distance of 120. If we reduce the administrative distance of RIP to a value lower than 110, r3 considers RIP updates more believable than OSPF updates and thus goes through Router r2 in order to reach network 192.168.1.0.

on the **job**

Remember that manipulating the administrative distance not only has repercussions on the paths you want to force—it could also have impacts on the valid paths that are already in service. Make sure you understand the ramifications of making one protocol more desirable than another before you make changes to a production environment.

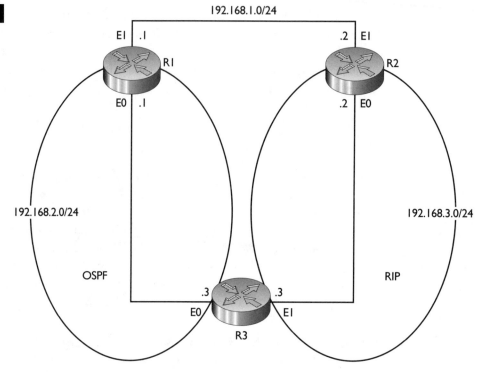

FIGURE 10-21

An OSPF- and RIP-advertised network

192.168.1.0/24

E1 .1   R1   .2 E1   R2

E0 .1   .2 E0

192.168.2.0/24   192.168.3.0/24

OSPF   RIP

.3   .3
EO   E1
R3

EXERCISE 10-3

To Loop or Not to Loop?

Something is amiss. You are called to investigate a possible topology issue and are asked to determine if the proposed configuration will have adverse impacts on routing paths. You are presented with the network topology shown in Figure 10-22. Networks from the RIP cloud are injected into IGRP, whereas a default route is injected into RIP. Using your knowledge of route redistribution, determine weather or not a routing loop is likely, define where it would occur, and explain the measure you would take to prevent it.

Solution: Yes, there is a likely chance that the network will form a routing loop. The reason is that the administrative distance of IGRP makes IGRP routes look more appealing to the routers. In this case, Router R1 sends an update for network

FIGURE 10-22

Is there a loop here?

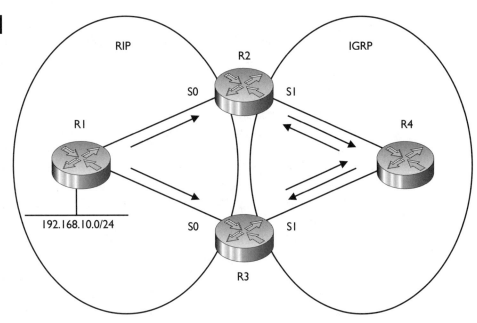

192.168.10.0 to Routers R2 and R3 via RIP. Routers R2 and R3 redistribute this route into IGRP and forward these routes to their neighbor, Router R4. Keep in mind that the route for 192.169.10.0 in Routers R2 and R3 are RIP learned routes (Type R) in the routing table, not IGRP (Type I). The route remains a RIP route, even though it is redistributed into IGRP, because the route was originally learned through RIP, not IGRP. This fact will become significant in a moment.

Router R4 receives equal cost advertisements for 192.168.10.0 from Routers R2 and R3 over IGRP. It installs both routes in its routing table, since the cost to reach that network through R2 or R3 is the same. R4 forwards the advertisement received from R2 onto R3 and the advertisement received from R3 back to R2. Notice the arrows in the figure. This process does not break the split-horizon rule, since R4 advertises updates it received via another interface. When R2 and R3 receive the IGRP update from R4, they compare it to the entry they have in their routing tables. Since the route entered in the routing tables was learned through RIP (distance 120), the new route received from IGRP (100) is more appealing to the routers. Both routers replace the RIP route pointing to R1 with the IGRP route pointing to R4. The next packet destined for network 192.168.10.0 that enters R2, R3, or R4 will see itself bounce from router to router until the TTL expires. This is because R2 and R3 point toward R4 to reach that network, but R4 points back to R2 and R3.

The solution to this problem is to install an inbound route filter on the Serial 1 interfaces of Routers R2 and R3 so that advertisements for network 192.168.10.0 are not accepted by these routers through IGRP. This solves the problem of routing loops, but what if the link between R1 and R2 goes down? R4 would advertise another possible path to R1 via R3, but R2 is filtering out this advertisement. A more elegant solution would be to change the administrative distance of IGRP to make RIP more interesting. Router R4 runs only IGRP, so this doesn't affect it. Routers R2 and R3, however, would always prefer the route learned through RIP for network 192.168.10.0. Since no IGRP route is redistributed into RIP, there is no chance for Routers R2 and R2 to learn about routes in the IGRP cloud through RIP. If the link between R1 and R2 were to fail, the RIP process on R2 would time out, and the IGRP advertisement coming from R4 for network 192.168.10.0 would then be adopted by R2, restoring connectivity to the destination network. The resulting configuration of R2 is shown in the following code listing. R3 has a similar manipulation of the administrative distance for RIP.

```
!
router rip
 redistribute igrp 100 metric 5
 network 192.168.20.0
 default distance 95
!
router igrp 100
 redistribute rip metric 1500 1 255 1 1500
 network 192.168.10.0
 network 192.168.30.0
!
```

In this case, the administrative distance of RIP was reduced from its default value of 120 down to 95, which is lower than the default administrative distance for IGRP, which is 100.

CERTIFICATION OBJECTIVE 10.04

Verifying Route Redistribution

Once a route filter has been configured on a router, it is necessary to verify the resulting connectivity. The following set of tools will aid you in the verification process.

The SHOW IP ROUTE Command

This is the most useful tool for troubleshooting routing issues. The output of this command is used to confirm the validity of routing tables. The standard syntax SHOW IP ROUTE displays the entire routing table of the router. In some situations, a router's routing table could be several pages long, but all you need to see are specific route entries. You might want to view only static routes or routes learned via a dynamic process such as RIP or EIGRP. Table 10-7 displays several variations of the SHOW IP ROUTE command. These SHOW IP ROUTE command alternatives could save you time and confusion by displaying only those routes of which you require knowledge.

TABLE 10-7   SHOW Commands

SHOW Command	SHOW Command Output
SHOW IP ROUTE	Shows all IP routes learned either dynamically or statically. Also shows floating static routes and directly connected interfaces.
SHOW IP ROUTE STATIC	Shows all IP static routes.
SHOW IP ROUTE EIGRP	Shows all EIGRP (or any IP protocol that is substituted for EIGRP) learned routes.
SHOW IP ROUTE 10.0.0.0 LONGER PREFIXES	Shows all 10.0.0.0 routes, including those that are subnetted.

EXERCISE 10-4

Selective Route Display

You are the newly hired network administrator for a large company. This company has a large internetwork, which, according to what you have heard, uses many different routing protocols. After looking at the output of the command SHOW IP PROTOCOLS, you determine that the following protocols are in operation on the router: RIP, IGRP, EIGRP, and OSPF. You imagine that there must be a way to simplify the network by consolidating the routing process into one or two routing protocols. For now, however, you need to take an inventory of what routes are handled by what protocols. Your first attempt with the command SHOW IP ROUTE dumps a huge routing table on your screen, with no apparent order to the entries shown. Which commands would you enter to display only the routes learned through the protocols on your list?

Solution: You would enter the following commands:

- SHOW IP ROUTE RIP
- SHOW IP ROUTE IGRP
- SHOW IP ROUTE EIGRP
- SHOW IP ROUTE OSPF

These four commands would list the routing entries handled by each of these protocols. You could subdivide the commands for IGRP, OSPF, and EIGRP even further by specifying the specific routing process ID of the protocol, if more than one instance is operating on the router.

The TRACEROUTE Command

TRACEROUTE does exactly what its name implies—it traces the path that your data will travel to a specified network and reports the given path back to you. TRACEROUTE is usually used for troubleshooting a route that has become unreachable. A failed ping to a destination does not isolate where the problem could lie in the internetwork. The TRACEROUTE command traces every router along the way, showing the response time for each router as the trace progresses through the entire path. Should a link be down in the path, TRACEROUTE shows the last link that responded to the trace process before it failed. This information can help you isolate the location from which a problem might originate.

The following code shows the output of the PING and TRACEROUTE commands, which fail somewhere along the way. Notice that compared to PING, the output of TRACEROUTE gives you much more information as to where the problem might be:

```
r1#ping www.redemptionmud.com
Translating "www.redemptionmud.com"...domain server (172.21.1.200) [OK]

Type escape sequence to abort.
Sending 5, 100-byte ICMP Echos to 64.240.60.51, timeout is 2 seconds:
.....
Success rate is 0 percent (0/5)
r1#
r1#traceroute www.redemptionmud.com

Type escape sequence to abort.
Tracing the route to www.redemptionmud.com (64.240.60.51)
Type escape sequence to abort.
Tracing the route to 64.240.60.51

  1 10.20.1.1 8 msec 8 msec 8 msec
  2 89.88.162.201.208.in-addr.arpa (208.201.162.89) 12 msec 12 msec 12 msec
  3 500.Serial2-3.GW6.ATL1.alter.net (157.130.87.141) 12 msec 16 msec 12 msec
  4 125.ATM3-0.XR2.ATL1.ALTER.NET (146.188.233.22) 12 msec 12 msec 12 msec
  5 294.ATM2-0.TR2.ATL1.ALTER.NET (146.188.232.106) 12 msec 12 msec 12 msec
  6 109.at-6/0/0.TR2.DCA8.ALTER.NET (146.188.138.190) 28 msec 28 msec 28 msec
  7 152.63.35.250 28 msec 32 msec 28 msec
  8 188.ATM4-0.BR2.DCA8.ALTER.NET (152.63.35.193) 32 msec 28 msec 32 msec
  9 uu-gw.wswdc.ip.att.net (192.205.32.133) 32 msec 28 msec 32 msec
 10 gbr3-p50.wswdc.ip.att.net (12.123.9.50) 36 msec 40 msec 36 msec
 11 gbr3-p80.n54ny.ip.att.net (12.122.2.165) 36 msec 36 msec 36 msec
 12 gbr3-p10.cgcil.ip.att.net (12.122.2.2) 60 msec 56 msec 60 msec
 13 gbr6-p60.cgcil.ip.att.net (12.122.5.9) 56 msec 60 msec 60 msec
 14 ar1-p3110.ipsin.ip.att.net (12.123.193.133) 60 msec 64 msec 64 msec
 15 12.126.250.174 !A  !A  *
r1#
```

We can clearly see that although PING does not tell us much other than the target can't be reach, TRACEROUTE shows us that the problem possibly comes from hop 15. That is where you should start troubleshooting the problem.

Even though routes are reachable through PING, that does not mean that the packet uses the optimal path. TRACEROUTE can also be used to verify the path employed by packets in order to reach their final destination. Another use of TRACEROUTE is to identify where routing loops occur in an internetwork. Take, for example, the TRACEROUTE output shown in Figure 10-23:

We can clearly see in that TRACEROUTE output that the packet gets bounced back and forth between the same two destinations, 192.168.1.1 and 192.168.1.2. The routing tables of these two routers point to each other as the next hop to be

FIGURE 10-23

A routing loop

```
Type escape sequence to abort.
Tracing the route to 192.168.3.3
  1 192.168.1.1 4 msec 4 msec 0 msec
  2 192.168.1.2 4 msec 4 msec 4 msec
  3 192.168.1.1 4 msec 4 msec 4 msec
  4 192.168.1.2 4 msec 4 msec 4 msec
  5 192.168.1.1 4 msec 4 msec 4 msec
  6 192.168.1.2 4 msec 4 msec 4 msec
  7 192.168.1.1 4 msec 4 msec 4 msec
  8 192.168.1.2 4 msec 4 msec 4 msec
  9 192.168.1.1 4 msec 4 msec 4 msec
 10 192.168.1.2 4 msec 8 msec 4 msec
 11 192.168.1.1 8 msec 4 msec 8 msec
 12 192.168.1.2 4 msec 8 msec 4 msec
 13 192.168.1.1 8 msec 4 msec 4 msec
 14 192.168.1.2 8 msec 4 msec 4 msec
 15 192.168.1.1 8 msec 8 msec 4 msec
 16 192.168.1.2 8 msec 8 msec 8 msec
 17 192.168.1.1 8 msec 4 msec 4 msec
 18 192.168.1.2 4 msec 8 msec 8 msec
 19 192.168.1.1 8 msec 8 msec 8 msec
 20 192.168.1.2 8 msec 4 msec 4 msec
 21 192.168.1.1 8 msec 8 msec 8 msec
 22 192.168.1.2 8 msec 8 msec 8 msec
 23 192.168.1.1 8 msec 8 msec 8 msec
 24 192.168.1.2 8 msec 8 msec 8 msec
 25 192.168.1.1 8 msec 8 msec 8 msec
 26 192.168.1.2 8 msec 8 msec 8 msec
 27 192.168.1.1 8 msec 8 msec 8 msec
 28 192.168.1.2 8 msec 8 msec 8 msec
 29 192.168.1.1 12 msec 8 msec 12 msec
 30 192.168.1.2 12 msec 8 msec 12 msec
r2#
```

FROM THE CLASSROOM

ICMP Restrictions By Network Administrators

You must understand the process used by the PING and TRACEROUTE commands. Many ISPs on the Internet block ICMP to prevent denial-of-service attacks on their systems. This blockage could result in the failure of the TRACEROUTE or PING process. Do not be confused by this situation. Overall, TCP/IP connectivity could very well be correct. When dealing with a PING or TRACEROUTE failure, never assume that the problem is on the local side. Your PING packet may very well reach the target host, but if that host does not know how to reach the originating network, it will not be able to return the PING packet to its point of origin. In this case, the routing process of the remote system must be investigated.

— *Benoit Durand, CCIE# 5754, CCDP, CCNP*

used to reach network 192.168.3.0. There is an obvious routing loop between these two routers.

We have covered a lot of information in this section. Try to answer the questions about redistribution and filtering in the following Scenario & Solution.

SCENARIO & SOLUTION

The value that gives a routing protocol its "believability" is called what?	Administrative distance
_____ performs a "quick" connectivity test between a source and a destination.	PING
What safeguard ensures that a route will not be advertised on the same interface on which it was learned?	Split horizon
True or false: TRACEROUTE always reports back the best path from the source to the destination.	False. It reports the actual path taken, which might not be the optimal path to the destination.

CERTIFICATION SUMMARY

In this chapter, you have learned the basics of redistribution, distribute lists, and passive interfaces. The chapter discussed many different scenarios in which each of these topics could play a role. Although none of these scenarios is a replica of what you might face while achieving your certification goals, the important thing to remember is that the concepts are the same. The same rules of redistribution with a single redistribution gateway apply in real-life networks. The network numbers, protocols, and router names might be different, but the issues that arise are generally consistent. Memorization of commands is important, but even more important, you must *understand* what is happening in your internetwork and understand the methods and tools at your disposal to ensure the proper routing path for all packets.

✓ TWO-MINUTE DRILL

Here are some of the key points from each certification objective in Chapter 10.

Selecting and Configuring Ways to Control Route Update Traffic

❑ The selection process for how to control route update traffic begins with studying the configuration, performance, and scalability of your network.

❑ Distribute lists are a simple way to control route updates entering or exiting on the router's interface.

❑ Expert knowledge of access lists is crucial in controlling route updates for medium-sized to large networks.

❑ The DEFAULT-NETWORK command is marked as an exterior route when used with IGRP or EIGRP.

Configuring Route Redistribution with a Single Redistribution Gateway

❑ Remember to watch for variable-length versus fixed-length subnet mask issues when you redistribute routing protocols.

❑ Mutual redistribution usually calls for configuring passive interfaces to each interface that does not need to advertise route updates.

❑ IGRP and EIGRP automatically redistribute between each other if the autonomous system number is the same.

❑ The SUBNET option must be included when you redistribute OSPF to include classless SUBNET information.

Configuring Route Redistribution with Multiple Redistribution Gateways

❑ Multiple redistribution points have multiple exit paths that can lead to path selection problems.

❑ Routing protocols use a "believability" value called *administrative distance* to determine which protocol is preferred over another.

❑ Static routes might be a more viable solution than dynamic routing protocols when multiple redistribution gateways are present.

Verifying Route Redistribution

❑ TRACEROUTE can verify that there is a path from the source router to the destination router.

❑ Remember that TRACEROUTE might not choose the best path during verification.

❑ The PING utility is the most commonly used tool for quickly testing connectivity between a source and destination or a locally connected interface.

❑ If your redistribution verification has failed, make sure that you have included the seed metric for each protocol that you are redistributing.

SELF TEST

The following questions will help you measure your understanding of the material presented in this chapter. Read all the choices carefully because there might be more than one correct answer. Choose all correct answers for each question.

Selecting and Configuring Ways to Control Route Update Traffic

1. Which of the following can be used to control route update traffic? Choose all that apply.

   A. Redistribution

   B. Variable-length subnet masks

   C. Distribute lists

   D. Passive interfaces

2. RIP and IGRP are examples of what type of routing protocol?

   A. Classful

   B. Classless

   C. Path-vector protocol

   D. Link-state protocol

3. Kasey, a network administrator, needs to redistribute a loop-back interface into her IGRP process. All other interfaces on the router except the loop-back interface are already being advertised by IGRP. Kasey does not want to include the network number in the IGRP. What option does she have to accomplish this task?

   A. Use a DISTRIBUTE-LIST OUT to force the network to be advertised.

   B. Redistribute connected routes into IGRP.

   C. Use a distribute list on other routers, forcing the entry of that network into IGRP.

   D. Configure a static route for that network pointing to loop-back 0. Static routes automatically get redistributed into IGRP, so the network will now be propagated.

4. When you perform mutual redistribution between two protocols, what tools are at your disposal in order to enforce the proper routing entries in the routing tables? Choose all that apply.

   A. Distribute lists

   B. TRACEROUTE

C. SHOW IP ROUTE

D. Administrative distance manipulation

5. Taylor, a new consultant, has been assigned to a financial institution to do some network engineering. The company is running IGRP 1 and wants to connect a new network to the existing router. The new network is to be kept isolated from the existing network for the time being. The new branch network will run under EIGRP 1. Taylor physically connects the new network cable to the router and configures EIGRP 1 as its advertising protocol. Taylor does not configure redistribution for any routing protocol. The lead network engineer calls Taylor and tells her that the two routing protocols are redistributing updates to each other and security has been compromised. What happened? Choose all that apply.

A. IGRP and EIGRP automatically redistribute updates when they are configured with the same autonomous system number.

B. Taylor inadvertently configured redistribution between the two protocols.

C. The lead network engineer is lying and is trying to get a date with Taylor.

D. Bridging is configured on the router and each network interface belongs to the same bridge group.

Configuring Route Redistribution with a Single Redistribution Gateway

6. Using a static route on an edge router that points to the core of the network has which of the following effects? Choose all that apply.

A. Enhances performance

B. Is more secure than a dynamic advertisement

C. Is easier to administer

D. Prevents the core from advertising the networks supported by the edge

7. Which command cannot be used to inject a default route into a dynamic routing protocol?

A. IP ROUTE 0.0.0.0 0.0.0.0 <NEXT-HOP>

B. IP DEFAULT-NETWORK <CLASSFUL_NETWORK>

C. DEFAULT-INFORMATION ORIGINATE

D. DISTRIBUTE-LIST 1 OUT

8. When you redistribute RIP into OSPF, which redistribution option(s) allows subnetted information pertaining to RIP to be passed to OSPF?

    A. DISTANCE

    B. IP CLASSFUL

    C. SUBNET

    D. METRIC-TYPE

9. Which of the following is *not* a metric used by EIGRP when calculating the proper path?

    A. MTU size

    B. Delay

    C. Bandwidth

    D. Cost

    E. Reliability

10. Kathy is a network administrator for a small school. The school consists of three locations in northern California connected via point-to-point Frame Relay circuits. Two of the remote locations have Frame Relay connections to the main location. All of the routers are configured with static routes. Kathy wanted to configure some kind of redundant route plan in case one of the Frame Relay circuits failed. She has limited knowledge of routing protocols and would like to stay with static routes. With Kathy's scenario, which of the following would best fit the needs of her environment?

    A. Install OSPF and set up a multipoint-to-point configuration.

    B. Configure the central and each remote site with ISDN backup and use floating static routes to create a backup route to the central site.

    C. Install ISDN at the central and each remote site but install only static routes between each remote and the central site.

    D. Install BGP at the central site and use it as a route reflector for each remote location.

11. Declaring a static route using an outbound interface instead of a next-hop IP address causes which of the following?

    A. The static route to appear directly connected

    B. The static route to fail

    C. You cannot define an interface as the next hop

    D. The metric for the static route to change to 4

Configuring Route Redistribution with Multiple Redistribution Gateways

12. In configuring redistribution between two protocols using multiple redistribution points, routing loops can occur for which of the following reasons? Choose all that apply.

    A. Route feedback between the two protocols can create erroneous paths.

    B. If redistributing between FLSM and VLSM protocols, the information will not be interpreted correctly by the classful protocol.

    C. Routes can be injected back into the originating protocol through the second distribution point, making routes more appealing because of the difference in administrative distance of the protocols.

    D. The default metric was not configured in the redistribution process.

13. The primary reason that routing protocols send data down a suboptimal path and cause network performance degradation is which of the following?

    A. The protocol's administrative distance value

    B. Flapping Frame Relay circuits

    C. Broadcast storms

    D. Incorrect MAC address at the host router

14. A distribute list filters route updates that are defined in which of the following?

    A. A host file

    B. An access list

    C. The route table

    D. The ARP table

15. A static route, by default, is normally the most preferred route for which of the following reasons?

    A. The administrative distance of a static route is very low.

    B. The router is programmed to always trust manually entered routes over everything else.

    C. Static routes always provide the longest match when route entries are compared.

    D. They disable any routing protocol operating on the router.

Verifying Route Redistribution

16. What will the command PING show you?

    A. The latency between the source and destination

    B. The bandwidth between the source and destination

    C. Where the problem can be if the packet does not return from its destination

    D. That the remote host does not receive the PING packet

17. What will the command TRACEROUTE show you? Choose all that apply.

    A. The latency between the source and destination

    B. The latency between the source and each hop along the way

    C. Where the problem can be if the packet does not return from its destination

    D. That the remote host does not receive the PING packet

18. SHOW IP ROUTE can verify which of the following? Choose all that apply.

    A. That redistribution is functioning correctly

    B. What static routes are configured

    C. What default routes are configured

    D. Which routes are learned from a particular protocol

19. What tool could you use to verify the next hop for a dynamically learned or static route?

    A. SHOW IP ROUTE

    B. DEBUG ROUTE UPDATE

    C. SHOW INTERFACE

    D. SHOW IP PROTOCOL

20. Which of the following verifies that you have an established TCP connection from source to destination?

    A. PING

    B. TELNET

    C. DEBUG

    D. SHOW IP ROUTE

LAB QUESTION

This lab demonstrates how to set up a simple distribute list. The outcome of this lab will have one router blocking two network updates from the other router. After completing this lab exercise, you will have the knowledge and ability to set up more complex distribute lists on your own.

Our scenario consists of two routers connected back to back via Ethernet ports. You can simply use a crossover cable or connect each Ethernet interface to a hub. Table 10-8 describes the step-by-step actions that you are required to take for each of the routers.

TABLE 10-8   Lab Table

R1	R2
1. conf t (Enter configure mode)	1. conf t (Enter configure mode)
2. write erase (Erase old configuration)	2. write erase (Erase old configuration)
3. reload (Reload router)	3. reload (Reload router)
4. connect Ethernet to other routers e0	4. connect Ethernet to other routers e0
5. conf t (Enter configure mode)	5. conf t (Enter configure mode)
6. int e0	6. int e0
7. no shutdown	7. no shutdown
8. ip add 192.168.1.1 255.255.255.0	8. ip add 192.168.1.2 255.255.255.0
9. int loopback 0	9. router eigrp 1
10. ip add 172.16.1.1 255.255.255.0	10. network 192.168.1.0
11. int loopback 1	11. no auto-summary
12. ip add 172.16.2.1 255.255.255.0	12. exit
13. router eigrp 1	13. no ip classless
14. network 192.168.1.0	14. exit
15. network 172.16.0.0	15. write memory
16. no auto-summary	16. show ip route -* you can see r1's updates for 172.16.1 and .2 networks*
17. exit	17. conf t
18. no ip classless	18. access-list 1 permit 172.16.2.0 0.0.0.0
19. write memory	19. router eigrp 1
	20. distribute-list 1 in Ethernet 0
	21. exit
	22. clear ip route *
	23. write memory
	24. show ip route

SELF TEST ANSWERS

Selecting and Configuring Ways to Control Route Update Traffic

1. ☑ **A, C, and D.** Redistribution, distribute lists, and passive interfaces are all methods used in controlling route update traffic.
    ☒ **B** is incorrect because VLSM describes a nonfixed-length subnet mask.

2. ☑ **A.** RIP and IGRP are both classful routing protocols.
    ☒ **B** is incorrect because RIP and IGRP are not classless protocols. **C** and **D** are incorrect because RIP and IGRP are both distance-vector protocols.

3. ☑ **B.** Redistribute connected routes into IGRP. Redistributing connected interfaces will redistribute the network of the loop-back interface into IGRP.
    ☒ **A** and **C** are incorrect because distribute lists do not force entries into a routing protocol. They are used to filter inbound or outbound routing advertisements. **D** is incorrect because static routes are not automatically redistributed into IGRP.

4. ☑ **A and D.** Distribute lists and administrative distance manipulation are correct because they are both tools used to ensure that the proper routing entries are accepted by the router.
    ☒ **B and C** are incorrect because, although they are valid tools for troubleshooting redistribution issues, they enforce no restrictions on the router's routing table.

5. ☑ **A and B.** When you configure IGRP and EIGRP to use the same process number, the two protocols automatically redistribute between themselves. **B** is also correct because Taylor did configure redistribution between the two protocols but was unaware of the rule defined in answer **A.**
    ☒ **C,** although plausible, it not the likely answer. He would not have cause to call Taylor if no routes showed up on his side of the network. **D** is incorrect because no bridging command has been entered. Furthermore, the remote router would also need to be configured for bridging, at which point the network would become one large broadcast domain instead of a routed environment.

Configuring Route Redistribution with a Single Redistribution Gateway

6. ☑ **A, B, and C.** Static routes use no processor time because there are no routes to advertise or learn, so performance is enhanced. The network is more secure because the core's networks are not being advertised to the edge routers. Because of network topology changes, dynamic routes are easier to administer.

☒   **D** is incorrect because, although the edge router is pointing to the core as a default route, the core still needs to advertise the networks supported by the edge to other edge routers in order for them to be able to reach these networks.

7. ☑   **D. DISTRIBUTE-LIST 1 OUT.** The DISTRIBUTE-LIST command injects no routes into the routing process. It is used to filter inbound and outbound advertisements.
☒   **A, B,** and **C** are incorrect because they are all valid methods used to inject default routes into dynamic routing protocols. Their use varies depending on the protocol.

8. ☑   **C.** The SUBNET parameter ensures that OSPF correctly interprets the subnet mask received through redistribution.
☒   **A** is incorrect because DISTANCE deals with the believability of a routing protocol, not the attributes passed from one routing protocol to another. **B** is incorrect because the IP CLASSFUL command does not exist in IOS. **D** is incorrect because METRIC-TYPE defines the type of metric that OSPF uses for this route once in the OSPF process. It does not deal with the subnet issue of the question.

9. ☑   **D.** Cost is a metric used by OSPF, not EIGRP.
☒   **A, B, C,** and **E** are incorrect since they all represent metrics used by EIGRP.

10. ☑   **B.** Configure the central and each remote site with ISDN backup and use floating static routes to create a backup route to the central site. Floating static routes are routes configured with an administrative distance higher than the current active route from your source to the specific destination. **C** would also work, but would cause the ISDN circuit to act as a parallel path to the Frame Relay circuit, so it is not the best answer. Active ISDN circuits can cost a lot of money.
☒   **A** is incorrect because a point-to-multipoint scenario would provide no redundancy over the existing topology. **C** is incorrect because using normal static routes would keep the ISDN links up due to the administrative distance of static routes being more attractive than OSPF. **D** is incorrect because route reflectors provide no link redundancy.

11. ☑   **A.** The static route to appear directly connected. Defining a physical interface as the next hop makes the static route "connected."
☒   **B** is incorrect because the static route will not fail due to the way it was entered. **C** is incorrect because you can indeed use an outbound interface as the next-hop parameter of a static route entry. **D** is incorrect because the command has no impact on the metrics used by the router.

Configuring Route Redistribution with Multiple Redistribution Gateways

12. ☑ **A and C.** Route feedback between the two protocols can create erroneous paths, and routes can be injected back into the originating protocol through the second distribution point, making routes more appealing because of the difference in administrative distance of the protocols. Both answers represent situations in which routing loops can occur in a multiple redistribution point scenario.

☒ **B** is incorrect because in redistributing into a classful routing protocol, route entries can be lost, but this will not cause a routing loop in the topology. **D** is also incorrect because, if the default metric is not defined, the routing protocol simply does not inject the redistributed routes into the routing protocol. This is a problem, but it does not cause a routing loop to occur.

13. ☑ **A.** The protocol's administrative distance value. The administrative distance defines the "believability" of the routing protocol and can cause suboptimal routing issues.

☒ **B** is incorrect because a flapping circuit would cause a recomputation of routes but not necessarily cause the router to chose a suboptimal path. **C** is incorrect because, although broadcast storms are a problem, they are not a problem related to routing. **D** is incorrect because incorrect MAC addresses do not pertain to the routing process. They are a Data-Link Layer issue that is resolved by the Address Resolution Protocol (ARP).

14. ☑ **B.** A distribute list filters routes that are defined by an access list.

☒ **A, C, and D** are incorrect because host files, route tables, and ARP tables are not valid tools used to define the traffic to be filtered by distribution lists.

15. ☑ **A.** Static routes have an administrative distance of 1, which is the lowest value after connected routes, which have an administrative distance of 0. This forces the router to prefer these routes over routes learned via a dynamic routing protocol.

☒ **B** is incorrect because, if the administrative distance of a static route is changed, the router can use a dynamic route over a static route to reach the target destination. **C** is incorrect because static routes do not always provide the longest match. **D** is incorrect because static routes do not disable any routing protocol running on a router. They can work in cooperation quite easily.

Verifying Route Redistribution

16. ☑ **A.** The latency between the source and destination. As the PING results are displayed, the time that the ICMP packet took to travel to the destination and back is displayed.

☒ **B** is incorrect because PING does not show the bandwidth of links between the source and destination. **C** is incorrect because if PING fails, no indication is given of where the problem could be. **D** is incorrect because a PING packet can reach its destination but not be able to return to the originating point. In those cases, the routing tables of the remote systems could be at fault.

17. ☑ **A, B,** and **C.** The latency between the source and destination, the latency between the source and each hop along the way, and where the problem can be if the packet does not return from its destination. TRACEROUTE provides all this information while tracing the path of a packet throughout the internetwork.

    ☒ **D** is incorrect because the packet could very well reach the target but not be able to return to its point of origin. In this case, TRACEROUTE will show the trace as failing 1 hop before reaching the target.

18. ☑ **A, B, C,** and **D** are all correct answers because they are all parameters that are displayed by the command SHOW IP ROUTE.

    ☒ There are no incorrect answers to this question.

19. ☑ **A.** SHOW IP ROUTE displays the content of the routing table, which includes the next hop for each route that was dynamically learned.

    ☒ **B** is incorrect because DEBUG ROUTE UPDATE is not a valid IOS command. **C** is incorrect because the SHOW INTERFACE command displays only status information about a specific interface. It does not give any information about routing paths. **D** is incorrect because although SHOW IP PROTOCOL shows information about the routing protocol operating on the router, it does not show any routing information.

20. ☑ **B.** TELNET is a TCP protocol and is a great tool to verify that you have end-to-end connectivity.

    ☒ **A** is incorrect because PING uses the ICMP protocol, which is different from TCP. **C** and **D** are both incorrect because DEBUG and SHOW IP ROUTE are IOS commands on the router that do not cause any form of connection to occur.

LAB ANSWER

Now look at your route table on r2. You should see r1's advertisements for the 172.16.2.0 network only. You have blocked the 172.16.1.0 network with the distribute list.

You can expand this lab by adding more loop-back interfaces to r1 and modifying the access list on r2 to allow different networks through. You can also add loop-back interfaces on r2 and then create filters on r1 to block those networks.

11

Policy-Based Routing and Route Maps

P olicy-based routing and route maps are the most powerful tools available to a
network administrator. Configuring routing policies and redistribution based on route
maps allows for complete manipulation and control of route tables and preferred data
paths. This chapter briefly defines queuing and then discusses in detail the topics of policy
routing and route maps.

Helping you understand when, where, and how to use policy routing and route
maps is the goal of this chapter. A route map ensures that the only route updates
that are passed into or out of your route table are the exact updates that you want.
After reading this chapter you will be in full control of your routers' facilities with
regard to route updates. Once you master the topic of policy-based routing, your
value as a CCNP and network engineer will skyrocket.

If you grasp this concept now while studying for the CCNP certification, you will
be way ahead of the game when you begin to study for your CCIE. If you are using
this guide to study for your CCIE, you have come to the right place. Remember,
during certification testing you will need to reroute, reengineer, and "perform
miracles" with route advertisements and data paths. This guide—more specifically,
this chapter—will aid your development of the skill and proficiency required to
master policy-based routing. It's easy, and it's fun, so let's get started.

CERTIFICATION OBJECTIVE 11.01

Understanding Policy-Based Routing

Policy-based routing allows an administrator to manipulate a router's incoming
packets based on the packet's source address. Like distribute lists and route maps
(the latter of which is discussed later in this chapter), policy routes use access lists to
define which incoming packets will be affected by the policy statement. Those
packets that do not match the access list criteria referenced by the policy route
match statements are routed normally.

Policy routes use a set of set and match statements within a route map to
influence the path taken by each packet. A packet is "matched" by its source address
and then "set" or directed to follow a particular path or interface.

FROM THE CLASSROOM

Traffic-Directing Power Tools

As you read this chapter, you will realize that directing traffic in and out of a router is not difficult. Keep the following points in mind to help maintain perspective with regard to policy routing and route maps:

■ **Policy routing**   Remember that policy routing is nothing more than routing in or out of an interface, following particular rules. If you are required to influence the path of specific packets at the interface level, you need to consider using a policy route.

■ **Route maps**   A route map is used with the policy route to define the actions taken when a packet or packets match your defined IP address definitions. The route map is where you define your *set* and *match* definitions that will influence the path your interfaces inbound or outbound packets might or might not follow.

■ **Verification**   Typical with most everything that you will do as a network engineer, it is always a smart next step to verify, after completing each task, that your configuration operates as planned. Never skip this step.

■ **Practice, practice, and more practice**   After you think that you have the concept down, practice that concept to make sure. Change the configuration around, write down what you think the new results will be, and try it out. If your results match what you have on paper, try it again to make sure. If the results do not match, look at the configuration again. Set up the configuration at the point at which it did last work and try to better understand what is happening, why this configuration works and the changed configuration does not.

—*Ron Panus, CCIE 5823, CCNP, CCDA, MCSE, CNA*

Let's take a look at an example of when and why we would use a policy route. Figure 11-1 depicts a simple network with LAN traffic flowing outbound to the serial interfaces. OSPF chooses to use the T1 circuit because it is faster. This leaves the 256k circuit unused, which is a big waste of company funds.

Not only does this strategy waste company dollars, it also provides the least optimal scenario with regard to network performance. Policy routing allows us to fix

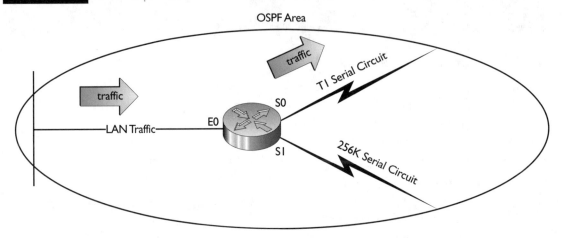

FIGURE 11-1   OSPF chooses the T1 because of its speed, leaving the 256k circuit unused

this problem by specifying that any traffic without a valid destination present in the route tables should utilize serial interface 1. All other traffic will use the T1 circuit attached to serial interface 0. The access list and policy route would look like the following code samples. In Global Configuration mode:

```
Access-list 1 permit any
Route-map use_256 permit 10
Match ip address 1
Set default-interface serial 1
```

In Interface Configuration mode:

```
Interface Ethernet 0
Ip policy route route-map use_256
```

As you can see in Figure 11-2, specific traffic now uses the 256k circuit and improves network performance over the T1 connection. You will also see a big smile on your boss's face.

Defining Policy-Based Routing

So far, we have learned that policy routing is used to manipulate certain characteristics with regard to a router's incoming packets. The command to enable a policy route is IP POLICY ROUTE-MAP. An access list defines the source IP

FIGURE 11-2   The effects of our policy route

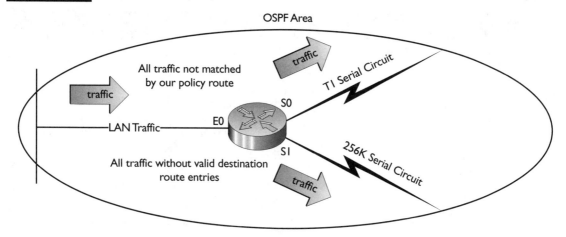

addresses that the route map must match. If an address is matched, a policy is set for that packet, which then follows the set parameter. Policy routes are valid for only the router on which they are configured. Table 11-1 displays the MATCH commands that can be used with policy routing.

As you can see from Table 11-1, the MATCH statement is pretty simple. If a source address matches an address defined in your access list, you are guided down a different path. Sort of sounds like a static route, doesn't it? Table 11-2 displays the SET commands that pertain to policy routes.

Once again, the commands are straightforward. If an incoming source IP address matches an address defined in our access list, direct (set) that packet to follow the instructions. The SET and MATCH commands are defined in a route map. We

TABLE 11-1   MATCH Commands Used in Policy Routing

Command	Description
MATCH IP ADDRESS {*ACCESS-LIST #*} (Example: MATCH IP ADDRESS 1)	Matches all packets that are defined in the corresponding access list.
MATCH LENGTH {MIN | MAX}	Matches the level 3 length of a packet (that is, the size in bytes of the datagram). Use this command if, for example, you want all packets less than and equal to 100 bytes to go out serial 1 and all packets equal to or greater than 101 bytes to go out serial 2.

| TABLE 11-2 | SET Commands Used in Policy Routing |

Command	Description
SET INTERFACE *TYPE NUMBER* (Example: SET INTERFACE e0)	This command defines the interface that each matched packet must traverse, providing that a route to the destination exists.
SET DEFAULT INTERFACE *TYPE NUMBER* (Example: SET DEFAULT INTERFACE e1)	This command defines the default interface that all packets must traverse if no route exists to the packet destination (kind of like a default route with an interface defined as the next hop).
SET IP NEXT-HOP *IP-ADDRESS*	This command defines the next hop router address, providing a route to the destination exists.
SET IP DEFAULT NEXT-HOP *IP-ADDRESS*	This command defines the next hop router address, providing a route to the destination does not exist.
SET IP PRECEDENCE *PRECEDENCE*	This command sets the precedence bits in the Type of Service field for each matched source IP address.
SET IP TOS *TYPE-OF-SERVICE*	This command sets the Type of Service field of every matching IP address.

discuss route maps in more detail later in this chapter. We also review policy routes and route maps in detail.

Reasons to Use Policy-Based Routing

Let's briefly discuss some of the reasons that we might use policy routing; then we will take a look at the types of policy-based routing we can implement.

Policy-based routing allows an administrator to control several data traffic characteristics, such as:

■ Which packets are serviced first according to the setting of the precedence bit

■ Which packets are filtered based on an access list that corresponds to a particular route map

■ Whether a packet will be dropped or will follow a data path that it would ordinarily not have chosen

It is very important that you understand every aspect of policy-based routing. This subject is one that will show up in one form or another during your certification endeavors. First we take a quick look at queuing as it pertains to IP policy routing, and then we delve deeply into the topics of filtering and path manipulation.

on the

◑ o b

The function I like best in policy routing is the IP NEXT-HOP command. This is an easy way to set an identified source IP address's next hop to either a router's IP address or a defined local interface.

Types of Policy-Based Routing

There are two methods of policy-based routing: queuing and filtering. *Queuing* helps control packets based on quality of service parameters. *Filtering* allows us to policy route packets based on particular filters that we create for specific scenarios. Let's look at these two concepts in more depth.

Queuing

Queuing with regard to policy routing covers the area of *quality of service*. This topic revolves around setting the IP precedence bit to allow certain packets precedence over others. The precedence bit can be set if policy routing is enabled, but the router ignores the precedence bit if queuing is not enabled. Queuing is worth mentioning but is not as relevant as filtering or path manipulation. Table 11-3 shows the IP precedence values.

TABLE 11-3	Number Value	Name
IP Precedence Numeric Values and Characteristics	0	Routine
	1	Priority
	2	Immediate
	3	Flash
	4	Flash-override
	5	Critical
	6	Internet
	7	Network

Filtering

Filtering, as discussed in Chapter 10, primarily deals with controlling route advertisements as they enter a router's interface. The control mechanism primarily used in this capacity is a *distribute list*. You should recall that each route update can be either permitted or denied when it enters a router's interface. If the update is permitted, the advertisement will update the router's route table. If the update is denied, the advertisement is dropped.

Path Manipulation

We now focus on the subject of path manipulation. A *route map* is the primary tool used to manipulate traffic path selection. Route maps can be applied in a number of areas to allow tight control of advertisements or traffic path selection. Some of the areas to which route maps can be applied are as follows:

- When configuring redistribution to allow or not allow certain networks to be redistributed to other protocols

SCENARIO & SOLUTION

Policy routing allows packet manipulation based on the packet's _____ _____?	Source address.
With regard to IP policy routing, if a packet is not defined in the corresponding access list of a route map, what happens to the incoming packet?	The packet is not policy routed but is routed normally.
Route maps for redistribution and policy routing use ____ and ____ commands to define the addresses that are recognized and the actions that will be performed upon their recognition.	MATCH and SET.
When redistributing route updates, what happens to a route update that does not meet the requirements defined in a route map and the corresponding access list?	The route update packet is dropped completely.
What function of policy-based routing allows certain packets precedence over others?	Setting the IP precedence bit in queuing.

■ When configuring IP policy routing to manipulate a packet path selection or which interface the packet will traverse

These are just two examples for the use of a route map. As we discuss here, route maps allow an administrator to set the metric, the metric type, and even the next-hop value for a defined IP source address.

EXERCISE 11-1

Creating a Policy Route to Force the Next-Hop Address

Follow these steps to create a policy route that will force a next-hop IP address of 192.168.1.1 for any route updates received on interface Serial 0 from network 10.1.1.0.

1. Log on to the router and enter Privileged Exec mode.

2. Create an access list to match route updates from network 10.1.1.0 by typing **access-list 1 permit 10.1.1.0 0.0.0.255** and then press Enter.

3. Create a route map by typing **route-map next_hop permit 10** and then pressing Enter, then type **match ip address 1** and press Enter. Finally, type **set ip next-hop 192.168.1.1** and press Enter.

4. Type **interface serial 0** and press Enter in order to enter the Interface Configuration mode for serial 0.

5. Now apply the policy to interface serial 0 by typing **ip policy route-map next_hop** and pressing Enter.

That's all there is to it. Any traffic with any source address from network 10.1.1.0 will be forced to use a next-hop address of 192.168.1.1. Policy routing is very powerful. Now let's move on to the operations of route maps.

Operations of Route Maps

A *route map* is an essential component of policy-routing configuration. Route maps are a required component of policy routing and should always be used to ensure that the traffic that needs to be directed is directed. As stated before, route maps can be used with various router administrative tasks, but this section focuses on using route maps with policy routing.

First let's familiarize ourselves with the functions of route maps and how they work. Additionally, this section discusses the functions of the MATCH and SET commands (these commands differ from those used with redistribution) and when and where to use each of the commands. We demonstrate the use of route maps with policy routing in several scenarios taken from real-world examples. We also examine several examples that you can use to set up and test your own policy routes. Finally, we construct and review scenarios in which route maps play a vital role when applying policy routes to local router interfaces.

Make sure that you completely understand route maps and policy routing before you move on from this chapter. If you are unclear on any part of this topic, go back and look at and try some of the example scenarios. Questions are posed throughout this chapter to make sure you stay on track. If you come across a question that does not make sense, go back and reread the section to which the question pertains until you fully grasp the concept. Make full use of the scenarios contained in this chapter and modify them to challenge yourself to the fullest.

Defining Route Maps

A route map is a multipurpose tool that gives a network administrator great flexibility in performing certain tasks. The route map's power depends on what you are going to use the route map for. The following are various functions that a route map can perform:

- Control route updates during redistribution
- Define specific connected interfaces for redistribution

■ Manipulate the path a packet or packets may follow, depending on the packet's source address

■ Assign default interfaces or default gateways to allow packets different destinations, depending on the packet's source address

Route maps are also used extensively in BGP. BGP goes beyond the scope of this chapter, but keep in mind that route maps provide the same functionality no matter where they are used.

MATCH and SET function

Every route map contains a set of commands and directives in the form of MATCH and SET commands. The functions of these commands are simple to learn and understand. When used with redistribution, a route map merely states that if an IP address is matched, you should have it do something. An IP address is matched from a corresponding access list that the route map references. For example, if network 10.1.1.0 is matched from the corresponding access list, set that network's next-hop router address to 20.1.1.1. (This address is just an example; it could be any valid router address.)

Table 11-4 displays the ROUTE-MAP command and each available option.

on the ***job*** *Remember to name each route map so that at a quick glance you will know what the route map is intended to do. It is also useful to keep written documentation with regard to route maps configured for each router.*

To define a route map for redistribution, use the commands shown in Table 11-5 in Global Configuration mode. Table 11-5 displays all of the match parameters that can be used to define a route map that will be used for redistribution. The route map is defined in Route-Map Configuration mode. You must specify at least one MATCH command for each route map. If you do not specify a SET command, by default nothing is done.

TABLE 11-4   The ROUTE-MAP Command

Command	Description
ROUTE-MAP *NAME VALUE* PERMIT | DENY {SEQUENCE NUMBER}	Defines a route map to be used with redistribution.

| TABLE 11-5 | Route Map MATCH Commands Used with Redistribution |

Command	Description
MATCH IP ADDRESS *ACCESS-LIST #	NAME*	Matches one or more of the destination IP addresses defined by the specified access list.
MATCH IP ROUTE-SOURCE *ACCESS-LIST #	NAME*	Matches one or more of the route update advertisements advertised by the router with a source address defined by the specified access list.
MATCH INTERFACE *TYPE NUMBER*	Matches each route that has a designated next hop out of the specified interface.
MATCH METRIC *METRIC-VALUE*	Matches each route that has a metric value specified in the *METRIC-VALUE* parameter.
MATCH IP NEXT-HOP *ACCESS-LIST #	NAME*	Matches each route that has a defined next-hop router address defined by the corresponding access list.
MATCH TAG *TAG-VALUE*	Matches each route with the tag value specified in the TAG-VALUE parameter.
MATCH ROUTE-TYPE *INTERNAL/EXTERNAL |TYPE 1 TYPE 2| LEVEL 1 LEVEL 2*	Matches the specific route type for EIGRP, OSPF, and IS-IS routing protocols.

Table 11-6 shows the SET commands for a route map that is used for redistribution. Remember that the SET command manipulates and directs the IP addresses or route advertisements that have been matched by the MATCH statement.

Additional SET commands used with BGP are not shown in Table 11-6. BGP is beyond the scope of this chapter, so we will not get into the additional commands here.

Sequence Number

A route map maintains a big advantage over an access list in that an administrator can easily insert or delete individual statements in the route map. This editing flexibility allows administrators the option of testing individual statements in a route map and then deleting the statements if the desired outcome is not met.

The default sequence number is 10. A good rule of thumb is to sequence each route map statement by 10. The first line might be permit 10, the second statement might be permit 20, and so on. For example, let's say you want to create a route map that is involved with redistributing IGRP into OSPF. Your route map will reference access list number 1 and permit the network to be redistributed. The route

TABLE 11-6   Route Map SET Commands Used for Redistribution

Command	Description
SET NEXT-HOP *NEXT-HOP*	Sets the specified next-hop router address for each matched route.
SET METRIC *METRIC-VALUE	BANDWIDTH DELAY RELIABILITY LOADING MTU*	Sets the specified metric value for each matched route.
SET METRIC-TYPE *INTERNAL	EXTERNAL TYPE 1 TYPE 2*	Sets the specified metric value for each route matched and redistributed into ISIS or OSPF.
SET TAG *TAG-VALUE*	Sets the tag value for each route that is matched.
SET LEVEL	*LEVEL 1 LEVEL 2 LEVEL 1-2| BACKBONE STUB-AREA*	Sets the level value for IS-IS or the OSPF area for each route matched and redistributed.

map would drop all other traffic with regard to the redistribution from IGRP into OSPF. Your route map would look like the following:

```
Route-map igrp_ospf permit 10
Match ip address 1
```

If you had omitted *permit 10* from the end of line one, the default of 10 would have been inserted for you. Notice also that there is no SET statement in the route map. Since all you want to do is allow the networks stated in access list one to be redistributed, you do not need a SET statement.

Route maps work in sequential order. If the routed packets are not matched in statement 10, they are passed on to the next statement (if there is a next statement). If a packet passes through all the statements and is not matched by any of them, those packets are dropped (as in this example). Remember that this process differs from policy routing. Packets that are not matched in policy routing are passed back to the normal routing process. The latter statement is also true for DENY statements that are met for either a route map or a policy route. A DENY statement performs the same action as a packet that has not been matched: the packet is either dropped or sent back to the normal route process.

The sequential numbers used with route maps allow you to delete individual statements from the route map. For example, let's say you have a route map with an additional statement (statement 20). It would look like the following:

```
Route-map igrp_ospf permit 10
Match ip address 1
```

```
Set metric 120
Route map igrp_ospf permit 20
Match ip address 2
Set next-hop 10.1.1.1
```

If you wanted to remove statement 20 from the route map, you would use the following command:

```
No route-map igrp_ospf 20
```

This command removes line 20 from the route map IGRP_OSPF. If you omitted the number 20 from the end of the route map, you would have deleted the whole IGRP_OSPF route map. Remember that route maps are configured in Global Configuration mode and policy routes are configured under the interface where the policy needs to be applied.

on the **job**

Many route maps that deal with redistribution look like the latter example. You usually need to allow one or two networks to pass for redistribution and drop the rest. This scenario is typical, and as you can see, it is short and sweet. This ROUTE-MAP statement merely states that you want to let network x.x.x.x be redistributed from IGRP into OSPF but no other networks. It is that simple!

Comparison Between Route Maps and Access Lists

A route map has some of the same attributes as an access list. For example:

- Both use PERMIT and DENY statements to allow or not allow identified traffic to pass.

- Both lists are followed sequentially from top to bottom. Once a match occurs for a packet, the specified action is taken and the packet ignores the rest of the route map or access list.

- Both lists maintain an implicit DENY ANY at the end of each list.

- A route map allows you to inject statements "in between" ROUTE-MAP statements, but you can only add commands to the end of an access list.

Now that you have a basic understanding of route maps, let's try to answer a few scenario questions before we move on to configuring route maps.

SCENARIO & SOLUTION

A route map is configured in _____ _____ _____.	Global Configuration mode.
What is the first default sequence number you use when configuring a route map?	10.
What happens to a packet that is not matched by a route map?	It is dropped.
A good rule of thumb is to increment each route map statement by how much?	10.
A route map, by default, has an implicit ____ ____ at the end of the route map.	DENY ANY.
During redistribution, a route map is a great tool to stop route-_____.	Feedback.

EXERCISE 11-2

Setting the Default Next-Hop IP Address with a Policy Route

Follow these steps to create a policy route that will set a default next-hop IP address for any packet that arrives via interface Ethernet 0 and does not have a route to its destination.

1. Log on onto the router and enter Privileged Exec mode.

2. Enter Configuration mode by typing **config term** and pressing Enter.

3. Create an access list that defines a policy route "match" as any traffic that enters interface Ethernet 0 with a source network address of 10.1.1.0 by typing **access-list 1 permit 10.1.1.0 0.0.0.255** and pressing Enter.

4. Create a route map that we will use with the policy route by typing **route-map set_default permit 10** followed by pressing Enter, then **match ip address 1** followed by pressing Enter and **set ip default next-hop 192.168.1.1** followed by pressing Enter.

5. Next, create the policy route for interface Ethernet 0 by typing **interface Ethernet 0** and pressing Enter. Then type **ip policy route-map set_default** and press Enter.

6. Press Ctrl-z to exit Configuration mode.

You have just created a policy route that forces any traffic that enters interface Ethernet 0 with any source IP address from network 10.1.1.0 that does not have a route to its destination to use IP address 192.168.1.1 as its default next-hop address.

CERTIFICATION OBJECTIVE 11.03

Configuring Route Maps

During the last exercise we created a policy route using a route map to get some experience using these maps. Now we break down the route map a little further with more complex examples.

We should stress the importance of understanding what happens to unmatched packets in either a policy route or route map situation. A policy route packet that is not matched by the access list is sent on to the routing table and will be routed normally. A packet that is not matched by a route map will be dropped. Make sure that you know and understand this fact.

Creating a Route-Map Command

Some of the previous tables showed us the proper definitions for each SET and MATCH command used with a route map. Now let's break it down further with command definitions that will make a little more sense.

ROUTE-MAP MAP-TAG {PERMIT|DENY} [SEQUENCE-NUMBER]

This command is where the route map begins. From Global Configuration mode, choose a route map name that coincides with some aspect of what you are using the route map for—in other words, what are you trying to filter, or what route updates do you need to influence? For example, if your route map sets a default interface for serial 0, you should name your route map in this fashion:

```
r2(config)#route-map default_s0 permit 10
```

This command names, or *tags,* your route map with the name DEFAULT_S0 and allows you at a quick glance to get a good idea of what the route map is used for. *Permit 10* was added to the end of the route map so that we'd have no misconceptions of the sequence number with which the route map begins. Keep in mind that *permit 10* is the default and it could have been left off. Also remember that once you enter an initial ROUTE-MAP configuration command, like the preceding one, you are put into Route-Map Configuration mode, where you will have access to the SET and MATCH commands.

MATCH {CONDITION}

The MATCH command, when used with policy routing, has two options: we can either match the IP address that corresponds to the access list we created, or we can match the level 3 length of the packet. You will most likely use the first option the majority of the time.

MATCH IP ADDRESS   Let's say that we need to match a single IP address of 172.16.2.2. Our access list would look like this:

```
r2(config)#access-list 1 permit 172.16.2.2 0.0.0.0
```

This access list defines the IP address of only 172.16.2.2 and nothing else. Notice the number 1 that defines the access list number. That is the number we will use in the MATCH statement of our route map. The command would look like this:

```
r2(config-route-map)#match ip address 1
```

This statement directs the route map to look for the IP addresses that I have defined with access-list 1. If the condition or IP address is matched, get ready to perform an action. (We use the SET command to perform the action, as we discuss later in this chapter.)

MATCH LENGTH MIN MAX   The ROUTE-MAP command MATCH LENGTH allows us to set a condition so that a packet will match if the packet is a certain minimum or maximum length. The command looks like the following:

```
r2(config-route-map)#match length 1300 1600
```

This command defines that we want to match packets that are no smaller than 1300 bytes but no larger than 1600 bytes.

SET {ACTION}

We have looked at the MATCH commands and understand that any update for which we want to set a specific condition must first be recognized, or matched, as it enters a specific interface. The SET commands, with regard to policy routing, control the action that the router will take if the packet matches our definition specified in the access list. Simply stated, if the packet is "matched" by our policy route statement, the packet is forced to do something. That "something" that we forced to the packet to do is covered immediately below this definition.

SET IP NEXT-HOP   The first SET command we will look at is the SET IP NEXT-HOP command. This command forces the packet to our defined next-hop IP address if the packet matches the specific source address in our policy route statement. The next-hop address specified by this command must be reachable and must possess a valid route. The following is an example of the command:

```
Set ip next-hop 10.1.1.1
```

If the packet is matched by our policy route statement, that particular packet must use 10.1.1.1 as its next-hop address.

exam
ⓦatch

If you need to set up a default route but do not or cannot use a default route command in your configuration, the SET IP NEXT-HOP command is the way to go.

SET INTERFACE   The SET INTERFACE command is much like the SET IP NEXT-HOP command in that the command forces a packet to follow an administratively determined pathway. The difference between the two commands is that the SET INTERFACE command specifies an interface instead of an IP address. The following is an example of how the command line looks:

```
Set interface E0
```

Any packet that matches our policy route statement is forced to follow a path out of interface Ethernet 0.

SET IP DEFAULT NEXT-HOP   The SET IP DEFAULT NEXT-HOP command is useful for setting a default next-hop IP address for packets that meet the requirements specified in the policy route statement and have no path in the route table to its destination. In other words, if the packet matches the policy route statement, this command presents the packet's default next-hop IP address. You might already have one default route configured on the router. This command allows you to create a second default route only for specified source addressed packets. The following is an example of the command line used to implement this feature:

```
Set ip default next-hop 172.16.1.1
```

Again, if any packet matches our policy route statement, this command sets the default gateway to 172.16.1.1 for those specific source addressed IP packets.

on the *job*

As a consultant I have seen many router configurations that accomplished a company's routing requirements, but did so in a suboptimal fashion. In particular, I have seen many creative router configurations that an administrator created in order to force packets, from several different source locations, to use individual default gateways. Some of these configurations included changing the administrative distance, using floating static routes—even using extended access lists in one fashion or another. Many of these network administrators and network engineers were good at their jobs, but they lacked some advanced router design skills, such as proficient understanding of policy routing. This situation will be a great advantage to readers of this book. You will know that a policy route such as SET IP DEFAULT NEXT-HOP will force packets from specific source addresses to use a predetermined default gateway.

SET DEFAULT INTERFACE   The SET DEFAULT INTERFACE command is very similar to the SET DEFAULT NEXT-HOP command in that any packet that matches the policy route statement is forced to use a specific interface as its default gateway. The packet must not have a valid, routable path defined in the route table for this command to function properly. The default gateway that the packet is forced to use is defined by an interface instead of an IP address. The following is an example of this command in use:

```
Set default interface Serial 0
```

This configuration sets any packet that matches our policy route statement to use interface Serial 0 as its default gateway.

exam
Ⓦatch

Remember a very important fact when you are deciding which configuration commands to use in your policy routes. If, and only if, the packets that you are going to policy route have no known destination in the routing table, you must include the default component for the given command. This goes for both the SET IP DEFAULT NEXT-HOP and SET DEFAULT INTERFACE commands.

Linking a Route Map to an Interface

Now we take a look at the procedure used to implement a policy route map. If you have thoughts of burning the late-night candle in order to master creating or implementing policy route maps, you can rest easy. Linking a policy route map to an interface is a very simple process. And if you think about it, policy routing makes a lot of sense.

Many of you are in situations in which you must direct certain traffic down specific paths that the packet might normally not choose or even know about. For others who are not in that position today, the fact that you are reading this book and are pursuing a Cisco certification means that your day is coming. When given the task of forcing traffic patterns that best fit the needs of your company, you will possess the knowledge to do it. That is when you think, "I need packets from this network to go out this interface and packets from all other networks to go out the other interface. How should I go about accomplishing this task?" Policy routing is your answer. Now let's move on and learn how to implement an IP policy route map.

IP POLICY ROUTE-MAP

As we said, this process is easy. Only a few steps are involved in implementing your policy route map. The steps are as follows:

1. For source IP addresses we need to match, we will use 10.1.1.0 network for our example. We have created an access list that contains the address. Let's use access-list 1 for our example.

2. We will use route map SET_NEXT_HOP for our example; it contains the SET and MATCH statements. Let's say that any address that matches our route map MATCH statement of match IP address 1 will be forced to use an IP next-hop address of 172.16.1.1 using the SET IP NEXT-HOP 172.16.1.1 command.

3. We have identified the interface that the identified traffic will enter. Let's use E0 for our example.

The following are the commands used to put our IP policy route map into action, beginning in Global Configuration mode:

```
Interface e0
Ip policy route-map set_next_hop
Exit
```

Are you ready for the rest of the commands to implement our policy route map? Some of you will be disappointed, but that is all there is to it! All traffic that enters interface E0 and that matches access-list 1 is assigned a gateway of 172.16.1.1.

IP ROUTE-CACHE POLICY

The IP ROUTE-CACHE POLICY command allows policy-based routing to be fast-switched instead of the traditional process-switched method. Policy-based routing must be enabled before the IP ROUTE-CACHE POLICY command can be enabled. The default for this command is disabled. This command can be used with Cisco IOS version 12.0 and later. Furthermore, this command does not support the SET IP DEFAULT NEXT-HOP and SET DEFAULT INTERFACE commands.

Conclusion

We learned a lot in the "Configuring Route Maps" section. Some of the topics we discussed were:

- Creating a route map
- Route map SET commands
- Route map MATCH commands
- Linking a route map to an interface
- IP route-cache policies

In addition, we also learned that a policy route is a great tool to allow us to influence a packet data path following its entrance into a specific router interface. A policy route is much like a distribute list in that a policy route filters at the interface level. Just keep in mind that a distribute list updates incoming and outgoing route updates and a policy route sets the policy on how packets are routed and which data path the packets should follow.

Remember to keep a list of every access list, policy route, and route map that you configure. In that list, make a short note as to what the policy or map is for and what interface you applied it to. Following this rule can be a life saver during written and hands-on exams.

You might be starting to think that you have a pretty good handle on policy routing. Why shouldn't you be feeling like you have a grasp on this topic? You have accomplished a lot by reading this section and learning the various functions of a policy route. With that in mind, let's answer some Scenario & Solution questions regarding what we have learned in this chapter. Following these questions, we move on to verifying route maps.

Follow the steps in Exercise 11-3 to create a policy route that will force packets from two individual network source addresses to use two different physical interfaces as a default gateway. This exercise assumes that our router is accepting inward-bound packets via interface Serial 0 and uses interfaces Ethernet 0 and Ethernet 1 as

SCENARIO & SOLUTION	
Route maps are configured in which configuration mode?	Route-Map Configuration mode.
Policy routes are configured to filter incoming or outgoing packets for a specific _____?	Interface.
In which configuration mode is a policy route linked to an interface?	Interface Configuration mode.
True or false: A policy route consists of various SET and START commands.	False. A policy route is configured with SET and MATCH commands.
True or false: A well-defined policy route can help maintain an optimized route table.	False. Remember that a policy route allows you to influence the path a packet will follow based on its source address. Policy routes do not influence route update advertisements.

gateway exit points. Packets from network 10.1.1.0 will be policy routed out of Ethernet 0. Packets from network 20.1.1.0 will be policy routed out of Ethernet 1.

EXERCISE 11-3

Using IP Policy Routing to Assign a Physical Interface as a Default Gateway

1. Log on to the router and enter Privileged Exec mode (Enable mode).

2. Type **config t** to enter Configuration mode.

3. Create two access lists that will determine which packets will be policy routed and which packets will be routed normally. (Remember that any packet that is not policy routed will be routed under the normal routing process.)

   ```
   Access-list 1 permit 10.1.1.0 0.0.0.255
   Access-list 2 permit 20.1.1.0 0.0.0.255
   ```

4. Create an IP policy route map that will define what actions will be taken to packets that meet our policy route definitions.

   ```
   route-map set_default_gw permit 10
   match ip address 1
   set ip default interface Ethernet 0
   route-map set_default_gw permit 20
   match ip address 2
   set ip default interface Ethernet 1
   exit
   ```

5. Now we link our policy route to the serial interface.

   ```
   Interface serial 0
   Ip policy-route route-map set_default_gw
   Press control-z
   ```

That finishes the policy route configuration. All incoming packets traversing interface serial 0 will be policy routed if they meet our definitions created in our policy route configuration. Any packet that has a source network IP address of 10.1.1.x will use Ethernet 0 for any packets that do not have a destination addressed in our router's route table. The same will occur for any incoming packets on Serial 0 with a source network address of 20.1.1.x.

CERTIFICATION OBJECTIVE 11.04

Verifying Route Maps

Creating a network from beginning to end involves several responsibilities. As a network engineer, you might be asked to assist or even lead in many or all of these tasks. These tasks might include:

■ Network needs and assessment

■ Network design and architecture

■ Router and switch hardware provisioning and configuration

■ Router and switch IOS configuration

■ Network hardware installation and implementation

■ Functional network testing and verification

Network engineers involved with consulting firms can have similar tasks and responsibilities. You could acquire the title of professional services consultant or network field engineer. Whatever your professional title, the function of a network professional working "in the field" is to perform tasks such as assisting customers with any or all of the job responsibilities outlined previously. You could also find yourself involved in a lot of network troubleshooting.

The basic functions of troubleshooting network problems are:

■ Assess exactly what the problem is

■ Locate where the trouble seems to have stemmed from

■ Find out the time the problem first occurred and who was doing what when the problem was first noticed

■ Perform the proper steps needed to render a solution to the problem

■ Verify that the problem has been corrected

This section pertains to the verification of route maps. You might be wondering what job responsibilities and troubleshooting have to do with verifying a route map.

In most everything you do as a network engineer will end with you verifying that the task you just completed is operating as it should. It is vital to understand how to verify that your policy route works correctly after you have applied a route map to a policy route. The rest of this section shows you the tools that are in your arsenal to ensure that your policy route maps are working as you need them to.

Here are a couple of study tips that I followed in order to achieve my CCIE. First, you will succeed much faster by understanding the technology—not only understanding the commands to make the technology work. Most of us possess the ability to memorize a scenario. If a curve ball is thrown into the scenario, true experts have the ability to understand the change and still make the hit. The second tip is practice, practice, practice. Did I mention practice? Practice makes perfect, and perfect practice will help make you certified.

The SHOW IP POLICY Command

The first policy-route verification tool we will look at is the SHOW IP POLICY command. This command, executed from Privileged Exec mode, displays the route map used for a policy route. To use this command, type:

```
Show ip policy
```

The SHOW ROUTE-MAP Command

The next verification tool is the SHOW ROUTE-MAP command. This command is also executed from the Privileged Exec mode and displays all configured route maps. The command uses the following format:

```
Show route-map map name
```

The *MAP NAME* is the name of a particular route map that you might want to view. If you omit the *MAP NAME* option, the router displays all route maps configured on that router.

Let's test the two commands we just learned about in a simple exercise. This exercise can be used on any Cisco router that has a route map and a policy route already in place.

Using the SHOW IP POLICY and SHOW ROUTE-MAP Commands

1. Log on to the router and enter Privileged Exec mode.

2. Type **show ip policy**. This command displays the route map used for policy routing.

3. Now type **show route-map** to display all the route maps configured on the router.

This exercise is short but to the point. You can use these commands to quickly view policy route and route map information.

Now that we have covered route map verification, let's answer a couple of questions to make sure that you understand the verification commands.

SCENARIO & SOLUTION

True or false: you must specify the route map name when using the SHOW ROUTE-MAP command.	False. If you omit the route map name, the router will display all the configured route maps.
True or false: policy routes can use standard and extended access lists.	True. You can specify the source and destination IP addresses in a policy route as a requirement for packets to match.

CERTIFICATION SUMMARY

Congratulations! You have come a long way since the beginning of this chapter. You have made great strides in the technical arena with regard to policy routing and route maps. By understanding the material covered in this chapter, you have excelled far beyond many in your field.

With your newfound knowledge, you now possess the ability to control whatever traffic enters or exits your router. Do you need to assign multiple default gateways on a single router, dependent on a source IP address? Now you can do it. Do you need to direct some traffic out of one interface while the remaining traffic uses a different interface? Again, you have the ability to do that now.

The knowledge you have gained and will gain in the remaining chapters of this book will aid you not only on the certification exams but on the job. Basic routing functionality will change very little. Technological enhancements to router hardware or IOS will always continue to optimize routing. By reading this study guide, you are building the foundation that will allow a smoother transition to whatever router technology you need to learn and master.

✓ TWO-MINUTE DRILL

Here are some of the key points from each certification objective in Chapter 11.

Understanding Policy-Based Routing

❑ Policy routes route traffic based on the IP source address.

❑ Policy routes can control inbound or outbound traffic.

❑ Packets are process-switched when utilizing policy routing.

❑ Policy routes control traffic per interface.

Operations of Route Maps

❑ Route maps use SET and MATCH commands to control traffic.

❑ Route maps match the source address of each IP packet as defined by a corresponding access list.

❑ Route maps follow each line in sequence until a match is made.

❑ Route maps can permit or deny matched packets.

Configuring Route Maps

❑ Each route map is configured in Route-Map Configuration mode.

❑ *Permit 10* is the default action and sequence number if omitted during route map configuration.

❑ Keep the name of each route map synonymous with what you are using the route map for.

❑ Line a route map to an interface with a policy route.

Verifying Route Maps

❑ Verification is *always* the final step when you are configuring a route map.

❑ Use the SHOW commands to display which route maps are linked to your policy routes.

❑ Use the TRACEROUTE command to verify that each route map is controlling your packets as you intended.

❑ Use the SHOW ROUTE-MAP command to display all route maps configured on a router.

SELF TEST

The following questions will help you measure your understanding of the material presented in this chapter. Read all of the choices carefully because there might be more than one correct answer. Choose all correct answers for each question.

Understanding Policy-Based Routing

1. By default, policy-based routing can negatively impact network performance for what reason? Choose all that apply.

   A. Because policy routing uses fast switching

   B. Because policy routing uses process switching

   C. Because policy route match definitions are based on an access list

   D. Policy-based routing does not negatively impact network performance

2. Policy routing allows you to direct traffic to what element? Choose all that apply.

   A. An interface

   B. A default interface

   C. A next-hop IP address

   D. A default next-hop IP address

   E. All of the above

3. Policy routing allows you to match packets based on:

   A. The packet length

   B. The packet encapsulation type

   C. The packet encryption methodology

   D. The packet subnet mask

4. Packets that are policy routed and are fast-switched will perform in what way?

   A. Better than process-switched packets

   B. Worse than process-switched packets

   C. The same as packets that are process switched

5. To control the path destination for packets received from another router, you would do which of the following? Choose all that apply.

    A. Configure an access list to match the source IP address

    B. Create a route map that identified the access-list definition with a MATCH statement

    C. Link the policy route to the inbound direction of the interface that the packet would enter

    D. All of the above

Operations of Route Maps

6. Route maps, by default, use a sequence number in multiples of what number?

    A. 5

    B. 10

    C. 15

    D. 20

7. If a packet is not matched in a route map used for redistribution, what happens to the packet?

    A. It is routed anyway

    B. It is dropped

    C. It is sent to a null device

    D. It is sent back to the originating router

8. If a packet is not matched in a route map used for policy routing, what happens to the packet?

    A. The packet is processed normally

    B. The packet is dropped

    C. The packet is sent to a null device

    D. The packet is sent back to the originating router

9. The command to send packets to an interface if no route exists in the routing table for that packet is:

    A. SET IP DEFAULT NEXT-HOP

    B. SET IP PRECEDENCE

    C. SET DEFAULT INTERFACE

    D. SET IP DEFAULT LENGTH

10. What is the command to enable fast switching of policy-based routing?

    A. IP ROUTE-CACHE POLICY

    B. ENABLE ROUTE-CACHE

    C. ENABLE FAST-SWITCHING

    D. FAST POLICY-ROUTING ENABLE

Configuring Route Maps

11. What is a route map "tag"?

    A. A game played at recess

    B. The name you apply to a route map

    C. What you define to be matched in your policy route

    D. The name of the interface to which you are linking the policy route

12. You must be in what configuration mode to begin defining a route map?

    A. Exec mode

    B. Privileged Exec mode

    C. Supervisor mode

    D. All of the above

13. To define a next-hop route for specific packets that have a valid route to the destination in the route table, which ROUTE-MAP command would you use? Choose all that apply.

    A. SET IP NEXT-HOP *IP-ADDRESS*

    B. SET NEXT-HOP INTERFACE *TYPE NUMBER*

    C. SET INTERFACE *TYPE NUMBER*

    D. SET IP DEFAULT NEXT-HOP *IP-ADDRESS*

14. We want to send all traffic that has a source IP network address from 10.1.1.0 out of our local Ethernet 0 interface. A valid route to the destination network is present in the route table. Our route map is named 10x_out_e0 and we will assume it is configured correctly. Assume our policy route is also configured correctly. Which of the following access lists would allow any traffic from network 10.1.1.0 to pass?

    A. ACCESS-LIST 1 PERMIT 10.0.0.0 0.0.0.255

    B. ACCESS-LIST 99 PERMIT 10.1.1.0 0.0.0.255

C. ACCESS-LIST 99 PERMIT 10.1.1.0 0.0.0.0

D. ACCESS-LIST 1 PERMIT 10.1.1.0 0.0.0.0

Verifying Route Maps

15. Which of the following IP policy route commands would you use if you wanted to match all packets with a length between 1100 and 1300 bytes?

A. MATCH LENGTH 1100 1300

B. MATCH LENGTH 1100

C. MATCH LENGTH + 1100 / 1300

D. MATCH LENGTH < 1300

16. The final step you should perform after configuring a policy route is:

A. Create a route map

B. Create a policy route

C. Create an access list

D. Verify that your configuration works

17. Which of the following tools can you use to verify that your policy route is functioning correctly? Choose all that apply.

A. SHOW VERSION

B. PING

C. TRACEROUTE

D. SHOW USER

18. When using a route map for redistribution, what is the quickest method of verifying that your route map is functioning correctly?

A. PING

B. TRACEROUTE

C. SHOW IP ROUTE

D. All of the above

19. Which of the following are the proper method(s) available to control any type of traffic entering or exiting your router? Choose all that apply.

A. Distribute lists

B. Policy routes

C. Route maps

D. Access lists

E. Redistribution

F. All of the above

LAB QUESTION

This exercise demonstrates how to send packets from three separate networks to three separate gateway interfaces. You could see this requirement often in the real world in small or large network environments. Practice this scenario enough so that you are very comfortable with this use of IP policy routing.

The following are the commands necessary to set up our scenario on a single router. If you do not have other routers to perform the PING verification at the end of this exercise, you can try using loopback interfaces as your gateway interfaces.

1. Log on to your router and enter Privileged Exec mode.

2. Type **config term** to enter Configuration mode.

3. Create three access lists that define which source IP addresses we want to match. Type **access-list 1 permit 10.1.1.0** and press Enter, **access-list 2 permit 10.1.2.0** and press Enter, and **access-list 3 permit 10.1.3.0** and press Enter.

4. Create the IP policy route map that defines which IP addresses to match and what to do with them if they do match. Type **route-map send_out_gateway permit 10** and press Enter. The type **match ip address 1** and press Enter. Then type **set interface ethernet 1** and press Enter. Type **match ip address 2** and press Enter. Type **set interface ethernet 2** and press Enter. Type **match ip address 3** and press Enter. Finally, type **set interface ethernet 3** and press Enter.

5. Create the IP policy route and link the policy route to the desired interface on which the packets to match will come in. Type **interface ethernet 0** and press Enter. Type **ip policy route route-map send_out_gateway** and press Enter.

SELF TEST ANSWERS

Understanding Policy-Based Routing

1. ☑ **B and C.** Because policy routing uses process switching and because policy route match definitions are based on an access list. When an access list is applied, each packet is process switched. Process switching examines each packet as it enters the interface and looks for a match to the access list.

☒ **A** is incorrect because process switching is enabled by default during policy-based routing. **D** in incorrect because the Cisco IOS uses process switching by default. Any time the router uses process switching, it must examine each packet as it arrives at an interface. This process then causes performance degradation within the router.

2. ☑ **E.** All of the above. Each of these exit points can be defined as to where you want traffic, based on the packet source IP address, to exit the router.

☒ There are no incorrect choices.

3. ☑ **A.** The packet length. Policy routing includes two match functions. One is to match each packet based on the source IP address. The second match function is to match the length of the packet.

☒ **B, C, and D** are incorrect because policy routing does not include packets to match the IP addresses defined by an access list by any of these choices.

4. ☑ **A.** Better than process-switched packets. This is the correct answer because process-switched packets are processed more slowly than any other switching methodology. Each packet header is examined on an individual basis, which slows down the routing process. Fast-switched packets are blindly sent to the specified interface without checking the validity of the path.

☒ **B and C** are incorrect because process switching checks the validity of the specified path before sending the packet on their way; fast switching does not.

5. ☑ **D.** All of the above is the correct answer because each of the answers combined would create a working policy route that would manipulate a packet's destination path that has entered a specific local interface.

☒ There are no incorrect choices.

Operations of Route Maps

6. ☑ **B.** 10 is the correct answer. By default, each route map MATCH statement is sequenced by 10. The first line will begin with 10, the second line 20, and so on. This system allows you to edit your route map and insert other MATCH statements between existing statements.
   ☒ **A, C,** and **D** are incorrect because 10 is the default sequence numbering scheme.

7. ☑ **B.** It is dropped. During redistribution, packets that do not match your access list are dropped completely. No other action is performed.
   ☒ **A, C,** and **D** are incorrect because if the packet is not matched by an access list, the packet is dropped and no other action is performed.

8. ☑ **A.** The packet is processed normally. Unlike route maps used with redistribution, any packet that is not matched by the corresponding access list is processed normally.
   ☒ **B, C,** and **D** are all incorrect because any packet that does not match the defined criteria is processed normally.

9. ☑ **C.** SET DEFAULT INTERFACE. Use this command to define a packet with a particular source IP address and that does not have a valid destination path in the routing table, to be matched and then sent to an interface of your choosing.
   ☒ **A** is not correct because the SET IP DEFAULT NEXT-HOP command, under the same circumstances, sends a packet to a valid next-hop IP address. **B** is not correct because the SET IP PRECEDENCE command sets the IP precedence bit if a match occurs. **D** is not correct because the SET IP DEFAULT LENGTH command does not exist.

10. ☑ **A.** IP ROUTE-CACHE POLICY. Cisco IOS version 12.0 and later allows you to configure a router to use fast switching in conjunction with policy-based routing. Prior to version 12.0, your only option was to use the slower process switching. Process switching is still the default method.
    ☒ **B, C,** and **D** are all incorrect answers because these commands do not exist.

Configuring Route Maps

11. ☑ **B.** The name you apply to a route map. The command ROUTE-MAP *BRANDY* tells the router that you are defining a route map with the name Brandy, which is the "tag" function.
    ☒ **A** is incorrect because kids in grade school usually are not configuring routers. **C** is incorrect because you use the MATCH command defined in your route map to specify which packets meet the match criteria. **D** is incorrect because you define which interface you want to send specific packets to using a SET command in the route map.

12. ☑ **B**. Privileged mode. When you begin to configure a route map, you will be in Privileged Exec mode (Enable mode). After you type the ROUTE-MAP command and give the route map a name, you will automatically enter Route-Map Configuration mode.

    ☒ **A** is incorrect because you cannot configure a route map from Exec mode. **C** is incorrect because Supervisor mode is not a valid Configuration mode on a Cisco router. **D** is incorrect because there is only one correct answer.

13. ☑ **A** and **C**. SET IP NEXT-HOP *IP-ADDRESS* and SET INTERFACE *TYPE NUMBER*. As long as a valid route to the destination exists, you could use either answer. **A** specifies the next-hop router IP address; **C** specifies the local interface from which you want the packet to exit.

    ☒ **B** is not a correct answer because the *IP* is missing from the command line and would be invalid. **D** is not correct because the SET IP DEFAULT NEXT-HOP *IP-ADDRESS* command would be used if there was not a valid route to the destination (the word *DEFAULT* is the giveaway).

14. ☑ **B**. ACCESS-LIST 99 PERMIT 10.1.1.0 0.0.0.255. A standard access list is numbered 1–99, which all the choices fall under. The network of 10.1.1.0 is followed by the correct wildcard mask that would allow any IP address from network 10.1.1.0 to pass and match our requirements.

    ☒ **A** is incorrect because the wildcard would allow any packets from network 10.0.0.0. **C** is incorrect because the wildcard would allow only the exact network address of 10.1.1.0 to pass and none of the hosts on that network. **D** is incorrect because, like **C**, it would allow only the exact network address of 10.1.1.0 to pass. The only difference between **C** and **D** is the access list number.

Verifying Route Maps

15. ☑ **A**. MATCH LENGTH 1100 1300. This command matches any packet with a length from 1100 to 1300 bytes.

    ☒ **B** is incorrect because the MATCH LENGTH 1100 command would only match packets that were 1100 bytes in length. Our requirement was to match packets that fell between 1100 and 1300 bytes in length. **C** and **D** are incorrect because MATCH LENGTH + 1100 / 1300 and MATCH LENGTH < 1300 are not valid command-line functions.

16. ☑ **D**. Verify that your configuration works. Verification should always be the final step after configuring a policy route—or anything else you configure, for that matter.

    ☒ **A**, **B**, and **C** are incorrect because they are all steps used to configure a policy route.

17. ☑ **B** and **C**. PING and TRACEROUTE. Each of these commands allows you to test the path from your destination to the source. PING verifies that you have connectivity between two hosts and the amount of time the packets take to reach one another. TRACEROUTE shows you the actual path the packet uses to get from source to destination.

    ☒ **A** is incorrect because SHOW VERSION shows the Cisco IOS version currently in use on the router. **D** is incorrect because the SHOW USER command shows what users are currently logged in to the console or virtual terminals.

18. ☑ **C**. SHOW IP ROUTE. Redistribution deals with route tables so that your route map would allow whatever route updates to be permitted or denied. The SHOW IP ROUTE command is the quickest means available to ensure that your route table is updated as intended.

    ☒ **A**, PING, could be used to test the connectivity between two hosts that are attached to the networks for which you have permitted updates, but it is not the method that makes the most sense. **B**, TRACEROUTE, could be used, but like **A**, it is not the optimal method to test for a proper redistribution configuration.

19. ☑ **F**. All of the above is the correct answer. Each of these tools ensures that you allow only the packets that are required to traverse your router.

    ☒ There are no incorrect choices.

LAB ANSWER

What you have created is very similar to three individual static routes that would have directed packets from each network to a local interface. Policy routing is a clean, well-defined method of directing packets based on specific source IP addresses.

CISCO® CERTIFIED NETWORK PROFESSIONAL

A

About the CD

Thi CD-ROM contains the CertTrainer software. CertTrainer comes complete with ExamSim, Skill Assessment tests, and the e-book (electronic version of the book), and DriveTime. CertTrainer is easy to install on any Windows 98/NT/2000 computer and must be installed to access these features. You may, however, browse the e-book directly from the CD without installation.

Installing CertTrainer

If your computer CD-ROM drive is configured to autorun, the CD-ROM will automatically start up upon inserting the disk. From the opening screen you may either browse the e-book or install CertTrainer by pressing the *Install Now* button. This will begin the installation process and create a program group named "CertTrainer." To run CertTrainer use START | PROGRAMS | CERTTRAINER.

System Requirements

CertTrainer requires Windows 98 or higher and Internet Explorer 4.0 or above and 600 MB of hard disk space for full installation.

CertTrainer

CertTrainer provides a complete review of each exam objective, organized by chapter. You should read each objective summary and make certain that you understand it before proceeding to the SkillAssessor. If you still need more practice on the concepts of any objective, use the "In Depth" button to link to the corresponding section from the Study Guide.

Once you have completed the review(s) and feel comfortable with the material, launch the SkillAssessor quiz to test your grasp of each objective. Once you complete the quiz, you will be presented with your score for that chapter.

ExamSim

As its name implies, ExamSim provides you with a simulation of the actual exam. The number of questions, the type of questions, and the time allowed are intended to be an accurate representation of the exam environment. You will see the following screen when you are ready to begin ExamSim:

When you launch ExamSim, a digital clock display will appear in the upper left-hand corner of your screen. The clock will continue to count down to zero unless you choose to end the exam before the time expires.

There are three types of questions on the exam:

- **Multiple Choice** These questions have a single correct answer that you indicate by selecting the appropriate check box.

- **Multiple-Multiple Choice** These questions require more than one correct answer. Indicate each correct answer by selecting the appropriate check boxes.

- **Simulations** These questions simulate actual Windows 2000 menus and dialog boxes. After reading the question, you are required to select the appropriate settings to most accurately meet the objectives for that question.

Saving Scores as Cookies

Your ExamSim score is stored as a browser cookie. If you've configured your browser to accept cookies, your score will be stored in a file named *History*. If your browser is not configured to accept cookies, you cannot permanently save your scores. If you delete this History cookie, the scores will be deleted permanently.

E-Book

The entire contents of the Study Guide are provided in HTML form, as shown in the following screen. Although the files are optimized for Internet Explorer, they can also be viewed with other browsers including Netscape.

DriveTime

DriveTime audio tracks will automatically play when you insert the CD ROM into a standard CD player, such as the one in your car or home stereo. There is one track for each chapter. These tracks provide you with certification summaries for each chapter and are the perfect way to study while commuting.

Help

A help file is provided through a help button on the main ExamSim Gold screen in the lower right hand corner.

Upgrading

A button is provided on the main ExamSim screen for upgrades. This button will take you to www.syngress.com where you can download any available upgrades.

Glossary

10Base2   Ethernet specification using 50-ohm thin coaxial cable and a signaling rate of 10-Mbps baseband.

10Base5   Ethernet specification using standard (thick) 50-ohm baseband coaxial cable and a signaling rate of 10-Mbps baseband.

10BaseFL   Ethernet specification using fiber-optic cabling and a signaling rate of 10-Mbps baseband.

10BaseT   Ethernet specification using two pairs of twisted-pair cabling (Category 3, 4, or 5): one pair for transmitting data and the other for receiving data, and a signaling rate of 10-Mbps baseband.

10Broad36   Ethernet specification using broadband coaxial cable and a signaling rate of 10-Mbps.

100BaseFX   Fast Ethernet specification using two strands of multimode fiber-optic cable per link and a signaling rate of 100-Mbps baseband. A 100BaseFX link cannot exceed 400 meters in length.

100BaseT   Fast Ethernet specification using UTP wiring and a signaling rate of 100-Mbps baseband. 100BaseT sends link pulses out on the wire when there is no data traffic present.

100BaseT4   Fast Ethernet specification using four pairs of Category 3, 4, or 5 UTP wiring and a signaling rate of 100-Mbps baseband. The maximum length of a 100BaseT4 segment is 100 meters.

100BaseTX   Fast Ethernet specification using two pairs of UTP or STP wiring and 100-Mbps baseband signaling. One pair of wires is used to receive data; the other is used to transmit. A 100BaseTX segment cannot exceed 100 meters in length.

100BaseX   100-Mbps baseband Fast Ethernet specification based on the IEEE 802.3 standard. 100BaseX refers to the 100BaseFX and 100BaseTX standards for Fast Ethernet over fiber-optic cabling.

AAA (authentication, authorization, and accounting) A security approach.

AAL (ATM adaptation layer) Service-dependent sublayer of the data-link layer. The function of the AAL is to accept data from different applications and present it to the ATM layer in 48-byte ATM segments.

AARP (AppleTalk Address Resolution Protocol) The protocol that maps a data-link address to an AppleTalk network address.

ABR (area border router) Router located on the border of an OSPF area, which connects that area to the backbone network. An ABR would be a member of both the OSPF backbone and the attached area. It maintains routing tables describing both the backbone topology and the topology of the other area.

Access layer Provides access to the network from remote segments.

access list A sequential list of statements in a router configuration that identify network traffic for various purposes, including traffic and route filtering.

ACK (acknowledgment) Notification sent from one network device to another to acknowledge that a message or group of messages has been received. Sometimes abbreviated ACK. Opposite of **NAK.**

Acknowledge (Type 5) Packets Acknowledge (ACK) packets are sent by the receiving router of a LSA to let the sending router know that the LSA was received. More than one LSA can be acknowledged in a single ACK. The ACK packet format is similar to that of the DD packet. The ACK can be sent to a multicast address for all routers (224.0.0.5), to DRs (224.0.0.6), or unicast to the sender. How the ACK is sent depends on the state of the sending router's interface and the sending router.

active hub A multiport device that repeats and amplifies LAN signals at the physical layer.

active monitor   A network device on a Token Ring that is responsible for managing ring operations. The active monitor ensures that tokens are not lost, or that frames do not circulate indefinitely on the ring.

address   A numbering convention used to identify a unique entity or location on a network.

address mapping   Technique that allows different protocols to operate together by associating addresses from one format with those of another.

address mask   A string of bits, which, when combined with an address, describes which portion of an address refers to the network or subnet and which part refers to the host. *See also* **subnet mask**.

address resolution   A technique for resolving differences between computer addressing schemes. Address resolution most often specifies a method for mapping network layer addresses to data-link layer addresses. *See also* **address mapping**.

Adjacency   Adjacency is achieved when the router has successfully built it topology database and routing tables via link-state advertisements exchanged with its neighbors. In order to become adjacent, the router and its neighbors must agree and go through a structured process to become full neighbors. Unless this occurs, routers will not become neighbors and will not exchange routing updates.

administrative distance   A rating of the preferability of a routing information source. Administrative distance is expressed as a value between 0 and 255. The higher the value, the lower the preference.

Administrative distance control   Administrative distance controls are one tool to force the router to determine one path is favored over another. Modifying the administrative distance is an alternative to filtering in some instances. Adding a higher administrative distance to a static route creates a floating static route entry. Remember that floating static routes are often used in dial backup situations with regards to analog or ISDN environments.

ADSL (asymmetric digital subscriber line) A technology that delivers more bandwidth downstream (from a central site to a remote site) than upstream.

Advertised distance Since each router passes its lowest calculated metric, or its feasible distance to its direct neighbors, this metric becomes the advertised distance for the neighbors. That is to say the advertised distance is the metric it received from R2, or R2's *own* feasible distance.

advertising A process in which a router sends routing or service updates at frequent intervals so that other routers on the network can maintain lists of usable routes or services.

AFI (Address-Family Identifier) This indicates the type of address being used; when IP is in use, the AFI is 2.

Aggregate route An advertised CIDR block is commonly referred to as an *aggregate route*. Supernetting, mentioned earlier, involves shortening the bits of the network portion of an address to encompass more networks, creating an aggregate.

Aggregation A benefit of BGP 4 support of CIDR is aggregation. This is the capability to take several networks, and condense them into one advertisement. This reduces CPU cycles, memory, and table size; this is possible because CIDR enables the advertisement of an IP prefix (really several IP network addresses summarized into one network address with the correct mask).

algorithm A specific process for arriving at a solution to a problem.

AMI (alternate mark inversion) The line-code type that is used on T1 and E1 circuits. In this code, zeros are represented by 01 during each bit cell, and ones are represented by 11 or 00, alternately, during each bit cell.

AND function The AND function compares two bits. The result is one and only one if the two bits are one; otherwise, the result is zero.

ANSI (American National Standards Institute) An organization of representatives of corporate, government, and other entities that coordinates standards-related activities, approves U.S. national standards, and develops positions for the United States in international standards organizations.

AppleTalk A suite of communications protocols developed by Apple Computer for allowing communication among their devices over a network.

application layer Layer 7 of the OSI reference model. This layer provides services to end user application processes such as electronic mail, file transfer, and terminal emulation.

ARP (Address Resolution Protocol) Internet protocol used to map an IP address to a MAC address.

AS_PATH Type Code 2 attribute This is a well-known mandatory attribute that identifies the ASs that this UPDATE message has passed through to reach this point. It contains the sequence of ASs, with the first AS being last in the list. It can be modified directly by the network engineer using route maps and regular expressions that can change its length.

ASBR (autonomous system boundary router) An ASBR is an ABR connecting an OSPF autonomous system to a non-OSPF network. ASBRs run two protocols: OSPF and another routing protocol. ASBRs must be located in a nonstub OSPF area.

ASN (Autonomous System Number) Identifies an AS in the Internet and maintained by the RADB.

asynchronous transmission Describes digital signals that are transmitted without precise clocking or synchronization.

ATM (Asynchronous Transfer Mode) An international standard for cell relay suitable for carrying multiple service types (such as voice, video, or data) in fixed-length (53-byte) cells. Fixed-length cells allow cell processing to occur in hardware, thereby reducing latency.

ATM adaptation layer   *See* AAL.

ATM Forum   International organization founded in 1991 by Cisco Systems, NET/ADAPTIVE, Northern Telecom, and Sprint to develop and promote standards-based implementation agreements for ATM technology.

AUI (attachment unit interface)   An interface between an MAU and a NIC (network interface card) described in the IEEE 802.3 specification. AUI often refers to the physical port to which an AUI cable attaches.

Automatic redistribution   Automatic redistribution occurs under a couple of different scenarios. First, when a single protocol is used throughout the infrastructure the protocol will automatically redistribute advertisements. If the protocol uses an antonymous system designation such as BGP, OSPF, EIGRP, and IGRP, the process number (or identifier) must be the same for automatic redistribution to occur. One technique to isolate routing advertisements on a single router when utilizing a single routing protocol is to define separate antonymous systems for each environment you wish to isolate.

AS (autonomous system)   A group of networks under a common administration that share in a common routing strategy.

AS (Autonomous system) External LSA   Autonomous system (AS) external LSAs are originated by autonomous system boundary routers (ASBRs). Type 5 LSAs describe particular destinations external to the AS and are also used to describe a default route. When carrying information about a default route, the LSID is always set to a default destination of 0.0.0.0 with a mask of 0.0.0.0. Another way to think of AS external LSAs is that they pull information into the AS from foreign autonomous systems.

B8ZS (binary 8-zero substitution)   The line-code type that used on T1 and E1 circuits. With B8ZS, a special code is substituted whenever eight consecutive zeros are sent over the link. This code is then interpreted at the remote end of the connection.

Backbone area   The backbone area is always designated as 0, or 0.0.0.0. All areas must be directly connected to the backbone or have a virtual link to this area. Area 0 characteristically contains high-speed routers and redundant links forming the core of a hierarchical network. Due to its nature, it is wise to keep all hosts off the backbone.

Backbone router   A router that has at least one interface connected to area 0. ABRs qualify as backbone routers, but not all backbone routers are ABRs. When all interfaces are in area 0, the router is not an ABR.

backoff   The retransmission delay used by contention-based MAC protocols such as Ethernet, after a network node determines that the physical medium is already in use.

bandwidth   The difference between the highest and lowest frequencies available for network signals. The term may also describe the throughput capacity of a network link or segment.

baseband   A network technology in which a single carrier frequency is used. Ethernet is a common example of a baseband network technology.

baud   Unit of signaling speed equal to the number of separate signal elements transmitted in one second. Baud is synonymous with bits per second (bps), as long as each signal element represents exactly one bit.

B channel (bearer channel)   An ISDN term meaning a full-duplex, 64-kbps channel used to send user data.

BECN (Backward Explicit Congestion Notification)   A Frame Relay network facility that allows switches in the network to advise DTE devices of congestion. The BECN bit is set in frames traveling in the opposite direction of frames encountering a congested path.

best-effort delivery   Describes a network system that does not use a system of acknowledgment to guarantee reliable delivery of information.

BGP (Border Gateway Protocol)   An interdomain path-vector routing protocol. BGP exchanges reachability information with other BGP systems. It is defined by RFC 1163.

bgp cluster-id <x> command   The bgp cluster-id command is used to identify the cluster ID when multiple route reflectors are utilized in a cluster. If a single route reflector is used, the router ID is used as the cluster ID. The bgp cluster-id command is configured under the bgp protocol configuration and should only be configured on the Route Reflectors, not the Route Reflector Clients.

bgp default local-preference <value> command   This command will set the Local Preference for all route prefixes advertised through IBGP to all other internal neighbors. The Local Preference attribute will be carried through the entire autonomous system. In order to apply Local Preference with greater granularity, a route-map must be used on a per neighbor basis. It is important to remember that the default local preference is 100.

binary   A numbering system in which there are only two digits, ones and zeros.

BIND (Berkeley Internet Name Domain)   The University of California at Berkeley implementation of DNS, which is run by many Internet hosts.

Black holes   There is nothing worse than an organization that gets a block of addresses, multihomes, uses BGP to advertise its networks, and advertises an aggregate describing networks not in their CIDR blocks. This creates "black holes" in the Internet, which occur when a router would route a packet to your AS, hoping to get to a destination your aggregate routers advertised to it, only to have the packet dropped by your routers because that network really isn't on your network.

BNC connector   Standard connector used to connect coaxial cable to an MAU or line card.

BOOTP (Bootstrap Protocol)   Part of the TCP/IP suite of protocols, used by a network node to determine the IP address of its Ethernet interfaces, in order to boot from a network server.

bps   Bits per second.

BRI (Basic Rate Interface)   ISDN interface consisting of two B channels and one D channel for circuit-switched communication. ISDN BRI can carry voice, video, and data.

bridge   Device that connects and forwards packets between two network segments that use the same data-link communications protocol. Bridges operate at the data link layer of the OSI reference model. A bridge will filter, forward, or flood an incoming frame based on the MAC address of the frame.

broadband   A data transmission system that multiplexes multiple independent signals onto one cable. Also, in telecommunications, any channel with a bandwidth greater than 4 KHz. In LAN terminology, a coaxial cable using analog signaling.

broadcast   Data packet addressed to all nodes on a network. Broadcasts are identified by a broadcast address that matches all addresses on the network.

broadcast address   Special address reserved for sending a message to all stations. At the data-link layer, a broadcast address is a MAC destination address of all 1s.

broadcast domain   The group of all devices that will receive the same broadcast frame originating from any device within the group. Because routers do not forward broadcast frames, broadcast domains are typically bounded by routers.

buffer   A memory storage area used for handling data in transit. Buffers are used in internetworking to compensate for differences in processing speed between network devices or signaling rates of segments. Bursts of packets can be stored in buffers until they can be handled by slower devices.

bus   Common physical path composed of wires or other media, across which signals are sent from one part of a computer to another.

bus topology   A topology used in LANs. Transmissions from network stations propagate the length of the medium and are then received by all other stations.

byte   A series of consecutive binary digits that are operated upon as a unit, usually eight bits.

cable   Transmission medium of copper wire or optical fiber wrapped in a protective cover.

cable range   A range of network numbers on an extended AppleTalk network. The cable range value can be a single network number or a contiguous sequence of several network numbers. Nodes assign addresses within the cable range values provided.

carrier   Electromagnetic wave or alternating current of a single frequency, suitable for modulation by another, data-bearing signal.

Category 5 cabling   One of five grades of UTP cabling described in the EIA/TIA-586 standard. Category 5 cabling can transmit data at speeds up to 100 Mbps.

CCITT (Consultative Committee for International Telegraphy and Telephony)   International organization responsible for the development of communications standards. Now called the ITU-T. *See* ITU-T.

CD (Carrier Detect)   Signal that indicates whether an interface is active.

CDDI (Copper Distributed Data Interface)   The implementation of FDDI protocols over STP and UTP cabling. CDDI transmits over distances of approximately 100 meters, providing data rates of 100 Mbps. CDDI uses a dual-ring architecture to provide redundancy.

cell   The basic data unit for ATM switching and multiplexing. A cell consists of a five-byte header and 48 bytes of payload. Cells contain fields in their headers that identify the data stream to which they belong.

CHAP (Challenge Handshake Authentication Protocol)   Security feature used with PPP encapsulation, which prevents unauthorized access by identifying the remote end. The router or access server determines whether that user is allowed access.

checksum   Method for checking the integrity of transmitted data. A checksum is an integer value computed from a sequence of octets taken through a series of arithmetic operations. The value is recomputed at the receiving end and compared for verification.

CIDR (classless interdomain routing)   Technique supported by BGP4 and based on route aggregation. CIDR allows routers to group routes together in order to cut down on the quantity of routing information carried by the core routers. With CIDR, several IP networks appear to networks outside the group as a single, larger entity. With CIDR, IP addresses and their subnet masks are written as four octets, separated by periods, followed by a forward slash and a two-digit number that represents the subnet mask.

CIR (committed information rate)   The rate at which a Frame Relay network agrees to transfer information under normal conditions, averaged over a minimum increment of time. CIR, measured in bits per second, is one of the key negotiated tariff metrics.

circuit switching   A system in which a dedicated physical path must exist between sender and receiver for the entire duration of a call. Used heavily in telephone networks.

Class A range   The Class A address space uses 8 bits for the network portion, giving us 128 total networks, each having 16,777,214 allowed hosts. Remember, 0 and 127 are reserved, so we really have 126 Class A networks. Within these networks are 24 host bits, which give us 16,777,216 hosts, but each network needs a network number and broadcast address, so, not counting these two addresses, we have 16,777,216 allowed hosts.

Class B range   The Class B address space uses 16 bits of network address space, giving us 16,384 networks, each having 65,534 allowed hosts. A Class B address is smaller than a Class A address, yet you are still allowed quite a large number of hosts. Class B addresses are suitable for medium-sized organizations.

Class C range   The Class C address space uses a 24-bit network address space, giving us 2,097,152 networks, each having 256 allowed hosts. The Class C address is perfect for small businesses and organizations; 2,097,152 networks is a pretty large number, but thinking globally, you can see how this number could be eaten up quickly.

Class D range   Class D addresses' first four bits are 1110, giving us 11100000 through 11100000 (224–239). Class D address space is used for multicast applications.

Class E range   Class E addresses have their first four bits set to 1111, giving us 11110000 through 11111111 (240–255). Class E address space is for experimental use only. You probably won't run into these addresses often.

Classful routing   Classful routing is the process of sending routing updates without advertising the subnet masks as an explicit part of the routing update per network. Classful routing protocols read the starting bit pattern of the IP address to determine its class. The subnet mask is automatically assigned to the IP address based on class standards. This means that a network with an IP address of 10.1.1.0 and a subnet mask of 255.255.255.0 would be advertised as 10.0.0.0 by classful routing protocols. The subnet mask would not be in the routing update.

Classless routing   Classless routing provides routers with the ability to advertise the subnet mask with each network address. This advertisement prevents classless routing protocols from making assumptions about the subnet mask. A Class B network with an IP address of 128.10.32.0 and a subnet mask of 255.255.224.0 would be advertised as 128.10.32.0/19 by classless routing protocols.

Clear ip bgp command   BGP provides sufficient mechanisms to report and recover from problems with neighbors, such as error notifications and automatic resets. There are times, however, when the network engineer needs to intervene directly, and manually reset or clear the neighbor peerings. Cisco provides the clear ip bgp command to do this and more. The purpose of CLEAR IP BGP is to reset a BGP connection. When you reset a BGP connection, you clear entries obtained via that connection, and restart the BGP peering process all over, from neighbor negotiations to routing information exchange (including full table updates).

client   Node or software program, or front-end device, that requests services from a server.

CLNS (Connectionless Network Service)   An OSI network layer service, for which no circuit need be established before data can be transmitted. Routing of messages to their destinations is independent of other messages.

Cluster ID   The cluster ID is a four byte value that is appended to a CLUSTER-LIST by route reflectors. If a cluster contains a single route reflector, the router ID is used as the cluster IDIf multiple route reflectors exist in a cluster, they all share the same CLUSTER-ID which must be manually configured.

CLUSTER-LIST   The CLUSTER-LIST is a BGP attribute that is optional and non transitive. This is a variable length field that identifies the route reflectors this prefix has passed through. The purpose of this attribute is to prevent routing information loops when multiple levels of hierarchy are used for route reflection.

collision   In Ethernet, the result of two nodes transmitting simultaneously. The frames from each device cause an increase in voltage when they meet on the physical media, and are damaged.

COMMUNITY Type Code 8 attribute   COMMUNITY is a variable-length optional nontransitive attribute. A community consists of destinations logically grouped that share a common set of attributes or characteristics. Of particular interest are two well-known communities used to control updates. The NO_EXPORT COMMUNITY (0xFFFFFF01) means that this route should only be advertised within the AS. It should not be advertised to any other AS. The NO_ADVERTISE COMMUNITY (0xFFFFFF02) indicates that the route should not be advertised to any BGP router within the receiving AS. The COMMUNITY attribute is designed to simplify routing policy, and to enhance control over how routes should be handled when passed to another AS.

Complex subnetting Complex subnetting involves using host bits to extend the network portion of the subnet of a given class or IP address space.

congestion Traffic in excess of network capacity.

connectionless Term used to describe data transfer without the prior existence of a circuit.

connectionless communication Connectionless communication occurs when using UDP with IP, which means stations receiving data do not send an acknowledgment back to the sender. The sending station has no way of knowing whether or not the data arrived successfully.

connection-oriented communication Connection-oriented communication occurs when TCP is used with IP to cause receiving stations to send an acknowledgment back to the sender.

console A DTE device, usually consisting of a keyboard and display unit, through which users interact with a host.

contention Access method in which network devices compete for permission to access the physical medium. Compare with **circuit switching** and **token passing**.

Convergence Convergence is the time it takes for a link change to be detected and updated on every router in the internetwork.

Core layer The central backbone of the network. Provides stability and reliability to an internetwork.

Core routing protocol   The core protocol is usually used in the backbone of a corporate infrastructure. Generally speaking, the core routing protocol is where you would redistribute an edge protocol. Core protocols are usually configured with EIGRP, OSPF, and BGP.

cost   A value, typically based on media bandwidth or other measures, that is assigned by a network administrator and used by routing protocols to compare various paths through an internetwork environment. Cost values are used to determine the most favorable path to a particular destination—the lower the cost, the better the path.

count to infinity   A condition in which routers continuously increment the hop count to particular networks. Often occurs in routing algorithms that are slow to converge. Usually, a some arbitrary hop count ceiling is imposed to limit the extent of this problem.

CPE (customer premises equipment)   Terminating equipment, such as terminals, telephones, and modems, installed at customer sites and connected to the telephone company network.

CRC (cyclic redundancy check)   An error-checking technique in which the receiving device performs a calculation on the frame contents and compares the calculated number to a value stored in the frame by the sending node.

CSMA/CD (carrier sense multiple access collision detect)
Media-access mechanism used by Ethernet and IEEE 802.3. Devices use CSMA/CD to check the channel for a carrier before transmitting data. If no carrier is sensed, the device transmits. If two devices transmit at the same time, the collision is detected by all colliding devices. Collisions delay retransmissions from those devices for a randomly chosen length of time.

CSU (channel service unit)   Digital interface device that connects end user equipment to the local digital telephone loop. Often referred to together with DSU, as CSU/DSU.

DACS (Digital Access and Crossconnect System)   A digital crossconnect system (in AT&T terminology).

datagram   Logical unit of information sent as a network layer unit over a transmission medium without prior establishment of a circuit.

data-link layer   Layer 2 of the OSI reference model. This layer provides reliable transit of data across a physical link. The data link layer is concerned with physical addressing, network topology, access to the network medium, error detection, sequential delivery of frames, and flow control. The data link layer is divided into two sublayers: the MAC sublayer and the LLC sublayer.

DCE (data circuit-terminating equipment)   The devices and connections of a communications network that represent the network end of the user-to-network interface. The DCE provides a physical connection to the network and provides a clocking signal used to synchronize transmission between DCE and DTE devices. Modems and interface cards are examples of DCE devices.

D channel   Data channel. Full-duplex, 16-kbps (BRI) or 64-kbps (PRI) ISDN channel.

DD (Database Description) (Type 2) Packet   Database description (DD) packets are sent during the formation of the adjacency. DD packets summarize the contents of the link-state database of the sending router. The exchange of DD packets uses a poll-response model during which one router is the master and the other router is the slave. The master sends DD packets (polls) that are answered by the slave's DD packets (responses). DD sequence numbers link the polls to the responses.

DDR (dial-on-demand routing)   Technique whereby a router can automatically initiate and close a circuit-switched session as transmitting stations demand. The router spoofs keepalives so that end stations treat the session as active. DDR permits routing over ISDN or telephone lines using an external ISDN terminal adapter or modem.

dead timer   The dead timer shows how many seconds will elapse before a router is declared dead.

Debug IP BGP Updates command   When you are experiencing problems with BGP, Cisco provides a comprehensive debug facility that enables you to monitor and analyze BGP events as they occur. When you run debug, the output is sent to your screen; the output can be fast and voluminous, so turn on the text logging feature of what software you are using to connect to the router. BE WARNED! Debug can generate copious amounts of output, and can consume many CPU cycles. Use it sparingly on a production network ONLY to resolve specific problems; be sure you that debug is the correct tool for problem analysis before you use it.

DEBUG IP OSPF ADJ command   When the SHOW commands cannot show you what is happening, you need to use DEBUG. This command shows you what is happening behind the OSPF scenes. There are several DEBUG commands pertaining to OSPF, but we discuss only one, DEBUG IP OSPF ADJ, which shows the events relevant to adjacencies.

DECnet   Group of communications products (including a protocol suite) developed and supported by Digital Equipment Corporation. DECnet/OSI (also called DECnet Phase V) is the most recent iteration and supports both OSI protocols and proprietary Digital protocols. Phase IV Prime supports inherent MAC addresses that allow DECnet nodes to coexist with systems running other protocols that have MAC address restrictions. *See also* **DNA**.

dedicated line   Communications line that is indefinitely reserved for transmissions, rather than switched as transmission is required. *See also* **leased line**.

de facto standard   A standard that exists because of its widespread use.

default route   A default route is a routing table entry used to direct packets when there is no explicit route present in the routing table. Default routes can be static or dynamic. A default route is where all unknown traffic is sent, which is typically a router connected to the Internet. Most routing protocols have the ability to originate and propagate a default route within their AS. You can also enter a static route and use it as a default route. A default route pointing to the router connected to the Internet can be substituted for a full-scale BGP implementation throughout your AS. The only caveat is that you ensure that link to the Internet is reliable and robust; otherwise, traffic could make an unnecessary trip, only to find out the link is down.

de jure standard   Standard that exists because of its development or approval by an official standards body.

delay   The time between the initiation of a transaction by a sender and the first response received by the sender. Also, the time required to move a packet from source to destination over a network path.

demarc   The demarcation point between telephone carrier equipment and CPE.

demultiplexing   The separating of multiple streams of data that have been multiplexed into a common physical signal for transmission, back into multiple output streams. Opposite of multiplexing.

DES (Data Encryption Standard)   U.S. National Bureau of Standards' standard cryptographic algorithm.

destination address   Address of a network device to receive data.

DHCP (Dynamic Host Configuration Protocol)   Provides a mechanism for allocating IP addresses dynamically so that addresses can be reassigned instead of belonging to only one host.

Disabling Automatic Summarization   Disabling Automatic Summarization will display information of all routes regardless of subnet masks. This information could be useful in determining specific routes that could provide information needed for troubleshooting. Although the router would use more memory to hold such a large table without summarization, it could make troubleshooting a route issue in a network a lot easier.

discovery mode   Method by which an AppleTalk router acquires information about an attached network from an operational router and then uses this information to configure its own addressing information.

distance vector routing algorithm   Class of routing algorithms that use the number of hops in a route to find a shortest path to a destination network. Distance vector routing algorithms call for each router to send its entire routing table in each update to each of its neighbors. Also called Bellman-Ford routing algorithm.

Distribution layer   Provides access to services. Most commonly relates to the campus backbone.

DLCI (data-link connection identifier)   A value that specifies a virtual circuit in a Frame Relay network. Also, DLCIs identify Frame Relay circuits. These DLCIs must be mapped to the network address of whatever router is at the distant end.

DLSw+ (data-link switching plus)   Cisco's proprietary implementation of the DLSw standard for SNA and NetBIOS traffic forwarding. DLSw+'s enhancements to DLSw provide increased scalability of data-link switching.

DNA (Digital Network Architecture)   Network architecture that was developed by Digital Equipment Corporation. DECnet is the collective term for the products that comprise DNA (including communications protocols).

DNIC (Data Network Identification Code)   Part of an X.121 address. DNICs are divided into two parts: the first specifying the country in which the addressed PSN is located and the second specifying the PSN itself. *See also* **X.121**.

DNS (Domain Name System)   System used in the Internet for translating names of network nodes into addresses.

DOWN State   The *DOWN state* is the beginning of the neighbor formation. No router has yet exchanged any packets to start the process.

DR (Designated router)   The DR reduces the link-state update (LSU) propagation workload of non-DR (DROTHER) routers by forwarding and tracking acknowledgments.

DSL (digital subscriber line)   Public network technology for delivering high bandwidth over conventional copper wiring at a limited distance. The four types of DSL are ADSL, HDSL, SDSL, and VDSL.

DSP (domain specific part)   Part of an ATM address. A DSP is comprised of an area identifier, a station identifier, and a selector byte.

DSU (data service unit)   Device for adapting the physical interface on a DTE device to a transmission facility such as T1 or E1. DSU also controls functions such as signal timing. The term is most often used with CSU, as *CSU/DSU*.

DTE (data terminal equipment)   Device at the user end of a user-network interface that serves as a data source, destination, or both. DTE connects to a data network through a DCE device (for example, a modem) and typically uses clocking signals generated by the DCE. DTE includes such devices as computers, routers and multiplexers.

DUAL (Diffusing Update Algorithm)   The basic functions of DUAL include loop-avoidance, path selection, and metric calculation among all routers in the network. The word "diffusing" in the name of the algorithm is very appropriate in that these calculations spread across the network in a distributed fashion, allowing each router to arrive at metric values whilst taking into consideration the metric values of its neighbors without recalculating all the paths in its routing table. Also, DUAL is a convergence algorithm used in EIGRP. DUAL provides constant loop-free operation throughout a route computation by allowing routers involved in a topology change to synchronize at the same time, without involving routers that are unaffected by the change.

DVMRP (Distance Vector Multicast Routing Protocol)   DVMRP is an internetwork gateway protocol that implements a typical dense mode IP multicast scheme. Using IGMP, DVMRP exchanges routing datagrams with its neighbors.

dynamic routing   Routing that adjusts automatically to changes in network topology or traffic patterns.

E1   Wide-area digital transmission scheme used in Europe that carries data at a rate of 2.048 Mbps.

E channel (echo channel)   A 64-kbps ISDN circuit-switching control channel. This was dropped from the 1988 ITU-T ISDN specification.

EBGP/eBGP (External BGP) neighbor   Neighbors in other ASs are called External BGP Neighbors (EBGP). EBGP neighbors, by default, must be directly connected to each other. Cisco provides a command called `ebgp_multihop` to compensate for those situations where the EBGP peers cannot be directly connected.

Edge routing protocol   The edge protocol is normally configured with RIP, IGRP, or Static routes. An edge protocol, as well as a core protocol can be any routing protocol. The most common scenarios, however, involve using one of the three defined protocols listed above.

EIA/TIA-232   Common physical layer interface standard, developed by EIA and TIA, that supports unbalanced circuits at signal speeds of up to 64 kbps. Formerly known as RS-232.

EIGRP (Enhanced Interior Gateway Routing Protocol)   EIGRP is Cisco's proprietary hybrid routing protocol that operates at the Internet layer of the DOD model and the Network layer of the OSI model. It combines the advantages of distance-vector and link-state protocols. EIGRP is an enhancement over its predecessor, IGRP, because it sends incremental routing updates instead of the entire routing table. This method uses less network bandwidth than previous distance-vector protocols, making EIGRP more scalable than IGRP and much more scalable than RIP.

EIGRP (Enhanced Interior Gateway Routing Protocol) Manual Summarization   EIGRP allows you to summarize internal and external routes using any bit boundary. Below we will discuss Manual Summarization. Manual summarization will give added control to the way your network routes will be summarized. You can provide summarization to only those subnets in your network that consume a lot of your routing tables. Or, you simply just don't have a need to see the routes detailed in a summary.

encapsulation   The process of attaching a particular protocol header to a unit of data prior to transmission on the network. For example, a frame of Ethernet data is given a specific Ethernet header before network transit.

endpoint   Device at which a virtual circuit or virtual path begins or ends.

enterprise network   A privately maintained network connecting most major points in a company or other organization. Usually spans a large geographic area and supports multiple protocols and services.

entity   Generally, an individual, manageable network device. Sometimes called an alias.

error control   Technique for detecting and correcting errors in data transmissions.

ESF (Extended Superframe)   A T1 framing type consisting of 24 frames of 192 bits each. The 193rd bit provides timing, among other functions.

Ethernet   Baseband LAN specification invented by Xerox Corporation and developed jointly by Xerox, Intel, and Digital Equipment Corporation. Ethernet networks use the CSMA/CD method of media access control and run over a variety of cable types at 10 Mbps. Ethernet is similar to the IEEE 802.3 series of standards.

EtherTalk   Apple Computer's data-link product that allows an AppleTalk network to be connected by Ethernet cable.

explorer packet   Generated by an end station trying to find its way through a SRB network. Gathers a hop-by-hop description of a path through the network by being marked (updated) by each bridge that it traverses, thereby creating a complete topological map.

Exstart state   In the Exstart state, we elect the router that is in charge of the exchange (called the *master*) and which sequence number to start with for the exchange of the database summary.

Exterior gateway   The term *exterior gateway* defines routing protocols that perform routing between multiple autonomous systems. Due to BGP's scalability, it is the routing protocol of choice for the Internet.

External LSA   An autonomous system border router (ASBR) produces *external LSAs*. They advertise routes to destinations outside of the OSPF domain and are flooded to all areas of the network.

External Type 2 LSA   External Type 2 LSAs disregard the cost of the route to the ASBR and only advertise the cost of the external route. This is the default method on Cisco routers and can be changed by the administrator.

Fast Ethernet   Any of a number of 100-Mbps Ethernet specifications. Fast Ethernet offers a speed increase ten times that of the 10BaseT Ethernet specification, while preserving such qualities as frame format, MAC mechanisms, and MTU. Such similarities allow the use of existing 10BaseT applications and network management tools on Fast Ethernet networks. Based on an extension to the IEEE 802.3 specification. Compare with **Ethernet**. *See also* **100BaseFX; 100BaseT; 100BaseT4; 100BaseTX; 100BaseX; IEEE 802.3.**

FDDI (Fiber Distributed Data Interface)   LAN standard, defined by ANSI X3T9.5, specifying a 100-Mbps token-passing network using fiber-optic cable, with transmission distances of up to 2 km. FDDI uses a dual-ring architecture to provide redundancy. Compare with **CDDI.**

Feasible successor   Any neighbor which has an *advertised distance,* which is less than the router's *feasible distance* may become a feasible successor. That is to say, it meets the criteria necessary to possibly be selected as a next-hop router in the path to the destination network.

FECN (Forward Explicit Congestion Notification)   A facility in a Frame Relay network to inform DTE receiving the frame that congestion was experienced in the path from source to destination. DTE receiving frames with the FECN bit set can request that higher-level protocols take flow-control action as appropriate.

file transfer   Category of popular network applications that features movement of files from one network device to another.

filter   Generally, a process or device that screens network traffic for certain characteristics, such as source address, destination address, or protocol, and determines whether to forward or discard that traffic or routes based on the established criteria.

Filtering   *Filtering* allows us to policy route packets based on particular filters that we create for specific scenarios. Filtering primarily deals with controlling route advertisements as they enter a router's interface. The control mechanism primarily used in this capacity is a *distribute list*. You should recall that each route update can be either permitted or denied when it enters a router's interface. If the update is permitted, the advertisement will update the router's route table. If the update is denied, the advertisement is dropped.

firewall   Router or other computer designated as a buffer between public networks and a private network. A firewall router uses access lists and other methods to ensure the security of the private network.

Flash memory   Nonvolatile storage that can be electrically erased and reprogrammed as necessary.

flash update   Routing update sent asynchronously when a change in the network topology occurs.

flat addressing   A system of addressing that does not incorporate a hierarchy to determine location.

flooding   Traffic-passing technique used by switches and bridges in which traffic received on an interface is sent out all of the interfaces of that device except the interface on which the information was originally received.

flow control   Technique for ensuring that a transmitting device, such as a modem, does not overwhelm a receiving device with data. When the buffers on the receiving device are full, a message is sent to the sending device to suspend transmission until it has processed the data in the buffers.

flush timer   Specifies how long a router should wait without receiving a specific route update before flushing the route from the routing table. The default is seven times the update timer.

forwarding   The process of sending a frame or packet toward its destination.

fragment   Piece of a larger packet that has been broken down to smaller units.

fragmentation   Process of breaking a packet into smaller units when transmitting over a network medium that is unable to support a transmission unit the original size of the packet.

frame   Logical grouping of information sent as a data-link layer unit over a transmission medium. Sometimes refers to the header and trailer, used for synchronization and error control, which surround the user data contained in the unit. The terms cell, datagram, message, packet, and segment are also used to describe logical information groupings at various layers of the OSI reference model and in various technology circles.

Frame Relay   Industry-standard, switched data-link layer protocol that handles multiple virtual circuits over a single physical interface. Frame Relay is more efficient than X.25, for which it is generally considered a replacement.

frequency   Number of cycles, measured in hertz, of an alternating current signal per unit of time.

FST (Fast Sequenced Transport)   Cisco's connectionless, sequenced transport protocol, which runs on top of the IP protocol. Encapsulates SRB traffic inside of IP datagrams and passes it over an FST connection between two network devices (such as routers). Advantages of FST include faster data delivery, reduced overhead, and improved response time of SRB traffic.

FTP (File Transfer Protocol)   An application protocol, part of the TCP/IP protocol stack, used for transferring files between hosts on a network.

Full BGP table   This common method involves accepting full Internet routing tables from all of your upstream providers. The resource requirements for this method are significant. At the time this was written, the full Internet routing table was approximately 80,000 routes. This means that any router accepting full Internet routes should have at least 128MB of RAM. Accepting full routes does not require a default route because any destination that exists on the Internet should have a specific entry in the table. This method also provides the most optimal routing of any method for multihoming, because it has the most granularity available, allowing for complex policy to be defined. Policy is often defined on incoming routing updates using the Cisco specific Weight attribute and the RFC defined Local Preference attribute.

full duplex   Capability for simultaneous data transmission and receipt of data between two devices.

full mesh   A network topology in which each network node has either a physical circuit or a virtual circuit connecting it to every other network node.

Full state   This state indicates that a successful router adjacency has been established. To maintain this status, OSPF routers exchange hello packets periodically.

Fully Meshed Networks   When you use a fully meshed network, all routers have a connection to each other. The greatest advantage of a fully meshed network is that there is no single link of failure: should a link fail in a network of N links, there will still be N–1 links to use. In the real world, fully meshed networks can be expensive and difficult to troubleshoot.

Gateway   In the IP community, an older term referring to a routing device. Today, the term router is used to describe devices that perform this function, and gateway refers to a special-purpose device that performs an application layer conversion of information from one protocol stack to another.

GB   Gigabyte. Approximately 1,000,000,000 bytes.

GBps   Gigabytes per second.

Gb   Gigabit. Approximately 1,000,000,000 bits.

Gbps   Gigabits per second.

Gigabit Ethernet   Ethernet technology. Raises the transmission speed in your backbone to 1 Gbps.

GNS (Get Nearest Server)   Request packet sent by a client on an IPX network to locate the nearest active server of a particular type. An IPX network client issues a GNS request to solicit either a direct response from a connected server or a response from a router that tells it where on the internetwork the service can be located. GNS is part of the IPX SAP.

half duplex   Capability for data transmission in only one direction at a time between a sending station and a receiving station.

handshake   Sequence of messages exchanged between two or more network devices to ensure transmission synchronization.

hardware address   *See* MAC address.

HDLC (High-Level Data Link Control)   Bit-oriented synchronous data-link layer protocol developed by ISO and derived from SDLC. HDLC specifies a data encapsulation method for synchronous serial links and includes frame characters and checksums in its headers.

header   Control information placed before data when encapsulating that data for network transmission.

Hello (Type 1) Packets   The EIGRP HELLO packet is sent by each router at regular intervals. These intervals depend on the default HELLO intervals outlined in the previous section, but may also be manually configured. They serve as sort of a heartbeat, allowing all routers within the same media domain to know that there is another EIGRP router alive on the network with which it can share routing information. The HELLO packet is vital both for establishing a neighbor relationship between routers, as well as for determining if a neighbor has died or is no longer available. Remember that if a HELLO packet is not received from a neighbor before its hold-time expires, that neighbor will be declared dead. Hello packets are used to initiate OSPF operations and routing information exchanges with neighboring routers. They also identify each router's settings as far as hello timers and other options are concerned. Hello packets are sent periodically; this is a configurable option, but the default setting set by the OSPF standards is 10 seconds for a multiaccess or point-to-point network.

Hello protocol   Protocol used by OSPF and other routing protocols for establishing and maintaining neighbor relationships.

Hello timer   The hello timer determines how often a router sends hellos to its neighbors.

hierarchical addressing   A scheme of addressing that uses a logical hierarchy to determine location. For example, IP addresses consist of network numbers, subnet numbers, and host numbers, which IP routing algorithms use to route the packet to the appropriate location.

hold-down   State of a routing table entry in which routers will neither advertise the route nor accept advertisements about the route for a specific length of time (known as the hold-down period).

hold-down timer   Specifies the hold-down period. The default is 280, or 10 plus 3 x the update timer.

hop   Term describing the passage of a data packet between two network nodes (for example, between two routers). *See also* **hop count**.

hop count   Routing metric used to measure the distance between a source and a destination. RIP uses hop count as its metric. *See also* **Maximum hop count**.

host   A computer system on a network. Similar to the term node except that host usually implies a computer system, whereas node can refer to any networked system, including routers.

Host entries   Host entries are routing table entries generated by OSPF when it is run over a point-to-multipoint network. They are basically host addresses with a /32 mask (255.255.255.255) that point to a specific neighbor.

host number   Part of an IP address that designates which node is being addressed. Also called a host address.

hub   A term used to describe a device that serves as the center of a star topology network; or, an Ethernet multiport repeater, sometimes referred to as a concentrator.

IBGP/iBGP (Internal BGP) neighbor   BGP speakers in the same AS can become neighbors with the other BGP speakers in the AS. This is called an Internal BGP (IBGP) peer connection, and is used to ensure that all BGP speakers in the same AS have the same BGP database. IBGP neighbors must already be reachable via an IGP route (or static). IBGP peers do not have to be directly connected to each other. IBGP neighbors must be fully meshed with each other because while an IBGP neighbor will propagate any information it receives over its EBGP links, it will not propagate any information it receives over its IBGP links. Also, IBGP neighbor will propagate any information it receives over its IBGP peer connections to its EBGP links. Some alternatives to the full mesh requirement are route reflectors and confederations.

ICMP (Internet Control Message Protocol)   A network layer Internet protocol that provides reports of errors and other information about IP packet processing. ICMP is documented in RFC 792.

IEEE (Institute of Electrical and Electronics Engineers)   A professional organization among whose activities are the development of communications and networking standards. IEEE LAN standards are the most common LAN standards today.

IEEE 802.3   IEEE LAN protocol for the implementation of the physical layer and the MAC sublayer of the data-link layer. IEEE 802.3 uses CSMA/CD access at various speeds over various physical media.

IEEE 802.5   IEEE LAN protocol for the implementation of the physical layer and MAC sublayer of the data-link layer. Similar to Token Ring, IEEE 802.5 uses token passing access over STP cabling.

IETF (Internet Engineering Task Force)   The organization providing standard coordination and specification development for TCP/IP networking.

IGP (Interior Gateway Protocol)   A generic term for an Internet routing protocol used to exchange routing information within an autonomous system. Examples of common Interior IGPs include IGRP, OSPF, and RIP.

IGRP (Interior Gateway Routing Protocol)   IGRP is Cisco's proprietary distance-vector protocol that operates at the Internet layer of the DOD model and the Network layer of the OSI model. IGRP was designed to replace RIP in Cisco internetworks by providing a more scalable routing protocol. IGRP supports a maximum of 255 hops, surpassing the 15-hop limitation of RIP. Another enhancement of IGRP over RIP is the additional routing metrics available to calculate route selection. IGRP metrics consist of bandwidth, delay, reliability, load, and Maximum Transmission Unit (MTU).

Incremental updates   Once neighbor negotiation has completed successfully, BGP peers will initially exchange their entire database. After that, they will perform incremental updates upon any network changes, rather than sending the entire database again. Incremental updates conserve bandwidth and CPU cycles.

INIT state   This means that the new OSPF router is added to the OSPF adjacency table of the listening routers. In the INIT state, the router has sent a hello packet out its OSPF interfaces and is awaiting a response from its neighbor(s). The hello packet is sent to the multicast IP address of 224.0.0.5, which will be received by all OSPF-enabled routers on the network. The sending router puts out its area number, router ID, and source IP address.

interface   A connection between two systems or devices; or in routing terminology, a network connection.

Internal router   These routers have all interfaces located within a single area and only require one link state database.

Internet   Term used to refer to the global internetwork that evolved from the ARPANET, that now connects tens of thousands of networks worldwide.

Internet protocol   Any protocol that is part of the TCP/IP protocol stack. *See* TCP/IP.

internetwork   Collection of networks interconnected by routers and other devices that functions (generally) as a single network.

internetworking   General term used to refer to the industry that has arisen around the problem of connecting networks together. The term may be used to refer to products, procedures, and technologies.

invalid timer   Specifies how long a router should wait without receiving a specific route update before declaring a route invalid. The default is 270, or three times the update timer.

Inverse ARP (Inverse Address Resolution Protocol)   Method of building dynamic address mappings in a Frame Relay network. Allows a device to discover the network address of a device associated with a virtual circuit.

IP (Internet Protocol)   Network layer protocol in the TCP/IP stack offering a connectionless datagram service. IP provides features for addressing, type-of-service specification, fragmentation and reassembly, and security. Documented in RFC 791.

IP address   A 32-bit address assigned to hosts using the TCP/IP suite of protocols. An IP address is written as four octets separated by dots (dotted decimal format). Each address consists of a network number, an optional subnetwork number, and a host number. The network and subnetwork numbers together are used for routing, while the host number is used to address an individual host within the network or subnetwork. A subnet mask is often used with the address to extract network and subnetwork information from the IP address.

IP FORWARD-PROTOCOL command   You can use the IP FORWARD-PROTOCOL {UDP [*PORT*] | ND | SDNS } address to pick and choose what you want forwarded.

IP HELPER-ADDRESS command   The IP HELPER-ADDRESS *ADDRESS* command forwards certain UDP packets to *ADDRESS*.

IP OSPF NETWORK BROADCAST command   Cisco enables you to treat an NBMA network as a broadcast network. This is achieved via the IP OSPF NETWORK BROADCAST interface command. On Frame Relay and X.25 networks, ensure that you have enabled support for broadcasts appropriately enough; otherwise, OSPF multicasts will not function. In order to use this network type, you must ensure that the network is either fully meshed or that all routers on the network have connectivity to each other. Since this is a "broadcast network," the

NEIGHBOR command is not necessary, because setting the network type to broadcast indicates that the network can and will provide broadcast capabilities.

IP OSPF PRIORITY command   The IP OSPF PRIORITY command is an interface command used to influence, and if used in conjunction with a well-thought-out IP addressing scheme for loop-back interfaces, to determine what routers will be the DR and the BDR.

IP ROUTE-CACHE POLICY command   The IP ROUTE-CACHE POLICY command allows policy-based routing to be fast-switched instead of the traditional process-switched method. Policy-based routing must be enabled before the IP ROUTE-CACHE POLICY command can be enabled. The default for this command is disabled. This command can be used with Cisco IOS version 12.0 and later. Furthermore, this command does not support the SET IP DEFAULT NEXT-HOP and SET DEFAULT INTERFACE commands.

IP stack   An IP protocol stack is a group of protocols used to transport data from one location to another. Different combinations of protocols within the stack can provide this function.

IP UNNUMBERED command   The IP UNNUMBERED command is commonly used in point-to-point environments to cut down on IP address usage. For any point-to-point serial link or point-to-point subinterface, IP UNNUMBERED lets you borrow the address of some LAN interface to use as a source address for routing updates and packets from that interface. No network is wasted, and precious address space is conserved. The syntax of IP UNNUMBERED is, in the interface's configuration mode.

IPX (Internetwork Packet Exchange)   NetWare network layer (Layer 3) protocol used for transferring data from servers to workstations. IPX is similar to IP in that it is a connectionless datagram service.

IPXCP (IPX Control Protocol)   The protocol that establishes and configures IPX over PPP.

IPXWAN A protocol that negotiates end-to-end options for new links on startup. When a link comes up, the first IPX packets sent across are IPXWAN packets negotiating the options for the link. When the IPXWAN options have been successfully determined, normal IPX transmission begins, and no more IPXWAN packets are sent. Defined by RFC 1362.

ISDN (Integrated Services Digital Network) Communication protocol, offered by telephone companies, that permits telephone networks to carry data, voice, and other source traffic.

IS-IS (Intermediate System-to-Intermediate System) OSI's link-state hierarchical routing protocol. Intermediate systems (routers) exchange routing information based on a single metric, for the purpose of determining network topology.

ITU-T (International Telecommunication Union Telecommunication Standardization Sector) International body dedicated to the development of worldwide standards for telecommunications technologies. ITU-T is the successor to CCITT.

KB Kilobyte. Approximately 1,000 bytes.

Kb Kilobit. Approximately 1,000 bits.

KBps Kilobytes per second.

Kbps Kilobits per second.

keepalive interval Period of time between keepalive messages sent by a network device.

KEEPALIVE message The KEEPALIVE message is nothing more than the 19-byte header. It is sent between peers at regular intervals to maintain their connection. BGP does not use TCP keepalives to maintain its peer connections. KEEPALIVES cannot be sent more than one a second; instead, they are sent just enough that the Hold Timer will not expire; typically one-third (1/3) of the Hold Timer is sufficient.

LAN (local area network)   High-speed, low-error data network covering a relatively small geographic area. LANs connect workstations, peripherals, terminals, and other devices in a single building or other geographically limited area. LAN standards specify cabling and signaling at the physical and data-link layers of the OSI model. Ethernet, FDDI, and Token Ring are the most widely used LAN technologies.

LANE (LAN emulation)   Technology that allows an ATM network to function as a LAN backbone. In this situation LANE provides multicast and broadcast support, address mapping (MAC-to-ATM), and virtual circuit management.

LAPB (Link Access Procedure, Balanced)   The data-link layer protocol in the X.25 protocol stack. LAPB is a bit-oriented protocol derived from HDLC.

LAPD (Link Access Procedure on the D channel)   ISDN data link layer protocol for the D channel. LAPD was derived from the LAPB protocol and is designed to satisfy the signaling requirements of ISDN basic access. Defined by ITU-T Recommendations Q.920 and Q.921.

latency   The amount of time elapsed between the time a device requests access to a network and the time it is allowed to transmit; or, amount of time between the point at which a device receives a frame and the time that frame is forwarded out the destination port.

LCP (Link Control Protocol)   A protocol used with PPP, which establishes, configures, and tests data-link connections.

leased line   Transmission line reserved by a communications carrier for the private use of a customer. A leased line is a type of dedicated line.

Limited BGP table   The Limited BGP Table with Default routes is a very popular method for multihoming. The resource requirements are less then that of carrying a full table, but greater granularity is available. This method involves having your ISP advertise all of their local networks and usually those of their customers in addition to the default route. This method is also referred to as Partial Routes and requires configuration on the ISP side to implement.

link   Network communications channel consisting of a circuit or transmission path and all related equipment between a sender and a receiver. Most often used to refer to a WAN connection. Sometimes called a line or a transmission link.

link-state routing algorithm   Routing algorithm in which each router broadcasts or multicasts information regarding the cost of reaching each of its neighbors to all nodes in the internetwork. Link state algorithms require that routers maintain a consistent view of the network and are therefore not prone to routing loops.

LLC (Logical Link Control)   Higher of two data-link layer sublayers defined by the IEEE. The LLC sublayer handles error control, flow control, framing, and MAC-sublayer addressing. The most common LLC protocol is IEEE 802.2, which includes both connectionless and connection-oriented types.

LMI (Local Management Interface)   A set of enhancements to the basic Frame Relay specification. LMI includes support for keepalives, a multicast mechanism; global addressing, and a status mechanism.

load balancing   In routing, the ability of a router to distribute traffic over all its network ports that are the same distance from the destination address. Load balancing increases the utilization of network segments, thus increasing total effective network bandwidth.

local loop   A line from the premises of a telephone subscriber to the telephone company central office.

Local_Pref Attribute   BGP 4 also added the Local_Pref attribute, which facilitates the selection of routes for the BGP routing table. A BGP router generates Local_Pref for its internal peers; it tells the peers the degree of preference for external routes (routes outside the AS). Prior to this, a BGP router did not have a simple way to pass this information along.

LOCAL_PREF Type Code 5 attribute   Local preference is a mandatory discretionary attribute that is included in all UPDATE messages that BGP speakers sends to all BGP speakers in its own AS. It will NOT be sent to EBGP peer. This attribute is restricted to the AS of the BGP router.

LocalTalk   Apple Computer's proprietary baseband protocol that operates at the data link and physical layers of the OSI reference model. LocalTalk uses CSMA/CA and supports transmissions at speeds of 230.4 Kbps.

Logical interface   A *logical interface* is a logical division of the physical Frame Relay interface into one or more virtual interfaces, such as dividing serial 0 into serial 0.1, serial 0.2, and so on. Logical interfaces can be configured as though they were actually physical interfaces.

Longest Match Rule   Route lookups are matched from the *longest math rule*, which means that the router will find the route that most closely matches the destination's bit count. For example, if a packet came in destined to 10.1.4.4, the router would match it to the route learned via Ethernet0 because it matches the first 26 bits with 10.1.4.0. On the other hand, if a packet came in destined to 10.1.5.2, the router would match it up with the route learned via Serial2 because it doesn't match the first 26 bits with 10.1.4.0, but it does match the first 16 bits of 10.1.0.0. If a packet came in destined for 10.2.2.2, it would be matched to the route on Serial0 because it doesn't match the first 26 or 16 bits of the other two routes, but it does match the first 8 bits of 10.0.0.0. This rule needs to be kept in mind when you are designing subnetted networks.

loop   A situation in which packets never reach their destination, but are forwarded in a cycle repeatedly through a group of network nodes.

Loop-back interfaces   Loop-back interfaces can introduce some measure of stability in OSPF operations, but they involve some tradeoffs. For starters, you must assign at least a /32 IP address to a loop-back interface (that is, an IP address with a 255.255.255.255 mask).

LSA (Link-state advertisement)   OSPF routers send routing updates with the use of *link-state advertisements*, or *LSAs*. LSAs contain a list of active links and are sent to neighboring routers.

LSP (Link-state packet)   Link-state protocols send *link-state packets (LSPs)* to other routers to inform them about the state of their links. This allows routers running link-state protocols to compile all of the LSPs received to create a complete topology map of the entire internetwork.

LSR (Link-State Request) (Type 3) Packets   Link-state request (LSR) packets are sent after a successful exchange of DD packets. After receiving another router's DD packets, the receiving router analyzes the contents of the DD packets and compares them to its link-state database. If there are unknown OSPF routers or updated database entries described by the DD packets it has received, the router generates LSR packets to request this new information. In other words, the router uses the DD packets to determine whether its information is out of date, and if it is, it sends the LSR packets necessary to bring itself up to date.

LSU (Link-State Update) (Type 4) Packets   Link-state update (LSU) packets are the "delivery boys" of OPSF. LSUs deliver link-state advertisements (LSAs) to the OSPF routers on the network. LSAs are the sections of the LSU containing the actual link information (the routing information).

MAC (Media Access Control)   Lower of the two sublayers of the data link layer defined by the IEEE. The MAC sublayer handles access to shared media.

MAC (Media Access Control) address   Standardized data-link layer address that is required for every port or device that connects to a LAN. Other devices in the network use these addresses to locate specific ports in the network and to create and update routing tables and data structures. MAC addresses are 48 bits long and are controlled by the IEEE. Also known as a hardware address, a MAC-layer address, or a physical address.

MAN (metropolitan-area network)   A network that spans a metropolitan area. Generally, a MAN spans a larger geographic area than a LAN, but a smaller geographic area than a WAN.

MATCH {CONDITION} command   The MATCH command, when used with policy routing, has two options: we can either match the IP address that corresponds to the access list we created, or we can match the level 3 length of the packet. You will most likely use the first option the majority of the time.

Maximum hop count   One method that distance-vector routing protocols use to manage routing loops is a maximum hop count. What this means for RIP is that a packet that has reached more than 15 hops in a routing loop will cause the router to mark the destination network as down in its routing table. This does not prevent a routing loop from occurring. It does, however, prevent a routing loop from continuing into infinity.

Mb   Megabit. Approximately 1,000,000 bits.

Mbps   Megabits per second.

media   The various physical environments through which transmission signals pass. Common network media include cable (twisted-pair, coaxial, and fiber optic) and the atmosphere (through which microwave, laser, and infrared transmission occurs). Sometimes referred to as physical media.

Mesh   Network topology in which devices are organized in a segmented manner with redundant interconnections strategically placed between network nodes. Mesh also refers to the amount of connectivity between all routers on a network. A network topology can be likened to a template for meshing.

message   Application layer logical grouping of information, often composed of a number of lower-layer logical groupings such as packets.

metric   Indicates the number of routers, or hops, that have to be crossed through this advertising router on the way to the destination; 16 indicates that the destination was unreachable.

MSAU (multistation access unit)   A wiring concentrator to which all end stations in a Token Ring network connect. Sometimes abbreviated MAU.

MTU (maximum transmission unit)   Maximum packet size that a given interface can handle; expressed in bytes.

MULTI_EXIT_DISC (MED)   MULTI_EXIT_DISC (MED) provides hints to external neighbors about the entry and exit points of the AS. This is an attempt of one AS to influence the decision of another AS: the AS receiving the MED is not required to factor it into its routing decisions. The MED is exchanged between ASs, and when it enters an AS, it does not get propagated out of that AS: it is a one-shot arrangement from one AS to another.

MULTI_EXIT_DISC Type Code 4 attribute   The multi_exit_discriminator (MED) is an optional nontransitive attribute that provides a hint to the receiving EBGP router what route it should take to reach the destination. It is exchanged between ASs, but does not leave the AS that it enters. It is used to make a decision within the AS that it enters. When passed to another AS, the MED, since it is nontransitive is reset to 0.

multiaccess network   A network that allows multiple devices to connect and communicate by sharing the same medium, such as a LAN.

multicast   A single packet copied by the network and sent to a specific subset of network addresses. These addresses are specified in the Destination Address field.

multicast address   A single address that refers to multiple network devices. Sometimes called a group address.

multiplexing   A technique that allows multiple logical signals to be transmitted simultaneously across a single physical channel.

Mutual redistribution   When two protocols are set up to redistribute their known routes to each other, the process is called mutual redistribution. Special consideration must be given to a router configured to mutually redistribute two protocols.

mux   A multiplexing device. A mux combines multiple input signals for transmission over a single line. The signals are demultiplexed, or separated, before they are used at the receiving end.

NAK (Negative acknowledgment)   A response sent from a receiving device to a sending device indicating that the information received contained errors.

name resolution   The process of associating a symbolic name with a network location or address.

NAT (Network Address Translation)   A technique for reducing the need for globally unique IP addresses. NAT allows an organization with addresses may conflict with others in the IP address space, to connect to the Internet by translating those addresses into unique ones within the globally routable address space.

NAU (network addressable unit)   An addressable entity that provides upper-level network services. Examples of NAUs include LUs, PUs, and SSCPs.

NBMA (nonbroadcast multiaccess)   Term describing a multiaccess network that either does not support broadcasting (such as X.25) or in which broadcasting is not feasible.

NBP (Name Binding Protocol)   AppleTalk transport level protocol that translates a character string name into the DDP address of the corresponding socket client.

NCP (Network Control Protocol)   Protocols that establish and configure various network layer protocols. Used for AppleTalk over PPP.

NEIGHBOR command   The NEIGHBOR command was developed for use on networks lacking broadcast and multicast capabilities. Prior to IOS version 12.0, this command could be used only on NBMA networks. With version 12.0 or later, it can be used on NBMA and point-to-multipoint networks. It should not be used or required on a point-to-point or broadcast network (such as an Ethernet). The NEIGHBOR command can also be used to set the priority (not applicable to point-to-multipoint interfaces), the poll interval (which should be larger than the hello interval; not applicable to point-to-multipoint networks), and cost (applicable to point to-multipoint networks; not applicable to NBMA networks).

Neighbor database   This database lists and details the neighbors of this router. The SHOW IP OSPF NEIGHBOR command can view it. This table keeps information on the neighbor's router ID, priority, state, dead time, address, and the interface through which this router connects to the neighbor.

Neighbor table   Stores information about other EIGRP neighbor routers. In addition the neighbor table is a router configured for EIGRP maintains a table of neighbors with which it is exchanging routing information. This table also includes other details such as on which interface or interfaces the neighbor is seen, hold timers, the address of that neighbor, time of activity, and update sequence numbers. The neighbor table can be viewed using the **show ip eigrp neighbors** EXEC command.

NetBIOS (Network Basic Input/Output System)   An application programming interface used by applications on an IBM LAN to request services from lower-level network processes such as session establishment and termination, and information transfer.

NetWare   A network operating system developed by Novell, Inc. Provides remote file access, print services, and numerous other distributed network services.

network   Collection of computers, printers, routers, switches, and other devices that are able to communicate with each other over some transmission medium.

Network command   The network command is used to specifically define prefixes to inject into the BGP process. The network command allows you to specific a network and optionally a network mask. There must be a route in the IGP that matches the network and mask exactly for that prefix to be injected into BGP. Routes that are injected into BGP using the network command have their ORIGIN attribute set to IGP.

network interface   Border between a carrier network and a privately owned installation.

network layer   Layer 3 of the OSI reference model. This layer provides connectivity and path selection between two end systems. The network layer is the layer at which routing takes place.

Network LSAs   The most important information you should understand and remember about network LSAs is that they are generated by a DR for broadcast and NBMA networks. Given the nature of these types of networks, it will come as no surprise that network LSAs are generated by the DR of that particular network.

Network Summary LSA   Type 3 LSAs are produced by ABRs and advertise destinations outside of the local area. When flooded to an attached area, they tell that area all the destinations it can reach within the OSPF domain. When flooded to the backbone, a *network summary LSA* contains all networks that are attached to the ABR.

Network topology   Network topology is the logical or physical structure of the network on which OSPF is running; that is, it is the geometry of the network.

Network type   Network type is simply how OSPF identifies the network on which it is running. The type does not necessarily have to match the underlying network topology or technology.

NEXT_HOP Type Code 3 attribute   NEXT_HOP is a well-known mandatory attribute that identifies the border router (by IP address) that is the next hop to the destination listed in the UPDATE message. What gets identified as the "border router" will depend on what router is receiving the UPDATE message. An IBGP router receiving the UPDATE message will see its IBGP peer as the next hop, rather than the EBGP router that actually originated. An EBGP router receiving the

UPDATE message from an EBGP peer will see that EBGP peer as the next hop. An IBGP router receiving the update from an IBGP peer will see the EBGP that originated the message. A peer should never advertise back to its peer the route it learned from its peer with its peer as the next hop. On multi-access networks, with the peers on the same subnet, the NEXT_HOP will be passed along unaltered, regardless of whether the network is broadcast or nonbroadcast. On NBMA networks running in point to multipoint, the spoke router will be responsible for disseminating the next hop information, with its IBGP peer that it learned the route from as the next hop, or passing the EBGP peer along as the next hop.

Nexterior   The number of networks outside the autonomous system (AS).

NFS (Network File System)   A UNIX networking protocol which controls sharing of files and printers.

Ninterior   The number of subnets in local network.

NLSP (NetWare Link Services Protocol)   Link-state routing protocol for IPX based on IS-IS.

NNI (Network-to-Network Interface)   The interface between two ATM switches that are both located in a private network or are both located in a public network, as defined by the ATM Forum standard. (The interface between a public switch and private switch is defined by the UNI standard.) NNI is the standard interface between two Frame Relay switches meeting the same criteria.

NO IP FORWARD-PROTOCOL command   We can use the NO IP FORWARD-PROTOCOL command to specify that something should *not* be broadcast; otherwise, the eight protocols are always forwarded when we specify a helper address.

node   Endpoint of a network connection or a junction common to two or more lines in a network. Nodes can be processors, controllers, or workstations. Nodes, which vary in their functional capabilities, can be interconnected by links, and serve as control points in the network.

Nonclient peer   A nonclient peer is any BGP speaker, which is a part of the IBGP network, that is not a route reflector client. This would include route reflectors and regular IBGP peers that are fully meshed with the route reflectors.

No-summary modifier   The no-summary modifier at the end of a stub command turns a stub area into a totally stubby area. This command is only needed at the ABR since it does not affect the hello packet like the stub command.

NOTIFICATION message   NOTIFICATION messages are sent immediately upon an error, and the peer connection is terminated after sending it. The ability to decipher the error codes contained in NOTIFICATIONS messages can expedite troubleshooting, and aid in resolving problems with BGP. It has the same fixed 19-byte header that the other messages have, and its minimum length it 21 bytes.

Nsystem   Number of networks within the autonomous system (AS).

NVRAM (nonvolatile RAM)   RAM that retains its contents when a device is powered off.

ones density   CSU/DSU's scheme to recover data clock reliably, for which it uses the data passing through. In order to recover the clock, the CSU/DSU hardware has to receive at least one 1-bit value for every eight bits of data that pass through it.

opcode   Indicates the message type: 1 = Update message, 2 = Request message.

OPEN message   Each side sends an OPEN message after the TCP connection is established between the peers. A KEEPALIVE is sent if the OPEN message is deemed acceptable. The OPEN message starts and completes the neighbor negotiations. The minimum length of an OPEN Message is 29 bytes.

ORIGIN Type Code I attribute   ORIGIN is a well-known mandatory attribute. It is generated by the AS that originated the route(s) in the UPDATE message. The ORIGIN information is propagated to BGP speakers.

ORIGINATOR-ID The ORIGINATOR-ID is a BGP attribute that is optional and nontransitive. This is a four byte value that is used to identify the BGP speaker that originated the prefix. The route reflector applies the ORIGINATOR-ID to prefixes it receives from its route reflector clients. The value the route reflector uses is the router ID of the client that advertised the prefix.

OSI reference model (Open System Interconnection reference model) A network architectural framework developed by ISO and ITU-T. The model describes seven layers, each of which specifies a particular network. The lowest layer, called the physical layer, is closest to the media technology. The highest layer, the application layer, is closest to the user. The OSI reference model is widely used as a way of understanding network functionality.

OSPF (Open Shortest Path First) A link-state, hierarchical IGP routing algorithm, which includes features such as least-cost routing, multipath routing, and load balancing. OSPF was based on an early version of the IS-IS protocol.

OSPF (Open Shortest Path First) Virtual Link A virtual link allows an area that is not connected to the backbone to communicate with the rest of the network.

out-of-band signaling Transmission using frequencies or channels outside the frequencies or channels used for transfer of normal data. Out-of-band signaling is often used for error reporting when normal channels are unusable for communicating with network devices.

packet Logical grouping of information that includes a header containing control information and (usually) user data. Packets are most often used to refer to network layer units of data. The terms datagram, frame, message, and segment are also used to describe logical information groupings at various layers of the OSI reference model, and in various technology circles. *See also* **PDU**.

PAM (pulse amplitude modulation) Modulation scheme by which the modulating wave is caused to modulate the amplitude of a pulse stream.

PAP   Password Authentication Protocol. Authentication protocol that allows PPP peers to authenticate one another. The remote router attempting to connect to the local router is required to send an authentication request. Unlike CHAP, PAP passes the password and host name or username in the clear (unencrypted). PAP does not itself prevent unauthorized access, but merely identifies the remote end. The router or access server then determines if that user is allowed access. PAP is supported only on PPP lines.

partial mesh   Term describing a network in which devices are organized in a mesh topology, with some network nodes organized in a full mesh, but with others that are only connected to one or two other nodes in the network. A partial mesh does not provide the level of redundancy of a full mesh topology, but is less expensive to implement. Partial mesh topologies are generally used in the peripheral networks that connect to a fully meshed backbone. *See also* **full mesh**; **mesh**.

Partially meshed networks   Partially meshed networks have some routers that have links to some of the other routers in the network.

Passive interface   A passive interface will listen for and receive routing advertisements on a designated interface for a particular routing protocol but will not advertise routing advertisement out of that same interface.

Passive interface command   A passive interface is a great tool to help ensure you do not advertise route updates out an interface for a particular protocol. We use the passive interface command to stop RIP from advertising the same routes out of interface serial 0 that OSPF is already advertising for RIP (remember that we are redistributing the two RIP advertisements via OSPF and OSPF is advertising the updates out interface serial 0). RIP can still learn updates that come in through interface serial 0 but simply will not attempt to advertise out of that same interface.

Path vector   Path vector means that the routing protocol does not route link by link (or hop by hop). Instead, it routes AS by AS.

PCM (pulse code modulation)   Analog information transmitted in digital form by sampling and then encoding the samples with a fixed number of bits.

PDU (protocol data unit)   The OSI term for a packet.

Peering   Peering is the act of forming a relationship with another BGP speaker, either in the same AS system, or in an external AS. Until they peer (that is, become neighbors), BGP routers will not become neighbors, and will not exchange routing updates.

Physical interface   A *physical interface* is an interface, such as a serial interface, that actually exists on the router.

physical layer   Layer 1 of the OSI reference model; it corresponds with the physical control layer in the SNA model. The physical layer defines the specifications for activating, maintaining, and deactivating the physical link between end systems.

Ping (packet internet groper)   ICMP echo message and its reply. Often used in IP networks to test the reachability of a network device.

Point-to-multipoint circuit   A point-to-multipoint circuit consists of a link between a core router and two or more other routers. It is the design that works best with partially meshed NBMA networks. At least one router (the hub) in this configuration must have either physical or logical connectivity to all other routers (the spokes). This configuration is sometimes referred to as the hub-and-spoke topology. In a point-to-multipoint configuration, no DR/BDR is elected; the links are treated as a collection of point-to-point circuits.

POINT-TO-MULTIPOINT NONBROADCAST command   The POINT-TO-MULTIPOINT NONBROADCAST command is also recommended for situations in which you do not or cannot have either a fully meshed topology or connectivity between all routers—in other words, when you have a point-to-multipoint network that does not provide any type of broadcast support.

POINT-TO-POINT command   NBMA networks can be configured as point-to-point networks using a combination of Frame Relay (for example) and OSPF commands. The command IP OPSF NETWORK POINT-TO-POINT tells

OPSF that the underlying NBMA is a point-to-point network. OSPF will then act accordingly: no DR is elected, and the two routers on the network will become neighbors (and adjacent). Frame Relay or X.25 mappings must be done accordingly to match what you actually have.

Point-to-Point configuration   Point-to-Point configuration allows for more control over virtual circuits. Interfaces can be divided into subinterfaces, thus allowing bandwidth to be configured separately for each virtual circuit. Each interface should have the bandwidth configured with a value no greater than the actual available bandwidth. If the interface is oversubscribed, bandwidth must be divided among the subinterfaces not to exceed the overall bandwidth associated with the interface.

Poison reverse updates   Routing updates that explicitly indicate that a network or subnet is unreachable, rather than implying that a network is unreachable by not including it in updates. Poison reverse updates are sent to defeat large routing loops.

Policy routing   Policy routing is nothing more than routing in or out of an interface, following particular rules. If you are required to influence the path of specific packets at the interface level, you need to consider using a policy route.

Policy-based routing   Policy-based routing allows an administrator to manipulate a router's incoming packets based on the packet's source address. Like distribute lists and route maps (the latter of which is discussed later in this chapter), policy routes use access lists to define which incoming packets will be affected by the policy statement. Those packets that do not match the access list criteria referenced by the policy route match statements are routed normally.

port   1. Interface on an internetworking device (such as a router). 2. In IP terminology, an upper-layer process that receives information from lower layers. Ports are numbered, and each numbered port is associated with a specific process. For example, SMTP is associated with port 25. A port number is also known as a well-known address. 3. To rewrite software or microcode so that it will run on a different hardware platform or in a different software environment than that for which it was originally designed.

PPP (Point-to-Point Protocol)   A successor to SLIP that provides router-to-router and host-to-network connections over synchronous and asynchronous circuits. Whereas SLIP was designed to work with IP, PPP was designed to work with several network layer protocols, such as IP, IPX, and ARA. PPP also has built-in security mechanisms, such as CHAP and PAP. PPP relies on two protocols: LCP and NCP. *See also* **CHAP; LCP; NCP; PAP; SLIP.**

Prefix lists   A prefix list is a feature that provides route prefix filtering capabilities. This feature was introduced into Cisco IOS in 11.1CC, 11.3, and is in 12.0 and later IOS code. This feature is only to filter routing updates and is not supported for filtering data packets. Prefix lists can be used with BGP to filter routing information inbound and outbound and also for distribute-lists with distance vector IGPs (RIP/IGRP/EIGRP).

presentation layer   Layer 6 of the OSI reference model. This layer ensures that information sent by the application layer of one system will be readable by the application layer of another. The presentation layer is also concerned with the data structures used by programs and therefore negotiates data transfer syntax for the application layer.

PRI (Primary Rate Interface)   ISDN interface to primary rate access. Primary rate access consists of a single 64-kbps D channel plus 23 (T1) or 30 (E1) B channels for voice or data. Compare to **BRI.**

protocol   Formal description of a set of rules and conventions that govern how devices on a network exchange information.

protocol stack   Set of related communications protocols that operate together and, as a group, address communication at some or all of the seven layers of the OSI reference model. Not every protocol stack covers each layer of the model, and often a single protocol in the stack will address a number of layers at once. TCP/IP is a typical protocol stack.

proxy ARP (proxy Address Resolution Protocol)   Variation of the ARP protocol in which an intermediate device (for example, a router) sends an ARP response on behalf of an end node to the requesting host. Proxy ARP can lessen bandwidth use on slow-speed WAN links. *See also* **ARP**.

PVC (Permanent Virtual Circuit)   Permanently established virtual circuits save bandwidth in situations where certain virtual circuits must exist all the time, such as during circuit establishment and tear down.

query   Message used to inquire about the value of some variable or set of variables.

queue   A backlog of packets stored in buffers and waiting to be forwarded over a router interface.

Queuing   *Queuing* helps control packets based on quality of service parameters. Queuing with regard to policy routing covers the area of *quality of service*. This topic revolves around setting the IP precedence bit to allow certain packets precedence over others. The precedence bit can be set if policy routing is enabled, but the router ignores the precedence bit if queuing is not enabled.

Query packets   The Query packet is used by the DUAL algorithm to manage diffusing metric calculations. Remember that EIGRP uses a topology table in which it maintains a listing of successors, feasible distance, and the feasible successor to the destination network. If the successor becomes unavailable, EIGRP then looks in the topology table for an alternative feasible successor. If none are available, the router will send a Query to attempt to find a path to the destination.

RADIUS (Remote Authentication Dial-In User Service)   A database used to authenticate modem and ISDN connections and to track connection time.

RAM   Random-access memory. Volatile memory that can be read and written by a computer.

RARP (Reverse ARP)   A TCP/IP protocol to allow a workstation to get its IP address.

reassembly   The putting back together of an IP datagram at the destination after it has been fragmented either at the source or at an intermediate node. *See also* **fragmentation.**

Redistribution   Redistribution is the process of advertising the routes learned by one routing protocol or process to another routing protocol or process. Normally, different routing protocols do not exchange route advertisements, even when the protocols are configured on the same router. Redistribution is essential in situations such as when merging an existing company with a newly acquired business and each company can not change their working routing protocol. Redistribution is a very powerful tool and should be used with careful consideration.

Reliable updates   BGP neighbors communicate over TCP port 179. TCP, a reliable transport layer protocol, is responsible for segmenting, reassembly, error detection, and error correction. BGP relies upon TCP to ensure the data arrive at its destination.

Reload   The event of a Cisco router rebooting, or the command that causes the router to reboot.

Reply packets   When a router sends a Query packet, in an attempt to find a path to a given destination, the other routers with which there is a neighbor relationship will send a reply packet indicating their route information for the queried path. Reply packets are always unicast, and use reliable delivery.

RFC (Request For Comments)   Document series used as the primary means for communicating information about the Internet. Some RFCs are designated by the IAB as Internet standards.

ring   Connection of two or more stations in a logically circular topology. Information is passed sequentially between active stations. Token Ring, FDDI, and CDDI are based on this topology.

ring topology   Network topology that consists of a series of repeaters connected to one another by unidirectional transmission links to form a single closed loop. Each station on the network connects to the network at a repeater.

RIP (Routing Information Protocol)   A routing protocol for TCP/IP networks. The most common routing protocol in the Internet. RIP uses hop count as a routing metric.

ROM (read-only memory)   Nonvolatile memory that can be read, but not written, by the computer.

root bridge   In a spanning-tree implementation, notifies all other bridges in a network when topology changes are required, by exchanging topology information with designated bridges. Prevents loops and defends against link failure.

Route feedback   Route feedback typically occurs at the point where the route is originally redistributed. Say, for instance, we redistribute a route from OSPF into RIP. Without the use of a passive interface, RIP will, after propagating the routes through the RIP routers, try to pass that same route back to the originating OSPF router. That is why it is called route feedback. The route is fed back to its originator. The majority of route feedback occurs on a router during mutual redistribution. Route feedback can happen in scenarios where a loop exists (for example BGP routing between two routers while both routers are also routing to two separate routers, all of which are communicating via an IGP).

Route maps   A *route map* is the primary tool used to manipulate traffic path selection. A route map is set with the policy route to define the actions taken when a packet or packets match your defined IP address definitions. The route map is where you define your *set* and *match* definitions that will influence the path your interfaces inbound or outbound packets might or might not follow.

Route reflectors   The route reflectors designate certain routers to act as reflectors and have the rest of the routers act as clients. The reflectors are all connected in a full mesh, with each client peering to one or more route reflector.

The reflector is responsible for receiving the update from the client and 'reflecting' it out to all its other clients and the other reflectors.

Route summarization   Route summarization is a method of advertising a block of networks as a single network address and mask. For example, if you had the Class A network 10.0.0.0 using a subnet mask of 255.255.255.0, a person could advertise 10.0.0.0/8 to routers in other networks, summarizing a large number of networks into a single route advertisement.

Route table   Stores the best routes from the topology table.

routed protocol   Protocol that carries user data so it can be routed by a router. A router must be able to interpret the logical internetwork as specified by that routed protocol. Examples of routed protocols include AppleTalk, DECnet, and IP.

router   Network layer device that uses one or more metrics to determine the optimal path along which network traffic should be forwarded. Routers forward packets from one network to another based on network layer information.

Route filtering   Route filtering is one method available to filter unwanted route advertisements from either entering or leaving a router. Each distribute-list is defined under the route process that requires filtering. The filtered network advertisements are defined in an access list that is then defined to the distribute-list.

Router LSA   Router LSAs are generated by each router in an area for each interface (also called a *link*) participating in the OSPF routing process. This LSA describes the state (up or down) and cost of each of the router's interfaces to an area. *All* of the router's links must be described in a single router LSA.

routing   Process of finding a path to a destination host.

routing loops   Routing loops occur because routers on an internetwork are not updated at close to the same time. This causes routers to send outdated route information as though the information were new.

routing metric   Method by which a routing algorithm determines preferability of one route over another. This information is stored in routing tables. Metrics include bandwidth, communication cost, delay, hop count, load, MTU, path cost, and reliability. Sometimes referred to simply as a metric.

routing protocol   Protocol that accomplishes routing through the implementation of a specific routing algorithm. Examples of routing protocols include IGRP, OSPF, and RIP.

routing table   Table stored in a router or some other internetworking device that keeps track of routes to particular network destinations and, in some cases, metrics associated with those routes.

Routing table entries   The routing table contains the actual routing entries. To view the entire routing table, use the SHOW IP ROUTE command. To view those routes learned specifically via OSPF, use the SHOW IP ROUTE OSPF command. OSPF routes are classified as intra-area, inter-area, or external area.

routing update   Message sent from a router to indicate network reachability and associated cost information. Routing updates are typically sent at regular intervals and after a change in network topology. Compare with **flash update**.

RSRB (remote source-route bridging)   Equivalent to an SRB over WAN links.

SAP (service access point)   1. Field defined by the IEEE 802.2 specification that is part of an address specification. Thus, the destination plus the DSAP define the recipient of a packet. The same applies to the SSAP. 2. Service Advertising Protocol. IPX protocol that provides a means of informing network routers and servers of the location of available network resources and services.

Seed metric   Each protocol uses its own defined metric for path selection. The lower the metric, the more preferred the path. When one protocol is redistributed into another protocol, the redistributed protocol's metric must be interpreted. The *seed metric* is the value that RIP understands and uses as the metric for EIGRP.

segment   1. Section of a network that is bounded by bridges, routers, or switches. 2. In a LAN using a bus topology, a segment is a continuous electrical circuit that is often connected to other such segments with repeaters. 3. Term used in the TCP specification to describe a single transport layer unit of information.

serial transmission   Method of data transmission in which the bits of a data character are transmitted sequentially over a single channel.

session   1. Related set of communications transactions between two or more network devices. 2. In SNA, a logical connection that enables two NAUs to communicate.

session layer   Layer 5 of the OSI reference model. This layer establishes, manages, and terminates sessions between applications and manages data exchange between presentation layer entities. Corresponds to the data flow control layer of the SNA model. *See also* **application layer; data-link layer; network layer; physical layer; presentation layer; transport layer.**

SET {ACTION} command   The SET commands, with regard to policy routing, control the action that the router will take if the packet matches our definition specified in the access list. Simply stated, if the packet is "matched" by our policy route statement, the packet is forced to do something.

SET DEFAULT INTERFACE command   The SET DEFAULT INTERFACE command is very similar to the SET DEFAULT NEXT-HOP command in that any packet that matches the policy route statement is forced to use a specific interface as its default gateway. The packet must not have a valid, routable path defined in the route table for this command to function properly. The default gateway that the packet is forced to use is defined by an interface instead of an IP address.

SET INTERFACE command   The SET INTERFACE command is much like the SET IP NEXT-HOP command in that the command forces a packet to follow an administratively determined pathway. The difference between the two commands is that the SET INTERFACE command specifies an interface instead of an IP address.

SET IP DEFAULT NEXT-HOP command   The SET IP DEFAULT NEXT-HOP command is useful for setting a default next-hop IP address for packets that meet the requirements specified in the policy route statement and have no path in the route table to its destination. In other words, if the packet matches the policy route statement, this command presents the packet's default next-hop IP address. You might already have one default route configured on the router. This command allows you to create a second default route only for specified source addressed packets.

SET IP NEXT-HOP command   The first SET command we will look at is the SET IP NEXT-HOP command. This command forces the packet to our defined next-hop IP address if the packet matches the specific source address in our policy route statement. The next-hop address specified by this command must be reachable and must possess a valid route.

Show IP bgp Neighbors command   The show ip bgp neighbors command displays very detailed information about a particular neighbor. You can focus the output of this command by using the argument shown below. This command will show how many connections have been established, any routes or filtering being performed, and the number of messages that have been exchanged with this neighbor.

Show IP bgp Summary command   Cisco provides a way to view snapshot statistics on all of a router's connections to its neighbor via the show ip bgp summary command. This command shows how many messages have been exchanged with a particular neighbor, and how long the peer connection has been up. It also shows the state of the connection.

Show IP OSPF Border-routers command   This command displays the internal routes to area border routers and autonomous system boundary routers.

SHOW IP OSPF command   The SHOW IP OSPF command shows what OSPF processes are running on this router, what areas this router is in, and how many interfaces are in this area. It also identifies whether the area has any authentication and how many times per area the SPF has been run.

Show IP OSPF Database command   This command displays the contents of the link-state database. It is useful in monitoring proper LSA propagation and troubleshooting DR issues. For example, the Net Link States section may be used to verify the router is receiving updates from the designated router. This command may also use variables to filter the output to just one type of LSA.

SHOW IP OSPF INTERFACE command   The SHOW IP OSPF INTERFACE command can be used to look at all OSPF interfaces. It shows you on what interfaces OSPF is operating. It also shows you the OSPF network type of this interface, which can be useful for troubleshooting OSPF failures.

SHOW IP OSPF NEIGHBOR command   The SHOW IP OSPF NEIGHBOR command lists the contents of the neighbor table and the states of each neighbor. It also identifies the type of router.

SHOW IP OSPF NEIGHBOR DETAIL command   The SHOW IP OSPF NEIGHBOR DETAIL command provides a continuous listing of all neighbors. The output is the same as a specific SHOW IP OSPF NEIGHBOR 1.1.1.2 command, only it shows the same information for all neighbors.

Show IP OSPF <process-id> command   This command shows a generic summary of all OSPF characteristics of the router. These include the process ID, router ID, type of router, redistributed protocols, and area information.

Show IP OSPF Virtual-links command   This command displays virtual links and detailed information about each connection. The output describes to which router ID the virtual link is connected, the interface used, and all OSPF timer intervals configured.

SHOW IP PROTOCOLS command   SHOW IP PROTOCOLS is the most basic and simple of routing commands; it merely shows what routing protocols are running on a router. It is best used to get a check summary of routing protocols on a router and to determine quickly whether OSPF is enabled. It also shows you what IP addresses are advertised via what protocol, what interfaces are participating in what protocol, and what redistribution, if any, is being performed.

Show IP ROUTE command   You can verify that the route to a given destination is installed in the routing table using the **show ip route** command. This command takes an optional argument of the destination host or network. If this argument is omitted, the command returns the entire routing table. When entered with no options, the SHOW IP ROUTE command shows the current entries in the routing tables as learned from all IP routing protocols.

SHOW ROUTE-MAP command   This command is also executed from the Privileged Exec mode and displays all configured route maps. The command uses the following format: show route-map *map name.*

SIA (Stuck in the Active) State   Slow convergence is usually what causes a network problem. In fact, slow convergence is usually why it takes a very long time for a query to be answered. This result in the router that issued the query gives up and just clears the adjacency to the router that isn't answering, forcing a restart of the neighbor session. This is known as Stuck in Active (SIA), or referred to as a Stuck in Active route. Basic examples of a SIA route is when a query is delayed traveling to the opposite end of the network therefore delaying a route traveling back.

Simple subnetting   Simple subnetting occurs when your subnet mask ends on the boundary of an octet. For example, if you were given the network address of 172.16.0.0, you could use a 24-bit mask to create several Class C addresses. Your subnet mask would be 11111111.11111111.11111111.00000000. You can see that the mask ends on the boundary. The reason this concept is so simple is that you're basically breaking a given class of address space into smaller classes, just as the above example splits a full Class B address into several Class C addresses.

Sliding window flow control   Method of flow control in which a receiver gives a transmitter permission to transmit data until a window is full. When the window is full, the transmitter must stop transmitting until the receiver acknowledges some of the data, or advertises a larger window. TCP, other transport protocols, and several data-link layer protocols use this method of flow control.

SLIP (Serial Line Internet Protocol)   Uses a variation of TCP/IP to make point-to-point serial connections. Succeeded by PPP.

SMDS (Switched Multimegabit Data Service)   WAN networking technology offered by telephone companies, which is high-speed and packet-switched, and uses datagrams.

SMTP (Simple Mail Tranfer Protocol)   A U.S. Department of Defense (DOD) standard for electronic mail systems (Military Standard 1781 or MIL-STD-1781) that have both host and user selections. User software is often included in TCP/IP PC packages; host software is available for exchanging SMTP mail with mail from proprietary systems.

SNAP (Subnetwork Access Protocol)   Internet protocol that operates between a network entity in the subnetwork and a network entity in the end system. SNAP specifies a standard method of encapsulating IP datagrams and ARP messages on IEEE networks.

SNMP (Simple Network Management Protocol)   Network management protocol used almost exclusively in TCP/IP networks. SNMP provides a means to monitor and control network devices, and to manage configurations, statistics collection, performance, and security.

socket   Software structure operating as a communications endpoint within a network device.

SONET (Synchronous Optical Network)   High-speed synchronous network specification developed by Bellcore and designed to run on optical fiber.

source address   Address of a network device that is sending data.

spanning tree   Loop-free subset of a network topology. *See also* **Spanning-Tree Protocol.**

Spanning-Tree Protocol   Developed to eliminate loops in the network. The Spanning-Tree Protocol ensures a loop-free path by placing one of the bridge ports in "blocking mode," preventing the forwarding of packets.

SPF (shortest path first) algorithm   Routing algorithm that sorts routes by length of path to determine a shortest-path spanning tree. Commonly used in link-state routing algorithms. Sometimes called Dijkstra's algorithm.

split horizon   Split horizon is another method that distance-vector protocols use to solve the routing loop problem. Split horizon is basically a rule that states that route information cannot be sent back in the direction from which that information was received.

split-horizon updates   Routing technique in which information about routes is prevented from being advertised out the router interface through which that information was received. Split-horizon updates are used to prevent routing loops.

SPX (Sequenced Packet Exchange)   Reliable, connection-oriented protocol at the transport layer that supplements the datagram service provided by IPX.

SRB (source-route bridging)   Method of bridging in Token Ring networks. In an SRB network, before data is sent to a destination, the entire route to that destination is predetermined in real time.

SRTT (Smooth round-trip time)   The SRTT is the smooth round-trip time, which refers to the average time between the transmission of a packet to the neighbor and the ACK received from the neighbor following that transmission. The SRTT is also used by the router to calculate the next field, the Retransmissions Timeout (RTO), which is the interval between unicast transmission attempts after switching to unicast mode following failure of the multicast method of transmission.

SSP (Switch-to-Switch Protocol)   Protocol used by routers to establish DLSw connections, locate resources, forward data, and handle flow control and error recovery. Specified in the DLSw standard.

SRT (source-route transparent bridging)   IBM's merging of SRB and transparent bridging into one bridging scheme, which requires no translation between bridging protocols.

SR/TLB (source-route translational bridging)   Method of bridging that allows source-route stations to communicate with transparent bridge stations, using an intermediate bridge that translates between the two bridge protocols.

Standard   Set of rules or procedures that are either widely used or officially specified.

Standard area   By default, any area connected to the backbone becomes a standard area. All LSAs are permitted and propagation takes place normally.

Star topology   LAN topology in which endpoints on a network are connected to a common central switch by point-to-point links. A ring topology that is organized as a star implements a unidirectional closed-loop star, instead of point-to-point links. Compare with **bus topology**, **ring topology**, and **tree topology**.

Static route   A static route is explicitly configured and entered into the routing table. Static routes take precedence over routes chosen by dynamic routing protocols. Static routes are routes entered by an engineer that point to a destination. Static entries are "always available" even when they are not. What that means if that link to the statically routed network goes down, the static route will not be removed from the routing table. This is a very important point to remember when configuring any routing, as is that fact that static routes have, by default, an administrative distance of 1. This is lower than the administrative distance of BGP and most routing protocols, and ensures that the static route will be the route placed in the routing table, even if a dynamic routing protocol offers a better route.

Stub area   The stub area prevents ASBR External LSAs (type 5) and ASBR Summary LSAs (type 4) from flooding to the routers contained within. The ABR for a stub area inserts a default route (0.0.0.0) that all stub area routers use when no routes are found for a destination. In networks where many external links are present, this causes a noticeable difference in performance by reducing the size of the routing table and database.

Subinterfaces   *Subinterfaces* offer great flexibility that might not be available with physical interfaces; this flexibility includes the ability to change the interface type from point to point to multipoint or to have multiple separate subnets off one interface and to route between them accordingly. A subinterface is also a virtual interface defined as a logical subdivision of a physical interface.

subnet address   Portion of an IP address that is specified as the subnetwork by the subnet mask. *See also* **IP address**; **subnet mask**; **subnetwork**.

subnet mask   32-bit address mask used in IP to indicate the bits of an IP address that are being used for the subnet address. Sometimes referred to simply as mask. *See also* **address mask**; **IP address**.

subnetting   Subnetting does not conform to the standard class subnet masks. Subnetting allows a network designer more flexibility with the network implementation. *See also* **Complex subnetting**; **Simple subnetting**.

subnetwork   1. In IP networks, a network sharing a particular subnet address. 2. Subnetworks are networks arbitrarily segmented by a network administrator in order to provide a multilevel, hierarchical routing structure while shielding the subnetwork from the addressing complexity of attached networks. Sometimes called a subnet.

Successor   When the topology table is built, a listing of possible feasible successors to the destination network is built. The feasible successor whose path yields the lowest cost, thus the lowest metric, becomes the successor. The successor may be defined as the selected next-hop router in the path to the destination.

Summary LSA   LSA types 3 and 4 are both summary links and, except for the obvious difference in their Type fields, deliver the same information to different destinations. A *type 3 summary LSA* is destined for IP networks, while a *type 4 summary LSA* is destined for an ASBR. The information content they carry is the same; only the destination types differ.

Supernet   A *supernet* occurs when the mask of a given address is smaller than the address's natural mask.

Supernetting   Supernetting involves taking several blocks of contiguous addresses and deriving one address with a network mask that will speak for them all.

SVC (Switched Virtual Circuit)   An SVC is temporary in nature and is created as needed.

switch   1. Network device that filters, forwards, and floods frames based on the destination address of each frame. The switch operates at the data-link layer of the OSI model. 2. General term applied to an electronic or mechanical device that allows a connection to be established as necessary and terminated when there is no longer a session to support.

T I   Digital WAN carrier facility. T1 transmits DS-1-formatted data at 1.544 Mbps through the telephone-switching network, using AMI or B8ZS coding. Compare with **E1**. *See also* **AMI**; **B8ZS**.

TCP (Transmission Control Protocol)   Connection-oriented transport layer protocol that provides reliable full-duplex data transmission. TCP is part of the TCP/IP protocol stack.

TCP/IP (Transmission Control Protocol/Internet Protocol)   Common name for the suite of protocols developed by the U.S. DoD in the 1970s to support the construction of worldwide internetworks. TCP and IP are the two best-known protocols in the suite.

TDM (time-division multiplexing)   Technique for allocating bandwidth on a single wire to information from multiple channels, based on preassigned time slots. Channels are allocated bandwidth regardless of whether the stations have data to transmit.

Telnet   A virtual terminal protocol from the U.S. Department of Defense (DOD) that interfaces terminal devices and terminal-oriented processes (MIL-STD-1782).

TFTP (Trivial File Transfer Protocol)   A simplified version of the File Transfer Protocol (FTP), associated with the Transmission Control Protocol/Internet Protocol (TCP/IP) family, that does not provide password protection or a user directory.

Throughput   Rate of information arriving at, and possibly passing through, a particular point in a network system.

Timeout   Event that occurs when one network device expects to hear from another network device within a specified period of time, but does not. A timeout usually results in a retransmission of information or the termination of the session between the two devices.

Token   Frame that contains only control information. Possession of the token allows a network device to transmit data onto the network. *See also* **token passing**.

Token passing   Method by which network devices' access the physical medium is based on possession of a small frame called a token. Compare this method to circuit switching and contention.

Token Ring   Token-passing LAN developed and supported by IBM. Token Ring runs at 4 or 16 Mbps over a ring topology. Similar to IEEE 802.5. *See also* **IEEE 802.5; ring topology; token passing**.

TokenTalk   Apple Computer's data-link product that allows an AppleTalk network to be connected by Token Ring cables.

Topology database   This database contains information about router relationships and types, links, types of links (router or network), advertising routers, and links contained in particular areas (except for summary links). It also holds information about external links and summary links. The whole OSPF database, sorted by area, can be viewed with the SHOW IP OSPF DATABASE command.

Topology table   A topology table stores information on all routes and keeps a record of all the paths available to the given destination, including all metric information as well as flags to indicate which path is actually installed into the routing table as the best path.

Totally stubby area   Cisco took the idea of a stub area one step further by eliminating type 3 LSAs from flooding into Totally Stubby Areas. The ABR inserts the default route again and all routers within the area send inter-area and external traffic to the border router.

Traceroute command   Traceroute does exactly what its name implies; it traces the router path that your data will travel to a specified network and reports the given path back to you. Traceroute is usually used when troubleshooting a route that has become unreachable. You will usually use the ping and traceroute commands during a troubleshooting session.

Transparent bridging   Bridging scheme used in Ethernet and IEEE 802.3 networks. Allows bridges to pass frames along one hop at a time, based on tables that associate end nodes with bridge ports. Bridges are transparent to network end nodes.

Transport layer   Layer 4 of the OSI reference model. This layer is responsible for reliable network communication between end nodes. The transport layer provides mechanisms for the establishment, maintenance, and termination of virtual circuits, transport fault detection and recovery, and information flow control.

Tree topology   A LAN topology that resembles a bus topology. Tree networks can contain branches with multiple nodes. In a tree topology, transmissions from a station propagate the length of the physical medium, and are received by all other stations.

Twisted-pair   Relatively low-speed transmission medium consisting of two insulated wires arranged in a regular spiral pattern. The wires can be shielded or unshielded. Twisted-pair is common in telephony applications and is increasingly common in data networks.

Two-way/EXCHANGE state   Routers send database description packets that describe their entire database in the two-way/EXCHANGE state. The receiving router uses these packets to see what LSAs it is missing or are out of date. This information will be used to generate *link state requests (LSRs)*.

Two-way/EXSTART state   In the two-way/EXSTART state, the router receives a response from other routers. It sees its RID in the hello packets that it receives (neighbor field), which indicates that the neighbor router has received the initial hello and is responding to it. The response is sent back to the originating router's source IP address—in other words, as a unicast packet.

Two-way/LOADING state   At the two-way/LOADING state point, the router has a list of LSRs that will be sent to ensure it gets all the information needed from its neighbor. After the LSRs are sent, the router receives *link state update (LSU)* packets containing the missing or out-of-date information. Once the LSUs have been received from the router's neighbors' databases, they will be installed into its topology tables.

Two-way state   This means that the new OSPF router adds all the replying routers to the adjacency tables.

UDP (User Datagram Protocol)   Connectionless transport layer protocol in the TCP/IP protocol stack. UDP is a simple protocol that exchanges datagrams without acknowledgments or guaranteed delivery, requiring that error processing and retransmission be handled by other protocols. UDP is defined in RFC 768.

Unnumbered interfaces   Unnumbered interfaces are a technique to avoid assigning IP addresses to a link in an effort to conserve IP addresses. They can also raise a number of interesting challenges. In Figure 4-2, the serial link between A and B does not have its own IP address. Instead, the serial interfaces linking the OSPF neighbors use the IP address of each respective router's Ethernet interface.

UPDATE message   UPDATE messages carry the routing information between neighbors. It advertises routes and identifies invalid routes for removal from the database.

Update packets   Update packets are used to send information concerning routes. These packets are sent only when there is a change to the network topology, such as a route becoming unavailable. They contain only the essential information concerning the route in question, and sent only to neighbors which are affected by the change. In other words, they are bounded updates, sent only to neighbors which need the information. If this update information is required by several neighbors, a multicast packet is sent. If the change only affects one router, however, a unicast packet is sent.

UTP (unshielded twisted-pair)   Four-pair wire medium used in a variety of networks. UTP does not require the fixed spacing between connections that is necessary with coaxial-type connections.

virtual circuit   Logical circuit created to ensure reliable communication between two network devices. A virtual circuit is defined by a VPI/VCI pair, and can be either permanent or switched. Virtual circuits are used in Frame Relay and X.25. In ATM, a virtual circuit is called a virtual channel. Sometimes abbreviated VC.

VLAN (virtual LAN)   Group of devices on one or more LANs that are configured (using management software) so that they can communicate as if they were attached to the same wire, when in fact they are located on a number of different LAN segments. Because VLANs are based on logical instead of physical connections, they are extremely flexible.

VLSM (variable-length subnet masking)   Capability to specify a different length subnet mask for the same network number at different locations in the network. VLSM can help optimize available address space.

VPN (Virtual Private Network)   Technique to enable IP traffic to travel securely over a public TCP/IP network. All traffic from one network to another is encrypted using tunneling.

Wait time   The wait time (always equal to the dead interval) is the amount of time that the router waits after the dead timer has elapsed before it flushes information about the dead router out of its tables.

WAN (Wide Area Network)   Data communications network that serves users across a broad geographic area and often uses transmission devices provided by common carriers. Frame Relay, SMDS, and X.25 are examples of WANs. Compare with **LAN** and **MAN**.

WEIGHT (Proprietary to Cisco) attribute   WEIGHT is an optional nontransitive attribute that is proprietary to Cisco products. A higher weight is more preferred, and can range from 0 to 65535; the default is 32768. It is used to help a BGP router to select the best route out of several routes to the same destination.

WFQ (weighted fair queuing)   Algorithm that manages congestion by identifying conversations (traffic streams), separating packets that belong to each conversation, and ensuring that capacity is shared fairly among conversations. By reducing retransmission, WFQ stabilizes network behavior during congestion.

wildcard mask   32-bit quantity used in conjunction with an IP address to determine which bits in an IP address should be matched and ignored when comparing that address with another IP address. A wildcard mask is specified when defining access list statements.

X.21   ITU-T standard for serial communications over synchronous digital lines. The X.21 protocol is used primarily in Europe and Japan.

X.25   ITU-T standard that defines how connections between DTE and DCE are maintained for remote terminal access and computer communications in public data networks. X.25 specifies LAPB, a data-link layer protocol, and PLP, a network layer protocol. Frame Relay has to some degree superseded X.25.

X.121   ITU-T standard describing an addressing scheme used in X.25 networks. X.121 addresses are sometimes called IDNs (International Data Numbers).

zone   In AppleTalk, a logical group of network devices.

INDEX

C

E

T

LICENSE AGREEMENT

THIS PRODUCT (THE "PRODUCT") CONTAINS PROPRIETARY SOFTWARE, DATA AND INFORMATION (INCLUDING DOCUMENTATION) OWNED BY THE McGRAW-HILL COMPANIES, INC. ("McGRAW-HILL") AND ITS LICENSORS. YOUR RIGHT TO USE THE PRODUCT IS GOVERNED BY THE TERMS AND CONDITIONS OF THIS AGREEMENT.

LICENSE: Throughout this License Agreement, "you" shall mean either the individual or the entity whose agent opens this package. You are granted a non-exclusive and non-transferable license to use the Product subject to the following terms:

(i) If you have licensed a single user version of the Product, the Product may only be used on a single computer (i.e., a single CPU). If you licensed and paid the fee applicable to a local area network or wide area network version of the Product, you are subject to the terms of the following subparagraph (ii).

(ii) If you have licensed a local area network version, you may use the Product on unlimited workstations located in one single building selected by you that is served by such local area network. If you have licensed a wide area network version, you may use the Product on unlimited workstations located in multiple buildings on the same site selected by you that is served by such wide area network; provided, however, that any building will not be considered located in the same site if it is more than five (5) miles away from any building included in such site. In addition, you may only use a local area or wide area network version of the Product on one single server. If you wish to use the Product on more than one server, you must obtain written authorization from McGraw-Hill and pay additional fees.

(iii) You may make one copy of the Product for back-up purposes only and you must maintain an accurate record as to the location of the back-up at all times.

COPYRIGHT; RESTRICTIONS ON USE AND TRANSFER: All rights (including copyright) in and to the Product are owned by McGraw-Hill and its licensors. You are the owner of the enclosed disc on which the Product is recorded. You may not use, copy, decompile, disassemble, reverse engineer, modify, reproduce, create derivative works, transmit, distribute, sublicense, store in a database or retrieval system of any kind, rent or transfer the Product, or any portion thereof, in any form or by any means (including electronically or otherwise) except as expressly provided for in this License Agreement. You must reproduce the copyright notices, trademark notices, legends and logos of McGraw-Hill and its licensors that appear on the Product on the back-up copy of the Product which you are permitted to make hereunder. All rights in the Product not expressly granted herein are reserved by McGraw-Hill and its licensors.

TERM: This License Agreement is effective until terminated. It will terminate if you fail to comply with any term or condition of this License Agreement. Upon termination, you are obligated to return to McGraw-Hill the Product together with all copies thereof and to purge all copies of the Product included in any and all servers and computer facilities.

DISCLAIMER OF WARRANTY: THE PRODUCT AND THE BACK-UP COPY OF THE PRODUCT ARE LICENSED "AS IS." McGRAW-HILL, ITS LICENSORS AND THE AUTHORS MAKE NO WARRANTIES, EXPRESS OR IMPLIED, AS TO RESULTS TO BE OBTAINED BY ANY PERSON OR ENTITY FROM USE OF THE PRODUCT AND/OR ANY INFORMATION OR DATA INCLUDED THEREIN. McGRAW-HILL, ITS LICENSORS, AND THE AUTHORS MAKE NO GUARANTEE THAT YOU WILL PASS ANY CERTIFICATION EXAM BY USING THIS PRODUCT. McGRAW-HILL, ITS LICENSORS AND THE AUTHORS MAKE NO EXPRESS OR IMPLIED WARRANTIES OF MERCHANTABILITY OR FITNESS FOR A PARTICULAR PURPOSE OR USE WITH RESPECT TO THE PRODUCT. NEITHER McGRAW-HILL, ANY OF ITS LICENSORS, NOR THE AUTHORS WARRANT THAT THE FUNCTIONS CONTAINED IN THE PRODUCT WILL MEET YOUR REQUIREMENTS OR THAT THE OPERATION OF THE PRODUCT WILL BE UNINTERRUPTED OR ERROR FREE. YOU ASSUME THE ENTIRE RISK WITH RESPECT TO THE QUALITY AND PERFORMANCE OF THE PRODUCT.

LIMITED WARRANTY FOR DISC: To the original licensee only, McGraw-Hill warrants that the enclosed disc on which the Product is recorded is free from defects in materials and workmanship under normal use and service for a period of ninety (90) days from the date of purchase. In the event of a defect in the disc covered by the foregoing warranty, McGraw-Hill will replace the disc.

LIMITATION OF LIABILITY: NEITHER McGRAW-HILL, ITS LICENSORS NOR THE AUTHORS SHALL BE LIABLE FOR ANY INDIRECT, SPECIAL OR CONSEQUENTIAL DAMAGES, SUCH AS BUT NOT LIMITED TO, LOSS OF ANTICIPATED PROFITS OR BENEFITS, RESULTING FROM THE USE OR INABILITY TO USE THE PRODUCT EVEN IF ANY OF THEM HAS BEEN ADVISED OF THE POSSIBILITY OF SUCH DAMAGES. THIS LIMITATION OF LIABILITY SHALL APPLY TO ANY CLAIM OR CAUSE WHATSOEVER WHETHER SUCH CLAIM OR CAUSE ARISES IN CONTRACT, TORT, OR OTHERWISE. Some states do not allow the exclusion or limitation of indirect, special or consequential damages, so the above limitation may not apply to you.

U.S. GOVERNMENT RESTRICTED RIGHTS: Any software included in the Product is provided with restricted rights subject to subparagraphs (c), (1) and (2) of the Commercial Computer Software-Restricted Rights clause at 48 C.F.R. 52.227-19. The terms of this Agreement applicable to the use of the data in the Product are those under which the data are generally made available to the general public by McGraw-Hill. Except as provided herein, no reproduction, use, or disclosure rights are granted with respect to the data included in the Product and no right to modify or create derivative works from any such data is hereby granted.

GENERAL: This License Agreement constitutes the entire agreement between the parties relating to the Product. The terms of any Purchase Order shall have no effect on the terms of this License Agreement. Failure of McGraw-Hill to insist at any time on strict compliance with this License Agreement shall not constitute a waiver of any rights under this License Agreement. This License Agreement shall be construed and governed in accordance with the laws of the State of New York. If any provision of this License Agreement is held to be contrary to law, that provision will be enforced to the maximum extent permissible and the remaining provisions will remain in full force and effect.